BRAZILIAN STUDIES

CENTER FOR THE STUDY OF THE FIRST AMERICANS

Oregon State University

Corvallis, Oregon

BRAZILIAN STUDIES

Typesetting and camera-ready preparations by C & C Wordsmiths of Blue Hill, Maine.
Printed in the United States of America by The Ellsworth American, Ellsworth, Maine.
Support for publication was provided by the Gruhn Research Trust.
This book is printed on 100% acid-free paper.

ISBN: 0-912933-10-0

The Sambaqui at Forte Marechal Luz, State of Santa Catarina, Brazil

Alan L. Bryan

Table of Contents

List of Figures

[1] Note that this and all other north arrows indicate magnetic north in 1960 (12° 35′ W). Datum (31.62 m) was established on the concrete water tank (circle at NE edge of the sambaqui). The *cassino* is on the beach west of the sambaqui. Small arrows on inset maps of Brazil and the Ilha de São Francisco do Sul indicate location of site.

List of Tables

Preface and Acknowledgments

Every archaeological project involves the cooperation and assistance of a great many people from its inception to the final stage of getting the report into print. The project was actually conceived by Professor Luiz de Castro Faria of the Museu Nacional in Rio de Janeiro. He had witnessed the destruction of many coastal shellmounds or sambaquis for industrial purposes and determined to do something about it. Among the things he did was to approach Professor Gordon R. Willey at Harvard University to see if he or one of his students might be interested in becoming involved in excavating a Brazilian shellmound. Professor Willey himself could not; but, knowing that I had written my master's thesis at the University of Washington on shellmound archaeology, he asked if I were interested in working in Brazil. I accepted the challenge because I wanted to broaden my experience and perspective, and because I recognized the special significance of the excellent preservation in shellmounds of bone and shell as well as stone artifacts to the question of what technology early people brought with them to the Americas.

In early May 1960 Professor Castro Faria arranged to show me a selection of known sambaquis, and Wilson Rauth of the Museu de Paranagua and Professor Castro Faria accompanied me on a rapid reconnaissance of many of the massive shellmounds in the southern part of the state of Paraná and northern Santa Catarina. By the time we reached the sambaqui at Forte Marechal Luz I was able to decide that this would be the best site for me to tackle. Rauth kindly stayed with me for a few days to help me over the hurdle of arranging for a crew and breaking them in to the special techniques of archaeology. Fortunately the site is on the grounds of a small coast artillery post which guards the entrance to the harbor of São Francisco do Sul. Tenente Coronel Osny Vasconcellos, then commander of the fort, arranged for a small number of men to help me dig; and a few weeks after commencement of the excavation he kindly arranged for me to move from the hotel in town to live in the bachelor officers' quarters (known as the *cassino*) which was very conveniently located on the beach at the foot of the sambaqui. This move eliminated the wasteful commuting time by bus.

With the excellent crew that I finally managed to train I acquired some basic Portuguese, but with my colleagues in the *cassino* I became a means for renewing their lagging acquaintance with English. Among my many unforgotten friends in the *cassino* I particularly wish to thank Tenente N. Tasso, who surveyed the site and prepared the site map for me. A few weeks after I started work at the site, John Gallovich arrived from Los Angeles and volunteered to help dig. I will be forever grateful that he was able to take over much of the time-consuming business of dealing with dozens of saturated human skeletons encountered in burials. Leonidas Boutin also drove down from Curitiba for several extended weekends to help excavate.

Most of the people who patiently identified the many bits I carried back to the Museu Nacional are acknowledged in the chapter on food; but I would specifically like to mention Professor Carlos de Paula Couto, who counselled me about many subjects as well as identifying my mammal bones. Also I want to thank Professor Walter da Silva Curvello of the Museu Nacional for identifying my rocks and Professor João J. Bigarella of the Universidade Federal de Paraná for advising me about geomorphological problems. Professor James B. Griffin of the University of Michigan kindly accepted eight radiocarbon samples for dating.

I would like to thank Drs. Betty Meggers and Clifford Evans of the Smithsonian Institution for taking an interest in my project and for suggesting that I apply to the

Organization of American States for a Latin American exchange fellowship and to the Grace Doherty Charitable Foundation for a supplementary grant which enabled me to do the field work in Brazil in 1960. Sabbatical leave from the University of Alberta and a Leave Fellowship from Canada Council during the academic year 1976/77 gave me the essential block of uninterrupted time necessary to complete the report so many years after the excavation.

Professor André Prous of the Universidade Federal de Minas Gerais translated and published a summary report in Portuguese (Bryan, 1977a). Finally, my heartfelt thanks go to my wife and colleague, Professor Ruth Gruhn of the University of Alberta, for critically editing the manuscript, which includes many paragraphs of artifact descriptions in boring detail in order to emphasize the significance of unshaped artifacts to the inhabitants of the sambaqui, and therefore also to the archaeologists who report on sambaqui excavations.

The basic artifact descriptions were finished in Rio de Janeiro in 1960. The bulk of the final report was written in Llao Llao, Argentina, in 1976. Subsequently, the report was considered by several publishers, who concluded that although it should be published, it would be too expensive for the few copies that would sell. The final version was finished in Edmonton, Canada, in 1992. Publication has been supported by the Gruhn Research Trust.

Foreword

Man is an ingenious creature; but more than that, he is a scrounger. When he needs a tool, he looks about him in the immediate vicinity for something that will suffice for the task. Not many campers carry a hammer with them for driving in tent pegs; it is much easier to pick up a rock, pound in the pegs, and discard the used implement, now an artifact. If necessary, a pedestrian will walk half a kilometer to search for something that can be used for the purpose at hand, rather than pack a finished tool with him for many days. Depending upon the situation, even a preform which can be fabricated into a special tool of proper size and shape may be too heavy or too awkward to carry very far. It is much easier and more efficient to pick up and use a natural object that may do the job adequately.

A person who lives near the ocean will comb the beach regularly looking for things that may be useful in some way—a stone, a bone, a tooth, a length of bamboo—and collect it for possible use. In a strict sense, all of these objects become artifacts when they are handled or put to use by man. As my friend J. M. Cruxent would say, "*Es un artefacto de fortuna.*" But how can the archaeologist be sure that the object was actually used by someone in the past? On a normal open site stones and bones can easily become incorporated into the site, or altered by agencies other than man. But, of course, the usual open site chosen by an archaeologist for excavation contains so many undoubted artifacts clearly shaped by man that there is little reason to be concerned with possible expediency tools.

Shellmounds, however, have notoriously poor yields of cultural information for the amount of material that must be excavated. In shellmounds, only rarely are actual living areas preserved intact for the archaeologist to excavate and try to reassemble original cultural contexts. The living areas have usually been disturbed, not so much by rodents or other digging animals, but by people; and usually by the inhabitants of the site, and for good reason. When the garbage around or in the house became too rank, either it was cleaned out or the house was moved. Occasionally the living area was covered over with clean shell; but more often the rotting garbage, including artifacts, was hauled away and dumped.

When confronted with disturbed situations such as these, the archaeologist must use his ingenuity to the utmost in order to realize his primary objective, which is to discern as much as possible about what the aboriginal people had been doing at the site he is excavating. At the same time he must remind himself that whatever he says about past human activities must be supportable by concrete evidence. Thus he cannot simply state that this rock was a hammerstone simply because it fits the hand nicely and has a suitable shape for such a purpose. He must be able to defend his statement that it was a hammerstone by noting that somewhere it retains evidence of use in the form of pecking or battering marks. If such evidence is not present it is the proverbial "unused hammerstone" that all archaeologists joke about. On an open site where such stones can occur naturally, nothing more can be said and the stone is discarded by the archaeologist on the spot. However, if the stone in question is found in direct association with an undoubted artifact or a cultural feature such as a burial, then it can be stated with some degree of certainty that it must have been placed in its position for some purpose, and therefore is an artifact that must be catalogued and described.

Excavation of a shellmound, or a site located on a sand dune, should be recognized as an extremely important endeavor because it gives the archaeologist special insight into what was actually used by the original inhabitants, not limited to what the archaeologist recognizes as formal types. Unless the stone was obviously brought to the site because it was attached to some shellfish, it must have been brought in by people for some purpose. In the case of a stone, that purpose may well have been simply for use as a hearthstone or boiling stone, examples of which are usually so abundant and heavy that no attempt is made by archaeologists to collect them, although in the strict sense of the word they are artifacts. In the case of stones unsuitable for use as cooking stones because they would shatter or disintegrate too easily, or other objects such as shark teeth or whalebone vertebrae, parts belonging to species unlikely to have been deliberately hunted for food, an argument is supportable that the objects were brought to the site to be used for some purpose as artifacts. They can help fill in the badly blurred and necessarily incomplete picture of what the people were doing at the site long ago.

As I excavated the sambaqui at Forte Marechal Luz I kept all unusual objects and examined them very carefully with a hand lens for evidence of use. At times I could find no evidence, or at least nothing that would be distinctive of human alteration; but still many objects were kept, although not counted as artifacts, simply because people must have intended to use them for some purpose. The exercise of careful scrutiny of all such objects was valuable, not only because it forced me to examine carefully all unusual objects, but also because I was able to discern unnatural patterns of use, such as on animal teeth, that must have been made by using the objects as tools. Ultimately I realized that these elusive marks of use on certain unshaped materials (stone, bone, teeth, and shell) fell into the very same distinctive patterns that I was finding on the artifacts which had obviously been altered intentionally in order to shape natural materials into tools. In other words the processes of altering raw materials accidentally or at least unintentionally were the same processes that were intentionally employed by people to shape tools for specific purposes.

Although it was not always possible to differentiate intentionally shaped artifacts from artifacts that were altered only by use, I found that the attempt to separate these two categories was valuable. It became clear thereby that both the identifiable *"artefactos de fortuna"* and the less-common shaped artifacts all exhibited the same marks of alteration; only applied in a different manner. With experience, it became possible to distinguish with little doubt when the particular process of alteration had been used intentionally to shape an object. Furthermore, it became clear that various major technological processes for shaping certain materials were innovated at different times at the site, and once put to use most techniques continued to be used. That is, the inventory of technological processes as well as formal types accumulated through time. Thus it became useful to think of these various technological processes as traditional manufacturing techniques, each of which was a discrete entity in a time/space grid in the same way that specific formal types exist in time and space. In fact, as specific taxonomic forms were relatively rarely encountered, because only a minor percentage of all the artifacts had been intentionally shaped, these technological processes became much more valuable as heuristic devices for visualizing material culture and the processes of culture change than trying to impose an arbitrary formal typology on the artifact collection.

As I had had previous experience excavating shellmounds on the Northwest Coast of North America I approached the sambaqui fully aware that there would undoubtedly be a low yield of well-shaped artifacts. Therefore, I was determined to get as much information out of artifact analysis as I could, and not be discouraged by the fact that higher-yield sites might seem more valuable; for if archaeologists excavate only high-yield sites, most of human prehistory will go unrecorded. I soon realized that with the exception of burials, there were very few cultural features that would yield much cultural information; so I concentrated on the artifacts, undistinguished as they were, describing them in considerable detail in the field laboratory with the intention of squeezing as much cultural information out of them as possible.

This foreword explains my philosophy of approach to the site and also serves as an introduction to my methodology of artifact analysis. The methodology will be amplified and hopefully will become clearer as the analysis of stone, bone, teeth, and shell artifacts proceeds. My approach to materials other than clay is analogous to the methodology used by a ceramics analyst who attempts to distinguish the various technological processes employed in fabricating a pottery collection. Each specific ceramic technique has its own developmental history and is therefore a discrete technological tradition.

The method of artifact analysis, based on the identification and description of specific technological processes employed in altering raw materials, fits into the theoretical framework which I have developed elsewhere (Bryan 1965, 1977b, 1988, 1991), where I discuss the importance of being able to distinguish technological traditions and to trace them in time and space. This descriptive report gives specific examples of how discrete fabrication techniques can be identified on various raw materials and used to define technological traditions. The next step, of tracing these defined technological traditions in time and space, will necessarily depend on other archaeologists who take the trouble to use and refine the methodology used here, in order to identify processing techniques as well as formal types in the artifact collections from other dated sites. The culture history of eastern South America—or of any other area or time period that lacks complex ceramic styles—can then be written with some degree of authority.

Meanwhile, this monograph purports to be the culture history of the people who lived at a particular site for nearly four millennia, as seen through the changes evident in their simple technology, or at least that portion of it which withstood destruction by time and by climate. But first of all the report attempts to reconstruct as much as possible about the daily activities of the occupants of the site. Specific events can rarely be captured; but it is possible to detect when the people were pecking, grinding, or flaking stone, and scrapping, cutting or grinding bone. Above all, I hope that it becomes obvious that the latter kind of paleo-ethnography or "anthropological archaeology" is part of the overall process of determining the history of a particular culture and ultimately the culture history of mankind on a more general level. Culture history is the ultimate objective of the paleo-ethnographer. Anthropological archaeology and culture history are two aspects of the same intellectual process and should not be thought of as discrete entities in opposition to each other.

I was uncomfortable with the idea of beginning an excavation without a preceding intensive reconnaissance of the island, but I had agreed that the intent of the extensive survey was to choose a known sambaquis for excavation. During the initial extensive survey we had visited the nearby site at Enseada, as well as several on the west side of the island and on the adjacent mainland upriver around Joinville. Although I encountered a couple of small campsites while walking near the fort, I never had access to a vehicle, nor time to carry out an intensive survey. I knew that a pattern of periodic removal to nearby shellmound sites within the same "tribal" territory had been historically recorded for Pacific Northwest Coast groups. For this reason I assumed that the smaller sites on the east side of the island were seasonal hunting/gathering campsites, while the other major site at Enseada was occupied by the same group of people for a few years while the garbage at Forte Marechal Luz decayed and became less aromatic.

Chapter 1
The Nature of the Site

The Environmental Context of Human Occupation

Forte Marechal Luz is a small army post situated at 27° 50′ S. Lat. and 48° 50′ W. Long. on the northern end of the Ilha de São Francisco do Sul, the second-largest island in the state of Santa Catarina, about 20 km south of the border with the state of Paraná. The island is separated from the mainland to the northwest by Babitonga Bay, which forms the entrance and the actual harbor of the port of São Francisco do Sul. To the west, Babitonga Bay merges with the narrower and shallower Barra do Sul or Araquari Channel which completes the separation of the island from the mainland. Babitonga Bay and Barra do Sul are old river channels degraded to a lower sea level and subsequently drowned by the transgressing sea in post-glacial times. Evidently both channels were incised through Pleistocene sediments which form a broad sandy plain east of the Precambrian crystalline foothills of the Serra do Mar. Actually the plain, the surface of which has been modelled into a series of sand ridges by waves and the wind, covers the bases of the outermost hills, the tops of which protrude as islands surrounded by sand or the sea. Most of the island of São Francisco is a nearly level sandy plain, but one of the several "islands" of crystalline rock projected above the plain is the Morro de João Dias forming the northern tip of the Ilha de São Francisco. The sambaqui of Forte Marechal Luz* was accumulated by people who lived on the leeward western side of this quartz-diorite hill, where there are three level steps or benches between about 19 and 24 m above present sea level. The sharply incised benches are of equivocal origin because no alluvial sediments were found on them, although they were identified as wave-cut terraces by Oliveira (1960:160).

The sambaqui at Forte Marechal Luz is situated in a small, fairly shallow sandy bay sheltered from the prevailing easterly winds and overlooking in the distance the mangrove swamps which line the sandy shores of Babitonga Bay to the west. Between the sambaqui and the point of the island, Cabo João Dias, are several fine-grained diabase dykes, oriented N 40° W, which intruded into the Precambrian bedrock during the Mesozoic (Figure 1). Beyond Cabo João Dias is the open ocean, which is actively eroding a steep cliff on the east side of the hill (*morro*). South of the *morro*, Ubatuba Bay fronts a rapidly building beach bar which arcs 6 km southeast to Enseada Point, a tiny crystalline hill, on which the sambaqui of Enseada accumulated. The Enseada sambaqui was excavated by Anamaria Beck in 1969 and 1970, and various reports on her work will be found in the bibliography.

The semi-tropical climate (Köppen type Cfa) is characterized as mesothermic with a mean annual temperature of 20.4° C. (*Atlas Geografico de Santa Catarina* 1985). Light frost is frequently recorded during the winter months. The relative humidity is high (86.6%), and precipitation is considerable (1851 mm). Even dur-

*In 1960 there was no uniform site designation system for Brazil, so I devised one, based on the Milionesimo map series. In this scheme, later published in Beltrão (1976:56–58), the Forte Marechal Luz sambaqui was designated 42-RB-1. Another system has been adopted by Brazilian archaeologists; and the site was redesignated SC.LJ.76 (Santa Catarina, Litoral de Joinville) by Beck (1968:90).

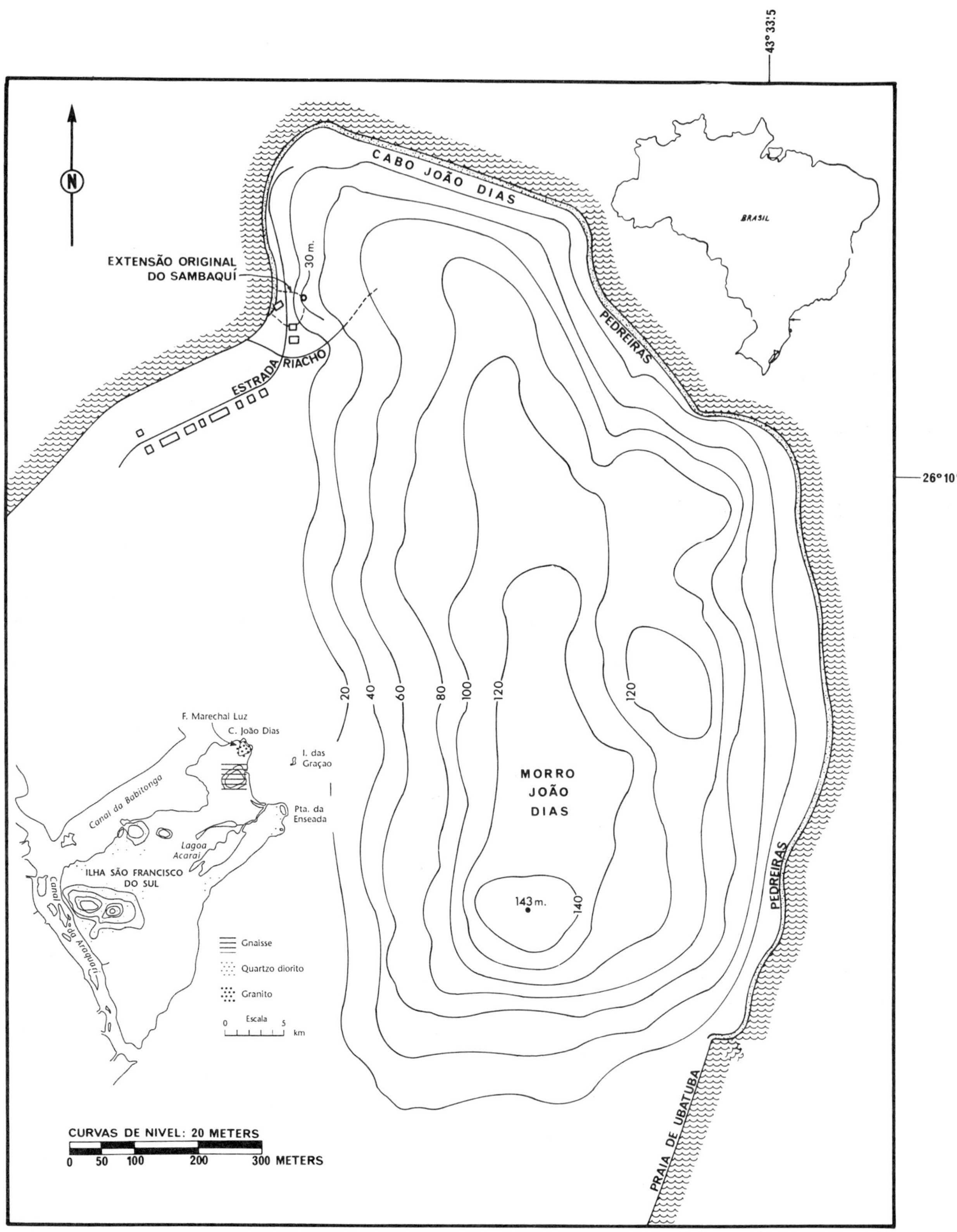

Figure 1. Map of Cape João Dias and Forte Marechal Luz.

ing the winter months, the driest season, there may be stormy periods with several consecutive days of heavy rainfall.

A dense rain forest must have covered the island in aboriginal times. Even now vegetation is abundant, and second-growth trees are quite high except on the windswept eastern side of the hill. The local terrestrial environment within easy walking distance of the site was quite varied because of differences in relief, shelter, and subsoil. Likewise, the site is located on a littoral ecotone with the nearby open ocean fronting on both rocks and beach bar, while in front of the site is a shallow sandy bay, beyond which is a deep channel which fronts mangrove swamps a short distance to the west. The local habitat for both animals and man must have been unusually favorable because of the varied natural resources so readily available in such an ecotone. The vegetation covering the sambaqui on the highest bench included *aroeira* (*Schinus terebinthifolius*) and *tucaneira* (*Vochysia tucanorum*), in addition to grass.

Methods of Excavation

After the trees and underbrush had been cut from the surface of the broadest bench, between 25 and 26 m above sea level, at the base of the steepest part of the bedrock hill, we laid out a grid of 2-m squares (Figure 2). The area chosen for excavation was the largest undisturbed area containing the deepest shell deposits exposed on the cut bank formed during quarrying operations for road material. Most of the sambaqui had already been removed, but fortunately a nearly complete section of the deep clean shell deposits was nicely exposed lying adjacent to and beneath more extensive layers of shell and dark organic occupation debris which covered the surface of the level bench. An area of 70 m^2 was excavated with trowels and dustpans.

At first it was hoped that the stratigraphy so well exposed on the cut bank could be used as a guide for excavating the squares by natural strata. But it soon became apparent that the deposits did not necessarily conform to what was visible a short distance away on the cut bank. I therefore attempted to adopt the system of digging in artificial 2-cm levels within a natural stratum. I could strip the material to that fine a thickness; but it soon became obvious that my untrained crew could not follow such levels consistently, nor were they able to tell when a new stratum commenced. I therefore let them dig in 10-cm levels as measured from the surface all around the square (as we maintained baulks for profile purposes). At first I tried to stop them whenever they penetrated a new stratum; but the frustration of trying to get the feel of the site by digging my own square as well as screening everything, while at the same time trying to control a group of untrained youths in a strange language, forced me to let them dig in controlled artificial levels of 10-cm thickness. After a few days I dug only occasionally, but continued to sift all material through a ¼-inch screen. After profiling, I keyed the level bags and the flake and sherd bags to the actual numbered strata. Although the underlying strata tended to conform to the surface relief, this was not always true; and therefore many level bags contain materials from two (rarely more) natural strata. All artifacts except flakes and potsherds were located precisely at the time of discovery *in situ*, or located approximately as soon as they were found in the screen. Thus I am confident that most artifacts were attributed to the proper natural stratum.

Because of the danger of collapsing walls, after the western pits reached depths beyond about 1.5 m, the baulks had to be profiled and eliminated. As it was no longer feasible to measure from the surface, we had to establish a datum level system for recording level bags. This dual system was awkward and sometimes confusing; but by that depth there were no potsherds, and the flakes were so rare each could be recorded precisely as artifacts, which were measured from datum as well as from the surface and keyed to the natural stratum. Although several walls did collapse, especially during heavy rains (Figure 3), all walls were profiled periodically as excavation proceeded, so very few profile sections went unrecorded.

Stratigraphic Units

Determination of the stratigraphy presented some problems. Forte Marechal Luz demonstrated the rule that stratigraphy in shellmound sites is very complex, and minor strata are difficult to follow during excavation; however, it was possible to identify and to number clearly marked major strata from the surface down as excavation proceeded, and to relate the artifacts and features uncovered to these natural strata.

Although the average depth was about 3 m, excavation reached a maximum depth below surface of approximately 6.5 m. Twenty-three major distinct natural strata were designated in the main trench. Minor subdivisions appearing on the profiles are in most cases self-explanatory and need not be described in detail.

For greater ease and conciseness of description these 23 strata will be grouped into seven "occupation zones," numbered with Roman numerals from bottom to top (Table 1). The term "occupation zones" was chosen to differentiate these units from physical strata and to suggest that there are identifiable cultural differences in mode of deposition as well as in artifact content throughout the span of occupation of the site. The term "occupation zone" does not imply occupation by new people; all evidence suggests that the same people continued to occupy the site, and there is no evidence for prolonged abandonment between occupation zones. If

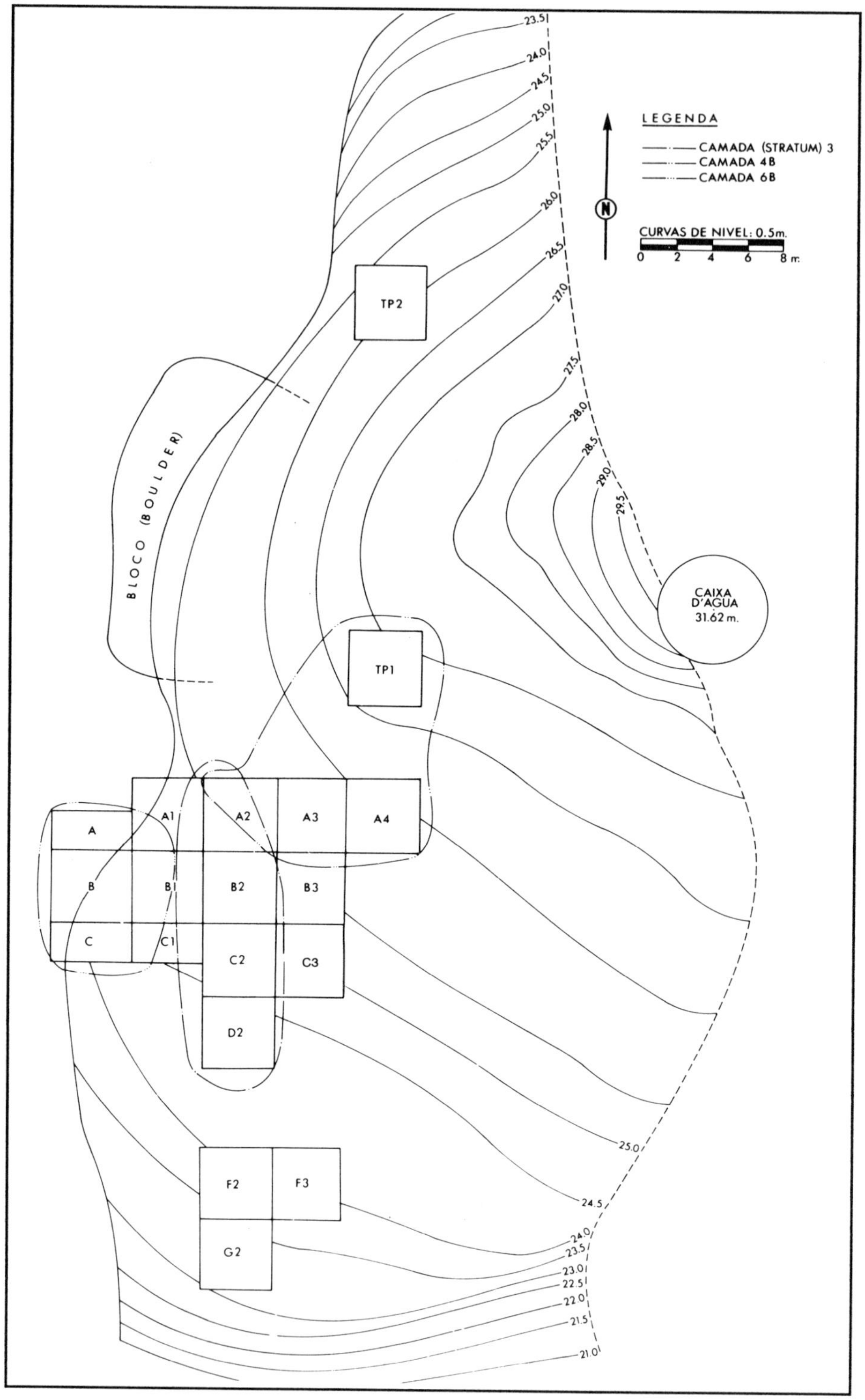

Figure 2. Contour map of Forte Marechal Luz sambaqui, showing excavation units.

every zone had yielded sufficient artifacts, or if the distinctive characteristics of each zone were confirmed at other sites in the region, the occupation zones could have been named as cultural phases. My criteria for believing that cultural stratigraphy has been separated from physical stratification are apparent changes in artifact types, fabrication techniques, and methods of disposal of the dead. Description of the zones will proceed

Table 1. Outline of Stratigraphy by Occupational Zones

Occupation Zone I	Dark brown residual clay; shell in upper portion.
Occupation Zone II	Strata 10 through 21: light color; stratified *berbigão* shell (*Anomalocardia brasiliana*), other clams, some oyster; with lenses of sand and univalues in lower levels. The "original" sambaqui.
Occupation Zone III	Stratum 9: light grey color; finely stratified *berbigão* shell, fish bone, and mussel; diffused with charcoal fragments. Deposit formed by redepositing and levelling the top of the original sambaqui.
Occupation Zone IV	Strata 6, 7, and 8: dark-brown color; *berbigão* shell and extensive deposits of oyster. Much of stratum 6 contains the lowermost deposit of dark organic material resulting from intensive occupation, and stratum 6 contains the earliest burials. Complex of unfired clay cooking basins in stratum 7. Earliest intentionally flaked stone.
Stratum 6B	Shell and dark organic matter. Ceremonial burial area intruded from strata 5 and 6.
Occupation Zone V	Stratum 5: heavy black organic deposit with lesser percentage of shells, still mainly *berbigão*, but including large oyster, mussel, and broken univalve columellas. Physically similar to strata 4B and 3, except pottery lacking. Mammal bone, especially comminuted fragments, common.
Occupation Zone VI	Stratum 4B: black organic deposit; shell; extensive areas of grey ash. Ceremonial burials covered with fired-rock cairns. First pottery.
Occupation Zone VII	Strata 1 through 4: dark organic deposits alternating with clean shell; much mussel and large fish bone in stratum 2, much fish bone in stratum 4. Pottery abundant. Most productive artifact-bearing occupation zone.

by means of recapitulation of the development of the stratigraphy at the site (see Figure 6).

Three quite level (wave-cut?) benches cut into the bedrock can be seen on the south wall profile of the main trench (squares B, B1, and B2: Figure 4). The base of the lower bench is about 19 m above sea level, and the middle bench about 20 m; while the upper wide bench appears to level off at about 23 m, although it is covered with talus boulders that have rolled down the steep hillside, the base of which intersects the water tank shown on the site map (Figure 2). Alluvial deposits were not present on the two lower benches, and excavations did not penetrate below the shell deposits on the upper bench. Possibly there are more benches, which appear to be beach notches, at lower elevations; but the slope was covered with disturbed shell deposits which we did not excavate.

Residual clay deposits, formed from natural weathering of the quartzdiorite bedrock, were found underlying the shell deposits in all places where bedrock was relatively level, or wherever depressions retarded downslope movement. Water seeping along the surface of the bedrock had often filled air spaces in the adjacent shell deposits with clay. Some large whalebone and stone artifacts were found with clay and some shell covering that portion of the piece closest to bedrock, while the remainder of the artifact was enclosed in its original shell matrix, a situation showing that the clay was later deposited around the artifacts.

The middle bedrock bench (about 20 m above sea level) was covered with a relatively thick deposit of residual clay which yielded shell only in the upper 10 cm; thus apparently this particular clay deposit had begun to form before the local deposition of shell by man. Several crude stone artifacts were found in the clay beneath the portion of the deposit containing some shells. The entire clay and shell stratum resting on the middle bench has been considered to be a separate earliest occupation, Occupation Zone I. A date of 4290 yr B.P. was obtained on a bone artifact from Zone I (see Table 2). Although possible, there was no evidence

Figure 3. Photograph of sambaqui near end of excavation showing slumping problem.

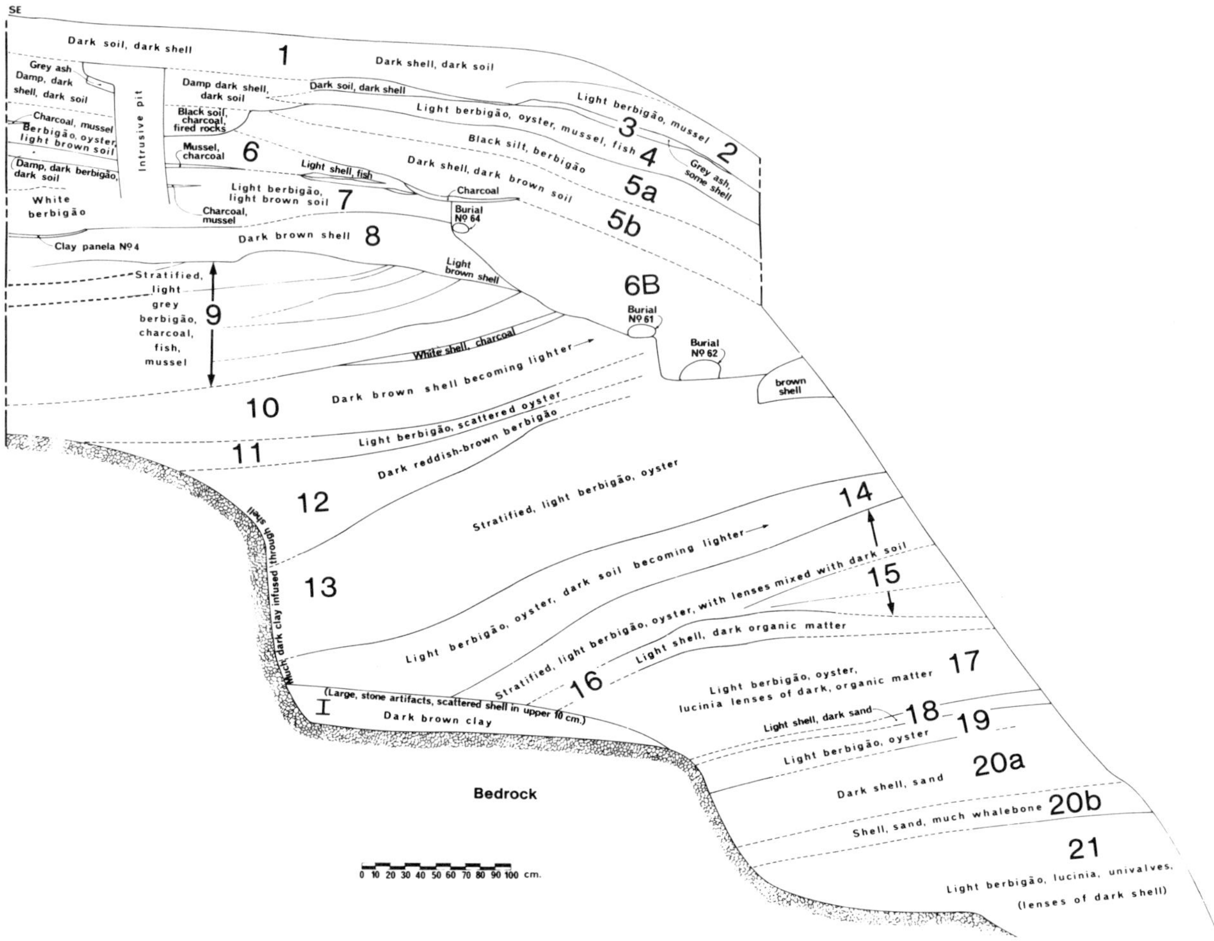

Figure 4. Profile of south wall of main trench, Forte Marechal Luz, Squares B, B1 & B2.

found that these people dumped shells over the bank in front of them, thereby initiating the original sambaqui. As occupation appears to have commenced prior to the deposition of any shell, the level bench 20 m above present sea level may have been a temporary campsite and lookout for hunters and fishermen before shellfish were collected locally.

More likely the first shell refuse deposits accumulated through the dumping activities of the next occupants, who lived on the hill slope just above the present beach level. As reconstructed in Figure 6b, the shellmound gradually expanded up the hillside as the occupants of the hillside dumped their shells over the bank toward the beach. Thus, unlike the typical sambaqui built on level ground, where the level area on top of the shellmound decreases as the shell deposits accumulate, the level living area expanded through time at Forte Marechal Luz. The reconstruction is partially conjectural because the main part of the original sambaqui had been almost completely removed for road cover by the time our excavations began. Because only a portion of the beach side of the original mound could be tested and so few artifacts were recovered, the strata from 10 to 21, the surviving portion of the main mound, were included within one occupation zone, II. In fact, people may have lived on the hilltop and carried the shells to form the original sambaqui. In the area of the main trench, the physical matrix of all of these strata appear to be quite similar. Rather thick layers of *berbigão* (a small clam), oyster, and other clam shells are differentiated from each other mainly by differences in the amount of reddish brown color produced by secondary iron staining. A thick lens of gastropod shells, indicating a temporary change of diet, was encountered near the bottom of the lowest stratum included in Occupation Zone II. Charcoal from this stratum (stratum 21) dated 3660 ± yr B.P. (see Table 2).

The steep dip of the deposits in the upper portion of Occupation Zone II gradually lessened with depth. Thus the back side or leeward slope of the original sambaqui gradually steepened upward and formed a depression between the mound and the hillside as the

Table 2. List of Radiocarbon Dates Arranged Stratigraphically

Description of Sample	Field No.	Lab No.	Date
Charcoal from fireplace associated with burials intruded from stratum 1 into stratum 5. Dates either final occupation of site (Zone VII), or post-occupational cemetery.	I	M-1203	620 ± 10 yr B.P.; A.D. 1340
Charcoal from stratum 1, from 10–30 cm below surface. Dates last occupation of site (Occupation Zone VII).	U	M-1200	640 ± 100 yr B.P.; A.D. 1320
Charcoal from ceremonial fireplace over Burial no. 5 in stratum 4B (Occupation Zone VI). Provides date for first occurrence of pottery.	F	M-1202	880 ± 100 yr B.P.; A.D. 1070
Charcoal from a fireplace associated with several burials in preceramic stratum 6B, probably relating to Occupation Zone V.	S	M-1205	850 ± 100 yr B.P.; A.D. 1110
Carbonized seeds *(Myrcia)* found in a large lens in stratum 6A. Dates burials at end of Occupation Zone IV.	K	M-1024	1110 ± 100 yr B.P.; A.D. 860
Charcoal found adjacent to unfired clay basin features in stratum 7. Dates Occupation Zone IV.	AA	M-1206	1440 ± 100 yr B.P.; A.D. 520
Charcoal from burned whale vertebra used as a brazier (artifact no. 901) from stratum 10. Dates end of Occupation Zone II.	V	M-1207	2060 ± 120 yr B.P.; 100 B.C.
Charcoal from stratum 21. Dates early part of Occupation Zone II.	Y	M-1208	3660 ± 130 yr B.P.; 1770 B.C.
Collagen extracted from whale bula artifact from Occupation Zone I.	Artifact No. 879	Birm-704	4290 ± 130 yr B.P.; 2340 B.C.

The Michigan solid-carbon dates were assayed gratis in 1962/63 with the cooperation of James B. Griffin and the University of Michigan Memorial Phoenix Project under the direction of H.R. Crane.

center of the sambaqui grew taller. Charcoal from a whale vertebra used as a brazier found in the uppermost stratum (10) in Occupation Zone II, dated 2060 yr B.P. (see Table 2); thus Occupation II lasted for about 1600 years.

The height of the original sambaqui can only be estimated from the dip of Occupation Zone II deposits and the contour of the base of the mound. The mound was probably once about 10 m higher than the level of the middle bedrock bench, so the top would have been about 29 m above present sea level. Pottery associated with the final occupation of Forte Marechal Luz was found far below in undisturbed shell deposits which fronted on the present beach a few meters above sea level; thus the shoreward extent of the original sambaqui had undoubtedly been continually truncated by wave action as all occupants dumped their shell over the bank onto the beach. Thus the slope of repose of the front of the shell mound was probably continually steepened by periodic storm waves sweeping up the beach.

The next stratum to be deposited, stratum 9, was composed of many thin lenses of shell and fish remains mixed with chunks of charcoal, apparently laid down as foreset beds building eastward from the main mound (Figure 6c). This stratum, although evidently not a separate occupation, was designated Occupation Zone III; it appears to have been intentionally redeposited in order to level the entire area from the top of the main shellmound to the upper bedrock bench. A visit to another large sambaqui being excavated for road cover led to consideration of an alternative interpretation, that formation of the peculiar charcoal-strewn matrix (which completely lacked fire-cracked rocks) reflected a cultural difference in the method of food preparation and/or refuse disposal. The entire visible deposit of this other large sambaqui was composed of the same peculiar type of thinly stratified matrix, and at first I found it difficult to believe that a whole shellmound would have been redeposited by aboriginal people. On the other hand it would be unreasonable to conclude that in this one instance of Occupation Zone III a different population with a different cultural heritage, living a few km away, camped at Forte Marechal Luz during the interval between deposition of the original shellmound and later reoccupation by people having a much richer non-perishable material culture. After due consideration I had to conclude that in some cases aboriginal people had moved large amounts of shell refuse in order to shape a mound. Tiburtius (1966) describes the process of intentionally shaping the Conquista sambaqui, located about 35 km southwest of Forte Marechal Luz. The archaeologist wishing to excavate primary cultural contexts must be aware of this potential problem, because original artifact contexts will obviously be absent in such deposits, and the people who moved the deposits also had the opportunity to collect any useful artifacts they encountered. Perhaps this is the reason why so few artifacts were found in Occupation Zone III. Despite the abundance of charcoal, none of it was localized in a fireplace; and therefore a radiocarbon sample was not collected. Thus Occupation Zone III is the only undated occupation zone in the site; but as it evidently was not a real living area, but rather a case of deliberate redeposition, an actual occupation would not be dated. After levelling the top in Zone II, an *in situ* cooking area was formed in the depression between the back of the mound and the hillside; this sheltered location in stratum 7 probably was intentional, in order to form a windbreak between the top of the mound and the hillside.

As the deposits of stratum 9 had been placed so as to fill the area between the rocky hillside and the earlier sambaqui, the deposits immediately overlying stratum 9 were fairly level for the first time since Occupation I. In fact, there was a striking disconformity in matrix as well as angle of deposition between stratum 9 and the overlying stratum 8. For the first time, people were able to expand their living area from the levelled top of the shellmound onto the highest bedrock bench (Figure 6d). At first they utilized the niches around the talus boulders on the bench as convenient windbreaks, but living debris accumulated fairly rapidly; so strata 8, 7, and 6, which now covered most of the talus boulders, were grouped together and designated Occupation Zone IV.

Much of the uppermost stratum of Occupation Zone IV, stratum 6, contains the lowermost deposits of dark organic matter, the result of intensive occupation; but stratum 6 is still physically more similar to the underlying strata, 7 and 8, composed largely of oyster shells, than to stratum 5 above. In some places, however, such as on the south wall profile of square B1, the line between stratum 5 and stratum 6 is barely discernible. The earliest burials at the site were enclosed within stratum 6 (see Figure 5, east wall of profile, square A2). A sample of charred *Myrcia* seeds over Burial no. 6 in stratum 6 yielded a radiocarbon date of 1100 yr B.P. (see Table 2). A date of 1440 yr B.P. on a clay basin feature in stratum 7 (see Table 2) indicates that the graves were dug in a temporarily unoccupied portion of the site. A set of unfired clay cooking basins was encountered in stratum 7 and on top of stratum 8. Strata 7 and 8 in the northern part of the site, as shown by test pits 1 and 2, were composed almost entirely of oyster shells. Occupation IV was the initial occupation in this outlying northern portion of the site on the uppermost bedrock bench.

The areally restricted stratum first encountered below stratum 6, and therefore designated 6B, was not deposited by occupation. This homogeneous layer consists of redeposited material disturbed by intrusive excavations for a cemetery. Evidently some graves were intruded from stratum 6, but most were dug by the occupants of stratum 5 (Occupation Zone V). As stratum 6B was a cemetery and not an occupation zone, it will be discussed as a separate entity (not part of an occupation zone) throughout the report. A total of 38 burials were encountered in this stratum within a restricted area of 18 m^2. As can be seen on the south wall profile (Figure 4), excavations for this burial area intruded through several older strata, including large portions of strata 6, 7, and 8. Charcoal from a ceremonial fireplace built over several burials provides a date of 850 yr B.P. (see Table 2) for this stratum 6B cemetery.

Although there is clear evidence for cultural continuity, significant innovations in artifact types and changes in burial complexes were the major reasons for separating Occupation Zones IV, V, VI, and VII. As a group, the three most recent occupation zones are characterized by the deposition of layers of shell mixed with very dark organic matter which contain relatively abundant cultural remains. Refuse deposition of this kind is not due to natural soil formation, which would indicate periodic abandonment; but rather this type of deposition indicates relatively intensive and prolonged occupation, with gradual accumulation of organic refuse in the living areas. Layers of almost clean shell are intercolated between the strata characterized by dark organic deposits containing much less shell. These pure shell strata (refuse layers) typically thicken in the downslope direction. Thus the main living area for the last three occupations was centered on the uppermost nearly level bench between the seaward slope of the earlier shellmound and the steep rock face rising abruptly upward to the east (Figure 6 d, e).

Stratum 5 ranges from a black to a dark-brown organic deposit, which is often physically similar to overlying strata, as well as to underlying stratum 6, except that oysters are less common and mammal bone more common than previously, so the contents of stratum 5 were designated as a separate occupation zone, Zone V. The previously discussed date of 850 yr B.P. on a burial intruded from Zone V is the only radiocarbon date applicable to this occupation zone.

Evidently stratum 4B (Figure 5) was deposited very soon after stratum 5, to judge by the slightly overlapping radiocarbon date of 880 yr B.P. from stratum 4B (see Table 2). As stratum 4B was mainly a burial area of limited extent, it was located after stratum 5 had been designated: the capital letter B is meant to show that this

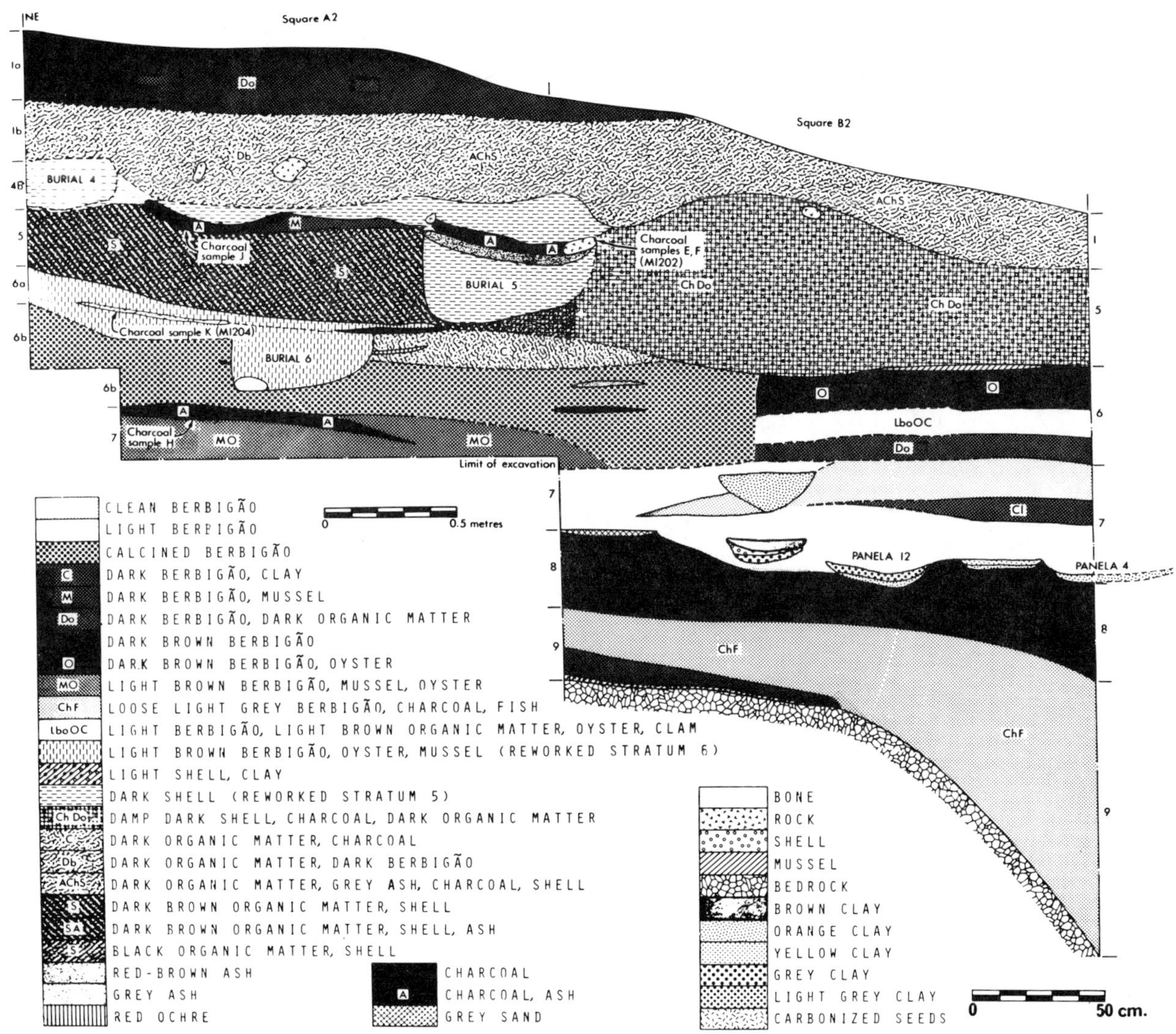

Figure 5. East wall profile, Squares A2–B2, Forte Marechal Luz.

stratum is distinct and not part of stratum 4, in the same way that stratum 6B is not part of stratum 6. Stratum 4B was designated Occupation Zone VI because it contains the first ceramics and because small rock cairns now mark the graves for the first time. The center of occupation was near the upslope (eastern) edges of the site, and in fact portions of this stratum directly overlie large talus boulders on the uppermost bench. As will be seen, the fact that many other artifact types continue across the line which separates the preceramic from ceramic strata suggests that the cultural changes brought with the introduction of pottery do not mean that a totally different and culturally advanced population immigrated into the area. All other technological traditions were retained after innovation of the tradition of making ceramics and a slightly changed burial complex.

A decompositional cycle of clean shell (stratum 4) covered by dark ashy organic matter mixed with shell (stratum 3) initiated the final prehistoric occupation zone at the site, Occupation VII. The last occupants, who deposited strata 1 through 4, left behind abundant potsherds. Ceramics were especially numerous in the lower portion of stratum 1b. This black organic layer represents the last intensive occupation of this portion of the site. The densest concentration of potsherds was found in stratum 1b in squares C2 and D2. The people dumped their refuse, composed of light-colored *berbigão* (a small clam) and mussel shells, towards the beach, forming stratum 2. The surficial stratum, 1a, contained relatively more shell and less pottery than stratum 1b. Stratum 1a was also the only stratum at the site that exhibited evidence for natural soil-

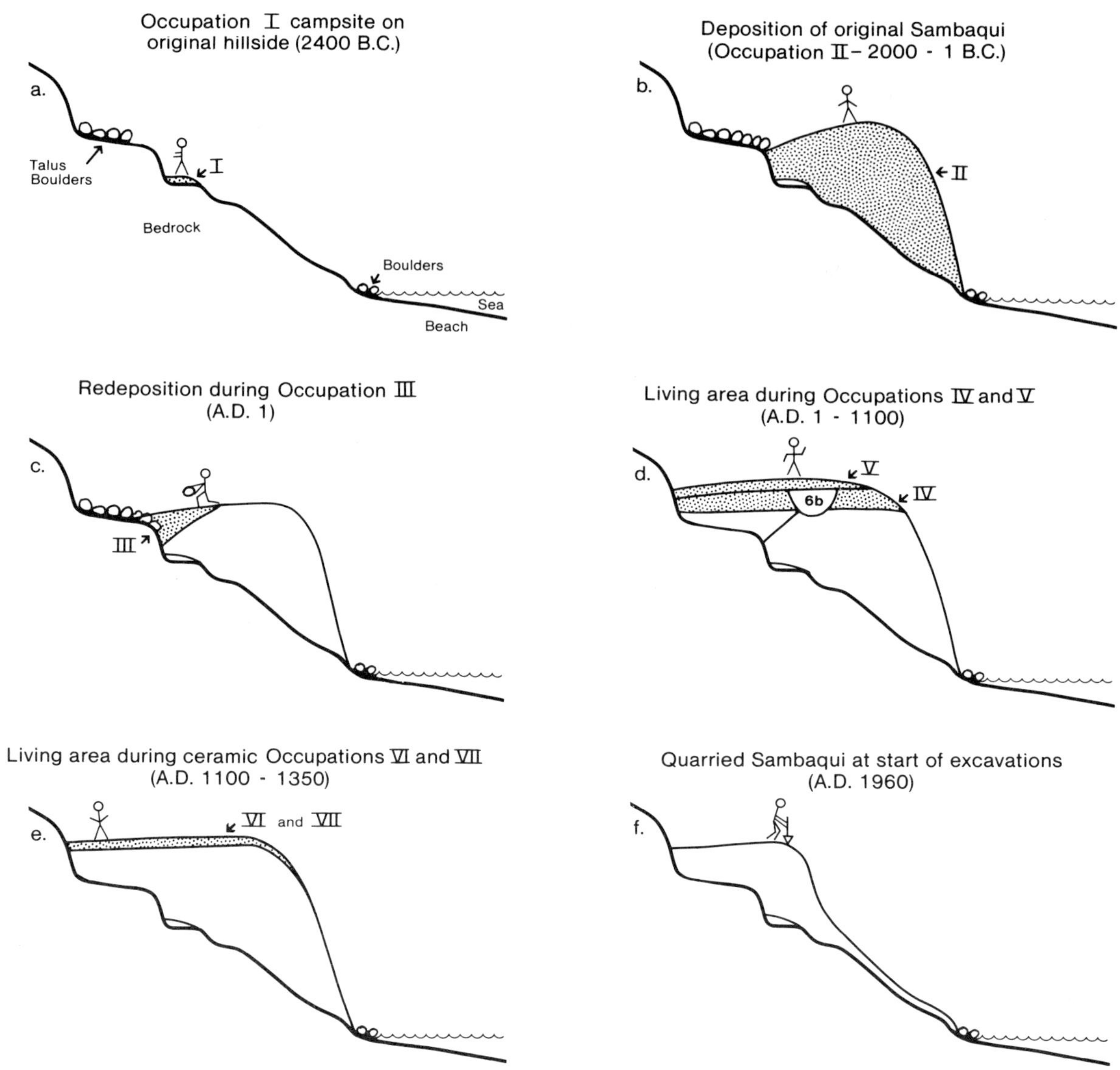

Figure 6. Sketches showing changing slope of hillside through time.

building processes, which suggests that the only prolonged period of abandonment of the site was after deposition of stratum 1a. A secondary burial complex was found in the southern squares, apparently incorporated within Occupation Zone VII; although possibly some interments were made soon after abandonment of the living area. One radiocarbon date of 640 yr B.P. (see Table 2) refers to the last primary occupation (undisturbed by burial pits) in stratum 1 in test pit 1, where substrata were not noted. A charcoal sample from a fireplace over a burial intruded from stratum 1 into stratum 5 assayed 620 yr B.P. (see Table 2).

Post-occupational disturbance of the site such as by recent gardeners utilizing the rich organic humus, was evidently minimal until the road building crews arrived to quarry the shell, followed by the archaeologists. The only post-occupational artifacts discovered were modern, associated with activities at the fort. At the time of my last visit in 1970 the site had been essentially completely destroyed by continued removal of shell for roadwork.

Chapter 2
The Raw and the Cooked at Forte Marechal Luz

What were the people eating and how did they prepare food at the Forte Marechal Luz sambaqui? The most obvious food resource is of course represented by the shells, which seem so overwhelmingly abundant that the first impression is that the people were simply shellfish collectors. But this would be a gross oversimplification. Unlike most sambaquis, shells accumulated quite slowly for more than three millennia at Forte Marechal Luz, a fact that suggests the population supported itself by other foods as well as shellfish. In fact, fish bones were very abundant throughout the shell deposits, and identification of the remains by Tania Andrade Lima has demonstrated the significance of fish in the diet. Crab claws and sea urchin spines commonly occurred in small lenses. Bird bones and sea-mammal bones were numerous, and land-mammal bones were also frequently encountered. Although few vegetal remains were preserved in the humid climate, plant foods may be assumed to have been very important; and there is some indirect evidence for horticulture in the latest occupation. The people of Forte Marechal Luz evidently had a much more varied diet than is commonly assumed for sambaqui-dwellers.

The shellfish were likely simply collected by hand and carried to the site in baskets. Most other animal foods required more effort to procure. It is assumed that most bones, whether or not made into artifacts, represent creatures that were hunted and eaten. However, there is no evidence that these people possessed a technology which would have allowed them to hunt whales or maneater sharks at sea. Rather, they probably scavenged beached animals, retrieving valuable oil and useful bones and teeth, plus the meat if the helpless animal were found alive or recently dead. The people may have been able to kill smaller sea mammals, especially seals when caught basking on shore; and they may occasionally have ventured out in canoes after sea turtles (*Chelonia* sp.), whose scutes occur in the shellmound. If they could be found fresh, sharks were undoubtedly eaten, but all that was preserved were vertebrae and teeth. Most teeth and vertebrae of two genera of sharks, *Carcharodon*, the white shark or maneater, and *Carcharias*, the sand shark, were probably collected on the beach as useful objects. A discussion of shark teeth will be found under the description of teeth artifacts. All teeth of the two shark families were identified by Professor Antenor Leitão de Carvalho at the Museu Nacional. Families cannot be distinguished by vertebrae.

Despite all the evidence for a varied diet, the tremendous amount of shell clearly indicates that gathering shellfish undoubtedly constituted a major food staple. As indicated earlier, the location of the site on a shallow sandy bay but not far from mangrove swamps and rocky cliffs facing the open ocean provided several types of microenvironments for different species of shellfish. For that reason, perhaps, there is little evidence of overexploitation of any species.

Among the shellfish species which fluctuated in frequency in the shellmound, oysters never died out completely, although both species were abundant in stratum 18 near the beginning of Occupation Zone II and again in the late preceramic occupation zones IV and V, about 2500 years later. Only periodic relative abundance certainly suggests the possibility of periodic overexploitation; but the microenvironment may also have been altered drastically on occasion, leading to population depletion by natural means. The giant oyster (*Ostrea arborea*), which lives on the roots of mangrove trees, although fairly common in Occupation Zone V, was always much rarer than small oyster shells.

For the small oysters, unfortunately it was not possible for Professor Arnaldo C. dos Santos Coelho of the Museu Nacional, who made all the shellfish identifications, to distinguish the species; so it is not known whether the people were collecting *Ostrea brasiliana* from the side of the open channel leading into the harbor of São Francisco do Sul, or the rock oyster (*Ostrea stentina*) from the rocky cliffs on the east side of the Morro do João Dias. Probably both species were utilized. The fact that oyster shells are present on the modern beach suggests that *Ostrea brasiliana* was readily available on the edges of the bay. Also, the lack of small pieces of rock which normally adhere to the shell when the rock oyster is collected (Hurt 1974:8) supports the conclusion that *O. brasiliana* was the oyster species most often exploited.

Likewise, it was not possible to distinguish the common rock mussel (*Mytilus perna*) from the mud mussel (*Modiolus brasiliensis*) which lives on the muddy floor of mangrove swamps, because none of these fragile shells were found that had not been totally fragmented and compacted by the weight of overburden in the shellmound. Mussels were particularly common in Occupation Zones IV, V, and VII; but were present in all zones.

The most common shell in all occupation zones was the ubiquitous small clam (*Anomalocardia brasiliana,*) which is locally known as *berbigão*. It lives in shallow sandy or silty bays. Presumably it was to be found in the sandy bay in front of the site; however, only one shell was seen on the modern beach, perhaps because the beach is now very actively aggrading, or perhaps because the species has been overexploited in modern times.

The other bivalves found in the shellmound were of much less importance, although the cockle, *Trachychardium muricatum*, and *Phacoides pectinatus*, a large shell which looks like a pecten, were fairly commonly found in Occupation Zones II, IV, and VII. *Phacoides* was also present in Zones V and VI. Both species live in the open waters of sandy bays. Cockles are not found on the modern beach, but one *Phacoides* was seen. Interestingly, three massive *Anadara brasiliana* shells were found on the modern beach, but only one was encountered in the sambaqui, in Occupation Zone IV. One *Anadara ovalis* and several *Anadara notabilis* were found in Occupation Zone II. *Anadara* are native to mangrove swamps, which are now within easy walking distance from the site.

Among the shells found on the modern beach were *Dosinia concentrica, Iphigenia brasiliensis*, and the large *Mactrella alata*; but all of these species were rare in the sambaqui, and apparently not eaten. Only one hinged pair of *Dosinia* shells was found in the sambaqui, in Occupation Zone V. From Occupation Zone VII were recovered three heavy *Mactrella* shells and six *Iphigenia* shells, two of which were worked artifacts. *Tivela fulminata*, found on the modern beach, occurred only in Occupation Zone VII.

Seven rare species identified from the sambaqui were not found on the modern beach. These include *Arca umbonata*, several of which were found in the lower strata of Occupation Zone II; one *Sangninolaria operculata* from Zone II and another from Zone IV; two *Chione pubera* shells from Zone V; one *Macoma constricta* from Zone III and another from Zone VII; a *Mactra fragilis* from Zone VI; a *Tagelus plebeius* from Zone V and two from Zone VII; and an *Amiantis purpurata* from Zone V and another from Zone VII.

Barnea costata was present in Occupation Zones V, VI, and VII. The barnacle, a crustacean, was especially abundant in Occupation Zone V. As their distinctive white shells are invariably crushed, undoubtedly many barnacles were present but not noted in other layers. Teredo worm tubes were also occasionally seen, especially in Occupation Zones III, IV, and V; while lenses of sea urchin spines were noted in Occupation Zones IV and VII. Even isolated sand dollars, another echinoderm, were noted in Occupation Zones V and VII, although probably they were not eaten but simply picked up by some child because of their interesting shape.

The keyhole limpet (*Diodara patagonica*) and three marine gastropods (*Conus* sp., *Oliva* sp., and *Olivancillaria brasiliensis)* were evidently brought in for use as jewelry, although two unaltered shells of the latter species were found isolated in Occupation Zone VII. The large *Lintricula auricularia* were also apparently desirable as grave goods, but two unaltered specimens were found in Occupation Zone VII and another in Zone V. The only other marine gastropod associated with a burial, in Occupation Zone VI, is the thick-walled *Strombus pugilis*, which evidently was also eaten, as they were found occasionally in all occupation zones except Zone I; and frequently were found broken probably to extract the meat. Broken shells and columellas of *Thais haemastoma* were also frequently found in Occupation Zones IV, V, and VII. Equally common were the shells of *Corithium atratum* and *Bulla striata* in Occupation Zones III, IV, V, and VII, even though the latter species lives in the open sea. *Polinices* sp., including some identifiable as *P. hepaticus*, were frequently encountered in Occupation Zones IV, V, and VII. Shells of both *Semicassis granulatum* and *Cymatium parthenopeum* were found in Occupation Zones IV through VII. The latter large shell was frequently found broken, sometimes with adhering oyster shells. Rare species include *Murex senegalensis* in Occupation Zones II, III, IV, and VII; *Nassa vibex* in Occupation Zones III, V, VI, and VII; *Hastula cinerea* in Occupation Zones V and VI; *Neritinea virginea* in Occupation Zones IV and VII; and examples of both *Astraea latispina* and *Cyprae zebra* in Occupation Zone VII.

Since no shells of terrestrial gastropods were found with patterned breaks, perhaps none were eaten, although such an assumption may be incorrect because the animal will emerge if placed near a fire. Isolated examples of *Strophocheilus oblongus*, the giant land snail, were found in Occupation Zones V and VI, in addition to several shells found on the surface of the site. Two *Odontostomus paulistus* shells were found in Occupation Zone V. Several small *Subulina octona* shells came from the surface, and there was a series of 22 *Subulina* shells found with Burial no. 15 in stratum 6B. It is interesting to note that *Subulina* is now a universal genus, usually thought to have been introduced to America with the arrival of Europeans; but their presence strung on a necklace about A.D. 1100 indicates that somehow they first came to America before Columbus.

Crabs were undoubtedly a much more important source of food than all the gastropods combined, but their remains are not as obvious when excavating. However, crab pincers were frequently encountered, often in lenses. They were particularly abundant in Occupation Zones II, IV, and VII; common in Zone V, and present in Zone III.

When identifications were being made, the Museu Nacional in Rio de Janeiro lacked comparative collections of fish remains. However, Tania Andrade Lima subsequently assembled a comparative collection from the State of Rio de Janeiro, and undertook the onerous task of identifying thousands of fish bones from 25-year-old level bags, many of which had been damaged by insects, which often had rendered many labels illegible. Because she lacked sufficient time to do an in-depth analysis, she considered her report to be superficial. Nevertheless, the report clearly shows the significance of fish in the diet in all but Occupation I, where bone did not preserve as well. It must be realized that there was always a tendency for the excavator to pick out large fish bones and ignore small ones, although this situation was partly counterbalanced by collecting more assiduously from the screen. No special attempt was made to recover otoliths, although some otoliths were identified, and others, as well as fish scales, were undoubtedly collected in some of the unanalysed "soil" samples (Table 3).

With the exception of Occupation I and the burial strata 4B and 6B, fish were always significant; although, as usual, the greatest abundance was in the final occupation zone, VII. The minimum number of individuals were determinable only for *Lagocephalus laevigatus* (70), *Chaetodipterus faber* (28), and *Caranx* (6). All other figures are estimates. Arbitrarily, to avoid overcounting, ten vertebrae from one level bag were counted as one individual, and other bones of the same species from the same bag were counted as the same individual. About half of the total number of fish bones collected were not identifiable, and do not appear on the chart. Interestingly, a mullet (*Mugil brasiliensis*) called *tainha*, now caught in abundance in the winter by local *caboclos* using dugout canoes to spread nets, were not identified in the collection. Their absence suggests the possibility of summer occupation; however, in conjunction with the paucity of *Anadara* shells, which live only in mangroves,

Table 3. Distribution of Unaltered Fish Bones by Occupation Zone. (Also see separate descriptions of bone and teeth artifacts.)

Specimen	II	III	IV	V	VI	VII
Bagre (catfish) (probably marine) (*Bagre* sp.)	2	1	1	2		4
Corcoroca (grunt) (*Haemulon* sp.)				1		2
Enchova (bluefish) (*Pomatomus saltratrix)*				1		2
Corvina (croaker) *(Micropogon furnieri)*				4		2
Baiacu (smooth puffer)(*Lagocephalus laevigatus)*		4	2	15	2	48
Baiacu de espinha (porcupine fish) (*Diodon hystrix)*						9
Sargo (porgy) (*Archosargus probatocephalus)*	2	2	1	6		29
Marimbá (porgy) *(Diplodus argenteus)*	1			3		11
Pargo (red porgy) *(Pagrus pagrus)*						1
Pirangiça (sea chub) (*Kyphosus sectratrix)*				1		
Enxada (spadefish) *(Chaetodipterus faber)*			4	8	2	20
Xaréu (jack) *(Caranx sp.)*				4		2
Espada (snakefish) *(Trichiuris sp.)*		1	1	5		14
Sea bass (Serranidae)	1			1		6
Unidentified teleost fish	12	8	6	26	3	110
Eagle ray *(Aetobatus sp.)*			1	4	1	9
Cow-nosed ray*(Rhinoptera)* or eagle ray *(Myliobatis)*	4	3	5	12	1	45
Unidentified ray	3	1	1	3		11
Unidentified shark vertebrae	8	6	5	20	3	71

the absence of *tainha*, who strain mangrove mud for edible plant and animal material, suggests the possibility that mangrove trees were not present near the site at the time of prehistoric occupation. Alternatively, perhaps this method of netting schools of mullet was unknown in prehistoric times; or perhaps many of the unidentified bones are from *tainha*. The most common fish, the smooth puffer (*Lagocephalus laevigatus*), attains a length of two feet, and is regularly caught on hook and line. The sheepshead porgy (*Archosargus probatocephalus*), and the Atlantic spadefish *(Chaetodipterus faber)*, are both easily caught on a hook baited with crabs or shrimps, their favorite food (Migdalski and Fichter 1976). In fact, most identifiable fish were medium-sized, shallow-water species which could have been obtained with bone fish hooks or fish arrow bipoints. Fish hooks first appeared in the shellmound in Occupation Zone V, at the same time these three species became more common. Bipoints made from bird bone, probably used as fish arrows, appeared in Occupation Zone IV, and both continued until the shellmound was finally abandoned. Only two possible net sinkers were found, in Occupation Zones IV and V. There is no material evidence for fishing techniques earlier, unless the ray spine projectile points, which first appear in Occupation Zone II and continue throughout (except in Occupation Zone IV), were used for taking fish. Nets and traps made of perishable materials may also have been important means for procuring fish. Probably the catfish *(Bagre)* lived in the bay; however, it is possible that some were caught in cylindrical fish traps placed in the small streams on the island.

Land mammals were hunted at inland localities, presumably by stalking or trapping, although little trace of the material equipment used, likely mainly of wood and fiber, has preserved in the humid climate. The mammal-bone projectile points may have been used to hunt land mammals. Land-mammal bones were never common. Only potentially identifiable unworked bones of mammals, birds, and reptiles were kept; but it was noted that comminuted fragments were not often encountered, and were noted as being abundant only in Occupation Zone V. Evidently mammal bones were too valuable for tool manufacture to pound up for soup. Land mammal bones, including those made into artifacts, were identified by the paleontologist, Professor Carlos de Paula Couto, then at the Museu Nacional. The distribution table indicates quite accurately the gradual increase in abundance of land mammals and birds through time. It is clear that these people were never able to eat meat regularly, however. One noteable absence from the faunal list at Forte Marechal Luz is the domestic dog. Evidently dogs were not kept, either as hunting aids, as pets, or for food. Very little of the material equipment used to hunt birds and land mammals was preserved. Most may have been trapped, and most projectiles were probably tipped with wooden points. None of the bird bones were identified specifically because of lack of comparative collections at the Museu Nacional (Table 4).

Professor Llewellyn Ivor Price of the Divisão de

Table 4. Distribution of Mammal, Reptile, and Bird Bones and Artifacts by Occupation Zone.

SPECIMEN	I	II	III	IV	V	VI	VII
Peccary *(Tayassu albirastris)*	1				11	2	25
Tapir *(Tapirus terrestris)*			2		2	1	8
Deer *(Hispardalis* sp.)				5	5		5
Deer *(Mazama* sp.)				2			
Jaguar *(Jaguar tirica)*							1
Puma *(Felis concolor)*						1	
Raccoon *(Procyon cancrivorus)*				1			
Capivara *(Hydrochoerus hydrochaeris)*							2
Paca *(Cuniculus paca)*			1	3	4	2	15
Agouti *(Dasyprocta agouti)*			1				
Unidentified land mammal		12	6	7	36	4	65
Seal				1			
Whale	5	16	3	30	26	3	29
Dolphin				1	1		3
Unidentified sea mammal		20	12	20	33	4	55
Turtle scutes *(Hydromedusa* sp.)				1			1
Sea turtle scutes *(Chelonia* sp.)		4		2	13		16
Unidentified turtle					5		9
Caiman *(Caiman latirostris)*				1			
Unidentified bird		8	6	19	19	7	49

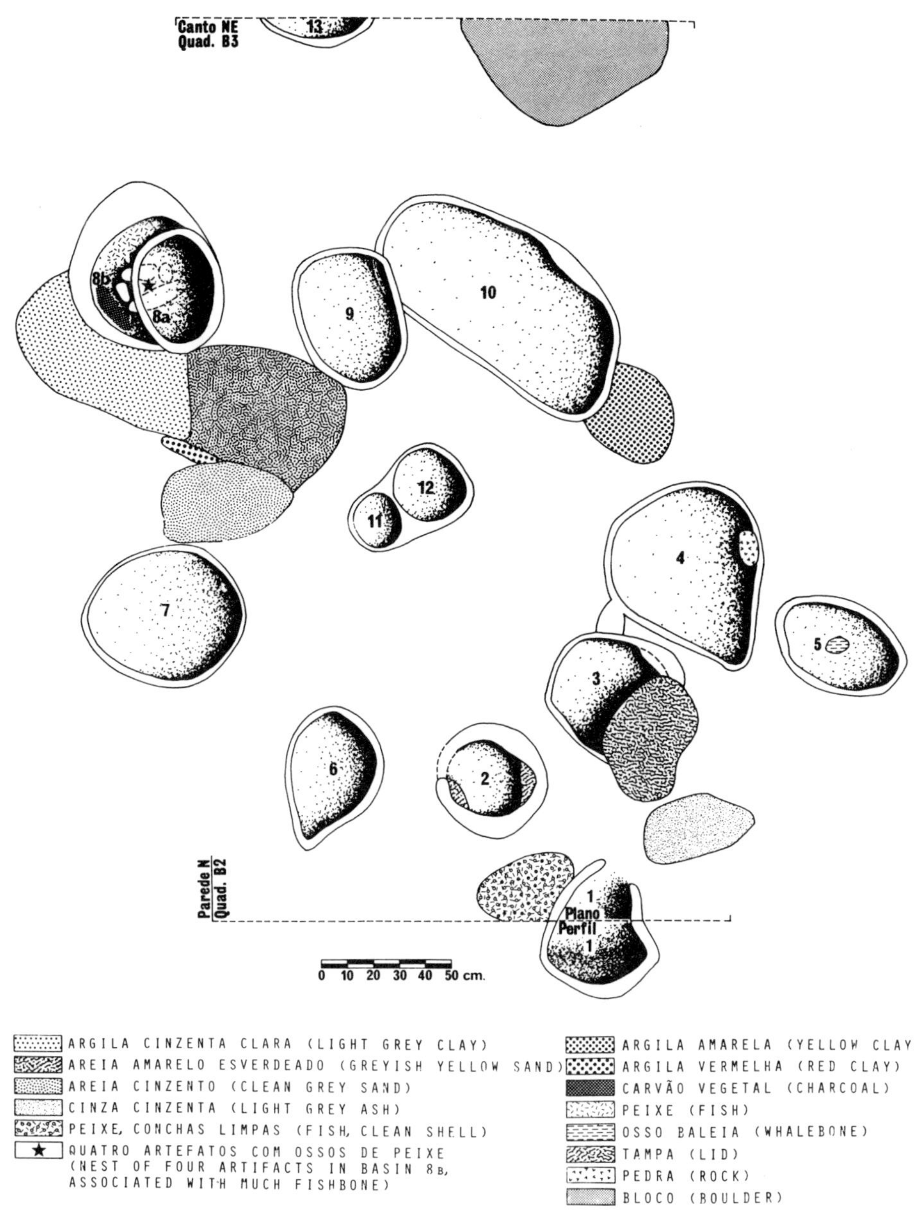

Figure 7. Kitchen area with unfired clay basins, Forte Marechal Luz.

Figure 8. Photo of unfired clay basins and lid.

Geologia e Paleontologia at Praia Vermelha in Rio de Janeiro was able to distinguish some of the seal, whale, and dolphin bones among the collection of bones of sea mammals. He also identified a caiman tooth, and distinguished the genera of land and sea turtles from the scutes. Professor Price noted that the sea turtles were all medium to small in size, except for one large individual. A few unidentified turtle scutes were later found in the fishbone level bags.

Plant foods must have formed a substantial part of the diet, but the only identifiable remains preserved were the occasionally charred seeds and shells of palms (Palmeira); zapotes (Sapotaceae); Mirtaceae, a family that includes delicious guayaba fruit; *Cabrolea*?

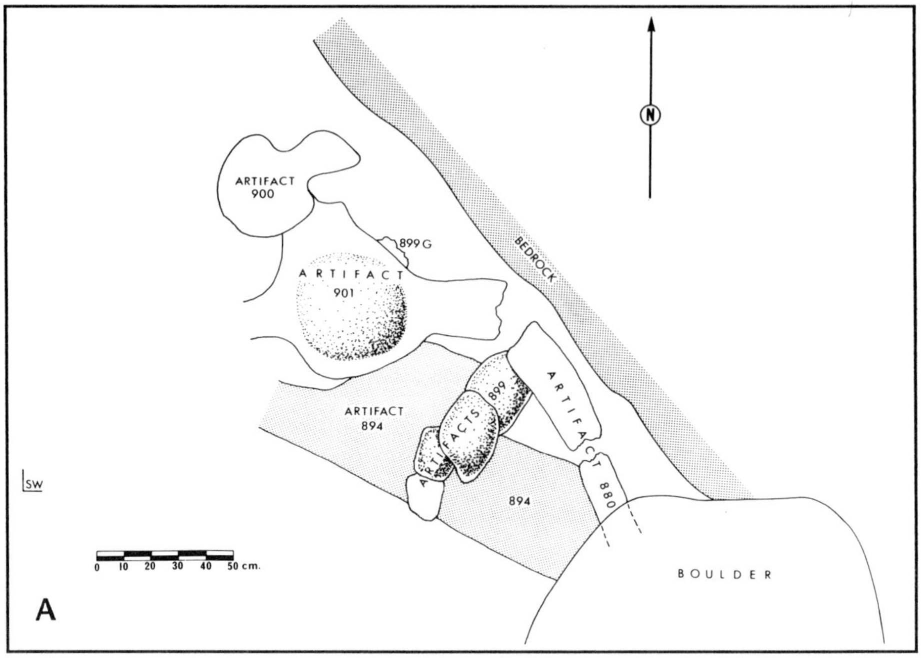

Figure 9. A) Whale-vertebra brazier (artifact 901) overlying calcined oyster shell (899 G) and partly covered by whale vertebra (900). Six giant oyster shells (899 A–F) placed in a line beneath a whale rib (880) and over a large whalebone chopping block (894). **B)** Whale-vertebra brazier (artifact 901) (trowel pointing to burned surface). Magnetic north arrow lying on oyster shell.

(Meliaceae); and Miristicaceae, a family that includes trees yielding nuts used for medicine. Palm seeds and shells were present in Occupation Zone IV, common in Zone V, and abundant in Zone VII, while *Virola,* a Miristicaceae, was present in Zones V and VII. Identifications, many tentative, were made by Profa. Graziela Maciel Barroso at the Jardim Botanico in Rio de Janeiro.

The only indirect evidence for domesticated plant foods are three heavily worn and striated bitted implements found in Occupation Zone VII, which were identified as probable digging stick blades for poking holes in the ground for seeds or cuttings. The only possible way to tell what these people living in a rain forest area may have been planting would be to try to collect pollen or phytoliths from the garden areas, if they could be located.

The fact that kitchen hearths had almost invariably been disturbed after a meal was prepared means that it is very difficult to describe cooking practices. The best preserved kitchen area encountered in the excavations was a set of unfired clay basins (*panelas*) found in stratum 7, Occupation Zone IV (Figures 5, 7, 8), and dated to A.D. 520. The basins themselves will be described in the chapter on clay artifacts. The 13 basins covered all of squares B2 and B3, and extended into neighboring squares. They were modelled into bowls of various sizes, but averaging about 50 cm in diameter and 15 cm in depth, from clay mixed with ash and possibly hematite, although the reddish orange color may have been caused by heating. The deepest basin, no. 1, about 25 cm in depth, was fashioned into a vessel with constricted neck. Three of the basins retained remnants of modelled clay lids which had been removed to obtain the cooked contents.

The kitchen area associated with the group of unfired clay basins extends to the north in square A2 north of basin no. 7, where a 16-cm-thick layer of red clay incorporating some burned and unburned fish bones was uncovered. The red clay area was about 60 cm in diameter; and both beneath and above this solid clay mass were a great many mussels, mixed with charcoal fragments. Mussels and charcoal were also spread more thickly over almost the entire 2-m square (A2); while half of square A1 to the west contained a mixture of ash, charcoal, burned shell, and burned and unburned fish bones beneath a layer of grey ash and clay.

This special kitchen area in Occupation Zone IV also extended to the south of the group of unfired clay basins. Basin no. 5 contained some brown ash mixed with mussel shell and burned whalebone fragments which were strewn out onto the lip of the basin. South of basin no. 5 was an extensive area strewn with a 5-cm-thick layer of charcoal, grey ash, and unburned fish bone (in square C2).

The two extensive areas of charcoal, ash, mussel shell, and fish bones strewn out to the north and south of the roughly circular group of unfired clay basins, plus concentrations of unburned fish bones next to basin no. 1 and inside basin no. 8 certainly indicate strongly that the main foods being cooked were fish and mussels. The presence of fire-cracked rocks in the area suggests that red-hot stones were placed in the basins filled with water, fish, mussels, and perhaps vegetable foods in order to boil soup. This conclusion is supported by the fact that very little shell beneath all these features was calcined, which would have occurred if the extensive ash and charcoal areas represented large bonfires made on the spot. The presence of burned whalebone in basin no. 5 seems strange. Perhaps it was being processed to extract oil.

This most elaborate kitchen exposed at Forte Marechal Luz poses the question as to why such an apparently efficient innovation as unfired clay basins was not employed at other times. The kitchen was constructed 500 years before the innovation of fired ceramics allowed easy boiling in portable pots. Perhaps the entire kitchen area was used only once, to prepare food for an important communal feast; whereas normally each family prepared its own meals over a simple small fire. Several meters away from this elaborate kitchen, still in stratum 7 of Occupation Zone IV, was a thin grey ash layer covering much fish bone. An area of mixed dark organic matter, shell, and large fish bones was located to one side, and beyond that was a concentration of small fish bones. Apparently this feature was the remains of a more modest feast.

Charcoal braziers made of whale vertebrae were a distinctive feature of Forte Marechal Luz culinary equipment. One occurred in Occupation Zone IV directly beneath the small kitchen area just described, but probably not in direct association with that feature. The uppermost face of the whale-vertebra centrum had been burned out, forming a shallow basin. Nearby was a piece of a large whalebone with a burned area of the same diameter as the burned area on the vertebra. Evidently the centrum of the large vertebra had been used as a charcoal brazier, while the other piece of whalebone was placed over it as a lid.

Late in Occupation Zone II (in stratum 10) a similar burned whalebone vertebra had been utilized. The charcoal remaining in the basin of this whalebone brazier yielded a radiocarbon date of 100 B.C. Near the brazier was a large flat whalebone which had evidently been used as a chopping block, with several giant oyster shells lying across it in a line as if they had been used as dishes (Figures 9 a, b). Another oyster shell, completely calcined, lay beneath the whalebone brazier; evidently this shell had been used as a container to cook something on the brazier. Two adjacent whalebones with burned areas may have been used as lids. Another possibility is that whalebone was being processed to extract oil.

In another part of stratum 10 a light grey ash lens about 35 cm in diameter was encountered. This is one of the few cases where the shell (clam and oyster) beneath the fire was calcined, showing that the fireplace had not been disturbed later. Actually, such a small fire that obviously had burned out may not have been for cooking, but simply for heating during a cold night. In many areas, some quite extensive, shells had been calcined to considerable depths, and there was no evidence of a fire on top. Either cooking fires or burial ceremonial fires must have caused the calcination. As will be seen in the chapter on disposition of the dead, materials from fires were usually moved after they burned out. Knowledge of such extreme disturbance by the actual occupants of the site makes it very difficult to interpret activity areas, although we were very fortunate to encounter the relatively well preserved area of unfired clay basins in Occupation Zone IV.

A badly disturbed feature, likely a cooking area, was exposed in stratum 4B (Occupation Zone VI). A very soft ash bed full of burned shell was found beneath a layer of mottled dark organic matter and charcoal, obviously mixed up. Over this was a compact layer of brown-grey ash and unburned shell. Obviously the shell had not been in the fire, so the layer below must have been mixed and compacted after the fire went out, probably by walking on it. The feature is not large enough to be a house floor, however; and in fact we never found any clear evidence for any kind of structure, although given the rainy climate the people must certainly have built shelters on the site. Perhaps the disturbance by living activities on the shellmound obliterated any evidence for perishable structures. Alternatively, it is possible that most houses were on the hilltop, which had been badly disturbed by gardening and modern structures.

In summary, one may conjecture that food was prepared by a variety of means at Forte Marechal Luz. The relative abundance of the so-called *"quebra-cocos,"* stones with pecked depressions used to crack nuts, in all occupation zones commencing with the earliest, Zone 1, suggests that much time was spent processing vegetable foods before cooking. For the cooking of food, it is evident that during Occupations IV, VI and VII food was boiled either in unfired clay basins or later in portable fired clay pots. Possibly some of the disturbed areas with layers of ash, charcoal, and fired rocks had been baking ovens; and of course the six charcoal braziers in Occupation Zones II and IV could have been used among other purposes for broiling fish or meat. We may conclude that the occupants of Forte Marechal Luz occupied a very productive ecosystem, and thereby enjoyed a varied menu indeed, especially during the later occupations as new technological innovations were added to their repertoire.

Chapter 3
The Methodology of Artifact Analysis

A total of 958 artifacts (plus five altered human bones) were recovered at Forte Marechal Luz, including 35 objects exhibiting no evidence of use but considered to have been artifacts because they were found directly associated with other artifacts or with burials. The artifacts include 430 pieces of bone (plus the five altered human bones which will be described in the chapter on the disposition of the dead), 137 teeth (not counting 61 shark teeth with no visible evidence of use), 96 shells, 17 fired and unfired clay objects (not including approximately 10,000 potsherds), and 278 stone artifacts (not counting 295 unused flakes, plus 12 unworked siltstone concretions that must have been carried up to the site for some purpose).

The oldest Occupation Zone I yielded 20 artifacts (five bone and 15 stone artifacts); while Occupation Zone II, the old sambaqui, yielded 62 artifacts (27 bone, seven shell, 27 stone, and one clay); and Occupation Zone III only 18 artifacts (nine bone, three shell, and six stone). The artifact yield increased significantly in Occupation Zone IV, with 104 artifacts (42 bone, four teeth, three shell, 42 stone, and 13 clay). The preceramic intrusive burial stratum 6B contained 161 artifacts (40 bone, six teeth, 64 shell, and 51 stone); while the last preceramic occupation, Zone V, yielded 135 artifacts (82 bone, 24 teeth, and 29 stone) plus 19 unused flakes. The early ceramic burial stratum 4B, Occupation Zone VI, yielded 77 artifacts (24 bone, 23 teeth, three shell, and 27 stone) plus 20 unused flakes and a few dozen potsherds. The final occupation, Zone VII, was the most productive, yielding a total of 306 artifacts (173 bone, 71 teeth, 14 shell, 45 stone, and three clay) plus 251 unused flakes and approximately 10,000 potsherds. The final occupation zone was the only zone that yielded a preponderance of bone relative to stone artifacts, although stone had not decreased in importance. In addition to the above listed artifacts, another 75 artifacts lacking provenience, found on the surface or screened from slumped walls, will be included in the artifact analyses.

As indicated in the foreword, most artifacts found at the site, excluding of course the pottery, had not been intentionally shaped. Although 50% of the stone artifacts (not counting unclassifiable fragments) had been deliberately shaped, only 22% of the worked bone, 15% of the teeth, and 5% of the shell artifacts had been intentionally shaped. All the other artifacts exhibiting evidence of human alteration had simply been used in their natural form without being shaped.

North American archaeologists are trained to establish typologies based on form and assumed function, so an assemblage with few recognizable formal types presents a methodological problem requiring a different approach. As the primary objective of an archaeological classification system should be to retrieve as much cultural information as possible from the artifact analysis, it follows that it is not very useful to force a typology based on form onto artifacts which have natural shapes. Not only were few artifacts intentionally shaped, but only a minor percentage of these had been shaped for specific functions, such as the series of bone fish hooks. Therefore, there is no value in attempting a functional classification either, as most artifacts were used for many purposes, depending on what was needed at the moment. Even deliberately shaped artifacts, such as the stone implements with bits, were evidently used for various purposes (e.g., chopping, adzing, wedging, digging) even though the basic form was the same. A formal typology and a functional terminology become useful only occasionally when dealing with a few of the artifacts from Forte Marechal Luz. The models employed in order to derive a useful descriptive classification system for all the artifacts is based upon the concept of identifying the particular manufacturing techniques used for altering natural materials. Each of these basic techniques for shaping natural materials was discovered by prehistoric experimenters who observed how each kind of useful natural material is altered when it is used. For example, cutting meat off an animal skeleton will occasionally cause accidental cuts and incisions on the bone. An observant person can experiment and discover that if the bone is intentionally incised more deeply in certain places, the bone can be shaped into a useful implement for a specific function. Bone can also be flaked, chopped, scraped, ground, and punctured. All of these technological processes can be identified on bones which are simply altered unintentionally by using the bone for some general purpose of the moment. The same techniques also can be identified on deliberately shaped bone implements. Thus both stages of development of each technological process are available to the analyst describing the artifacts. Each of the identified processes of working bone is a fabrication technique which was developed by the fabricator after observing the marks of accidental alteration. The technique was then applied to the fabrication of deliberately shaped objects. Undoubtedly this innovative process did not occur completely independently at Forte Marechal Luz. Most, if not all, innovations were the result of diffusion when contact was made with other human groups.

Discrete technological traditions of working stone are also evident at Forte Marechal Luz. Stone can be pecked, flaked, ground, and drilled. The first two technological processes were innovated by experimental man long before coming to America, and the tradition of grinding (termed polishing in Portuguese) has a long history in coastal Brazil; however, the technique of drilling, although frequently applied to perforating teeth, was not found on stone artifacts at Forte Marechal Luz.

For some reason, perhaps because pecking and grinding proved to be such efficient techniques for working locally available stones, the ancient technological tradition of percussion flaking was at a very primitive stage of development at Forte Marechal Luz. When the technique was reinvented about a millennium ago, the knappers evidently were not aware of any special techniques for preparing a platform in order to be able to remove bifacial thinning flakes. Instead they removed flakes from alternate faces of the bifacially flaked object using a naturally thick flat edge of a tabular diabase nodule as a platform from which to strike right-angled blows. Thus there are no overlapping flakes from alternate faces as in true bifacial flaking. If a natural platform was not available the knappers tried to square an irregular edge simply by battering it with forceful right-angled blows with a hammerstone. Such a battering technique rarely removed flakes but it did accomplish successfully what was intended, to straighten and square the side of the axe preform, which was meant to be as rectangular as possible. Such a primitive flaking technique is really more like the process of pecking, which powders the stone, than true percussion flaking. The even more complex technological tradition of pressure flaking was never innovated at Forte Marechal Luz. The late inception of intentional flaking of stone, and the lack of technical expertise in platform preparation suggest that local people reinvented the process of knapping, perhaps by observing finished implements made by knappers from neighboring cultural groups.

It can be deduced from the above discussion that there are many specific identifiable manufacturing techniques which compose the basic technological tradition of stone flaking. Whenever specific manufacturing techniques applied to any material can be identified, it is useful to conceive of them as discrete technological traditions. The archaeologist can then note how many of these technological traditions are present at the site being described, and how many significant traditions are notably absent. Beyond that it is useful to be able to trace their distributions in space and time in order to unravel the history of technological development and thereby infer the culture history of any region. As the study is concerned with manufacturing techniques, the majority of photographs are intended to show the marks of alteration rather than artifact shape. Because fabrication marks are more evident on bone, most photographs will be of bone artifacts. Very few stone artifacts are illustrated, but most of them are very similar to illustrated artifacts in available reports on other sambaquis. When relevant, the dimensions of artifacts will be given in millimeters in the order of length, width, and thickness. As a scale was not included in most photographs, the actual length in millimeters of one example will be given in the caption.

Chapter 4
Stone Artifacts

Forte Marechal Luz yielded many stone artifacts in all occupation zones (Table 5); although, as with bone artifacts, they were most abundant in the upper zones (the late preceramic Occupations IV and V plus stratum 6B, and the ceramic Occupations VI and VII). Before describing the artifacts, the three main processes of alteration of stone to produce artifacts must be defined. Except when assemblages of closely associated artifacts are described together, the relatively few intentionally shaped artifacts will be described separately from the naturally shaped pieces simply altered by use. Stone was unintentionally altered by the same processes that were only occasionally put to use to shape an artifact intentionally. The three processes of alteration involved in shaping stone at Forte Marechal Luz were, in chronological order of appearance at the site: *pecking*, *grinding*, and finally *percussion flaking*, the latter employed in nearly all cases to shape an artifact preparatory to grinding it.

Pecking is a slow, laborious process of carefully striking one stone ("hammerstone") against the stone to be shaped. During this process the hammerstone may also acquire characteristic shape because of the way it is held in the hand. In many cases it is difficult to tell for sure whether such shaping was intentional; i.e., whether the person intended to create a certain shape. Pecking is a slow process because only a minute fragment of stone can be removed with each blow. In fact, the detritus of manufacture is stone dust. Almost any kind of rock can be shaped by pecking, including the various metamorphic rock types which compose the coastal littoral of Brazil. Occasionally when a stone is struck too forcefully, a rough flake will be removed; but this is not intentional, and one can see that it is not because of the pecked surface remaining on the flake platform. The same is true when a ground stone object, like an axe, is struck too hard or is used too roughly on hard material. Normally it is easy to tell that flakes were removed accidentally by hard use after the object was finished by pecking or grinding because the flakes removed by accident will retain a much battered platform and one or more pecked or ground surfaces. Usually these accidental flakes are very thick relative to their overall size, and have especially thick platforms, because they were struck off the parent body with a direct blow at nearly a right angle. Unfortunately, however, the flaked axe "preforms," to be discussed below, were intentionally flaked with direct rather than angled percussion blows, so therefore some of the flakes removed from "preforms" also have battered platforms. It is imperative that the archaeologist attempt to differentiate very carefully between accidental flaking and percussion flaking that is intended to shape an object. Considerable unintentional flaking occurred in all occupation zones at Forte Marechal Luz because most of the pecked and ground stone objects were designed for heavy use.

Grinding is a much more efficient method for shaping stone, although it has its limitations. The stone to be ground cannot be a course-grained rock like granite, because crystals would pop out when the granite is pushed against the grinding platform. In other words, the locally available metamorphic rocks were really not suitable for grinding. Fortunately, however, there is a dyke of homogeneous medium-grained diabase outcropping on the beach less than 200 m from the site. Also, conveniently, several diabase boulders on the beach served as handy and most effective axe-grinding platforms (Figure 10), much more efficient than using portable grinding slabs, as had to be done at some sites (e.g., Tiburtius and Leprovost 1953, plates 39 and 40). The boulders contain several deep U-shaped grooves for grinding the edges and adjacent faces of axes by

Table 5. Stone Artifacts and Unused Flakes by Occupation Zone.

	I	II	III	IV	6B	V	VI	VII	No Prov.
Thermally fractured quartz pebbles								2	1
Flake from quartz pebble				1					
Natural quartz fragments		1				2		3	
Thermally fractured vein quartz				4		5			1
Flaked quartz fragments							7		
Flaked granite pebble						1			
Scorched stones (carbon stain)								2	
Use battered/flaked pebbles	2	1		2				1	
Unworked pebbles associated with burials/artifacts				1	1			1	
Polished pebbles		1	1	1	2			24	7
Facetted pebbles		1			1	1		1	
Pebbles with pecked and/or battered ends	1	6	1	5	12	6	3	29	2
Pebbles with ground faces	2	1				4	4	2	1
Same with pigment stain				1					
Angular slabs with ground faces				1	1	2	1		2
Pebbles with hematite stain (pestle)				1	5			2	
Pebbles with pecked depressions and ends	3	2		8	8	1	1	13	1
Same with pigment or food stain				2	3			1	
Striated/facetted hematite pebbles		5	2	4	4	1		1	4
Other worked hematite pebbles		2	1	1	1		1		
Iron ore pebble with depression					1				
Pecked spherical pebbles							1	1	
Spherical pebbles with hematite stain					2				
Pecked discoidal pebbles					3			3	
Pecked discoidal pebbles with hematite					2				
Axe fragment with hematite stain					1				
Pebbles with pecked depressions	6	2		2	1		1		
Other striated pebbles		1				1		3	
Pebble with pecked groove	1								
Pebble with pecked bilateral notches				1					
Pebble with flaked bilateral notches						1			
Cylindrical ground "plummet"									1
Stones with longitudinally ground facets				1				3	
Pebble with ground conical tip						1			
Tabular fragments flaked along flat side				2					
Bitted implements ground on flakes				1	1	1		7	1
Bitted implements ground on flaked "preforms"						5	3	15	7
Fragments of same						5	4	11	4
Flaked preforms without grinding						1		7	1
Pebbles with flaked then ground bits								2	1
Bitted implements ground on unflaked pebbles		2	1	3				1	
Bitted implement fragments lacking flaking					1			6	
Unworked siltstone concretions				4		3		5	
Reused preform flakes								1	
Reused unintentional flakes		2			1		1	3	2
Unused flakes removed from preforms						10	14	168	
Unused flakes spalled from artifacts	1	1		2	1	9	6	83	
Totals	16	28	6	48	52	60	47	401	36

Total No. of stone artifacts and flakes: 694 (plus 12 unused concretions)

Figure 10. Axe-grinding boulder on the beach west of the sambaqui.

pushing the piece to be shaped back and forth in the groove. Several adjacent shallow oval concavities were formed where the axe bits were sharpened. Only excurvate faces could be created on the incurvate depressions on the boulders, however. Apparently the earliest axes at Forte Marechal Luz were simply beach-worn pebbles of approximately the proper shape and size, most of which were finished by grinding them on a grooved boulder. Finishing the ground surface by polishing (such as with fine sand and a liquid) is rare at Forte Marechal Luz; only a few axe bits were really polished, perhaps more by use than by intention. The term *polido* in Portuguese refers to grinding as well as polishing.

Intentional *percussion flaking* appeared late at the Forte Marechal Luz site. Increased demand for axes must have created a local shortage of diabase beach pebbles of suitable shape and size; and knowledge of fabricating axe "preforms" by means of percussion flaking first became apparent during Occupation Zone IV. The idea of making bifacial preforms was probably introduced by diffusion, although the crude technique of direct battering to form a platform appears to have been a local innovation. By Occupation Zone V, about A.D. 1000, the basic techniques of percussion flaking, involving removal of a spall from a boulder and then shaping the spall, or more frequently simply selecting a weathered slab of diabase of about the right size and shaping it by direct percussion blows, had become common knowledge among the residents of the sambaqui of Forte Marechal Luz. These people fashioned their own preforms right on the sambaqui and then took properly shaped preforms down to the boulders on the beach for finishing by grinding. The problem of a shortage of axe blanks had been overcome, and it now took less time to make a functional axe from a flaked preform. Other than axe preforms, very few artifacts were shaped by percussion flaking at Forte Marechal Luz, and few of the sharp-edged reduction flakes show any evidence of use.

Natural Stones Altered by Use

Several important categories of stone artifacts were simply natural rocks and minerals altered by use, as distinguished from intentional shaping. The most numerous category of such tools are the hammerstones, which range from those with a protruding surface exhibiting a few pecking marks, and occasionally the scar of an accidentally removed flake, to objects with a thick discoidal form, caused by revolving the pebble in the hand as the pecking job on another object proceeded. Hammerstones will be dealt with last because they grade into the category of intentionally shaped artifacts.

On a normal open site many natural stones would be discarded by the archaeologist as having no clear evidence of use, but their mere presence in a shellmound indicates cultural selection for some purpose. As people must have carried them to the site for some reason, it should be the job of the archaeologist to try to determine what that purpose was; or at the least, to try to identify any evidence of use.

Quartz Artifacts

At Forte Marechal Luz the most readily accessible category of stones which required no intentional alteration to put the stones to useful purposes are the angular vein quartz fragments which could be obtained from the underlying metamorphic bedrock. Hypothetically it is possible that a few of these quartz fragments slid or rolled onto the shellmound from the slope behind, but the slope is well stabilized by vegetation and we found no evidence of a natural slide onto the parts of the shellmound we excavated. Thus it is almost certain that the scattered vein quartz fragments were intentionally brought to the site. A few water-worn quartz pebbles were also brought up from the beach. Many beach pebbles were also evidently carried up for use in fireplaces, either for cooking or ceremonial fires. Such fire-cracked rocks were not individually counted, although they were examined for possible use before being discarded.

Three quartz beach pebbles appear to have been used after they were thermally fractured, perhaps in a hearth. Two of these were associated with Burial no. 7 in Occupation VII. The high spots on one or more of the straight broken faces appear to exhibit wear polish; and the sharp pointed end of one fragment is considerably worn, as if it had been used as a reamer or punch. The sharp edges on both fragments also appear to be "nibbled" (i.e., tiny flakes were removed by use, most likely from scraping). On one piece, two of the sharp edges which intersect at a steep acute angle with the flat water-worn surface also appear to retain a dark organic coating, as some of the scraped material is still adhering to the scraper. The third piece, screened from a slumped wall, has much more irregular fire-broken edges; but two sharp projecting angles appear to have been worn by use. One fragment of a water-worn quartz pebble, from Occupation IV, is a flake, probably removed accidentally from a hammerstone. One short straight portion of the broken edge appears to be smoothed by use as a scraper; while two tiny flakes have been removed from another edge, perhaps by strong downward pressure exerted while scraping.

Two angular quartz fragments which evidently had been on the beach or in flowing water for a short time have projecting "noses" at one end which appear to have been used. A piece of quartz crystal from Occupation VII has several broken edges, all of which are quite sharp and unworn except for the projecting nose, which is worn and has use-flakes removed from it. The other smaller pebble from Occupation II has a rounded nose which appears to have been used as a reamer or drill; but unfortunately the amount of wear is about the same on all surfaces, so it is not possible to prove human alteration.

Ten of 22 remaining angular fragments of vein quartz have a pinkish tinge which appears to be the result of oxidation by heating. As a group, these fragments are much larger (ranging from 48 x 35 x 19 mm to 33 x 17 x 11 mm) than the uncolored natural fragments, which range from 20 x 12 x 8 mm to 28 x 17 x 10 mm. All are too small to have served as hearth stones, but it does seem possible that particularly large vein quartz chunks had been intentionally fractured by heating them in fires. The largest and sturdiest fragments could then be selected for use as scrapers, knives, gravers, and punches. That such a technique may indeed have been used to obtain useful sharp-edged pieces of quartz is supported by the fact that all of these fragments came from Occupation Zones IV (4 specimens) and V (5 specimens), (plus one from a slumped wall), at the time when there was a sudden increase in the number of bone objects that were scraped into shape.

Two smaller quartz fragments from Occupation Zone V have projecting tips which are differentially worn and "nibbled" as if they had been used for graving, grooving, or gouging. One similar fragment from Occupation VII has a tiny flake removed from the edge adjacent to a pointed tip. It could have been removed by using the object for reaming a hole. The only other quartz fragment from Occupation VII is so coarse grained that it is impossible to be sure that one excurving edge, which appears to be more worn than other edges, was indeed used.

A group of seven quartz fragments found near each other in Occupation VI are evidently the result of crude percussion flaking. Although this was a case of intentional percussion flaking, there is no evidence that the intent was to remove a specific flake; rather, it appears that someone simply bashed a larger piece of quartz, which was evidently resting on another rock, and picked out what he wanted from the resulting pile of fragments, which range in size between 19 x 19 x 7 mm and 39 x 23 x 14 mm. A little wear and use nibbling appears at the projecting portions of one flat face on one specimen. Evidently this wear occurred before the piece was shattered. Two much-battered straight edges suggest that the object was struck several times before it shattered. The battering is very like that which occurs with bipolar flaking (i.e., holding the piece to be flaked on an anvil while the piece is struck). However, the points of impact are not directly opposing each other, so there is no definite evidence that the true bipolar technique was used. Another fragment is a flake retaining both a negative and a positive bulb beneath a much-battered platform. Apparently when a large quartz artifact such as a scraper plane became disfunctional, it was bashed to pieces by throwing a stone at it; and the useful fragments were salvaged.

Utilized Pebbles and Slabs

Two large stones that were probably part of someone's kitchen equipment were found together in a slumped wall from Occupation Zone VII. One is a tabular piece of angular granite (193 x 58 x 38 mm) with a 100-mm-long and 25-mm-wide dark scorched stain on its flattest surface. Evidently some very hot object had been laid on it. That object could well have been a flattened oval fire-cracked syenite pebble (99 x 67 x 22 mm) with two parallel scorch streaks, one near each end of one face. The pebble had been fire-cracked, presumably in a hearth. Possibly both objects served as stands for cooking vessels, or possibly for firing a small pot.

A natural spall from a water-worn gneiss pebble exhibits a broad excurvate edge which appears to have been worn and "nibbled" by use as a scraper. This spall and a water-rounded pebble of vein quartz both came from Occupation Zone VII. Near one end of the ovoid quartz pebble (43 x 37 x 21 mm) is an iron stain which may have been caused by grinding or mixing hematite. It was found associated with Burial no. 57 and with a water-worn diabase pebble exhibiting wear polish on a flat face.

Water-worn flattened ovoid pebbles with polished faces were very frequently encountered, particularly in the ceramic levels, where many of them were likely used for polishing pots before firing. Two shiny black jasper pebbles with highly polished surfaces but no obvious evidence of use were found in preceramic stratum 6B associated with Burials no. 11 and no. 16. These are the kind of beautiful rare stone that was likely carried with a person as a charm or "medicine." But polished pebbles of locally available stones were also placed with burials. Ovoid diabase pebbles with both faces highly polished were associated with Burials no. 7 and 19 in stratum 1. Burial no. 19, at least, was identified as an adult woman. Perhaps these stones were the woman's favorite pot polishers. But another diabase pebble polished on one face, and a flattened oval quartz pebble highly polished on both faces were found associated with Burial no. 53, a male, so there is no consistent correlation between the presumed potters and polished stones.

Diabase pebbles have a naturally rough surface which becomes so rough when weathered that it looks and feels like sandstone. It is therefore quite likely that many of these pebbles with smoothed or polished surfaces were whetstones and files which had served for grinding and filing bone and wooden objects, but were discarded when the working surfaces became too smooth. One fire-cracked fragment of a diabase pebble from Occupation VII exhibits a pattern of ground and polished facets around its periphery, as well as smoothed faces. Three facets are present on the edge, one with a clear pattern of parallel grinding striations. This is the kind of pattern that one might suppose would result from use of the object as a file.

Five polished stones from preceramic levels obviously were not pot polishers. The high spots on both faces of a tabular diabase pebble (54 x 29 x 7 mm) from Occupation IV have been polished. A flattened ovoid pebble (68 x 42 x 29 mm) with a similar wear pattern came from Occupation II. A small (33 x 29 x 14 mm) pebble of unidentified material from Occupation III has been polished on one face and all around the adjacent edge. One irregularly round diabase pebble (69 x 63 x 49 mm) from Occupation II exhibits a polished facet on one face and use pecking near both ends of the other face. A similar pecked end is present on a diabase pebble with quadrangular cross-section (74 x 19 x 13 mm) from a slumped wall. The raised portions of one of the four faces were smoothed by use. Another pebble (80 x 60 x 42 mm) from an unknown preceramic occupation exhibits use polish on both faces and evidence of pecking near the center of one face as well as on the extremities. Evidently pebbles that were not pot polishers can be distinguished by the occasional pecked area (used as a hammerstone), and/or a pattern of smoothing the high spots only, rather than a completely polished surface. One large (91 x 59 x 52 mm) diabase pebble from Occupation II exhibited the pattern of smoothed high spots on one face; but the large concavity on the other face appeared to have been deliberately roughened, suggesting that overly smooth surfaces were occasionally resharpened by pecking with a hammerstone.

In addition to those already described, 21 polishing stones came from Occupation VII, while six more found while screening slumped sections probably came from these ceramic levels. Unless otherwise mentioned, they are diabase pebbles (20 examples). One has been used so much that there are highly polished facets on both faces. At the other end of the range are five pebbles with one face which is only slightly smoother than the other surfaces. Five specimens (one quartz) have one face that is highly polished. Two granite pebbles have been smoothed on both faces, but especially on one face. Five specimens (including one quartzite and one unidentified stone) have two highly polished faces, while the polishing is less evident on two harder quartz pebbles. Diabase pebbles may also exhibit only slight polish on two (five examples) or three faces (two examples). All of these flattened ovoid pebbles appear to exhibit a consistent pattern of polish only on slightly excurvate to nearly flat faces, but not on the edges. As they are associated with the ceramic levels, all, except possibly those that exhibit only slight polish, were likely pot polishers. Seventeen of these specimens range between 54 and 71 mm long; however, one is only 36 mm long and three range between 85 and 93 mm long. Possibly the three largest pebbles functioned as hand stones for grinding or filing material like bone, although they do not exhibit grinding striations.

Two pebbles of unidentified material have naturally flat faces exhibiting grinding striations. One piece, found on the surface of the site and measuring 76 x 57 x 32 mm, has a clear pattern of striations running at an oblique angle to the axis of the ovoid pebble. Grinding striations and polishing facets are on both faces of a pebble (72 x 42 x 15 mm) from Occupation VI. The same occupation zone yielded a similar-sized pebble slightly pecked on both ends and smoothed on one face.

One tabular diabase pebble (74 x 51 x 17 mm) from a slumped wall has been smoothed on both undulating faces. One face is quite concave, so another object must have been rubbed on it; therefore this pebble was a nether stone. The high spots have been ground on the concave surface of a rectangular broken stone of unidentified material found in apparent association with a male burial (no. 4) in Occupation VI. Another fragment of unidentified stone from the same area exhibits a rough surface which has been planed by grinding the high spots. A tabular fragment of fine-grained granite or diorite from Occupation VII has one plane surface and a concave surface, both of which were ground.

That grinding stones (hand stones) and nether stones are present but not readily distinguished from polishing stones is also indicated by the presence of several flat stones with shallow concave depressions which exhibit grinding striations. One broken diabase slab from Occupation V has a broad concave trough on one face with grinding striations running with the long axis of the natural depression. The high spots on the opposite face are also slightly polished. Another tabular piece of diabase (93 x 74 x 25 mm), with a natural elongated depression exhibiting grinding striations, was found in a fireplace in Occupation V directly associated with a large (115 x 52 x 34 mm) diabase pebble exhibiting three highly polished facets, but lacking evident grinding striations. Occupation V yielded another associated pair of pebbles, apparently also fired. The handstone (82 x 43 x 35 mm) has two polished faces, but no evidence of grinding striations. The possible nether stone (77 x 54 x 42 mm) has a slightly concave face which appears to have been deliberately roughened by pecking, while the opposite convex face is polished. There is also some evidence of pecking on the extremities, as if it had been used as a hammerstone. Although not in direct association, another pair of stones were found near each other in Occupation V. In this case the presumed handstone is a large (126 x 91 x 15 mm) tabular quartzite concretion with the high spots on both undulating faces smoothed by use. This is one of the few quartzite rocks found at Forte Marechal Luz; therefore this heavy piece must have been valuable enough to carry a considerable distance. The nether stone is even larger (197 x 118 x 86 mm). It is a tabular piece of granite with the high spots on the flattest face ground to a slightly concave surface by use. Collected from the surface was a naturally fractured rectanguloid chunk of diabase (74 x 47 x 16 mm) which exhibits grinding of the high spots on the two flattest faces and both ends. One edge and the corner of the opposing edge are also ground by use. After grinding, the smallest end has been battered, with a few flakes removed by use as a hammerstone.

Two large angular diabase slabs were probably brought to the site directly from the dyke about 200 m away (both exhibit many large irregular scratches on the surfaces from handling or dragging during transport). These pieces, which are similar to those illustrated by Tiburtius and Leprovost (1953:Figures 23, 24), probably were portable axe-grinding platforms. Three of the flattest faces on each of them exhibit minute grinding striations and smoothing of the high spots. The one from stratum 6B was found very near Burials no. 31 and no. 32, and in association with three hammerstones. One of its ground faces has large concavities which appear to have been made by use. Several percussion flakes were removed from the edges both before and after grinding. The piece measures 705 x 175 x 137 mm. The other slab, from Occupation Zone IV, is of similar size (790 x 141 x 130 mm); and exhibits even more obvious evidence of grinding facets. The edges have also been much battered.

Eight fire-broken fragments of a much larger diabase nether stone were found scattered in a ceremonial fireplace circle placed over a male burial (Burial no. 5) in Occupation Zone VI. Another piece of what appears to be the same large slab was found more than 2 m away in a slumped wall. Two of the pieces appear to have been battered by percussion, perhaps in an attempt to "kill" the piece ceremonially. Fragmentation of the slab had occurred elsewhere, as adjacent pieces did not fit together and much of the whole piece is missing; therefore the only dimension known is the thickness: 105 mm. Both faces of the slab exhibit fine grinding striations, but the grinding area was much more extensive on one face. As is true with the other pieces, grinding did not produce deep concavities. In other words, these grinding slabs are in no way similar to *metates* used to grind seeds. Possibly they were used for grinding bone and wooden tools and for sharpening axe bits, but their size suggests that it is possible that some softer food was ground on some of them.

Nether stones may also have been used for grinding hematite and perhaps manganese concretions and pebbles into powder. A quartz pebble with a red stain near one end was already mentioned as being associated with Burial no. 57. An ovoid diabase pebble (82 x 48 x 46 mm), also from Occupation Zone VII, has been use-polished on one face; and hematite is still adhering to one of its pecked ends. Probably both tools were used as pestles for powdering hematite. Two pebbles were associated with a young female burial (no. 32) in stratum 6B. One is a piece of red (burned?) mudstone exhibiting three smooth grinding facets, and the other is a water-rolled granite pebble with no evidence of alteration, although it is similar in shape to the quartz pebble with Burial no. 57. Is it possible that hematite was being processed by baking iron-rich mudstone concretions? Another piece of mudstone from a slumped wall also appears to have been worn on both faces, but this tabular piece is a more normal grey/brown color. Perhaps it was not red because it had not been baked. Twelve natural mudstone or siltstone concretions were catalogued but not described as artifacts because there was no evidence of alteration, but they must have been carried to the site for some purpose. Perhaps they were discarded because they were not the proper kind for obtaining hematite. Four of these concretions came from Occupation IV, three from V, and five from Occupation VII.

A Worked Pebble Assemblage Associated with Unfired Clay Basins in Occupation IV

Several pebble artifacts, three of which were evidently used for processing paint pigments, were found directly associated with unfired clay basins in stratum 7 (Occupation Zone IV). The basins are described under the category of clay artifacts. Three pebble implements were found inside basin no. 8, and another lay beside the same basin. A long quartzite pebble (127 x 174 x 68 mm) has a large pecked circular depression (28 mm diameter) on its flattest face. The opposite face has a natural trough which appears to have been smoothed by use. Both ends have been pecked; the smallest end was flattened by heavy pecking. The ends of the other quadrangular diabase pebble (87 x 66 x 59 mm) are only slightly pecked, while the very shallow central depression on one face retains a dark stain. Also cached in the same basin was a triangular diabase pebble (84 x 68 x 51 mm) with shallow polished depressions on both faces, and pecked areas on all three of its extremities. A burned pebble (72 x 47 x 15 mm), found just outside the same basin, was slightly battered on one end and slightly pecked near the center of a concave face which retains a hematite stain. A striated hematite pebble was found adjacent to clay basin no. 6, and an irregular diabase pebble (45 x 40 x 34 mm) with one highly polished concave face which is stained black was found inside clay basin no. 10. Although the main purpose of these clay basins appears to have been for cooking or at least for containing food, it is possible that there was a secondary association with baking iron-rich clay and/ or mudstone concretions to obtain ochre.

An Assemblage of Paint-Preparation Tools from Stratum 6B

The largest (68 x 54 x 51 mm) pebble of hematite found at the site came from stratum 6B along with a similar-sized pebble of an unidentified iron mineral which has a possibly artificial depression on one face. Unlike most of the tiny chunks of hematite, these two large pieces exhibit little evidence of use; but they were associated with a concentration of 12 hammerstones, four of which have pecked ends heavily stained with hematite. All 14 artifacts were found within 30 cm of each other at the same level in stratum 6B.

One diabase pebble hammerstone in this assemblage has been pecked into a sphere (diameter 62 x 58 mm) with several flat facets, four of which are stained with red ochre. Another hammerstone, a near sphere (diameter 56 x 51 mm), has one flat face with a pecked depression, but no ochre stain. A pair of pebble hammerstones were pecked into discs: the water-worn faces on one example (62 x 58 x 43 mm) have central depressions with red ochre on one face and an adjacent edge; the faces of the other example (65 x 62 x 52 mm) are unaltered, although ochre is adhering to one end of the pecked periphery. Two other discoidal pebble hammerstones (66 x 61 x 38 mm, and diameter 55 x 38 mm) have pecked depressions in the center of both water-worn faces, perhaps placed so as to afford a secure purchase of the thumb and an opposing finger while pecking (Figure 11). A similar quartz disc hammerstone (56 mm diameter x 44 mm) has unaltered water-worn faces. The fourth hammerstone which has an ochre stain on one end is flattened-oval in shape with pecked ends. One end and one side have been battered. The opposite side has a circular battered area, and there are smooth shallow depressions near the center of both faces. Two pebble hammerstones have triangular cross-sections: one granite piece (69 x 49 x 41 mm) has been pecked on one end, while the other end is broken; both ends of the diabase example (81 x 54 x 40 mm) are squared by fine pecking which continued into two edges. Another diabase pebble hammerstone (91 x 58 x 42 mm) has a triangular plan, the most pointed end of which has been pecked more than the two broad extremities. The last diabase pebble hammerstone in the associated group is ovoid with a planoconvex cross-section (89 x 64 x 54 mm). One end has been pecked more than the other, and one slightly concave face appears to be use-polished. The close association of these artifacts with each other strongly suggests that they were all used for processing pigment, although the paint is not now evident on several hammerstones.

Another ochre-stained diabase pebble hammerstone found nearby in stratum 6B was also pecked into a nearly spherical form (52 x 51 x 48 mm). Hematite is impregnated on both faces of the bit half of a rectangular axe (75 x 72 x 13 mm) from the same zone, as if it had been used as a paint palette after it broke.

Several other hammerstones and pebbles with pecked depressions, found nearby in stratum 6B, but not in immediate association with the concentration described above, will be described later. Quite possibly, all of these implements were pigment-processing tools used by the people who were preparing the many bodies for interment in stratum 6B. That iron ochre was consumed in considerable quantities during burial ceremonies is evident from the profile of the east wall of the square A2, where a thick lens of hematite mixed

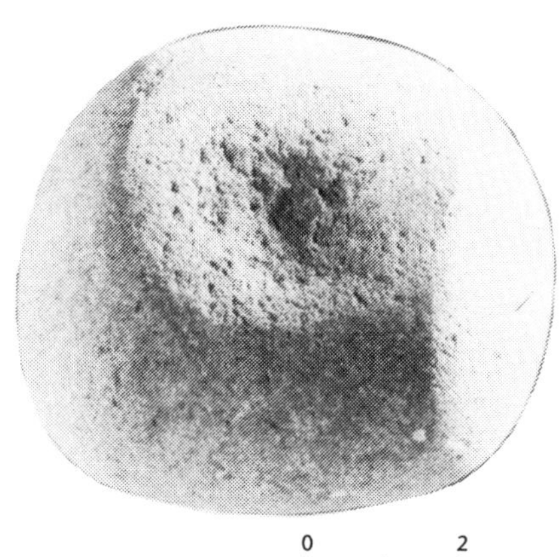

Figure 11. Hammerstone with pecked depressions.

with the ash is seen associated with Burial no. 6, one of the early burials in stratum 6B, dated A.D. 860. Hematite pebbles with striated facets were associated with Burials no. 22 and no. 32 in the same stratum. A hematite pebble with several cuts on one surface was also found with Burial no. 22 in stratum 6B, and a hematite pebble with two concave faces that had been scraped was associated with nearby Burial no. 23.

Paint Processing in Other Stratigraphic Levels

With the exception of one pebble from Occupation V and another from Occupation VII, all other hematite pebbles with striated facets came from earlier occupations than stratum 6B (three from IV, two from III, one from II), or lacked provenience (four examples). Most of these pebbles or chunks of hematite with striated facets range in size between 20–30 mm by 10–15 mm by 7–10 mm. Tiburtius and Leprovost (1952:151) include other specimens from Forte Marechal Luz in their study of paint pebbles.

Occupation II yielded three smooth facetted hematite pebbles which appear to have been rubbed directly on the body as they lack grinding striations. Evidently all later facetted hematite chunks either had been scraped with a tool having an irregular edge or ground on another stone, evidently to prepare ochre powder.

Three hematite pebbles exhibiting one worked but unfacetted and unstriated surface come from Occupation Zones III, IV, and VI. The upper levels of Occupation II also yielded two cylindrical pebbles of hematite, one with smooth surfaces, the other having four striated longitudinal facets. This striated pebble is 41 mm long, the largest of the paint pebbles exhibiting clearly worked surfaces.

Why were so many pieces of ochre discarded before all the paint was utilized? Certainly the chunks could easily have been powdered with a hammerstone used as a pestle. Was production so abundant that wastage was not a significant factor?

Other Striated Stones

Four striated stones do not fit into the preceding categories, nor do they form a consistent pattern by themselves. Three of these striated stones came from Occupation Zone VII. An irregular arkose pebble has some fine striations on one smooth slightly concave face and many crisscrossing incisions on one of its two excurving abraded ends. This piece (64 x 56 x 23 mm), apparently split in a fire, could have been a paint-grinding mortar or pestle. An elongated pointed pebble (62 x 22 x 20 cm) of weathered diabase has marked striations on its edges and faces. Possibly this implement with its sandpaper-like surface served as a file. A flattened water-worn silicified sandstone pebble (92 x 49 x 22 mm), with use-battering flakes removed from both ends and a portion of one edge, has a series of longitudinal scraping marks on another edge as well as scattered striations on both faces. As there is no evidence of platform preparation on the flaked bifaces (to be described later), this piece evidently did not receive its peculiar marks as a result of preparing edges for flaking, although the battered ends could have been caused by use as a percussion-flaking tool.

A tabular fragment of an unidentified stone (36 x 25 x 12 mm) with the high spots of one face polished by use came from Occupation Zone II. The opposite rough concave face has several straight line striations crisscrossing each other in three directions. Perhaps such marks were made by using the piece as a whetstone.

An Assemblage of Rough Stone Artifacts from Occupation Zone I

A discrete assemblage of rough stone artifacts found in Occupation Zone I in a rather restricted area within the deposit should be described together at this point for several reasons. They form an assemblage that was apparently used by the same people, the original occupants of the site about 4000 years ago. The assemblage not only differs from later less-closely associated assemblages, but some of the artifacts themselves are distinctive and difficult to discuss with later types. Two of the stones, as well as two whalebone tympanic bulae described elsewhere, were subjected to such heavy use that unintentional flakes were removed: thus the distinction between accidental flaking and intentional flaking can be further distinguished in discussing this assemblage. In addition, the use of pecking as a basic technique for shaping artifacts was innovated in Occupation I; so discussion of these artifacts will lead naturally into the category of pecked stone artifacts, including hammerstones.

Most of the artifacts from Occupation I were found in a clay matrix formed from weathered diorite bedrock. Probably most of this clay was deposited on the level bedrock bench long after this first occupation because the tops of several of the artifacts extended above the clay. Clay particles can easily move through the shell along the steep back slope west of the bench (see profile, Figure 4). As the bedrock is acidic and most movement occurred when the clay was saturated by rainwater, the stone and bone artifacts from this assemblage are more weathered than most of those from a shell matrix. Unless otherwise indicated, all the artifacts were fashioned from water-worn diabase pebbles.

One of the four artifacts from Occupation I most difficult to identify because of weathering was a diabase pebble fragment with one concave face which appears smoothed by use, while the other face appears to have been intentionally roughened. The extremities of another rhomboidal pebble (79 x 67 x 28 mm) have been battered, while the faces were smoothed by use. One naturally wedge-shaped pebble of unidentified stone has a concave face which has been smoothed on the high spots; also the short bit of the wedge appears to have been smoothed by use. Another wedge-shaped spall has several flakes removed from the bit end by use. The water-worn surface also has been smoothed on the high spots.

Three granite pebbles from Occupation I, although very weathered, exhibit evidence that they are definite artifacts. One is an angular piece (85 x 50 x 42 mm) with a quadrilateral cross-section, which apparently has been pecked all the way around the middle, forming a "waisted" object which could easily have been hafted. The other is a flattened ovoid pebble (82 x 60 x 26 mm) with battered ends and possibly pecked depressions on both faces. Another smaller pebble (69 x 69 x 46 mm) has a small pecked depression near the center of one face.

A badly weathered diorite pebble (79 x 61 x 35 mm) has been battered along one side, and in the process a flake was removed from one extremity. Superficially this object resembles a pebble chopper; but the flake was evidently not removed intentionally, and the object continued to be used for bashing something.

At this point it would be instructive to point out an ethnographic analogy recorded among the Waika of the Amazonian Territory of Venezuela by Cruxent (1967). The photograph illustrates an Indian striking a small palm nut placed in a central depression of a nether stone with the edge of a quadrangular hammerstone (Figure 12a). Several quadrangular-shaped hammerstones similar to the one used by the Waika occur in later occupation zones at Forte Marechal Luz (Figure 12b). There is one elongated pebble (78 x 21 x 18 mm) from Occupation I which has been much battered on one end. Even more closely analogous in Occupation I, however, are five pebbles with intentional depressions pecked on at least one flat face. These irregularly shaped pebbles range in size between 66–99 mm long, 45–84 mm wide, and 26–51 mm thick. The circular depressions may be quite shallow but range up to 4 mm deep and between 12 and 34 mm in diameter. The example with the deepest hole has a roughened, shallow depression on the opposite face, as if a new depression had just been pecked because the old depression had become too deep and too smooth to remain functional. The extremities of one pebble have been used as a hammerstone. It is difficult to escape the conclusion that one activity being carried out by the initial occupants of the site was the processing of palm nuts, although probably other materials were also pounded on these stones with pecked central depressions.

Hammerstones

The large and varied category of pebbles with pecked extremities will be described next, because, although most of them were simply pebbles picked up from the beach and put to use, a few examples exhibit sufficient patterning, such as squaring the extremities by pecking, to suggest that they were intentionally shaped. In addi-

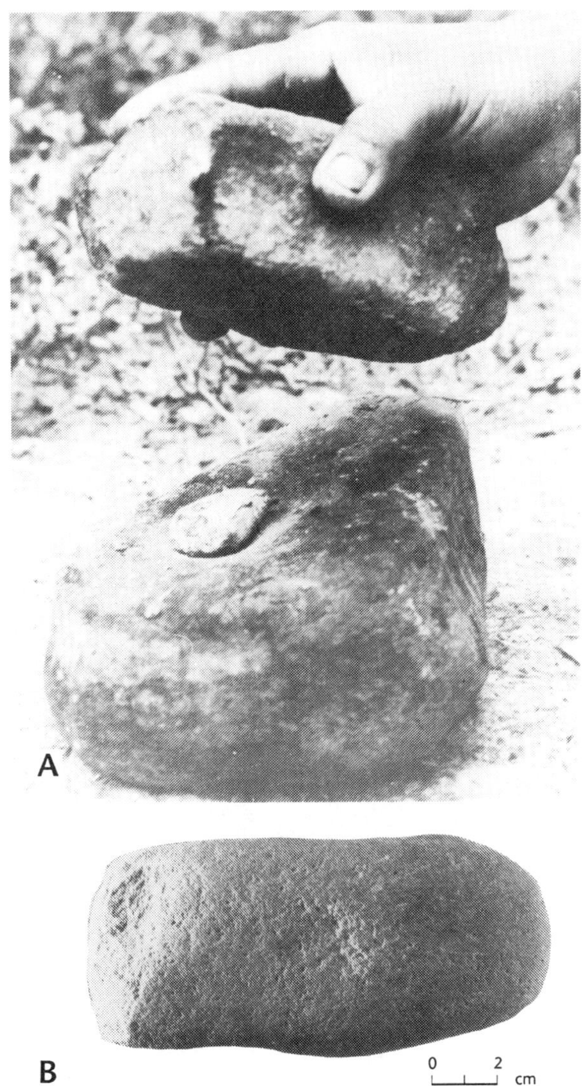

Figure 12 A) Photograph courtesy J. M. Cruxent of Waika Indian of Amazonas Territory, Venezuela: breaking a large seed with a pair of *quebra-cocos.* **B)** Similar *quebra-coco* from Forte Marechal Luz.

tion to the hammerstones with deliberately pecked depressions in the center of one or more faces, the most obvious shaped hammerstones are the well-formed discoidal and spherical specimens, most of which were found associated with the already described paint processing laboratory in stratum 6B. It will become obvious from the description of the many variations found at Forte Marechal Luz that hammerstones were used to grind, pound, peck, strike, and flake many different kinds of materials. To detail the evidence for varied uses to be found on most of these implements unfortunately will require tedious and repetitive descriptions.

Usually when a North American archaeologist uses the term "hammerstone" he is referring to an implement employed to flake other stones by direct percussion. Undoubtedly some of the hammerstones in the upper Occupation Zones (V, VI, and VII) were used as flaking tools; but evidently not in Zones I, II, III, and IV, because no intentionally removed percussion flakes were found in those zones. Hammerstones at all levels were undoubtedly used for pecking other stones into shape more often than for flaking. Hammerstones also were used for striking palm nuts (*cocos*) and other hard-shelled objects; and many of them also have pecked depressions on their faces, some of which undoubtedly functioned to secure the nut while it was being struck with another hammerstone. Others apparently served as mortars and pestles for pounding and grinding mineral paints. Many also exhibited more general facial grinding caused by use as handstones and nether stones probably for grinding seeds as well as pigments. But none of these functions appears to explain the evidence for extreme pounding leading to the accidental removal of flakes and sometimes larger spalls from the battered pounding surface. As will be seen, similar battering is evident on the poll ends of many ground-stone axes. It should not be forgotten that these people lived surrounded by forest. They must have worked wood a great deal, even though the wood is not preserved for us. The similar pattern of heavy battering on many hammerstones (including some with pecked depressions) and on axe polls suggests that many axes also served as pounding wedges, while many hammerstones were heavy-duty woodworking mauls which occasionally served for hammering wedged axe polls. The possibility that many stone implements were used as heavy-duty woodworking tools will be discussed at greater length near the end of the section on bitted implements.

As will be seen in the next section, most of the pebbles with pecked depressions were also used as hammerstones in addition to their related function as specialized anvil stones. Several hammerstones with pecked depressions will be described in this section because hammering appears to have been their major function. Thus this section on hammerstones forms a natural transition to the category of objects intentionally shaped by pecking.

Two flattened oval diabase beach pebbles from Zone VII have had battering flakes removed from both extremities, which were later flattened by less-rigorous pecking. One example (111 x 82 x 47 mm) also has shallow pecked central depressions on two slightly ground faces, while the other (81 x 66 x 55 mm) has a shallow polished depression on a polished face. A similarly shaped example (91 x 62 x 47 mm) from Occupation IV has been pecked smoothly on both ends and slightly near the center of one face. Occupation VII yielded another pebble (92 x 57 x 62 mm) with pecked extremities, and polished depressions on two flat faces which appear to have been polished and facetted by use as a handstone. Two flattened pebbles with triangular outline from Occupation VII exhibit small pecked areas near the center of one flat face. The diabase piece (76 x 58 x 21 mm) has had battering flakes removed from one pecked end, while the pebble from a quartz-feldspar vein (49 x 67 x 52 mm) has two pecked ends.

A water-worn gneiss pebble from Occupation VII with battered ends (87 x 71 x 42 mm) has been slightly used near the center of two faces. A similarly battered granite pebble (76 x 54 x 39 mm) from stratum 6B was also used slightly on one face. A flattened rectanguloid vein quartz pebble (75 x 59 x 25 mm) from Occupation III was pecked on its most protruding corner, while a natural depression near the center of one face was slightly roughened.

Four diabase hammerstones have dark stains near the center of one or two faces, possibly caused from crushing nuts. The one (62 x 60 x 52 mm) from Occupation VII has been slightly pecked on the edges and corners, while the centers of two faces were pecked, polished, and stained black. A small one (59 x 46 x 36 mm) from stratum 6B has been pecked on both ends and one face, the central portion of which was later smoothed, polished, and stained. Two larger examples (98 x 89 x 73 mm and 108 x 88 x 76 mm) from stratum 6B have slightly pecked and stained depressions on one face. On the smaller example the pecked depression was later polished, and the edge as well as two opposing ends was pecked. The larger example has been heavily pecked on one end, and slightly pecked on the other edges and corners.

The three examples noted above from stratum 6B were found very near but not directly associated with a concentration of hammerstones, two of which have centrally pecked depressions on their faces. Fourteen artifacts were found in square B1 within 50 cm of each other at the same depth. The presence of an iron-ore pebble and a large hematite pebble, in addition to hematite stain on four other pieces, suggested the probability that all of these tools were associated with a paint-processing laboratory. For that reason they have been described separately as an assemblage under the category of paint processing. It is quite possible that other hammerstones and pebbles with pecked depressions were also used for processing paint, and the dark stain noted on some examples could be from manganese rather than from plant juices. This possibility has already been suggested under the description in the previous section of the red and black stained pebbles with central depressions found associated with the unfired clay basins in Occupation IV.

The remaining hammerstones with no or minimal evidence of central depressions will be described by occupation zone, commencing with a heavily battered diabase pebble (108 x 93 x 56 mm) from Occupation II (stratum 14). Percussion flakes have been removed from both faces at one end by heavy chopping and hammering. As the flakes were apparently not intentionally removed, and as one face has completely spalled off, the piece is not a true "cobble chopper," although it looks like one. A diabase pebble (89 x 94 x 52 mm) from the same occupation has had two spalls removed from one end by heat, so it also superficially looks like a cobble chopper. The high spots of the water-worn surfaces appear to be slightly ground, and there is a shallow depression near the center of one concave face. The unbroken end is pecked slightly. Five water-worn pebble hammerstones came from stratum 10 in Occupation Zone II in square B2. They range in size between 85 x 59 x 26 mm and 57 x 36 x 19 mm. Two are of diabase, two of quartz, and one is granite. The granite pebble, with its smallest end pecked to a flat facet, was found directly associated with a naturally discoidal vein quartz pebble with a pecked depression in the center of one face, but little evidence of peripheral pecking. The other quartz pebble was use-battered on one corner. One diabase pebble was battered and pecked on both extremities, while both ends and the narrowest edge of the other diabase pebble have been pecked to excurvate surfaces. Elsewhere in the same occupation zone (II), a discoidal diabase pebble (81 x 63 x 19 mm) was apparently used as a chopper rather than a hammerstone, as three-quarters of its periphery has large flake scars removed by heavy use, and the flaked surfaces continued to be battered.

Occupation IV yielded two flattened water-worn vein quartz pebbles with flakes removed from one extremity by heavy hammering. These two objects (74 x 50 x 18 mm and 93 x 65 x 39 mm) were found directly associated with each other just above bedrock in stratum 8. Two water-worn diabase pebbles with pecking on both ends came from the same occupation zone in stratum 7. The largest one (186 x 98 x 69 mm) had apparently been cached under a large boulder. The small one (34 x 29 x 22 mm) had been pecked on the ends but in other areas as well. Three hammerstones fell from the wall of stratum 7 (Occupation IV). The largest one (109 x 55 x 49 mm), probably granite, is pecked on a conical extremity and around the periphery of the broader flat end; in other words it is naturally shaped like a conical pestle, but was not used as one. One of the two diabase pebbles is naturally spheroidal (62 x 50 x 49 mm), and has been pecked on two extremities; and one concave surface appears to have been ground by use. The other (65 x 56 x 46 mm) is quadrangular, and all protruding edges and both ends have been finely pecked. Although this is the "typical" shape for a "*quebra-coco*," the specimen lacks central depressions.

One of the six examples from Occupation V actually appears to be the discoidal broken end of a larger cylindrical hammerstone fashioned out of a pegmatite pebble (84 x 81 x 24 mm). Depressions have been pecked near the center of both the old pecked face and the broken face, so it could have been described with the hammerstones with pecked depressions.

An unidentified exfoliating rock (82 x 59 x 48 mm) has been pecked on both ends and slightly on one face. A naturally spheroidal diabase pebble (80 x 75 x 55 mm) has been slightly pecked on one extremity, and one face appears facetted by use-grinding. It was found directly associated in Occupation Zone V with a granite pebble (79 x 48 x 27 mm) with one percussion flake removed from its narrowest edge.

In addition to those already described under pigment processing, stratum 6B yielded 12 more hammerstones, all in square B1. Two ovoid diabase pebbles were associated with burials. The example (87 x 60 x 47 mm) with Burial no. 24 was pecked on both ends and slightly on one edge, while the one (58 x 48 x 33 mm) with Burial no. 16 was pecked only on the ends. Another irregularly diamond-shaped pebble (65 x 55 x 30 mm) of unidentified stone had also been placed with Burial no. 24. All four of the projecting ends were finely use-pecked, and later the pebble appears to have been cracked by fire.

Also from stratum 6B, a quartz pebble (81 x 62 x 37 mm) had been pecked on the three projecting ends of its triangular outline. A large ovoid diabase pebble (137 x 87 x 61 mm) was pecked on both ends, while one flat face appears to be use-polished. Three discoidal pebbles, two of diabase (60 x 57 x 35 mm and 78 x 72 x 29 mm), the other of gneiss (70 x 70 x 33 mm), had been finely pecked around most of their perimeters. The smaller diabase pebble has been slightly pecked near the center of the flattest face; while the large pebble was slightly pecked on both faces, and battering flakes were removed from both sides of the narrowest part of the perimeter.

Three large quadrangular pebbles from stratum 6B are similar in shape to the typical "*quebra-cocos*" to be described in the next section. One gneiss pebble (123 x 61 x 61 mm) has been pecked only on the ends, while a quartzite example (124 x 87 x 47 mm) was not pecked on the ends at all; rather, pecking extends along the ridge across one end, on one corner, and in an irregular circular area near the center of one face. Also large battering flakes had been removed from an opposite corner. The third pebble of diabase (127 x 80 x 59 mm) has had both ends flattened by much pecking. Large oval areas near one end of two faces and a large circular area (31 mm diameter) near the end of the flattest face have been pecked. The fourth face shows scattered pecking marks.

The last pecked hammerstone from stratum 6B, found associated with one of the discoidal hammerstones, is a diabase pebble truncated transversely along a cleavage plane (69 x 62 x 32 mm). The straight edges of the truncated face have been pecked, and battering flakes removed from it. The opposite rounded end has been finely pecked, forming an irregular bifacetted bit.

Unlike the people who left a total of 29 hammerstones in burial stratum 6B, the later people who buried during Occupation VI (Stratum 4B) left only four hammerstones, and two of these are so badly weathered that it is not possible to prove that they were used. One diabase pebble (39 x 28 x 18 mm) has small pecking scars scattered over its entire surface, while the other spherical diabase pebble (diameter 29–32 mm) appears to have been pecked into shape. One hammerstone (38 x 34 x 22 mm) with Burial no. 5 is a naturally rounded unidentified stone, use-battered on both ends and pecked along one facial ridge. A longer diabase pebble (93 x 39 x 28 mm) has been pecked on both ends.

Although 33 hammerstones were found in Occupation VII, they are not as carefully made, nor is there as much elaboration in form as in stratum 6B. Undoubtedly this fact is directly correlated with the relative scarcity of hematite in Occupations VI and VII. Two large diabase hammerstones were associated with burials in Occupation VII. One (116 x 79 x 67 mm), found between the flexed legs of Burial no. 33, was only slightly pecked on both ends, and one face appears to be slightly ground. The ends of the other (110 x 68 x 63 mm), found near Burial No. 19, were much pecked, and flakes had been removed by heavy battering, giving it the appearance of a double-ended cobble chopper. In addition to apparent facial grinding, there are irregular circular pecked areas on two opposing ridges near one end, and scattered pecking elsewhere on these edges.

Five diabase hammerstones were found very near each other in Occupation VII. A directly associated pair included a flattened ovoid pebble (99 x 93 x 64 mm) with squared ends produced by much pecking, and a parallel-sided loaf-shaped pebble (108 x 92 x 80 mm), also with pecked square ends. This and another quadrangular pebble (117 x 62 x 62 mm) with similarly squared ends would have made typical "*quebra-cocos*," but they lack depressions. The other two do have slight depressions, however. A rectanguloid pebble (92 x 88 x 55 mm) has very shallow depressions on both flat faces, while two corners and the opposite broad end have been pecked. An ovoid pebble (121 x 76 x 70 mm) has only one flat face containing a shallow central depression. The most pointed end is heavily pecked, but only slight pecking is found on the broad end.

The flattened spheroidal or discoidal pebbles pecked around the entire perimeter are still present in Occupation VII, as well as in stratum 6B. One diabase example (71 x 67 x 55 mm) has a slightly pecked depression on one face, while the other face is slightly polished. Another (66 x 92 x 52 mm) has been pecked on all high spots to create a dome-shaped hammerstome with one unused flatter surface. The piece was later fire-spalled, removing some of the worked surface. It was found with another badly fire-cracked diabase fragment (82 x 59 x 25 mm) which retains some evidence of pecking on one convex edge. A flattened oval example (77 x 71 x 37 mm) has been pecked around its entire perimeter and especially on its extremities, so that it approaches the discoidal form. Another discoidal pebble (60 x 53 x 29 mm) has also been heavily pecked on both ends, while the flat faces were polished by use. One flattened spheroidal granite pebble (54 x 54 x 40 mm) has been roughly pecked on its perimeter, and has a battering flake scar on one extremity.

Another rectanguloid granite pebble (59 x 54 x 63 mm) from Occupation VII has been pecked on both extremities, all along one edge, and on another corner. A longer diabase pebble (96 x 56 x 45 mm) has been battered on both ends, heavily pecked along one edge, and slightly on the faces. It was found directly associated with a naturally wedge-shaped piece of weathered diabase (120 x 39 x 23 mm). The only evidence of use is that the surfaces are smoothed on the end near the excurvate bit, as if it had been used as a wedge, or possibly to flatten fibers for basketry. A similarly shaped object was described from Occupation Zone I.

A diabase pebble (69 x 65 x 46 mm) from Occupation VII has been pecked along one long excurving edge but only slightly on one pointed end. Another diabase pebble (102 x 73 x 42 mm) has been slightly pecked along two edges and near the center of one flat face as well as being heavily battered on both ends, which accidentally removed flakes (Figure 13). A quartz pebble (84 x 68 x 45 mm) from Occupation VII has also had battering flakes removed from both ends. A large diabase pebble (126 x 81 x 76 mm) with both extremities much battered was found on the surface of the Occupation VII strata. Three diabase pebbles from Occupation VII have also been pecked on both ends. One example (77 x 47 x 35 mm) is battered on one end and pecked on the other. The largest example (104 x 70 x 52 mm) also has slight use-grinding on one concave and one flat face, while the smallest example (51 x 39 x 26 mm) exhibits use polish on one flat face. The latter specimen, and a larger one (102 x 80 x 51 mm) with slight pecking on both ends and over one convex face, came from a slumped wall and might have been associated with an earlier occupation.

The remaining hammerstones from Occupation VII

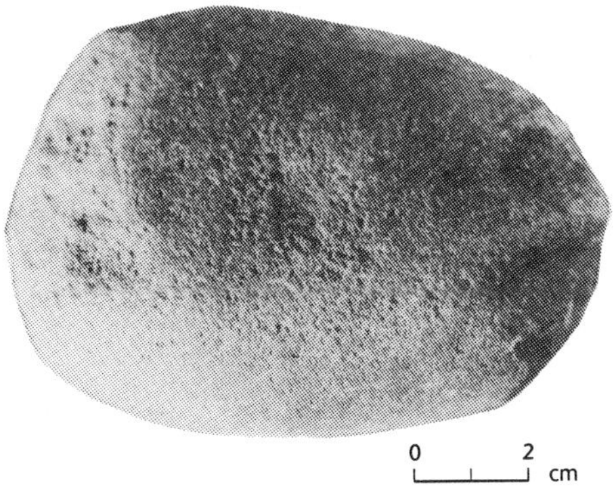

Figure 13. Hammerstone with battered ends.

have been pecked only on one end, although one diabase pebble (74 x 61 x 41 mm) was also pecked on an adjacent edge. This specimen is unusual because the pointed extremity was not pecked. One flat face was slightly use-polished. Another diabase specimen (68 x 76 x 33 mm), with an old transversely broken end, has been heavily battered on one end and polished on two faces. A pebble of amphibole gneiss (70 x 63 x 34 mm) has been battered on one end and use-polished on one face. One diabase pebble (70 x 51 x 39 mm) has been pecked on its most pointed end. One elongated diabase pebble (97 x 41 x 33 mm) with three longitudinal ridges has been pecked on one end, and facetted by use-polish on one rounded ridge and the opposite face. The unworked end appears to have broken before use as a hammerstone. One fire-broken diabase spall has a battered poll end, and two fragments of another fire-broken hammerstone pecked on one end were found near each other in Occupation VII. A long gneiss pebble (131 x 71 x 62 mm), pecked only on its most pointed end, was found standing vertically with its used end down, suggesting it had been used as a pestle.

Apparently one hammerstone (91 x 56 x 35 mm) from Occupation VII originally was intended to be an axe preform. One face is oxidized, unlike all the water-rounded diabase pebble hammerstones of diabase. The entire periphery has been percussion-flaked; but because the piece is wedge-shaped in cross-section, the knapper was unable to thin the thick edge. He therefore used the ends, edge, and center of one face as a hammerstone, and the opposite flat face as a rubbing stone. As the piece was impossible to shape by flaking, it cannot be included under the category of intentionally shaped flaked artifacts.

Chapter 4

Chapter 5
Intentionally Shaped Pecked Objects

Pebbles with Pecked Central Depressions

Other than the hammerstones, which are largely shaped by use, the most-numerous category of pecked stone artifacts was pebbles with central depressions on one or more faces. In most cases these depressions were obviously pecked intentionally in order to contain the object or material to be hit or ground by a hammerstone or pestle. These stones are often referred to in the literature as nutting stones, *"quebra cocos"* or *"quebra coquinhos"*; and an argument was presented when discussing the assemblage from Occupation I that breaking palm nuts was very likely the major function that these objects served. Nevertheless, they probably served other functions as well, so it is best to use a descriptive rather than a functional term. No matter what they were used for, it is evident that the depressions were intentionally pecked to their characteristic shape. The depressions, which vary from a rough to a polished surface, were periodically renewed by pecking when they had become too polished and thereby too slippery to hold the nut or other object securely in place. In the descriptions that follow, all the central depressions are quite smooth unless otherwise indicated.

Stones with intentional depressions shaped by pecking were the earliest type of intentionally shaped artifacts found at Forte Marechal Luz, as they occur in Occupation Zone I. All the other artifacts in this early assemblage were natural rocks, bones, and shells exhibiting only evidence of unintentional shaping by means of pecking, grinding, and flaking. Despite the presence of several stones with central depressions in Occupation Zone I, only one example came from the next two occupation zones. This specimen, from near the base of Occupation Zone II, has a "typical" shape and size; i.e., it is a quadrangular pebble (95 x 63 x 53 mm) with shallow central depressions on two opposing faces, although the extremities were not used as a hammerstone as on some later examples. In addition, this specimen has an 8-mm-deep depression, 34 mm in diameter, in the center of another face, all of which, including the depression, had been freshly resurfaced by pecking. Possibly this is an example of reworking an old artifact. The object could have been picked up from the old Occupation I surface, some of which must have been exposed along the wave-cut beach while stratum 21 was being deposited (see profile of main trench, Figure 4).

Eight of the 24 stones with pecked central depressions remaining to be described came from Occupation IV. (In addition, an assemblage of worked pebbles, including five with pecked central depressions or broader concave faces, was already described under the discussion of pigment processing in Occupation IV.) All but two of the eight pebbles with pecked depressions from Occupation IV have also been used as hammerstones; one of these is a rectanguloid pebble (102 x 72 x 47 mm) with one large (37 mm diameter) circular rough depression in the center of the flattest face. The other unbattered specimen is half of an associated pair of artifacts: hammerstone and nether stone. The hammerstone is a quartz pebble (100 x 65 x 53 mm) with planoconvex cross-section and a shallow diffuse pecked area in the center of the flat face. The directly associated quadrangular pebble (95 x 52 x 42 mm) exhibits large pecked depressions (4 mm deep and 24 mm in diameter) on opposing faces. Both ends have been squared by much battering and pecking (Figure 14). Another pair of pebbles directly associated with each other includes a similar example with shallow circular depressions 26 mm in diameter on opposing faces. Both ends are

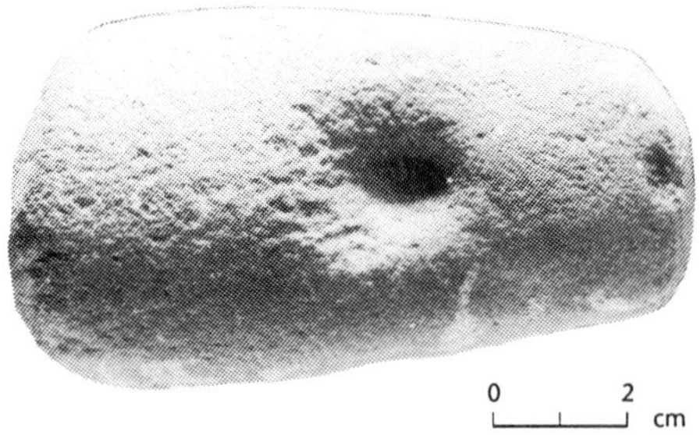

Figure 14. Quebra-coco.

pecked, and one flat edge has apparently been used for grinding. The associated mate is a smaller pebble with no apparent evidence of use whatever. It was catalogued as an artifact because of its direct association with the other piece. One long flat pebble (140 x 68 x 36 mm) has a shallow circular rough pecked area at the center of one face, and a smooth depression in the center of the opposing face (Figure 12b). Both ends have been pecked, and several flakes were removed from one end by heavy battering.

One long pebble (113 x 54 x 54 mm) from Occupation IV is of a soft chlorite with roughly pecked circular depressions on two adjacent faces. Pecking is also evident on one edge and one end. A small pebble (60 x 60 x 50 mm) with a deep circular depression on its flattest face appears to have been much used subsequently as a hammerstone on its convex face as well as on most edges. It would feel natural to hold a pecking hammerstone with the thumb placed in a depression, so this object may be an example of a discarded tool which later acquired a new function.

Two "typical *quebra-cocos*," quadrangular specimens of stone with central depressions, came from stratum 6B, in addition to the one already described with the assemblage of paint processing tools. One is quite large (136 x 68 x 53 mm), with pecked ends and edges; and large circular depressions pecked on both broad faces. The other (96 x 69 x 44 mm) is a water-worn pebble of stone that originally came from a quartz-feldspar vein. It has rough pecked depressions 34 mm in diameter near the center of two opposing faces, and the ends have been flattened by heavy pecking.

One of the two examples from Occupation VI, measuring 76 x 34 x 32 mm, is lightly pecked on the center of both faces, on both ends, and in the center of both edges. The other specimen is a fire-broken granite pebble with a round smooth depression on one face, and a roughly pecked area near the center of the opposing face.

One quadrangular pebble lacking provenience, measuring 102 x 73 x 61 mm, has shallow circular depressions in the center of the two largest faces. These and another face also exhibit tiny striations and polished areas, indicating that the stone was used for grinding and polishing. Both ends and two edges also show signs of pecking.

The remaining 11 pebbles with pecked depressions came from Occupation Zone VII. One pebble (95 x 68 x 56 mm) has a deep circular depression on its flattest face and slight pecking on its convex face (Figure 15). Both ends have been pecked, and battering flakes have been removed from one end by heavy use. A smaller granite pebble with one flat face that appears to be polished would not have been called an artifact except that it was found next to the previous specimen. Another example (70 x 54 x 54 mm), pecked on both ends and exhibiting pecked depressions on two flat faces, was found with Burial no. 7 in Occupation VII.

Only one "typical" quadrilateral diabase pebble *quebra-coco* with centrally pecked depression came from Occupation VII. It measures 97 x 56 x 49 mm; and has a shallow depression 12 mm in diameter on one face, a slightly used natural concavity on the opposite face, and a circular pecked area 20 mm in diameter near one end of the narrowest face (Figure 16). All faces exhibit areas with tiny striations visible, and both ends have been pecked and battered.

Also from Occupation VII, four ovoid pebbles, one of which is quartzite, have only one flat face exhibiting shallow depressions or diffuse areas of pecking. Both ends of three of these specimens have been pecked, and

Figure 15. Quebra-coco.

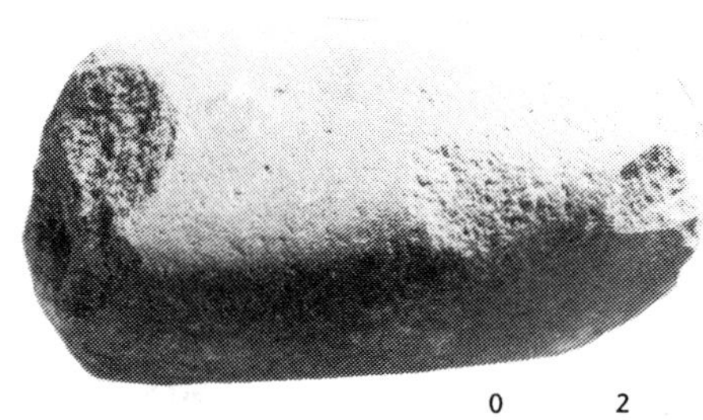

Figure 16. Quebra-coco/hammerstone.

one also has a pecked area near the end of a convex face. They range in size from 118 x 75 x 59 mm to 71 x 59 x 44 mm. A fire-broken pebble of unidentified material has shallow roughened depressions near the center of both faces. Another fire-cracked specimen (83 x 75 x 61 mm), with a triangular cross-section, has pecked ends, as well as two centrally pecked faces, and another circular pecked area near the end of one face. Actually, this type of shallow pecking would be classified as a special pattern of hammerstone use if it were not for the fact that there are so many stones with intentional central depressions on one or more faces. Certainly when the centrally pecked area is so shallow it is hard to defend its placement with intentionally pecked depressions. This is just one example of the natural overlap between artifacts arbitrarily placed in different categories, because so many artifacts were used for several purposes.

Other Intentionally Shaped Pecked Objects

Other than the grooved granite pebble from Occupation I, the many stones with pecked depressions, and possibly a few discoidal and spheroidal hammerstones, only three objects found at Forte Marechal Luz were pecked into deliberate shapes. It should be noted that bitted implements ("axes") were never intentionally pecked into shape. A granite pebble (55 x 51 x 26 mm) from Occupation IV has a flattened ovoid shape with a notch pecked on two opposing sides. This specimen is nearly identical to a series of objects identified as fishnet weights at the Itacoara site on the Rio Pira in Joinville 32 km from the coast (Tiburtius, Bigarella, and Bigarella 1951). At Itacoara the net weights occur only in the upper ceramic zone, but the example from Forte Marechal Luz came from preceramic stratum 6 in Occupation Zone IV. A similar object from stratum 5 (Occupation Zone V) will be described later as the only object at Forte Marechal Luz, other than axe preforms, which was intentionally shaped by flaking.

A tabular schist object from Occupation Zone V, measuring 59 x 29 x 13 mm, naturally has nearly parallel sides; while the two opposing ends appear to have been deliberately squared to form a quadrangular piece. The presence of net sinkers in the same stratum and the stratum immediately below suggests the possibility that this object served as a net gauge. A similar function is suggested for a rectangular whalebone object from Occupation Zone VI.

A naturally cylindrical weathered diabase cobble from Occupation Zone II, measuring 145 x 58 x 41 mm, has one concave face with a circular depression near the center. The broad end has been squared by pecking and battering, which removed several large use-flakes. The smaller end has also been pecked, as well as a small area along a ridge on the face opposite the central depression. Perhaps the object should be classed as a shaped hammerstone, or hand maul; but its conical form suggests that it was used as a pestle.

Chapter 6
Intentionally Shaped Ground and Flaked Objects

Introduction

I originally chose to excavate at Forte Marechal Luz because its upper layers obviously contained ceramics, which at that time had never been proven to be manufactured by prehistoric residents of sambaquis. An additional incentive was because I found a large percussion-flaked biface on the talus slope of shell near the base of the sambaqui. As the site was located high above Babitonga Bay and therefore had been protected from Holocene marine transgression, I hypothesized that I might get a long sequence from ancient bifaces to recent ceramics. It should be noted that at that time I was working with the model that the earliest Americans brought large bifaces with them from Asia. I was somewhat dismayed, therefore, when I started excavating similar crude bifaces in the upper ceramic levels, and realized that they were simply "blanks" or "preforms" designed to be finished into axes by grinding. But still I remained hopeful that the flaked bifaces would be found in the lower levels of the site as well, so everything was very carefully screened in order to retrieve every telltale flake. We discovered that the preformed axes and the flakes removed from them were still present in preceramic Occupation V before the innovation of pottery. But careful scrutiny of all material from earlier deposits revealed that, with the possible exception of a flake removed from a quartz pebble in Occupation IV, the only flakes were either thermal spalls, or percussion spalls accidentally removed from the working ends of axes or hammerstones.

We did find in Occupation IV two tabular pieces of diabase with intentional flakes removed from one naturally flat side, and one finished axe that had been percussion-flaked before grinding. However, there was no evidence of flaking on two broken axes from Occupation IV or on another from Occupation III. In addition to several flakes removed from ground axes by use in Occupation IV and II, a large section of a well-made axe from Occupation II exhibited a scar from a flake removed from the ground bit by heavy use. Analysis revealed that several axes in Occupation Zones IV through II, including the latter example, had been ground without any preliminary shaping by percussion; a water-worn pebble of approximately the proper size and shape was simply picked up from the beach and directly ground into a functional axe. In fact, to judge from the absence of intentional flakes and axe "preforms" in earlier zones, diabase was not intentionally flaked at the site before Occupation Zone V. Although the occupants of Zone IV were evidently aware of percussion flaking, the flaked objects evidently were brought in from elsewhere.

The apparent significance of these facts, especially the complete absence of intentional percussion flakes before Occupation Zone V, despite our careful search for them, did not occur to me until after I had completed the descriptive catalogue of artifacts. As a diabase dyke outcrops on the beach less than 200 m north of the sambaqui, the favorite material for making axes was readily available on the beach; but apparently nobody had deliberately percussion-flaked at the site until Occupation Zone V. Evidently the three flaked artifacts from Occupation IV were either brought in or traded in from elsewhere. The most common method of shaping stone in the earlier zones was by pecking with a hammerstone, although axes were not pecked, but rather ground directly from beach pebbles of about the right size and shape.

All shaping by grinding, whether on percussion-flaked axe blanks or simply on a beach pebble of suitable shape, was easily accomplished by using several large diorite and diabase boulders situated on the beach in front of the shellmound (Figure 10). These boulders have several deep parallel grooves and large oval depressions ground onto their upper surface. At a similar axe-grinding station on the Ilha de Santa Catarina I experimented and found that it took less than an hour to produce a crude but functional axe from a diabase beach pebble of approximately the right shape because the weathered surfaces of the stone are removed very readily by grinding. Thus, although percussion flaking is of great assistance for shaping preforms, a knowledge of flaking is not essential for making axes. And in fact there is no evidence that the occupants of the Forte Marechal Luz site had any knowledge of intentionally percussion-flaked artifacts before Occupation IV. Furthermore, apparently they did not innovate the actual techniques of flaking for themselves until Occupation Zone V.

We know very well, of course, that people living in the interior of southern Brazil who had access to several types of easily flakeable stone (mainly cherts and quartzites) were master flint knappers for many millennia before the inception of occupation of Forte Marechal Luz. Interestingly, however, these well-made pressure-flaked objects rarely appear in coastal sambaquis; and when they do, evidently they were traded in. In other words, some of the people living on coastal sambaquis appear to have been quite isolated from neighbors on the Planalto for a long time. If so, it is not difficult to suppose that the ancestors of some sambaqui-dwellers had lost the complex technological procedures for flaking stone, either when they moved through stoneless areas such as the lower Amazon Basin; or they had long inhabited the coastal littoral, which suffers a paucity of easily flakeable stone. Evidently the basic technique of percussion flaking was not reinnovated by the people who occupied Forte Marechal Luz until about A.D. 1000, and they always remained ignorant of the art of pressure flaking. It may be noted that an analogous pattern of the abandonment of flaking for the more expedient technique of grinding stone tools into shape occurred among the shellmound accumulators of some parts of the forested Northwest Coast of North America in late-prehistoric times where easily flakeable stone was not readily available (Bryan 1963). Archaeologists often assume that certain basic technologies, particularly flint knapping, once developed, were never abandoned, at least until they were superseded by modern technology. The evidence from Forte Marechal Luz evidently disproves that assumption.

In order to maintain the method of descriptive classification by reconstructing how artifacts were shaped, rather than by establishing a formal classification, it will be necessary to combine the description of intentionally shaped flaked and ground stone artifacts, because nearly all the percussion-flaked artifacts were preforms for axes which were intended to be finished by grinding. However, several axes were shaped directly by grinding. As noted above, before Occupation IV no axes were intentionally shaped by flaking, so temporally the technological process of grinding preceded intentional flaking at Forte Marechal Luz. Evidently pecking was never used to shape an axe into its overall form, although frequently the polls were squared by use as hammerstones.

Ground Stone Artifacts without Bits

Other than bitted implements, very few artifacts intentionally shaped by grinding and/or flaking were found at Forte Marechal Luz. The only nearly complete carefully shaped ground stone object was found on the road through the military post, so it may not have been associated with the sambaqui at all. It is a small symmetrically cylindrical object (Figure 17) broken at both ends, with an encircling raised band around its widest diameter. The shorter end was probably blunt and rounded; but the longer end tapered to a more pointed conical tip, which could have been perforated. In North America such an object would be called a "plummet." Its function is unknown.

A tabular fragment of schist from Occupation VII, measuring 69 x 42 x 8 mm, has been used on one projecting end and ground on two other edges. One short, excurving edge is unilaterally bevelled, while the longer straight edge has three parallel facets. The entire piece could have been considerably larger. A central fragment of an object of unidentified fine-grained stone with triangular cross-section (35 x 30 x 25 mm) came from Occupation VII. All three faces are carefully ground, and each angle subsequently had been facetted by grinding. A tabular green argillite (?) object from Occupation IV, measuring 52 x 32 x 7 mm, would be classified as the poll end of a small ground axe with converging sides and a flat face, except that the material is not suitable for heavy use. In fact, it was split longitudinally in half by a light blow, leaving a negative bulb but no mark at the point of impact.

A naturally cylindrical sandstone (?) concretion from

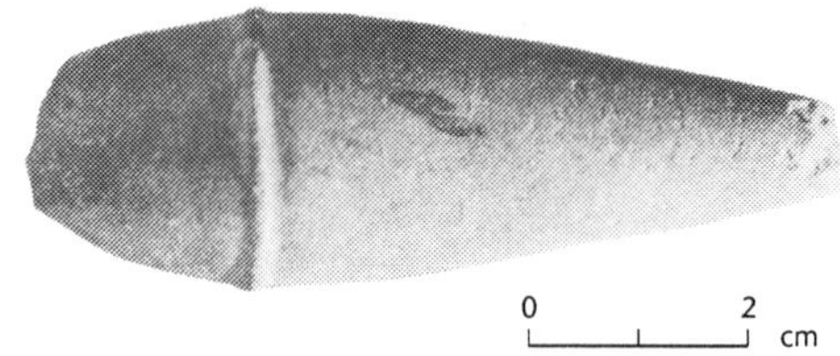

Figure 17. Cylindrical ground stone object.

Occupation V, measuring 54 x 16 mm in diameter, has one end which tapers abruptly and symmetrically to a conical tip. In this case the grinding probably was caused by use as a drill bit.

Other than axe preforms, the only object intentionally shaped by flaking alone also came from Occupation Zone V. It is an irregularly flattened quartzite pebble (86 x 61 x 32 mm) with notches formed near the center of two opposing edges by unifacial flaking. It is similar in form to an object with bilaterally pecked grooves, also from Occupation Zone V, which has been identified as a probable fishnet sinker.

A water-worn siltstone pebble (92 x 49 x 21 mm) from Occupation VII has a ground facet 4 mm wide along 39 mm of one edge. Both ends of the facet were later truncated by flaking, which also removed both ends of the pebble. The flaking appears to be intentional, but the function of the piece is unknown.

Bitted Implements

The largest category of intentionally shaped stone artifacts at Forte Marechal Luz includes the percussion-flaked axe "blanks" or "preforms"; and all other bitted implements finished by grinding, whether made directly on beach pebbles, or flaked preforms, or on flakes. Most of the reused flakes were removed from axes or hammerstones by heavy use. Except for one small preform of glassy basalt, all specimens were made of fine- to medium-grained diabase.

Because it is the earliest flaked axe, an implement from Occupation IV that was shaped from a side-blow flake will be described before discussion of the axes that lack any evidence of intentional flaking. Likewise, two tabular pieces from Occupation IV and a beach pebble which was minimally shaped by flaking will be mentioned before discussion of the bifacially flaked preforms, including those with evidence of further shaping by grinding. The finished axes will then be described, including those implements which show evidence of subsequent reshaping by flaking and grinding. Analysis of the flakes, both reused and unused, will be discussed at the end of the chapter.

As mentioned above, the bit half of one axe from Occupation IV, measuring 89 x 69 x 16 mm, was made on a large side-blow spall; and the parallel sides and excurvate bit were then shaped by flaking before the surfaces were ground; but there was no evidence of preliminary flaking on two other fire-broken axes from the same occupation zone. Only the bit was ground on one example (52 x 45 x 15 mm), while the edges and faces of this beach pebble show only use polish. Both faces and the edges of the other fragment (43 x 53 x 21 mm) have been ground with no evidence of flaking. Another fire-broken axe from Occupation III, which measures 58 x 78 x 27 mm, also lacks any evidence of preliminary shaping before grinding, although a use-flake was removed from the bit, which was then reground. Similarly, a use-flake was removed from the sharp bit of a carefully ground axe with convex faces (58 x 45 x 18 mm) from Occupation II. Thus there are four axes with no evidence of preliminary flaking from Occupations II, III, and IV. In addition, there are two diabase bitted implements to be described later as probable wedges. The one from Occupation IV was ground into shape, and the bit subsequently had flakes removed by use; while the implement from Occupation II was slightly ground on its surfaces, and one use-flake was removed from the wedge-shaped bit.

The available evidence indicates that the people at Forte Marechal Luz first became aware of percussion flaking during Occupation IV, but they did not begin to shape bifacial preforms at the site until Occupation V. Before Occupation IV they simply collected a suitably shaped beach pebble and ground the bit and faces directly without preliminary shaping. The latter method of making axes continued during later occupations whenever a suitably shaped pebble was found, as there is no evidence of flaking on the large bit half of a rectangular axe from stratum 6B. This piece was described earlier with an assemblage of paint-preparation tools because the ground surfaces are impregnated with red ochre; apparently it had been used as a paint palette. As burial stratum 6B is partially composed of disturbed deposits from Occupation V, this unflaked axe may well have been picked out of the older deposits by later people who were preparing ochre for burial ceremonies. In addition, one bit end from Occupation V, and two bit halves, three bit fragments, and the poll end of a small axe with converging sides from Occupation VII lack any evidence of preliminary flaking. The largest of these broken bits (48 x 46 x 15 mm), and the only one not showing heavy use, was associated with Burial no. 52 in Occupation VII.

Beach pebbles were occasionally shaped minimally by flaking before being ground. One example found on the shell talus slope was an irregularly oval pebble (136 x 68 x 31 mm), thickest at its naturally squared poll, which was not altered in any way. The other half was preliminarily flaked and then ground to an excurving bit which is bilaterally symmetrical in both cross-sections. It is possible that this presumed axe with its naturally constricted poll was hafted in the solid socketed type of haft (see later discussion of hafting).

Two tabular diabase pieces with parallel sides exhibiting minimal flaking came from Occupation Zone IV. As both retain old weathered surfaces, they may originally have been poll ends of axe preforms. The rectangular piece (97 x 87 x 46 mm) with naturally parallel sides and slightly convex faces came from stratum 8 in Occupation Zone IV; thereby it is the earliest intentionally flaked object at the site. A series of non-overlapping, short, shallow flakes have been removed alternately from both faces, using one naturally flat side as a striking platform.

The other piece from Occupation IV, which measures 63 x 48 x 16 mm, was originally classified as a whetstone because three flat sides and both faces (especially the face retaining the original sandstone-like weathered cortex) exhibit long grinding striations which appear to be from use rather than by intention. However, one of the parallel sides was further straightened by alternate flaking, similar to the previous example except that the flaking platform was deliberately battered in order to square the side. Finally the battered edge was ground to dull it, in the same manner as most axes were shaped, so probably the piece originally was intended to be an axe, although it may have been used as a whetstone after the bit end broke off. The pentagonal form of this piece is unusual, if indeed the original intention was to make an axe, because the poll is shaped like a gabled roof with two converging sides, both of which are ground.

The term "axe preform" is used for seven percussion-flaked pieces and four fragments made on weathered diabase nodules (never beach pebbles) because they were obviously preliminarily shaped to be made into bitted implements. They show no evidence of use. Oxidized (deeply weathered) cortex is still present on both faces and even on portions of the bits of all preforms, showing that they were unfinished and unused. Four of the largest ovoid to rectangular bifaces [the two unbroken examples are 215 x 111 x 61 mm from Occupation VII and 120 x 43 x 34 from Occupation V (Figures 18, 19); one broken example is from Occupation VII; the other from the talus] lack any evidence of grinding as does the small naturally rectangular basalt example (110 x 35 x 21 mm) from Occupation VII (Figure 20). The high spots of two other whole bifaces (256 x 110 x 46 mm from the base of the talus, and 146 x 75 x 21 mm from Occupation VII) have been ground to reduce thick ridges on both faces. The larger example (Figure 21) was slightly flaked again after grinding. Three of the four broken preforms, all from Occupation VII, lack any evidence of grinding; but the sides of the poll half of another nodule (94 x 70 x 21 mm) were flaked and then ground. Evidently the preforms were discarded before they were finished, either because they were too thick and/or heavy, or because they broke during the process of flaking.

Figure 18. Flaked axe preform.

Figure 19. Flaked axe preform.

With one possible exception there is no evidence that these bifaces were used as hand-held implements (cf. Tiburtius and Leprovost 1953:508–515). The exception, not counted above because it has been used, is the bit half of an implement made on a tabular oxidized nodule (80 x 64 x 15 mm). It was minimally flaked along both sides and the bit, which also retains a large portion of the oxidized cortex. The piece was never ground, but the naturally dull bit exhibits considerable wear polish; and both patinated faces have many crisscrossing striations from heavy use, as if the piece had been used as a digging implement. It will be mentioned again at the end of this section when the question of function of the bitted implements is discussed.

Flaking, only by percussion, was very crude in the sense that the knapper evidently did not know how to prepare a platform or how to hold the piece at an angle so that thinning flakes could be removed. Rather, he approached the problem as if he were pecking the stone. He relied on naturally flat thick edges for his platforms; and if he needed to straighten the side, he repeatedly battered it with direct right-angled blows, which removed thick flakes having battered platforms.

Axes were made on two kinds of flaked preforms: expanding side-blow flakes, wider than their length, and weathered nodules of approximately the correct shape which were further shaped by percussion flaking. No unfinished side-blow preforms were found; and only five axes ground into shape from broad side-blow flake spalls, all retaining the bulb of percussion. The bit half of a parallel-sided example has already been described from Occupation IV, one of the earliest intentionally flaked pieces at the site. Three other examples have irregular sides converging to irregularly rounded, unused polls and expanding bits. One from Occupation V measures 59 x 39 x 13 mm; one from stratum 6B measures 104 x 66 x 22 mm, and was associated with Burial no. 11; while the other, found on the road in front of the site, measures 157 x 102 x 22 mm. All are fashioned from relatively coarse-grained diabase, and only the high spots of the faces have been ground. Apparently these spalls were struck from flat-surfaced angular boulders, using a nearly right-angled corner as a striking platform. All lateral edges that were not already flat, thick, and fairly straight were battered and ground into that shape. The fifth example (64 x 39 x 11 mm), from Occupation VII, is more completely ground, almost obliterating the original cortex and the flaking scars. The faces are biconvex in both directions, creating unusually thin but dull edges. The square poll retains the old flake scars.

All of the unused preforms and most of the axes flaked from preforms retain the natural oxidized weathering crust on at least one surface, showing that the knapper preferred not to have to remove a flake from an angular boulder, but rather simply to select a natural spall or nodule of approximately the proper shape. Not only was this procedure easier; but also a naturally rectangular nodule more closely approximated the desired shape of the finished product than did a flaked spall, whose shape is difficult to control.

The only axes not retaining some rust-colored sandpaper-like weathering rind are those made from water-worn pebbles or those made on side-blow spalls. Oxidized pebbles might have been found in old raised beach deposits; but more likely these nodules came from the exposed portion of the diabase dyke above high-tide level, about 200 m north of the site. Some of the boulders and smaller fragments at the dyke exhibit incipient columnar structure, or they broke into angular and occasionally tabular pieces for other reasons. Such pieces with naturally straight edges were selected for use, especially if they had broken into tabular slabs of suitable thickness. The knappers had not perfected quarrying methods for reducing and quartering massive raw material; although as already noted, evidently occasionally they did strike a spall from a right-angled corner of a boulder. Actually, there is very little difference between the earlier method of simply picking up a beach pebble of more or less the proper shape and grinding the surfaces directly, and the later method of selecting a suitably shaped tabular nodule and shaping it further by percussion before grinding the surfaces. The later method must have been somewhat less time-consuming and thereby more efficient; at least it was more efficient if the flaking process did not break the preform.

As already mentioned, the knapper did not know how to thin the bifaces, and in fact there are no typical

Figure 20. Flaked axe preform.

Figure 21. Slightly ground axe preform.

bifacial thinning flakes in the collection of flakes. The thick sides were struck on alternate edges with solid direct blows, removing short flakes with broad platforms, which often exhibit stepped flaking due to repeated blows on the same spot before a flake was removed successfully. There is, of course, no evidence of grinding the edge to produce a platform. The edges of the axes and preforms that had to be shaped by flaking are battered by repeated heavy direct blows, producing a stepped platform from which it would be essentially impossible for even an expert knapper to remove a thinning flake by holding the piece to be flaked at a high angle relative to the direction of the blow. But despite the fact that the knapper was evidently ignorant of the technique of thinning a core or biface, he did accomplish what he intended to make—a thick flat side as similar as possible to a naturally thick straight side. The only sharp edge he wanted was the bit, and that could be ground down whenever necessary. He was after thick, straight, flat lateral sides, as parallel as possible; and in many cases an equally thick, straight butt which could be used for hammering. If the battered sides of the preform were still too sharp or rough, he could grind them, producing a sinuous ground side, retaining only the terminal ends of flake scars alternating from both edges (cf. Tiburtius and Leprovost 1953:Figure 12, last example).

Although the ideal was not always attainable, especially if the preform were a side-blow flake, evidently the most desired shape for the finished product was rectangular, both in plan and cross-section, with straight polls, flat or slightly convex faces, thick flat parallel or slightly expanding sides toward the bibevelled bit, which was excurvate to nearly straight (the common rectangular type of Tiburtius and Leprovost 1953:525–528). Unless they had been reshaped bilaterally (i.e., the width was reduced by further flaking and grinding), all axes are fairly thin relative to their overall size. Unless noted to the contrary, all of the bitted implements to be described below were evidently made on bifacially flaked preforms.

The only direct evidence suggesting hafting is the presence on two examples of pecked unilateral grooves near the poll end, although it could be argued that such pecked areas were caused by patterned use as a hammerstone. Other specimens could have been hafted if an encircling withe were fastened with good binding glue. Many axes have pecked or battered polls, so they could not have been inserted into a solid socketed haft. It is possible, however, that a solid socketed haft was used to mount some of the small axes with sides converging toward the poll; although two of these have been broken by striking the poll, at which time they could not have been mounted in such a haft. Actually, because of the lack of definite evidence for hafting, it could be argued that they were all hand-held. The best argument that they were hafted is the abundant evidence for heavy use, a fact which implies that strong sweeping blows were delivered with a full arm swing, a dangerous practice without a haft to absorb the shock and prevent bruises.

Two variants to the above generalities about form are both nearly square in plan, although rectangular in cross-section. Both were flaked from patinated nodules, then ground to make broad bits. One from Occupation V, which measures 114 x 94 x 18 mm, is widest at the bit, which has had a use-flake removed from it after grinding. The other, from Occupation VII, and measuring 62 x 52 x 15 mm, has an expanding bit which extends around one corner onto the long axis of the piece as well, while the other edge and the poll were ground square. The bit has been slightly battered by use, and the corner of the poll where the bit grinding converged has been broken by heavy use.

One axe was found near Burial no. 4 in stratum 4B (Occupation VI). It measures 135 x 68 x 20 mm; and except for the poll, all surfaces were carefully ground to a bilaterally symmetrical implement in three planes, including a squared oval outline and a lenticular cross-section with unusually rounded sides. A few small use-flakes have been removed from the bit, but the poll was not used.

Five symmetrically rectanguloid axes with straight square sides that expand slightly to an excurvate bit all have polls that were squared by grinding or pecking. One thin example with a ground poll from Occupation VII, measuring 86 x 48 x 10 mm, exhibits little evidence of subsequent use; but the polls of the others are much battered. One nodule from Occupation VI needed very little shaping by flaking and grinding, except on the bit; this axe measures 162 x 80 x 31 mm. Another large axe (138 x 81 x 36 mm) from the same occupation zone has small circular pecked areas near the center of both faces. The poll has been much pecked and battered, resulting in the removal of several flakes. Even more use-flakes were removed from the poll of an example from Occupation VII, which measures 121 x 63 x 60 mm. A specimen from Occupation V has been intentionally battered on one edge and the poll to square the piece; it measures 175 x 92 x 30 mm. During this process one corner of the poll accidentally flaked off. The high spots were then ground; and the poll as well as the bit show subsequent use, with the removal of tiny flakes.

The remaining whole pieces have all been altered even more significantly by use. One example found on the surface of the talus slope of shell was originally much like the above examples—a weathered nodule flaked and ground into a rectangular bibevelled axe with a pecked poll (Figure 22). It differs in shape only in that the widest portion is near the center rather than the bit; the piece measures 129 x 74 x 34 mm. It differs also because one whole side of the bit has been removed by dozens of overlapping stepped flakes, while only one flake was removed from the other side. Because the resultant edge is so sharp, I at first thought that the piece was intentionally retouched unilaterally by percussion to sharpen the bit. But as there is no evidence of a prepared platform or even a battered edge which would serve as an essential platform, I had to conclude that the stepped flaking was by use and not by intention. Dennis Stanford, an expert flintknapper, concurred; and we agreed that the peculiar use-flaking must have been caused by an adzing stroke; that is, the object must have been hafted at right angles and probably used to hollow out a log for a food trough or a canoe. In most parts of the world an adze blade is intentionally unibevelled, and thereby distinguishable from bibevelled axe blades; but in this case the apparent function of the piece was revealed by unintentional rebevelling of a bibevelled bit.

The adze blade provides a clue to the probable function of another larger specimen (194 x 82 x 36 mm), also found on the surface of the talus slope of shell. It is a tabular nodule with minimal preparation flaking, and grinding only on the bibevelled bit. A sequence of large flakes was then removed from one side of the bit, forming a gouge-shaped object. Very likely this implement was also hafted as an adze, as the edge of the bit is very sharp. Both of these sharp bitted implements would still seem to be quite functional.

The remaining whole bitted implements have been so heavily worn by use that attempts were obviously made to reshape and resharpen them, although apparently all of them were discarded because they were no longer functional. Three flaked, then ground, implements from Occupation VII were reshaped again by alternate flaking on all edges; but the battering type of flaking either squared the bit too much or broke the piece, so they were discarded. It is instructive to note that when the bit of one example (125 x 62 x 17 mm) broke off, forming an oblique transverse straight edge, the knapper evidently did not know how to utilize the resultant flat surface as a striking platform for removing bifacial thinning flakes. Instead of striking near the center of the platform with a high-angled blow, he struck several small flakes off with direct right-angled blows from the very edge of both sides, making it difficult to remove any more flakes. He then did the same thing on

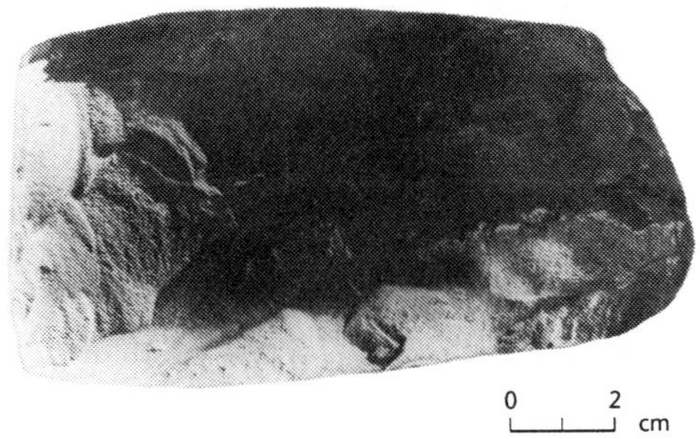

Figure 22. Ground and use-flaked adze.

one side of the ground poll, but he was evidently dissatisfied with the possibility of having an implement with a narrow bit and did not finish it by grinding. The bit half of a similar piece (74 x 52 x 17 mm) evidently broke in half because it was struck too hard while reshaping one edge. The bit of the third similar example (106 x 56 x 23 mm) was successfully reflaked, but the attempt to reshape one lateral edge was thwarted by a thick bulge which refused to be removed by repeated battering blows. The knapper then tried to grind down the bulge but evidently gave up and discarded the piece.

The bit of a rectangular implement with biconvex cross-section, recovered from the intrusive pit in square B2 (original stratum unknown), has been resharpened by grinding at a steeper angle, revealing old use-flake scars under the grinding surface. The irregularly squared poll was never used, but the new bit was subsequently dulled and flakes were removed from it by further hard use.

One implement from Occupation VII, made on a broken beach pebble (99 x 64 x 24 mm), shows a complicated sequence of use. First it was flaked, and the faces and poll were ground; the poll also received pecking marks on one corner. Then the sides and bit were reflaked and reground after heavy use. Both faces and especially the bit again received hard use, which created many crisscrossing striations, and a very dull bit. This final type of wear is not consistent with use as an axe, but strongly suggests that the implement had been hafted and used as the blade of a digging stick. Similarly shaped digging-stick blades were still used recently among the slash-and-burn horticulturists of the Rio Uaupes (Beltrão 1970:Figure 1). A flaked implement lacking grinding but with a similar pattern of wear has already been described from the same occupation zone. Another implement, measuring 103 x 56 x 17 mm, with slight evidence of bifacial grinding, has many striations near its use-flaked bit. The shape differs from the other two because the sides converge toward the poll; but the pattern of heavy use-flaking and striations, especially near the bit, is consistent with use as a digging implement. This last specimen was found on the surface of the site.

That implements with bibevelled bits were not always used as axes is also indicated by two thick narrow parallel-sided implements from Occupation VII. One example, measuring 105 x 46 x 26 mm, is a reshaped piece showing the following working sequence: (1) flaking; (2) grinding; (3) sides reshaped by flaking; (4) further shaping of parallel sides by grinding longitudinal facets, creating a lozenge-shaped cross-section; (5) pecking of the poll as well as an area on one side near the poll, creating a unilateral groove which might have been included for hafting; (6) dulling of the bit by heavy use before discarding. This specimen and another implement (82 x 24 x 24 mm), having a wedge-shaped longitudinal section and square cross-section (Figure 23), and with pecked poll, have shapes which strongly suggest that they were used as wedges.

The other possible wedges came from earlier occupations. A naturally wedge-shaped pebble of unidentified stone, measuring 40 x 52 x 14 mm, from Occupation V, exhibits many striations on both faces; and the edges of the faces and the bit are smoothed and worn by use, although it was never flaked or intentionally ground. A broken diabase object, from Occupation IV, and measuring 66 x 24 x 8 mm, was ground into shape with a plano-convex cross-section. The thin narrow end subsequently was flaked, evidently by heavy use as a chisel or a wedge, before the object broke. An irregularly shaped pebble of altered diabase, measuring 94 x 54 x 42 mm, from Occupation II, has evidence of slight grinding on its surfaces; and has had one use-flake removed from a wedge-shaped end.

Two small bitted objects from Occupation VII were made on naturally tabular spalls which were minimally flaked and ground into implements with straight converging sides. The bits were battered and much dulled by hard use. After the bit was rendered useless, another bit appears to have been ground onto the narrow poll of one implement, which measures 87 x 39 x 15 mm. This secondary bit was also heavily battered and flaked by use before the object was discarded. The other implement, which measures 103 x 56 x 17 mm, had been ground slightly on both faces; but most evidence of bit-grinding was removed by use-flaking (Figure 24).

Another atypical implement from Occupation VII is

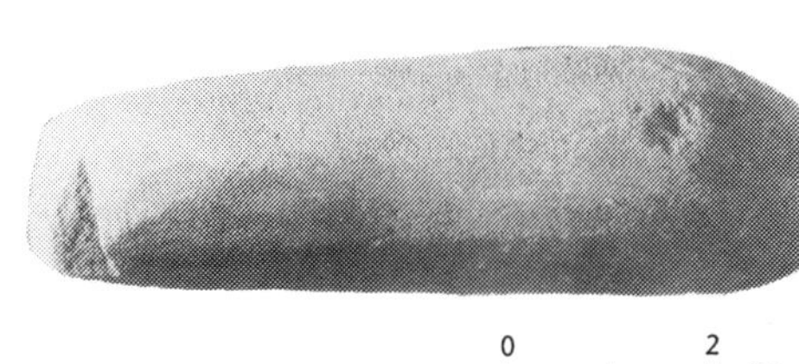

Figure 23. Ground stone wedge.

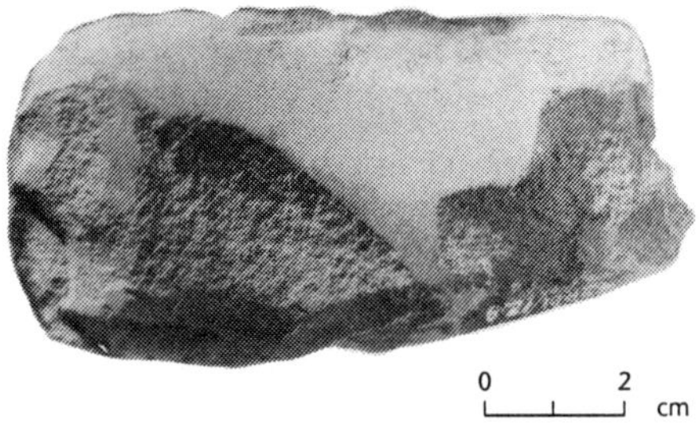

Figure 24. Use-flaked axe.

made on a tabular beach pebble with a natural transverse oblique poll end. The poll and the faces have been lightly ground, but the edges retain water-smoothed surfaces, and there is no evidence of flaking. The implement could hardly have served as an axe, but the bit could have been used for scraping.

Two of the bit halves evidently continued to be used after they broke transversely. The example from Occupation VII, which measures 71 x 63 x 18 mm with a biconvex cross-section, was shaped by flaking and grinding; and the expanding bit has been battered by heavy use, some of which was after the piece broke in half, to judge by the use-polish on the broken surface. The other example (85 x 64 x 29 mm), found on the surface of the site, exhibits a similar sequence of shaping; and use flakes have subsequently been removed from one corner of the bit. It was broken near the center by a hard blow which removed a hinge flake that took most of one face with it. The broken surface had been pecked by subsequent use as a hammerstone. A hinge fracture of this type could have been caused by a hard blow delivered while the piece was hafted as an adze.

Two bit ends from Occupation V show the usual sequence of shaping by flaking and grinding, as well as subsequent hard use of the blade. This pattern of heavy use is also found on the bit of an example from Occupation VII which measures 74 x 78 x 24 mm.

One poll end fragment from Occupation V was flaked, then ground and later reshaped by flaking again. A large tabular poll end (111 x 67 x 8 mm) from a disturbed area of Occupation VII is unusually thin and probably broke easily when used. Another poll end, measuring 66 x 40 x 17 mm, fell out of a trench wall, so lacks provenience. A similar-sized poll end, measuring 67 x 42 x 14 mm, was associated with Burial no. 52 in Occupation VII. All four of these poll ends were shaped by flaking and grinding.

Little new can be said about the two bit fragments which were recovered, one from Occupation VI, the other from a slumped wall; or the 18 other fragments of axes, all but two of which had been thermally fractured. Nine of these 18 came from Occupation VII, including two large fragments of the same axe from stratum 1. A surface find as well as two fragments from slumped walls probably came from the same zone. Two fragments came from Occupation Zone VI, three from V, and one from III. The latter, a large fragment which has a central depression on one face, has already been mentioned, in addition to one of the larger pieces from Occupation Zone VII, because they lacked any evidence of preliminary flaking. Four pieces included here as probable axe fragments (two from Zone VII, one from VI, and one from V) also lack evidence of preliminary flaking. Another small poll fragment from Occupation Zone V, too small to be sure if it was shaped by flaking, has had several flakes removed subsequently from the poll by heavy battering. All other fragments retain evidence of preliminary shaping by flaking before grinding. The bit fragments also exhibit dulling and/or battering by hard use. The example from Occupation VI is unusual as the bit is bevelled more from one face. None of the fire-broken fragments were actually found in a fireplace, so it is not possible to say for sure whether they were simply used as fireplace stones, after they were discarded as axes. It is also possible that some were deliberately burned in ceremonial fires.

Discussion of the Possible Functions of Bitted Implements

The question of function of the finished products with bibevelled bits requires further discussion. It appears obvious at first that bibevelled bitted implements were shaped to be used as axes, but we have seen that at least two and probably three of the bitted implements were dulled and striated by heavy use of a kind that would occur on a hafted digging-stick blade. Also, at least one and probably three implements exhibit evidence that they were hafted as adzes.

Some bitted implements may have been used for other purposes. Use-flakes have frequently been removed from the ground bits of "axes." Several examples show evidence of sharpening badly broken bits by grinding, and two examples of bit end fragments continued to be used after the poll was broken off by a heavy blow. Such heavy usage suggests that these implements were used for purposes other than chopping wood or even whalebones.

Two axes have pecked unilateral grooves near their poll ends, suggesting that they were hafted with an encircling withe. The type of hinge flakes removed from the poll end of one of these and from another similar example with a heavily battered poll (Figure 25) is very similar to the kind of use flakes removed from hafted (or actually bound) elk (wapiti—*Cervus canadensis*) antler wedges on the Northwest Coast of North America, where the poll end of antler wedges is tightly wrapped with an encircling binding to retard splitting and break-

Figure 25. Axe with use-flaked poll.

age when it is battered. This fact suggests, but of course cannot demonstrate, that some of the implements may also have been used as wedges for splitting logs of branches; while many of the heavily battered hammerstones served, among other functions, as hand mauls for striking the squared polls. An argument against this possible function is that the axes are not wedge-shaped in transverse section, a shape which would function more efficiently. Nevertheless, if the log to be split is not too big or too tough, the wedge-shaped bit by itself would function as a splitting tool. A naturally wedge-shaped piece of weathered diabase, found directly associated with a hammerstone in Occupation VII, had smoothed surfaces on its natural (unground) bit, as if it had been used as a wedge. In addition, several small chisel-like bitted implements were described, one of which in particular, with a nearly square thick cross-section and pecked poll, would serve quite readily as a wedge for splitting small pieces of wood, such as pickets. Several even smaller bitted implements made on detritus flakes, to be described next, most likely were used as small wedges, chisels, or scrapers.

Evidently most of the stone tools were used for many purposes during their active careers. Also, it seems probable that some implements were intentionally made quite long in the first place; and as they broke and were worn down, they were resharpened and used for similar or different functions. Perfectly shaped and carefully polished axes with sharp bits are rarely found in sambaquis, and they are usually associated with burials.

Reused and Unused Diabase Flakes

The rough bulbar surfaces of 11 thick flakes accidentally removed from ground diabase axes were probably reused as abrading stones or files for working bone and wood. On one small implement (31 x 15 x 4 mm) the lateral edges and one end have been carefully shaped by battering to create straight sides and a rectangular plan in the same way that full-sized axes were shaped. The sides of two other flakes also appear to have been deliberately straightened into steep edges, which were then used for scraping at a high angle. These tiny shaped tools as well as five larger flakes ranging in size from 48 x 26 x 5 mm to 80 x 41 x 10 mm came from Occupation Zone VII. All of them exhibit straight to slightly excurvate bibevelled bits formed by grinding a portion of the bulbar surface parallel to an old ground surface. The bits appear to be deliberately shaped by grinding; but it is possible that repeated pushing at a low angle on the surface to be abraded would naturally smooth the leading edge; and the other edge was already ground. One thick flake from Occupation VII, removed from an axe preform, exhibits two grinding facets on its positive bulbar surface, showing that this unshaped implement, which measures 73 x 30 x 10 mm, was also used as a file or abrading stone. Although a short section of the edge was smoothed, obviously the sharp edge was not as desirable as the rough emery paper-like flake surface. Another flake removed from a ground axe found in Occupation Zone VI has a grinding facet on its positive bulbar face. The thin distal edge exhibits smoothing and steep flaking caused by intensive scraping at a high angle. Certainly this flake would be ideal for filing and scraping a bone tool. Similarly, a rough diabase flake, measuring 59 x 36 x 13 mm, found on the surface, has been used as a file on one face; while the edges are all smoothed by use as a scraper.

One pentagonal flake from stratum 6B measuring 59 x 59 x 11 mm, with flat negative and positive bulbar faces, exhibits two steep battered edges and three equally steep edges which appear to have been deliberately formed by high-angled percussion blows delivered with considerable force. All of these nearly right-angled (70–85°) edges appear to have been heavily scraped on their sharpest angles by a pushing action (i. e., used as a scraper-plane) which removed stepped flakes from the adjacent flat face. All edges and faces are much worn, although the faces lack grinding facets.

Two large flakes removed from the battered poll ends of axes from Occupation VII exhibit subsequent use of their sharp excurving edges. A small flake from the same zone has use facets ground onto the bulbar surface as well as superimposed on the old ground surface of the axe. In addition, half of the perimeter of this nearly round flake is smoothed by use as a scraper.

A large flake (65 x 62 x 15 mm) from Occupation VII has smoothed edges and a grinding facet on the bulbar surface, suggesting that it was used as a scraper-plane. This diabase flake has a thin platform, and retains the original weathered cortex, so it probably was a decortication flake removed by the intentional flaking of an axe preform. One spall removed accidentally from the working end of a hammerstone shows evidence of subsequent use. The edges of this example from Occupation VII have been facetted by heavy use; and the exterior water-worn surface exhibits grinding striations at the battered end, which actually forms a dull axe or wedge bit. The high spots of the bulbar face of a crystalline flake, measuring 69 x 59 x 25 mm, from Occupation Zone II have been smoothed; and one excurving edge exhibits "nibbling" flake scars from heavy use. The flake apparently spalled off a hammerstone.

A large spall (144 x 120 x 55 mm) found on the talus slope has been slightly ground on the bulbar surface, while the sharp edge and pointed corner also exhibit use as a scraping tool. Two fragments of thermally fractured object from Occupation II exhibit ground faces and edges.

Unused Flakes

A total of 105 other flakes and spalls accidentally removed from hammerstones and axes lacked any evidence of subsequent use. These specimens and 192 intentional flakes were distributed as follows:

	I	II	III	IV	6B	V	VI	VII
Spalls from "hammerstones"	1				3		3	
Spalls from "axes"		1		1	1	6	6	83
Intentional flakes from preforms						10	14	168

Logically, one would think that some of the relatively sharp-edged flakes removed intentionally from shaping axe preforms in Occupations V, VI, and VII would have been used as knives for whittling wood or carving bone objects, but careful examination of the 192 intentional flakes removed from axe preforms failed to reveal any such evidence of use. A couple of these flakes have slightly "nibbled" edges which may have been caused from slicing something soft, like meat; but the evidence is too equivocal to classify these flakes as artifacts and the nibbling not accidentally or spontaneously removed.

Apparently the motor habits of the craftsmen did not change simply because an abundance of sharp-edged flakes suddenly became available; they continued to scrape, grind, and groove in the accustomed manner. Evidently the aboriginal people at Forte Marechal Luz were not aware of a technique to retouch the sharp edge of a thinning flake to make it suitable for scraping or for cutting resistant material. They therefore selected naturally thick sturdy edges which would not easily crumble when working resistant materials, like fibres, wood, and bone.

About 40% of the apparently unused flakes removed from preforms have repeatedly battered platforms. As discussed when the axe preforms were described, evidently the knappers did not know how to thin an object by grinding a platform and holding the piece to be struck so that a high-angled flake would be removed. Rather, using a forceful pecking motion, they repeatedly struck the platform at a near right angle, resulting in battered platforms.

The absence of typical bifacial thinning flakes (whose bulbs retain part of both converging flaked surfaces, thus forming a characteristic lip) helps to demonstrate that the usual kind of bifacial flaking was not known at Fort Marechal Luz. Instead, the knappers used the thick flat sides of their preforms as a platform for removing flakes from both faces, so the bulbar ends of the flakes are squared and often battered from repeated attempts to remove the flake.

Thus analysis of the unused flakes has supplemented the evidence from the finished artifacts themselves, and revealed that the people who occupied the Forte Marechal Luz sambaqui during the last 400 years of its accumulation lacked any real expertise with their recently acquired technique of percussion flaking. This situation is in stark contrast to the situation concerning the other major technological tradition—fired ceramics—which was exercised with considerable expertise, if not finesse, at the site during the last 250 years of occupation. Most likely, both traditions were obtained indirectly from neighboring groups. The striking difference in degree of expertise leads to a speculation admittedly difficult to test. Is it possible that local males went into the interior on trade missions which included a search for suitable wives? When they entered foreign villages, they obtained a few flaked bifaces in gift exchanges; but they did not have the opportunity to see how they were fabricated. Later, at home, the men attempted to copy the technique; but as they had not observed the knapper's art of preparing a platform by grinding the edge in order to thin a biface, nor the even more complicated art of pressure flaking, their percussion technology was only at an incipient stage. After a few generations, when they successfully obtained wives either by exchange or theft, the women brought with them their fully developed ceramic tradition, which is technologically the same as that found on the Planalto.

Chapter 7
The Processing of Bone

Marks of Alteration on Bone

Unintentional Marks

Butchering Marks.

As all potentially identifiable bones were saved in level bags, it was possible to recover essentially all specimens with any evidence of human alteration. One important category of alteration, albeit unintentional, is butchering marks, which may yield evidence for patterned human behavior if enough altered bones of one species are recovered. Unfortunately, this was not the case at Forte Marechal Luz, although enough evidence was found to show that these foragers did occasionally hunt and butcher large land mammals, especially in the upper occupation zones. Deep cuts, grooves, and fine incisions identified as butchering marks were found on mammal, bird, and fish bones. Even some human bones exhibit such marks, but they will be discussed with the chapter on the disposition of human remains. Gastropod columellas occasionally exhibit incisions where a sharp object has been used to extract the meat. Univalve columellas are discussed under shell artifacts.

Unfortunately, because of the paucity of comparative osteological material in Rio de Janeiro, the sea mammal and bird bones have not been identified as to species, and many fish bones remain unidentified.

a. **Fish Bone.** Striations identified as probably the result of butchering were noted on thirteen long fish bones. The most commonly observed evidence is two or more fine parallel incisions across the grain of the bone on one face. On one of the ten examples the cuts were made at an oblique angle. One example came from Occupation II, three from Occupation IV, two from Occupation V, and one from Occupation VI. Another incised cylindrical fragment from Occupation V is very hard because the bone has been heated. A similarly hardened vertebral spine is described with the fish-bone artifacts. Two other specimens from Occupation V exhibit a deep longitudinal groove along one face at right angles to the parallel striations, while one bone from Occupation VI has a deep cut which nearly encircles the perimeter, plus an adjacent shorter cut. The sample of butchered fish bones is insufficient to discern cultural patterns, although it does indicate that such patterns may be identifiable from the careful examination of larger series of identified species.

   One horny object from Occupation IV, shaped like a bird beak, is probably actually a fin spine of a fish. The tip end exhibits striations which may have been caused by use as a perforator, although it may be due to natural wear.

b. **Bird Bone.** Only four bird-bone fragments (one from Occupation V and three from Occupation VII) exhibit possible butchering marks. Parallel incisions on one fragment along the grain on the interior surface suggest that the bone may have been suspended. The third more-complete bone with the articulating end removed exhibits one transverse cut on the external surface. Possibly the latter piece, or even all four, are simply the detritus left from fabricating bird bone bipoints, a major industry from the upper levels to be described below.

c. **Land-mammal Bone.** Very few of the land-mammal bone fragments showing striations were identifiable as to species. The distal end of a left humerus of *Cuniculus paca* from Occupation IV exhibits fine parallel incisions on two areas near the head. The distal end of a right tibia of *Tapirus terrestris* also was striated, but in addition exhibits a series of short parallel cuts and chops with a blunt instrument, such as a stone axe. This broken end from Occupation VI may have been discarded after using the remainder for making bone tools. Both articular ends of a left second metatarsal were found together in Occupation VII. The distal end has three parallel incisions on the articular surface. In this case it is also likely that the thick-walled shaft had been removed for making tools. The distal end of what is probably the left femur of a tapir, from Occupation VII, has been crudely chopped off, probably with a stone axe. Scattered striations are visible on the surface, and a sharp broken tip shows evidence of use. Another mammal-bone splinter from the same occupation zone also has a sharp point which appears to have been worn by use. No other marks are evident on this splinter. Crude chopping with a dull instrument was found on one end of a splinter from Occupation VII, and a series of deep cuts from a similar blunt instrument is visible on a rib from Occupation V. A fragmentary large right femur of *Tapirus terrestris*, from Occupation III, exhibits many scattered striations and depressions made by a blunt instrument. Part of the distal end of a deer cannon bone from Occupation VII has some oblique striations on the ventral surface.

The remaining seven land-mammal bone fragments and two ribs all show striations, incisions, or short cuts on a face. Except for two from unknown provenience, and one splinter from Occupation IV, all of them come from the last occupation (VII), including one of them found in the fill with Burial no. 18. The only possible evidence for an intentional artistic design found at the site was an irregular diamond-shaped form made by four striations on one of these fragments.

Although no evidence of butchering marks was found, two long bone fragments exhibit conchoidal fractures caused by striking green bone by percussion. One example came from Occupation VII, the other from Occupation IV. As there is no evidence of further reduction, probably these bones were broken to remove the edible marrow. Other portions of these broken bones may have been chosen for further reduction into bone tools.

d. **Sea-Mammal Bone.** Sea-mammal bones constitute the majority of bones showing alteration marks which are not readily identified as due to the fabrication of tools. Detritus of manufacture will be dealt with separately in a discussion of the processes used in making bone tools.

Apparently flaking of dense bone was not a technique used for the preliminary reduction of bone, or there would have been much more evidence found. As mentioned above, only two long bones of land mammals were found that exhibited percussion bulbs. A knapper must have dense bone to flake it effectively, and most sea-mammal bone is too porous. The large tympanic bulae of whales are the notable exception to this generalization. As they are exceedingly dense as well as being thick-walled, they can be flaked very easily by use as a chopper. But although whalebone was commonly found in certain upper strata, all but one piece of tympanic bula came from Occupation I (the exception was an unflaked fragment from Occupation IV, exhibiting many cuts and incisions on its external surface). Two similar pieces, one of which exhibited a small burned section, came from Occupation I; while two other pieces had been flaked. As the flaked edges showed use, and as the associated stone objects in this early stratum were also occasionally flaked by heavy use, it was concluded that the flaking on these pieces was not intentional, but rather due to their use as expediency tools. One rectangular piece had been unifacially flaked at both ends. If one held or hafted the object and used it as an adze with a chopping action, use flakes would readily be removed. Similar unifacial flakes were removed from the excurving edge of the lip of a more-complete bula, evidently as a result of scraping or chopping while gripping the internal tuberosity of the bula. This artifact was sacrificed to obtain the radiocarbon date of 2340 B.C. on Occupation I. As very little shell was present in this basal stratum, porous bone did not preserve. The exception was a flat piece of whalebone hardened by fire, the external surface of which exhibited a polished depression (18 mm in diameter and 2 mm deep), perhaps used for breaking small palm nuts. With this exception, all bone tools from Occupation I were shaped by use rather than by intention. Similarly, with the exception of a pebble with a pecked groove, the only evidence of deliberate shaping found on the assemblage of stone tools from Occupation I is pecked depressions.

The difficulty of distinguishing butchering marks from marks of intentional fabrication, either of some part of the piece itself or of other objects held against the piece, as on an anvil or chopping block, is most notable when dealing with cut and incised whalebone. Whalebone is easy to distinguish from land-mammal bone by its porosity as well as by size, although some other sea-mammal bones may have been mistakenly identified as whale, because again the scarcity of comparative material made it impossible to identify species. Whales were probably never hunted off the coast of Brazil in prehistoric times, but the fairly abundant occurrence of worked bones in the deposits indicates that stranded whale carcasses were frequently utilized. Even several very large vertebrae were carried up to the site for use, and several smaller long bones were used as chopping blocks. Of the 37 whalebones with cuts and incisions originally classified as being the result of butchering, at least two of these could easily be the result of attempts to manufacture bone artifacts; but as nothing was removed from the pieces, it is difficult to be certain. For instance, one bone has a deep V-shaped cut across the grain made by two parallel cuts with a sharp instrument. The other fragment, also from Occupation VII, exhibits four parallel incisions which run the entire length of this calcined fragment at an oblique angle to the grain of the bone. Some other broad deep cuts, as distinguished from fine incisions, may also have been the result of trying to fabricate bone objects rather than removing meat, or dismembering a stranded whale to obtain valuable blubber and oil.

Nine sea-mammal bones, all from Occupation VII, exhibit from one to several deep, usually parallel, cuts across the grain. Usually the cuts are on the broader faces, but may also be on the thick edges of the bone. Although most of these pieces are too fragmentary to be able to identify the bone, at least three are ribs; and one is a scapula, perhaps of a seal, the associated mate of which exhibited no cuts. Interestingly, the articulating end of one cut bone appears to have been chewed.

One complete and three fragmentary dolphin (probably *Sotalia brasiliensis*) mandibles all lacked teeth, but exhibited parallel incisions on their exterior surfaces. The complete specimen, which also exhibited many scraping marks, was found in Occupation IV; while the broken section and the fragmentary pair of mandibles came from Occupation V. Three seal (?) long bones, one a femur, also probably from Occupation V, exhibit parallel cuts on the shafts. The femur also has a cut mark on an articular tuberosity.

Actually only nine incised whalebones are fairly obviously the result of butchering. The lateral processes of two vertebrae, found together in a slumped area, exhibit a series of fine parallel incisions at an oblique angle to the long axis of the processes. Six long bones (four from Occupation V; one from Occupation VII; and one with Burial no. 4, Occupation VI) exhibit striations parallel to an articulating or epiphyseal end. In addition to parallel striations, the cancellous area of the interior also appears to have been removed on another long bone from Occupation VI.

Chopping Blocks

Both faces of the dorsal portion of a large whale vertebra from Occupation VII are deeply incised as if something had been chopped on it. A large piece of whalebone from Occupation V and nine long bones (listed below) exhibit cuts, chops, and striations across the grain near the center of one or both faces, a pattern which suggests that they also were probably used as anvils or chopping blocks. Two illustrated phalanges show this pattern very well. Two specimens, including the smaller illustrated one (Figure 26) with two deep cuts, were found on the surface; while the larger one (Figure 27) came from Occupation III. Four came from Occupation VII; and two, which may be long bones of some other sea mammal, came from Occupation VI in test pit 1. The category of incisions and cuts so placed that they do not appear to be butchering marks, but nonetheless essentially unintentional marks made by using the objects as chopping blocks, is an intermediate category to deliberate chopping, apparently as a means of preliminary reduction of very large bones to a size where they can be more easily moved.

Intentional Processing Marks

Altered Whalebone

Evidence of chopping on a few large land-mammal bones has already been mentioned. Apparently blunt instruments, such as stone axes, were even more often used to break up large thick-walled whalebones. In several South American museum collections I have noticed very similar chopping marks on extinct animal bones, including mastodons and ground sloths (Bryan 1983; Prous 1986:Figures 1, 2, 3). Evidently the process of reducing and sectioning very large mammal bones by chopping them up with a blunt axe is an old cultural tradition on the continent.

Four objects have been sectioned by chopping across the grain in the manner that one sections a piece of firewood. Two pieces from Occupation V were chopped from both directions and severed by breaking the piece in the center where the oblique cuts converge. One cylindrical hollow section, from Occupation VII, was sectioned in this matter at both ends, possibly with the intention of using it as a haft for another object. A similar fragmentary cylindrical object from Occupation II was chopped at one end; and appears to have two deliberate circular depressions, 5 mm in diameter, on the interior cancellous side. Conceivably the depressions could somehow have helped to secure an object into the haft.

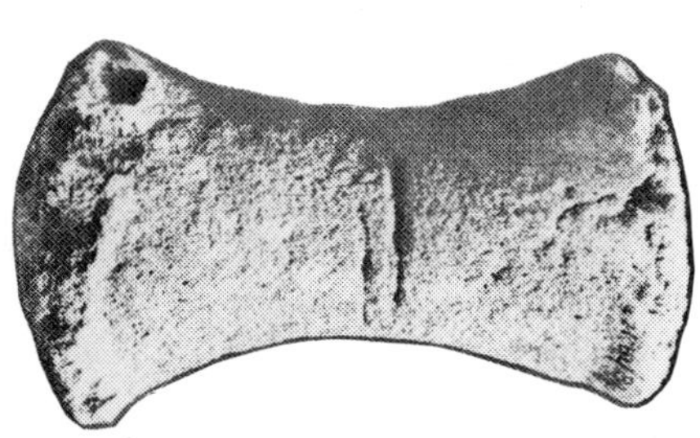

Figure 26. Whale-phalange chopping block.

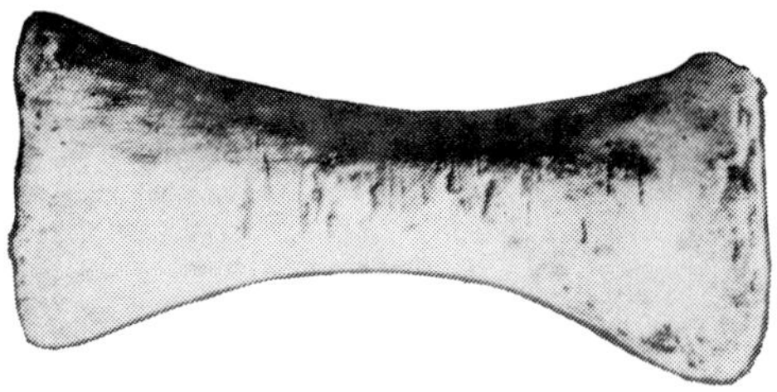

Figure 27. Whale-phalange chopping block.

Quite possibly, some of the sea-mammal long bones already identified as chopping blocks were used as anvils upon which to hold large bones while chopping them. In fact, one associated set of whalebone artifacts found in stratum 10 near the top of Occupation Zone II includes two bones chopped on their ends and edges (artifacts 880 and 900 in Figure 9a), lying near a large tabular chopping board exhibiting many nicks and cuts (artifact 894 in same Figure 9a). They are associated with a vertebra with a burned depression on its upper surface (artifact 901), and several giant oyster shells (artifacts 899).

Not shown in the plan drawing (Figure 9a), but found nearby and probably also associated, were the fragments of a large rib, another piece of chopped whalebone, and many fragments of a large bone burned on one face and lying next to another vertebra slightly burned on one face and with a V-shaped groove chopped into the other face with a sharp instrument. At first I thought that these associations were the remnants of cooking areas, but why would anyone carry so many heavy bones up to the site simply as cooking equipment? Possibly they are the remains of some sort of specialized processing of whalebone for rendering bone grease and oil by heating the bones, which thereby also became hardened and more useful as tools. With this thought, the presence of calcined whalebone fragments within and on the lip of basin no. 5 of the group of unfired clay basins (Figure 7) in stratum 7 (Occupation Zone IV) may achieve significance.

Although not directly associated, several fragments of at least three more very large bones (pelves?) with scorched areas on one of their surfaces also came from stratum 10 in a neighboring square. Two of these fragments, as well as pieces of a large unburned bone from the same stratum, had been chopped at one end. This concentration of large bones may well have come from dismembering one beached animal in order to carry the useful parts up to the site for further processing. Another less-obvious concentration from near the top of Occupation Zone IV (stratum 6) included four fragments of a long rib chopped cleanly at one end apparently with a single blow from an axe, a large fragmentary piece chopped at one end and burned on one surface, and a third piece which appears to have been deliberately broken at one end. Fragments of another large piece cut at one end were found in an older level of Occupation Zone IV.

One other concentration of whalebone was encountered. Contiguous burials nos. 22 and 23 were interred in stratum 6B with three large whalebones. In fact, the primary flexed skeleton of no. 22 appears to have been deliberately placed on a large flat unmodified whalebone. Fragments of a large rib with deep cuts near one end were found beneath both skeletons, while another piece with a burned exterior surface was associated with Burial no. 23. Calcination had hardened the bone and caused the surface to check. One wonders if divination by reading the pattern of check marks may have been practiced during the burial ceremony. Another fragmentary rib exhibiting scattered striations was found under the skull of nearby Burial no. 24. Certainly these associations must have had special cultural significance.

Sectioning of large bones by chopping, and shaping by whittling, perhaps with the same blunt axe, were very likely also the preliminary stages of reduction for the fabrication of bone tools, which will be discussed later. However, as the technological tradition of bone tool manufacture probably developed out of familiarity with the way bone breaks while people were butchering and breaking up bones for processing marrow and bone grease, it is impossible to segregate neatly those bones which exhibit essentially unintentional signs of alteration from bones that were being deliberately shaped for tool production.

Most of the carved and whittled pieces of whalebone were quite solid. Perhaps some were simply pieces of exceptionally dense bone, but others appear to have been deliberately hardened by heating. Many of these pieces are probably detritus of manufacture. None of these carved and whittled artifacts were fashioned of very dense tympanic bulae (cf. Tiburtius, Leprovost, and Bigarella 1949). Two from Occupation VII were bevelled at one end. One from a cave-in appears to have a carved concave edge, while a large piece found above the hands of Burial no. 44 (stratum 6B) appears to have a carved S-curving edge. The interior surface of a fragment from Occupation IV has been whittled, while three objects were probably finished artifacts. One large rhomboidal piece from Occupation V exhibits overall shaped surfaces which have been much worn. As the edges appear more worn than the faces it could have been used as a scraper or hide-preparation tool. A solid piece from Occupation II was chopped and worn on one end and three faces to produce a waisted effect, as if it might have been hafted, perhaps as a fish-line weight. One long cylindrical piece from Occupation IV was chopped at one end and burned on the other end. It could have been used as a poker with a brazier, although there was no close association. One solid bone, probably a scapula with a longitudinal ridge, from Occupation IV, had several marks made by dull implements on its concave surface. This large bone could have been used as a platter. Functional interpretations such as these probably have little value except that they may help the reader to visualize the objects better. Two pieces of a large object exhibit a scorched surface which was polished and haphazardly striated by use. Although not a vertebral epiphysis, this object from stratum 6B exhibits use patterns similar to those on ephiphyses.

Whalebone vertebrae and epiphyseal discs removed from vertebrae almost invariably show considerable evidence of use. In fact, only one fragmentary epiphysis from stratum 6B lacked any evidence of alteration. The incompletely fused epiphyseal discs appear to have been deliberately pried off in several cases. The centrum of one vertebra from Occupation VII retains portions of both epiphyses, but there are three parallel cuts on one edge which appear to have been made by trying to pry off one epiphysis. The epiphysis had been removed and a central depression made in the exposed cancellous portion of one vertebra from Occupation IV. The basin-shaped depression had then been charred. A large fragment (55 x 22 cm) of a larger bone was found nearby (Figure 28). Part of a circular burned area about the same diameter as the burned area on the vertebra suggests that this piece had been held over a fire built in the bowl-shaped depression. A smaller vertebra from the same occupation zone had been hollowed on one side and burned in the same manner. The only associated artifact is a whale patella or sesamoid (?) with four deep cuts near the edge of one face.

Two more vertebrae with similar burned depressions on their upper faces were found in stratum 10. Several associated whalebones exhibiting various kinds of alteration have already been discussed. Near a vertebra showing only slight burning were fragments of another large whalebone with a similar circular burned pattern. Both epiphyses are missing on this burned vertebra, and the base of one missing lateral process shows that it had been severed by several chopping strokes with a sharp axe. The other burned vertebra from stratum 10 (artifact 901 in Figure 9 a, b) still had charcoal in its central burned depression, which had a diameter of 20 cm. This charcoal was used to obtain a radiocarbon date of 100 B.C. for this uppermost stratum in Occupation II. In this feature the only associated object that had been burned was an oyster shell (artifact 899 G in Figure 9a) found beneath the vertebra. As the thick shell was completely calcined it must have originally been directly in the fire. Obviously considerable heat was generated in these charcoal braziers. These braziers were likely used for cooking food, but possibly also bone grease was being extracted and collected in the oyster shells. The two large fragments with circular burned areas may have been used as lids over the burning braziers to help retain the heat.

Apparently the removed ephiphyseal discs were useful for other purposes. One fragment exhibited several scorched areas, including a triangular pattern where something hot had been placed on it. It was found adjacent to an ash lens in Occupation IV. Six fragments exhibited only striations or cuts on their articular faces. Half of these came from Occupation V and the remainder from Occupation VII. The central segment of an ephiphysis which exhibited a broad semicircular gouge made by a fairly sharp implement like an axe bit was found in Occupation VII.

Four other fragments exhibit ground epiphyseal surfaces which partially expose the internal cancellous structure. Three of these were from Occupation V and the other from stratum 6B. Two were ground to a concave surface (Figure 29), while one has a flat surface and the other surface is undulating. The only complete ground whalebone object (128 mm long), a tabular rectangular piece with a central perforation (Figure 30) is obviously not made on a vertebral ephiphysis, so there is no evidence that these ground ephiphyses should be classed as detritus of manufacture. More likely, they are pieces of finished artifacts, perhaps porous dishes, which would readily drain the grease off food and at the same time retain the grease for other uses.

One fragmentary whalebone object from Occupation VII has a smooth polished surface which exhibits some

Figure 28. Whalebone with circular burned area.

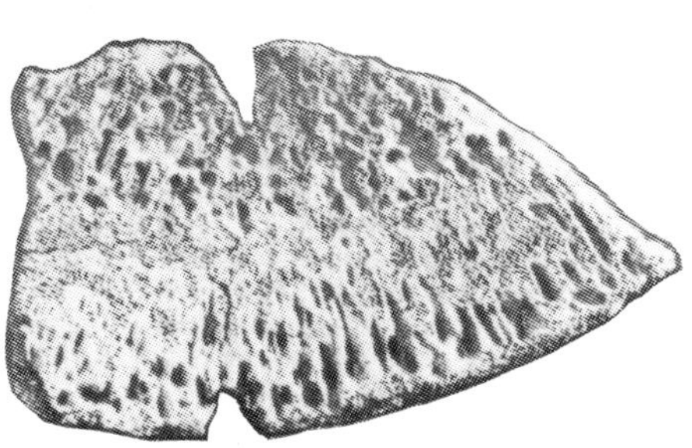

Figure 29. Ground whalebone object.

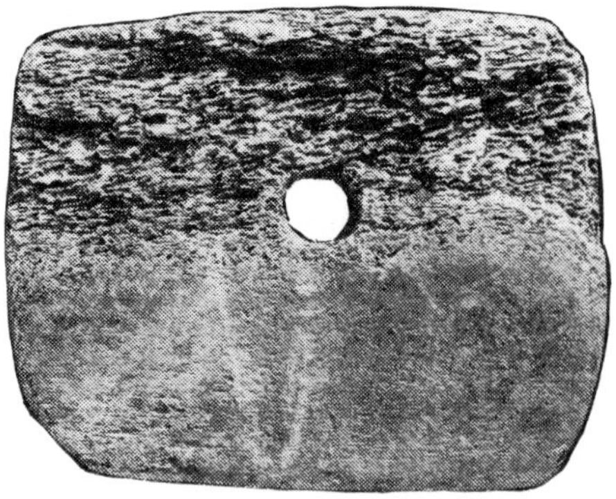

Figure 30. Perforated whalebone object.

grinding striations. An adjacent edge has been deeply cut across the grain and thereby intentionally broken. As most of the object is missing it is difficult to tell whether it was a completed artifact or merely a piece of detritus left from fabricating an artifact. One face of another fragment from stratum 6B has been ground flat with oblique strokes.

So far, this discussion of altered bone has ranged from unintentional incisions identified as butchering marks, through deliberate chopping apparently as a means for sectioning large bones, to whittling for further reduction, and finally to grinding as a means of shaping certain large bones. Also described was scorching, which may have been the result of processing chopped bones, or perhaps for the extraction of bone grease; but which incidentally resulted in hardening some bones, which could then be used more effectively for making tools. All of these technological processes for altering bone were evidently the result of many trial-and-error experiments carried out through the millennia by many generations of occupants of the site.

Detritus of Manufacture

The second part of this chapter will show how manufacturing processes were applied to make tools from bone and thick pieces of shell. In addition to the processing technique applied to whalebone—hardening by heating, incising and cutting, chopping, whittling, grooving, and grinding—the process of scraping and sawing bone will also be introduced as important techniques for shaping small bone objects from bird, land mammal, and certain fish bones. With the exception of some fish bones, perforations in bone were made by scraping or simply punching; and not by drilling, a technique reserved for perforating teeth.

Just as the systematic reduction of stone by flaking creates a residue of flakes, the study of which can yield useful clues about flaking techniques, the processes applied to the making of bone objects frequently results in small pieces and many fragments which contain the essential clues to understanding how bone objects were fabricated. Normally it is not necessary to use a binocular microscope to be able to see the marks of fabrication on these pieces of detritus because subsequent use has not worn the telltale marks. It is possible, of course, that some of these fragments are pieces of finished objects that broke soon after being put to use, but nevertheless they help to elucidate the techniques of manufacture.

Many of the tools used for cutting, scraping, grooving, and punching were made of teeth, particularly shark and paca teeth. Most cutting and scraping in the final occupations was evidently accomplished with thick diabase flakes; natural quartz fragments served the same purposes, but perhaps less efficiently, in Occupations IV and V.

Interestingly, all 56 of the bone objects classified as detritus of manufacture are from the later Occupations (IV to VII, and intrusive stratum 6B). The fact that such pieces apparently do not occur in the earlier three occupations implies that the processing of bone for the fabrication of artifacts was an industry less important in earlier occupations. Nevertheless, a few nicely finished bone artifacts did occur in the older occupations. Two broken objects from Occupation II and another from III will be included in this discussion as they illustrate the simple primary techniques of manufacture used at that time—cutting, scraping, and filing. Five splinters of a bird-bone tube from Occupation III show that the ends were cut transversely and then polished. A mammal-bone splinter was scraped, and then a straight edge was filed with an oblique stroke. Scraping marks also occur on the bird-bone fragments from Occupation II.

Before proceeding further, it is necessary to define terms. Cutting or deep incising is done with a knife in order to sever a piece of bone, much like a glass cutter is used to make a deep guide incision. Ideally, lateral pressure then causes the piece to break cleanly along the incision, although in most cases the break is rough or entirely unsuccessful on the detrital examples. On thick-walled mammal bone the cuts are often insufficiently deep to create a clean break, so parallel cuts from opposite faces are employed to increase the chances of successful breaking. Table 6 shows that all six pieces cut from both faces were successfully severed. Although most of the pieces with guide cuts only on one face are broken, the break was frequently not where it was intended. This fact may be the reason why some of these objects were discarded. Occasionally a flat thin piece of bone has been deliberately broken cleanly without a guide cut. One example came from Occupation IV, and another from Occupation VII.

Repeated back-and-forth thrusts with a thin serrated edge or a simple unretouched flake will create sawing marks. As no intentionally serrated saws were found, when sawing is identified it was probably done by repeated strokes with a dull flake. In other words there is no significant difference between cutting and sawing.

Scraping is similar to whittling except that the knife is held at a higher angle and usually drawn back as with a spokeshave or draw knife, instead of being pushed forward. Scraping with a dull blade does not create nicks or notches as does the strong pushing action of whittling, and scraping with a stone (or tooth?) knife shows all the irregularities on the knife blade as a series of tiny parallel grooves and ridges which generally run along the natural grain the length of the object. If only one regular series of parallel undulating grooves is found, one knows that the piece was scraped with a single stroke; but normally the grooves and ridges cross each other and eliminate most marks from the preceding stroke. Scraping is the most common technique for shaping a curving face on hard material. Many ethnographic objects carved out of hard wood, such as bows, clubs, and boomerangs, by people who did not have steel knives, exhibit scraping marks.

The three pieces of detritus illustrated in Figure 31 exhibit deep incisions intended to help snap the pieces into sections. In the case of the central long bone fragment, the incision was not deep enough to break it in the desired places. The same piece also illustrates the pattern made by scraping marks. The wall, especially of thin-walled bird bone, can be further thinned or even perforated by scraping. One piece of bird-bone detritus (not illustrated) from Occupation V was cut and broken at both ends after both longitudinal edges had been sawed in lengthwise grooves prepared by scraping. Thus the cut cross-section exhibits both scraped and sawed facets which run the entire length of the piece.

Grinding is the other primary technique for shaping bone. Usually the bone is ground by moving it on a whetstone, creating an overall pattern of parallel striations on a flat surface or straight edge. As with scraping, subsequent strokes may be at a different angle; and they tend to eliminate the previous pattern. Sometimes the whetstone is used as a file, creating a pattern of many short sections of parallel striations, usually at different oblique angles to the normal grain of the bone. Also the filed surface need not be flat, although usually it is. Again, there is really no significant difference between grinding and filing; and it is very difficult if not impossible to distinguish the two techniques on a finished object. The faces and edge of the object in Figure 32 exhibit ground facets in addition to a successfully sawed and broken end. The object illustrated in Figure 33 exhibits a filed lateral facet and a scraped excurvate face; these processes were applied before it was cut and sawed transversely in order to section it.

Table 6 shows that bone tool fabrication first became important in preceramic Occupation V (as stratum 6B was intruded from stratum 5) and reached its peak in the ceramic levels (VI and VII). This distribution is directly correlated with the stratigraphic occurrence of bone bipoints and fishhooks. In fact many of the pieces included in the tabulation were undoubtedly left over from fabricating these important items of fishing gear, and they will be mentioned again in the description of how these objects were made (Table 7).

Finishing the Bone Object

Artifacts Retaining Their Natural Form

Many bone tools did not require much work to make them functional objects. Some of these objects, mostly fragmentary, have already been described in the preceding discussion of alteration marks and pieces of detritus. Most finished objects, like most pieces of detritus, have been processed too much to allow species identification. An exception is the right frontal bone with attached antler of *Mazama*. The surface of this deer-antler tine, from stratum 6B, has been ground slightly and much worn and polished by use. The left frontal of another *Mazama*, found in Occupation IV, has had the tip end of its antler intentionally removed by breaking along an encircling cut (Figure 34). The point projecting

Figure 31. Incised bone detritus of manufacture.

Figure 32. Sawed and ground bone.

Table 6. Multiple Manufacturing Techniques Applied to Bone-Detritus Fragments.

	Total Number of Pieces	Cut from One Face	Cut from One Face, Broken	Cut from Both Faces, Broken	Encircling Cut	Encircling Cut, Broken
Occupation IV						
Bird bone	1				1	
Mammal bone	2					
Stratum 6B						
Bird bone	4	2	2			
Mammal bone	5		2			
Occupation V						
Bird Bone	4		3			
Mammal bone	13		5	4	1	
Occupation VI (Stratum 4B)						
Bird bone	2		1		1	
Mammal bone	1			1		
Occupation VII						
Bird bone	14	5	7		1	1
Mammal bone	10	1	4	1	1	
Total	56					

Figure 33. Cut and scraped bone.

from the broken edge shows subsequent use wear. No other antler objects were found at the site.

Fishbone

Fishbone objects required very little alteration to make them functional. One vertebral spine from Occupation II is superbly preserved, as if it had been specially cured, perhaps by heating it in oil. It is 10.5 cm long and has a natural hole at its proximal end. Many striations are visible on the highly polished surface, especially near the sharp tip. Probably this object was used as an awl or possibly even as a needle. One eroded cylindrical fishbone from Occupation Zone VII has been neatly drilled biconically to form a hole near one end (Figure 42o). An abortive drill hole can be seen adjacent to the perforation, which was probably intended for suspension.

A common type of fishbone object which has frequently been described from sambaquis is perforated vertebrae (Table 8). The perforation can be drilled; although if much worn, it is impossible to be sure unless it is obviously biconically drilled. Most often the holes were simply punctured with a punch, although in one case from Occupation Zone V the hole appears to have been carved out with a pointed knife. In Occupation Zone VII a line of 28 vertebrae was encountered. The smallest 20 had been perforated, with the largest hole in the smallest vertebra. Obviously the vertebrae had been rammed onto a long wooden rod or spit, which in the process broke the two smallest vertebrae. A few other vertebrae are also incompletely perforated. At first we thought that another 18 associated vertebrae from Occupation Zone V were similarly punctured; but six of these had no hole, and all but one of the remainder had

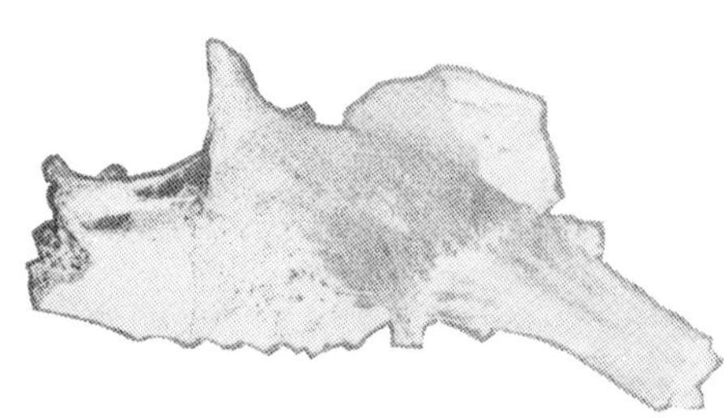

Figure 34. Deer antler attached to skull with encircling cut used to remove tine.

CUT EDGE(S) GROUND	CUT LONGITUDINALLY	FACES GROUND	EDGE(S GROUND	EDGE(S) SCRAPED	SCRAPED GROOVE	SCRAPED SURFACE	SCRAPED SURFACE (ACROSS GRAIN)
	1						
			1			1	
1	1			1	1	1	
	1	1	1		1	1	1
1				1		1	
5		5	5	1		2	
			1				
			3	2		2	
2	1	4	2		1	1	

pinholes in the exact center of the piece (the punctured holes are usually slightly off center). After further examination of many vertebrae it was realized that these pinholes are natural, and if they show no other evidence of alteration these vertebrae cannot be classified as artifacts. In this case someone may have collected several vertebrae together and gave up after puncturing only one of them. Some of the vertebrae which are very round in plan are also relatively soft. André Prous (personal communication) identified these as cartilaginous shark vertebrae which preserve in calcareous shell deposits.

Other than wear polish and occasional scratches, evidence of other kinds of intentional alteration of fish vertebrae is difficult to demonstrate. Two vertebrae exhibit apparently artificial paired grooves on opposite sides of the perimeter parallel to the faces (Figure 35). The illustrated object (39 mm in diameter and 25 mm thick) was found beneath Burial no. 4 in the bottom of stratum 4B, and may have been associated with that individual. The other object, also a large specimen (34 mm in diameter and 24 mm thick), came from Occupation V. A smaller vertebra from Occupation II has a similar cut which is not paired on the other side. One large example (40 mm in diameter and 25 mm thick) from Occupation VI has a large gouged depression on one side. All of these large vertebrae show considerable evidence of wear, especially in and around the perforation.

All except two perforated specimens are caudal vertebrae, which are disc-shaped with biconcave faces and nearly vertical sides (Figure 36, a–c). The two exceptions are spool-shaped (i.e., the sides are also concave) thoracic vertebrae. These are the kind with long vertebral spines, which had been removed. Both were excluded from the tabulation (table 132a) because the one from Occupation VII is thicker (36 mm) than its diameter (24 mm x 5 mm perforation), while the other, the only example found in Occupation III, had an irregular perforation 2 mm on one side and 5 mm on the other face. It was 20 mm in diameter and 17 mm thick. The 28 associated vertebrae in the process of being punctured were also excluded from the tabulation to stress the fact that all the other 112 perforated vertebrae were found

Figure 35. Perforated and grooved fish vertebra.

Table 7. Bone Artifacts.

	I	II	III	IV	6B	V	VI	VII	No Prov.
Fishbones with butchering marks		1		3		5	2		
Bird bones with butchering marks						1		3	
Land-mammal bones with butchering marks				1			1	2	
Worked land-mammal bone fragments			1	2		2		9	2
Worked fishbones		1						1	
Worked bird bones				2	1			2	
Worked tympanic bulae of whales	4			1					
Whalebone with polished depression	1								
Dolphin mandibles with incisions				1		3			
Cut seal (?) bones						3			
Whalebones with butchering marks						4	2	1	2
Whalebone chopping blocks			1			1	2	5	2
Chopped and/or cut whalebones		7		5		2		12	
Burned/chopped whalebones		5		1	2			3	
Whalebones associated with burials					4				
Carved and whittled whalebones		1		2	2	1		2	1
Whale vertebrae with burned depressions		4		2					
Worked whale vertebral epiphyses				1		3		5	
Epiphyses with ground surfaces					1	3			
Ground whalebone					1			1	
Detritus of Manufacture: Bird and Mammal Bone (Cut, ground and scraped detrital fragments)				3	9	17	3	24	
Worked deer-antler tines				1	1				
Perforated fish and shark vertebrae		2		8	1	20	5	61	13
Worked sting-ray spines		1	5		6	3		4	
Bone bipoints (mostly bird)				7	3	9	4	29	6
Points with unibevelled bases		1	2				1	3	
Tanged (pedunculated) points		2			1			3	
Socketed projectile points		2							
Point fragments				1			2	3	
Fishhooks and fragments					8	4	1	9	1
Longitudinally facetted and drilled bone						1			
Spatulate tool of tapir fibula								1	
Hollow cylindrical haft				1					
Perforated deer cannon bone								1	
Totals	5	27	9	42	40	82	23	184	27

Total No. of bone artifacts—439

Table 8. Perforated Fish Vertebrae.

	No Prov.	Occ. II	Occ. IV	Occ. V	Stratum 6B (Bur. #23)	Occ. VI	Occ. VII	Total
Total number of specimens	13	2	8	20	1	5	61	110
Drilled hole	2			1			5	8
Circular/oblong puncture	9	1	7	14	1	2	49	83
Angular puncture	2	1	1	5		3	7	19
Worn perforation	6	1	6	6		4	26	49
Large diam. (40–30 mm) Thickness (26–10 mm) Diam. of perf. (2–6 mm)	6		2	8		4	15	35[1]
Medium diam. (29–20 mm) Thickness (18–8 mm) Diam. of perf. (1–7 mm)	5	1	4	8	1	1	28	48[2]
Diam. (19–11 mm) Thickness (12–4 mm) Diam. of perf. (1–6 mm)	2	1	2	4			18	27[3]

[1]22 have worn holes
[2]19 have worn holes
[3] 8 have worn holes

isolated, and only two of these were associated with burials. The only evidence suggesting that any might have been strung as beads is the one found beneath the skull of Burial no. 23 near an *Oliva* bead.

The tabulation shows that fewer than a quarter of the total fish vertebrae have holes that are worn smooth, although the larger examples exhibit a higher percentage of wear. If they had been strung as beads, more evidence of wear would be expected. The range in diameter of the artificial perforation is quite constant regardless of the total diameter of selected vertebrae. Also thickness does not vary in proportion to size as much as would be expected, and this feature may well reflect cultural selection. If the vertebrae were not strung as beads, they could have been used as spindle whorls; toy tops; ear or lip plugs with holes for the insertion of feathers or some other ornament; or possibly charms worn on the penis string by fishermen, thus explaining why two specimens were found beneath skeletons.

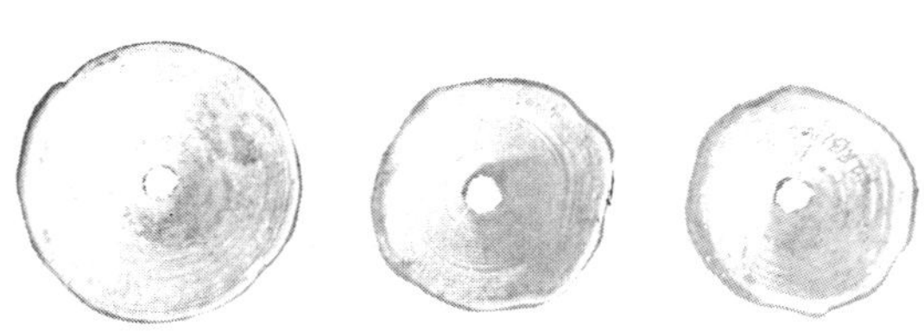

Figure 36. Perforated and polished fish vertebrae.

Stingray-Spine Projectile Points

The last category of artifacts fashioned from fish bones is the naturally serrated tail spines of stingrays, which have been made into projectile points. All that had to be done to create a functional projectile point was to cut and break the base off squarely, file off a few barbs at the base end for hafting, and grind a symmetrical point on the tip. Figure 37 is a complete full-sized example exhibiting all these alterations. On this example the convex face (the opposite face is variable and can be con-

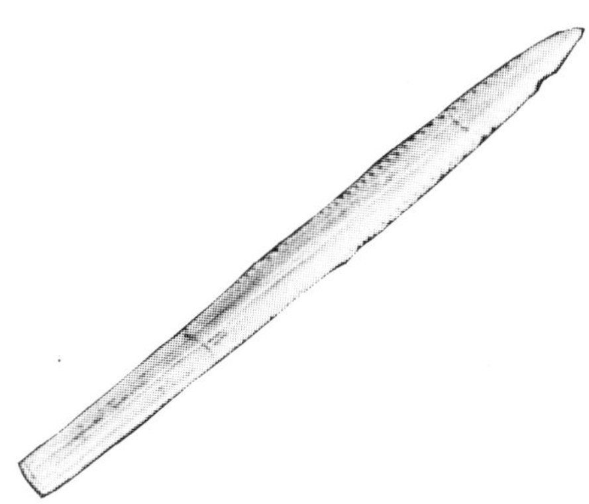

Figure 37. Ray-spine projectile point.

cave) of the base (not illustrated) has been slightly thinned by grinding in a manner well illustrated by Figure 38A. Apparently a uniform thickness of between 3 and 5 mm and a width of 4 to 6 mm was desired for hafting into a rectangular socket. If the projectile point broke it was an easy matter to grind a new tip (Figure 38 A, B). In fact, another short point could also be fashioned from a broken central section. Including the one without a squared base in Figure 39, six short sections were squared and retipped, including one former basal section where all the natural barbs had previously been filed down. The latter example came from Occupation III, the one lacking a squared base from Occupation V, while the remaining five (including the long complete example) came from Stratum 6B. Another specimen from Stratum 6B had a broken base, but again the basal section with previously filed barbs had been retipped. Evidently the presence of naturally sharp barbs was not essential for use.

The tips were broken off five fragmentary specimens by end pressure, presumably by impact when the hafted point hit something. Two of these nearly complete specimens, one from Occupation III and one from II, had finished cut and ground bases; while another from Occupation VII had apparently been used without squaring or grinding the base. The broken tip of the example from Occupation II shows use polish. The other two (one from Occupation III and one from VII) were central sections, lacking any evidence of use except the impact breaks. Two more central sections had not been broken by impact: one from Occupation VII exhibits a few striations near the tip, while a section from Occupation V shows that one face had been ground. Three basal fragments were found: the one from Occupation III had been cut and broken transversely, the one from V had facial grinding and one scraped edge, while the base from Occupation VII had only one transverse striation. Only one broken tip end,

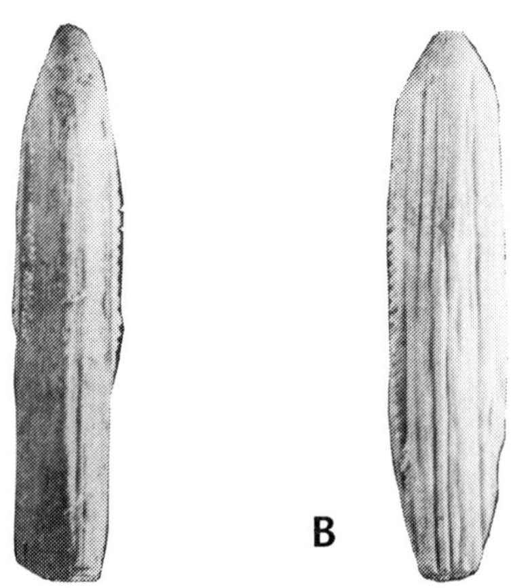

A B

Figure 38. Ray-spine projectile points.

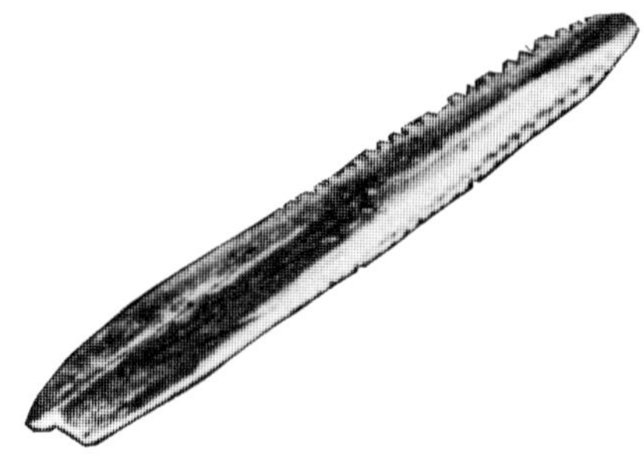

Figure 39. Ray-spine projectile point.

having a grooved conical point, was recovered, from Occupation III.

Of the seven complete and 12 broken pieces, probably all but one of the seven complete stingray spine projectile points had been refinished after breaking. It is worth noting that five of the complete specimens came from Stratum 6B. In fact, two of these were found associated with each other; but none were found with burials. This is one type of bone artifact which diminishes in importance in the ceramic levels. In fact the four fragments from the ceramic levels (all in Occupation VII) exhibit only striations or impact breaks. As the typical marks of alteration were absent, it is difficult to prove that they were used, although the base of the one whose tip was broken by end pressure appears to have been cleanly broken transversely without any evidence of preliminary cutting of a guide incision. In other words, although probably they were still used, much less effort was expended on finishing them in the upper levels. Evidently they had been superseded by more efficient shaped projectile points.

Shaped Bone Artifacts

Bipointed Objects

Other than perforated fish vertebrae, the most common class of finished bone artifacts was bipointed objects. Most of the 58 nearly complete examples were made of bird bone, although 12 of them with a concavo-convex cross-section and sharp points at both ends may have been fashioned from mammal bone or possibly very large birds. At first it was considered that they might possibly have been tied to a line a bit off center and thereby served as toggling fish gorges. But it is better to have a solid cross-section and an encircling groove to avoid slippage if a bipoint is to serve efficiently as a fishhook. When it was noticed that 20 of them have one tip that was broken by end pressure, evidently from an impact blow, it was realized that they must have served as projectile points. Emperaire and Laming (1956:151) had previously observed that similar bone bipoints are mounted onto bevelled arrow shafts by the Indians of the Alto Xingu so that one point serves to penetrate while the other point serves as a lateral barb which prevents the fish from falling off when it is lifted (Emperaire and Laming (1956:Figure 155). Also Tiburtius had deduced from the patterns of discoloration evidently caused by binding that similar points from the riverine shell deposit at Itacoara, near Joinville, had been mounted as unilaterally barbed points (Tiburtius, Bigarella, and Bigarella 1951:Figures 7, 33, pp. 329–330). The Enseada sambaqui, 6 km south of Forte Marechal Luz, yielded 150 bipoints in addition to several simple points made of ray spines and mammal bone (Beck, Araujo, Duarte, Fossari, Belani 1970:39–43, fotos 6, 7, 12).

Obviously the bipoint with its built-in barb is a much more effective type of projectile point than the straight ray-spine projectile point, which would allow the fish to slip off too easily. The barbs would be too short for any purpose except to aid in penetration. Perhaps ray-spine projectile points were still used by boys for practice and for the hunting of small land animals during later occupations; but as already mentioned, their use tended to be superseded by this innovation, which is so much more effective for catching fish. A short table of comparative frequencies illustrates this fact very well:

	II	III	IV	6B	V	VI	VII	Unk.
Ray-spine projectile points	1	5	0	6	3	0	4	0
Bipointed projectile points	0	0	7	3	9	4	29	6

As there is no apparent evidence for morphological change through time, the associated occupation zones will not be mentioned further. Interestingly, none of the 58 bipoints were associated with burials. Bird-bone bipoints are also quite easy to make, although a good deal of care seems to have been expended on finishing most of them. Apparently a straight bird-bone shaft was first sectioned at both ends by cutting and breaking a section (possible examples at this stage of manufacture were already discussed under detritus) ranging between 26 and 74 mm long, to judge from the 17 complete specimens. Some of the shorter ones have been resharpened after breaking, however; so the most-desired range of length was probably between about 35 and 65 mm. The segment was then incised, or more often grooved by scraping lengthwise, and then broken, yielding a piece with the desired concavo-convex cross-section. The broken edges were then scraped or filed smooth and the tips were bevelled, also by scraping and/or grinding. Most retain parallel sides in plan view (Figure 40, a–h); but a few short examples, perhaps because of resharpening, exhibit sides that converge gradually to both tips (Figure 40, i–l). Thick-walled bone was thinned by scraping over all exterior and sometimes the interior surfaces. In fact, the exterior surface of one mammal bone exhibited three longitudinally ground planes, creating a tri-facetted cross-section. All edges, particularly near the tips, were smoothed and polished, probably by use. In longitudinal section there is no notable difference in length between the two ends, so one cannot guess which point was intended to be the barb. On some examples the craftsmen evidently utilized to advantage the natural curvature of the bone to form a naturally projecting barb (Figure 41 b, g, i), which would evidently serve even if mounted on a straight cylindrical shaft.

If the penetration tip shattered it could easily be resharpened while still hafted, and after repeated breaks, removed from the shaft and mounted the other way around. As the collection contains many broken and resharpened points, a detailed typology of the variations in form would be superfluous because it would not reflect the original intent of the craftsman.

Some variations in method of manufacture or repair are of interest, however. The longitudinal edges may be ground to the same plane, but more often are scraped and/or ground to planes at or near a right angle to the cross-section. The edges are double-facetted by relatively crude filing and/or scraping on four examples which also exhibit repaired broken tips. A simple way to resharpen a broken tip was to file it across the grain from the interior surface (seven examples), the exterior surface (three examples), or both (one example). In such cases it was not necessary to remove the point from the haft in order to resharpen it.

Two examples included in the tabulation had one end cut and broken transversely, which means that in fact they were not bipoints. As both had been repaired, probably the shattered penetration tips had simply been squared off and mounted the other way around. If indeed it was not essential to have a sharp barb, but merely something that would catch the fish as it was lifted, then two similar examples should be included in the total count. They were apparently made from the same bone, and were found associated with each other in Occupation IV. For that reason it was originally assumed that they may have mounted together on some composite instrument, but there is no other evidence for such a type of implement. The squared base of one of these pieces has what appears to be an intentional notch removed by end pressure. As two of the bipoints had tiny burin spalls removed from the center of one tip by impact, it is probable that this unpointed specimen had also been burinated by accident, and the other point squared off simply to prevent shattering cracks from spreading, as when one files a broken fingernail. In fact several of the objects illustrated in Figure 40 exhibit notches, and a lateral burin scar can be seen on one object (Figure 41b).

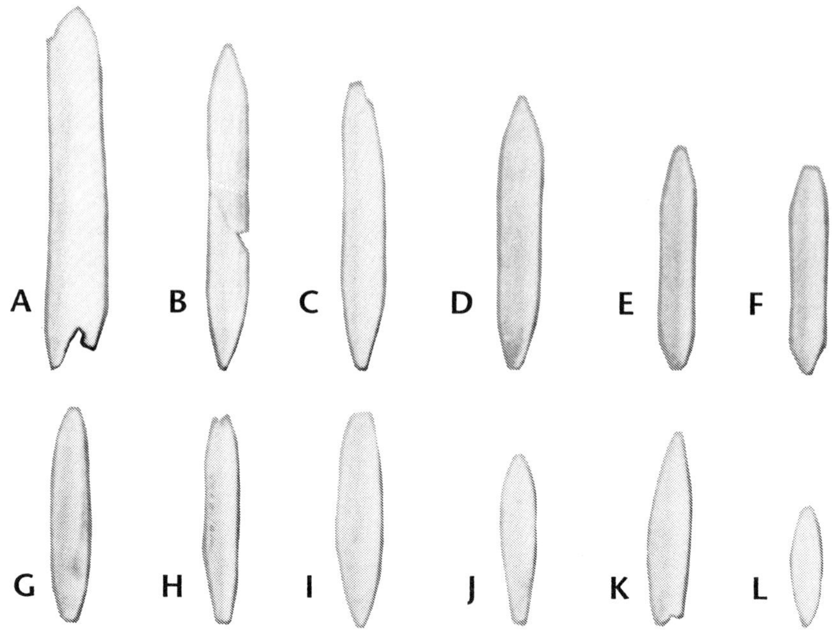

Figure 40. Plan view of bird-bone projectile points.

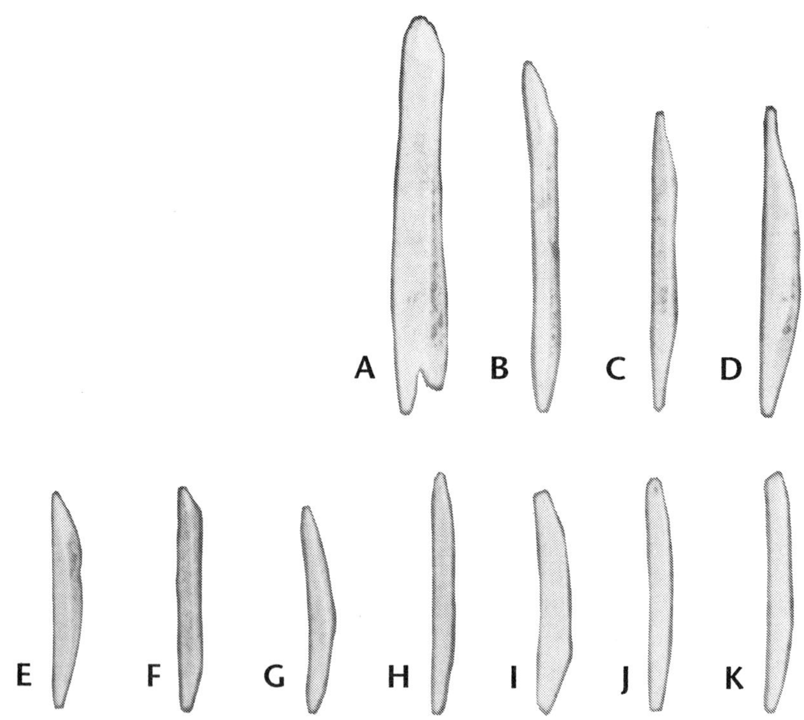

Figure 41. Bird-bone projectile points.

Projectile Points with Bevelled Bases

Apparently the occupants of the site experimented for a long time with several types of projectile points made of mammal bones in addition to the simple stingray spines before the bipoint became the most common type in use. One class of mammal-bone points have bevelled bases apparently for hafting onto scarfed shafts in a manner similar to the way the bipoints are hafted, except that after mounting they apparently did not have projecting pointed barbs (Table 9).

Among the most carefully made bone objects found at the site are the projectile points from Occupation II, the original sambaqui. One of these examples, illustrated in Figure 50a, is shaped somewhat like the bipoints although it is circular in cross-section near its sharp conical point and plano-convex near the blunt end. All surfaces including the butt have been ground and/or scraped. The conical tip appears to have been resharpened by grinding after it had been broken by an impact blow. Apparently the point was meant to be mounted on a shaft having a flat surface; if that surface were bevelled or scarfed the tip end would project straight ahead. A nearly complete central section of what appears to be the same type of point with all faces carefully scraped to a plano-convex cross-section came from Occupation III. Another central fragment of a larger point with the same carefully finished cross-section came from Occupation V. The complete short point illustrated in Figure 24d is another example of this type in Occupation Zone III. The tip end of this point is semiconical with one flat face, while the blunt base appears never to have been finished.

Possibly two basal sections from stratum 1 (Occupation VII) with butts squared by filing should be classified with the bipoints with one point squared off, because they are all concavo-convex in cross-section. On these examples, however, there is no suggestion that a shattered point tip was simply squared off to prevent further splitting. They appear to be deliberately made with square bases, and their exterior surfaces are carefully ground and scraped into two longitudinal facets (Figure 42 a, n). The edges are also ground to a flat plane which would fit onto a scarfed shaft in the same way that the bevelled points with solid plano-convex cross-sections presumably were fitted. As they have thinner walls they would not withstand an impact blow as well as a solid object, and that may explain why there are no complete examples. Another central section of a similarly prepared object had been warped in a fire associated with Burial no. 53 in Occupation VII. On this specimen a previously broken tip was evidently resharpened by transverse filing of the edges.

Tanged Projectile Points

Another beautifully finished projectile point from Occupation Zone II appears to be deliberately shouldered for hafting (Figure 43). As the entire object has a modified plano-convex cross-section, the socket into which the tang was meant to fit must have been a flattened cylinder, similar in shape to the socket in which the ray-spine points were fitted. On its tip end there is a dorsal ridge formed by two ground planes, while a longitudinal natural groove is found on the opposing nearly flat face. The base half is much more roughly filed, probably to facilitate bonding by gluing into its socketed haft.

Two other shorter points lack shoulders but are also broadest near the tip end, so they also could be called tanged points. All surfaces have been carefully facetted by grinding, and the base of the example with a rectangular cross-section from Occupation Zone VII (Figure 44) has been thinned bifacially for hafting. The body of the one from stratum 6B has a flattened ovoid cross-section (Figure 45), but the base has a square cross-section.

Three other less carefully made projectile points are not tanged, but are included in this category because they are also designed to fit into a socket. The bullet-shaped example illustrated in Figure 46 has a flattened oval cross-section with deliberately squared base. As can be seen in the illustration, this simple point from Occupation Zone II is very similar in shape to many of the short ray-spine points. Two examples from Occupation Zone VII also exhibit overall grinding except that the bases appear not to have been finished. Both have a plano-convex cross-section near the base end.

Similar mammal-bone points, as well as ray-spine points, were found at the Itacoara site, near Joinville (Tiburtius, Bigarella, and Bigarella 1951:Figure 28). At the Enseada site, 38 tanged points, most of which have broad triangular blades and abrupt shoulders, were recovered (Beck, Aruajo, Duarte, Fossari, Belani 1970:38–39, foto 5). Although quite similar to the first point described, this is the only major variety of bone artifact from Enseada which was not found at Forte Marechal Luz.

Table 9. Bone Projectile Points.

	Occ. II	Occ. III	Occ. IV	Stratum 6B	Occ. V	Occ. VI	Occ. VII
A. Scarfed shaft	1	2	0	0	1	0	3
Barbed bipoints	0	0	7	3	9	4	29
B. Socketed shaft	2	0	0	1	0	0	3
Ray-spine points	1	5	0	5	3	0	4
C. Pointed shaft	2	0	0	0	0	0	0

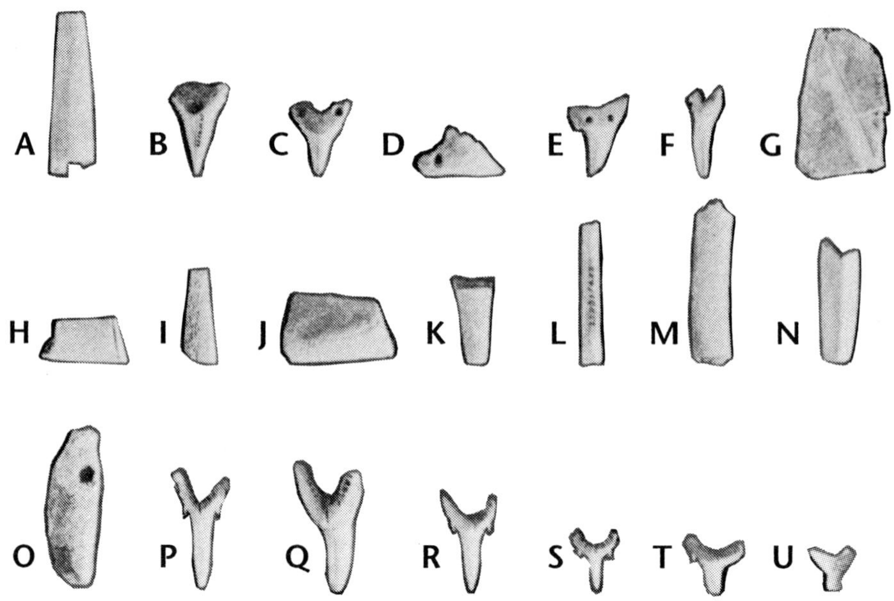

Figure 42. Bone and shark-tooth artifacts.

Socketed Projectile Points

One complete and one nearly complete conical socketed bone projectile point came from stratum 10 in Occupation Zone II. These are short examples of a similar type of point frequently made of conical antler tines with the center hollowed out to fit over a pointed shaft. On these examples a conical hole for the insertion of the shaft has been carved out by the removal of cancellous bone from the marrow cavity near an articular end. The external surfaces have been scraped and the tip sharpened by scraping a unilateral bevelled facet (Figure 47). The squared bases were scraped transversely and then cut cleanly along the thinned groove. Obviously the artisan took no chances that the object might not break cleanly along a partial guide cut.

Despite the fact that these alternative projectile points evidently shattered less easily, none of them ever went into mass production as did the fragile but easily fashioned and readily resharpened bipoints with their built-in effective feature of simple unilateral barbs to assist in retrieving a pierced fish. The more solid types of projectile points, none of which were obviously barbed, may have served for hunting land mammals.

Table 9 categorizes all projectile points found at the site into three basic types according to hafting technique.

The occupants of the original sambaqui (Occupation Zone II) were aware of all forms of hafting; but the socketed points, fashioned to fit over a simple pointed shaft (type C), were not found in later occupations. The bevelled base points with solid cross-sections meant to fit onto a scarfed shaft were used occasionally throughout the occupation of the site; while the

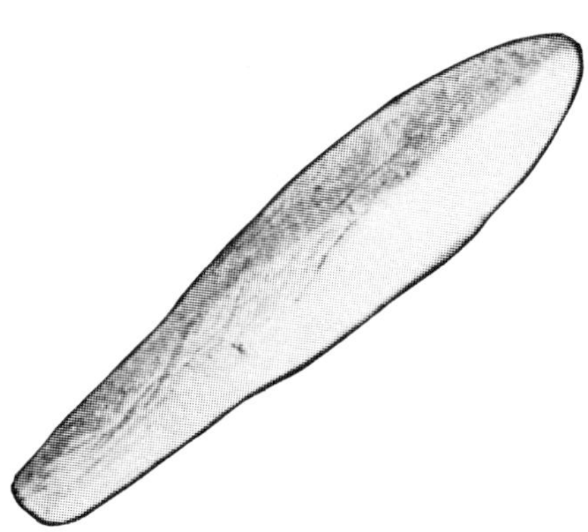

Figure 43. Shouldered mammal-bone projectile point.

Figure 44. Tanged projectile point.

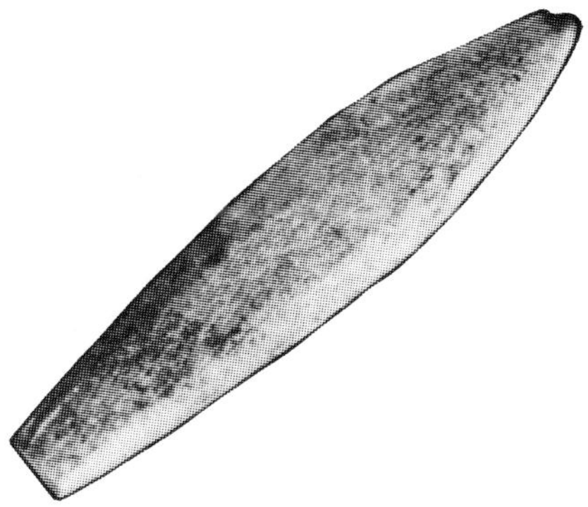

Figure 45. Tanged projectile point.

related bevelled bipoints, which apparently were innovated in Occupation IV as an efficient subtype with the addition of barbs, went on to become the dominant projectile-point type used at the site. Type B, straight shank points, designed to fit into a socketed shaft, including the simple ray-spine points, were used quite consistently throughout time without ever becoming dominant.

Four fragments of carefully finished objects were probably broken pieces of unclassifiable projectile points. Two of these (Figure 42 i, k) from Occupation VII, appear to be discarded portions of finished or nearly finished objects deliberately removed by cutting and breaking off projecting ends, despite the fact that all surfaces had been carefully finished by scraping and grinding. Perhaps broken objects were frequently refashioned into new objects and unnecessary segments were simply cut off and discarded. A central section of an object from Occupation IV has a flattened cylindrical cross-section. Both are probably designed to be fitted into sockets. Another fragment with ground butt and crudely filed lateral edges from Occupation VI may also be the broken base of a point.

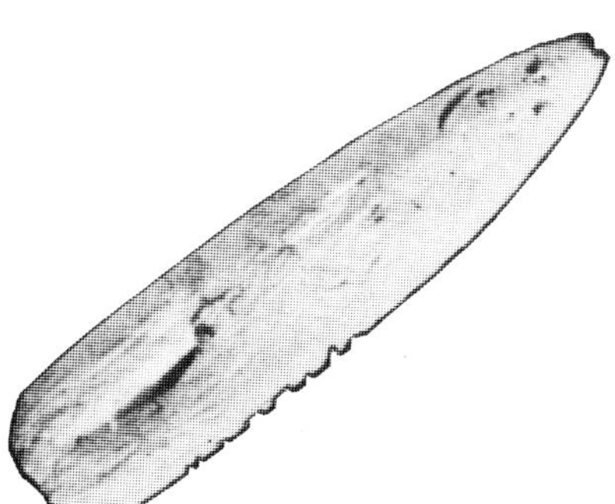

Figure 46. Ovoid projectile point.

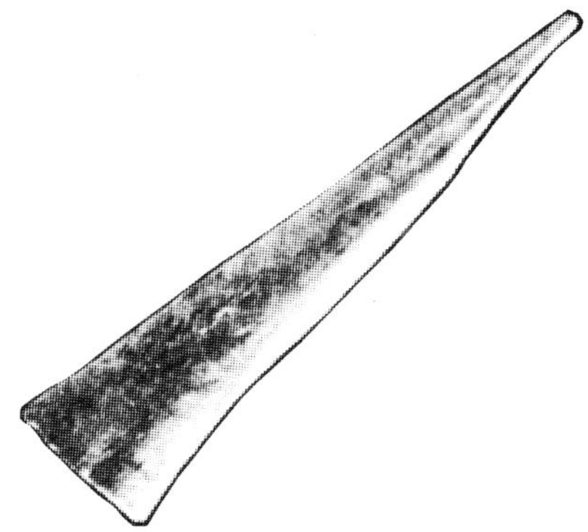

Figure 47. Socketed projectile point.

Fishhooks

The most carefully made class of bone objects in the upper layers at Forte Marechal Luz is fishhooks of a type first described from the interior riverine site of Itacoara about 30 km west, near Joinville (Tiburtius, Bigarella, and Bigarella 1951:327–328; Figures 7, 28); Bigarella and Tiburtius 1953). Beck also recovered 28 whole and 36 fragmentary fishhooks from the Enseada site (Beck, Araujo, Duarte, Fossari, Belani 1970:39; foto 4). All 16 nearly complete and seven fragments of fishhooks from Forte Marechal Luz came from stratum 6B and Occupation Zones V, VI, and VII. Thus, evidently they were innovated by diffusion after the initial appearance of deliberately flaked stone in Occupation Zone IV and before the initial appearance of pottery in Occupation Zone VI.

Despite the short span of time these objects were being made at the site, there is a significant alteration in type which evidently reflects a change to a more secure method of tying the hook to the line by strengthening the fragile knob at the proximal end of Type I (Figure 42, a–f). On the three nearly complete examples of Type II (Figure 48, g–i), the central gouged hole is not so extensive, leaving a much broader and stronger end to which to tie the line. In this case, the distribution by stratum is significant, as seen by Table 10.

The abrupt change from Type I to Type II occurred after the deposition of stratum 4 and before the excavations were made for interments in stratum 4B. One type I specimen from stratum 4B was apparently associated with Burial 10; and four others from stratum 6B were apparently associated with each other, although not as a cache. The fact that the points were missing on all of them (Figure 48 a, d), and the proximal end was also missing on the two fragments, suggests that someone discarded them all at the same time.

Essentially the same process of fabrication was followed to make all the fishhooks. Most variations in shape, especially the size and curvature of the hook,

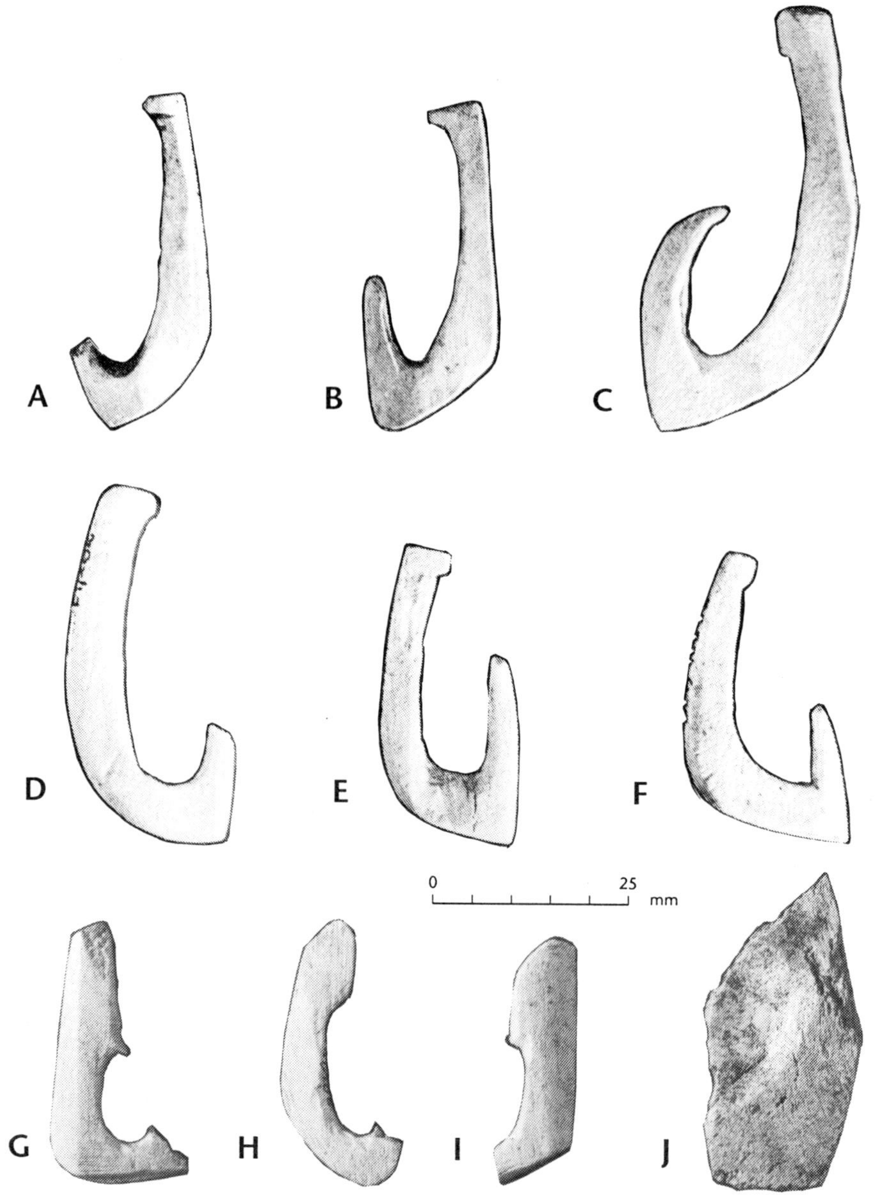

Figure 48. Ground bone fishhooks: a–f, Type I with small attachment knob; g–i, Type II with broad attachment knob; j, Fishhook blank.

reflect the natural curvature of the original piece of mammal bone. One broken hook appears to have been resharpened by grinding, and three broken knobs evidently were repaired by notching the shank. Apparently most broken hooks were simply discarded without attempting to repair them.

First a relatively flat plaque of fairly thin (3–4 mm) mammal bone was cut and broken into a rectangular section about 40 mm long and from 10 to 20 mm wide. Care had to be taken that the grain of the bone was parallel to the long axis, so that the axis of the shank and the hook run with the grain. Two rectangular pieces from stratum 5 (one illustrated in Figure 42j) are still too thick, but nevertheless they are probably sectioned preforms for making fishhooks. As is evident on some hooks and on another roughly ovoid section from the upper part of Occupation VII, both faces could be ground until the proper thickness was reached. The latter piece (Figure 48j), the most obvious fishhook blank, appears to have been made from a tough piece of skull; but it may have been abandoned because the grain of the bone runs in various directions, which could create weakness at the vital stress points. In order to finish a hook, only the perforation remained to be carved out. Two more pieces of detritus which may well be fishhook blanks are illustrated in Figure 42 g, h. The latter of these, accidentally broken at one end, came from stratum 6B, the other from stratum 5.

Table 10. Bone Fishhooks.

	TYPE I	TYPE II	UNCLASSIFIABLE FRAGMENTS
Stratum 1	0	1	2
Stratum 3	0	1	0
Stratum 4B	0	1	0
Stratum 4	5	0	0
Stratum 6B	6	0	2
Stratum 5	1	0	3
Screened from slumped area	1	0	0

Another partially worked fragment from stratum 6B also broke before finishing. Even a weathered rectanguloid plaque of thick skull squared across the grain on two ends from stratum 3 may have been a fishhook blank. Probably several other pieces of detritus of manufacture already discussed were partially finished fishhook blanks.

Continuing with the process of manufacture of fishhooks, a large oval perforation or indentation was then made near the center of the thinned piece by scraping and gouging with a flake or perhaps a paca tooth. Remnants of these gouge marks can be seen at the bottom of the central cavity on the hooks illustrated in Figure 48 e, g, h. The outer edges were then trimmed by filing and scraping so that the shank was of regular width, and the hook end tapered to a conical point. On Type I examples a cut was made parallel to the previously cut straight top to fashion a projecting knob to which the line was secured. Evidently the knob on the example in Figure 48f broke off and the haft was repaired by notching the shank; the same repair was made on two other examples. In fact the attachment knob is the most vital weak point in the overall design. One can easily imagine that many fishhooks broke at the knob and disappeared with the fish.

To remedy this frustrating problem, the design was changed to Type II. On these three examples the attachment end of the shank was filed into two facets, but more significantly the fragile knob was eliminated and replaced by a larger attachment surface simply by making the central gouged cavity smaller and more circular. Unfortunately the hook ends were broken off all three examples; it is possible that this new design resulted in a weaker hook.

One suspects that, relative to the amount of effort expended in fabricating them, these fragile implements were not as efficient for obtaining fish as were the spear shafts mounted with simple barbed bipoints. Nevertheless, they do form a significant percentage of the recovered artifacts, which suggests that certain species of fish could more effectively be lured by a baited hook than by spearing (see discussion of fish remains in chapter I). The evidence certainly demonstrates that the later occupants of the site were industrious fishermen and not just shellfish gatherers.

Miscellaneous Mammal-Bone Objects

Three absolutely unrelated mammal-bone objects were completely finished with great care to make an archaeologist speculate as to their respective functions. The smallest object (29 x 11 mm) is a longitudinally bisected section of a small long bone carefully ground to four longitudinal facets on the exterior surface in addition to planing the edges and the ends to make a house-shaped cross-section. The most notable feature is that the interior (medullary) canal contains two adjacent cup-shaped depressions, apparently drilled with a 6-mm bit. One depression is central, the other off center. Without finished perforations on this object from Occupation V, it is difficult even to speculate about a possible function.

The shaft of a left fibula of *Tapirus terrestris* from Occupation Zone VII is highly polished but only slightly altered by grinding. The proximal end had been carefully filed to create a spatulate tool with rounded corners (Figure 49), although one corner was broken during removal. A spatula can have many uses; the one that first comes to mind is a tool for shaping pottery vessels.

Certainly the most impressive single bone artifact recovered from the site is a large tabular rectangular whalebone object (128 x 105 x 17 mm) with a 15-mm-diameter hole drilled slightly off center (Figure 30). The sides of the hole as well as the faces and edges are slightly worn on this object from Occupation Zone VI. Considerable cancellous structure has been ground off one face (the scapular ridge?) to make the faces irregu-

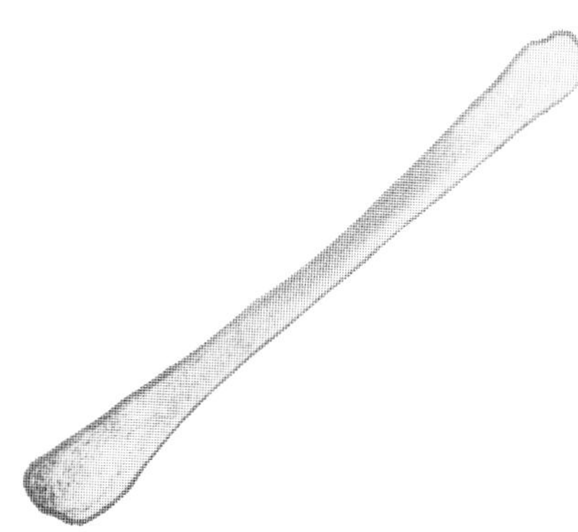

Figure 49. Tapir fibula spatula.

larly parallel, although the solid (non-cancellous) side is still thinner, creating a wedge-shaped cross-section. All edges had been carefully rounded by grinding. Two half-size objects of the same shape, but made of whale tympanic bulae, are known from other sambaquis (Tiburtius, Leprovost, and Bigarella 1949:Figure 12). My first thought was that the object was a large spindle whorl, but it would not spin properly with its off-center hole. Perhaps it was a net gauge; but the hole would seem to be unnecessary, and a net of that gauge could catch only very large fish. Perhaps the Indians used nets for retaining beached sea mammals or turtles, or for trapping large land mammals; and the object served not only as a gauge but at the same time as a functional part of a trap, perhaps as a triggering device.

Three other mammal-bone object fragments require separate attention. There is a notable absence of mammal-bone awls, which normally make up a large proportion of bone tools from North American sites. A much-used fish vertebra spine and a polished deer-antler tine, both already described, may have served as punches or awls for poking holes in some material like skin. The tip end of a fire-hardened conical point with a symmetrical diameter of 4 mm from Occupation VI may also have been an awl tip, again possibly for working skins. The paucity or near absence of awls may be correlated with an absence of coiled basketry and tailored skin clothing.

Another fragmentary object from Occupation IV appears to have been a haft. Two possible hafts made of whalebone, and the paca tooth hafted into a large bird bone have already been described. A paca-tooth chisel could also have been mounted into this hollow cylindrical object, which appears to have broken under downward pressure. The lower 15 mm of the outer surface has been filed transversely into several facets as if to roughen the surface in order to facilitate bonding. A dark stain is visible where the bonding material squeezed out at the base and along the edge of the roughened surface. The remainder of the exterior surface exhibits scattered striations and small grinding facets.

The final object, the broken half of the distal end of a deer cannon-bone from Occupation Zone VII, has two apparently intentional perforations punched through the walls. The larger perforation (7 mm in diameter) is on the dorsal surface near the epiphysis, while a 2-mm-diameter hole had been knocked into the ventral surface farther from the end. The perforations were not made by teeth of an animal like a dog, as the holes are not opposing each other. Apparently it was not suspended, as there is no wear on the edges of the holes; but the surfaces, especially on the medial groove, do show wear polish. Perhaps the object was intended to be a whistle.

Bird-Bone Objects

Some hollow bird bones were used for purposes other than for the fabrication of bipoints. Unfortunately, however, all of them were broken; and their functions can only be surmised. All but one of them were intentional tubular objects; and as two items were associated with burials, they may have served ceremonial functions. The non-tubular object was associated with Burial no. 26, Occupation VII. It is a splinter with a straight longitudinal polished edge with parallel striations and use-polish extending onto adjacent surfaces. The fragment does not appear to be a bipoint.

Two tubes, both unfortunately broken at one end while troweling, were cut and broken cleanly at the other end. One from stratum 6B is only 41 mm long and could be a bead. The other is 138 mm long and evidently nearly complete, as there is a ground facet adjacent to the break. As it was found between the legs of Burial no. 33 in Occupation VII it may be a shaman's sucking tube or more prosaically a drinking tube. Several fragments of mammal bone, one calcined, but none showing evidence of alteration, were also associated with this burial.

Two badly eroded sections of what appear to be the same long bird bone were found together in Occupation IV. Evidently seven holes were scraped through the surface. One of these is an oblong depression with only partial perforation, two are complete circular holes, while remnants of four more circular holes can be seen on each of the broken ends. Perhaps these are the fragmentary remains of a bone flute. The combined length of the two pieces is nearly 11 cm, but if it was a flute the object must have been considerably longer as all ends were broken at perforations.

Chapter 8
Tooth Artifacts

The teeth of certain mammals, sharks, as well as some fish and a caiman, were readily adaptable as tools and ornaments with little or no intentional alteration and minimal evidence of use. Unfortunately for the archaeologist, normally the most useful working edge is the same edge that was used previously by the living animal. Likewise, many teeth can be strung as beads or pendants from the unaltered bulbous roots by the careful tying of cordage, which never preserves under natural conditions in a shellmound.

Despite these handicaps to analysis, I concluded after careful examination (with hand lens and binocular microscope) of the many isolated teeth we encountered, that most of them had been used and that it is frequently possible to demonstrate such use. All of the teeth discussed below were originally catalogued as artifacts, using the basic assumption that when mammal or shark teeth were found isolated, the chances are very good that these durable and beautiful objects had been removed by man from their natural context for some special purpose. Of the teeth originally catalogued as artifacts, 10 peccary canines, 62 shark teeth, and one caiman incisor have been excluded from the list of artifacts, for reasons to be discussed.

Twenty-six mammal teeth, many of which have obviously been altered by drilling and/or grinding; and eleven rodent incisors, some still hafted, will be described first. Two unidentified reptilian and fish teeth, and a large number of shark teeth which have probably been used will then be discussed.

The canines of peccaries (*Tayassu albirostris*) frequently exhibited ground facets and sometimes drilled holes. Three canines which were ground into unusual triangular objects are the only shaped artifacts of peccary teeth; all others retain their natural form. An upper canine associated with Burial no. 51 in Occupation Zone VII has been completely ground into a triangular object in both plane- and cross-sections, and then drilled through the wall of the root cavity (Figure 50c). A similar object, except that it lacks a drill hole and comes to a conical point at the enamel end (Figure 50b), was ground from a lower canine, while an upper canine was even more completely reduced (Figure 50e). The root tip of the latter object is broken off, perhaps as a result of attempting to drill a hole in it. If it were not for the fact

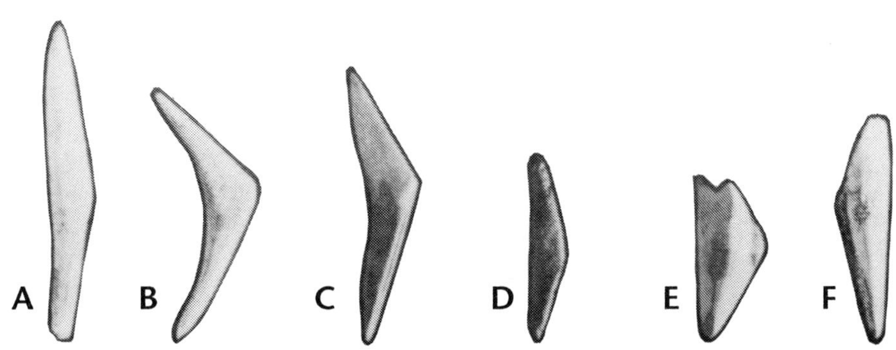

Figure 50. Ground mammal-bone and peccary-canine artifacts.

Table 11. Tooth Artifacts.

	I	II	III	IV	6B	V	VI	VII	No Prov.
Ground and/or drilled peccary canines						1		3	2
Altered peccary canines							2	3	
Altered peccary mandible						1			
Drilled tapir molar								1	
Ground and/or drilled carnivore canines				1			2	1	
Ground capivara incisor								1	
Hafted paca incisors						1	1	1	
Bone hafts for incisor tools								3	
Used paca incisors				1				3	
Used fish tooth						1			
Ground and/or drilled shark teeth					1	2	1	9	1
Used shark teeth				2	5	18	17	46	6
Totals				4	6	24	23	71	9
Total number of tooth artifacts: 137									
(Shark teeth with no evidence of use)				1		27	1	32	

that one of these objects had been drilled, one would suspect from the similarly shaped bone objects illustrated in the same figure, that they all were shaped so as to form sharp barbs projecting from a scarfed shaft of a projectile. As the drilled tooth has a square countersink on the interior root cavity surface it is possible that the hole was made to fit over a projection carved onto a wooden projectile shaft; however, its association with a burial tends to strengthen the probability that the piece was drilled for suspension. Actually, another upper canine, from Occupation V, with no other evidence of use, exhibits the remnants of perforations of the same diameter (2 mm) through both the root walls. Two lower canines of piglets, unfortunately found after a wall collapsed, were also drilled at the root ends, which are worn and polished by suspension (Fig 50 d, f).

Two upper canines, at the left in Figure 51, although they appeared to be intentionally bevelled, according to Professor Carlos de Paula Couto, are normally found in that condition in old individuals, especially if there is some malocclusion. Three more specimens (one from Occupation V and two from Occupation VII) were simi-

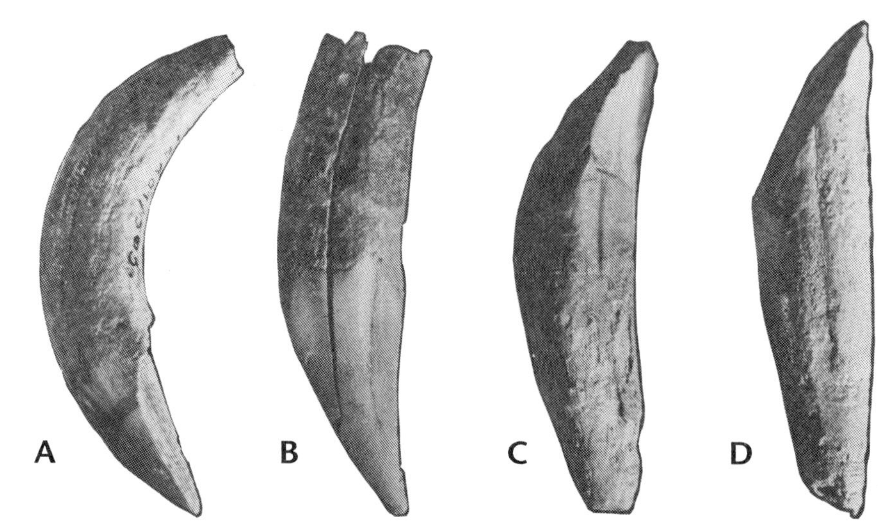

Figure 51. Peccary canines with natural occlusal surfaces.

larly identified as normal wear on teeth of old pigs, while five others exhibited no proof of use by man.

The much-worn lower left peccary canine illustrated at the right in Figure 51 also lacks any apparent evidence of use except that the occlusal surface appears to be abnormally pitted. Nevertheless it apparently is an artifact because it was found in Occupation Zone VII on top of the skull of Burial no. 55. As an *Olivancillaria* shell was beneath the skull, both pieces may have formed parts of a headband. Two more right canines with similar pitting which perforated the enamel and dentine of the grinding surface also came from Occupation Zone VII. One of these exhibits scattered striations and use polishing on the root surfaces. A lower left canine from the surface of the talus slope of shell exhibits a series of parallel striations near the tip of the occlusal surface opposite to the direction of normal wear. Finally, two lower canines, one right and one left, found near each other in Occupation Zone VI, exhibit some evidence for use. One has an extra wear facet near the tip. The tip of the other example was broken, but there are transverse striations near the break. Such features could be due to malocclusion, but several striations on the root surface of the latter tooth suggest that people used it.

In summary, of the 22 peccary canines we found, six were carefully ground and/or drilled, one must be an artifact by association, five are probably artifacts because of unusual striation patterns, while ten are not demonstrably artifacts. In Occupation Zone V we found a fragmentary right mandible of a peccary with one end deeply cut and broken to expose the molar root sockets, which have been worn, probably by using the naturally hafted teeth, since broken out, as a tool.

The lower left molar of a *Tapirus terrestris* had been drilled for suspension (Figure 52). After the root tips had been squared off by grinding, conical holes (3 mm in diameter tapering to 2 mm) were carefully drilled from opposite directions through both roots. The piece was found isolated in Occupation Zone VII.

The cylindrical canines of carnivores make spectacular pendants, and for that reason it seems odd that only four were found. Unfortunately they are difficult to identify as to species. One from Occupation VI was identified as probably the upper canine of a puma (*Felis concolor*). After the root tip had been ground to a flat

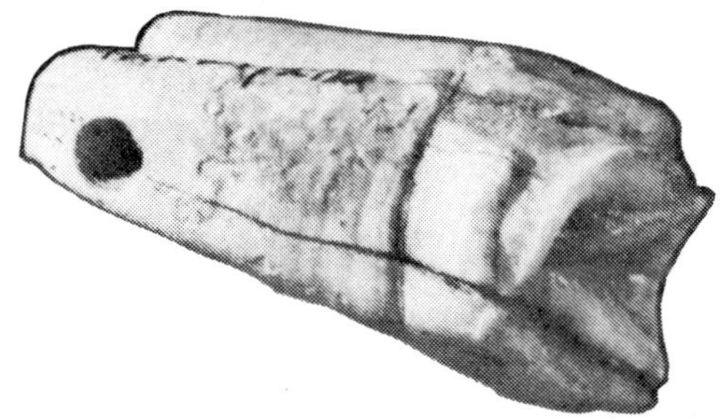

Figure 52. Drilled tapir molar.

plane the root was biconically drilled from opposing ground facets with a 2-mm-diameter bit (Figure 53d). The canine of what may be a seal was also found in Occupation VI near, but not directly associated, with Burial no. 5. Four facets were ground into the base of the root to form a flattened knob with rectangular cross-section and a rounded base (Figure 53c). Without a drilled hole, the constrictions above the knob seem too shallow for successful suspension unless the object was used as a *tembetá* lip ornament. One unidentified mammal canine from Occupation VII exhibits many tiny scratches running in various directions on the wear surface. Such a haphazard wear pattern suggests that it may have been used as a tool. The canine of what may be *Procyon cancrivorus*, a raccoon, from Occupation IV, has two short striations on the root. In addition, the tip was broken by pressure and subsequently polished, as if it also had been used as a tool.

All but one of the eleven rodent incisors belong to the medium-sized *Cuniculus paca*. The exception was the lower left incisor of a capivara (*Hydrochoerus hydrochaeris*) from Occupation VII. Although there may be an abnormal wear pattern on the occlusal surface of the rodent incisors, the other end of the capivara tooth obviously had been used, as it also was ground and polished. As with the peccary canines, if evidence of reuse is limited to the normal wear surface of rodent incisors it is difficult to prove human alteration. Interestingly, the best example demonstrating the hand of man is a lower left paca tooth from Occupation VII. There is some evidence of grinding across the normal grain; but the original concave occlusal surface is preserved, sug-

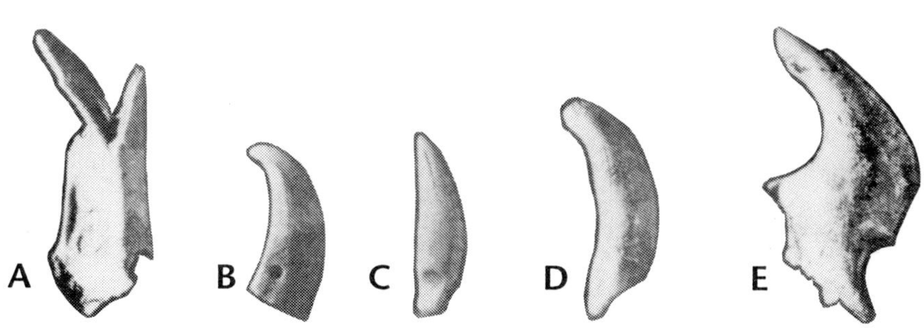

Figure 53. Mammal-tooth artifacts.

gesting that is was little used. The fact that it was found inserted inside a large hollow bird bone (Figure 53a) demonstrates the presence of human alteration beyond any doubt. No evidence of use was found on the haft except for slight wear polish; a similar bird bone from the same occupation zone, with articulating end broken off and the other end cut and broken, could also have served as a haft.

Another paca incisor, the occlusal surface of which was ground to a flat plane across the normal grain, was found still hafted in the right mandible. In this case its association with Burial no. 4 (Occupation VI), an adult male, suggests that it was a woodworking tool. A right mandible of a paca from Occupation VII was missing its canine tooth, which apparently had been broken out of the socket by downward pressure. Evidence of use includes several striations on the lateral surface and a worn symphyseal surface. Exactly the same use patterns, except for the presence of more striations, were found on the left mandible of another individual from the same occupation zone, VII. The left mandible of a young individual from Occupation V lacks evidence of use, although the tooth had been ground to a flat plane like the one illustrated in Figure 53e.

Apparently the presence of a flat rather than a normal incurvate occlusal surface, and the pattern of lateral or transverse grinding across the normal grain are the best characteristics for identifying human use if only the tooth is preserved. On one lower left incisor from Occupation VII part of the original occlusal surface is preserved adjacent to a new bevelled plane caused by subsequent transverse grinding. The occlusal surface on the tooth of a young individual also was ground transversely to a flat plane, while the occlusal surface on an upper left incisor has extra wear facets on both lateral edges. In the latter case all three facets were formed by up and down movements, which could be one type of normal pattern on upper incisors. All three examples so far discussed in this paragraph came from Occupation VII. Another upper left incisor, the only one from Occupation IV, exhibits a normal concave wear pattern on its occlusal surface, but the presence of several tiny flakes removed from the external tip of the occlusal surface suggests that it may have been used in a different manner as a punch or chisel.

Unfortunately the presence of only one paca incisor from an earlier occupation than V through VII is not sufficient to establish a different cultural pattern of use. Apparently all the incisor tools from later levels were not used as chisels, but were pushed with a strong downward movement. Perhaps they were used for scraping or planing bone or long pieces of wood, such as bows or projectile shafts.

Two hollow cylindrical teeth were catalogued as artifacts because it occurred to me that they would make excellent hard tips for wooden arrow shafts. One *Caiman latirostris* incisor from Occupation IV shows no evidence of use, and is probably not straight enough to serve the purpose suggested. The other, a fish tooth from Occupation V, proved under the microscope to have fine incisions which partially encircle the tip end, which has a diameter of 11 mm. Such a pattern suggests that it may have been used as a drill bit for working wood, and the missing tip may have broken off while being used.

It was assumed that, like any other foreign object in a shellmound, all shark teeth were carried there by man; so all such manuports were carefully examined for human alteration. Shark teeth were commonly encountered isolated in the midden. In fact it seemed surprising that there was no indication that any of them were closely enough associated with each other to suggest that they were strung as beads or mounted so as to create the edge of a sword or other weapon.

Only two kinds of shark are represented in the collection, both commonly found in southern Brazilian waters. The white shark, "man-eater," or *tubarão* (*Carcharodon carcharias*) has flat triangular teeth, many with natural fine serrations (*v.* perforated examples in the top row of Figure 42). As these teeth are quite straight in longitudinal section, they could easily serve as projectile points and/or knives with some modification of the slightly thickened roots. *Carcharias taurus*, the more common sand shark or sand tiger *(cação de areia)* has less dangerous unserrated teeth which are nonetheless very sharp. These teeth have more bulbous roots which can easily be hafted, while the exposed enamel curves to form a pointed cylinder flattened on one side (*v.* bottom row of Figure 42). Without modification, these thicker teeth would readily serve as awls, punches, or drill bits for working bone or wood. Teeth which have obviously been altered by grinding and drilling will first be described. Unaltered teeth will be discussed on the basis of the compilation in Table 12 because most are sand-shark teeth.

Interestingly, two of the four recovered white-shark (*Carcharodon*) teeth which were not altered by grinding facets were associated with Burial no. 26, stratum 6B. One of these specimens has a broken and worn tip with tiny striations visible on one face; the other has no visible evidence of use. The roots of the remaining eight complete examples of white-shark teeth have all been carefully thinned by grinding (Figure 42 b, u), and three of these also have paired sets of biconical perforations through the flattened bases (Figure 42 c–e; also see examples from the Enseada sambaqui in Beck, Araujo, Duarte, Fossari and Belani, 1970:foto no. 13). Such a pattern suggests the likelihood that these artifacts were not intended as ornaments, but rather as small tools hafted onto bifurcated wooden handles with some sort of glue. The carefully paired perforations would be superfluous for suspension, but would serve admirably to keep a mounted knife from slipping sideways under lateral pressure. The root face containing the bulging tuberosity has to be ground down completely, while the opposite root face needs relatively slight facetting in order to make plane parallel faces. The ends of the wings may also be rounded or neatly truncated as in Figure 42u. The ground facets frequently show considerable use-polishing. All of these artifacts exhibit many fine striations on their faces; but the tip, although sometimes worn and polished, is rarely broken. On two examples (Figure 42c) the broken tip was subsequently ground to a conical point. One side of the tip of another example also exhibits a grinding facet. This example and most others show many striations and much use polish over all enamel surfaces. The tip and base are missing on one calcined tooth, but one face is covered with fine striations.

Thus, of the 13 white-shark teeth, only three lack any evidence of workmanship; and one of these justifiably may be called an artifact because of its association with a burial. Three of the white-shark teeth came from stratum 6B associated with two burials; two from Occupation Zone V; one from Occupation Zone VI (stratum 4B); and six (including two unmodified teeth) from the last occupation, VII; one was screened from a slumped wall.

The sand-shark teeth are tabulated according to provenience and evidence for use (Table 12). All five specimens which had been facetted and/or drilled came from Occupation VII. Only one tooth exhibits both a grinding facet and remnants of drill holes. In this case, however, the facet was not used as a platform for drilling; and the direction of drilling was from the sides of the root wings, at right angles to the drilled holes on the white-shark teeth. The conical holes had been completed, but the outer margins of the holes broke off (Figure 54). The broken edges are very worn and polished, as is the facet ground to reduce the central tuberosity. The tip was broken and worn, and both enamel faces exhibit striations. A similar ground facet to reduce the large tuberosity was found on another example from Occupation VII. One root wing as well as the tip had broken off this specimen, which also shows many use-striations on the faces. Perhaps the wing was broken during an attempt to drill it. An evident attempt was made to drill a hole in one side of the root wing of an unusually large specimen (Figure 55). When the edge of the depression started fragmenting, the attempt was

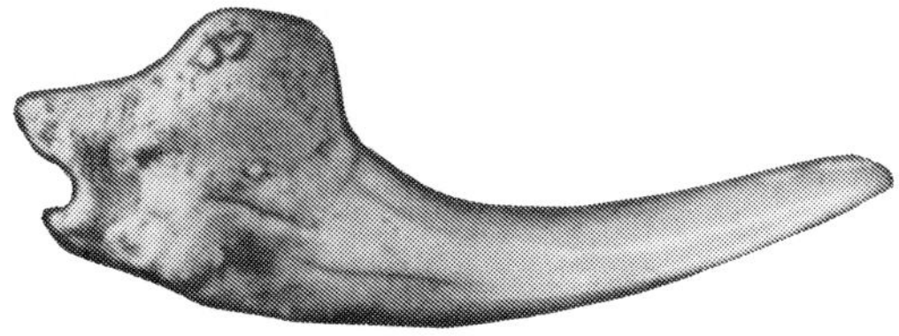

Figure 54. Sand-shark tooth with transverse drill holes (later broken).

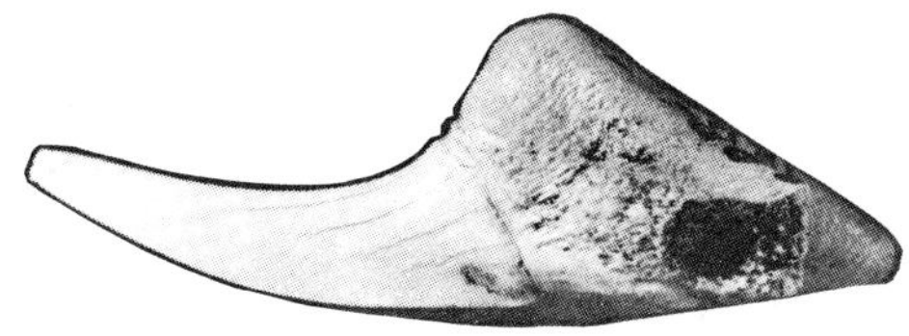

Figure 55. Sand-shark tooth with attempted transverse drill hole.

abandoned. The broken tip was worn, and striations are evident on both faces; but the root is unaltered.

The fact that the broken edges of the drilled holes are worn and polished in the first example suggests subsequent use other than by suspension. Also it would appear to be unnecessary to reduce the thickness of the central tuberosity if one intended only to suspend the object, unless the platform were designed for drilling a central hole. The fact that instead there are two laterally directed holes plus the evidence for considerable use on the enamel faces, suggests that this type of tooth also served as hafted small tools. In this case, however, the thick cross-section of the working end and the laterally directed holes suggest that the objects were meant to be secured for a pushing or perforating action, such as a graver, a punch, a reamer, or a drill.

That some teeth in fact were used for reaming or drilling is indicated on five examples with broken lateral edges and particularly on three other examples where the lateral edges near the tip were broken or deliberately facetted to form a conical tip, which was then worn. The root wings were broken off one of these specimens, perhaps by heavy use. Actually, the root wings are broken or the root is missing on a total of 15 specimens. In one case there is obvious lopsided wear on the tip, wear which indicates that it was used as a graver, perhaps to make a groove in a bone or wooden object. Another example, found with Burial no. 7, has a different pattern of root facetting. In this case the lateral surface of one wing and the tips of both wings were ground flat. The only other evidence of use is that both faces are striated. Two other teeth, unaltered except that both had broken and subsequently worn tips, and many facial striations on one example, were also encountered with this burial. Two much-used teeth were found with Burial no. 4, two with Burial no. 53, and one with Burial no. 52. One of the specimens from Burial no. 4 was calcined black, as was another example from Occupation Zone VII. The fact that two teeth were burned may be of no special significance.

The possibility must be considered that some of the evidence for use on the recovered sample of 155 sand-shark teeth might have been created by the natural habits of the living sharks. Sharks have rows of teeth which move forward as the animal ages, eventually projecting vertically at the mouth opening. Depending on what is

Table 12. Sand-shark Teeth *(Carcharias taurus).*

Association		Broken Tip	Worn Tip	Striations near Tip	Striations on Face(s)	Root Wing(s) Broken	Remarks
Occup.	IV	X	X				
	IV				X		
	IV						No evidence of use on one specimen.
Strat.	6B	X			X		
	6B	X	X		X		
Occup.	V			X			Lateral edges broken near tip.
	V		X	X			
	V	2					Two specimens.
	V				2		Two specimens.
	V	X		X			
	V			X			
	V		X		X	X	
	V		X			X	Edges broken and smoothed to form conical tip.
	V	X	X		X	X	
	V	4			4		Four specimens.
	V						Edge near tip serrated.
	V						No evidence of use on 27 specimens.
Occup.	VI	X					Lateral edges broken near tip.
	VI			X			
	VI	X	X		X	X	Ends of both wings worn after breaking.
	VI		X		X		
	VI	X	X		X		
	VI				2	2	Two specimens.
	VI	X		X			
	VI				5		Five specimens.
	VI				2		Only one striation near tip. Two specimens.
	VI						No evidence of use on one specimen.
(Bur. 4)	VI	X	X	X	X		
(Bur. 4)	VI	X					Lateral edges broken near tip.
Occup.	VII	8			8		Eight specimens.
	VII	X			X		Striations across grain on one face.
	VII				7		Most of root missing on one of seven specimens.
	VII				X		Root missing. Striations near base only.

Table 12 (continued).

Association	Broken Tip	Worn Tip	Striations Near Tip	Striations on Face(s)	Root Wing(s) Broken	Remarks
Occup. VII	2	2				Two specimens.
VII	X	X				Root missing.
VII						Root missing. Tip rounded and worn to conical point.
VII		2		2		Two specimens.
VII					X	
VII	2					Two specimens; one with single flake removed from tip.
VII	X		X			
VII	X	X	X			
VII		X	X			Much-worn face with striations.
VII	2	2		2		Striated facets across grain on both faces of one specimen.
VII	2	2		2		Lateral edge broken on one specimen.
VII	X	X		X		Conical drill hole on one root wing (Figure 55).
VII		X	X	X		
VII	X			X		Striations on one face near base.
VII				X	X	
VII			4			Four specimens.
VII	X			X	X	Central root tuberosity ground flat.
VII		X				Lopsided wear on tip.
VII	X	X		X	X	Both wings uniconically drilled, and central tuberosity ground flat (Figure 54).
VII				X	X	Only one striation. Calcined.
VII						No evidence of use on 37 specimens.
(Bur. 7) VII	X	X				
(Bur. 7) VII				X		Tips of wings and lateral surface of one wing facetted by grinding.
(Bur. 7) VII	X	X		X		
(Bur. 52) VII				X		Root missing.
(Bur. 53) VII			X	X		
(Bur. 53) VII	X	X		X		
Unknown	X	X				Lateral edges facetted near tip.
Unknown				3		Three specimens.
Unknown	X			X		
Unknown	X	X		X		

grasped, the vertical row of teeth can become scratched, broken, and even reworn by further use before being replaced in due time. That such natural marks are not always present is shown by the fact the no evidence of use whatever was visible on 62 specimens encountered in the shellmound, while three have only one scratch on an enamel face. Thirty of the 47 teeth with broken tips show subsequent wear. Use striations are found only near the base on two examples, only near the tip on 13 examples, on one or both faces on 64 examples, and over all exposed surfaces on three examples. On two specimens the striations extend only across the grain, a pattern which suggests but does not demonstrate human intervention. It could also be argued that the seven unfacetted examples associated with burials were not placed in position but accidentally included in the backfill of the grave. Similarly, it can be argued that the broken or missing roots on 15 specimens do not demonstrate tool use. Nevertheless, there is definite evidence for human alteration of 15 sand-shark teeth; and a suggestion has been made that most if not all of these alterations were caused by the fabrication and use of these teeth as small tools for working wood and bone. It seems likely, therefore, that the remaining teeth were also brought to the shellmound to serve some useful purpose, which probably resulted in artificial scratches and broken tips on many of these specimens.

Little particular significance can be deduced from the fact that no teeth artifacts were found in the earliest three occupation zones. The lack of land-mammal teeth in the early zones is probably directly correlated with the paucity of land-mammal bones in these same deposits. But dead sharks were presumably always available on the beach even if they were never intentionally caught, so their absence in the early zones combined with their increasing abundance in later zones tends to support the argument that the shark teeth were intentionally brought up to the site for some purpose.

Chapter 9
Shell Artifacts

Valves of shellfish undoubtedly were used for hundreds of routine daily tasks. When excavating a shellmound it is not possible to check all shells for evidence of use other than for food; normally only the unusual species, or shape, or association is noted. If we had had the time to look at all shells, the inventory of shell artifacts would undoubtedly have been increased severalfold by deducing unusual patterns of use from the examination of large series. A detailed description of the large range of shell artifacts that has been found in a sambaqui farther north in the state of Rio de Janeiro will give the reader some idea of the many shell artifacts we may have overlooked (Lima et al. 1986). Several giant oyster (*Ostrea arborea*) and large *Lucina* clam shells could have been numbered as artifacts because they were useful objects as plates and were found isolated, but they were not designated as artifacts because there was no visible trace of use. However, in the kitchen feature in stratum 10, Occupation II, even large *Ostrea arborea* were considered to be artifacts as they were found directly associated with several whalebone artifacts (artifacts 899 in Figure 9a). Likewise, when 22 small terrestrial gastropod (*Subulina octona*) shells (Figure 56, upper row) were found associated with 33 worked *Oliva* beads (Figure 56, lower row) in Burial no. 15, stratum 6B, there can be little doubt that the unaltered shells served some cultural function. The apices of the *Oliva* shells had all been truncated for suspension. An unsuccessful attempt had even been made to drill a hole in the one in the center of the photograph (Tables 13, 15).

The most common evidence of alteration of shells is by perforation. Included in this category as an equivocal example is one *berbigão* (*Anomalocardia*) clam valve tentatively numbered as an artifact, which evidently was the victim of a gastropod that made its living by drilling

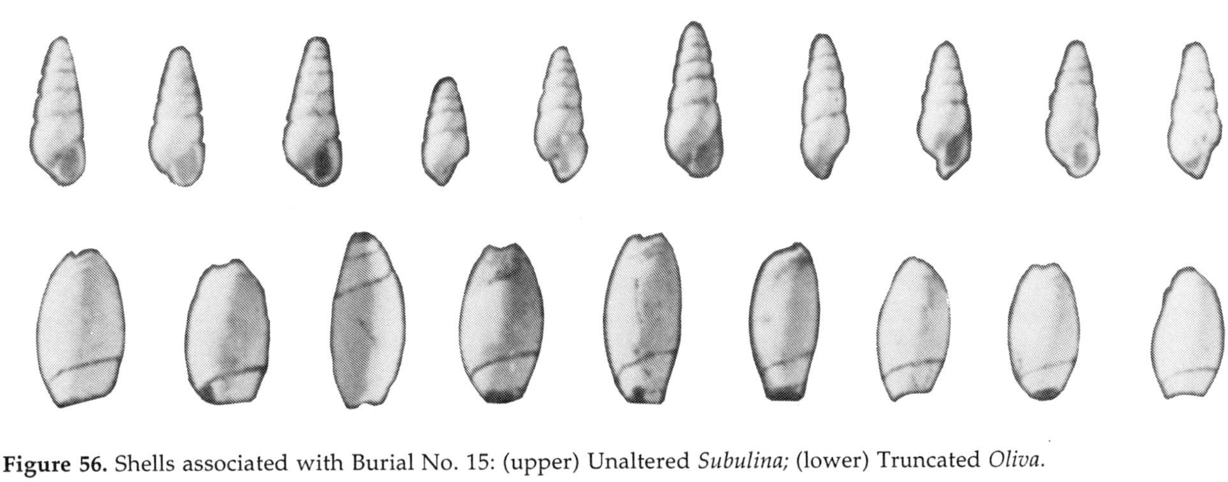

Figure 56. Shells associated with Burial No. 15: (upper) Unaltered *Subulina;* (lower) Truncated *Oliva.*

holes in succulent shellfish. But why would the human shellfish collector bother to bring in the shell of a dead animal, unless perhaps the drill hole became a useful means of suspending an ornament? (Perforated shells are tabulated in Tables 14a and b.)

If the perforation is apparently made by puncturing a hole with several percussion blows, especially if the resultant flakes are removed from the outside face by blows directed from the inside, one is on somewhat more secure ground when the object is dubbed an artifact. While excavating, I assumed that it would be possible to puncture a hole in a thick-walled valve by the pressure of walking on the convex outer face. I later tested this assumption by experimenting at another Santa Catarina shellmound, and found that I was unable to break the natural arch of the umbo unless I stomped heavily on a shell placed on a level hard surface; and then the shell would break in half or shatter without creating a perforation. Of course, thin-walled shells, such as mussels and some clams (e.g., *Atrina rigida*), shatter into tiny fragments under pressure; and thereby become difficult or impossible to identify in a shellmound. Most clams, cockles, univalves, and oysters have thick arched valves which withstand tremendous pressure under many meters of overlying deposits without breaking. On the other hand, shells weakened by burning or weathering may fragment quite easily.

I found that it is easy to puncture a hole in a valve with several carefully directed blows with a hammerstone. Expanding conchoidal flake scars on the face opposite the point of percussion indicate the direction of percussion. As indicated above, before performing these experiments I had discarded many valves whose direction of impact was from the external face. Consequently, except for the obviously used large *Mactrella* shells, only one externally punctured valve (of *Anomalocardia*) was saved. The large (diameter up to 8 x 11 cm) *Mactrella* shells and perhaps the *Iphigenia* shell which also exhibits fine striations adjacent to the perforation, may have been used as graters or peelers. As three of the four perforated "pectens" (*Phacoides*) were associated with burials; these relatively thin-walled shells were likely used as ornaments.

The most carefully shaped shell artifacts were four univalve columellas, from 3 to 4 cm long, which had been ground into irregularly conical shapes (Figure 57). Too much of the valves had been removed to be able to identify the species, although they were solid near their thick apices. As they are so asymmetrical it seems unlikely that they were fashioned for use as projectile points. Possibly they were used as *tembetás* (lip ornaments). Although Cunha (1973) does not suggest a cylindrical shape, evidence was found for the use of *tembetás* at Forte Marechal Luz from analysis of the peculiar longitudinal abrasion found on the root of an inferior molar of a burial. Two of these objects tapered to a slender conical point at one end. One of the latter, from Occupation III, has a thick truncated conical tip at the other end. The thick conical end of the natural shell on the other piece was retained. This and the other two objects, which are flatter in transverse section and have squared bases, came from Occupation VII. The surfaces of all pieces had been chemically eroded and polished by use, obliterating most grinding marks.

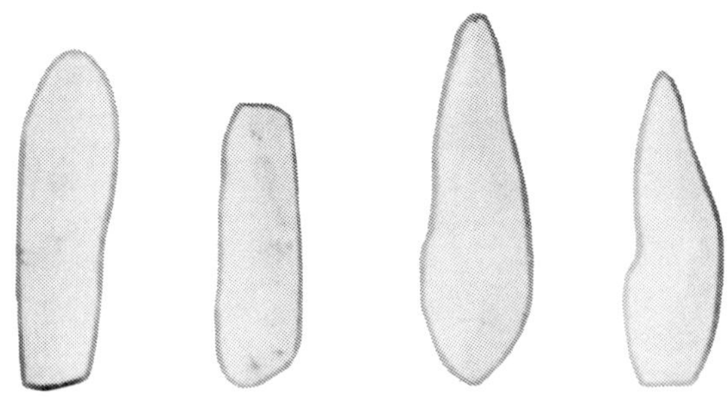

Figure 57. Cylindrical ground gastropod columella artifacts.

Three large *Oliva* beads truncated for suspension (Figure 58 left) were found in the intrusive burial stratum 6B. A similarly truncated *Conus* shell (Figure 58 right) was associated with Burial No. 7. Other associations of unusual shells with burials are tabulated in Tables 13 and 14; and their associations are discussed in the chapter on the Disposition of the Dead.

Although not strictly speaking artifacts in the sense of serving a cultural function as a tool or ornament, we occasionally noted lenses or concentrations of gastropod columellas (probably *Thais*) which had evidently been broken to remove the meat. Only a few of these columellas were saved in the level bags. One large *Strombus pugilis* columella from Occupation V exhibited several fine striations near the mouth where a sharp object had been inserted to extract the meat. Evidently no other shellfish had to be broken to remove the meat. The occasional giant land snail (*Strophocheilus oblongus*) shell was found, particularly near the surface; but there was no indication that they had been eaten.

Five large marine gastropods exhibited worn (Figure 59) or flaked lips which appeared to have been altered by use as tools. These shells will be discussed further in the final chapter.

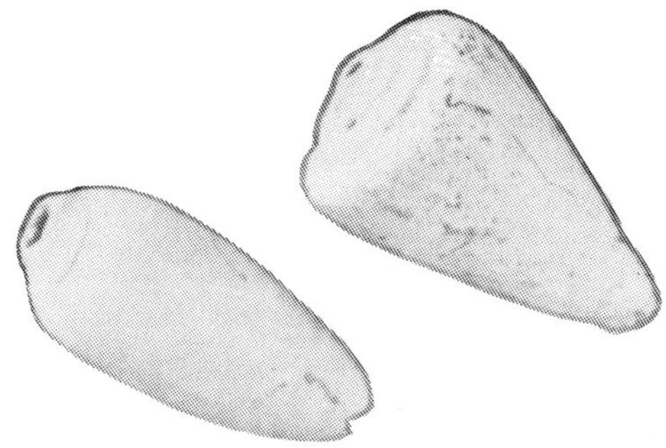

Figure 58. Perforated shells.

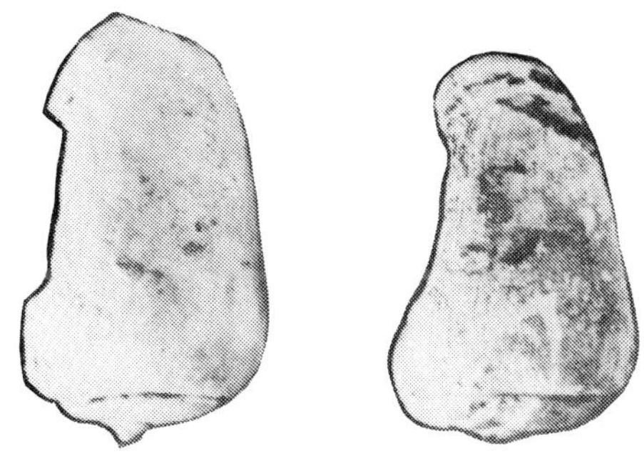

Figure 59. *Olivancillaria* shells with worn lips.

Table 13. Shell Artifacts.

	II	III	IV	6B	V	VI	VII	NO PROV.
Ground shell artifacts of unknown use		1					4	
Truncated *Oliva* beads				2				
Truncated *Oliva* beads with Burial No. 15				33				
Associated terrestrial *(Subulina)* shells				22				
Associated *Lintricula auricularia*				2				
Truncated *Conus* bead with Burial No. 7							1	
Strombus pugilis associated with Burial No. 5						1		
Olivancillaria with worn lip							2	
Worn lip of *Semicassis granulatum*							1	
Tivela fulminata with flaked lip								1
Lintricula auricularis with worn lip							1	
Perforated *Lintricula auricularis*							1	
Perforated *Olivancillaria*							1	
Diodara patagonica with Burial No. 13				2				
Perforated *Mactrella alata*			1				2	
Perforated *Ostrea* shells			1			1		
Used giant *Ostrea arborea* shells	7	2		1				
Perforated *Anomalocardia brasiliana*			1					
Perforated *Phacoides pectinatus* with burials				2		1	1	
Perforated *Iphigenia brasiliensis*								1
Totals	7	3	3	64	—	3	14	2

Total number of shell artifacts: 95

Table 14a. Perforated Shells (Bivalves).

Association	Species	Perf. from Outside	Perf. from Inside	Remarks
Occup. IV	*Mactrella alata*	X		Part of distal edge broken and smoothed.
Occup. IV	*Anomalocardia brasiliana*	X		1-mm-square hole near umbo.
Occup. IV	*Ostrea arborea*			Oblong perforation near center.
Strat. 6B, Bur. #39	*Phacoides pectinatus*		X	Oblong hold near center of face.
Strat. 6B, Bur. #44	*Phacoides pectinatus*		X	Round hole near umbo.
Occup. VI, Bur. #5	*Phacoides pectinatus*		X	Most of distal edge broken away
Occup. VI	*Ostrea* sp.			Small oyster lamina with round hole punctured from outside near center.
Occup. VII	*Iphigenia brasiliensis*		X	Oblong hole near center.
Occup. VII	*Mactrella alata*	X		Round hole near center. External edge of hole ground smooth. Very fine unidirectional striations on umbo edge.
Occup. VII	*Mactrella alata*	X		Oval hole near center. Striations on external edge of perforation and adjacent face.
Occup. VII	*Anomalocardia brasiliana*			Round drilled hole (natural) near edge.
Occup. VII	*Phacoides pectinatus*		X	Oblong hole on umbo.
Surface	*Iphigenia brasiliensis*	X		Uniconical perforation near umbo. Striations on external surface. Distal edge flaked by use.

Table 14b. Perforated Shells (Univalves).

Association	Species	Illustration	Remarks
Strat. 6B	*Oliva* sp.	Figure 58	Tip removed for suspension.
Strat. 6B, Bur. #15	*Oliva* sp.	Figure 56	33 small beads with tips broken off. No evidence of wear, but probably strung as necklace as found amongst ribs.
Strat. 6B, Bur. #23	*Oliva* sp.		Tip removed. Near perforated fish vertebra.
Strat. 6B, Bur. #13	*Diodara patagonica*		Natural apical perforations on two conical limpets. No evidence of wear.
Occup. VII, Bur. #7 (under surface mound)	*Conus spurius*	Figure 58	Tip removed.
Occup. VII	*Lintricula auricularia*		Perforation on ventral surface.
Occup. VII	*Olivancillaria brasiliensis*		Narrow oval puncture on dorsal surface with grooves radiating from one end of puncture presumably from being strung. Lip broken away.

Table 15. Miscellaneous Shell Artifacts.

ASSOCIATION	SPECIES	ILLUSTRATION	REMARKS
Occup. II, Strat. 10	*Ostrea arborea*	Plate 9A	Six shells (four with concave surface up as if used as dishes) placed in a line on top of whalebone chopping block (Artifact 894 in Figure 9A). Another calcined shell (possibly used to carry hot coals) found beneath whale vertebra brazier (Artifact 901).
Occup. III	*Ostrea arborea*		Remnants of hematite paint in concavity.
Occup. III (?)	*Ostrea* sp.		Thick shell apparently use-flaked on one end.
Occup. IV	*Ostrea arborea*		Very large isolated oyster with deep concavity. No evidence of use.
Strat. 6B, Bur. #16	*Ostrea arborea*		Sitting with concave surface up. Probably a food offering to the dead (?).
Strat. 6B, Bur. #15	*Lintricula auricularia*		Two large unaltered shells.
Strat. 6B, Bur. #15	*Subulina*	Figure 56	22 unaltered terrestrial gastropod shells.
Occup. V	Section of *Teredo* worm tube (?)		Ring of shell (no evidence of working).
Occup. V or VII(?)	Section of *Teredo* worm tube (?)		Same
Occup. VII	Section of *Teredo* worm tube (?)		Same
Occup. VI, Bur. #5	*Strombus pugilis*		Partially calcined. Found on maxilla.
Occup. VII	*Lintricula auricularia*		Section of lip worn.
Occup. VII	*Olivancillaria brasiliensis*	Figure 59	Lip worn.
Occup. VII, Bur. #55 & 56	*Olivancillaria brasiliensis*	Figure 59	Section of lip worn. Adjacent to humerus of Burial #56 and beneath skull of #55.
Occup. VII	Unidentified		Weathered piece of thick shell, the ends of which appear to have been ground across the grain, perhaps to make a fishhook.
Occup. VII	*Semicassis granulatum*		Thick lip apparently broken to form a sharp polished tip.
Surface	*Tivela fulminata*		Excurving edge serrated as if for use as a saw.

Chapter 9

Chapter 10
Clay Artifacts

Introduction

In 1960, when the Forte Marechal Luz sambaqui was excavated, a perceived problem was whether or not pottery was ever manufactured by the occupants of sambaquis, as it was generally believed that all of the coastal shellmound people had a simple preceramic material culture. Ceramics had already been excavated from the black humus level of the small riverine shellmound of Itacoara in Joinville, 32 km upriver from the coast and a similar distance southwest of Forte Marechal Luz (Tiburtius, Bigarella, and Bigarella 1951). Tiburtius, Bigarella, and Bigarella (1954) had also found similar pottery in two layers at least 50 cm below the surface of the sambaqui do Rio Pinheiros, about 1 km from the Canal de Araquari (or Barra do Sul) on the mainland opposite the Ilha de São Francisco (v. inset map on Figure 1). Despite the lack of European trade goods, many archaeologists argued that it was possible that these surficial layers with much organic debris and relatively little shell had been deposited by semi-acculturated *caboclos* in early post-contact times.

When Professor Luiz de Castro Faria, Wilson Rauth, and I visited the sambaqui at Forte Marechal Luz, we observed that potsherds were present in several upper layers of shell, in addition to the surficial layer of humus. As the problem of whether or not unacculturated Indians had made the pots could evidently be resolved here, this site was selected for excavation.

The upper layers were excavated particularly carefully, although mostly in arbitrary 10-cm levels. Everything was screened, and all potsherds were saved in order to resolve the problem beyond all doubt. The only post-contact artifacts, all modern, were found in the black humus and shell layer, never more than 10 cm below the surface, except in a recent pit excavated for the nearby water tank (circle on Figure 2). In my excavations, potsherds were found to be abundant in the upper four strata, up to 80 cm below the surface, including two layers (strata 2 and 4) of predominantly clean shell, which is generally conceded to be a typical kind of sambaqui deposit. Up to 1 m below the surface, in stratum 4B, later much disturbed for burials, but dating before the deposition of strata 1 through 3, we found the earliest potsherds: one sherd was found on the right foot of Burial no. 5 in stratum 4B (Occupation Zone VI). Charcoal from a ceremonial fire built over Burial no. 5 provided a date (M-1202) of 880 ± 100 yr B.P. (A.D. 1070) for stratum 4B and the earliest pottery at Forte Marechal Luz. Obviously, the stratigraphy and the radiocarbon date clearly demonstrated that ceramics were introduced to Forte Marechal Luz in late-prehistoric times, at least four hundred years before European contact. Also, it should be emphasized that there is no evidence that the sambaqui was ever occupied as a living site after the European conquest, although the rich organic humus likely had been used for gardens by *caboclos* in post-contact times. Two dates in the 14th century A.D. (M-1200: A.D. 1320 and M-1203: A.D. 1340) refer to the last occupation of the sambaqui, so ceramics were produced at the site for at least 300 years before the site was abandoned (Table 16).

Unfired Clay Basins

Fired pots were not the earliest clay objects used at the site, however. A most interesting set of unfired clay cooking vessels was found in stratum 7 (Occupation Zone IV). Charcoal found adjacent to one of these *panelas* was dated (M-1206) to 1440 ± 110 yr B.P. (A.D. 520), or 500 years before the introduction of ceramics. A

Table 16. Clay Artifacts.

	II	III	IV	6B	V	VI	VII	NO PROV.
Unfired clay basins			13					
Fired clayball	1							
Fired perforated clayball							1	
Fired square-cornered object							1	
Unfired square-cornered object							1	
Undecorated ceramics						rare	abundant	abundant
Totals	1		13				3	

Total number of clay artifacts: 17 (plus ca. 10,000 sherds)

concentration of unfired and untempered clay basins and bowls had been excavated into the top of stratum 8 by the depositors of stratum 7 (Occupation Zone VI). This group of basins, made of a red clay evidently mixed with ash, covered all of Squares B2 and B3 and extended into all neighboring squares. See the plan (Figure 7) and the profile of the east wall of Square B2 (Figure 5) for all the features that were excavated.

A total of 13 vessels were exposed. They were quite irregular in shape, although only the deepest one (no. 1) expanded below the mouth; the others were simple basins. Size also varied between a diameter of 20 cm (no. 11) to 110 x 55 cm (no. 10). Interior depth was usually between 10 and 15 cm, but no. 1 (see in profile as well as plan view in Figure 7) was 25 cm and no. 2 was 22 cm deep. The walls varied from 3 to 10 cm in thickness. The red color is probably the result of heating, although hematite may have been mixed with the clay and ash. Flat-topped concentrations of grey and yellow clay in the vicinity of the basins appear to have been put in place but not yet molded into shape; also the small but thick-walled double broiler (no. 11 and no. 12) sat on a bed of grey clay mixed with shell. The presumed function, for boiling fish, was deduced from the scatter of thermally fractured pebbles, evidently boiling stones, and the concentration of uncalcined fish bones found lying on a bed of clean shell next to no. 1, and another concentration of fish bones and charcoal found inside no. 8. A concentration of calcined whalebone fragments in and on the lip of no. 5 suggests the possibility that oil may have been extracted from whalebones by heating them in the basins.

The worked pebbles associated with the unfired clay basins have been described under the section on pigment processing because a pebble found inside no. 10 retains a dark (manganese?) stain on its concave face, as does one of the three pebbles with central depressions found nested inside no. 8. Another pebble found adjacent to no. 8 retains a hematite stain on its concave face. A striated hematite pebble was found adjacent to no. 6. Actually the red clay itself could have been used directly for painting bodies, either live or dead.

The artifacts inside no. 8 were apparently cached beneath a lid constructed of the same clay. Evidently the lid had been moved aside to extract its original contents, presumably fish soup. No. 3 also had a lid partially moved aside and broken away, while no. 2 retains the remnants of a lid that was constructed after the basin itself. In other words, the basins evidently were reused simply by constructing a new lid.

Although most of the basins are quite level, no. 7 and no. 10 both slope down to the southwest; presumably when they had lids any liquid in them would not spill out. The pile of clean grey sand near no. 7 could have functioned for retaining heat.

Rohr (1960:Figures 10 and 11; p. 20) found similar clay vessels at the Praia Grande sambaqui near the northern end of Santa Catarina Island. The red clay vessels at Praia Grande are somewhat different, as they are higher (30 to 63 cm); and one had a whalebone lid. Perhaps the piece of whalebone in no. 5 at Forte Marechal Luz was the remnant of such a lid. Rohr indicates that the red clay used for the vessels was the same as that used to paint human skeletons at that site.

Fired Clay

An irregular fired clay ball (75 x 50 x 45 mm) came from stratum 12 (Occupation Zone II), some centuries before the time of Christ, to judge from the date of 2060 ± 120 yr B.P. (100 B.C.) on charcoal from the overlying stratum 10 (M-1207). The ball appears to have been deliberately molded into shape, but of course it could have been fired accidentally.

Obviously, neither the 2000-year-old fired clay ball nor the 1500-year-old unfired clay basins led directly to the innovation of fired ceramics a millennium ago at Forte Marechal Luz. When pottery was finally innovated, it was well tempered and well finished, although not decorated; obviously the result of a well-developed ceramic tradition of long duration which came from elsewhere, perhaps as a result of local men taking wives from another village, or perhaps as a result of trade. It should be emphasized that there was no apparent break in occupation at Forte Marechal Luz at the time of the introduction of pottery. This fact was evident when digging because whenever ceramic stratum 3 directly overlay preceramic stratum 5, the only way to distinguish the two dark shell strata was by the presence or absence of pottery; there was no disconformity, humus nor other kind of physical change, and all other artifact types continued through both layers. Obviously, ceramics were not introduced to Forte Marechal Luz by an invading group of people.

Examination of a small sample (ca. 100) of the total sherd collection (ca. 10,000) revealed that the pottery assemblage comprises two basic types. The minority type (ca. 5%) is a black ware which sometimes features a polished black slip. The vast majority of the sherds pertain to a dark plain unslipped ware which varies in surface color from dark brown through grey to reddish brown or orange buff, depending on firing. About 20% were in the lighter end of the color range. The sherds are hard, fairly thick (5–10 mm), and most have a black or grey core, indicating incomplete oxidation. The vessel forms are simple jars and bowls with vertical or flaring mouths and round or rarely flat bases. Several sherds have a black (food?) encrustation on the interior surface. Examination of a thin section of the most common type by Charles Schweger revealed feldspar and angular to slightly rounded quartz fragments, the grain boundaries of which are sutured, suggesting a metaquartzite source. The quartz temper is coarse and unsorted, with grain size ranging from less than 1 mm to 3 mm. The temper makes up an estimated 30% of the paste. Paste, sherd thickness, and rim and vessel forms seem to conform to the description of Enseada wares published by Beck (1968). Beck (1968:93) had the opportunity to examine the collection from Forte Marechal Luz, and concurred with this opinion

In manufacturing, the pots were apparently held in one hand and twirled while balancing on the thumb (to judge from the thumb-impressed dimple on the bottom of many pots) while the vessel sides were extended by coiling. The vessel lips, which feature the only decorative variation applied to the pots, were frequently thickened and rounded; but occasionally thinned by carving oblique angles on the interior and/or the exterior. Most often, however, the lips were simply rounded and everted. The pots were smoothed, usually with a pebble, but occasionally with a stick or spatula. The pots were then incompletely fired in an open fire, or a very simple kiln, as the interiors of sherds are usually dark and reduced while the exteriors are generally more oxidized and occasionally fire-clouded.

A nearly complete pot, a small flat-bottomed bowl, was found next to the cranium of Burial no. 52 in Occupation Zone VII (Figure 60). The exterior is dark red with fire clouds, while the interior is black and semipolished. Some alkaline mineral apparently accumulated on and beneath the surface, causing exfoliation and a platy texture. The pot is 80 mm high with a base diameter of 162 mm, expanding to a rim diameter of 192 mm. The wall, which thickens a bit below the lip on the exterior, averages 5 mm in thickness. The temper, which includes other minerals in addition to angular quartz, evidently did not come from the beach.

Several short segments of fired clay coils were found. An unusual piece was the corner of a square-cornered box-like container with four straight faces intersecting to form a right-angled corner with surfaces nearly parallel with the exterior faces. The object was 58 mm high, but the other original dimensions are unknown. Nearby, and also associated with the same ash concentration excavated into the top of stratum 2, was an unfired piece of red-brown clay, tempered and molded into two plane faces intersecting at a right angle. Possibly the ash area in the northwest corner of square F3 was the remnant of an open fire for baking pots, although there were also unburned fish bones in the ash, suggesting that the fish was boiled in a pot.

A spherical baked clay object (36 mm long and 22 mm in diameter) pinched at two opposing ends to make sharp conical points, one of which was perforated transversely by poking a hole 2 mm in diameter through the soft clay, was found in clean shell in Test Pit 2. Such an object could have been used as a fish-line weight.

Discussion of Ceramic Traditions in Southern Brazil

The ultimate source of the dark plain ware of Forte Marechal Luz is not known, although two dates (800 yr B.P. and 1140 yr B.P.) on a plain black ware tradition

Figure 60. Burial with associated flat-bottomed pot.

from northwestern Rio Grande do Sul (Schmitz 1968:131) suggest that the tradition was somewhat earlier in the southern interior. A plain brown ware variety from the same state is associated with even earlier dates (1380 yr B.P. and 1190 yr B.P.); so it is possible that the more widespread black variety may have developed originally in the northern interior of Rio Grande do Sul.

Essentially identical ceramics to those at Forte Marechal Luz were found by Beck (1968) at the nearby site of Enseada, a sambaqui located on the Ilha de São Francisco only 6 km south of Forte Marechal Luz. Beck et al. (1970:26) divided all sites in the São Francisco area into a preceramic Morro do Ouro phase characterised by abundant stone tools; and a ceramic Enseada phase characterised by abundant bone tools. Her Enseada phase included the ceramic levels at Itacoara, Rio Pinheiros, and Forte Marechal Luz, as well as Enseada. Beck (1968:89–99) hypothesized that the pottery complex intruded into the area with a new population which occupied ten abandoned sambaquis.

Piazza (1974), aware of the published date of A.D. 1070 on the early ceramic layer at Forte Marechal Luz, set up a different series of phases for the north coast of Santa Catarina. His Saguaçu phase, the oldest, is characterised by flaked stone, which he found at two preceramic sambaquis; and the use of mussels as the predominant shellfish. His preceramic Sai phase (dated 970 B.C. to 270 B.C.), is characterized by ground stone, flexed burials, and *Anomalocardia (berbigão)* as the predominant shellfish. His Araquari phase, featuring plain pottery and polished stone, starts about A.D. 1100; while his final Pirai phase includes the plain ware as well as some intrusive Tupi-Guarani ware, as both occurred together in the surface layer of two sites, including Itacoara, near Joinville.

Chmyz (1968) recognized that the dark plain ware from the north coast of Santa Catarina, as well as from two sites (not typical sambaquis) farther south on the Ilha de Santa Catarina, was related to his Itararé ceramic tradition, defined from the river of the same name on the Planalto that divides the states of Paraná and São Paulo. The Itararé tradition includes a variety of simple bowls and globular or egg-shaped vessels with slightly flaring rims, frequently thickened lips, and round flat bases (Chmyz 1968:Figure 1). All vessels are small in size; and they are red to dark grey in color, with abundant quartz sand temper, which causes many sherds to crumble easily. Chmyz considered the presence of such pottery in the surface layers of sambaquis on the coast of Paraná to be "accidental" and/or intrusive from the interior (Chmyz 1968:117). Unlike coastal sites, the interior Itararé Phase sites are associated with abundant flaked stone and no ground stone tools at all.

It is clear from the Forte Marechal Luz data that the dark plain ceramics were not introduced to the coast by invading people, who would have brought their stone-flaking tradition with them; but rather the discrete ceramic tradition was introduced by diffusion to the coastal people. At Forte Marechal Luz, the only coastal sambaqui with quite precise radiocarbon dating for the appearance of pottery, there is no evidence of any new population intrusion or invasion; for the total artifact assemblage remains essentially the same at Forte Marechal Luz except for the addition of pottery, in the same way that flaked bifacial axe preforms and bone fishhooks had been added to the artifact inventory as discrete technological traditions during earlier occupations.

Schmitz (1968) recognized three great pottery "complexes" in southern Brazil: (1) the late Tupi-Guarani expansion from the north; (2) another complex of painted wares associated with small mounds *(cerritos)* and probably related to the Carrua of Uruguay, who apparently moved up the coast of Rio Grande do Sul; and (3) the coiled plain ware tradition of well-smoothed to polished wares, egg-shaped or globular pots with excurving lips, or simple bowls, all made with a fine, quartz-tempered paste. Schmitz divided this third complex into three varieties on the basis of color: (I) brown ware associated with a flake industry on open sites in northern Rio Grande do Sul (the previously mentioned dates of 1380 and 1190 yr B.P. are associated); (II) predominantly black ware of northwestern Rio Grande do Sul, dated between 800 and 1140 yr B.P., and most closely related to Chmyz's (1968) Itararé tradition farther north on the Planalto; (III) the black to red ware of Beck's Enseada phase, closely related to Schmitz's second variety. Interestingly, Schmitz was able to associate this second variety of the plain ware complex with the ethnographic Kaingang, and considered all three varieties of plain ware to be associated with Gê-speaking peoples. Schmitz noted that the black to red plain ware is found throughout the interior states of southern Brazil, as well as in Mato Grosso.

I perceive that the pattern of ceramic traditions in southern Brazil is quite analogous to the situation in eastern North America, where two great ceramic traditions have become established in the archaeological literature during the last half century. The earliest ceramic tradition is the Woodland Tradition, which features egg-shaped and globular pots and simple bowls. In comparison, the main difference with the Brazilian plain ware is that Woodland pots are frequently decorated by impressions; but as in Brazil the vessels are almost never painted. Although the mere presence of pottery was at first used to define the Woodland time "period" and later a Woodland "stage" of cultural development, it was recognized very early by archaeologists that there was no sudden change in the way of life between the preceding non-ceramic culture of the "Archaic" "period" or "stage." Pots were simply added to the total cultural inventory, whatever that may have been in different places. It appears to be earliest (perhaps dating 4000 years ago) in coastal Georgia, but it did not reach the northern Plains provinces of Canada until about A.D. 1000. Soon after A.D. 800, a new tradition of making large decorated pots of more complicated forms, including painted vessels and carinated vessels, developed in the lower Mississippi Valley region. The new tradition became known as Mississippian, a term also used to define a "period" or "stage." Characteristic Mississippian pottery is fairly consistently associated with pyramid mounds, arranged around plazas in sizeable towns apparently supported by intensive maize agriculture. The Mississippian tradition spread rapidly wherever the associated farming techniques could be maintained. In some areas the people established colonies, and in many cases ultimately subdued the people with Woodland ceramic tradition, either by warfare or assimilation. But in marginal areas, like New England or large parts of southern Canada, the old Woodland tradition persisted until the Europeans arrived, with minimal influence from the Mississippian tradition. Thus it became clear that "Woodland" and "Mississippian" could not be used to define "periods," except in a local sense. The terms can be used to define stages of cultural development, but such a concept is really most useful only when one is thinking about culture history in broad general terms. Actually, it is best to conceive of Woodland and Mississippian, with their many local variations, simply as ceramic traditions; and whatever other technological traditions of different kinds that may or may not be associated with them must be defined for each site, each area, and each region. Only in this way will the prehistory of an area of whatever size be determined. In other words it cannot be assumed that a particular ceramic tradition is necessarily associated with a particular technological tradition of working stone or a particular tradition of shaping bone artifacts, any more than one can assume that ceramics or ground stone axes are always associated with agriculture.

The direct analogy with southern Brazil now becomes quite apparent. The early widespread ceramic tradition of egg-shaped or globular vessels in dark plain ware is directly analogous to the Woodland ceramic tradition, not only in vessel forms and construction, but more importantly in the fact that the ceramic tradition may be adopted by inland hunters with a well-developed flaked-stone industry who lacked ground stone tools, or by the accumulators of coastal shell-mounds who emphasized pecked and ground stone tools and neglected finely flaked tools. The story of the colonizing farmers with the Mississippian ceramic tradition is directly analogous to the Tupi-Guarani expansion along the fertile alluvial valleys and coasts of Brazil. However, the most important analogy is that, like the Woodland tradition in North America, the earlier simple ceramic tradition of southern Brazil, which might be identified with Gê-speaking peoples, persisted into ethnographic times in certain marginal areas.

Chapter 11
Disposition of the Dead

Human bones preserved very poorly in the constantly saturated sambaqui even when the shell matrix contained relatively little dark organic material, which would be more acidic than the shell. Most whalebone was also found in the same mushy state because all porous bones acted like sponges, absorbing the abundant rain water, which became quite acidic as it percolated through the humus mantle that developed over the site after its abandonment. The poor condition of the bones was exasperating for us because it meant that a great deal of time had to be spent exposing the soggy fragmentary remains which then had to be thoroughly dried before packing. It was depressing to learn later that only 19 of the skulls recovered were sufficiently reconstructable to be useful to the physical anthropologists (Mello e Alvim and Mello Filho 1967–68).

The earliest interments were three children in stratum 6 of Occupation Zone IV, 500 years before the last dated burial associated with Occupation VII. Although only one burial came from stratum 5, about a third of the graves had been excavated from stratum 5 through earlier strata: this intrusive stratum 6B contained 38 burials. Stratum 4B contained two burials and the first pottery. The remaining 21 interments were enclosed within the four strata composing Occupation Zone VII.

As is normally the case among prehistoric human societies, dead bodies were not all disposed of in exactly the same way. The only set pattern discernible at Forte Marechal Luz is that all of the single interments were placed into a roughly circular pit in a flexed position. Although only the legs of most individuals were flexed while the head and trunk were extended straight, the bodies were never fully extended, even when the pit was large enough to hold several skeletons. Also there was no consistent patterned orientation, either to cardinal directions or to local topographic features such as the hillside or the beach. Bodies in multiple graves were only occasionally placed in the same direction, and in one case they were placed crossways on top of one another. Such variations might be explainable if the bodies of individuals belonging to different clans or moieties were consistently oriented to certain directions.

The remains of 79 individuals (26 of whom were children under five years of age; while only one individual had reached old age) were distinguishable in the collection from Forte Marechal Luz (Mello e Alvim and Mello Filho 1967–68). Only 21 of the burials came from ceramic layers. Significantly, reconstructable skulls from both preceramic and ceramic strata formed a consistent and distinctive morphological type which is closest to a type described from coastal Patagonia, and very unlike other known skeletal populations from Brazilian coastal sambaquis. We uncovered and numbered only 65 burials, and several of these numbered burials were exposed in profiles and not recovered. The discrepancy between number of individuals and number of burials is accounted for by the fact that there were many isolated bones, mostly of infants, found within and adjacent to the burial pits. In addition, we catalogued separately 76 isolated teeth and fragmentary human bones, including several concentrations of bone fragments. Some of these isolated bones may have been scattered by animals; however, there are no chewing marks, either by rodents or canids, so it is quite likely that human activity was responsible for most of the scattering. As many of the scattered remains were near the surface, post-depositional disturbance by modern gardeners may have moved some bones; although there was no evidence of plowing, it is possible that hoeing had penetrated some shallow graves. Very likely, repeated reexcavations for new graves had disturbed skeletons and scattered some bones, although at least in one instance it seemed fairly clear that many fragments had been deliberately scattered over a burial (no. 10). Possibly the large number of fragments found near the mass grave (Burials 22–25) also had been deliberately scattered by man rather than by animals.

To judge from the unnaturally tight position into which a few skeletons had been squeezed, as well as the presence of alteration marks on some human bones, and the fact that several skeletons were headless or otherwise incomplete, either post-mortem exposure of the body for prolonged periods and/or secondary burial was evidently practiced. Such cultural practices could easily account for many of the human remains found scattered in the strata of the sambaqui. The earliest human fragment, the head of a femur, was found in stratum 10, near the top of Occupation Zone II, the old sambaqui.

Skulls evidently were often accorded special attention. Of the scattered bones or concentrations of bones, 27 were cranial fragments, in addition to the eleven instances where one or more teeth were encountered isolated from skulls. Obviously, isolated teeth need not have come from dead bodies; but as will be seen when the burials are discussed, several skulls did receive special attention prior to final disposal. Certainly something unusual had occurred to the fragmentary right parietal of an infant encountered in the north wall of square A2 in stratum 5 (Occupation Zone V). Each of two reconstructible pieces of the bone exhibits parallel scratches on the external surface, and the larger piece also has two small depressed fractures which appear to have been caused by a blunt instrument. An occipital fragment of an adult found in a slumped portion of stratum 6B exhibits an artificial bevel which shows some evidence of healing; this may be an example of trepanation. Interestingly, three cranial fragments came from strata 7 and 8, beneath the earliest burials in stratum 6.

Some long bones also had been altered. Stratum 5 yielded the central section (112 mm long) of a very large femur with a massive bifurcating linea aspera. The bone had been broken at both ends when it was green; also two surface areas had been cut and incised. Another central section of a femur from stratum 6B, measuring 128 x 27 x 17 mm, had been broken in the same places in the same manner; and parallel incisions are visible in two areas of one face. The latter worked human bone was associated with several fragments of other human bones which lacked any evidence of alteration. Also it should be mentioned that the right femur of Burial no. 4 in Occupation Zone VII had two cuts on it, and the shaft of the right femur of Burial no. 5 in the same zone was unaccountably missing. A humerus shaft fragment of another individual also exhibited a series of small parallel incisions across the grain. It was found near several other bone fragments exposed in stratum 1 of the cut bank 150 cm north of square A1.

The only other evidence of direct cultural alteration of the human bones themselves is an isolated phalange from stratum 6B that had been stained with hematite. Hematite staining was not noted on any bones of complete skeletons. Other cultural practices include artifact associations in the graves, unnatural associations of bones within a single grave; and evidence for various kinds of ceremonials, especially involving fires, either before or after placement of the body in the grave. To allow interpretation of the discernible cultural patterns in handling the dead, a descriptive summary will be made of those burials yielding significant information. The burials will be grouped by occupation zone, commencing with the earliest in Zone IV.

Three children had been buried tightly flexed in small individual graves in stratum 6 of Occupation Zone IV. No artifacts were associated with these earliest interments; but as seen on the east-wall profile of square A2, evidently the area of the grave for Burial no. 6 had been prepared by spreading out a lens of hematite mixed with clay and ash. The grave was then excavated through the ochre lens into stratum 6b (not the same as later stratum 6B), and a layer of small round carbonized seeds (identified as probably *Myrcia*, a Mirtaceae related to the cherry-like *jaboticaba*) was spread over the backfilled pit. The seeds provided a radiocarbon date of 1100 ± 100 yr B.P. (M-1204) for these earliest interments at Forte Marechal Luz.

Stratum 6B was in a restricted area intruded mainly from stratum 5 (Occupation Zone V). It contained more than half of all the human skeletons uncovered at the site, mostly in multiple graves. Burial no. 1, a rare single burial, was an adult male lying on his right side and headed west. The legs were tightly flexed, but the upper part of the body was straight. No artifacts had been placed in the grave. After the grave was backfilled a 20-mm-thick lens of ochre mixed with clay and ash was spread over the grave. Burial no. 34 was an even more unusual single grave because it contained only an adult skull, two vertebrae, a humerus, and phalanges. The skull was sitting upright on its mandible, atlas, and axis over a lens of white ash and charcoal. There is little doubt that this was an instance of decapitation.

Not far from Burial no. 1, an adult male and an adult female (Burials no. 8 and 11) had been placed on their left sides in the same grave. Burial no. 11, the female, was first placed in the pit headed east and lying on top of some infant bones (Burial no. 15). A lot of fish bones, probably representing a food offering, mixed with some shells, were found over the female skeleton. Then Burial no. 8, the male, was placed crossways on top with his head to the north. Possibly this was a family group, and the pattern evidently was repeated in another area: two more adults (Burials no. 43 and 44), one identifiable as a female, had also been placed on top of each other in the same grave, along with a juvenile (Burial no. 45). A perforated pecten shell and a carved whalebone were found with Burial no. 44.

Perhaps contemporaneously, and certainly within a short time of the cross-shaped interment of Burials 8 and 11, a child (Burial no. 9) was interred 1 m to the southeast in the same position, on the left side, headed east. Halfway between Burials 8 and 9 was an isolated fragment of a femur. Four more skeletons (Burials no. 10, 12, 13, and 14), two of which were adults, were found grouped together and headed in various directions between 2 and 3 m south of the cross-shaped interment (Burials 8 and 11). The only objects found with these skeletons were two unworked limpet shells with Burial no.13. Although the legs of all these burials were flexed, as usual the upper portions of the bodies were extended straight. Between the two groups of skeletons was a 15-cm-thick concentration of fired rocks mixed with charcoal and black organic matter. Evidently this pile had been dumped from an extensive charcoal and ash lens, the remnants of a fire which had been built over the backfilled pit for Burial no. 12. The charcoal lens eventually yielded a radiocarbon date of 850 ± 100 yr B.P. (M-1205) for this multiple burial complex, which evidently had been intruded from Occupation Zone V.

Also in stratum 6B, fired rocks were found between the feet and the pelvis of an adult male (Burial no. 36) who had been interred in the same grave with the incomplete remains of three children (Burials no. 37, 38 and 39). The only associated artifacts were a worked whalebone and a perforated pecten shell (*Phacoides*) placed nearest Burial no. 39.

Other group burials from stratum 6B were more productive of artifacts. Although one of the three children (Burials no. 15, 16, and 17) in one grave had no associations; no. 15 had 33 *Oliva* shell beads with apices broken off for suspension, plus 22 unaltered *Subulina* and two *Lintricula* shells on its chest beneath an arm. A younger child (Burial no. 16) was associated with a polished black jasper pebble; a hammerstone; and a giant oyster shell with its cup facing up, probably to contain a food offering. This triple burial of children was found beneath and evidently preceding the multiple burials no. 10 through 14. A group of five skeletons plus fragments of others in one grave includes a child's skull (Burial no. 29) which had been placed on top of an adult male skull (Burial no. 23). A small charcoal lens was located just north of the two skulls. A truncated *Oliva* shell and a perforated fish vertebra had apparently been suspended together as a pendant, while a whalebone and a scraped hematite pebble were placed with the complete skeleton of the man. Another adult male skeleton (Burial no. 22) had been placed into the same grave on a slab of whalebone, along with a striated chunk of ochre and a cut hematite pebble. Another charcoal lens was located near his skull. Another child's skull (Burial no. 25) had been placed next to the skull of the third adult (Burial no. 24) in the same grave. A whalebone rib was under the adult's skull, and two hammerstones were lying next to the skeleton.

Finally in stratum 6B, a young adult female (Burial no. 32) had been placed in her own grave near a cache of three hammerstones, a large diabase grinding slab, a granite pebble, a red (baked?) mudstone concretion and a chunk of hematite. Many other pigment processing tools were found nearby, so possibly the artifacts were not actually burial offerings. Four children and an adult in stratum 6B, and an adult burial in stratum 5 (Occupation Zone V), were not notable for any reason; while the remaining numbered burials were either partial skeletons, or not removed from the field.

The two burials (nos. 4 and 5) from Occupation Zone VI, found near each other but in separate graves, were both adult males lying on their left sides with heads pointing north. The legs were tightly flexed, but the upper parts of the body were extended. Both had been buried with considerable grave offerings. An axe, a whetstone, an incised whalebone, a paca-mandible tool, two sand-shark teeth, a perforated fish vertebra, and several potsherds were found with Burial no. 4. Burial no. 5 contained a potsherd, a perforated pecten shell, a burned *Strombus* shell found in the nasal sinus, a cut bone, and a hammerstone; plus several pieces of a large diabase grinding slab placed in a circle on top of the backfilled grave. The visceral cavity of Burial no. 5 contained a great many small fish bones, as if a basket of fish had been left on the abdomen. This grave had been excavated from stratum 4B to the bottom of stratum 6. A layer of ash and charcoal was then laid on the bottom of the pit and the center of the ash was reexcavated before depositing the body. The grave was then filled with shell and the area covered over with ash. A circular pile of charcoal and fired rocks, including several broken pieces of a large grinding slab, was then placed over the grave. Evidently a fire was not actually built on the grave itself because several of the grinding stone fragments are missing. Probably a fire was built nearby during the burial ceremony, and ash plus some charcoal provided the initial grave fill while the stones were saved to place over the grave in the form of a cairn. The fact that the shaft of the right femur is missing would not be remarked upon except for the possibly related fact that the shaft of the right femur of Burial no. 4 has two cut marks on it. Possibly there was some burial custom involving the working of femora of deceased persons.

The sequence of events in preparation for Burial no. 4 was similar but more complex than with Burial no. 5. Evidently a small pit containing fired rocks and charcoal had been dug into stratum 5 and backfilled with the shells that had been removed. Two large burned rocks were then placed on edge to form a partial ring marking the empty pit. One wonders if this feature was a false grave intended to mislead evil spirits. Nearby, another larger pit was dug, partially filled with fired rocks and charcoal, and then expanded into a grave for Burial no. 4. After backfilling, a mixture of shell, charcoal, and fired rocks was placed over the entire area of both graves, evidently forming a low mound, which was subsequently obliterated when the occupants of stratum 4 (Occupation Zone VII) dumped clean shell over the east end of the mound.

The concept of a low burial mound persisted in Occupation Zone VII, where two low eminences became visible after the surface vegetation had been cleared from the site. Burial no. 7 was a child lying on its left side, headed west. The skeleton was incomplete; and as some bones of an adult were associated, it probably was a secondary burial, evidently placed on or near the surface with a low mound of shell piled over the bones. In addition to many potsherds, a polished pebble, a worked quartz fragment, a *Conus* shell truncated for suspension, and three sand-shark teeth (one of which had ground facets on the root) were associated with this burial. Beneath the other low mound was the skull of a juvenile with an adult man's limbs, so evidently this also was a secondary burial (no. 18). A piece of cut bone and several potsherds, some partially reconstructable as a small pot 10 cm in diameter, were found in the grave.

Another similar secondary burial in Occupation Zone VII (Burial no. 27) included the skull, ribs, and femur of a child and the ulna and legs of an adult. Headless Burial no. 30 had been placed into its grave on top of a bed of clean shell that had been thrown in first. A small ash lens was found in the pit adjacent to the thorax. No artifacts but many fish bones, presumably the remains of a food offering, were associated. Another headless burial (no. 33) of a young adult contained two skull fragments adjacent to its knees. A bed of clean oyster shells had been placed over a thin ash lens in the bottom of the grave. Associations included many potsherds, a hammerstone, a grinding stone, and a bird bone tube which may have been a shaman's sucking tube. The isolated skull and mandible with articulated atlas and axis of an adult female (Burial no. 19) was found with a hammerstone and a polished pebble, while an isolated infant's skull and mandible (Burial no. 21) was associated with a broken bone-projectile point. Evidently the practice of decapitation persisted into Occupation VII.

A child (Burial no. 51) was found in the same grave with an adult male (Burial no. 53). Both skeletons were oriented in the same direction, toward the west; and the knees only were flexed. A perforated peccary tooth ground into a triangular form was found with the child; while a polished quartz pebble, two sand-shark teeth, and a calcined bone projectile point were found with the man. Nearby, another adult (Burial no. 52) was headed east with knees flexed (Figure 60). In addition to a sand-shark tooth, a nearby complete small flat bottomed pot with a rim diameter of 19 mm was lying upright next to the skull, while an axe bit was under a tibia and the poll end of another axe was nearby.

A juvenile (Burial no. 26), headed northeast with legs flexed and trunk extended in the usual way, was found with two unaltered white-shark teeth, a worked bird bone, many potsherds, and many fish bones probably representing a food offering. Burial no. 54, a child, was lying face down with head to the east. No artifacts were associated with this individual, with an adult female (Burial no. 28), or with an infant (Burial no. 42).

A large whalebone had been placed vertically to mark one end of the grave of an adult (Burial no. 41). Two children (Burials no. 2 and 3) had been placed in the same grave lying parallel on their left sides, headed southeast. Potsherds and fish bones were the only associations.

The only other multiple burial in Occupation Zone VII contained two adult males placed tightly flexed in semi-sitting positions but tilted on their right sides with heads to the west. The skull of Burial no. 55 was on top of the feet of Burial no. 56 (Figure 61). An *Olivancillaria* shell was lying beneath and a peccary canine above the skull of Burial no. 55, as if the two objects had formed parts of a headband. No artifacts were associated with Burial no. 56, although its mandible had evidently been removed after death and placed upside down. Two more adults were buried in individual graves less than 2 m away: Burial no. 59 contained only the pelvis and vertebrae, but both individuals had been tightly flexed in semi-sitting positions, heading southeast. A quartz pebble with a red stain on one end and a diabase pebble had been placed with Burial no. 57, the complete skeleton of the adult. After backfilling, shallow basins had been formed over the latter grave and the double interment, evidently in preparation for spreading a sheet of grey ash over the entire area.

Evidently ceremonial fires were frequently a part of the burial ritual during the last three occupations at Forte Marechal Luz (Zone V including stratum 6B,

Figure 61. Double burial showing typical state of preservation.

Zones VI and VII). Some combination of ochre, clay, ash, charcoal, and/or fired rocks was either placed in the grave pit or spread over the top of the backfilled grave. In one case, in stratum 6B, a layer of hematite was first laid over the grave area; and after the grave was dug through the hematite lens and backfilled, a layer of charred seeds was either placed on top of the grave or burned in place. The same stratum contained the only grave where evidently a fire had been built over the backfilled grave, although the remnants of the fire were later spread over a large area of multiple graves. Small charcoal lenses with a multiple grave next to two pairs of skulls are probably remnants of small ritual fires *in situ*. This particular multiple burial also contains several associated whalebones. The absence of hematite and the presence of low mounds, composed of fired rocks in Occupation Zone VI and shell in Zone VII, evidently signify changes from stratum 6B, where the fired rocks and charcoal were spread out thinly, as were hematite lenses.

In sum, changes in burial customs appear to have been minimal through time. In support of the morphological evidence for continuity of a distinctive population, the conclusion must be reached that the same people had buried in the site for several hundred years; and there is no evidence that these were not the same group of people who had occupied the site earlier.

In conclusion, certain interpretations may be made about disposal of the dead at Forte Marechal Luz, as several patterns correspond in general to ethnographic data on the peoples of southern Brazil. Secondary burials were common, suggesting that corpses were exposed before burial; and parts of the skeleton may have been preserved for some time before final interment. Ceremonial fires over the body, and the construction of low mounds in some cases, are reported from interior groups. Of special interest are the cases of the association of parts of a child's skeleton with parts of the skeleton of one or more adults. Gê-speaking peoples of southern and eastern Brazil, as well as many tropical forest tribes, believe that there is a close association, both in spirit and in bodily substance, between a child and its parents: this belief is the basis for the practice of *couvade*. One may speculate that parts of a child's skeleton might have been preserved until the death of the parent, at which time both were interred together as being of one substance. No specific ethnographic examples of such practice are known to me, however. At any rate, the evidence for decapitation does not imply that captives or criminals were being beheaded. What seems like a grisly custom to us for keeping special parts of bodies around the house may have had deep spiritual significance to the people who lived on the sambaqui of Forte Marechal Luz.

Chapter 12
Summary, Conclusions, and General Discussion

Introduction

Forte Marechal Luz was a large sambaqui located on the northern end of the second-largest island in the state of Santa Catarina. As the well-dated site was situated on the bedrock hillside between about 19 and 36 m above sea level, occupation was allowed to continue for more than 3600 years, to within a century or so of European contact. Its location in a sheltered and relatively shallow sandy bay was favorable because it was within easy walking distance in one direction across a sandy plain to a mangrove swamp bordering a large sheltered inlet; while the deep ocean was nearby, over the hill in the other direction. Thus the immediate environment provided at least three types of marine habitat (shallow sandy bay, mangrove swamp, and ocean abutting on rock cliff and sand ridges) for varied maritime food resources (shellfish, fish, and sea mammals). Also available were four types of floral microenvironment—scrub forest on the windward side of the hill, rain forest on the leeward side, and a different type of rain forest on the sandy plain; plus the mangrove swamp. Birds and land mammals, including deer, tapir, paca, and capivara, were also available on this island, providing food as well as raw material for making tools. About 200 m north of the site, a fine-grained diabase dyke had intruded through the quartz-diorite bedrock, so three useful kinds of rocks, especially the diabase and vein quartz, were immediately available to the occupants of the site.

Although most of the shell had been quarried for road cover before the time of excavation, we excavated a 6.5-m-deep section of the mound, which was originally about 10 m high. The strata were numbered downward as excavated, but later were grouped into occupation zones. The earliest, Occupation Zone I, radiocarbon-dated about 4300 years ago, was on a narrow bench (probably an old beach notch) about 20 m above sea level. A typical shell dump which began accumulating on the hillslope below the bench about 3700 years ago gradually became a large sambaqui, which continued to accumulate for 1600 years. This original sambaqui was designated Occupation Zone II. Occupation Zone III was a series of thin, dipping layers of shells probably moved from the top of the original mound in order to make the mound level with the next higher bedrock bench about 23 m above mean sea level. Because of the broadened level area about 1400 years ago, Occupation Zone IV was the first extensive occupation in the remaining portion of the site; but unfortunately much of it was disturbed between 800 and 1100 years ago by people digging graves. Most of the gravediggers lived during the time of Occupation Zone V; but most of Zone V was in turn disturbed by more graves in stratum 4B, which was designated Occupation Zone VI, dating about 850 years ago. The final occupation, Zone VII, lasted until about 600 years ago, to judge from two radiocarbon dates plus the fact that there is no evidence for European trade goods or any evidence of the presumed late prehistoric Tupi-Guarani invasion of the area.

Methodology of Description: Manufacturing Techniques and Technological Traditions

Except for fire-broken hearthstones and boiling stones, all recovered raw materials (stone, bone, teeth, shell, and clay) which showed any human alteration have been described in the body of the report, using a classification system based upon the identification and analysis of the artificial marks left by human alteration. A further distinction has been made between marks of alteration which were accidentally or unintentionally applied and those that were intentionally applied in order to shape the material into an implement. Thus simply picking up and using stones for various purposes often caused detectable alteration by pecking, grinding, and flaking. These same technological processes were less often applied to shape stone implements intentionally. Likewise, bone was ground, scraped, cut, grooved, and burned while working with it in various ways. In addition, these same technological processes were applied to shape bone deliberately.

Obviously a classification system based only on form would not be valid for describing those artifacts altered only by use. Also, because the overall form of most of the intentionally shaped stone artifacts was little changed from the shape of the original pebble or nodule, a strictly formal classification would yield little cultural information except which natural forms tended to be collected for further shaping. An inclusive classification of most shaped stone artifacts such as hammerstones and axes by function is also useless because most implements, particularly the pebbles with pecked ends and facial depressions, and the bitted implements, were obviously used for many purposes. The same problems confront the analyst working with most other altered materials, except for ceramic vessels and certain bone implements such as projectile points and fishhooks, which were fairly obviously shaped for specific purposes. In these few instances a functional terminology and formal typology became useful.

The only way that all the artifacts found at the site could be encompassed within a single comprehensive classification scheme was to base the classification upon the manufacturing processes that were employed in altering the basic raw materials and in fabricating shaped implements. Certain other advantages soon became obvious when this method of classification was employed. Most importantly, it yielded a great deal of insight into what the people living on the Forte Marechal Luz sambaqui were actually doing during their daily activities. When pertinent, such deductions and speculations about human behavior are liberally sprinkled throughout the body of the descriptive sections of the report.

Another advantage, of interest to the culture historian as well as to the archaeologist interested in paleoethnography, also derived from this initial stage of analysis. As a result of classifying the processes of alteration of raw materials, distinguishing the next step of shaping tools, and discovering the stage of fabricating finished implements, as well as detecting various stages of reshaping and reuse of many implements, I became fully aware of the fact that the processes of manufacture as well as the forms and apparent functions of the finished implements were all reflections of traditional cultural means for utilizing raw materials and making objects from these materials. That is, the occupants employed reduction and manufacturing techniques in a traditional manner, and these fabrication techniques were passed on to new generations of toolmakers. With this conception in mind it became more obvious that certain technological traditions were not present throughout all occupation zones. Also, it was obvious that, for the most part, new techniques did not replace old ones; rather, there was a process of gradual accumulation of new techniques and new technological traditions which allowed for increasingly effective adaptations to the productive local ecosystem.

Although most of the basic technological processes for altering stone and bone were already evident in the earliest levels, utilization of these fabrication techniques for actually shaping artifacts was innovated periodically through time. Indeed, all the various discrete technological traditions accumulated gradually through time; although this innovation process apparently accelerated during Occupation Zones IV and V, before ceramics were innovated. Despite the fact that technologically the occupants of the sambaqui always remained at a primitive stage of development relative to the many technologically more advanced peoples in America, evidently they continued to be receptive to new ideas that fitted into their traditional thought patterns as reflected by their tools. At the same time, local ingenuity and experimentation to resolve a problem are evident, recognizable especially in changing the shape of a fishhook to attach a line, and invention of a distinctive process to remove flakes from diabase cores.

Nevertheless, evidently nearly all of the most significant technological traditions found at Forte Marechal Luz were introduced by diffusion as a result of contact with other cultures. If the innovation of these same technological traditions can be identified and dated in stratigraphic contexts elsewhere in southern Brazil, future archaeologists will be able to outline the prehistoric culture history of southern Brazil and neighboring regions.

Summary of Occupation Zones

The most useful way to summarize the detailed artifact analysis presented in the body of the report is to assemble all of the artifacts found in each occupation zone, and thereby illustrate more vividly how most of the discrete technological traditions were gradually added to the simple artifact assemblage found in Occupation Zone I. Thus, in effect, this section details the history of technological development that occurred at the sambaqui of Forte Marechal Luz (Table 17).

Although the technological processes of pecking, flaking, and grinding stone as well as flaking bone were already evident on the rough artifact assemblage from Occupation Zone I, the only process then used in any

Table 17. Outline of Cultural Development at Forte Marechal Luz.

Occupation Zone I (2400 B.C.)

First shaping of stone by pecking.

First use-alteration of stone by pecking, grinding, and flaking.

First shaped whalebone (polished depression after hardening by calcination).

Use-flaking of bone.

Occupation Zone II (1700–100 B.C.)

First bitted implements shaped by grinding.

First striated hematite pebbles (pigment processing).

First mammal-bone projectile points shaped by cutting, scraping, and grinding.

First ray-spine projectile point.

First whalebones processed by chopping, cutting, carving (in addition to calcining).

Whalebone braziers.

First perforation by puncturing (bone).

Fired clay ball (accidental?).

Occupation Zone III (ca. 100 B.C.–A.D. 400)

First shell shaped by grinding.

First whalebone chopping block.

Occupation Zone IV (A.D. 500–900)

First shaping of stone by percussion flaking.

First bitted implement made on a stone flake.

First bone detritus of manufacture, exhibiting cutting, grooving, scraping, grinding.

First bipointed projectile points of bird bone.

Last whalebone braziers.

Unfired clay basins (restricted to this zone).

First burials (flexed).

Occupation Zone V (A.D. 900–1100)

First intentional percussion flaking (first flakes).

First bifacial preforms shaped by percussion flaking.

First bone fishhooks.

First perforation by drilling (bone).

Stratum 6B (A.D. 1100)

First teeth perforated by drilling.

Multiple burials associated with ceremonial fires.

Emphasis on processing paint pigments for ceremonial interments.

Occupation Zone VI (A.D. 1100–1200)

First fired ceramics.

Burials with stone cairns.

Occupation Zone VII (A.D. 1200–1350)

Synthesis of all earlier technological innovations.

Increase in ceramics and use of bone artifacts.

Bitted stone implements used as digging-stick blades.

way deliberately to shape a stone artifact was pecking, used to form depressions of limited area near the center of pebble faces. Likewise, a fire-hardened whalebone from Occupation I exhibited a polished depression, evidently made by the basic techniques of scraping and grinding. Thus pebbles and a bone with pecked central depressions (or *quebra-cocos*, to refer to an assumed functional term) are the earliest deliberately shaped artifacts at the site. The earliest shaping of stone was done by the laborious process of pecking with a pebble hammerstone.

Twenty artifacts were found in Occupation Zone I. Six of these were pebbles with pecked depressions; and one evidently had a pecked encircling groove, perhaps intended for hafting the piece. Three pebbles with pecked ends ("hammerstones") also had pecked depressions on their faces; while three other hammerstones had been much battered by pecking and pounding, to the extent that some use-flakes had been removed accidentally. One such flake, clearly identifiable as an accidental flake because it retains the old pecked surface on its striking platform, was also found in Occupation Zone I. The surfaces of two other weathered diabase pebbles, which look and feel like sandstone, had been smoothed by use. Although subsequent weathering in the saturated acidic clay had removed most surficial evidence of working, including grinding striations, it is evident that the high spots on one naturally wedge-shaped pebble had been smoothed by rubbing, perhaps by using the object as a wedge. Among the few bones that preserved in the acidic clay was a tabular piece of calcined whalebone which had been hardened in a fire. Calcination appears to have been an intentional technique used to harden porous whalebone so it became more durable. A much-used polished central depression had been formed on the surface. Unfortunately, subsequent use had obliterated evidence of the technological process used to form this depression, although it probably was made by scraping or filing (a form of grinding). The other four bones were pieces of exceedingly dense tympanic bulae of whales. Two of these fragments exhibited cuts and incisions from use; the other two had in addition been unifacially use-flaked with a chopping action. Use-flaking is recognizable because the sharp flaked edge does not retain any evidence of a striking platform. One rectangular piece of bula was flaked at both ends as if it had been hafted and used as an adze. The lip of the nearly complete tympanic bula was flaked, evidently by gripping the internal tuberosity in the hand and using it for chopping or adzing. The latter artifact was sacrificed to obtain the radiocarbon date of 2,340 B.C. for Occupation I.

Occupation Zone II, the original sambaqui, yielded 27 stone artifacts, an equal number of bone artifacts, seven giant oyster (*Ostrea arborea*) shells found either isolated or associated with a kitchen feature, and an irregular clay ball which had been fire-hardened. The technological process of grinding stone was added in Zone II to shape two implements with bibevelled bits, including a wedge-shaped implement with slightly ground surfaces, and a well-shaped ground axe with convex faces.

Although flakes had been removed by heavy use from the ground bits of both implements, there was no evidence of preliminary shaping by flaking. Instead, diabase beach pebbles of approximately the proper size and shape had been selected and shaped directly by grinding them, probably on the several grooved boulders lying on the beach between the dyke and the base of the sambaqui.

Five of the seven worked chunks of hematite from Occupation Zone II exhibit grinding striations where they have been rubbed on a stone, such as on the pebble with a ground face found nearby. Among other worked pebbles is one exhibiting grinding striations; one with grinding facets; and one with polished surfaces, evidently made by grinding softer materials than stone. Six pebble hammerstones have pecked and battered ends, and a use-flake had been removed from another diabase pebble. Two of the four pebbles with pecked facial depressions also have pecked ends. The edges of natural vein quartz fragments and two unintentional thick flakes, one of which obviously had spalled from a hammerstone, were used as scrapers, perhaps from shaping bone artifacts. Another unused flake, retaining a ground surface, had obviously spalled off an axe during heavy use.

Altered bone from Occupation II ranges from two worked fish bones (one with butchering marks) and two perforated fish vertebrae to a series of projectile points. The simplest point type is a naturally barbed ray spine, with the tip ground to a conical point and the base of which had been cut off squarely, while the adjacent lateral edges were ground to shape it for insertion into a socketed shaft. The other projectile points from Occupation II were made of mammal bone. Two carefully scraped and ground tanged (pedunculated) points with slight shoulders also had bases shaped to fit into a hollow socketed shaft. Two cylindrical naturally hollow mammal-bone projectile points had been scraped and ground so as to form sharp unibevelled tips. In this case the socketed bases were fashioned to fit onto a solid cylindrical shaft. A third method of hafting is evident on the carefully shaped point with a conical tip and a scraped and ground unibevelled base fashioned to fit onto a scarfed unibevelled shaft so that the point would be directed forward.

Whalebones were much used in Occupation Zone II, but not for fabricating carefully shaped artifacts such as the series of mammal-bone projectile points. Evidently the bones of beached whales were utilized in various ways. One piece had been carved and whittled as if it were wood, while seven other bones had been sectioned by chopping them with an axe. Five other bones with chopping marks evidently caused by use as chopping blocks had also been burned. Calcination may sometimes have been intended to harden the bones so that they could be worked into durable implements, but also partially burned pieces of whalebone were found associated with four vertebrae with charred depressions on their centra. The latter were evidently charcoal braziers, and the partially burned pieces were lids placed over the burning coals. One of these whalebone vertebra braziers was found in a kitchen area built in a sheltered spot between the side of the sambaqui and the bedrock hillside. This kitchen feature (Figure 9) was the only undisturbed activity area found in Occupation Zone II. In the figure, artifact no. 901 is the brazier which still had some charcoal in its depression. Artifact no. 894 was a large slab of bone which evidently had been used as a chopping block. Portions of its undersurface had been burned, and the shell underneath had been toasted to a brown color. Artifacts no. 880 and 900 were chopped whalebones; while four giant oyster shells (artifact 899) had been placed in a line with cupped faces up, evidently for use as containers.

Occupation Zone III followed. The thin layers of shell interspersed with chunks of charcoal, that apparently had been redeposited from the top of the old sambaqui to level the entire area from the top of the original sambaqui across to the edge of the highest and broadest bedrock bench (about 23 m above sea level), did not contain evidence for any technological traditions for processing raw materials, although grinding was now applied to shaping a shell artifact. Occupation III contained two more bone points with bevelled bases, five ray-spine points, one whalebone chopping block, and a piece of worked land-mammal bone. Two more giant oyster shells were found, in addition to a completely ground columella of an unidentifiable univalve. The latter piece, of irregular cylindrical form, had been ground to a conical point at both ends. The technique for grinding thick shell was the same as for grinding bone. The object itself is evidently a new tool type, as two similar artifacts were found later in Occupation Zone VII. Perhaps they were labrets (*tembetás*) attached somehow to wooden bits. No new tool types were found in the small stone artifact assemblage, which includes a polished pebble, three hematite pebbles (two of them striated), a pebble with pecked ends, and a broken axe directly ground into shape from a beach pebble.

The newly prepared broad level area was occupied by people who deposited strata 6, 7, and 8; also the first three interments found at the site were made in stratum 6. These strata, constituting Occupation Zone IV, contained 41 stone artifacts and 42 bone artifacts; in addition to four worked teeth and three shells which had been intentionally perforated by puncturing, perhaps for suspension. Two shark teeth and one paca incisor show evidence of alteration from use, probably from grooving wood or scraping bone. As there are use striations on the base of a raccoon (*Procyon*) canine, the use-wear on the broken tip of the tooth must also have been made by man. Butchering marks appear on three fish and one land-mammal bone; while a dolphin mandible has some patterned incisions, perhaps from using the object as a tool. An altered piece of whale tympanic bula, two pieces of a bird bone with a series of holes scraped into it (a flute?), and two used land-mammal bone fragments were also found. In addition, there are two carved whalebones; six chopped whalebones, one of which was calcined; two more whale-vertebra braziers with burned depressions; and a whale vertebral epiphysis which had been scorched where something hot had been placed on it. Perforated fish and shark vertebrae appear again, with eight examples. The left frontal of a deer (*Mazama*) had had the tip end of its attached antler removed by cutting an encircling groove and breaking the tine (Figure 34). The broken edge of the tine was subsequently worn. Probably the tine had been removed to make a tool for a specific purpose.

The increased fabrication of small bone tools in Occupation Zone IV is evident from the three pieces of detritus of manufacture exhibiting the processes of cutting, scraping, and grinding. The fragment of a mammal-bone projectile point was also found. The most significant innovation at this time was represented by seven easily made bird-bone bipoints, which tended to supersede the old laboriously ground-mammal bone points with unibevelled bases. The bird-bone bipoints also have unibevelled bases, but the basal point is designed to protrude as a built-in barb when the concave surface of the point is tied onto a cylindrical shaft. Thus the tip end serves to penetrate the quarry (probably fish), while the unilateral barb keeps the shaft of the projectile in the quarry. Thus the hunter can grasp the projectile shaft and haul in the fish. The entire procedure, from the manufacture of the simple points by scraping and grinding to shooting the fish, could now be accomplished much more quickly and efficiently.

Most of the 42 stone artifacts from Occupation Zone IV illustrate that old technological traditions persisted. Thus there are two use-battered pebbles, a polished pebble, five pebbles with pecked and battered ends, two spalls removed by much battering, two pebbles with pecked central depressions, and ten pebbles with both pecked ends and depressions. For the first time, though, two of the latter retain a dark stain in the pecked depression. One of these dark-stained pebbles was located inside one of the 13 unfired clay basins found together in stratum 7 (Figure 7). Two other pebbles with pecked extremities and facial depressions were found cached in the same clay basin; while a fourth, which retained a hematite stain on its polished concave face, was located on the lip of the same basin. One of the five facetted hematite chunks from Occupation IV was found between two clay basins, while a pebble with a polished concave face which is stained black was found inside another basin. Although the association of fire-cracked rocks and piles of unburned fish bones with the clay basins suggests that the primary activity was stone-boiling fish stew, evidently the kitchen area was also used as a pigment-processing laboratory.

A ground tabular piece of argillite found in Occupation IV looks like a small axe poll fragment; but, if so, the experiment with this fragile material was unsuccessful, because it not only broke transversely but split longitudinally from a slight impact blow. The old technique of pecking was used to form bilateral grooves on a flattened pebble. This ground artifact, obviously shaped for a specific purpose, was very likely a fish-net sinker.

Evidently during Occupation IV a new technique was innovated for obtaining vein quartz fragments with the high angles so useful for scraping bone and wooden tools into shape. Four large quartz fragments had apparently been fractured in a fire, and several thermally fractured edges show evidence of use. Evidently the people had built fires over thick quartz veins in the bedrock and simply selected the most useful fragments.

The people who lived at Forte Marechal Luz during Occupation IV also became aware of the significant technological tradition of percussion flaking, but evidently their ability to shape a stone by flaking was not integrated into their cultural repertoire until Occupation V, when the first intentional flakes occur at the site. Two of the three bitted implements found in Zone IV were still shaped only by grinding; however, another axe was ground into final shape from a percussion spall intentionally removed with a forceful side blow from the corner of an angular diabase boulder. The diabase is somewhat more coarse grained than the stone in the dyke near the site, a fact which suggests that this earliest flaked and ground axe was obtained from another group by trade.

Two tabular diabase nodules, retaining the characteristic oxidized weathering patina which is present on all later flaked axe "preforms," also came from Occupation Zone IV. Both pieces lack bits; but they may have been designed to be the poll ends of axe preforms, which were not made on large flakes but rather on naturally tabular nodules of about the right size and shape. Presumably these nodules were collected at the nearby diabase dyke; certainly not from the beach, because there is no evidence of water-rolling, which would remove the weathering patina. One rectangular piece with naturally squared parallel sides has had a series of non-overlapping short shallow flakes removed from both faces, using one of the naturally flat sides as a striking platform. Evidently the piece was never used, perhaps because it broke during the process of flaking. The other piece, from a later stratum in Zone IV, had only one naturally straight side, so the irregular side was straightened by removing flakes from the platform at right angles with a forceful pecking action in order to flatten and square the side. Finally, the battered side was ground to dull it and make it parallel to the naturally straight side. Possibly this piece was finished and actually used as an axe, but when it broke the remnant was evidently used as a whetstone because the rough oxidized patina exhibits many isolated long grinding striations.

Sometime during Occupation IV a large diabase slab was evidently hauled to the site with great effort from the diabase dyke 200 m away. The faces and edges had been battered during the move, but also perhaps in the attempt to remove useful spalls. Many grinding facets and concavities on its surface suggest that the slab was used as a portable axe-grinding platform, and probably it was equally useful for grinding bone artifacts.

By Occupation V the technological tradition of percussion flaking had been adopted by the people of Forte Marechal Luz, who used it almost exclusively to prepare preforms subsequently ground into bitted implements. The artifacts indicate that the knappers had only rudimentary knowledge of percussion flaking techniques. A number of preforms have been ground in order to reduce particularly thick ridges because the knappers did not know how to prepare a platform for the purpose of thinning a biface. As the "mental template" for all finished axes was rectangular, both in outline and in cross-section, the knappers directed forceful percussion blows at right angles to any irregular edges in order to straighten and square the sides. One of the finished ground axes from Occupation Zone V had been battered so hard while trying to shape the preform that one corner of the poll broke off; nevertheless, the axe including the broken poll, was subsequently used. All five axe fragments from Zone V had been broken by heavy use. All the broken axes and five of the six whole axes were finished from flaked preforms; the other example had been fashioned from a side blow spall.

The first flakes intentionally removed from axe preforms by percussion were readily identified in Occupation Zone V because they retain oxidized patina. Some of these ten flakes were struck from battered platforms; but most of them quickly feather out to thin edges which were unsuitable for use as scraping tools. Evidently the thin sharp edges were never used as knives for cutting resistant materials, and careful examination revealed no evidence that any were used to cut soft foods. In addition to the intentional but unused flakes, there were nine unused flakes spalled from axes and hammerstones.

Other than axe preforms, the only artifact intentionally shaped by flaking at Forte Marechal Luz came from Occupation Zone V. It is a flattened pebble with bilateral notches, having the same form and presumably serving the same function (a net sinker?) as the pebble with pecked bilateral notches found in Zone IV. An unshaped granite pebble had a flake removed from one edge. A small cylindrical sandstone concretion had a ground conical tip which may have attained its shape by use as a drill bit. All other worked stones illustrate the persistence of old traditions: two naturally fractured and five thermally fractured vein quartz fragments with evidence of use; a facetted pebble; seven pebbles with pecked or battered ends, one of which also had pecked facial depressions; four pebbles with ground faces; two angular slabs with ground faces; a striated chunk of hematite; and another striated pebble.

The number (83 total) of bone artifacts increased considerably in Occupation Zone V, although there was only one new significant innovation—fishhooks. Fishhooks were the most carefully shaped bone objects since the projectile points in Occupation II; and they illustrate very well a kind of complexly shaped artifact which was made for a special purpose by the traditional processes of cutting, scraping, and grinding. Unlike the vast majority of artifacts at Forte Marechal Luz which served multipurpose functions, the still-rare but increasing number of special purpose tools demonstrates that people were adjusting themselves ever more closely to the specific economic opportunities available to them in their immediate environment. Bird-bone bipoints, of which there are nine examples in Occupation Zone V, were probably used to catch certain fish that lived in shallow water; while fishhooks were used to catch fish in deeper waters. The net sinkers from Occupation Zones IV and V demonstrate yet another method for catching fish. Obviously the people were adjusting more closely to their environment with ever more efficient tools for specific purposes. The four bone fishhooks in Occupation Zone V are all of one type, with a narrow lateral projection at the proximal end for retaining a tied line.

Also from Occupation Zone V, three epiphyses of whale vertebrae which have concavities ground onto their internal (epiphyseal) faces constitute an unusual kind of object shaped for an unknown purpose. Three more whale epiphyses have been worked in other ways. Two whalebones sectioned by chopping, a carved whalebone, and a whalebone used as a chopping block demonstrate continuation of the old tradition of working whalebones by chopping. Four whalebones, three seal bones, three dolphin mandibles, five fish bones, and a bird bone exhibit cuts and incisions; most of which are probably butchering marks. There are two worked mammal bone fragments; and 17 cut, ground, and scraped detrital fragments left from making bird- and mammal-bone tools. Twenty perforated fish and shark vertebrae and three ray-spine projectile points complete the assemblage of bone artifacts from Occupation Zone V.

Another significant innovation in Occupation Zone V was the technique of perforating teeth by drilling. An immature peccary canine with holes drilled through both root walls for suspension was found. Two of the 20 utilized shark teeth had facets ground on their roots as platforms for drilling two holes. Such careful preparation suggests that the unnecessary double perforations were not intended for suspension but rather for keeping a small graving tool made of shark teeth from wobbling in a haft. In support of the hypothesis that the teeth were tools for making other objects, these two white-shark teeth, as well as the other sand-shark teeth, exhibit use striations on the enamel faces, especially near the sharp tips. Also catalogued were 27 sand-shark teeth that showed no evidence of alteration, but which must have been brought up to the site for some purpose. A cylindrical fish tooth exhibits a series of fine incisions which partially encircle its conical tip, as if it had been mounted as a drill bit. A paca incisor still mounted in the rodent's mandible exhibits an unnatural planed surface probably from use as a graving or grooving tool. A peccary mandible with the molar root sockets exposed by cutting and breaking the bone transversely shows much use as a tool on the cut edge.

Stratum 6B, a cemetery area containing one half of the human skeletons interred at the site, intruded through several lower strata. Evidently stratum 6B was redeposited mainly by the occupants of Occupation Zone V. Stratum 6B yielded the first definite evidence for ornaments. Of the 63 shell artifacts, 33 are *Oliva* shells with the tips broken off for suspension (Figure 56), all found on the chest of Burial no. 15, a child. Interestingly, an experimental attempt had been made to drill a hole laterally through the tip of one shell. As the apex of the shell broke off while drilling, the craftsman simply broke the apices off the other 32 shells as well and threaded the suspension string through the entire shell. Two large marine gastropods (*Lintricula auricularia*) and 22 small terrestrial gastropod shells (*Subulina*), although lacking any evidence of alteration, must also have been part of the jewelry placed with the dead body. Similarly, two limpet shells (*Diodara patagonica*), lacking use marks, were found with Burial no. 13; and a giant oyster shell (*Ostrea arborea*) lacking use marks, was found with Burial no. 16. The grave of Burial no. 39 and no. 44 each contained a large and beautiful *Phacoides pectinatus* shell that had been perforated for suspension by puncturing a hole from the interior. Three white-shark (*Carcharodon*) teeth were also associated with burials, including the only two white-shark teeth found at the site without ground and/or drilled roots. Three used sand-shark (*Carcharias*) teeth found in stratum 6B were not associated with burials.

Four of the ten whalebone artifacts found in stratum 6B were associated with burials. All were cut and chopped except one epiphysis with a ground face, one large slab that lay beneath Burial no. 22, and a piece with Burial no. 23 which had been calcined so that there was a cracked pattern on one face. One wonders if the cracks were made intentionally for purposes of ceremonial divination.

Only one perforated fish vertebra (Figure 35) came from stratum 6B, next to an *Oliva* shell bead with Burial no. 23. This is the only instance where there is good evidence that a perforated fish vertebra had actually been strung as a bead.

The other worked bones are evidently not associated with burial ceremonialism. They include nine pieces of detritus of manufacture, a worked bird bone, a deer (*Mazama*) frontal bone with attached antler which is much polished on its tip, six sting-ray spine projectile points, three bird-bone bipoints, a short mammal-bone projectile point ground to fit into a socketed shaft, and eight fishhooks.

Most of the stone tools from stratum 6B were not directly associated with burials; but they were associated with the processing of paint pigments, mainly hematite. Not only was hematite directly staining a few of the human bones; but, as can be seen on the east wall profile (Burial no. 6), a thick ochre lens was sometimes laid down either before the grave pit was dug, or placed directly over the pit. Hematite chunks with striated facets were found with Burials no. 32 and 22; and the latter grave also contained a hematite pebble with cuts on its surface, while another pebble with scraping marks on its surface was found with Burial no. 32.

A large hematite pebble and an unidentified iron mineral pebble with a depression on one face were found directly associated with 12 hammerstones, four of which have been used so much that, perhaps by intention, they had assumed spherical and discoidal forms. One spherical pebble had ochre adhering to its periphery; while a discoidal hammerstone has bifacial depressions, one of which retains red ochre. Ochre is also adhering to one end of a hammerstone with pecked ends and facial depressions. Another ochre-stained spherical hammerstone was found nearby; and both faces of the bit half of a rectangular axe from the same stratum are impregnated with hematite, evidently because the fragments had been used as a paint palette. Stratum 6B yielded 22 more hammerstones, including three discoidal forms and three large quadrangular forms; plus a pebble with pecked facial depressions. Although none of these implements were directly associated with hematite, very likely most also had been used for processing pigments. In addition, there is an angular slab with ground faces, a facetted pebble, two polished pebbles; plus a granite pebble with no evidence of alteration but nevertheless considered to be an artifact because it was associated with Burial no. 32.

Although stratum 4B, designated Occupation Zone VI, was used for interments soon after people stopped burying in stratum 6B, evidently the associated ceremonies had changed somewhat. There are no lenses of hematite, and only one worked hematite pebble. Evidently none of the four simple hammerstones or the single pebble with pecked depressions and ends was used for processing paint. Perhaps in the interim a red vegetable dye had been substituted for the mineral pigment. Although there were still ceremonial fires built before the interment, in one case there was also constructed a small circular cairn over the grave. Eight pieces of a large metate-like angular slab with a ground face (a manioc griddle?) had evidently been ceremonially "killed" and placed in a circular cairn over Burial no. 5.

Among the seven bitted implements and fragments from Occupation Zone V was the most carefully shaped axe found at Forte Marechal Luz. Except for the unused poll, all surfaces had been carefully ground. The axe was found near Burial no. 4, and probably had been interred with the body. Also found in stratum 4B were four pebbles with ground or polished faces, and one with a pecked facial depression.

A unique event occurred in Occupation VI when someone evidently placed a chunk or possibly an old artifact of vein quartz on a rock, bashed it with another rock, and then selected a few fragments to be used for scraping. It seems strange that this simple method of obtaining useful high-angle flakes was never repeated at the site. In addition, there were one reused and nine unused accidental flakes spalled from artifacts; and 14 thin unused flakes removed from preforms.

Only three shell artifacts were found in stratum 4B. A partially burned *Strombus pugilis* shell was found on the maxilla of Burial no. 5, and a *Phacoides pectinatus* shell with most of its edge broken away was associated with the same burial. An unassociated small, thin oyster shell lamina has a hole punctured near its center, perhaps by accident.

One puma (?) canine had been biconically drilled; and the root of a seal (?) canine had been ground into a facetted knob, presumably for suspension. Two peccary canines show some evidence of use, including striations on one of the roots. A paca mandible with its incisor ground to a flat plane was found with Burial no. 4. Only one root of the 18 used shark teeth had been ground for drilling.

Likewise, there were no significant innovations among the bone artifacts, although perhaps the most spectacular shaped bone tool excavated at the site came from Occupation Zone VI. This is a large, thin rectangular piece of ground whalebone with a circular perforation slightly off center (Figure 30). It must have been made for a specific function, but that purpose remains conjectural. The other shaped artifacts include four bone bipoints, a mammal-bone point with a bevelled base, two point fragments, and one fishhook. There were only five perforated fish vertebrae, three pieces of detritus of manufacture, two whalebone chopping blocks; plus two whalebones, two fish bones, and one land-mammal bone with butchering marks.

Except for the initial occurrence of ceramics, including a few sherds incorporated with burials, Occupation VI was not notable for any significant innovation. All other technological innovations had already been introduced during earlier occupations; and persisted through the last occupation, Occupation VII.

Once introduced, the useful art of making undecorated fired clay vessels for many utilitarian purposes became readily integrated into the abundant material cultural assemblage that characterized Occupation VII. Partly because a greater area of strata 1 through 4 was excavated, but mostly because all of the significant innovations of techniques for working stone, bone, teeth, shell, and clay detailed above for earlier occupations were now functioning in a balanced manner, Occupation Zone VII yielded nearly a third of all the artifacts recovered at the site plus most of the approximately 10,000 potsherds.

One nearly complete small flat-bottomed bowl, apparently deliberately "killed," had been placed next to the head of Burial no. 52 (Figure 60) in Occupation Zone VII. Even in this case the pot was probably serving a utilitarian function, to provide food for the dead, as had the oyster shell with Burial no. 16 in Stratum 6B. The potters occasionally experimented by making distinctive clay artifacts. One person made a ball, pinched two ends of it into pointed tips, and poked a lateral hole through one of the tips before firing it. This small object could have served as a sinker for a fish line or net. But evidently the experiment was never repeated, just as the potential significance of the isolated fired clay ball found in Occupation II was never recognized by the person who made it. Elsewhere in Occupation Zone VII someone was experimenting with making square-cornered clay vessels, probably in imitation of wooden boxes or bowls; but although one of the two fragmentary objects had been baked, evidently the experiment failed and the idea was abandoned.

Innovative occupants of Zone VII also experimented with stone. Three pebbles had several longitudinal facets ground onto their surfaces for unknown reasons. One experiment, however, may have been quite significant to the innovators; certainly it is to the archaeologist. One flaked then ground bitted implement was reflaked and reground after heavy use. The bit was then dulled and gouged by rugged use and the faces gouged with many deep crisscrossing striations before the piece was finally abandoned. This type of wear would not be consistent with use as an axe; rather it was probably the result of mounting the piece on the end of a digging stick and using the implement to jab holes in the ground, perhaps for planting. Another piece, which appears to be the bit half of a flaked preform, also exhibits considerable wear polish on the dull bit, and similar crisscrossing striations on its faces. A third object with the same pattern of heavy use and striations, especially near the bit, was found on the surface of stratum 1. This suggestive evidence for horticulture does not necessarily imply that gardening was innovated at this time; rather, it simply suggests that wooden digging sticks, which perhaps had been in use for a long time, were now made more useful and durable by mounting a stone bitted implement like a hoe.

Several other bitted implements from Occupation Zone VII appear to have been used as wedges for splitting wood (e.g., Figure 23); and several small bitted implements, mostly on thick accidental flakes removed from ground axes, were evidently used as scrapers for working wood and bone. Two bitted implements, unfortunately found out of context on the shell talus slope, exhibit a pattern of unifacial stepped flaking (Figure 22) on the bit which must have been caused by mounting the implements as adzes hafted at right angles to the shaft.

Thus, in addition to using bitted implements for chopping, hammering, pounding, and occasionally grinding, some were evidently employed for digging earth; while some were used for wedging, gouging, and adzing wood; and still others for scraping and chiseling wood and bone. All these varied functions render it impossible to employ a functional terminology, like "axe," for the broad category of bitted implements shaped by grinding and flaking. Altogether there were found in Occupation Zone VII seven flaked preforms; 26 bitted implements ground on flaked preforms; seven bitted implements ground on flakes; four other reused flakes; two pebbles with flaked and ground bits (not made on bifacially flaked preforms); one bitted implement ground on an unflaked pebble; and six fragments of bitted implements which also showed no evidence of preliminary percussion flaking before being ground into shape. Evidently, whenever a suitably shaped pebble was found, the preliminary shaping step was omitted, as it had been before Occupation IV. Increased activity in shaping and using bitted implements is indicated by the 168 flakes intentionally removed from preforms and 83 flakes removed accidentally by hard use from finished bitted implements and three from hammerstones.

Occupation Zone VII also yielded 29 pebbles with pecked and battered ends, from which flakes had been removed; a flattened pebble with use-flakes removed around its entire periphery; one spheroidal hammerstone; three discoidal hammerstones; 14 pebbles with pecked depressions and ends, including one with a black stain in one facial depression; two pebbles with hematite stains; one striated chunk of hematite; three other striated pebbles; one facetted pebble; two pebbles with ground faces; and 24 polishing pebbles, most of which had probably been used for smoothing and polishing the surfaces of pots. A tabular slab of granite with a long carbon scorch stain on one face was found associated with a smaller syenite pebble with two parallel scorch streaks on one face. Evidently these scorch marks had been caused by something very hot laid upon them. There were also two thermally fractured quartz pebbles, which may have simply been hearthstones, although usually diorite and diabase pebbles were used for that purpose. Perhaps someone was experimenting with breaking up quartz beach pebbles to see if the fractured edges were useful. Three natural fragments of vein quartz appear to have used edges, but another pebble showed no evidence of use except that it had been placed with a burial. There are also five siltstone concretions which had been carried up to the site for some reason.

Although the proportion of bone relative to stone artifacts increased significantly, except for a tapir fibula which had been carefully ground into a useful spatulate tool (Figure 49) perhaps for shaping pots, there was nothing new in the assemblage of bone artifacts from Occupation Zone VII. Among the large number of worked whalebones were five chopping blocks, five worked vertebral epiphyses, 12 chopped and cut bones, three burned and chopped pieces, two carved and whittled bones, plus a piece that had been ground. Six bird and mammal bones exhibited butchering marks. Also two bird bones, one fish bone, and nine mammal-bone fragments had been worked; in addition to 24 cut, ground, and scraped detrital fragments of bird and mammal bone. There were 61 perforated fish and shark vertebrae, 28 of which had been found strung out in their original articulated column. The smallest 20 of these vertebrae had been punctured, evidently with a stick pushed through their centers, as the smallest vertebra had the largest punctured hole, and the diameter decreased up the line. Interestingly, this instance, which shows how at times vertebrae were mass perforated, is the only case where more than one perforated vertebrae were found together. This fact suggests that many perforated fish and shark vertebrae were not simply strung on necklaces. Perhaps they served as spindle whorls, toy tops, or fishermen's charms.

Four minimally worked sting-ray spines showed that these simple projectile points were still being used, as were all the other earlier kinds of bone projectile points, including 29 bipoints, three mammal-bone points with bevelled and scarfed bases, three tanged (pedunculated) points, and three point fragments. Fish were still being caught with fishhooks, although interestingly three of the nine examples now had sturdier lateral projections for the retention of the line. As seen from several broken examples of the old type with thin lateral knobs, this spot constituted a major structural weakness. Evidently the problem was solved by making the attachment knobs wider, because none of the example of that type from Occupation Zone VII were broken at that spot.

The same story of continuation of old fabrication techniques, occasionally applied in new ways, is found on the tooth artifacts from Occupation Zone VII. Thus, of the six altered peccary canines, three have been ground into objects with triangular longitudinal sections. One of the three carefully shaped objects had a drilled hole, presumably for suspension; perhaps the other two were lost before they were perforated. Both roots of a tapir molar had been carefully drilled for suspension. A capivara incisor had been slightly ground and polished but without any intention to shape it. The canine of an unidentified mammal exhibits many tiny striations running in various directions over its enamel surfaces.

Evidently paca incisors were more often used for working wood during Occupation VII. Although deliberate facets had been ground on the occlusal surfaces of three paca incisors, paradoxically the best piece of evidence for human use lacked any obvious marks of alteration. In this case the tooth was found inserted inside a large hollow bird bone which exhibited only slight wear polish; but obviously it was a makeshift haft for the incisor tool. A similar bird bone from the same occupation zone was probably another haft. Two paca mandibles with surficial striations were broken next to the incisor tooth socket as if the tooth had fallen out because of too much downward pressure applied while scraping or grooving wood or bone. Perhaps the bird bones were then put to use to haft the still useful teeth.

Of the 87 shark teeth that had been brought to the site for some reason during Occupation VII, 32 showed no obvious evidence of use. Four white-shark teeth had been ground and drilled, as in earlier occupations; but five sand-shark teeth, which have quite a different shape, were also experimented with. An unsuccessful attempt was made to perforate the roots of one exceptionally large white-shark tooth by drilling, and all five exhibited grinding facets.

The thick columellas of three marine gastropods were ground into cylindrical objects with squared bases. Although intentionally shaped for some purpose, they were too irregular to have been used as projectile points; but conceivably they could have been mounted onto wooden flanges and used as lip or ear ornaments. The external edge of a punctured *Mactrella* shell had been ground smooth, and there were five unidirectional striations radiating from the hole of this example, as well as another one; this is the kind of wear that would occur from suspension as a necklace. Another perforated *Phacoides pectinatis* shell was found with a burial, similar to those in both earlier burial strata 6B and 4B. Three new genera of shells were either perforated (one *Lintricula*, one *Olivancillaria)* or truncated (one *Conus)*, presumably for suspension. In addition, two *Olivancillaria*, one *Lintricula*, and one *Semicassis*, all univalves, had broken and worn lips, obviously much used.

Discussion of Comparisons with Other Sambaquis

This is a report of the analysis of excavation results, and it will not include a synthesis of sambaquis archaeology, mainly because most relationships with sambaquis in other areas would mainly be generalities because many summary reports but very few complete site reports have been published. One major difference between Forte Marechal Luz, which was occupied for nearly 4000 years, is that most of the 26 radiocarbon-dated south Brazilian littoral sites were occupied for only a few hundred years; very few for more than a millennium (Schmitz 1981:128). Concise summaries of many of these sites may be found in Neves (1988:62–73). Even partially contemporary sites in other areas have few similarities in detail. From the literature available to me, it seems that there was a great deal of cultural diversity along the south Brazilian coast in late-Holocene times. As I do not have access to much of the primary literature, I must therefore rely on syntheses and overviews of scholars familiar with the literature who are more competent to perform this task (e.g., Hurt 1974; Neves 1988; Prous and Piazza 1977; Schmitz 1981, 1984, 1987; Schmitz et al. 1992).

At the time of my excavation in 1960, not many sambaquis had been excavated and reported upon. Several archaeologists were actively working in the states of São Paulo, Paraná, and Santa Catarina throughout the 1960s and 1970s. Even before that period of intensive field work, Guilherme Tiburtius, the exceptional avocational archaeologist who lived in Joinville, had recorded and tested many sites in the river valley, and along the Araquari Channel that divides the mainland from the west side of the Ilha de São Francisco. He also had recorded many sites on the island, including Forte Marechal Luz. Tiburtius' reports were my major sources of comparative information in 1960 when I described the artifacts from Forte Marechal Luz. Padre João Rohr was also actively working farther south on the Ilha de Santa Catarina. Reports of his numerous excavations on this large island are still being published several years after his death (e.g., Schmitz et al. 1992).

The proliferation of fieldwork led to several syntheses of sambaqui archaeology, and more broadly of the archaeology of southern Brazil, beginning in the 1970s, and intensifying in the 1980s. The first synthesis was produced by Anamaria Beck (1972) as her doctoral dissertation, which I have only seen summarized (Neves 1988; Schmitz et al. 1992). She attempted to establish five phases for the northern littoral of Santa Catarina. Based mainly on her work at Morro de Ouro in Babitonga Bay and Enseada 1 on a headland fronting the open ocean only 6 km from Forte Marechal Luz, she distinguished the preceramic Morro de Ouro Phase from the ceramic Enseada Phase, which she related to the undecorated Itararé ceramic tradition. She also concluded that the Enseada Phase represented an intrusive population from the interior that displaced the earlier population. At the time she wrote, I had published only a preliminary report (Bryan 1961), so Beck (1972, 1974) did not include Forte Marechal Luz in her studies, although it is located between the two sites she excavated. She included bone fishhooks as well as pottery to define the Enseada Phase, and indicated that the Enseada Phase was not a true sambaqui because the upper humic layer contained mainly organic material and relatively few shells. When André Prous condensed my final report into a summary report (Bryan 1977a) I was not aware of her conclusions. My report on a site located between her two sites, and yielding similar artifacts, clearly contradicted Beck's conclusion that there was population displacement associated with the introduction of ceramics and fishhooks. Piazza (1974, and in Prous and Piazza 1977) proposed a different set of phases based more on composition of shellfish species and less on artifact changes. Prous himself later pointed out that fishhooks had been innovated at Forte Marechal Luz before the introduction of pottery; and he even questioned the usefulness of trying to set up phases (In: Schmitz, Barbosa and Ribeiro, eds. 1978/79/80:15). I must agree with Prous that trying to force highly diverse cultural entities into arbitrary pigeonholes can create more confusion than enlightenment. In my opinion, definition of various technological traditions, in addition to ceramic traditions, would be a much more useful exercise, at least until considerably more basic research has been published.

Several authors have emphasized the obvious diversity found within both culture and biology associated with sambaquis, even at partially contemporary sites not far from each other. After reviewing the literature available to me in the light of this final report, I have come to some tentative conclusions. The old idea that there was a homogeneous coastal population ("sambaqui man") has certainly been proven wrong by modern excavations. Clearly, there was tremendous cultural diversity and significant biological diversity along the southern Brazilian coast. Coastal groups had extensive trade contacts with each other and with interior people, but there is no clear evidence for migrations or conquering peoples, except possibly for the Tupi-Guaraní, who were able to penetrate the south coast only in limited areas. The introduction of Itararé plainware to the Ilha de São Francisco may well have been by the social process of exogamy, with local men marrying women potters from neighboring groups in a patrilocal system, as Neves (1988) suggested. Certain morphological differences between the sexes noted by Mello e Alvim (1967/68) would fit this model. Pottery could also have been obtained by trade. Perhaps less likely because the technology is so complex, pottery could simply have been accepted as a useful new technique just as fishhooks and the idea of bifacial axe preforms had previously been adopted from neighboring groups. However it was innovated, I fail to see any evidence for violent population disruptions or displacements as Beck suggested. Rather, the stratigraphic evidence at Forte Marechal Luz indicates that the same cultural group continued to occupy the site for almost four millennia, but that their cultural adaptations to the productive local ecosystem were periodically improved by the acquisition of new technological concepts from neighboring groups by means of a well-established exchange system.

I think my original working hypothesis that the Enseada site was another locality occupied periodically by the same cultural group that occupied Forte Marechal Luz has not been disproven by Beck's work; although it is possible that the stratigraphic sequence at Enseada 1 was more condensed (and therefore misled Beck) than at Forte Marechal Luz. Sites on the west side of the island along the Araquari Channel and up the river near Joinville were probably occupied by different, but socially related, groups, who were among those who supplied new ideas to their western neighbors living on the outer coast. The highly distinctive morphological features of people living at Forte Marechal Luz, quite different from other populations, described by Mello e Alvim (1967/8), suggest not only biological relationships with Patagonia, as she suggested, but also the possibility that an early coastal population had expanded southward along the South Atlantic littoral before the early-Holocene sea-level rise forced them to move inland. Eventually, earlier submerged sites should be found on the continental shelf to test this hypothesis.

Conclusions

By developing a methodology for identifying and defining the processes of alteration and manufacture of all artifacts (not just ceramics and stone artifact reduction), rather than adopting a formal classification scheme, certain other kinds of significant cultural processes became evident. New technological processes clearly were innovated at different times, and almost all technological processes persisted once they were innovated. Thus, there is no evidence for abrupt population change during the nearly four millennia of occupation of the site. The only evidence for periodic abandonment of the site is the two periods when the site was used intensively as a cemetery, when the people may have occupied the hilltop adjacent to the sambaqui. The fact that they sometimes lived on their own garbage dump means that it is unlikely that the site was occupied continuously. The nearby Enseada 1 site with its similar technology was very likely occupied by the same population. One of these two sites (and perhaps others?) may have become the major village for a few years, to give the garbage a chance to decompose. The lack of buried humus layers, such as formed on the surface of the site after final abandonment sometime after A.D. 1300, indicates that periodic abandonment was never prolonged.

The preserved technology of the people who first occupied the Forte Marechal site was very simple. Of course, perishable material culture, including basketry, woodworking, and featherwork, may have been highly developed. Four millennia ago, the only evident technique for shaping artifacts was the pecking of depressions on the faces of *quebra-cocos*, although stone was altered by grinding and accidental flaking. Bone was also flaked during heavy use, and a whalebone was hardened by calcination; also a depression similar to that on facially pitted stones was made, perhaps also by pecking.

A pattern of gradual accumulation of new technological traditions was established in Occupation Zone II and accelerated during Occupation Zone IV. By Zone VII the occupants of the sambaqui at Forte Marechal Luz had developed an integrated synthesis of many discrete technological traditions which was functioning very successfully as an agent for coping with their environment until the time of abandonment of the site. The people were, as before, collecting several kinds of shellfish, including crabs, but especially small clams, small oysters, and mussels; and they were quite successful fishermen, to judge by the abundance of fish bones. There was also a notable increase in the numbers of land-mammal bones in Occupation V which became even more evident in Occupation VII. At the same time there was a notable increase in the number of sea-turtle scutes, while sea-mammal bones remain as abundant as ever. Identifiable remains of plant foods include charred shells of palms (*Palmae*) and nuts of Sapotaceae, Miristicaceae, and Mirtaceae. These plant foods were especially common in Occupation Zone VII, but already present by Occupation IV; and, of course, the presence of "*quebra-cocos*" in all occupation zones implies that such nuts were always a staple food. Charred food remains baked onto the interior of cooking vessels were very common, but the means were unavailable for analysis of the charred material.

Evidently the people of Forte Marechal Luz ate quite well with a varied diet, so why did they abandon this site and presumably the area which had sustained them for nearly four millennia? One possibility is that aggressive Tupi-Guarani groups had pushed them out of the coastal region; but if so, these intruders did not occupy the sambaqui, as their distinctive ceramics are absent even on the surface. Perhaps the answer was disease, against which they lacked immunity, introduced to South America by European explorers. As in North America, diseases undoubtedly swept in advance of the first European explorers. The semi-legendary *Carijos*, who were encountered by the first Europeans to reach southern Brazil, are supposed to have spoken a Tupi-Guarani language; and they reportedly referred to the people who previously had lived on the coast as savages ignorant of technologically advanced culture. Will we ever know who the earlier people were and what happened to them? Perhaps they were Gê speakers, as some have suggested on the basis of their ceramic tradition, but possibly they belonged to some other group distantly related to coastal Patagonians, as the skeletal morphology suggests.

General Discussion of the Relevance of Sambaqui Archaeology

The archaeology of Brazilian shell mounds has universal as well as local relevance. Hurt (1974) and others have pursued the problem of the positions of sambaquis relative to changes in world-wide sea level. The Forte Marechal Luz site cannot contribute to this problem because it was situated on a hillside, apparently well above the level of the sea throughout the prolonged time of occupation.

Because the Forte Marechal Luz site was relatively protected from marine erosion, occupational evidence was preserved for an extended period of time (about four millennia). As the artifact yield was relatively rich for a sambaqui, a clear story of cultural change can be reconstructed in the form of gradual but accelerating accumulation of new technological innovations. For archaeologists, the most significant innovations were the addition of pottery about A.D. 1100 and the local innovation of percussion flaking sometime between A.D. 900

and 400. Prior to that time the occupants of the site did not make pottery nor did they flake stone. Evidently they retained a marginal technology long after many other groups in southern Brazil had innovated these highly diagnostic technological traditions, which are more significant for the archaeologist than they were for the prehistoric occupants of the site. If so, it is instructive to realize that these technologically marginal people illustrate a case of persistence into recent times of a simple but effective technological complex which likely characterized Pleistocene man in America and East Asia before more standardized (and therefore diagnostic) tool traditions (including bifacially flaked stone projectile points) were developed in certain areas in response to local environmental conditions and opportunities.

Although the occupants of the Forte Marechal Luz site always maintained a relatively simple technology, the analysis of fabricating techniques has demonstrated that their technology was not stagnant. The people were ingenious and innovative. They accepted new ideas from other cultural groups, and they experimented on their own (e.g., with unfired clay cooking vessels, square-cornered fired clay containers, and stone breaking by heating vein quartz). They were obviously alert to accept innovations that increased efficiency with less expenditure of effort. This trait is evident when the easily made yet highly efficient bird-bone bipointed projectile points superseded the scarfed mammal-bone points which required much more labor to make. The later innovation of bone fishhooks seems like a paradox in this regard because they took considerable effort to make, although evidently the fishhooks allowed greater success in catching certain species of deeper-water fish that may not have been obtainable previously by spearing. Experimental ingenuity is evident, however, when a sturdier method of attaching the line was innovated after many of the previous hooks broke under stress at the weak line attachment knob at the proximal end.

Perhaps the greatest increase in efficiency was attained by the innovation of percussion flaking in order to preform bitted implements ("axes"). Previously an axemaker had simply chosen a beach pebble of approximately the right natural shape and had laboriously ground it on a boulder into a finished form. With the innovation of percussion-flaked preforms the amount of labor expended in grinding was significantly reduced. Although they got what they wanted—a better-shaped axe preform—close analysis of all the evidence for flaking revealed several inescapable conclusions: (1) They were very inexpert flint knappers, as they did not know how to thin a thick flake or nodule—they simply battered the thick edge forcefully at right angles, using their tradition of forceful pecking, which occasionally would result in the removal of a flake. (2) They made very little if any use of the few thin and sharp-edged percussion flakes they did remove; none were ever retouched, and most flakes show no evidence that they used the naturally sharp edges for cutting. All identifiable utilized flakes were thick in cross-section and evidently had been used for scraping or chiseling and not for cutting. Cutting implements may have been made out of sharp teeth or hard bamboo and palm wood. (3) The most striking fact is that the occupants of the site evidently did not flake stone intentionally themselves until Occupation V. It appears that they taught themselves how to flake by observing evidently imported axes made on thick side-blow flakes that were found only in Occupation IV. They examined these imported axes but did not copy the special technique of striking off a side-blow flake. Instead, they reduced naturally tabular pieces of diabase from a nearby dyke by removing flakes from both faces by direct battering using their traditional pecking action; and they never prepared a striking platform in the way an experienced knapper would do. With these limitations, they created a rectangular biface preform; but they still had to expend a great deal of effort to reduce the preform to a useful bitted implement by grinding.

Is there any special significance to the fact that the early occupants of the site did not know how to flake stone? Most archaeologists assume that once an advanced flaking technology was innovated, that technology would never be abandoned, but the evidence from Forte Marechal Luz disproves that assumption. There is considerable evidence elsewhere in South America that many groups did not flake stone bifacially (see discussion in Bryan, 1978), but there is little archaeological evidence that some cultural groups did not know how to flake stone at all. Many sites on the coast and especially in the interior of southern Brazil contain intentionally flaked stone artifacts, some quite expertly fabricated. However, a few other sambaquis do not contain intentionally flaked stone artifacts, just as most sambaquis lack any evidence of ceramics. Obviously, if it were not for the fact that sambaquis are clearly accumulations of human refuse, the archaeologist would have an exceedingly difficult time locating sites that lack both ceramics and flaked stone, especially in a heavily vegetated region. So the paucity of evidence for people who did not flake stone (or fire ceramics) in large part may be because the archaeologist has difficulty locating such sites. This is certainly one of the most compelling reasons why shellmound archaeology is significant. Without excavations of sambaquis a most important segment of the prehistory of South America would remain unrecorded simply because most of the cultural groups that accumulated the huge shell deposits possessed an exceedingly simple non-perishable material culture.

When one looks at recorded ethnographies of most Brazilian Indians, and, for that matter, of much of the ceramic archaeology of lowland South America, one finds that the paucity or absence of flaked-stone artifacts is the rule and not the exception. Even when flakeable stone was available many lowland South American Indian groups used flakes only for fabricating manioc graters. Bone and wood were always preferred for projectile points and even knives. When stone was used for tools it was normally ground into shape. The technological tradition of grinding stone artifacts was well established and had a long duration in many parts of lowland South America. Perhaps the tradition of grinding replaced the much older tradition of flaking stone; but possibly some groups had lost the art of stone flaking much earlier.

For the archaeologist, imbued with the classic European three-stage model of technological development (Paleolithic, Neolithic, and the Metal Ages), the paradox presented by the evidence from some South American sambaquis is the occasional lack of a flaked-stone industry when ground stone tools were commonly used. Everyone knows that the art of flaking stone was well developed nearly 2,000,000 years ago in Africa and probably a million years ago in Europe, so if the dilemma of finding ground stone tools without flaked stone tools is discussed at all, it is simply assumed that some people lost the art of stone flaking in relatively recent times, perhaps because they or their ancestors lived in territory lacking flakeable stone, or because other materials were more easily worked into the desired tool forms. But perhaps this ready assumption is begging the question. Although one or both of these facile explanations must have been true at some time in the history of groups of prehistoric people who did not flake stone, the question remains unanswered as to when some populations may have lost the art of stone flaking. Perhaps it was only "recently" after the ancestors of these people adapted themselves to various parts of South America, but it is also possible that their ancestors had lost the art of stone flaking even before they entered South America. My experience excavating sites in several South American countries has led me to the conclusion that the question is an important one for archaeologists to consider and should not be dismissed lightly. My main reason for discussing this possibility is because of my interest in identifying the archaeological evidence for really early man in America. As noted above it would be difficult for any archaeologist to locate a non-ceramic, non-flaked-stone site except when the matrix includes obvious occupational debris, such as food remains, hearths, etc.

Recognizing the potential relevance of excavating such sites to my primary interest in locating verifiable cultural evidence for human occupation in America during the Pleistocene, I have developed a logical set of criteria for locating early sites that may retain relatively undisturbed cultural contexts, such as contained in a sambaquis, but at a time before shellmounds that may have accumulated along sea coasts before the final Pleistocene rise in sea level submerged them. The inexorable processes of erosion and deposition have disturbed most cultural contexts in late-Pleistocene occupation sites. If the occupants of these sites made abundant well-shaped flaked-stone tools, subsequent disturbance may not be a devastating factor if the stratigraphic contexts are secure, but obviously it is best to find undisturbed contexts if the occupants did not flake stone tools, because the only evidence preserved may be hearths, bone objects, food remains such as smashed bone or coco shells, and perhaps human hair. Such elusive evidence may be present in open sites, but it would be difficult to locate such sites. Logically, limestone caves or rockshelters are best because bone should be well preserved; but it is essential to select sites carefully to find those that would be regularly occupied, as well as having minimal evidence of erosion and slow deposition. Because the available evidence from Brazil indicates clearly that certain marginal foraging groups retained a simple technology into protohistoric times, we should consider the possibility that this technology reflects their ancient cultural heritage as descendants of early immigrants to America. As Pleistocene shellmounds would be preserved only along tectonically rising coasts, I have concluded that caves, which retain the closest available set of conditions for preservation of elusive cultural evidence such as can be found in sambaquis, constitute one of the best possible places to look for conclusive evidence for Pleistocene Americans.

References Cited

Atlas Geográfico de Santa Catarina
1958 Departmento Estadual de Geográfia e Cartográfia. Florianópolis.

Beck, A.
1968 A cerámica dos sambaquis do Litoral Norte de Santa Catarina. *Pesquisas,* Antropologia, no. 18: 89-99. Instituto Anchietano de Pesquisas, São Leopoldo RS.
1972 A Variação do Conteúdo Cultural dos Sambaquis do Litoral de Santa Catarina. Tese de Doutorado, Universidade de São Paulo. (Not seen.)
1974 O Sambaqui de Enseada 1-SC-LN-71:um Estudo sobre Tecnologia Pré-Histórica. Tese de Livre Docencia, Universidade Federal de Santa Catarina, Florianópolis. (Not seen.)

Beck, A., E. M. Araújo, and G. M. Duarte
1970 Sintese da arqueólogia do Litoral Norte de Santa Catarina. *Anais do Museu de Antropologia,* Ano 3:23–29. Florianópolis.

Beck, A., E. M. Araújo, G. M. Duarte, T. D. Fossari, and E. M. Belani
1970 A indústria ossea do sambaquis do Litoral Norte—Fase Enseada. *Anais do Museu de Antropologia,* Ano 3:35–55. Florianópolis.

Beltrão, M.
1970 A Propósito de Coleções Líticas Desprovides de Dados Estratigráficos. *Publicações Avulsas do Museu Nacional,* no. 52. Rio de Janeiro.
1976 Documentos sobre a Pre-história dos Estados do Rio de Janeiro e Guanabara (1500–1963). *Coleção Museu Paulista, Series de Arqueologia,* vol. 2. São Paulo.

Bryan, A. L.
1961 Excavation of a Brazilian Shell Mound. *Science of Man* 1 (5):148–151, 174–175. Mentone, California.
1963 An Archaeological Survey of Northern Puget Sound. *Occasional Papers of the Idaho State College Museum,* no. 11. Pocatello.
1965 Paleo-American Prehistory. *Occasional Papers of the Idaho State University Museum,* no. 16. Pocatello.
1977a Resumo da Arqueologia do Sambaqui de Forte Marechal Luz. *Arquivos do Museu de História Natural* 11:9–30. Belo Horizonte.
1977b Developmental Stages and Technological Traditions. *Annals of the New York Academy of Sciences* 288:355–368.
1978 An Overview of Paleo-American Prehistory from a Circum-Pacific Perspective. In *Early Man in America from a Circum-Pacific Perspective,* edited by Alan L. Bryan, pp. 306–327. Occasional Paper no. 1, Department of Anthropology, University of Alberta, Edmonton.
1983 Bone Alteration Patterns as Clues for the Identification of Early Man Sites; or, An Attempt to Demythify the Search for Early Americans. In *Carnivores, Human Scavengers, and Predators: a Question of Bone Technology,* pp. 193–217. Proceedings of the Fifteenth Chacmool Conference, Archaeological Association of the University of Calgary.

Chmyz, I.
1968 Considerações sobre duas novas tradições ceramistas arqueológicas no estado do Paraná. *Pesquisas,* Antropologia, no. 18:115–125.

Instituto Anchietano de Pesquisas, São Leopoldo, RS.

Cruxent, J. M.
1967 Litos con hoyuelos. *Boletín Informativo* 5:4–5. Instituto Venezolano de Investigaciones Científicas, Departamento de Antropologia, Caracas.

Cunha, E. S.
1973 Sobre um caso particular de abrasão dentaria em homem do sambaquis. *Arquivos Fluminenses de Odontologia* 6 (4):107–111. Niteroi, RJ.

Emperaire, J., and A. Laming
1956 Les sambaquis de la Cote Méridionale du Brésil (campagnes de fouilles), 1954–1957. *Journal de la Societé des Americanistes*, n.s. t. XLV:5–163.

Hurt, W. R.
1974 The Interrelationships between the Natural Environment and Four Sambaquis, Coast of Santa Catarina, Brazil. *Occasional Papers and Monographs, Indiana University Museum*, no. 1. Bloomington.

Laming, A.
1960 Novas perspectivas sobre a pré-história do Sul do Brasil. *Anhembi* 38 (113):31–40. São Paulo.

Lima, T. A., E. M. Botelho de Mello, and R. C. Pinheiro da Silva
1986 Analysis of Molluscan Remains from the Ilha de Santa Site, Macaé, Brazil. *Journal of Field Archaeology* 13 (1):83–97.

Mello e Alvim, M. C. de; e D. Pereira de Mello Filho
1967/68 Morfologia da População do Sambaqui do Forte Marechal Luz (Santa Catarina). *Revista de Antropologia* 15/16:5–12. São Paulo.

Migdalski, E. C., and G. S. Fichter
1976 *The Fresh and Salt Water Fishes of the World.* Alfred A Knopf, N.Y.

Neves, W. A.
1988 Paleogenética dos Grupos Pré-Históricos do Litoral Sul do Brasil (Paraná e Santa Catarina). *Pesquisas*, Antropologia, no. 43. Instituto Anchietano de Pesquisas, São Leopoldo RS.

Oliveira, B.
1960 Geologia, petrologia, e geomorfologia da Ilha de São Francisco do Sul. *Revista Brasileira de Geografia* XXII (2):133–168. Rio de Janeiro.

Piazza, W.
1974 Dados a arqueologia do Litoral Norte e do Planalto de Canoinhas. PRONAPA no. 5 (ano 1969/70), *Publicações Avulsas, Museu Goeldi*, no. 26:53–66. Belém.

Prous, A.
1986 Os mais antigos vestígios arqueológicos no Brasil Central. In *New Evidence for the Pleistocene Peopling of the Americas*, edited by Alan L. Bryan, pp. 173–182. Center for the Study of Early Man, University of Maine at Orono.

Prous, A., and W. Piazza
1977 Documents pour la préhistoire du Brésil Méridional 2—L'etat de Santa Catarina. *Cahiers d'Archéologie d'Amérique du Sud* 4. Paris.

Rohr, J. A.
1960 Pesquisas Paleo-etnográficas na Ilha de Santa Catarina, no. 11. *Pesquisas*, Antropologia, no. 8. Instituto Anchietano de Pesquisas, Porto Alegre RS.

Schmitz, P. I.
1968 Grandes complexos da ceramica indigena no Sul do Brasil. *Pesquisas*, Antropologia, no. 18:127–140. Instituto Anchietano de Pesquisas, São Leopoldo RS.

1981 Contribuciones a la Prehistoria de Brasil. *Pesquisas*, Antropologia, no. 32. Instituto Anchietano de Pesquisas, São Leopoldo RS.

1984 *Caçadores e Coletores da Pré-história do Brasil.* Instituto Anchietano de Pesquisas, São Leopoldo RS.

1987 Prehistoric hunters and gatherers of Brasil. *Journal of World Prehistory* 1 (1):53–126.

Schmitz, P. I., A. S. Barbosa, and M. B. Ribeiro (editors)
1978–80 Temas de Arqueologia Brasileira 3: Arcaico do Litoral. *Anuário de Divulgação Científica* no. 7, Instituto Goiano de Pré-História e Antropologia, Universidade Católica de Goias, Goiania.

Schmitz, P. I., M. A. Nadal De Masi, I. Verardi, R. Lavina, and A. L. Jacobus
1992 Escavações Arqueológicas do Pe. João Alfredo Rohr, S.J. *Pesquisas*, no. 48. Instituto Anchietano de Pesquisas, São Leopoldo RS.

Tiburtius, G.
1966 O Sambaqui Conquista (Nr. 9). *Boletim Paranaense de Geografia* nos. 18/20:71–126. Curitiba.

Tiburtius, G., I. Koehler Bigarella, e J. J. Bigarella
1951 Nota previa sobre a jazida paleoetnográfica de Itacoara (Joinville, Estado de Santa Catarina). *Arquivos de Biologia e Tecnologia* VI:315–346. Instituto de Biologia e Pesquisas Tecnológicas, Curitiba.

1954 Contribução ao estudo das sambaquis do Litoral Norte de Santa Catarina II, Sambaqui do Rio Pinheiros (no. 8). *Arquivos de Biologia e Tecnologia* IX:141–197. Instituto de Biologia e Pesquisas Tecnológicas, Curitiba.

Tiburtius, G., e A. Leprovost
1952 Sobre a ocurrencia de pedras corantes e esqueletas pintadas nos sambaquis dos estados do Paraná e Santa Catarina. *Arquivos de Biologia e Tecnologia* VII:149–155. Instituto de Biologia e Pesquisas Tecnológicas, Curitiba.
1953 Nota sobre a ocurrencia de machados de pedra nos estados do Paraná e Santa Catarina. *Arquivos de Biologia e Tecnologia* VIII:503–554. Instituto de Biologia e Pesquisas Tecnológicas, Curitiba.

Tiburtius, G., A. Leprovost, e J. J. Bigarella
1949 Sobre a ocurrencia de bula timpanica de baleia e artefatos derivados nos sambaquis dos estados do Paraná e Santa Catarina. *Arquivos de Biologia e Tecnologia* IV:87–94. Instituto de Biologia e Pesquisas Tecnológicas, Curitiba.

Index

Archaeological Research at Six Cave or Rockshelter Sites in Interior Bahia, Brazil

Alan L. Bryan and Ruth Gruhn

Table of Contents

List of Tables

List of Figures

Chapter 1
Introduction

THE FIELDWORK

Our work in Bahia was part of the Projeto Central, an interdisciplinary research project formulated by Profa. Maria de Conceição de Moraes Coutinho Beltrão of the Museu Nacional. This project, to involve Brazilian experts in geology and paleontology as well as Brazilian and foreign archaeologists, was to determine aspects of prehistory in the region of the town of Central, an area already known for its many caves and rock overhangs with rich rock art; and for an abundance of fossilized remains of Pleistocene fauna, commonly found in the excavations of waterholes. The primary objective of the project was to discover evidence of human presence in the area during the Pleistocene.

The project was initiated by Beltrão and Brazilian associates in 1983, with a preliminary extensive reconnaissance of the region for two weeks in June. We arrived in Brazil in July 1983 to carry out a year's fieldwork under a research grant from the Social Sciences and Humanities Research Council of Canada, and were requested by Beltrão to conduct an intensive site survey and test excavations in the Central area. We were based in Central from 12 July to 15 August 1983. During this month of intensive fieldwork, an excavation begun by Beltrão at Toca dos Buzios was expanded, and a test excavation at Toca de Manoel Latão was undertaken. An extensive archaeological site survey was carried out, focusing on a series of limestone ridges, locally termed *serras,* in the area 6 to 15 km north of the town center of Central; and over 100 caves were recorded. Among them, a small number of promising archaeological sites were noted for future excavation.

In October 1983 we returned to Central; and, with the assistance of Fabiano Lopez da Paula of the Universidade Federal de Minas Gerais, we undertook excavations at the small limestone rockshelter called the Abrigo da Lesma. The excavations extended from 2 to 24 October. We spent the ensuing months in Rio de Janeiro, analysing the materials recovered from the excavations in Toca dos Buzios, Toca de Manoel Latão, and Abrigo da Lesma. In early May 1984 we returned to Central. Further excavations were carried out in Toca dos Buzios from 5 to 6 May and Toca de Manoel Latão from 4 to 25 June. The major excavation program was undertaken at a large limestone rockshelter, Abrigo do Pilão, from 7 to 23 May. Afterwards, we spent several days on an extensive survey of the Rio Verde valley. The following two months were spent in Rio de Janeiro, analysing the materials recovered.

The Social Sciences and Humanities Research Council of Canada research grant was extended to 1985; and in June and July 1985, assisted by Canadian students Keary Walde and Max Friesen, we excavated in two limestone caves in the Rio Verde region of the *municipio* of Xique-Xique, Toca do Cosmos and Toca da Gameleira. The analysis of materials recovered from these sites was completed in Rio de Janeiro in the month of August.

At intervals from 1984 to 1987 excavations were also carried out in caves and rockshelters in the Central region by Wesley R. Hurt of Indiana University. Hurt will publish a report on his sites in the future. The present report provides the detailed description and analysis of the stratigraphy and archaeological materials recovered at our sites: Toca dos Buzios (BA-CE-1), Toca de Manoel Latão (BA-CE-2), Abrigo da Lesma (BA-CE-3), Abrigo do Pilão (BA-CE-17), Toca do Cosmos (BA-XX-1, and Toca da Gameleira (BA-XX-2) (map, Figure 1-1). A description of major features of the environment of the Central region will be provided in this introductory section of the report, and there

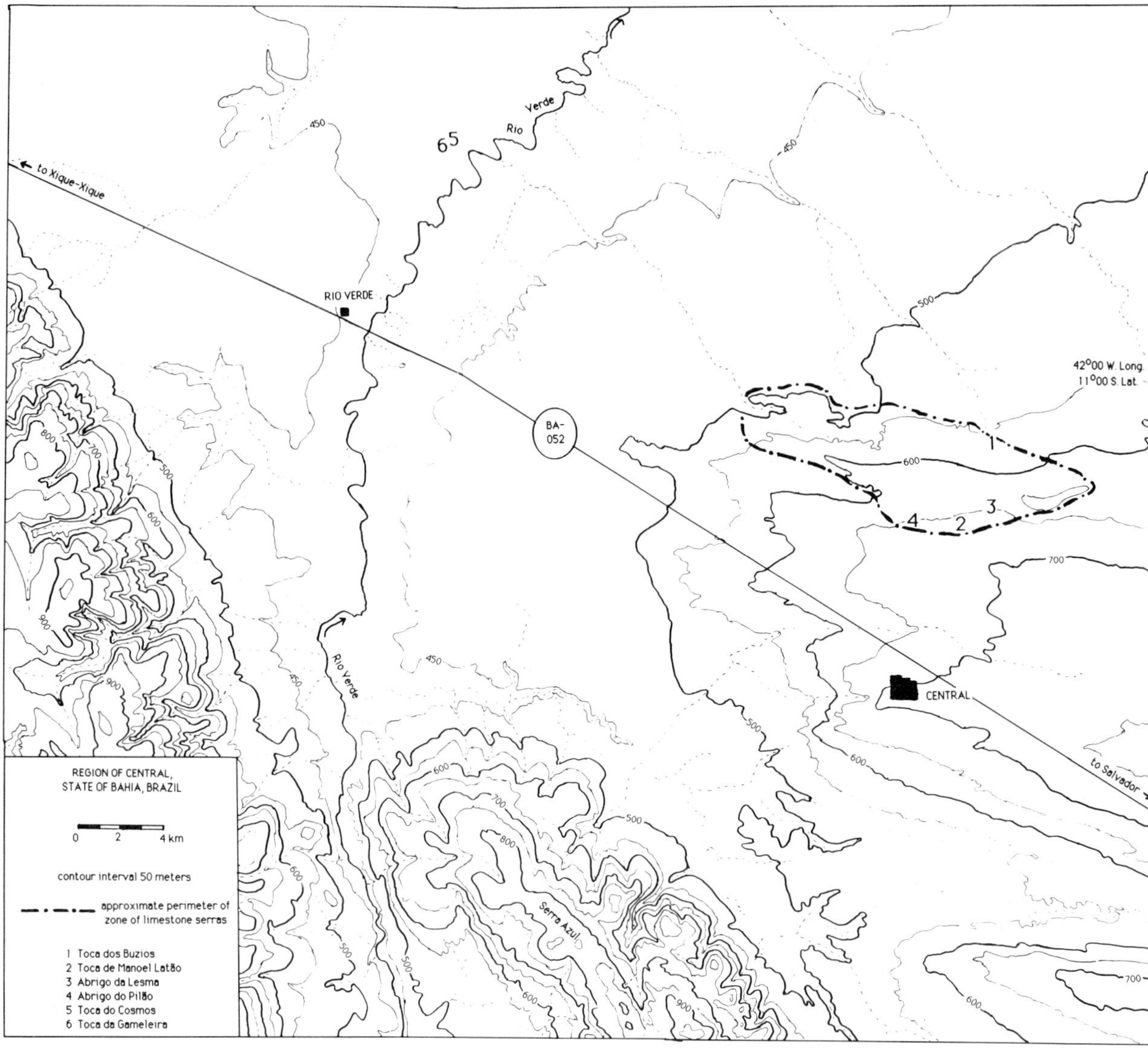

Figure 1-1. Map of the Central region, redrawn from 1:100,000 topographic maps Folha SC-23-X-II (Central) and Folha SC-23-Z-B-VI (Rio Verde).

will be a general discussion of the nature of the archaeological situation and our methodological approach. Following the site reports, a concluding analysis of the record of prehistory in the region will be presented.

THE REGION

The Town of Central, as the name was meant to imply, is located in the central part of the state of Bahia. Via the state highway BA-052, it is approximately 520 km northwest of the city of Salvador; and approximately 75 km southeast of the old town of Xique-Xique, which is situated on the Rio São Francisco. The town center of Central is situated at approximately 42° 07′ West Longitude and 11° 08′ South Latitude.

According to local history (Duarte 1978b), this region was first penetrated by Portuguese mineral prospectors in the late 16th century. The first *fazenda,* part of a large land grant, was established at Santo Eusebio about 15 km north of the present town center of Central in 1825. In time the large land grants were broken up into much smaller parcels. European settlement in the 19th century, however, was focussed along the relatively well watered northeastern skirts of a high quartzite ridge about 15 km to the southwest, the Serra Azul (map, Figure 1-1). The town now known as Central grew up around an isolated large waterhole which was discovered out in the forest in 1885. Most of the region of Central was not settled until the 1920s. Even now, the area projects a frontier atmosphere. Until 1928, when it became a new *municipio* separated from the *municipio* of Xique-Xique, the town center of Central was known as Roça de Dentro. In 1978, the population of the town center was put at approximately 4000; and the rural population of the *municipio,* which is 476 km^2 in area, was approximately 16,000 (Duarte 1978a). The present population is supported by commercial and subsistence farming, cattle ranching, and trade.

The bedrock of the Central area is very ancient. Prominent on the horizon to the southwest is a high northwest-trending quartzite ridge, the Serra Azul, an eastern fold of the massive Chapada Diamantina, which extends south into Minas Gerais. The Chapada Diamantina is Middle Proterozoic, with an estimated age of 1.4–1.2 billion years (Inda et al. 1984). It is composed of ancient coastal sands, metamorphized into consolidated sandstone or quartzite beds, with some argillite or conglomerate deposits. The beds are folded and uplifted. The Serra Azul reaches a maximum elevation of about 1000 meters a.s.l. Its flanks are dissected by a series of steep-walled canyons with intermittent streams (map, Figure 1-1).

The bedrock to the northeast of the Serra Azul is a very extensive limestone formation which is part of the widely distributed Bambui Group, of Precambrian age, (Inda et al. 1984). This limestone, believed to have been deposited on a stable epicontinental platform, was subject to subsequent deformation and metamorphoses. In most areas it is covered with well-weathered silt.

The town of Central sits on the northwest end of a very broad limestone ridge at an elevation of about 700 meters a.s.l. To the west of the town center the ridge drops gradually to a broad limestone area of very low relief, about 500–450 m in elevation. Appearing about 6 km north of the town center, however, is a large and distinctive limestone outcrop, extending through an area measuring about 16 km east-west by 8 km north-south (map, Figure 1-1). On the Central quadrangle (Folha SC-23-X-11) this area is simply labeled the "Serra da Pedra Calcária." In fact, there is a series of steep-walled, eroded limestone ridges or *serras* trending east-west, with narrow forested valleys or canyons intervening: over a dozen *serras* are distinguished in this area and named separately by the local people. The *serras* rise 25 to 50 m above the surrounding countryside (Figure 1-2a). This area was the major focus of our archaeological research, as the limestone *serras* are riddled with complex cave systems.

The entire limestone area of Central is karstic. On the broad ridges and flats are numerous sinkholes. These sinkholes may be called *tocas* (a generic name for any hole in the rock) or *cacimbas.* Large deep sinkholes hold water during the rainy season; when dug out to enhance their capacity, they are called *tanques.* The larger waterholes were centers of population concentration in the early history of European settlement of the Central area; as, with the exception of the Rio Verde to the west, there are no permanent streams.

The Rio Verde originates deep in the Chapada Diamantina and flows north, in a narrow valley directly west of the Serra Azul, emerging onto the low limestone platform at the north end of the Serra Azul (map, Figure 1-1). It then follows a strongly meandering course through a shallow valley north to the Rio São Francisco. It has low volume and low velocity, especially in the dry season; but it is a permanent stream. Its few tributaries in the Central area are ephemeral, active only in the rainy season. Even the streams draining the east side of the Serra Azul are short and ephemeral; although there is flow well into the dry season, and at the peak of the drought water may be retained well up in the canyons.

Interior Bahia is within the dry belt of northeast Brazil. The dry season is usually about seven months in duration, from April through October; and all too often the drought may last a year or more. The actual amount of rainfall from November through March varies unpredictably: a figure of 488.7 mm annually given by Duarte (1978a) for Central in only a long-term average. As well, the climate is hot. Daytime temperatures may climb above 40° C in the summer, although 25–30° C is usual. In the winter (May through August), the usual daytime temperature is between 20° and 25° C; but the temperature may drop to 13° C at night (Duarte 1978a).

The natural vegetation reflects the hot, dry climate. The vegetation throughout the Central area is *caatinga,* low scrub thorn forest characteristic of the vast semi-arid interior of northeast Brazil (Figure 1-2b). In the long dry season the trees and shrubs drop their leaves, leaving the forest bare and stark in appearance; when the rains come the forest greens quickly. *Caatinga* forest is difficult to penetrate. Many of the trees and shrubs bear thorns, and are draped with entangling vines; and there are many cacti of varying size, and spiny succulents underfoot. Passage is through open fields, roads, and cattle trails. Local people mentioned remote areas in which, because cattle could not enter over rocks to establish trails, the forest is closed to human passage.

No botanist or zoologist has done a detailed study of the flora and fauna of the Central area, but some particular plants and animals readily identifiable by local people may be mentioned (Duarte 1978a). Local species of trees and shrubs (scientific names from IBGE 1980 and Ferri 1980) include (among many) *angico* (*Piptadenia* sp.), *aroeira* (*Astronium urundeuva*), *imburana* (*Bursera leptophloeos*), *juazeiro* (*Zizyphus joazeiro*), *pau ferro* (*Caesalpina ferrea*), *jurema* (*Mimosa hostilis*), *pau d'arco* (*Tecoma* sp.), *caatinga de porco* (*Caesalpinia microphylia*), and *gameleira* (*Ficus doliaria*). Prominent cacti are the tall, tree-like *mandacaru* (*Cereus jamacaru*) and *faxeiro* (*Cereus squamosus*), the

Figure 1-2. Regional features of the Central area: **A)** a limestone *serra;* **B)** *caatinga* forest.

medium-sized *xique-xique* (*Pilocereus gounellei*), and the small barrel-shaped *cabeça de frado* (*Melocactus bahiensis*). The modern native fauna includes deer (*Mazama* sp.), peccary (*Tayassu* sp.), jaguar (*Leo onca*), small felids, armadillo, marmosets, various small rodents and marsupials, and lizards and snakes. There is quite a variety of birds, including some fairly large species. The larger native animals and birds are rarely encountered now.

Soils on the limestone platform in the Central area may be quite fertile, especially the *terra avermelha* or red soil, prized by farmers. Beans and maize are widely cultivated in the area for subsistence and commercial production, and there is also some cultivation of manioc (Duarte 1978a). Sisal and castor bean (mamona—*Ricinus communis*) are now important commercial crops.

It is most unfortunate that a systematic ethnoecological study was not carried out in the Central area as part of the Projeto Central. A two-day preliminary survey by the American anthropologist Darrell Posey in 1984 indicated that a vast amount of ecological information could be gained from the local population of the area, but Beltrão was unable to come up with the resources necessary for an in-depth, long-term scientific study. Posey's brief survey, however, and our own experiences with local people, make it clear that an abundance of valuable natural resources was available to the aboriginal people of the Central region.

The *caatinga* forest features a variety of plant species which yield edible or useful products: wood, fibres, bark, fruits, nuts, roots, pith. Our local guides frequently related how useful certain plants of the *caatinga* were for food, medicine, and cordage, as well as providing emergency water sources. Posey (pers. comm.) found that even cacti provided not only fruit in season but edible pulp. As our guide Valdemar once commented, no one who knows the forest need suffer hunger. Game was previously abundant in the forest. Indeed, a local historian (Duarte 1978b) commented that in the years of the earliest settlement, in the early part of this century, the population depended primarily upon hunting. Deer and peccary were the largest game, now rare; but many local people still hunt regularly for armadillo, small rodents and marsupials, and a variety of birds.

Another valuable resource of the area was molluscs. Giant edible terrestrial gastropods, *Megalobulimus* sp. and *Strophocheilus* sp., are common in the limestone area. The snails are 10–20 cm long. André Prous, archaeologist at the Universidade Federal de Minas Gerais, has studied the use of these snails (Prous 1980). A nutritionist reported to him that the snails are high in protein, although they contain some toxic substances which will build up in one's body if only snails are consumed for food. The easiest way to procure the snail is to place the shell near a fire for a few minutes, and the snail will emerge. This food resource is seasonal, as the gastropods hibernate deep in crevices or under the ground during the dry season. They appear in abundance during the wet season; although with first emergence the flesh is too stringy to chew, and one must wait until they fatten. Shells of large terrestrial gastropods are common in prehistoric occupation sites in the Central area.

Available year-round in the Rio Verde, a permanent stream, was the bivalve *Diplodon delodontus*, which reaches a diameter of 5 cm. Shells of these fresh water mussels are abundant in archaeological sites in the Rio Verde area, and a few were found on prehistoric occupation sites over 30 km from the river.

In this semi-arid region of periodic severe drought, reliable water sources are essential. The permanent waterholes scattered in the limestone area are well known to local people now and were no doubt known and exploited by occupants of the region in prehistoric times. Good natural shelters were provided by numerous caverns in the limestone *serras* of the area north of Central, and by rock overhangs in the canyons of the Serra Azul. The region also provided lithic raw materials to aboriginal peoples. Vein quartz, chert, and flakeable limestone were available in the limestone area, and quartzite in the Serra Azul and the gravels of the Rio Verde. All of these materials were found on prehistoric occupation sites.

THE ARCHAEOLOGICAL SITUATION

The region of Central, then, offered a variety of valuable resources to prehistoric inhabitants. A comprehensive scientific archaeological research program would have gathered detailed evidence for ecology and economy, and for settlement systems as well as technology at various periods in the history of cultural development in the region. Our archaeological research, however, was not complete. It must be stressed that our particular research was focussed upon the evidence for the initial human occupation. Certainly the attempt was made to determine the evolution of cultural traditions in the region by analysis of stratified sites; but a complete regional reconnaissance incorporating all open occupation sites was not attempted, so that an analysis of settlement systems is not possible; and as will be seen, faunal analyses failed to be completed, so that interpretations of economic pursuits at the various excavated sites are not formalized.

As described above, two-thirds of the region of Central sits on a limestone karstic platform; the remainder, in the southwest, is older folded quartzite, forming the high ridge of the Serra Azul. Canyons on the northeast slope of the Serra Azul feature spectacular rock art, indicating much aboriginal interest in the area; but rockshelters in the quartzite were shallow, narrow, and very close to the intermittent streams, with little earth fill preserved. The major focus of archaeological excavations in the Central region, then, was the limestone caves concentrated in the 16-by-8-km area of low east-west trending limestone ridges or *serras* beginning about 6 km north of the town center of Central (map, Figure 1-1). Outside of this area, limestone caves worthy of excavation were very rare: Toca do Cosmos and Toca da Gameleira were the only two good limestone-cave sites discovered in the Rio Verde area to the northwest of the limestone *serra*.

A foot survey of the series of limestone *serras* north of the town center of Central was rendered difficult by the dense *caatinga* forest covering the land intervening between the *serras*. Even during the dry season, when the trees shed their leaves, low bushes and vines hanging from the trees reduce visibility significantly. The only practical way to carry out a survey under such conditions was to rely on local guides who had an intimate knowledge of the location of all the caves in the area they were familiar with. The most frustrating problem on the reconnaissance was the inadequacy of the only available topographic map, the Central quadrangle (Folha SC-23-X-11), which is 1:100,000 in scale, and does not distinguish the separate limestone *serras* in the region. It proved to be impossible to place accurately most of the caves located on the survey on the topographic map. A large-scale map would have to be constructed from low aerial photos of the limestone region. Therefore, the only sure way to relocate the sites described in this report is by consultation with our local guides: Dilton Pires de Souza, a resident of the town center of Central; and Valdemar Fausto de Silva, a resident of the settlement of Pau d'Arco.

As mentioned above, locally the term *toca* is used to refer to any hole in the rock; and of particular importance to the local people are those *tocas,* sinkholes or caverns, which hold water. Most such places are uninhabitable, but an interest in particular ones by aboriginal people may be demonstrated by the presence of a few pictographs placed at the entrance or mouth of the cavern or waterhole. Caverns in the limestone *serras* varied in size; but many were very large, extensive, and complex cave systems. Large well-lighted chambers would have been habitable; but all too commonly the chambers were situated low, often below the level of the surrounding ground; and thus subject to flooding, with periodic severe disturbance of cave deposits. Because of the indications of severe seasonal flooding and disturbance, many a good-sized cave had to be considered not worthy of excavation. In fact, the vast majority of the caverns seen, even those no doubt occupied in prehistoric times, with pictographs on the walls and/or artifacts on the surface, presented obvious problems in stratigraphic interpretation because of periodic flooding.

The best archaeological sites are high and dry rockshelters or *abrigos,* but very few sites of this type were seen on the reconnaissance. Although we outlined the criteria for the most desirable sites to our local guides, it was almost two weeks in the initial 1983 survey before we were shown any rockshelters, because simple rockshelters or *abrigos* are now of no importance to the local people. Only one of these rockshelters, the Abrigo do Pilão, had a local name.

Open sites were rarely identified on the survey of the limestone *serra* region north of Central. A few places seen in the inter-*serra* canyons were likely quarry locations, with extensive outcrops of fractured vein quartz fragments which were probably exploited by the aboriginal people. As will be seen, very few stone artifacts in the area are shaped, and there are no stone points or indeed any bifacial tools, so familiar and useful to North American archaeologists in identifying open sites. Although we found occasional lithic artifacts and/or ceramics in fields, trails or roadways, we did not identify any definite open settlement site in the Central area.

The valley of the Rio Verde west and northwest of Central, however, is much more productive of open sites. Indeed, on the edge of the low limestone platform enclosing Toca do Cosmos and Toca da Gameleira, about 100 m from Toca do Cosmos, is a thin but extensive spread of crushed riverine mussel shell with lithic artifacts scattered throughout; likely marking an open settlement. On one afternoon's hike along the east bank of the Rio Verde we discovered extensive open sites marked by dense scatters of stone flakes, lithic artifacts, potsherds, and shell fragments in the cultivated fields; suggesting sizable villages. A systematic intensive survey of the Rio Verde valley would no doubt prove very productive.

Certainly a deficiency of the Projeto Central which must be acknowledged is the lack of a thorough, systematic site survey intended to recover data on settlement systems in correlation with all ecological microzones. Another serious problem in terms of making a formal interpretation of prehistoric economic patterns was the incomplete analysis of the mammalian remains recovered from the six sites we excavated. The Setor da Arqueologia of the Museu Nacional had no facilities at all for faunal analysis; so we engaged a student in the Setor da Zoologia, Martha Locks, to make species identification of the bones of modern fauna we recovered. Unfortunately her work was delayed until after we had left Rio de Janeiro, and she failed to follow our instructions to maintain the segregation of bone lots by excavation unit and stratigraphic level. As a result, all that she produced were simple lists of the species represented at a given site; and we have no record of differences in frequency of species in different places and at different times. Worst of all, our major collection of modern mammalian remains, from the Abrigo do Pilão, has been misplaced in the museum collections; so it has not been examined at all, and we have only our field notes to indicate the larger and most obvious animals represented. We do have the proper identification of extinct species, by Fausto Luiz de Souza Cunha of the Museu Nacional and Diogenes de Almeida Campos of the Departamento Nacional da Produção Mineral; and the identification of molluscs by the Setor da Malacologia of the Museu Nacional.

It also proved very difficult to have mechanical and chemical analyses of sediment samples done in Brazil. A stratigraphic column of sediment samples was collected at the Abrigo da Lesma and given to a geology student for analyses; but no report was ever sent to us. A stratigraphic column of sediment samples from Toca de Manoel Latão was processed in Edmonton by Keary Walde, so there is some record of the mechanical and chemical properties of common cave deposits provided in this site report.

At least we ourselves could deal with the artifact analyses, which were carried out in Central or in our apartment in Rio de Janeiro. The problem here was to produce a meaningful analysis of essentially shapeless tools and utensils. We took the approach of description of morphology, process of manufacture, and evidence of use in very fine detail.

Traditionally, artifact classification has been based

on form. Careful description of the shape of an artifact is very useful if there are many artifacts which were intentionally produced to conform to a preconceived shape (i.e., the mental template of the artisan). In most parts of the Americas, including some parts of Brazil, diagnostic artifacts, including bifacially flaked stone projectile points and the early unifacially retouched *lesmas* or *limaces,* are easily classifiable by outline and proportion. Descriptions of such formal classes are valuable to the archaeologist who is searching for possible relationships with other sites and other areas.

In many parts of South America formal types are rare or absent in the archaeological inventory. In most cases this fact is probably largely a matter of lack of preservation of the items of material culture that were chosen to be shaped into formal types. If materials such as wood, fibre, hide, and feathers were fashioned into formal preconceived shapes while stone was not, the recoverable material culture may not include any formal types.

The lack of formal types and diagnostic artifacts for comparative purposes is seen by most archaeologists as a handicap to proper comparative research. If a choice is available, only sites that contain diagnostic artifact types are selected for excavation; and an excavation may be abandoned if diagnostic artifacts are not recovered from deeper levels of a site, especially if the conditions of excavation are difficult. The preselection of sites for presence of diagnostic artifacts, and the premature abandonment of sites when very few artifacts (and none diagnostic) are being recovered, are important reasons why more archaeological sites dating to the Pleistocene have not been reported in the Americas.

The paucity of formal artifact types and diagnostic artifacts recoverable from the archaeological sites in the Central region should not be seen as a handicap. Although the primary objective of the Projeto Central was to find evidence for Early Man, the cultural remains from all later deposits were also studied carefully because it is essential to understand how people at all times adapted themselves to this area. Knowledge of the economic and technological adaptation of more recent populations will assist in the interpretation of how their predecessors adapted themselves to the local environment during the Pleistocene.

Clues for proper interpretation will come from many sources, the most important of which will be from the contextual associations (both artifactual and sedimentary), and from the artifact analyses. The primary objective of all analyses and especially of the artifact analyses should be to reveal as many clues as possible about the behavior of the prehistoric inhabitants of the area. Therefore, instead of a formal artifact typology, which would yield very little insight into what the people were actually doing, the artifact descriptions presented in our site reports emphasize evidence of how the artifact was made and how it was used. Shape will be mentioned as part of the procedure of describing the process of manufacture in such a way that the reader can get a feeling for what the fabricator was doing as he proceeded with minimum effort to obtain an effective tool or utensil for the purpose in mind. Culturally patterned sequences of individual decisions are involved in selection of raw material, reducing a block of material to a workable size and form, determining how best to convert the piece into a useful object, using and reusing a tool by careful selection of effective edges and surfaces, and finally discarding an artifact after it has served its usefulness. These behavior patterns are characteristic features of the way of life of the prehistoric people, and an artifact description emphasizing the human behavior involved in production and use of the artifact may help to gain a better understanding of the prehistoric society and its relationship to the environment of the Central region.

In this report, then, individual artifacts are described in detail. Unfortunately, illustrations are rather limited. The Setor da Arqueologia of the Museu Nacional had no facilities for artifact photography, so it was carried out in our apartment, using natural light; and some distinctive artifacts, it turns out, were overlooked or inadequately photographed. Drawings would have been ideal, especially of unphotogenic quartz artifacts; but time and skill were lacking. We hope that the artifacts illustrated at least provide a sample of the material recovered from archaeological sites in interior Bahia.

Chapter 2
Toca dos Buzios

INTRODUCTION

Location and Description of the Site

Toca dos Buzios is part of a large multi-chambered cavern about 12 km north of the town center of Central; and it is situated on the north side of the Serra Pé do Morro, a large high limestone outcrop on the Fazenda Pé do Morro, to the south of the main fazenda buildings. The cavern is approached from the north or northeast by climbing over a low eroded part of the *serra*. The mouth of the cavern faces out to the northwest, into a narrow rock-strewn defile (Figure 2-1a). There is very heavy rock fall at the mouth of the cavern, and a high mound of large boulders has accumulated at the mouth.

The cavern has two principal chambers, separated by a sloping ridge of rock. The lower chamber (now known as Toca da Esperança) is the larger, continuing deep into the *serra*, with a tributary chamber running south into darkness. The lower chamber has an outward-sloping flowstone floor, broken in many places, revealing an underlying silt deposit. The surface of the flowstone floor of the lower chamber was strewn with rock rubble, and there was little evidence of prehistoric occupation. Toca dos Buzios, the higher chamber to the north, is smaller, measuring approximately 10 x 8 m, with the ceiling reaching a maximum height of about 6 m at the mouth (map, Figure 2-2). The basin-like floor of this northern chamber contained earth and rubble fill in the northern third. The fill in the northern sector was excavated by us at brief intervals in July 1983, and in early May 1984.

The walls of the northern chamber feature a number of pictographs in white, red, black, and (rarely) yellow paint (Figure 2-1b). The principal design elements are circles of various forms, and clusters or lines of dots. There are also a few anthropomorphs and zoomorphs. A study of the pictographs was to be done by other researchers on the Projeto Central.

The Excavations

The relative accessibility of the site and the abundant evidence of prehistoric occupation in Toca dos Buzios led Maria Beltrão and Tania Andrade Lima to place two test pits about 2 x 1.5 m in extent in the central part of the chamber in June 1983. The discovery of a deposit of yellow silt sealed beneath a flowstone floor under the upper ashy midden containing many gastropod shells (locally called *buzios)* suggested a great antiquity for the lower deposits. In July 1983 we saw that much of the yellow silt remained, so the excavations were pursued.

Our excavations in July 1983 expanded the area of the earlier test pits (map, Figure 2-2). Datum was established on the surface of the floor fill at the southeast corner of excavation unit C3 at a point 210 cm directly below a distinctive circular barred white pictograph; and a grid system of four units, each measuring 2 x 1.5 m, was imposed. Excavation was carried out using hand picks, trowels, and dustpans. Excavated earth was loaded into buckets and the material examined on a 4-mm screen (a 1-mm screen was tried briefly but failed to increase sufficiently the recovery of very small bones or floral material to warrant the extra time). All bones, and samples of shell, were collected. At the completion of work at the site in July 1983 the excavation was left open. No profiles were drawn in July, due to collapse of the walls of the excavation.

When bone fragments collected from the yellow silt zone were cleaned by mechanically removing a thin layer of calcium carbonate, and examined in the labora-

Figure 2-1. A) view of mouth of Toca dos Buzios, from northwest; **B)** pictographs on north wall/ceiling of Toca dos Buzios.

tory in Rio de Janeiro, a number of fragments revealed marks of scraping, cutting, or wear polish. These modified bones were associated in the yellow silt zone with bones or teeth which could be identified as horse, giant peccary, and a large cervid. As a Pleistocene age was indicated for the modified bones, it was decided to pursue further excavations in Toca dos Buzios in hopes of recovering more possible evidence of man, and bones of extinct fauna.

In early May 1984, when we returned to the Central area for more field work, two days were spent at Toca dos Buzios, excavating the yellow silt zone in the area at the front of the cavern, just below the inner edge of the high lip mound of large boulders. The overlying rock rubble was removed by pick and shovel, and excavation proceeded into the yellow silt zone using trowel and hand pick. All material was screened, and all quartz and bone fragments collected. The yellow silt was cleared from the bedrock channel in Units B5 and C5; and a good profile of the stratigraphy of the fill in the northern chamber of the cavern was exposed on the south face of Unit B5 (Figure 2-3). Again the excavated area was left open.

STRATIGRAPHY

Field Description of the Sediments

Two major stratigraphic units were encountered in Toca dos Buzios: an upper unconsolidated zone of ash, shell, and rubble; and a lower zone of compact coarse yellow silt (profile, Figure 2-3). Also a factor in the stratigraphy towards the back of the chamber was a 10–15 cm thick layer of flowstone/breccia which in this area underlay the upper zone of ash, shell, and rubble; and unconformably overlay the lower zone of yellow silt.

Ash, Shell, and Rubble Zone

The upper zone, composed of ash, shell, and limestone rubble, varied in thickness from about 10 cm at the rear of the chamber, over the flowstone/breccia floor, to about 50 cm at the front of the chamber, where this zone directly overlay the basal zone of yellow silt. It consisted of abundant angular limestone fragments in a matrix of fine grey silt and ash. About 10 cm below surface the rubble became very loose, with many voids around large rocks. Rocks ranged in size up to 40 cm or more, and lay at odd angles. The rocks became larger on the average with depth. A few very large rocks, over 50 cm in size, occurred in the south sector of the excavated area. Near the front of the chamber, in the lower 10 cm of this zone, many of the flowstone fragments featured one smooth surface, while the opposite surface was rough with calcium carbonate precipitate ("popcorn"), apparently derived from broken flowstone/breccia which had collapsed.

Gastropod shells and fragments of gastropod shells were very abundant in the ash, shell, and rubble zone. As identified by the Setor da Malacologia of the Museu Nacional, three principal genera were represented: the large *Megalobulimus* sp., a medium-sized gastropod (*Protoglyptus durus*), and a small species (*Cyclodontina* sp.). All these snails are edible, and the shells are common on archaeological sites in the Central region. Partially intact *Megalobulimus* shells commonly featured a

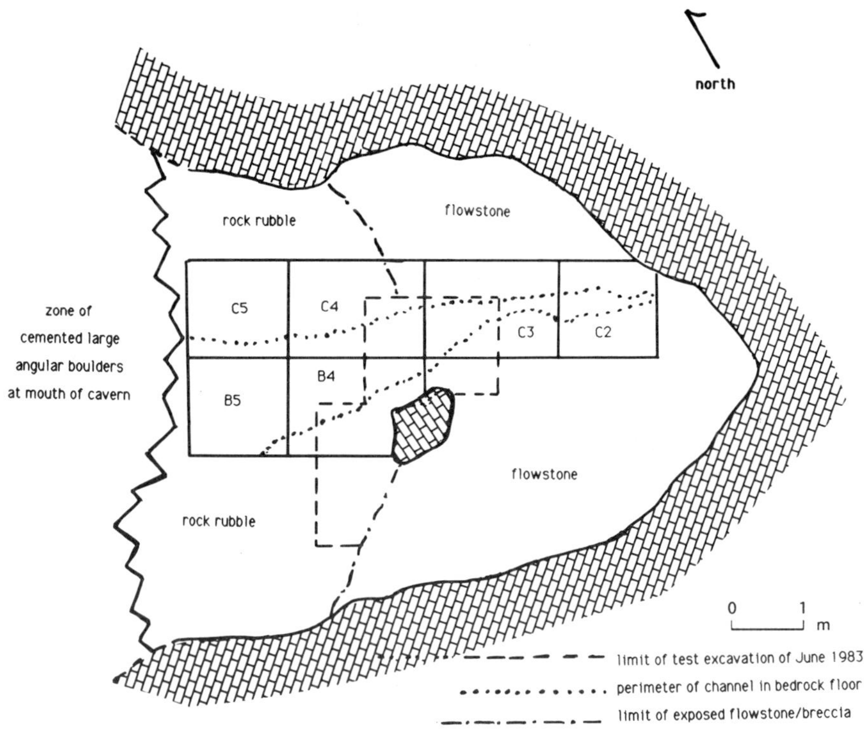

Figure 2-2. Plan of Toca dos Buzios.

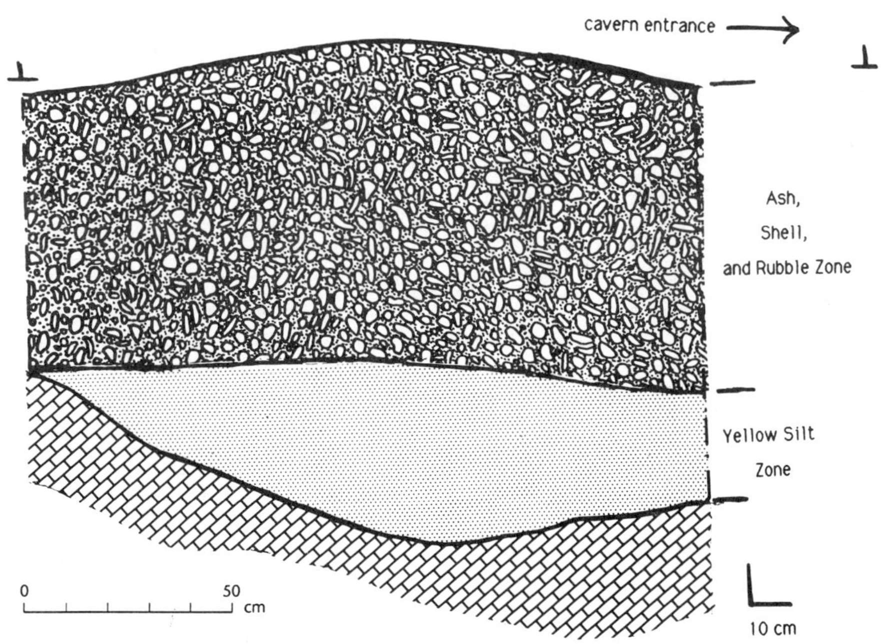

Figure 2-3. Profile of south face of Unit B5, Toca dos Buzios.

broken apex, or a hole in the side near the lip. Shells of smaller species were often smashed.

Bones of small mammals and birds also commonly occurred in this zone. Mammalian species identified by Martha Locks of the Museu Nacional include *Euphractus sexcinctus* (armadillo) and *Kerodon rupestris* (*mocó*, a rat-sized rodent that frequents caves). The articular ends of small bones were often burned, suggesting that the animals were a food resource for the prehistoric occupants of the cavern.

Wood ash was abundant in the ash, shell, and rubble zone; and scattered charcoal fragments also occurred.

With the shell and bone, it is obvious that human occupation was intensive during the period of accumulation of the limestone rubble in this upper sedimentary zone. However, only five artifacts were recovered from the ash, shell, and rubble zone: a quartz crystal flake, a chert flake-blade, a large limestone flake, a bone point, and a shell bead.

Flowstone/Breccia Zone

In the rear part of the cavern, in Unit C2 and the eastern half of Unit C3, a flowstone floor directly underlay the ash, shell, and rubble zone. The "flowstone" is not travertine but actually a cemented breccia, composed of angular limestone fragments cemented in a matrix of yellowish-white silt and calcium carbonate (Figures 2-4a, 2-4b).

The average thickness of the flowstone/breccia was 10–15 cm, and it was broken up with a hand pick and removed in Units C2 and C3. It was found to be directly underlain by a 10-cm-thick zone of "popcorn," a precipitate of calcium carbonate. In most areas this "popcorn" zone directly overlay the bedrock floor of the cavern. However, it was discovered that a narrow channel cut into the bedrock was filled with coarse yellow silt. In Unit C2 there was a void or gap about 25 cm in height between the upper surface of the yellow silt and the under surface of the flowstone/breccia: "popcorn" flanked this void on either side, but directly above the void the under surface of the flowstone/breccia was free of "popcorn." In two places there was an open gap or hole in the flowstone/breccia which allowed debris to fall onto the surface of the yellow silt underlying; and close to the rear wall of the chamber, a hole about 10 cm in diameter opened into a drip pool with small rounded and polished limestone pebbles and fragments of bone of small mammals, resting on the surface of the yellow silt. When the site was visited in October 1983 after a rainfall, it was observed that much water had come through the rear ceiling of the cavern and passed through this hole and followed along the route of the bedrock channel which had been filled with yellow silt.

Figure 2-4. A) interior of Toca dos Buzios in 1984; **B)** section of flowstone/breccia in Toca dos Buzios.

Yellow Silt Zone

The coarse yellow silt deposit was restricted to a water-eroded channel in the bedrock floor of Toca dos Buzios. This channel extended from a point about 80 cm west of the rear wall of the cave through Units C2, C3, C4, C5, B4, and B5; and continued west-southwestward under the high mound of heavy cemented rock debris at the mouth of the chamber (Figure 2-5a). At the rear the channel is very narrow and deep, but it broadens and shallows in the area near the mouth of the cavern (map, Figure 2-2). The floor of the bedrock channel is irregular in contour, with longitudinal ridges of limestone (Figure 2-5a). The yellow silt deposit enclosed in the bedrock channel varied in thickness from a maximum of 50 cm in the narrow deep part of the channel at the rear, where it underlay the flowstone/breccia floor, to a minimum of 15 cm in the shallow part of the channel at the front of the cavern, where the yellow silt lay directly underneath the ash, shell, and rubble zone (Figure 2-5b).

Within the bedrock channel the yellow silt zone varied in texture and content. At the rearward end of the channel, in Units C2 and C3, the yellow silt was porous in texture although compact; and in restricted areas in Units C3, C5, and B5 on the side of the bedrock channel, the yellow silt was locally very cemented. Angular rock fragments within the yellow silt zone were most numerous within the channel at the rear of the cavern and also at the front, in Units B5 and C5. The fragments ranged in size up to 15 cm. Many rock fragments from the yellow silt zone featured well-smoothed surfaces and rounded edges, suggesting in situ chemical weathering rather than rolling.

Permineralized fragments of bones of large mammals, broken naturally by desiccation, were recovered in the yellow silt zone in a restricted area toward the front of the cavern, in Units C4, B4, C5, and B5. The bones were highly fragmented; but teeth or bones of two sizes of horse, a giant peccary, and a large cervid could be recognized by the paleontologist Fausto da Souza

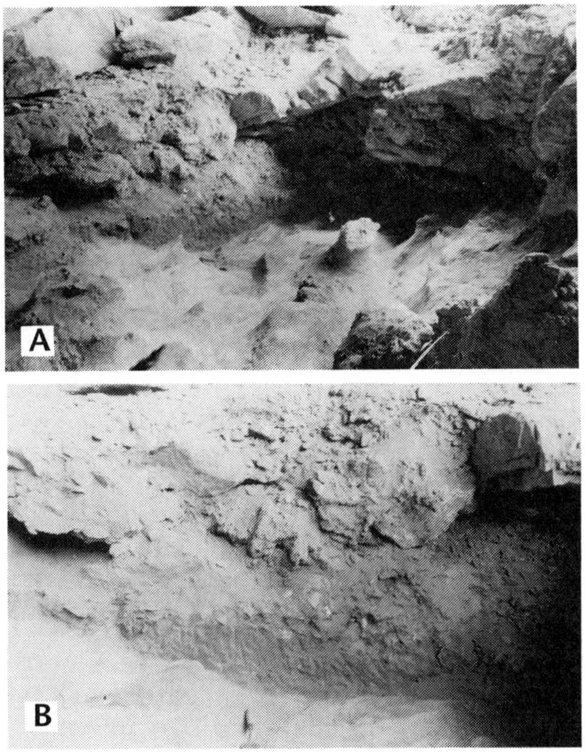

Figure 2-5. A) floor of bedrock channel extending under cemented rock fall near mouth of Toca dos Buzios; **B)** Yellow Silt zone in bedrock channel, underlying Ash, Silt, and Rubble Zone near mouth of Toca dos Buzios.

Cunha of the Museu Nacional. The collection from the yellow silt zone near the front of the cavern also included a well-preserved parrot beak, but other bird bones were not recognized. Elsewhere in the cavern only bones of unidentified small mammals occurred in the yellow silt zone. In some cases bone fragments were cemented to rock fragments. Thirty-one of the fragments of bone of large mammals plus two teeth show evidence of modification. Also found in the yellow silt zone, in Units B5 and C5 at the front of the cavern, were nine small fragments of quartz, an exotic stone in the Toca dos Buzios area. Seven of these fragments were flaked or utilized by man.

ARTIFACTS

Artifacts from the Ash, Shell, and Rubble Zone

Stone Artifacts

The tip of a clear quartz crystal (BA-CE-1/1), found in the 20–30 cm level in the ashy midden, had been decapitated by holding one crystal facet on an anvil and striking the opposing edge near the crystal apex. The sharp bipolar blow split the cone, causing three flakes to peel off in addition to the head of the crystal. One sharp edge is duller than the other, suggesting possible use; however, the most useful pieces were evidently transported elsewhere. This quartz artifact measures 53 x 41 x 9 mm.

A thick wedge-shaped limestone flake (BA-CE-1/3), measuring 75 x 60 x 29 mm, was found in the 40–50 cm level of the ashy midden. Lines of force point to a positive bulb on the ventral surface. Additional lines of force lead to two separate points of impact on the same platform, creating a broad negative bulb on the dorsal face. The thin excurvate distal edge formed by the intersection of the two flake surfaces appears to be use-nibbled and worn.

A completely patinated cream-colored chert flake-blade (BA-CE-1/2), measuring 53 x 41 x 19 mm, and a thermally spalled piece of grey chert (BA-CE-1/35), measuring 24 x 11 x 4 mm, were recovered in the screen from the top of the yellow silt deposit. Evidently they came from the ashy midden zone, to judge from the adhering matrix and lack of yellow stain. Possibly the pieces lay on the surface of the yellow silt zone for a long time, thus accounting for the heavy patination of the flake-blade; and they were later covered by ashy midden deposit. After recovery, the edges of the flake-blade began to exfoliate in the plastic sack; so it could not be washed. Ripple marks and lines of force on the ventral surface point to the bulbar end, which is missing. The distal end terminates in a hinge fracture. The dorsal face has a central ridge. Some use-nibbling is present on one edge. One negative flake scar on the grey chert piece is visible on a 90° edge, which also appears to be use-crushed.

The surface of the yellow silt zone yielded three possible limestone artifacts. One (BA-CE-1/21), measuring 45 x 22 x 10 mm, is simply a flake with a positive bulb that hinged off. No evidence of use is discernible. Two subangular fragments of limestone rubble found near a concentration of charcoal reported by Beltrão and Lima on the surface of the yellow silt zone appear to show some evidence of use. One, a rhomboidal fragment (BA-CE-1/20) measuring 89 x 33 x 25 mm, may have been flaked by use as a chopper, forming a bi-bevelled bit on one end. The other, an irregular chunk of limestone (BA-CE-1/20) measuring 112 x 67 x 41 mm, with a red-stained carbonate coating, is differentially polished in the central section of one face and part of the adjacent excurvate edge. The polish may have been caused by use, perhaps as an anvil or chopper. Many other fragments of limestone rubble were examined without finding any evidence of flaking or use.

Bone Artifacts

A medium-sized mammal-bone splinter bipoint (BA-

CE-1/4) with one end broken off came from a depth of 50 cm, near the base of the ash, shell, and rubble zone, under a very large rock. It measures 74 x 19 x 14 mm. The naturally pointed end was minimally shaped by scraping to a symmetrical point. The edges of the point and another section near the base end were polished by use.

A short fragment of a medium-sized mammal bone (BA-CE-1/22) with spirally fractured edges has a negative bulb scar showing a large point of impact from the external surface. The specimen, which measures 43 x 17 x 4 mm, was noticed in a level bag for the upper yellow silt zone; but as it has not been permineralized as are all other bones from the yellow silt zone, it probably came from the surface of the yellow silt.

Shell Artifacts

Two fragments of utilized freshwater mussel shell were found on the surface in the Toca dos Buzios. The genus is probably *Diplodon*, which occurs in permanent watercourses, the nearest of which (the Rio Verde) is 30 km distant from the site. The most complete specimen (BA-CE-1/7) measures 67 x 55 x 5 mm. The interior appears to have been deliberately perforated by flaking from the center of the external face, resulting in a rough-edged elliptical hole about 30 cm in diameter. The edge of this perforation has a thick coating of calcium carbonate, so it was impossible to detect evidence of use. There was no obvious evidence of use on the outer rim of the valve. The other specimen BA-CE-1/8) measured 72 x 29 x 6 mm. It was a very large valve before breakage. There is faint evidence of use as a scraper on the internal edge. The external face is covered with a thick coating of calcium carbonate, so possible marks of use could not be observed.

One shell bead (BA-CE-1/5) was found in the ash, shell, and rubble zone at a depth of 50 cm. A short section of the twisted coil of a *Megalobulimus* (?) shell near its mouth was evidently ground on three broken edges to form a spiral bead with a natural longitudinal perforation. The specimen measures 23 x 18 x 13 mm. Most grinding marks have been worn away, but some are visible on one end and on the edge.

Ceramics

One large potsherd (BA-CE-1/6), broken in two pieces, was evidently found on the surface in Toca dos Buzios in June 1983. The sherd measured 80 x 75 x 6 mm. It is apparently derived from a large bowl or jar. The exterior (convex) surface is coated with a thick white deposit, probably calcium carbonate. The interior is smooth, with probably a thin slip, pale pinkish brown in color. The sherd has heavy coarse temper, with rare quartz fragments but mainly fragments of a dark mineral, up to 1 mm in diameter. Another large potsherd (BA-CE-1/55) was found on the surface of the lower chamber of the cavern in May 1984. This sherd measured 58 x 41 x 8 mm. The exterior surface is brown in color, and brushed; the interior is grey. Temper could not be discerned.

Artifacts from the Yellow Silt Zone

Stone Artifacts

Nine subangular-to-subrounded chunks of vein quartz were recovered from the yellow silt zone in Units B5 and C5 at the front of the cavern. Seven of these show evidence of use and were considered to be artifacts. The only other piece of quartz seen in the area of Toca dos Buzios was a flaked chunk of quartz crystal from the overlying ash, shell, and rubble zone, already described above. No other pieces of quartz were encountered in the cavern or anywhere along the trails near the site. All of the recovered quartz chunks had been rolled to some extent by water; and one fragment (BA-CE-1/52) is a piece of rounded quartz pebble exhibiting semilunar scars of partial cones produced only by percussion in a fast-moving stream, which is not present anywhere in the region. Evidently people carried all of the subangular quartz chunks and the more rounded pebbles into the cavern. Therefore the two subrounded chunks that show no evidence of use could be considered as artifacts because they must have been manuports.

The surfaces of all quartz chunks acquired a yellow stain from the yellow silt. This iron stain could not be removed by washing, even in an acid bath. All chips removed by digging tools are therefore clearly evident, so recent unstained flake scars cannot possibly be confused with ancient flaking. Close examination of the quartz artifacts indicates that the bipolar anvil technique was used in some cases, but usually a flake was simply removed from an edge or corner by percussion. Another flaking technique was patterned resharpening of worn edges and projections by removing small retouch flakes from the face adjacent to the original flake scar.

BA-CE-1/24, a quartz chunk measuring 23 x 21 x 17 mm, was unfortunately flaked by a pick; but close inspection revealed ancient flaking, which is visible under high magnification (Figure 2-6a). The piece was anciently split bipolarly on one end by placing a flat face on an anvil and striking the opposite apex, creating a central ridge extending from the point of impact and a hinged flake scar created by rebound from the anvil. The recent flaking by the pick evidently obliterated another old flake scar. A coating of silica possibly derived from cutting of vegetation with high silica content was observed on this piece under high magnification.

Three utilized quartz chunks were apparently asso-

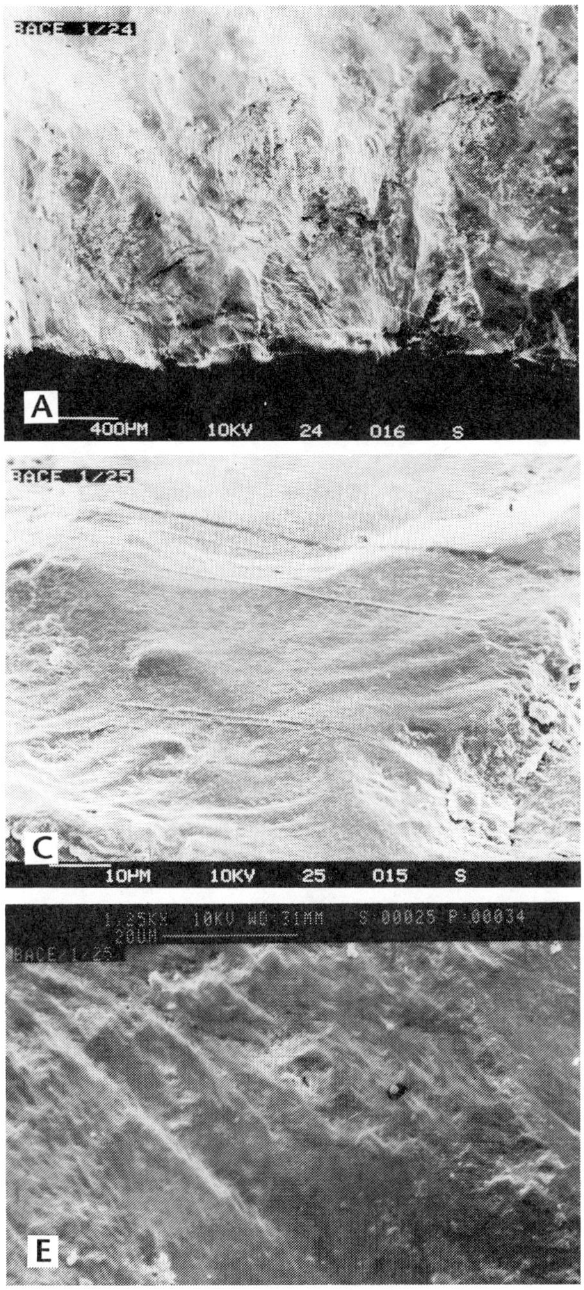

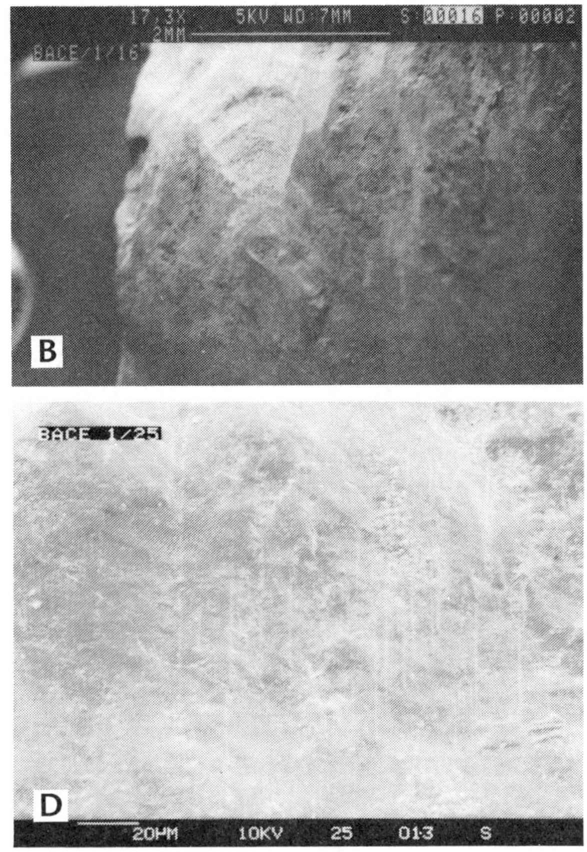

Figure 2-6. A) flaked edge of quartz artifact BA-CE-1/24; **B)** quartz artifact BA-CE-1/26; **C–E)** polish and striations on flaked surface of quartz artifact BA-CE-1/25.

ciated with each other in the north-central part of Unit B5, BA-CE-1/26, which measures 17 x 16 x 16 mm, is a very much used quartz chunk which is flaked on all but one weathered surface (Figure 2-6b). All four other surfaces were percussion-flaked in order to create steep sharp working edges (85–90° edge angles) with useful projections. Two adjacent edges and two corners were later resharpened by removing small flakes from the opposite faces. Although heavy use and repeated resharpening have obliterated most of the original flake scars, apparently two nearly flat faces were originally created by bipolar flaking which split the cone of percussion. Artifact BA-CE-1/25, which measures 21 x 19 x 17 mm, exhibits one negative flake scar removed from a projecting corner to create two 90° angle working edges. Under the scanning electron microscope, a patterned set of parallel scratches is visible extending at right angles from one edge of the flake scar (Figures 2-6, c–e). An adjacent smaller flake scar created a sharp projection. All other edges had been previously rounded by water action. The third associated quartz chunk (BA-CE-1/28), which measures 29 x 21 x 19 mm, also has weathered surfaces, except for a naturally sharp projection at one end created by intersecting crystal faces. This 3-mm-wide edge had apparently been crushed and stained by use, and there is a long narrow negative flake scar extending from the crushed edge. The high parts of the flake scar exhibit polish under the scanning electron microscope (Figure 2-7a), while under 431 power the surface of the flake scar exhibits polish and very fine striations (Figure 2-7b).

Unfortunately artifact BA-CE-1/23, which measures 42 x 32 x 26 mm, was ticked several times with a hand pick while excavating the cemented yellow silt. Nevertheless, three distinctively old (stained) negative flake scars created three separate steep working edges with angles of 90, 90, and 110°. Step-flaking from heavy use is evident on one projection adjacent to one concave flake edge. Under the scanning electron microscope, high magnification of the step-flaked surface revealed a pattern of cross-hatched scratches on a use-polished face (Figure 2-7d). The photograph was taken at the point indicated about 2 mm from the edge (Figure 2-7c). Another part of the heavily used surface shows a similar alteration pattern (Figure 2-7e). Resharpening flakes were removed from the opposite face of the other 90° edge to create two projections, which were also subsequently heavily used.

BA-CE-1/51 is a subangular chunk of quartz measuring 22 x 17 x 14 mm. It has two sharp edges (angles of 60 and 75°) at one end, created by intersecting crystal faces which appear to be use-crushed and stained. The flaked surface does not exhibit striations under the scanning electron microscope.

The last quartz artifact is a rounded quartz pebble fragment (BA-CE-1/52) which broke longitudinally along an old crystal face. It may have been deliberately snapped so as to create a blunt end which appears to be use-crushed. The pointed tip end has several tiny use-flake scars removed from the crystal face. The artifact measures 15 x 9 x 5 mm.

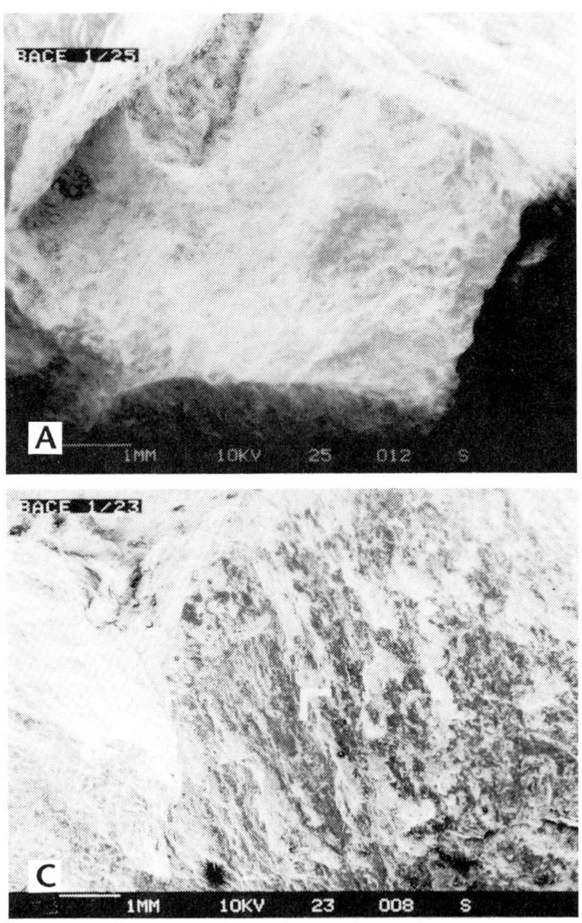

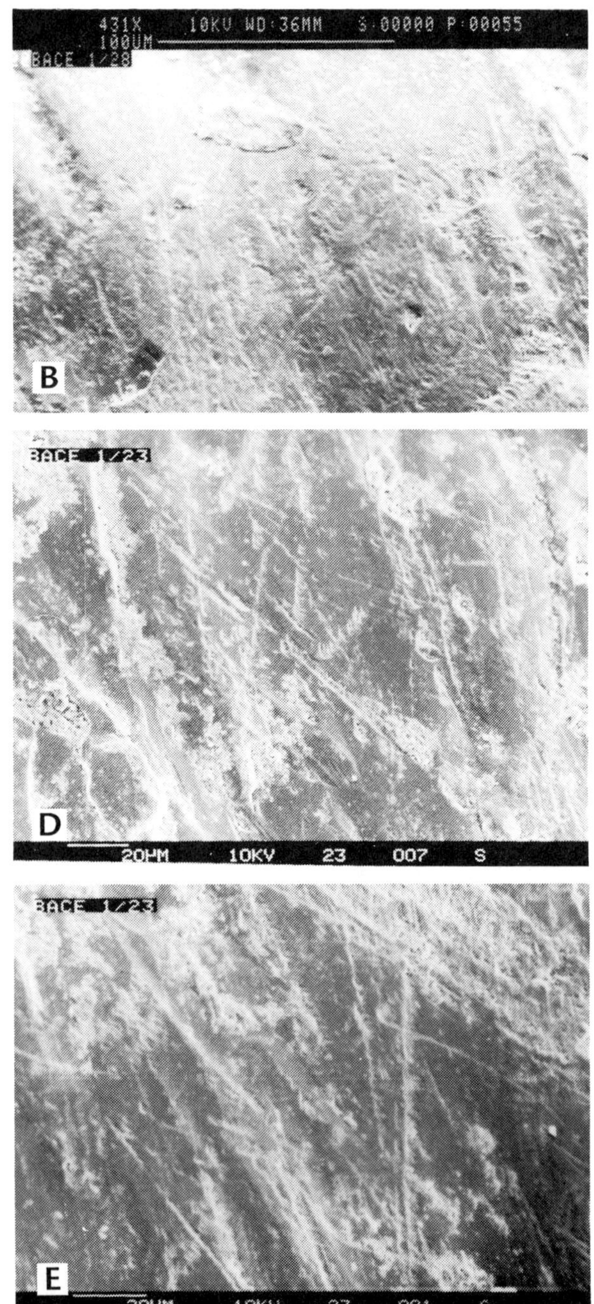

Figure 2-7. A) flaked edges of quartz artifact BA-CE-1/28; **B)** polish and striations on flaked surface of BA-CE-1/28 at 431X SEM magnification; **C)** flaked surface of quartz artifact BA-CE-1/23; **D, E)** polish and striations on flaked surface of BA-CE-1/23.

Modified Bone Fragments

A localized concentration of broken and heavily permineralized bones of large to medium-sized mammals was also found in the lower (western) part of the channel fill of yellow silt. The hundreds of small fragments exhibited angular desiccation breaks but no evidence of green-bone spiral fracture, chewing, or water-rounding. There is a notable absence of whole bones or bones with articular ends (except for a few foot bones). In fact, there are no large fragments: the fragments range in size from 67 x 32 x 19 mm to 12 x 4 x 2 mm, with a mode of 25 x 10 x 3 mm.

Probably the bones recovered in excavation had been fragmented naturally, either by the process of alternate wetting and drying or by the pressure of overlying sediments after the bone had desiccated. Lack of time prevented any effort to try to fit fragments in the collection together, but in a few cases unmodified fragments which fit together were found near each other or cemented together in calcium carbonate or iron concretions. This fact, as well as the lack of rounding of the edges, indicates that bones were not subsequently moved by water after fragmentation.

Clearly, many individual large and medium-sized mammals of several different species are represented in the collection, but most of the bones of these many individual animals are absent. As very little area of the yellow silt was left unexcavated, their absence is not due to sampling error. Despite careful examination no evidence was seen of carnivore activity in the form of teeth marks or chewed areas on any of the bone fragments. The lack of whole bones or large bone fragments suggests that large mammals did not inhabit the cave. The simplest and most reasonable explanation for the unnatural taphonomic pattern at Toca dos Buzios is that people had selected objects with potentially useful edges elsewhere, and transported the bones and teeth along with the quartz to the cavern.

Most of the bone fragments from the yellow silt zone at Toca dos Buzios had been heavily encrusted with iron salts and calcium carbonate deposits, so they had to be cleaned for examination by soaking in water for several days and then removing the coating mechanically by pressing the incrustations with a dull dental pick. The dental pick rarely marked the surface; and as on the quartz pieces, recent marks or flakes clearly differ in appearance from ancient marks. The surfaces of many fragments were pitted by chemical erosion. Fortunately, about a third of the bone fragments had surfaces well enough preserved by the process of permineralization and the subsequent calcium carbonate encrustation so that old marks were visible with the naked eye or with a hand lens.

Examination with a hand lens of the surfaces of about 2000 bone fragments revealed obvious alteration of the external surfaces of 31 fragments and two broken canine teeth. These obviously altered fragments were transported to Edmonton for examination under a scanning electron microscope, and later returned to the Museu Nacional. The other fragments were left in level bags in the Toca dos Buzios collection in the Setor da Arqueologia of the Museu Nacional. Perhaps if all fragments had been examined under the SEM, more alteration patterns would have been discovered. The fact that all alterations are confined to the original exterior surfaces and adjacent edges of the bones supports the hypothesis that they were not produced by some natural means after the fragments were in the depositional matrix in the cave, a situation which would have created marks on all exposed surfaces. However, it is possible that unpatterned marks on some bones had been caused by trampling of whole bones before the fragments were collected for use.

The only artifact (BA-CE-1/53) from the yellow silt zone which may have been intentionally shaped is a broken section of a solid bone rod with a triangular cross-section (dimensions 22 x 5 x 4 mm). The lack of cancellous bone suggests that all three faces may have been worked, although possibly it is a horse splint bone, which lacks cancellous tissue. Although all faces are polished, only the most concave face exhibits evidence of workmanship. A longitudinal incision extends the entire length of the piece, and a roughly parallel incision extends nearly half the length. Two short cuts intersect the main groove at right angles near the end, which appears to have impact flake scars extending down two faces from the end. The opposite end was evidently snapped when the bone was green. This fragment could be the central section of a projectile point. We were not allowed to transport this artifact to Edmonton for microscopic study, and unfortunately a photograph could not be found for publication.

Three kinds of patterned alteration marks are evident on the rest of the altered bones found in the yellow silt deposits. (1) Differential polish and a pattern of short parallel grooves was found on one bone fragment, part of a metapodial. (2) A pattern of short shallow incisions, often appearing as a set of parallel scratches that extend onto the external surface of the bone from a broken edge or side, is most frequent in the collection of artifacts. The short scratches, generally across the grain of the bone, are too shallow to be butchering marks. They appear to have been made by using the broken edge of bone for working some other material. (3) A pattern of broader and more shallow incisions and scrape marks which occur in linear undulating arrangements is also common in the collection. These linear patterns most often occur as parallel sets that generally run with the long axis and natural grain of the bone. Often superimposed on the original set of marks are one or more overlapping sets of incisions at somewhat different angles. The more random longitudinal scrape marks that do not extend onto the adjacent edge might be ascribed to trampling, although we were able to replicate the undulating and overlapping pattern of long parallel incisions by running an unretouched flake or quartz fragment over the surface of a green cow bone. The specimens constituting each group will now be described in detail.

(1) Differential polish combined with a pattern of short parallel grooves was found on one bone (BA-CE-1/13). This is a fragment of the distal end of an unidentified metapodial, measuring 32 x 18 x 11 mm. It exhibits a limited area (12 x 6 mm) of high polish on the lateral corner of the articular surface (Figure 2-8a). An integral part of the polished area is a pattern of short shallow grooves at an oblique angle to the axis of the edge of the bone. Under the scanning electron microscope, only the polished surface exhibits any evidence of alteration. Under low magnification (6.75 power), polished striations are barely visible where marked with a rectangle (Figure 2-8b). At 88.7 power two cross-hatched sets of parallel scratches are clearly visible (Figure 2-8c). At 163 power the same spot exhibits parallel grooves with some scratches at right angles (Figure 2-8d). At 581 power there are several sets of grooves and scratches visible (Figure 2-8e). This bone fragment was clearly utilized to rub something such as a hide.

(2) The second group of modified bone fragments fea-

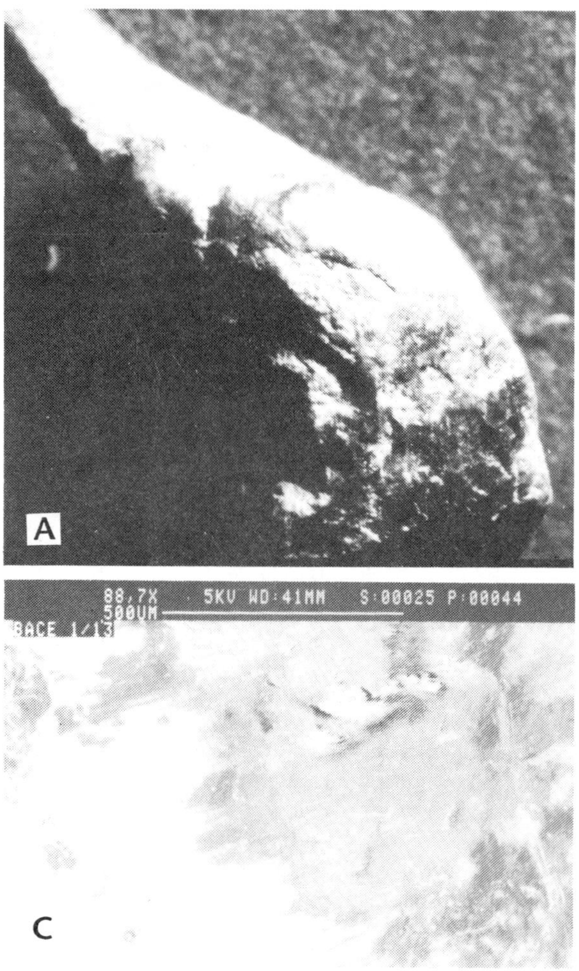

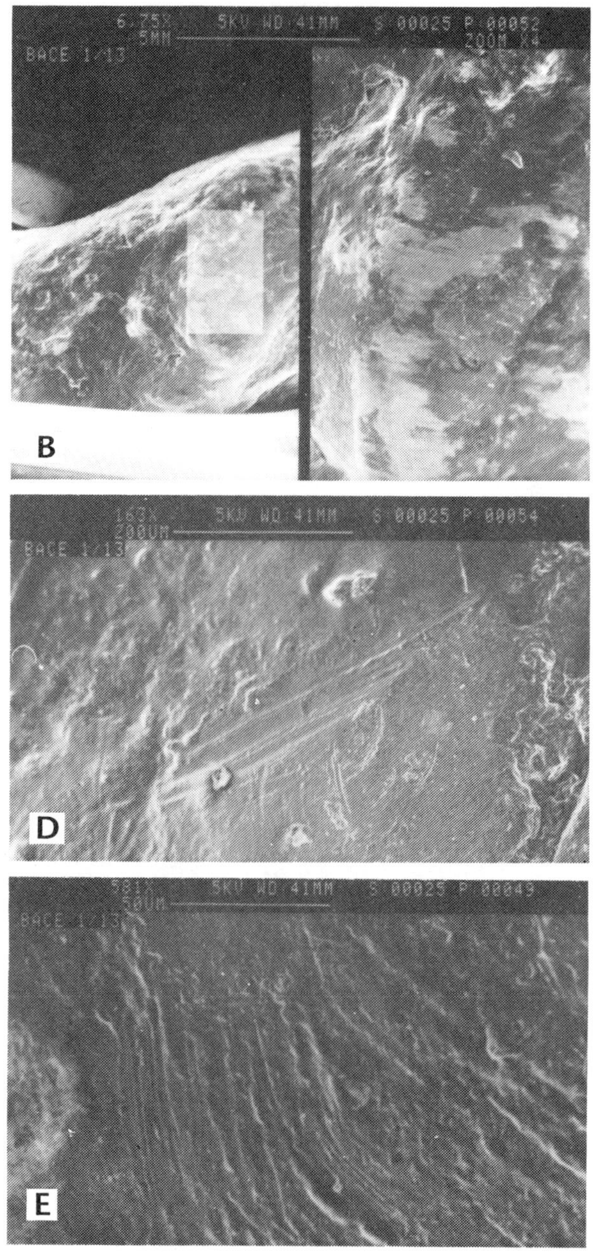

Figure 2-8. A) BA-CE-1/13, metapodial with area of high polish on distal end; **B)** polish and striations on BA-CE-1/13, at 6.75X SEM magnification; **C)** at 88.7X SEM magnification; **D)** at 163X SEM magnification; **E)** at 581X SEM magnification.

tures incisions, scratches, and gouges. A pattern of concentrations of incisions and scratches extending from a straight edge or a pointed end is most similar to the patterned scratches seen on the quartz artifacts, and these bones with rough right-angled edges may have been used in the same way. Parallel incisions extend obliquely from near an edge of BA-CE-1/42, which measures 38 x 16 x 5 mm. The pattern, with a long groove parallel to the edge, is visible at 32.1 power (Figure 2-9a). A similar pattern is seen on BA-CE-1/50, which measures 18 x 8 x 3 mm. The edges and/or ends of five other bone fragments from which sets of scratches and incisions extend are also polished and worn. Two deep parallel incisions and several faint scratches extend at an oblique angle from the polished edge of BA-CE-1/45, which measures 27 x 9 x 6 mm (Figure 2-9b). The pattern is clearly visible under 19.5 power (Figure 2-9c), while an older pattern of striations may be seen at 128 power (Figure 2-9d). A set of fine parallel oblique scratches extends across the face from the smoothed broken edge of BA-CE-1/27, a rib fragment which measures 34 x 7 x 3 mm. At 22.6 power the pattern of parallel scratches extending from the rounded edge is very clear (Figure 2-10a). On BA-CE-1/34, which measures 43 x 13 x 7 mm (Figure 2-10b), a concentrated set of parallel scratches and one groove extends obliquely from one edge, visible at 11.7 power under the scanning electron microscope (Figure 2-10c); and another irregular set of short incisions extend from a polished end. Under 225 power the polished surface exhibits cross-hatched sets of fine striations or scrape marks (Figure 2-10d). A set of parallel oblique scratches and one deep gouge, in addition to many other scratches, isolated in sets, is visible on the face of BA-CE-1/36, which measures 52 x 18 x 5 mm (Figure 2-11a). Several short scratches and incisions extending obliquely from a polished lateral edge of this piece are visible at 8.1 power (Figure 2-11b), 77.8 power (Figure 2-11c), and 170 power (Figure 2-11d). A clear set of fine sub-parallel incisions extends obliquely from a lateral edge of BA-CE-1/46, an unusually broad fragment which measures 64 x 32 x 7 mm (Figure 2-12a). Several scratches are clearly visible at 9.28 power (Figure 2-12b) and 32.5 power (Figure 2-12c), while a pattern of short incisions appears at 134 power (Figure 2-12d). Many shallow depressions may have been pecked into the surface of this tabular piece by use as an anvil. Another set of scratches extends between two polished edges that converge to a point.

Three incised bone fragments have flaked as well as polished edges. The largest specimen (BA-

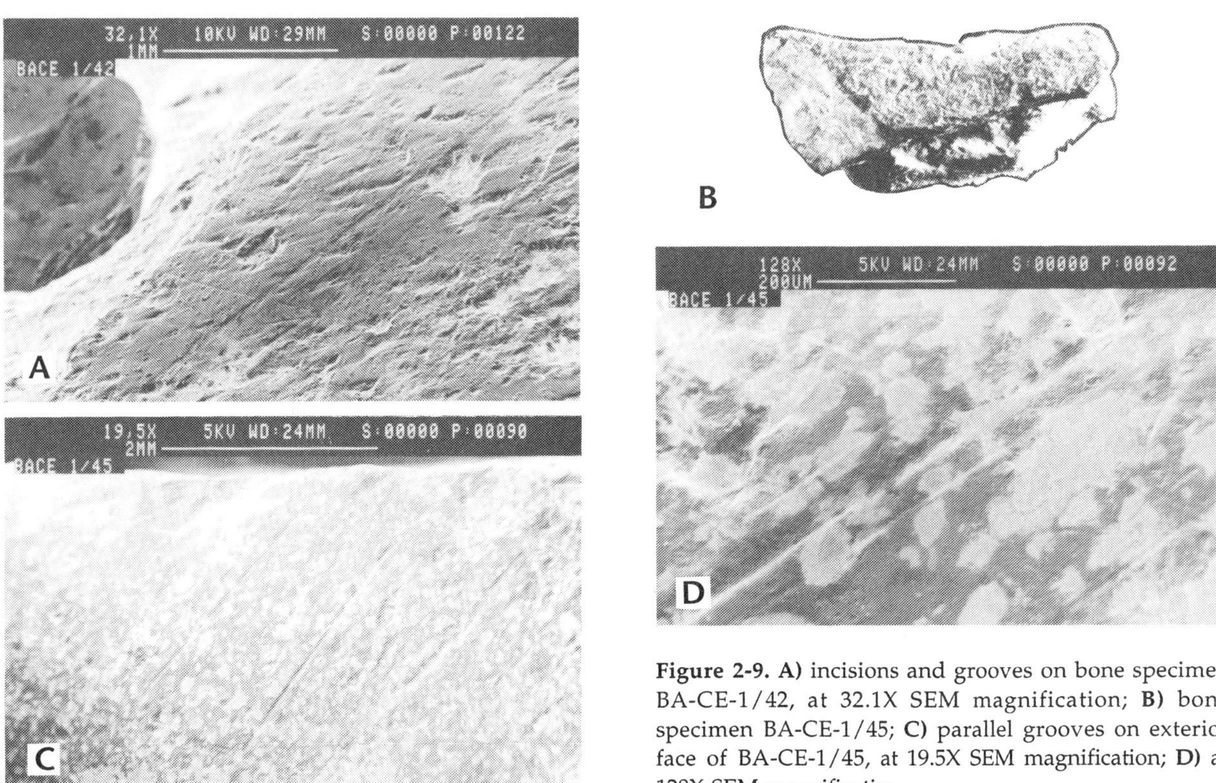

Figure 2-9. A) incisions and grooves on bone specimen BA-CE-1/42, at 32.1X SEM magnification; **B)** bone specimen BA-CE-1/45; **C)** parallel grooves on exterior face of BA-CE-1/45, at 19.5X SEM magnification; **D)** at 128X SEM magnification.

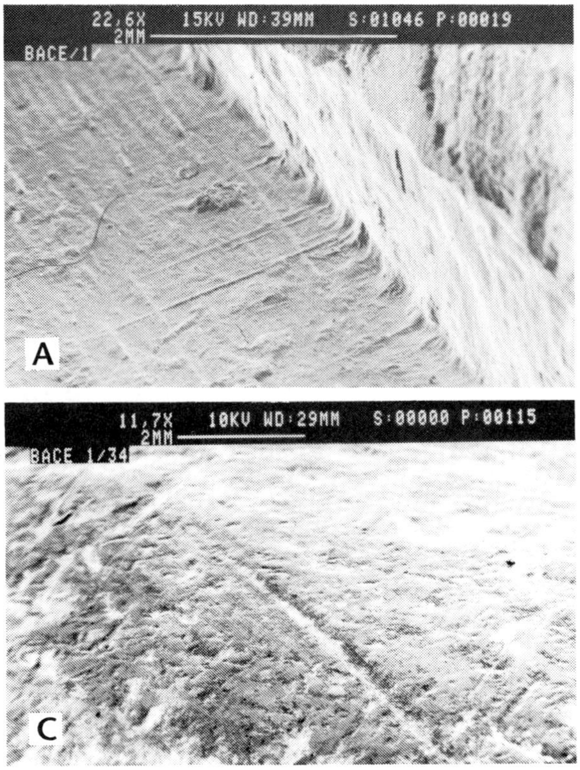

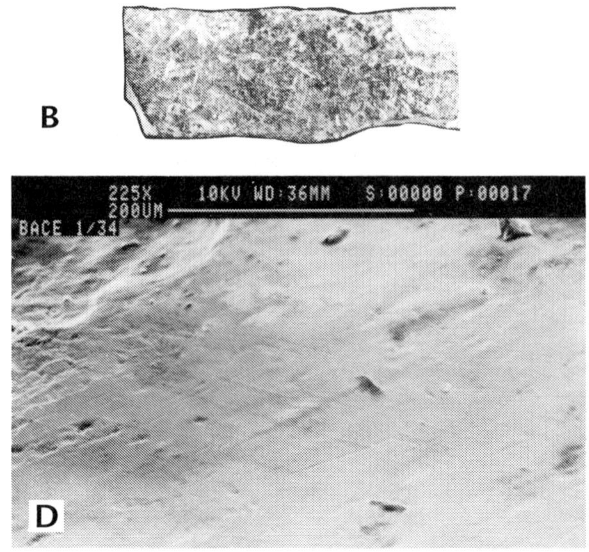

Figure 2-10. A) parallel scratches extending from edge of bone specimen BA-CE-1/27, at 22.6 X SEM magnification; **B)** bone specimen BA-CE-1/34; **C)** scratches and grooves on exterior surface of BA-CE-1/34, at 11.7X SEM magnification; **D)** fine striations and polish at 225X SEM magnification.

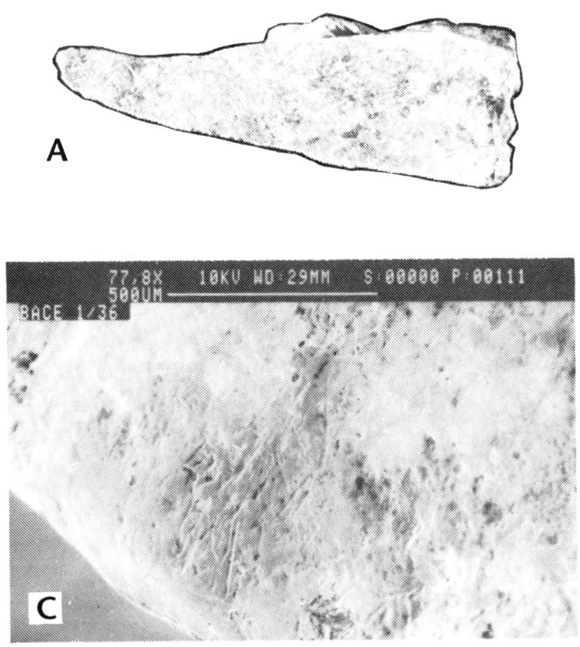

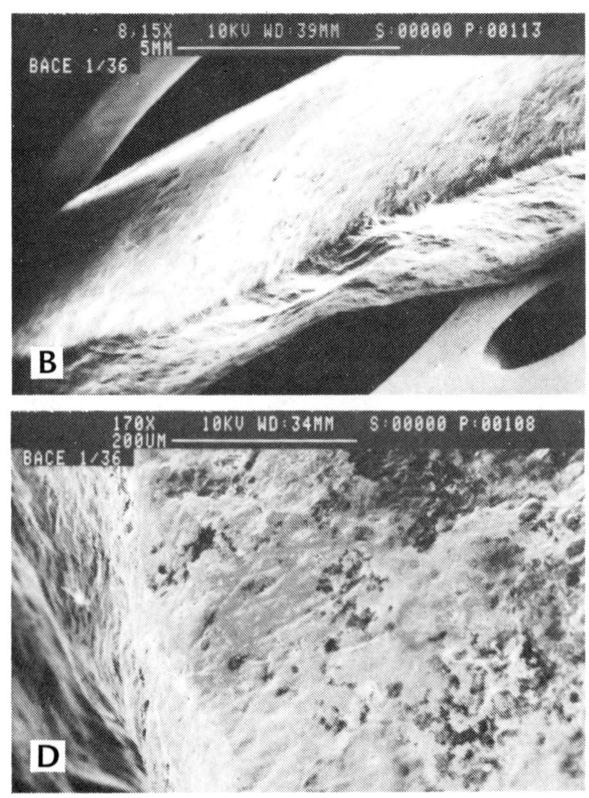

Figure 2-11. A) bone specimen BA-CE-1/36; **B)** scratches extending from edge of BA-CE-1/36, at 8.1X SEM magnification; **C)** at 77.8X SEM magnification; **D)** at 170X SEM magnification.

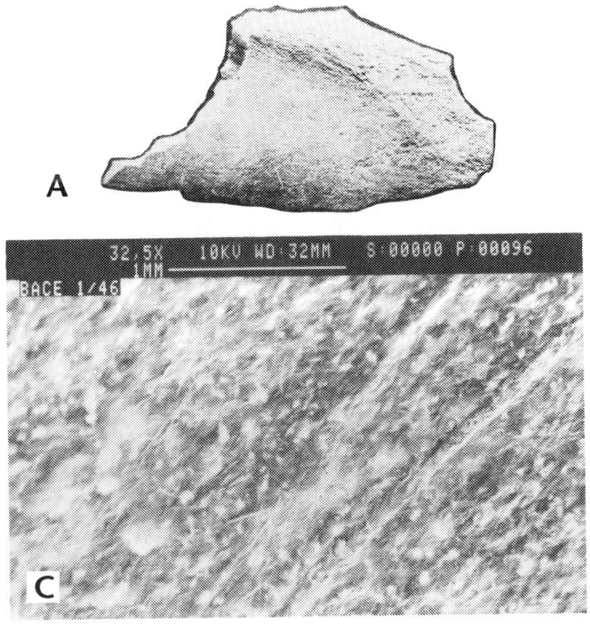

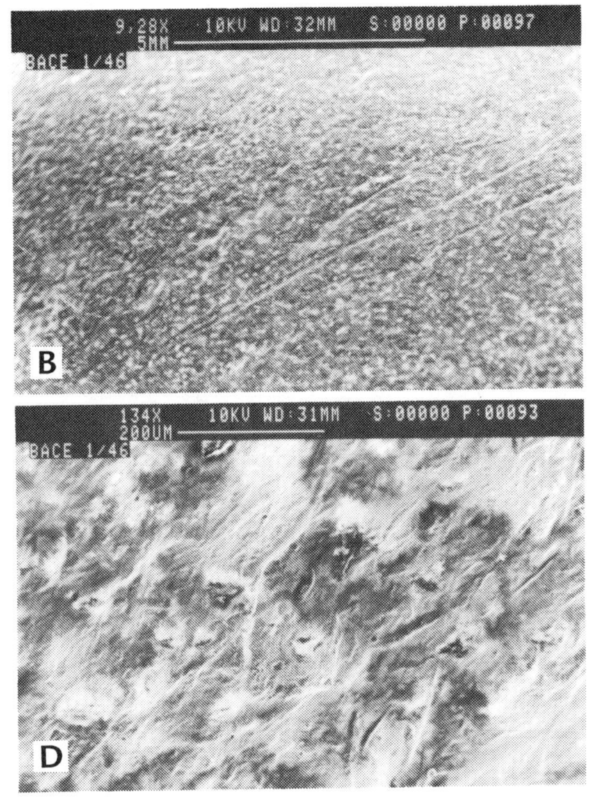

Figure 2-12. A) bone specimen BA-CE-1/46; **B)** scratches on exterior surface of BA-CE-1/46, at 9.28X SEM magnification; **C)** at 32.5X SEM magnification; **D)** at 134X SEM magnification.

CE-1/41), which measures 65 x 18 x 7 mm, exhibits several sets of cross-hatched scratches and incisions extending from one polished edge. Two other broken edges which converge to a pointed tip appear to be use-flaked and polished. Two flake scars extend from the tip as if caused by an impact blow. The opposite squarely broken end also appears to have a flake scar on the concave interior face. Deep incisions extend from a concave worn section of an edge of BA-CE-1/27, which measures 25 x 17 x 7 mm. The most pointed end appears to be use-flaked. Deep broad gouges and fine scratches are visible on a triangular fragment of bone (BA-CE-1/32) adjacent to an edge which may have been use-flaked. The piece measures 31 x 14 x 5 mm. A broad excurvate end has apparently been polished and flaked by use, perhaps as an end scraper.

Seven fragments of large mammal bone feature short incisions on the external surface. One of these artifacts (BA-CE-1/14), which measures 32 x 13 x 5 mm, has one short cut (3 mm long) adjacent to two faint parallel incisions across the grain of the bone near one end. On another artifact (BA-CE-1/15), measuring 43 x 15 x 10 mm, two sets of short incisions against the grain and at an angle to each other are evident near one end. A third artifact (BA-CE-1/16), measuring 29 x 14 x 4 mm, features a set of short (3.5 mm long) incisions extending from a broken edge parallel to one broken end. Near the center of another bone fragment (BA-CE-1/17), which measures 24 x 14 x 4 mm, is a set of short (3 mm) cut lines across the grain of the bone. The pattern is visible at 36 power (Figure 2-13a) and at 266 power (Figure 2-13b) under the scanning electron microscope. Other less definite short scratches are also visible on this artifact. A very thick walled fragment of bone (BA-CE-1/40), which measures 35 x 14 x 12 mm, exhibits several short incisions across the grain of the bone. Several overlapping sets of incisions, scratches, and scrape marks across the grain cover much of the surface of BA-CE-1/31 (Figure 2-13c), which measures 41 x 19 x 6 mm. Under 192 power, the surface is seen to be eroded after it was scraped (Figure 2-13d). The rounded and scratched edge is visible at 149 power under the scanning electron microscope (Figure 2-13e). Several short incisions across the grain are visible on the edge near the most pointed end of BA-CE-1/27, which measures 33 x 16 x 6 mm.

(3) The third group of modified bones to be described features both short cut marks and linear scrape marks. Three fragments of large mammal bone (BA-CE-1/10, 11, 12) exhibit both cuts and scrape marks over their entire surfaces (figs. 2-14 a, b).

The size range of these three fragments is quite limited (48 x 18 x 7 mm, 36 x 19 x 8 mm, and 36 x 19 x 5 mm). The marks consist of overlapping sets of short parallel straight incisions, and longer scrape marks criss-crossing the external surfaces in various directions. The pattern is clearly visible on BA-CE-1/11 at 11.7 power (Figure 2-14c). Unlike other fragments, the lines of alteration on these three pieces appear to have continued onto adjacent parts of the bone before fragmentation occurred. Small areas on the surfaces of these bones have subsequently been etched away by acid action. As the same alteration marks continue on both sides of the etched sections, alteration must have occurred before etching by the ground water. These three specimens are quite similar in form, color, and surface markings, so it is possible that they were all part of the same bone before it fragmented. The evidence for alteration on these three pieces could be explained by the hypothesis that they were parts of an anvil used for working other materials such as meat, hide, bone, feathers, wood, or plant fiber. If something that had to be cut or scraped was held on a bone anvil, some of the working thrusts of the flake would slip onto the surface of the anvil and leave marks. The flattest face of a large tabular bone (BA-CE-1/54), which measures 59 x 42 x 22 mm, also exhibits linear incisions and scrape marks in various directions as if the piece had been used as an anvil. The more random nature of alterations on these four specimens, especially on the three pieces that may be parts of a larger bone, might also be explained as trampling marks. This possibility will be discussed later.

Six bone fragments exhibit both linear scrape marks and shorter parallel scratches or incisions. They could be complete tools used for preparing some other material, because the patterned alteration marks are con-

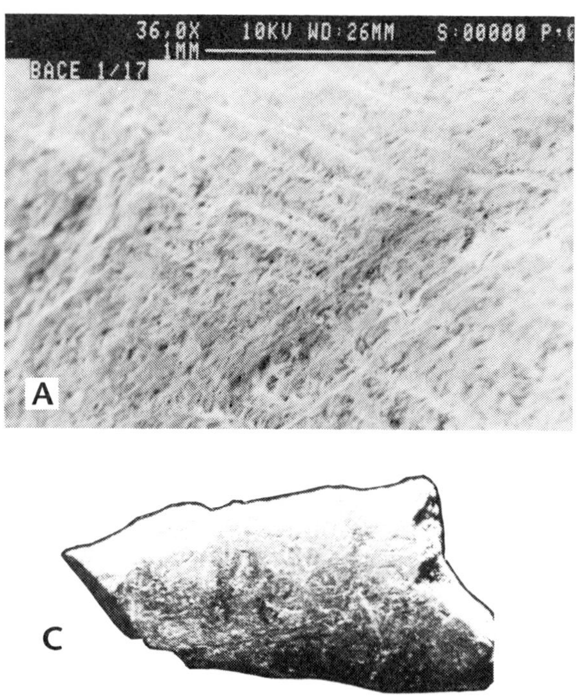

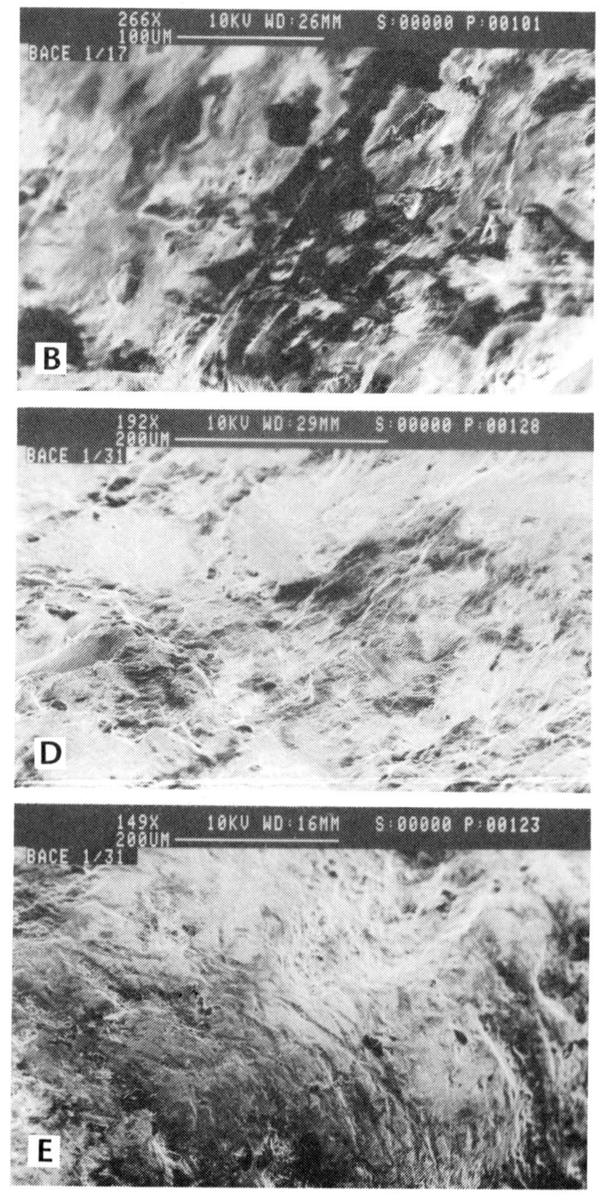

Figure 2-13. A) parallel scratches on exterior surface of bone specimen BA-CE-1/17, at 36X SEM magnification; **B)** at 266X SEM magnification; **C)** bone specimen BA-CE-1/31; **D)** scratches and polish on exterior surface of BA-CE-1/31, at 192X SEM magnification; **E)** on edge of exterior surface at 149X SEM magnification.

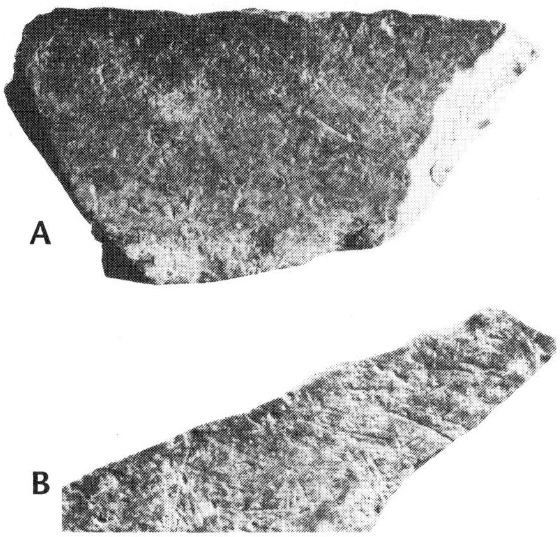

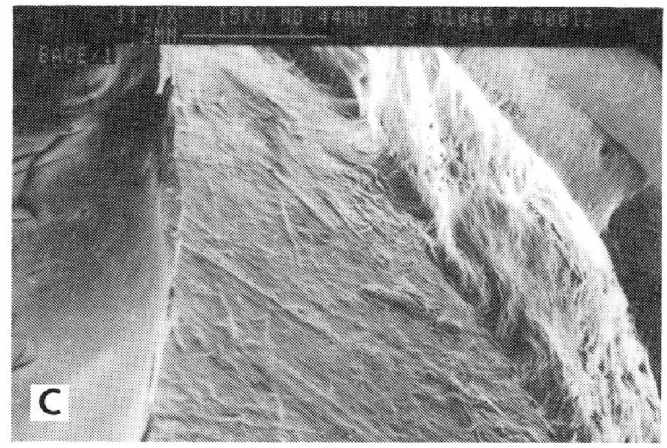

Figure 2-14. A) bone specimen BA-CE-1/10; **B)** bone specimen BA-CE-1/11; **C)** scrape marks on surface of BA-CE-1/11, at 11.7X SEM magnification.

fined to the piece and usually extend from a utilized edge. A fragment of a large mammal bone (BA-CE-1/9), measuring 45 x 30 x 9 mm, exhibits one short incision (4 mm long) across the grain of the bone. Also visible are two sets of long scrape marks across the central portion of the broadest face. The external edge of one broken end appears be battered, flaked, and differentially polished by use. The parallel incisions, scratches, and in a few cases the scrape marks on the other five examples extend from an edge, usually near one end; and/or from a pointed end. The relevant end or edge of the bone is usually lightly polished. A set of long nearly parallel incisions extends obliquely from one pointed end across the external face of BA-CE-1/31 (Figure 2-15a). The pattern is clearly visible under the scanning electron microscope at 27.5 power (Figure 2-15b), while under 615 power one of the incisions is seen as a groove having fine parallel lines within it (Figure 2-15c). Other more random sets of scratches and scrape marks are visible across the grain of this bone fragment, which measures 47 x 18 x 5 mm. Many scrape marks extend in various directions from a broken end across much of the flattest face of BA-CE-1/47 (Figure 2-15d), which measures 18 x 15 x 11 mm. A pattern of parallel scratches adjacent to an unaltered surface is seen at 24.9 power under the scanning electron microscope (Figure 2-15e). The external surface of BA-CE-1/33 is covered with scrape marks and incisions in various directions (Figure 2-16a). A concentration of parallel scratches extends from a broken and polished end. The piece measures 33 x 18 x 8 mm. Two parallel gouges extend obliquely from a broken end of BA-CE-1/27, which measures 26 x 15 x 5 mm (Figure 2-16b). Other more random incisions and scratches extend from the adjacent broken edge, and a set of parallel scrape marks extends from the opposite end. A close set of deep parallel scrape marks is visible on the face of BA-CE-1/27, which measures 42 x 10 x 7 mm (Figure 2-17a). Another set of shorter scrape marks crosses at right angles and connects with a set of scratches extending from a polished edge near one end. The scrape mark is clearly visible at 11.7 power under the scanning electron microscope (Figure 2-17b). At 141 power the deep furrow is seen to be ridged (Figure 2-17c).

The outer surfaces of three other bone fragments are badly eroded; but short scratches and longer scrape marks are visible on the high spots of the eroded surfaces of BA-CE-1/30, which measures 53 x 22 x 13 mm; BA-CE-1/43, which measures 18 x 13 x 7 mm; and BA-CE-1/44, which measures 42 x 15 x 6 mm.

The upper left canine of a peccary, measuring 54 x 17 x 10 mm, was compared with a modern peccary tooth, which is much more slender in proportion. The extinct peccary tooth is considered to be an artifact (BA-CE-1/18) because the wear facet of the tooth exhibits not only the natural wear pattern of fine parallel oblique striations but also two long irregular grooves which Martha Locks, mammalogist at the Museu Nacional, believes must have been produced artificially. Unfortunately, the tip of this tooth was broken off and lost during excavation. The tip of another peccary tooth (BA-CE-1/29) was found in an adjacent excavation unit. The tip end is much worn and rounded by use. That this use was after the animal's death is indicated by a short deep incision across the pattern of natural wear. Two irregularly parallel grooves begin in a deeply gouged area and extend longitudinally beyond the broken edge.

Were all the bone fragments modified before or after permineralization? This question is relevant to the question of whether people lived in the cave contemporary with Pleistocene animals; or whether later people may have utilized ancient fossil bones, a situation we discovered in 1985 at Toca da Gameleira. Certainly the fragments would have been more durable if they had already turned to stone. On the other hand, the straight

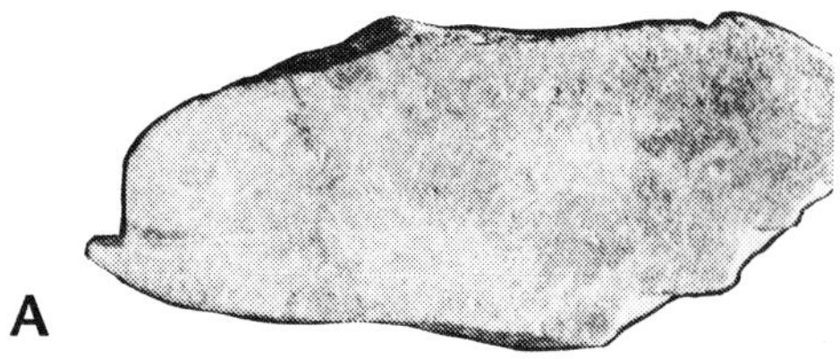

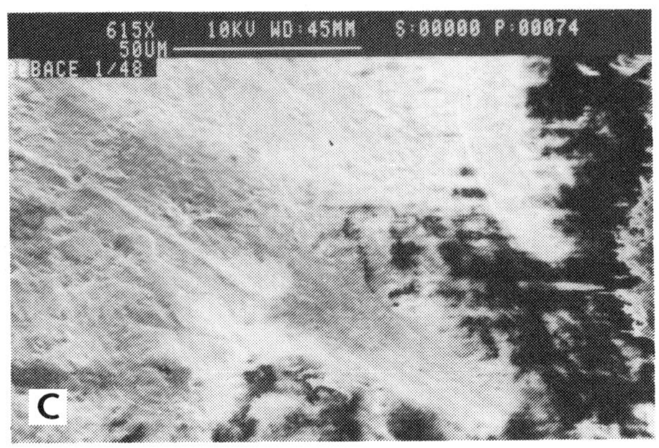

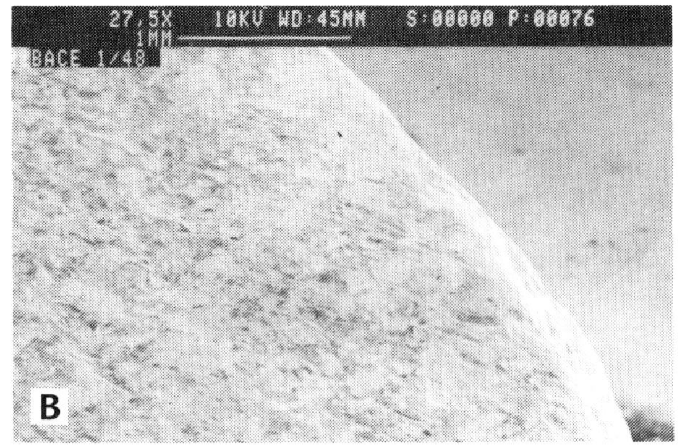

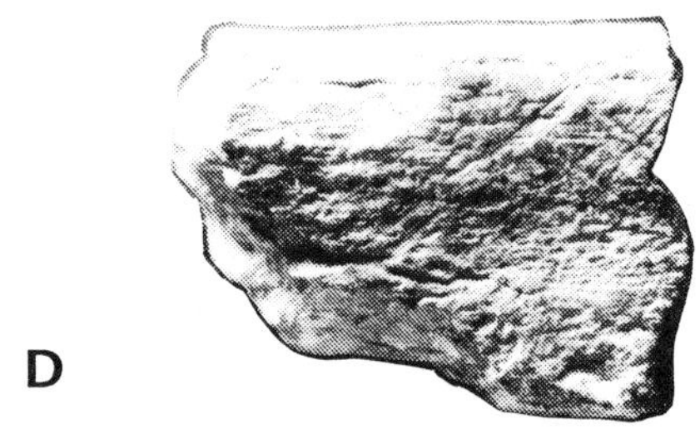

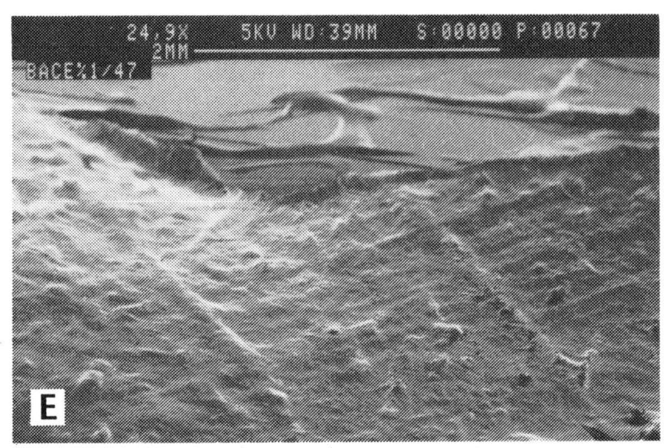

Figure 2-15. A) bone specimen BA-CE-1/48; **B)** parallel scratches on exterior surface of BA-CE-1/48, at 27.5X SEM magnification; **C)** groove on BA-CE-1/48, at 615X SEM magnification; **D)** bone specimen BA-CE-1/47; **E)** parellel grooves on exterior surface of BA-CE-1/47, at 24.9X SEM magnification.

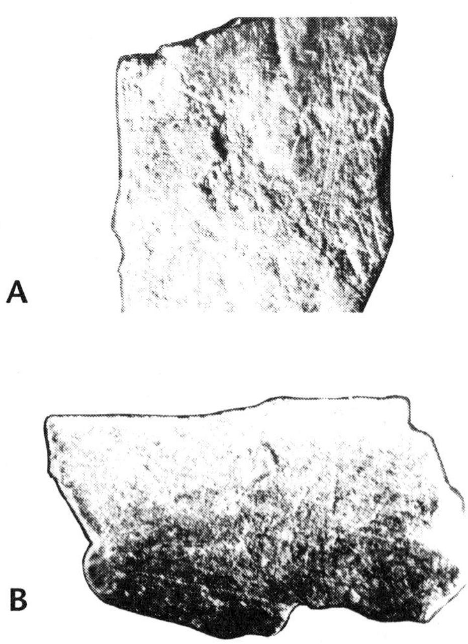

Figure 2-16. A) bone specimen BA-CE-1/33; **B)** bone specimen BA-CE-1/37.

rough edge of a recently desiccated bone might be preferable to stone for certain purposes, as it would not cut a skin being dehaired or plant fibre being scraped and flattened to make cordage or basketry.

The bones are completely permineralized. A test for potential radiocarbon dating determined that no collagen remained. When they were being examined, we had the impression that the modification scars would have looked fresher if they had been made after permineralization. The microphotographs show that many of the incisions, grooves, and scrape marks are partially filled by minerals after they were made; however, this feature can be ascribed to the later formation of the encrustation. The fact that the modifications are sometimes etched by (carbonic?) acid also suggests that modification had occurred before permineralization, but the etching could have occurred by groundwater action on permineralized bones prior to formation of the encrus-

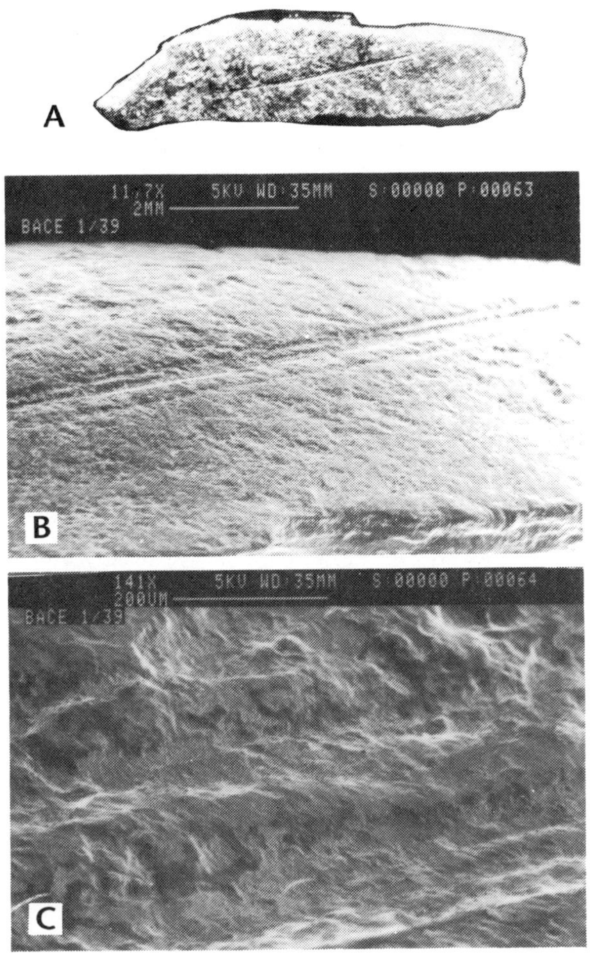

Figure 2-17. A) bone specimen BA-CE-1/39; **B)** parallel scrape marks on exterior surface, at 11.7X SEM magnification; **C)** at 141X SEM magnification.

tation. The extreme rounding of the modified edges of a few examples supports the hypothesis that modification occurred before permineralization: if already permineralized, the right-angled edges should have fragmented and crushed instead of becoming rounded by heavy use. It seems impossible to be absolutely certain that the bones were modified before permineralization, but the weight of evidence suggests the likelihood that people collected and modified desiccated but not yet completely permineralized bone.

DISCUSSION AND CONCLUSIONS

The potential for discovery of evidence for early man in Toca dos Buzios was recognized by Profa. Maria Beltrão during her initial extensive survey of the Central area in June 1983. When we saw the site a month later, we also thought that the cave looked promising, especially with the possibility that evidence for occupation might be present in the yellow silt zone stratigraphically beneath the ash, silt, and rubble zone.

Excavation of the upper ashy zone, with so much loose rock, was frustrating but nevertheless instructive because, although the deposit included obviously human midden, very few artifacts showing any evidence of alteration were recovered. We learned how few identifiable artifacts might be recovered from midden deposits left by people who rarely shaped artifacts of stone or bone. Many pieces of limestone rubble with potentially useful edges and points were carefully examined. Although many of these might have been used for some purpose, we concluded that unless actual evidence for workmanship could be identified, they were not demonstrably artifacts. The paucity of artifacts in the ashy midden led us to conclude that most artifacts used by these later occupants had been fashioned of perishable materials.

Two potsherds and two probably utilized mussel shells came from the surface of the site. Evidently the ashy midden was preceramic; but the flaked quartz crystal, the limestone flake, and the shell bead recovered from the midden gave no clue as to cultural affiliation.

A case could be made that the other artifacts recovered on or near the base of the ashy midden zone had been deposited on the surface of the yellow silt before the ashy midden began to accumulate. These artifacts include a use-retouched chert flake blade, a minimally flaked chert chunk, three probable limestone artifacts, and a spirally fractured mammal bone. A segment of bone ground to a point at both ends was the only shaped artifact. Amazonian Indians still mount bipoints like this one as projectile points with one pointed end extending backward as a barb.

The evidence for a Pleistocene occupation came from the yellow silt stratigraphically beneath the ashy midden and an intervening discontinuous flowstone/breccia which may mark a depositional interval of increased rainfall between the two cultural deposits. The yellow silt was deposited in an ancient channel cut into the cave floor. The yellow silt deposit could originally have been thicker and more extensive, expanding beyond the bedrock channel in which it is now preserved; but removed through erosion by water flowing across the cave floor during the period of increased rainfall. If so, most of the original silt was redeposited outside the cave. The silt within the bedrock channel evidently was not redeposited by water at this time, as no fluvial structures were seen, and the enclosed bone fragments were not waterworn.

At first, excavation of the yellow silt deposit seemed unproductive until we recovered an obviously shaped bone rod (BA-CE-1/53) and a few vein quartz fragments which evidently do not occur naturally in the area of Toca dos Buzios. We also recovered a horse tooth and phalange, so we knew the yellow silt sediments were old. Unfortunately, all bone from the yellow silt zone was covered with a coating of iron-stained calcium carbonate that was difficult and time-consuming to remove. We therefore kept all bone fragments in level bags for more careful examination later, and concentrated on cleaning and describing the vein quartz chunks.

It was easily seen that seven of the nine quartz fragments recovered from the yellow silt zone been flaked. Although some of these quartz chunks were reflaked during excavation, which required hand-picking to break up the cemented silt, it was easy to distinguish unstained recent flaking from ancient flake scars which were stained yellow. None of the quartz chunks had been shaped. They had simply been broken by placing them on an anvil and bashing them, or flakes had been removed from one or more fractured edges to produce or resharpen a useful edge. Only later, when several of the quartz specimens were examined and photographed in a scanning electron microscope, was it realized that scratches from use are clearly visible along several of these flaked edges. The fact that the pattern of scratches, usually extending at or near right angles from a steep sharp edge, is very similar to the pattern of scratches found on several bone fragments suggests that all of these stone and bone fragments were probably used in a similar way, as scrapers. Also, if the obviously worked quartz chunks had not been found, the directly associated modified bone fragments would probably have been ascribed to some natural action, such as gnawing, trampling, or differential movement in the deposits. It is possible that some of the 31 altered bone fragments were scratched by trampling because the marks are random, and on two examples the marks originally extended beyond the broken edges in several directions. However, the shaped bone rod could not be caused by trampling. It is obviously an artifact, as demonstrated by long incisions and cut marks at right angles. Most of the rest of the altered bone fragments have patterned sets of parallel scratches, incisions, and grooves which typically extend at or near right angles from an edge or end which is lightly polished and/or use flaked. Evidently the irregularly straight but rough edges were held at a steep angle and pushed or pulled against the material to be worked.

Other than the cylindrical bone rod, which could have been the central section of a projectile point, the artifacts recovered from the yellow silt zone evidently were chunks of stone and bone picked up to be used as small hand tools for scraping other materials, probably mostly wood and fibre, but also bone. The original cultural contexts have evidently been disturbed, so there is no evidence that the Pleistocene animals, including horse and giant peccary, were hunted. Possibly the skeletons of dead animals were simply scavenged for desiccated bone fragments with useful edges, in the same way that vein quartz was broken up and pieces with useful edges were selected. Together, these altered stone and bone fragments indicate that people occupied Toca dos Buzios sometime during the late Pleistocene.

Chapter 3
Toca de Manoel Latão

INTRODUCTION

Location and Description of the Site

Toca de Manoel Latão is a large cavern located on the Fazenda Grota, about 8 km north of the town center of Central. The cavern is at the base of the Serra da Pedra Branca, and it opens to the south (Figure 3-1a). The *toca* is an extensive and complex cave system which extends along a 200-m front on the south side of the *serra*. There are three principal chambers which are readily accessible by descending 3 to 5 m over a heavy rock fall at the easiest entrance to the cavern. The so-called central chamber, with large stalagmitic columns on either side, presently features a large pool of water at the rear (Figure 3-1b). This pool was deepened by excavations by local people in the recent past; and the backdirt was piled to the west of the pool, against a large stalagmitic formation, and also to the southeast, near the main entrance to the cavern. Water is available in the pool until the height of the dry season. To the west of this chamber of the cavern is a complex series of small rooms, with low ceiling and flowstone floors at different levels. This area is accessible by passing a large stalagmitic column and crawling down a flowstone-covered slope from the rear of the central chamber. Even farther to the west, separated by heavy rock fall from a collapse that opened the cavern, are two additional large low deep chambers which are very difficult of access, and were not explored.

The eastern chamber is the highest chamber in the cavern: the surface of the earth deposits on its floor is approximately 40 cm higher than the unexcavated floor of the central chamber. The eastern chamber is elongate in form, with a high ceiling (Figures 3-2a, 3-2b). It features a level floor of earth extending a maximum 12 m north-south, with a maximum width of 6 m at the base of the slope of large boulders at the mouth of the cavern (map, Figure 3-3). The ceiling of the eastern chamber is irregular in form, but extends to a maximum height of about 6 m at the south end. There are several small chimneys in the roof, with staining indicating an entrance for water into the chamber; and there is a small drip basin at the rear. Along the east-central wall of the chamber, at the entrance to a very low passage leading east, an area of the floor is covered by fragmented sinter which was redeposited from the passage. Evidence of standing water in the past is presented by a level line of calcareous deposit on the walls about 70 cm above the surface of the earth fill, and desiccation cracks on the surface of the fill. After several months of rain in season, the floor of the eastern chamber becomes very moist; and water collects in low areas. The sediments dry out by the middle of the dry season.

The Excavations

Features of the eastern chamber of Toca de Manoel Latão are typical of many of the limestone *tocas* seen on our July/August 1983 survey of the Central region: a deep cavern situated relatively low in relation to the level of the surrounding land, and presenting evidence of standing water in the past. A broken quartzite pebble and a few flakes of quartz and quartzite were seen on the surface within the eastern chamber, and there is some rock art (a few indistinct red marks at the entrance to the central chamber; and a rectangular grid pattern in red, unfortunately vandalized, at the junction of the eastern chamber with the central chamber); but otherwise, as at other similar sites, there was no really encouraging evidence of human occupation. However,

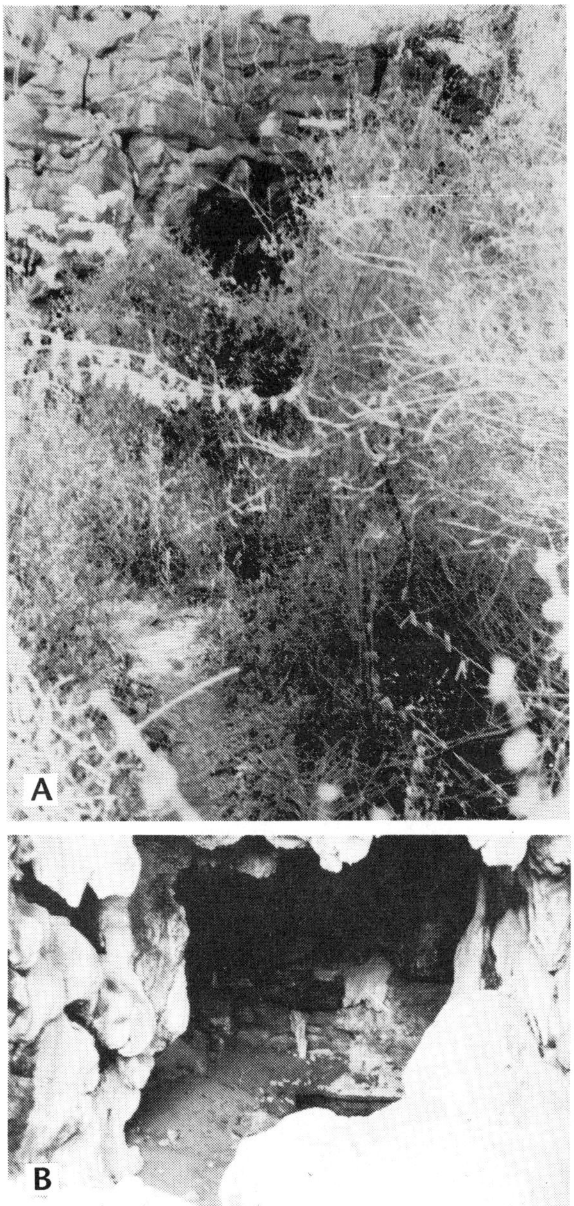

Figure 3-1. A) entrance to Toca de Manoel Latão; **B)** central chamber of Toca de Manoel Latão, with waterhole excavated by local people.

fragments of permineralized bone of large mammals were observed in the backdirt from the recent excavation of the waterhole in the central chamber. It was decided to place an excavation in order to test the hypothesis that such kinds of sites might contain remains of Pleistocene fauna in association with evidence of man.

The first excavations in Toca de Manoel Latão were carried out from 31 July to 14 August 1983. A plan was made of the floor of the eastern chamber, and a grid system was imposed (map, Figure 3-3). Excavation began by arbitrary 10-cm levels in the 2-m square designated C4. When a depth of 50 cm below surface was attained, the dearth of artifacts and the great difficulty in excavating stiff clayey sediment, combined with a shortage of time, forced restriction of excavation in Square C4 to the northern half (2 x 1 m). Excavation in the northern half of Square C4 was carried in arbitrary 10-cm levels to bedrock, at approximately 150 cm depth. The northern half (2 x 1 m) of Square C5 was also excavated in arbitrary 10-cm levels to a depth of 50 cm below surface, in order to increase the yield of artifacts and associated bones.

Further excavations in June 1984 were stimulated by the evidence discovered in 1983 for the association of artifacts with remains of extinct fauna. Squares D4, C3, and B4 were opened; and also the northern sectors of Squares B5 and D5. However, grave difficulties in excavation and screening of the sediments caused by moist conditions in the cavern in early June restricted excavation to the upper 60 cm of deposit.

Excavation of all units in the eastern chamber began with trowel and dustpan; but the compactness of the

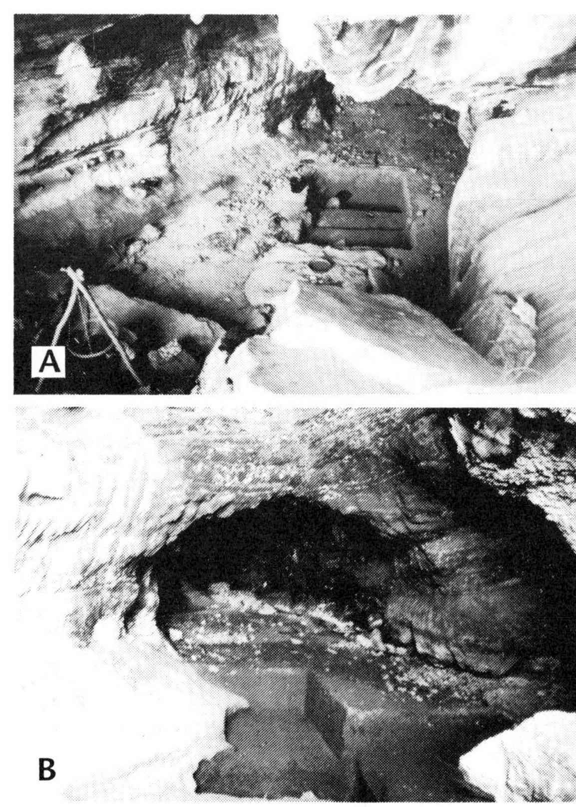

Figure 3-2. Eastern chamber of Toca de Manoel Latão: **A)** in 1983 season; **B)** in 1984 season.

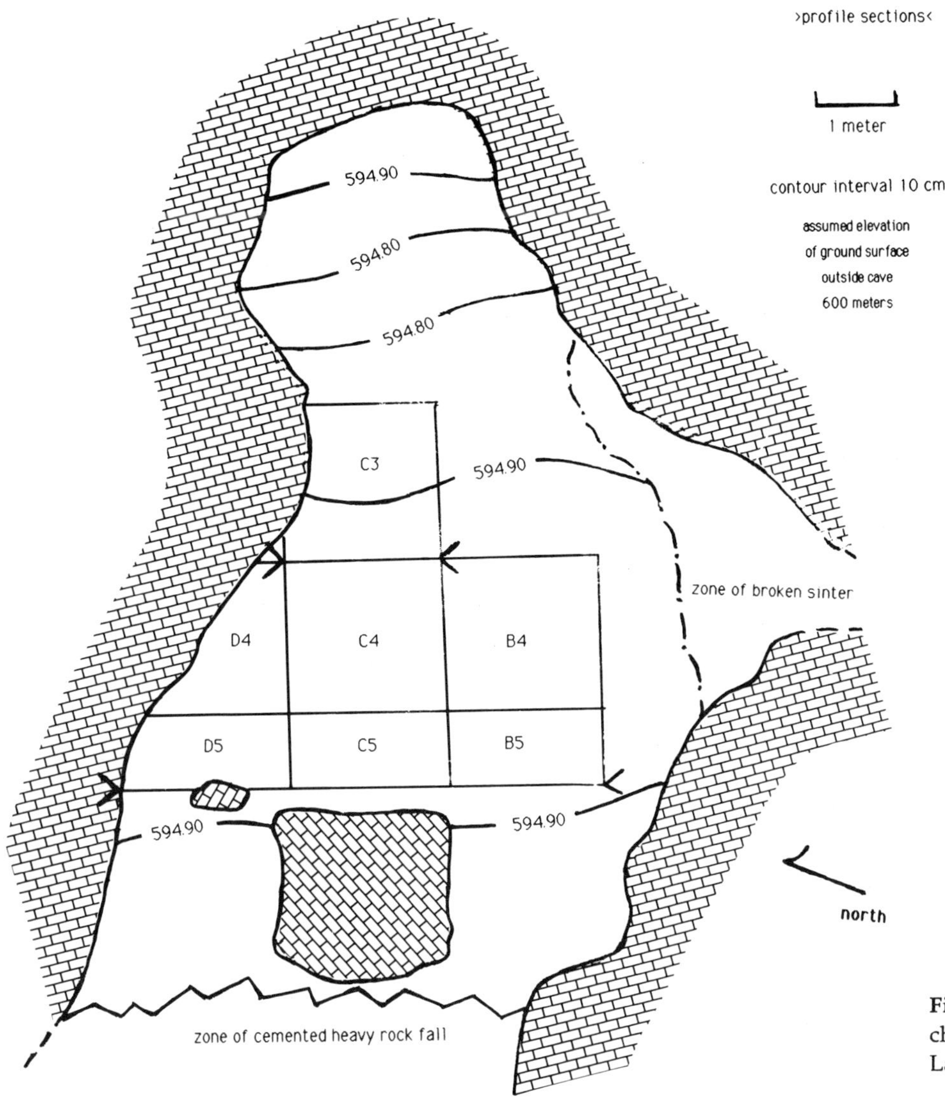

Figure 3-3. Plan of eastern chamber of Toca de Manoel Latão.

deposit forced the use of a geologist's pick below 20 cm, and below 30 cm depth a long pick with sharp narrow blade had to be used to loosen the earth. Lumps of earth had to be broken up before loading into buckets for screening. All excavated material was examined in a 4-mm screen. In 1984, when the sediment was wet, the stiff clay matrix had to be soaked and then kneaded before screening in a large tub of water.

Photographs were taken of the excavation in progress. At the conclusion of excavations in August 1983, the north face of Square C4 was profiled. Samples of the sediment were extracted in columns from this profile near the center of the east chamber for mechanical and chemical analyses. In 1984, profiles were obtained of all faces of excavated units; and cross-sections of the cavern fill were made available.

In 1985, paleomagnetic samples were collected but have not been analysed.

STRATIGRAPHY

Natural Stratigraphy

Field Description of the Sediments

The earth fill in the eastern chamber of Toca de Manoel Latão was found to be essentially a massive clay/silt deposit, with several major horizons distinguished by differences in color, texture, degree of cementation, and size and frequency of concretions. Change in these properties, however, was gradual from one level to another (profiles, Figures 3-4, 3-5).

The upper 20 to 30 cm of the deposit was distinguished as a brown clay/silt, compact but light and very porous in texture, relatively easy to excavate and to screen. Desiccation polygons, about 10 cm in diameter and 5 cm deep, were observable on the surface. On the

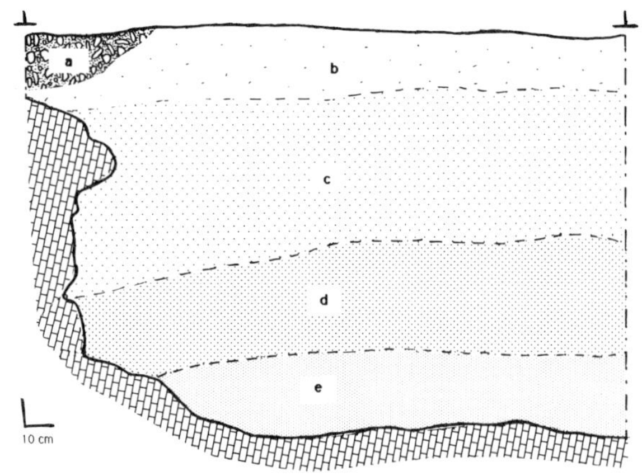

Figure 3-4. Profile of north face of Square C4; **A)** brown clay/silt with rubble; **B)** brown clay/silt; **C)** stiff reddish brown clay/silt with ironstone nodules; **D)** stiff reddish brown clay/silt with abundant large ironstone nodules and calcareous concretions; **E)** cemented brown clay/silt with abundant large ironstone nodules and calcareous concretions.

western side of the excavation, near the west wall of the chamber, angular limestone rubble was a prominent component of the upper 10–20 cm of the brown clay/silt zone; and on the east side of the chamber limestone and flowstone rubble also occurred in the upper 10–20 cm. Many tree roots of varying size extended horizontally through this zone.

Below a depth of approximately 20 cm the matrix gradually became reddish brown in color; and increasingly more compact or stiff, more clayey in texture, making excavation difficult. Limestone fragments became very rare; and very small in size, with smooth surfaces or rounded edges indicating chemical erosion. A few very small quartz pebbles, including some waterworn crystals, occurred scattered. Small ironstone nodules appeared in the matrix at a depth of approximately 20 cm below surface. Ironstone nodules became increasingly abundant, and increased in average size from 2 mm diameter to over 10 mm in the lowest levels. Small lumps of breccia, nodules of cemented coarse reddish brown silt with ironstone inclusions, apparently formed in situ by local cementation of the matrix, also appeared at the 20–30 cm level and increased in size and abundance with depth. The breccia nodules were most abundant in the zone within 30 cm of the west wall of the chamber. White calcareous concretions became common in the matrix below a depth of approximately 70 cm below surface. A restricted zone of less clayey matrix, yellow/brown in color and containing fewer breccia nodules, occurred on the west side of the excavation from 70 to 120 cm depth. Below a depth of approximately 120 cm the matrix became brown in color; and virtually cemented, with abundant large ironstone nodules and calcareous concretions.

The bedrock floor of the chamber, encountered at an approximate depth of 150 cm below surface, was irregular in contour. It featured a very rough surface, coated with hard white calcareous material.

In May 1984 the excavations in the area toward the front part of the eastern chamber (in the north sectors of Squares B5 and D5) revealed a stratigraphic horizon of roof fall, marked by the presence of several large flat slabs of limestone (up to 175 cm in size) lying horizontally at the 20–25 cm level in the clay/silt (Figure 3-5). A large rock previously exposed in the south side of Square C5 (northern sector) may be associated with this roof fall, as indeed may be a huge rock slab exposed lying flat on the surface in the south sector of Square C5. All of these rock slabs evidently were detached from the ceiling directly overhead, which is now thickly coated with calcareous precipitate ("popcorn"). In Square D5 (northern sector), two rock slabs at this level were covered with a thick stalagmitic deposit.

Results of Soils Analysis

Chemical analyses and particle-size analyses were carried out on a stratigraphic series of 15 samples of sediment collected at 10-cm intervals to bedrock at 150 cm in Square C4. The results are presented in Tables 3-1 and 3-2.

Particle-size analyses showed a predominance of clay and silt grade in all samples. In all but three samples, the clay grade ranged from approximately 62% to 68%; and the silt grade from 20% to 29%. Coarser

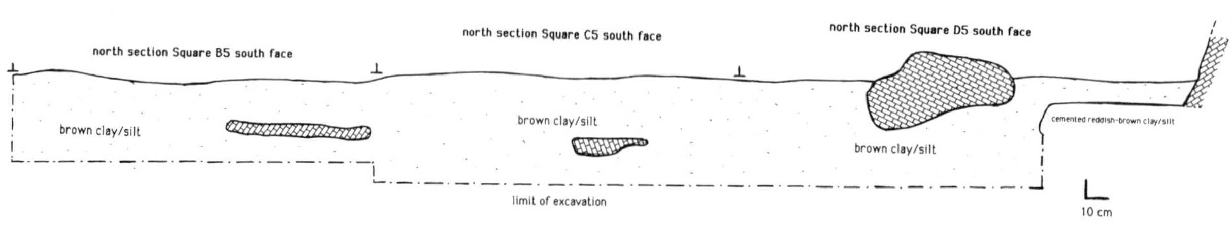

Figure 3-5. Profile of south face of north sections of Squares B5, C5, and D5. Large rock protruding above surface of Square D5 is covered with a stalagmitic deposit.

Table 3-1. Particle-Size Analysis of Sediment Samples from Square C4 in Toca de Manoel Latão.

Depth	Percent Content					
	Clay	Silt	Fine Sand	Medium Sand	Coarse Sand	Gravel
0–10 cm	67.08	28.92	3.20	0.80	0.0	0.0
10–20 cm	64.03	26.36	8.01	1.40	0.2	0.0
20–30 cm	63.00	25.28	7.32	3.60	0.8	0.0
30–40 cm	65.06	24.64	6.50	3.00	0.8	0.0
40–50 cm	63.00	28.00	5.60	2.80	0.6	0.0
50–60 cm	64.03	25.04	7.13	3.20	0.6	0.0
60–70 cm	67.09	22.84	6.47	3.00	0.6	0.0
70–80 cm	67.18	21.87	7.00	3.40	0.6	0.0
80–90 cm	55.92	28.01	10.47	3.40	2.2	0.0
90–100 cm	65.11	23.47	6.82	3.60	1.0	0.0
100–110 cm	65.11	23.29	6.80	3.80	1.0	0.0
110–120 cm	66.13	20.07	7.80	4.60	1.4	0.0
120–130 cm	62.04	18.56	8.60	8.00	2.8	0.0
130–140 cm	55.88	19.59	10.13	10.40	4.0	0.0
140–150 cm	57.96	18.44	10.20	9.80	3.6	0.0

Table 3-2. Chemical Analyses of Sediment Samples from Square C4 in Toca de Manoel Latão.

Depth	Dithionite (%)		Oxalate (%)		Hematite/Geothite (%)		pH	L.I. (%)	$CaCO_3$ (%)
	Al (%)	Fe (%)	Al (%)	Fe (%)	Al (%)	Fe (%)			
0–10 cm	0.53	4.8	0.33	0.21	0.20	4.6	7.6	9.0	9.3
10–20 cm	0.50	5.3	0.32	0.23	0.18	5.1	7.6	9.0	5.3
20–30 cm	0.54	5.2	0.22	0.22	0.32	4.9	7.8	11.1	8.7
30–40 cm	0.48	6.0	0.18	0.25	0.30	5.7	7.6	8.7	3.3
40–50 cm	0.42	5.8	0.20	0.27	0.22	5.5	8.0	9.0	5.3
50–60 cm	0.51	5.7	0.17	0.27	0.34	5.4	7.8	10.2	8.0
60–70 cm	0.52	6.0	0.16	0.24	0.36	5.8	7.8	8.6	9.3
70–80 cm	0.61	5.8	0.16	0.30	0.45	5.5	7.8	10.3	4.0
80–90 cm	0.62	6.3	0.15	0.23	0.47	6.1	7.8	8.9	6.7
90–100 cm	0.51	5.9	0.15	0.25	0.36	5.7	8.0	4.7	12.0
100–110 cm	0.54	6.1	0.13	0.21	0.41	5.9	7.8	17.2	8.7
110–120 cm	0.50	6.1	0.13	0.19	0.37	5.9	7.8	10.2	12.7
120–130 cm	0.52	5.7	0.13	0.24	0.39	5.5	7.6	13.0	12.0
130–140 cm	0.39	5.1	0.13	0.17	0.26	4.9	7.8	9.8	10.6
140–150 cm	0.36	5.4	0.13	0.25	0.23	5.2	7.8	11.8	8.0

particles increased in frequency in the lower part of the section; with approximately 20% fine sand and medium sand grades, and 4% coarse sand grade at the 130–140 cm level and 140–150 cm level. These levels are just above bedrock, so that particles of decomposing bedrock may be included. At the 80–90 cm level there was also an increase in coarseness of particle size grade, with 56% clay, 28% silt, 10% fine sand, 3% medium sand, and 2% coarse sand grades. The particle-size analyses confirmed the field identification of a fairly homogeneous clay/silt deposit in the cavern. The settling out of fine sediment in quiet water, likely in a pool formed during the rainy season, is indicated.

Chemical analyses indicated, as expected, a high carbonate content; with the percentage of $CaCO_3$ fluctuating between 3.3% and 9.3% in all but four lower samples, in which the percentage ranged from 10.6% to 12.7%. The pH of the 15 sediment samples fluctuated from 7.6 to 8.0. As an indication of organic content, the percentage of loss on ignition in the upper part of the stratigraphic section varied, with readings above 10% at the 20–30 cm level, the 50–60 cm level, and the 70–80 cm level. Below 100 cm depth, percentage of loss on ignition was above 9.8% in all levels, with a high reading of 17.2% at the 100–110 cm level. Aluminium content tended to decrease with depth, but there was no marked change in iron content throughout the section.

Interpretation of the Natural Stratigraphy

The gradual change with depth in the color, texture, and chemistry of the deposit in Toca de Manoel Latão was due to gradual weathering and groundwater fluctuation, the latter responsible for the precipitation of calcium-carbonate concretions and ironstone nodules, which are large and abundant in the lower levels. Neither sedimentary structures nor unconformities were visible in the sediment profile, so running water did not cause deposition or erosion. Evidently the deposition of the clay/silt was slow, by precipitation from muddy standing water in the pools which formed in the chamber during the rainy season.

The fact that limestone rubble is abundant near the walls in the upper 20 cm of deposit but practically nonexistent in lower levels might have paleoenvironmental significance. Periodic saturation and desiccation of the limestone roof would occur during the present climatic regime of heavy rains and prolonged drought. Limestone will expand and shatter when hydrated during a rainy period after a warm dry period (Farrand 1985:28). As remains of extinct fauna occur below the rubble zone, the implication is that the Pleistocene climatic regime did not experience the extreme wet/dry cycles of modern times. The widely accepted model proposing that interior Brazil should have been drier than now during the late Pleistocene (e.g., Ab'Saber 1977) may be supported by the evidence from Toca de Manoel Latão.

Faunal Remains

A few gastropod tests and shell fragments were mixed among the rubble in the upper part of the brown clay/silt zone, but shell fragments rarely occurred below 20 cm depth. Bones of small mammals and fragments of bone of large mammals were recovered from all levels of the clay/silt deposit. In general, bone fragments were most abundant on the west side of the excavated area, with a marked decrease in the central part of the chamber; but localized concentrations also occurred on the east side. Fragments of bone of large mammals were commonly found near rock slabs, and many concentrations were encountered in other areas as well. Fragments of bone of large mammals were found in the clay/silt directly underlying rock slabs at the 20–40 cm level. In terms of vertical distribution, bone fragments were most abundant from 10 to 40 cm depth, becoming less frequent below this depth. Other than a few glyptodon scutes, only small mammal bones, mostly of bats or microtines regurgitated from owl pellets, were found below 60 cm depth.

Fragments of bone of large or medium-sized mammals were small; few specimens exceeded 30 mm in length. Species identification was possible only with preserved podials, teeth, and scutes. Modern species which were identified by the zoologist Martha Locks are listed in Table 3-3. Unfortunately the provenience and frequency of the modern faunal remains were not recorded at the time of species identification. The field notes suggest that remains of apparently modern small mammals were distributed in the silt deposits to bedrock. The distribution of remains of extinct taxa, including equid, giant armadillo *(Pampatherium)*, giant sloth *(Nothrotherium)*, camelid *(Paleolama)*, and glyptodon is given in Table 3-4. These remains were identified by the paleontologist Diogenes de Almeida Campos.

Cultural Stratigraphy

No definite cultural features—no hearths, ash lenses, or pits—were encountered in the deposits in the eastern chamber at Toca de Manoel Latão. Indeed, not even fragments of charcoal were found in the clay/silt deposits. Nevertheless, there is clear evidence of sporadic human occupation of the cavern in the form of 78 stone or bone artifacts, found to a depth of 50–60 cm below surface .

Thirty-nine stone artifacts were recovered from the clay/silt deposits. The 0–10 cm level yielded 11 utilized quartz fragments, two utilized limestone flakes, three fragments of quartzite pebble hammerstones, and one fragment of hematite. The 10–20 cm level produced four utilized quartz fragments, one spall of a quartzite hammerstone, one utilized quartzite flake, two chert scrapers, and two hematite fragments. The 20–30 cm level yielded six utilized quartz fragments. The 30–40 cm level produced four utilized quartz fragments and a utilized quartzite flake. A utilized chert fragment was

Table 3-3. List of Modern Species of Mammals Identified in Sediments in Toca de Manoel Latão.

Mazama gouazubira	caatinga deer
Mazama americana	forest deer
Tayassu albirostris	peccary
Tayassu tajacu	peccary
Euphractus sexcinctus	armadillo
Tolypeutes tricinctus	armadillo
Felis pardalis	ocelot
Nasua nasua	coatimundi
Kerodon rupestris	*mocó*, a rat-sized rodent
Cebus apella	monkey

Table 3-4. Distribution of Remains of Extinct Taxa by Stratigraphic Level in Toca de Manoel Latão.

depth 10–20 cm	
Square B4	*Nothrotherium* sp., 1 complete molar
Square D5 north	*Pampatherium* sp., 1 left distal phalanx, digit 4; 1 left medial phalanx, digit 4
depth 20–30 cm	
Square D4	*Pampatherium* sp., 1 juvenile tooth; 1 tooth
Square C4	1 large edentate scute probably *Pampatherium*
depth 30–40 cm	
Square D4	*Equus* sp., 2 left astragalus fragments, same individual
Square C5	1 large edentate scute probably *Pampatherium*
depth 40–50 cm	
Square B5	*Equus* sp., 1 carpal
Square C5	6 large edentate scutes probably *Pampatherium*
depth 50–60 cm	
Square C4/C5	*Paleolama* sp., 1 right mandibular 1st molar
depth 80–90 cm	
Square C4	4 fragmentary scutes of large edentate
depth 120–130 cm	
Square C4	1 large thick edentate scute probably glyptodon

found in the 50–60 cm level. In addition, 93 unmodified flakes of quartz, quartzite, chert, or limestone were distributed in the sediments to a maximum depth of 50 cm below surface (Table 3-5).

Twenty-eight bone artifacts were also recovered from the clay/silt deposits. Three definite bone artifacts were found at the 40–50 cm level: one a fragment of a long bone of a small mammal with a cut and bevelled end, one an equid podial with two well-defined deep short cut marks, and the other a broken bone bipoint. Six fragments of possible bone points were recovered from the 30–40 cm level; and 15 fragments of possible bone points from the 20–30 cm level along with one scratched bone fragment and one possibly worked tooth. Two other possibly worked fragments of bone were recovered from the 0–10 cm level.

Thus simple but definite stone and bone artifacts occurred in the consolidated clay/silt deposits of Toca de Manoel Latão at the same level and below bones of extinct species. A late-Pleistocene dating is indicated for the earlier human occupations of the cavern.

ARTIFACTS

Surface Finds

At the time of the first visit to Toca de Manoel Latão, a broken quartzite pebble hammerstone was noted but not collected from the surface of the eastern chamber. The only bones on the surface of the eastern chamber were small mammal bones, most of which were in drip pools, where they had been rolled and polished. However, three fragments of heavily permineralized and iron-stained large mammal bones (BA-CE-2/29, 30, 31) were collected from the surface of the backdirt pile in the central chamber. These fossilized bone fragments range in size from 46 x 32 x 14 mm to 18 x 13 x 7 mm. Short incisions and scrape marks across the grain of the bone were visible on the external surfaces only of these fragments. Also the piece with the largest number of cross-hatched incisions and scrape marks exhibits two negative bulbs from blows evidently directed before permineralization. The presence of incisions and scrape marks on fossilized large mammal bones was the major factor that prompted excavation of the undisturbed eastern chamber.

Worked Bone

Unfortunately the conditions for permineralization of bone were different in the upper part of the deposits in the eastern chamber: surface marks of workmanship were rarely visible on bone from the latter zone. In fact, most bones from the cultural zone (up to 60 cm depth in the clay/silt) are very similar in color to fresh bone; although we discovered later, when some bones were sent for radiocarbon analysis, that no collagen was present. Evidently most of the collagen in most bones from this zone had been replaced with calcium carbonate, rather than iron compounds; so the surface of these bones was soft and friable when still wet. Perhaps the deeply iron-stained bones had become permineralized in constantly damp deposits, while the buff-colored bones had been subject to periodic drying.

At the time of the first excavation in August 1983, bones that appeared to be of interest were washed with fingers only, in water from the pond in the central chamber. Nineteen bone fragments were selected and called artifacts on the basis of shape or because scratches appeared to be visible on them. Later, when the pieces were examined in the museum, neither striations nor scrape marks were visible. Possibly the alkaline cave water (pH 7, normal for the area) had eroded all surface indications of workmanship. At the start of

Table 3-5. Distribution of Unmodified Stone Flakes in Sediments in Toca de Manoel Latão.

	Quartz	Quartzite	Limestone	Chert	Total
Square B4					
0–10 cm	7	2	1	0	10
10–20 cm	2	1	1	0	4
20–30 cm	1	0	0	0	1
30–40 cm	0	0	0	0	0
40–50 cm	0	0	0	0	0
				total	15
Square B5 north					
0–10 cm	4	0	0	0	4
10–20 cm	1	1	0	0	2
20–30 cm	0	1	0	0	1
30–40 cm	0	0	0	0	0
40–50 cm	0	0	0	0	0
				total	7
Square C3					
0–10 cm	8	5	0	1	14
10–20 cm	13	1	0	0	14
20–30 cm	8	2	0	0	10
30–40 cm	7	1	0	0	8
40–50 cm	9	3	0	0	12
				total	58
Square D4					
0–10 cm	0	0	2	0	2
10–20 cm	0	0	3	0	3
20–30 cm	0	0	0	0	0
30–40 cm	1	0	2	0	3
40–50 cm	0	0	0	0	0
				total	8
Square D5 north					
0–10 cm	0	1	3	0	4
10–20 cm	0	0	1	0	1
20–30 cm	0	0	0	0	0
30–40 cm	0	0	0	0	0
40–50 cm	0	0	0	0	0
				total	5
Total flakes: 93					

the second season of excavations in June 1984, interesting bones were washed in bottled mineral water; but fine scratches were still not visible, so we reverted to washing with cave water and resigned ourselves to the identification of bone artifacts by shape alone, without being able to identify fabrication marks. Nevertheless, three artifacts with surface marks were identified in 1984, in addition to one from the 1983 excavations. Interestingly, the bones with definite cuts and clear striations are amongst the deepest artifacts recovered, between 40 and 60 cm below surface, well below the 10- to 20-cm level which yielded the youngest remains of extinct fauna.

One end of a small mammal phalange (BA-CE-2/26), found in the northern sector of Square C5 at a depth of 40–50 cm, was intentionally bisected with an encircling incision; and broken squarely by snapping (Figure 3-6a). The piece, which measures 29 x 9 x 5 mm, could have been a bead. The cut marks are visible adjacent to the smooth square end. The other end was more roughly broken off squarely.

Another early artifact (BA-CE-2/76), an equid carpal found in the 40–50 cm level near the south wall of Square B5, exhibits two definite deep butchering cuts, the only such marks thus far found on any Pleistocene bones from the Central area. Dimensions of the bone are

56 x 32 x 17 mm. The presence of two short parallel V-shaped cuts, 4 mm and 8 mm in length, near and at right angles to a corner of this central carpal bone (Figures 3-6, b–e), was considered definite evidence for human occupation of the cavern in late Pleistocene times. The cuts are in a logical place for separating the foot from the radius of the horse's front leg.

A fragment of a porous large mammal bone (BA-CE-2/35) was recovered from a slumped part of the west wall of the northern sector of Square C5, and probably came from the lower part of the section. Two intersecting deep parallel cuts (10 cm long) or chop marks (the margins of the cuts are depressed) are present at an angle to the grain of the bone, which measures 32 x 19 x 9 mm.

One of the deepest specimens (BA-CE-2/69), from the 50–60 cm level, is a medium-sized mammal bone fragment (13 x 12 x 4 mm) which is stained dark brown because it was permineralized by iron compounds. The external surface of the piece exhibits many scratches in various directions, only two of which are parallel.

Another bone artifact (BA-CE-2/32), part of the articular distal end of a long bone of a large mammal, measures 48 x 32 x 24 mm. As the bone was well permineralized, clear evidence of workmanship is visible on the largest articular surface in the form of several long cut-and-scrape marks at various angles, with a concentration of short incisions near the most pointed end. The artifact came from the 20–30 cm level in the northern sector of Square C5.

The tip end of a felid (?) canine (BA-CE-2/70), which measures 12 x 5 x 4 mm with the root roughly broken off, came from the 0–10 cm level in the northern sector of Square D5. The edge of the break is smooth and polished. Several short striations and one deep incision, 2 mm long, visible at right angles to the axis of the tooth and parallel with the break, cannot have been caused by natural wear. Two other mammal teeth, found in the northern sector of Square C5 at the 20–30 cm level, were segregated as appearing unusual, although no definite evidence that they were artifacts could be seen. A broken canine tooth (BA-CE-2/20) from the 20–30 cm level in Square C5 was naturally split longitudinally, creating a point which could feasibly have been hafted. The tooth fragment measures 22 x 7 x 4 mm. One peccary (?) molar (BA-CE-2/19) from the same area appeared to

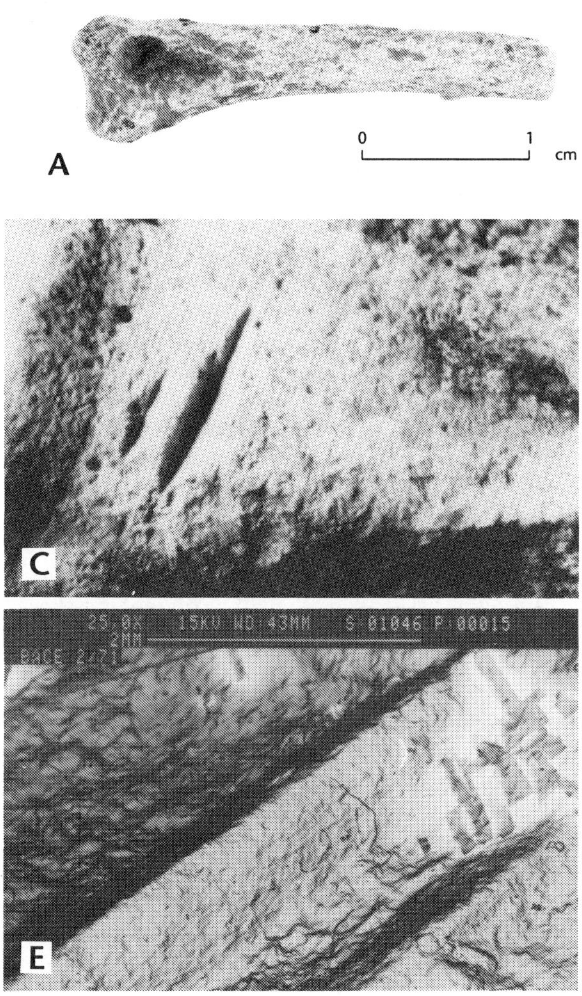

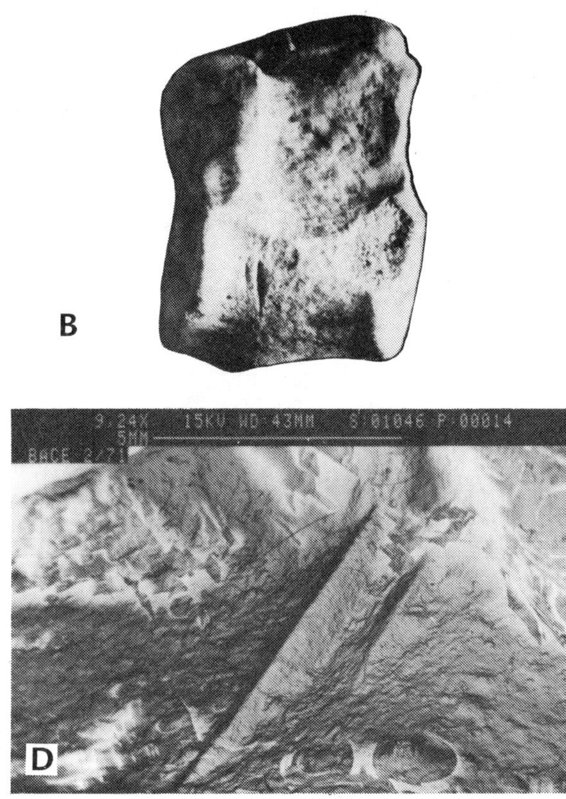

Figure 3-6. A) bone artifact BA-CE-2/26, a small mammal phalange with cut end; **B)** horse carpal (BA-CE-2/76) with two deep cut marks on exterior surface; **C)** detail of cut marks; **D)** cut marks at 9.24X SEM magnification; **E)** at 25X SEM magnification.

have its roots worn off flat at the base of the enamel, possibly by use as a tool; but no marks of wear are visible and the flat base may be a natural feature of a deciduous tooth.

Another more definite bone artifact from the 40–50 cm level in the northern sector of Square C5 is the broken half of a bone-splinter bipoint (BA-CE-2/25), with symmetrically pointed tip (Figure 3-7a); and deliberately fashioned from near the expanding end of a small mammal or large bird bone so that in cross-section the tip "bends" naturally outward. The specimen measures 20 x 6 x 2 mm. The piece has been snapped transversely with a hinge break. Evidently the point was tied onto a projectile shaft with the pointed basal end protruding as a barb. The tip end snapped off upon impact, and was probably left in the field. The base end was removed and replaced with a new point in the cavern. Possibly a complete although short (dimensions 23 x 7 x 3 mm) symmetrical point (BA-CE-2/34) was found in the slump from the west wall of the northern sector of Square C5 (depth 0–50 cm). This piece of a medium-sized mammal bone is not "bent," but it could have been hafted onto a bevelled wooden shaft so that one point protruded in front while the other formed a barb. Such projectile points are still used by some lowland South American Indians. Three larger fragments of medium-sized mammal bone, ranging from 42 to 28 mm in length, also could be segments of bone-splinter bipoints. Two (BA-CE-2/7, 8) are from the 20–30 cm level in Square C4, and one (BA-CE-2/22) is from the 20–30 cm level in the northern sector of Square C5.

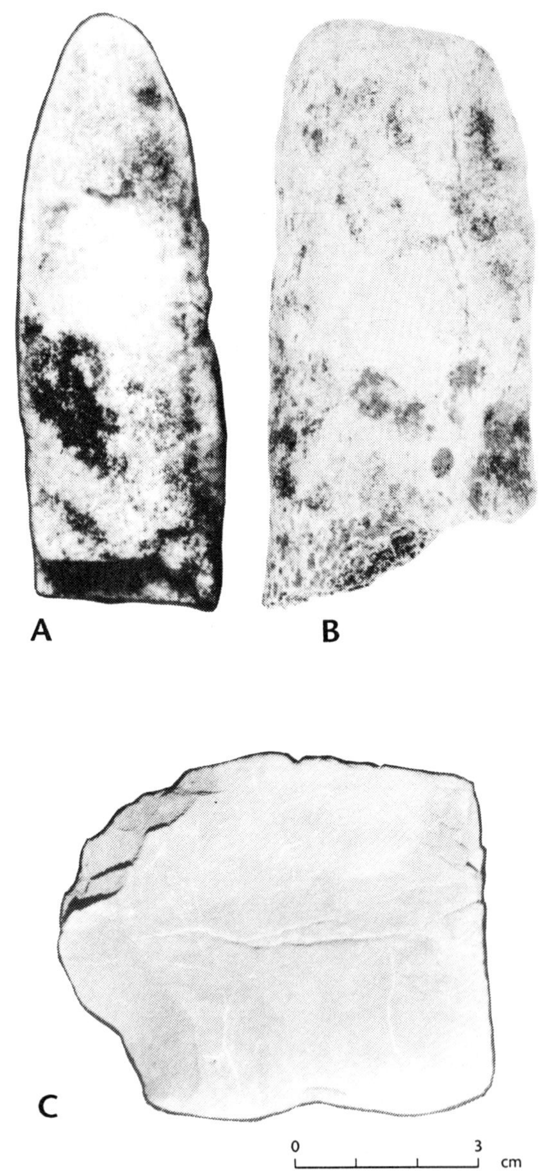

Figure 3-7. A) fragment of bone bipoint (BA-CE-2/25), magnified; **B)** base of bone point (BA-CE-2/10), magnified; **C)** limestone chopper (BA-CE-2/2).

Eleven fragments of medium-sized mammal bones ranging in length from 29 to 12 mm are possible fragments of projectile points. All but one were found in Square C4. Six occurred on the 20–30 cm level and five on the 30–40 cm level. Most appear to be one end of a bone-splinter bipoint (BA-CE-2/4, 5, 6, 9, 12, 13, 14, 17, 24), but two (BA-CE-2/11, 16) may be central sections of flattened cylindrical points. A 43-mm-long central section of a medium-sized mammal long bone (BA-CE-2/23), found at a depth of 28 cm in the northern sector of Square C5, appears to be the central section of a flattened cylindrical bone projectile point; but there is no definite evidence of workmanship on the surface of this bone or the other probable bone point fragments.

One base of a probable projectile point (BA-CE-2/10) was found in the 20–30 cm level in Square C4, and another (BA-CE-2/70) in the 30–40 cm level of the northern sector of Square D5. Evidently sections of long bone of large mammal were intentionally shaped into points with squared bases and an oval cross-section. The specimens measure 35 x 17 x 12 mm and 13 x 13 x 4 mm respectively. The broken end of the longest fragment (BA-CE-2/10; Figure 3-7b) reveals a fine network of cancellous tissue such as might be present in the head of a femur.

Two badly eroded central segments of solid bone apparently shaped into oval sections of points were found in the northern sector of Square D5 in the 20–30 cm level. BA-CE-2/65 measures 17 x 17 x 8 mm, while BA-CE-2/66 is 23 x 12 x 6 mm. The break at the larger end of the latter tapering piece is more eroded than at the smaller end, indicating that the ends broke at different times. The other artifact does not taper; but again one end appears to have an older break, suggesting that both could have been bases of hafted points, the tips of which broke off in the field. The symmetrically tapering tip end of another possible bone point (BA-CE-2/74) came from the 20–30 cm level in the northern part of Square B5. It measures 12 x 6 x 1 mm. All these fragments feature the proper form for parts of bone projectile points, but any evidence of workmanship has been obliterated by erosion of the surface of the bone.

An unusual cylindrical bone rod (BA-CE-2/53) which expands symmetrically to a blunt tip could have been a bird bunt point. It measures 24 x 7 x 7 mm. The base is broken, providing a cross-section of a solid large mammal bone which was shaped across the coarse grain. All surfaces except the broken end are polished, although again there are no surface marks of manufacture. The artifact was found in Square B4 at a depth of 0–10 cm.

Stone Artifacts

Flaked stone occurred in the upper third of the 150-cm-deep deposits of clay/silt in the eastern chamber. Utilized quartz, quartzite, chert, limestone, and hematite flakes or fragments were recovered. Very small weathered chunks of quartz and black chert occur scattered throughout the sediments, evidently redeposited into the cavern when heavy rains flooded the area. Dense fine-grained limestone occurs within the cavern. Two of the tabular slabs of roof fall south of the excavated area exhibit apparently intentional negative flake scars on their edges. As these isolated slabs evidently fell flat onto the silt sediments from the roof, and there was minimal roof fall thereafter, natural flaking by roof fall cannot explain the abundant flake scars on these slabs which are in the most intensively occupied part of the cave.

One large limestone flake (BA-CE-2/60), which measures 76 x 44 x 22 mm, was considered to be an artifact because the prominent excurving lip on the positive bulbar platform edge (120° angle) is differentially worn where it was evidently used for scraping or rubbing something soft, like hide. This artifact came from the 0–10 cm level in Square D4. Probably there would be more limestone flake artifacts recognized if this type of stone did not weather so rapidly.

A naturally horse-hoof-shaped piece of weathered limestone (BA-CE-2/2) which does not appear to be derived from the roof of the cavern was found in the upper 5 cm of deposit in Square C4. It measures 64 x 52 x 38 mm (Figure 3-7c). The wedge-shaped end of the piece exhibits a series of four flake scars removed probably by use as a chopper. Also one corner was used as a chopper, removing a series of split cone spalls with one blow.

Although only one red pictograph is visible in Toca de Manoel Latão, three pieces of hematite nodules striated on their external faces were recovered from near the west wall in Square C3, one in the 0–10 cm level and two in the 10–20 cm level. Two of these fragments are small (33 x 22 x 18 mm and 16 x 8 x 2 mm), and exhibit overlapping striations and scrape marks on one side of the smallest piece (BA-CE-2/54) and on three intersecting facets on the thicker chunk (BA-CE-2/39). The most unusual piece (BA-CE-2/40) is a large hinged flake fragment (58 x 38 x 13 mm) with the outer smooth face heavily striated by grinding generally in one direction. After the surface was ground, the nodule was evidently broken open by removing a large flake that hinged. The bulbar end was then truncated and removed by placing the flat flake on an anvil and striking the outer surface, creating a 90° angle break. To judge from the polish and wear on the broken edges, particularly the hinge break, the edges were then used for scraping or rubbing something soft, such as skin. The polish extends onto the face over the older grinding striations.

Three quite different kinds of chert, none occurring naturally in the cavern, were used to make scrapers. Two flake scrapers came from Square C3 in the 10–20 cm level. A flat secondary flake (43 x 35 x 11 mm) of dark-brown chert (BA-CE-2/43) with an eraillure scar on its positive bulbar face was unidirectionally retouched to create a serrated lateral edge (edge angle 40°) 20 cm long (Figure 3-8a). A steep keeled scraper (BA-CE-2/45) was step-flaked from the flat face by heavy use along nearly all irregular edges (edge angles from 55° to 90°). The artifact, also from the 10–20 cm level in Square C3, measures 56 x 46 x 20 mm (Figure 3-8b). This chert is a very distinctive banded black and yellowish pink stone composed of cemented oolites. One flake was removed from the planar face to resharpen a very worn projection. Four other projections of various sizes and shapes, as well as several concave edges, also show considerable wear. This scraper was probably used to shape bone and wooden artifacts. A natural chunk of grey chert (BA-CE-2/49) with a triangular cross-section (dimensions 38 x 20 x 12 mm) was unidirectionally use-retouched along the sharpest edge (33 mm long, with an edge angle of 40°). Flakes removed from the opposite face of two projecting corners (with edge angles of 40° and 55°) were evidently intentionally removed to resharpen these worn corners (Figure 3-8c). This artifact came from the 50–60 cm level in Square C4/C5.

Quartzite does not occur naturally in the limestone region in the northern part of the *municipio* of Central, although flakeable quartzite occurs about 30 km away in the Serra Azul, and dark-red quartzite occurs in the *serras* flanking the Rio São Francisco 100 km or more north of the area. One of the nearest sources of quartzite pebbles would be the Rio Verde, about 30 km west of Toca de Manoel Latão. Quartzite, in the form of river pebbles, was a material favored by the occupants of the Central area; and its presence on the surface is one of the easiest means of locating an archaeological site in the limestone area. Complete quartzite tools were carefully curated; usually only broken or expended tools and flakes are encountered by the archaeologist.

The collection of quartzite artifacts recovered from Toca de Manoel Latão includes a pebble chopper, two broken hammerstones, a spall from a hammerstone, four utilized flakes, and a flaked pebble fragment. Most of the quartzite artifacts came from the upper 20 cm in the clay/silt deposit. All are pieces of pebbles which had become rounded in a river. The oval pebble tool (BA-CE-2/33), found on the surface of Square B4, was unidirectionally flaked along one side (rather than an end) to create a 55-mm-long working edge (with a 70° angle) which is slightly worn (Figure 3-9a). The overall dimensions are 69 x 40 x 26 mm. Half of a hammerstone (BA-CE-2/37), evidently broken by a heavy blow near the center of a face, probably while being used as an anvil, was found in Square C3 at a depth of 3 cm below surface. The remaining end exhibits battering on the tip, and two areas of concentrated peck marks on the flattest lateral faces near the battered end (Figure 3-9b). There are also scattered peck marks elsewhere on the surface of this ovoid, originally white quartzite hammerstone,

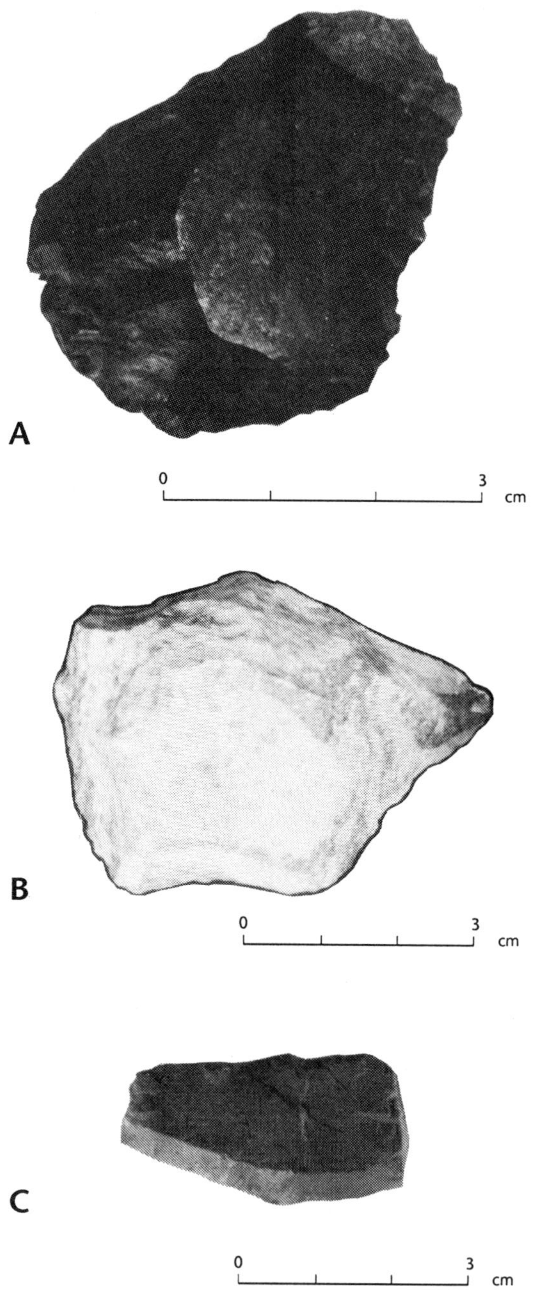

Figure 3-8. A) chert flake scraper (BA-CE-2/43); **B)** chert steep keeled scraper (BA-CE-2/45); **C)** utilized chert fragment (BA-CE-2/49).

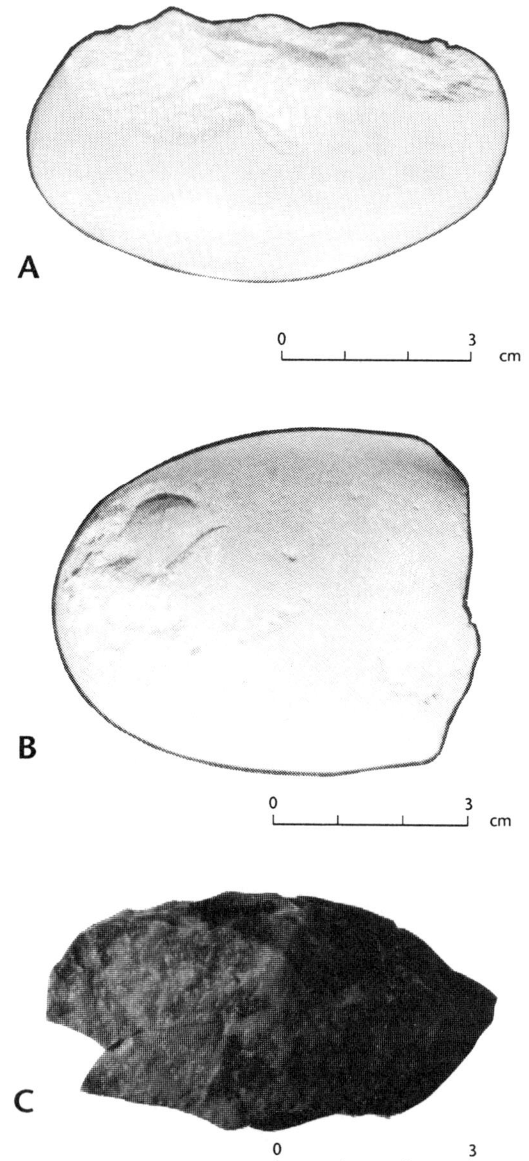

Figure 3-9. A) quartzite pebble tool (BA-CE-2/33); **B)** quartzite hammerstone fragment (BA-CE-2/37); **C)** utilized quartzite flake (BA-CE-2/78).

which now measures 56 x 52 x 50 mm. An ovoid heavily weathered disintegrating buff quartzite (or sandstone?) pebble (BA-CE-2/46), exhibiting fine bedding planes, was heavily battered on both ends and pecked on two faces. This hammerstone, which measures 82 x 80 x 51 mm, was found in Square D4 at a depth of 8 cm. A small (28 x 23 x 7 mm) quartzite spall (BA-CE-2/44) removed by a heavy blow from a red quartzite hammerstone was excavated from Square C3 in the 10–20 cm level. The original face exhibits a pecked depression, but there is no evidence of subsequent use. Another flaked section of a red quartzite pebble hammerstone (BA-CE-2/51), exhibiting peck marks on its original rounded surface, was split by a heavy blow into a flake looking like the segment of an orange (dimensions 58 x 43 x 22 mm). The wedge-shaped projection formed by the intersection of the positive bulb and a cleavage plane exhibits differential use-wear as if someone had used it to groove a piece of wood. Also the excurvate edge (50° angle) has several use-flake scars removed from the cortex surface. This unusual artifact was recovered from the 0–10 cm level in Square B4.

There are a variety of flake tools of quartzite in the collection. The excurvate edge of a thick flake (BA-CE-2/28), found on the surface of Square C5, had been retouched to form a steep irregular working edge with graver spurs and a concave (spokeshave) section which have been worn and polished. Evidently this scraper, measuring 47 x 48 x 18 mm, broke in half and was discarded. A section of a white sugary quartzite pebble (BA-CE-2/36) was recovered from Square C3 in the 0–10 cm level. One irregular edge (45° edge angle), created by intersecting breaks, appears to be use-flaked and worn, as if the fragment had been used briefly as a chopper. This artifact measures 72 x 69 x 29 mm. A thick utilized flake of white quartzite (BA-CE-2/3) was found at a depth of 10 cm in Square C4. It measures 57 x 54 x 22 mm. The dorsal face has a central ridge, so it may have been a flake-blade before the distal end broke off. Both lateral edges exhibit use flaking and polishing. This piece is unusual in that most of the thick platform (which still exhibits a bit of the original waterworn surface of a pebble) has been removed by a blow directed from the corner of the dorsal ridge. This retouch blow was intended to create two sharp (but steeper) working edges, one of which exhibits heavy use-wear.

Two secondary quartzite flakes with both positive and negative bulbs on the same cortical platform exhibit subsequent use flaking on their distal edges. The distal edge of BA-CE-2/42 was snapped to create two 90° angle edges, one of which is worn smooth while the other exhibits several use-flake scars removed from the dorsal surface. This artifact, measuring 62 x 37 x 17 mm, also exhibits use flaking on a lateral 25° edge. It was recovered from the 10–20 cm level in Square C3. The deepest quartzite artifact (BA-CE-2/78) came from the 30–40 cm level in the northern sector of Square B5 (Figure 3-9c). The prominent positive bulb on this yellow-stained flake (dimensions 62 x 37 x 17 mm) is differentially worn, and the distal edge was subsequently unidirectionally steeply retouched (to a 70° angle) on a 28-mm-long section to reveal the original white color. This flake evidently was retouched long after it was originally created. The presence of some yellow stain on the retouched surface indicates that the flaking was not done by a pick in excavation.

Quartz was the favorite stone material used for cutting, scraping, graving, or whittling various materials because it is very hard and the working edges retain their usefulness longer than other kinds of stone. Clear quartz crystal was the best for cutting because it can be flaked in a normal way after the crystal faces are carefully broken open by bipolar flaking. Most vein quartz crystals have too many immature crystal faces for easy flaking. Clear crystal does not occur in the Central area, however; so it is not surprising that only one obviously utilized clear crystal flake was found at Toca de Manoel Latão. This small (15 x 13 x 5 mm) secondary flake-blade (BA-CE-2/47) with a central ridge came from the 20–30 cm level in Square C3. This microtool, which retains a crystal facet on its striking platform, exhibits considerable evidence of use. The sharpest lateral edge (30° angle) and the opposite projecting corner are use-flaked and worn. The distal end, which was snapped by downward pressure, has subsequently been used to scrape something containing quartz grit because the action ground the edge and left it stained reddish brown. Even the 90° edges of the thick platform exhibit use flaking.

Another retouched quartz flake (BA-CE-2/15), found at 35 cm depth in Square C4, exhibits both positive and negative bulbs struck from the same platform but at different times. One end of this artifact, which measures 29 x 27 x 7 mm, has been intentionally formed into a blunt graver (?) point by retouching on either side of the point from alternate faces (Figures 3-10, a–b).

Stream-rolled quartz pebbles also had to be transported from elsewhere to Toca de Manoel Latão. Artifact BA-CE-2/79 is a segment (measuring 18 x 13 x 4 mm) of a fairly clear crystal pebble which was quartered along crystal faces to create an excurvate end (80° angle) useful for scraping, a sharp (40° angle) lateral edge, and three 90° angle edges at the other end. All edges feel somewhat worn, and a use flake was removed from one of the right-angled edges. This artifact was recovered from the 30–40 cm level in Square B5.

Vein quartz does occur naturally in the Central area. Irregular milky-white crystals were observed extruding through calcite veins at Maxixe, about 6 km west of Toca de Manoel Latão; and concentrations of broken chunks of poorly crystallized vein quartz were found in various places along trails where prehistoric people evidently had broken up pieces that were eroding out of the limestone. The presence of small weathered chunks and vein

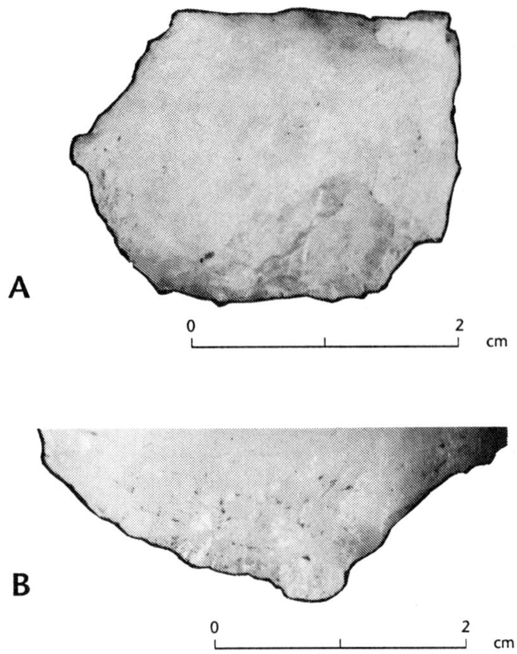

Figure 3-10. A) retouched quartz flake (BA-CE-2/15); **B)** closeup of graver point on retouched quartz flake (BA-CE-2/15).

quartz crystals throughout the cave sediments indicates that there was a source somewhere near the cavern.

Three different but intergrading forms of vein quartz were used at Toca de Manoel Latão. Irregular milky-white crystals, usually broken apart by bipolar flaking, are the form on which the evidence for alteration and use was most easily seen. More massive chunks of vein quartz, that often were broken open haphazardly simply by bashing them with another rock, nevertheless can contain many useful edges and projections. These grade into a third form of angular and tabular chunks, often composed of interlocking tiny crystals, which grew to fill a narrow vein. These latter pieces are the most difficult to analyse.

Two small irregular vein quartz crystals, which have acquired a yellow stain from sediment, evidently were broken open by bipolar flaking and used. Artifact BA-CE-2/77 is the central section of a vein quartz crystal with one naturally rough end. The apex of the crystal at the opposite end was bipolarly split by holding one crystal facet on an anvil and striking the opposing broken edge. One corner of the concave split cone face was later renewed to create a sharp projection with an 85° angle working edge. The steep opposite edge (90° angle) of the split cone face was also use-worn. This artifact, which measures 11 x 11 x 10 mm, came from the 30–40 cm level in Square B4. The other small naturally worn crystal (BA-CE-2/55) was split open obliquely by holding one flat surface on an anvil and striking an opposite crystal face, creating a useful 50° angle end which would serve as a tiny endscraper. This end is heavily worn, and many use flakes were removed from the crystal faces by a pushing action, such as planing wood. This small tool, measuring 18 x 12 x 8 mm, came from the 10–20 cm level in Square C3.

Eight vein quartz crystals evidently were split open bipolarly by holding one crystal face or flat edge on an anvil and striking an opposing crystal face. This careful flaking technique yielded many edges and projections useful for working other materials. Five of these split crystals came from the upper 10 cm of the clay/silt deposit. An elongated chunk of vein quartz (BA-CE-2/18) with a triangular pointed apex at one end came from 10 cm below surface in Square C5. This specimen measures 30 x 13 x 14 mm (Figure 3-11a). All three edges of the pointed end appear to be use-worn (Figure 3-11b). A chunk of vein quartz (BA-CE-2/1) from the upper 5 cm in Square C4 measures 48 x 28 x 7 mm. All edges of the flat face show use wear and flaking, evidently to form a point at one end and a nose at one corner. Both the point and the nose show evidence of use wear. Two opposing 80° edges are worn and use-flaked on artifact BA-CE-2/57, which came from the 0–10 cm level in Square C3. This artifact measures 28 x 18 x 14 mm. A concave broken edge (60° angle) is also apparently use-flaked and worn, as if it had been used as a spokeshave. The upper 10 cm of the clay/silt in Square D4 yielded artifact BA-CE-2/64, two faces of which were split

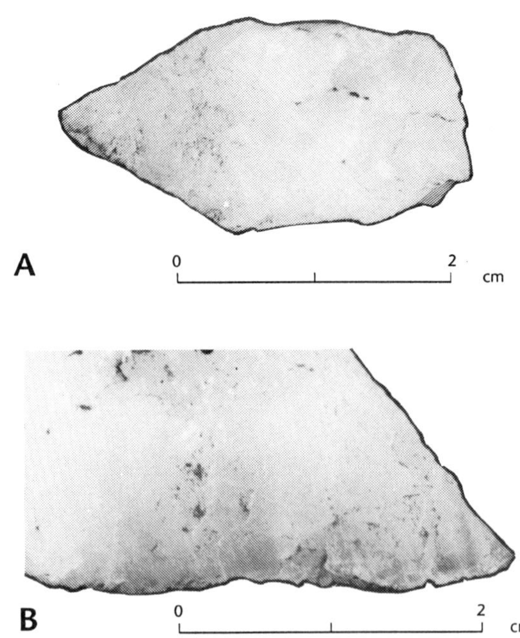

Figure 3-11. A) utilized quartz flake (BA-CE-2/18); **B)** closeup of utilized quartz flake (BA-CE-2/18).

bipolarly. At least one lateral edge (55° angle) of this artifact, which measures 19 x 18 x 12 mm, exhibits use flaking; and all edges feel worn. Artifact BA-CE-2/52, from the 0–10 cm level in Square B4, is split along a crystal face. One 21-mm-long straight edge (55° angle) feels differentially smooth, and a use flake was removed from a pointed end. Artifact BA-CE-2/75 came from the 10–20 cm level in the northern sector of Square B5. An 80° angle edge of this piece, which measures 23 x 19 x 12 mm, was step-flaked by heavy use. One projecting end (4 mm wide, with an edge angle of 40°) of BA-CE-2/61 is use-flaked and worn. An adjacent edge of this artifact, from the 20–30 cm level of Square C3, is use-flaked from the other direction. Both flaked edges of this piece, which measures 35 x 17 x 12 mm, are differentially worn. Another fragment (BA-CE-2/73) from the 20–30 cm level of Square B4 exhibits use flaking and wear on an excurving end (80° edge angle), which was used like an endscraper. The used edge is 10 mm long, and the piece measures 25 x 14 x 13 mm.

A retouched pyramidal chunk of vein quartz crystal (BA-CE-2/21) with use-battered apex was recovered from 20 cm depth in the northern sector of Square C5. This specimen measures 19 x 15 x 9 mm. Traces of probable use wear and crushing are visible along one steep edge and adjacent to a graver spur which appears to have been broken by use.

Careful intentional bipolar flaking is not evident on the remainder of the vein quartz chunks which show evidence of use. All 12 of them could have be formed simply by throwing another rock at large vein quartz chunks while they were lying on a hard surface. One edge of a vein quartz fragment (BA-CE-2/72), from the 0–10 cm level in the northern sector of Square B5, was used and then intentionally resharpened by removing several flakes from the flattest broken face to create a serrated scraping edge (65° edge angle). This piece measures 24 x 22 x 15 mm. An excurving projection (50° edge angle) on one corner of BA-CE-2/68 has evidently been use-flaked. This artifact, which measures 37 x 31 x 18 mm, came from the 0–10 cm level in Square B4. The same uppermost level of Square C3 yielded BA-CE-2/59, which measures 33 x 24 x 13 mm. Two negative flake scars removed from one edge (60° angle) were evidently placed to form a serrated edge with several worn projections. Another utilized quartz chunk (BA-CE-2/41) came from the 10–20 cm level in Square C3. There are several worn edges and projections (edge angles of 80° to 90°) resharpened by carefully placed negative flake scars. This multi-purpose tool measures 38 x 43 x 33 mm. Another vein quartz chunk (BA-CE-2/48), from the 20–30 cm level in Square C3, has a small sharp projection on one 65° edge which evidently was intentionally created by removing two lateral flakes. This artifact measures 27 x 22 x 18 mm.

The most projecting end of an angular quartz chunk (BA-CE-2/62) from the 20–30 cm level in Square C3 appears to be use-flaked from one direction. A long narrow resharpening flake that looks like a burin spall scar was removed from the opposite face of the projecting end (edge angle 90°). This artifact measures 35 x 24 x 22 mm. A naturally rhomboidal chunk of vein quartz (BA-CE-2/67) that broke along jointing planes was recovered from the 30–40 cm level in Square C3. One irregularly straight edge (80° angle), culminating in a pointed projection at one corner, appears to be use-flaked and worn. This piece measures 34 x 28 x 17 mm. The naturally projecting gouge-like end of BA-CE-2/58, 11 mm long with an edge angle of 60°, is use-flaked and worn. This piece, which measures 44 x 27 x 20 mm, is an example of a naturally useful-shaped object which probably was picked up and used without any alterations. It was found in the 0–10 cm level of Square C3. Another example is a naturally tabular piece (BA-CE-2/63), measuring 67 x 48 x 14 mm, which was first thought to be a piece of flowstone. Three edges, with angles varying from 50° to 90°, and the high spots on one convex face of this artifact have been differentially worn. The center of the smooth face of this piece, from the 20–30 cm level in Square C3, also retains a red stain, presumably from hematite. Possibly this artifact was used to prepare red ochre or perhaps to apply it to some material such as hide.

The last two pieces of tabular vein quartz exhibit minimal evidence of use flaking or wear. Both came from just below the surface of Square C3. One piece (BA-CE-2/56) appears to be a flake with a positive bulb, and it measures 57 x 43 x 17 mm. The irregular distal end, with an edge angle of 65° to 80°, is differentially worn; and a rounded lateral projection (8 mm wide with an edge angle of 40°) is use-flaked and heavily worn. An irregular tabular chunk (BA-CE-2/38) exhibits rough stepped flaking from use along one edge, which is 18 mm long with an edge angle of 50°. There may be use flaking on other edges of this large chunk, which measures 72 x 59 x 30 mm.

Unmodified Stone Flakes

A total of 93 flakes were identified from excavated levels to a depth of 50 cm below surface in the clay/silt. Data on the distribution of the flakes are given in Table 3-5. The 0–10 cm level was most productive, with 34 flakes; 12 flakes occurred in the deepest level at 40–50 cm below surface. Square C3, in the midpart of the cavern, was most productive of flakes at all levels, yielding 62% of the total collection from the site.

Quartz flakes were the most common on all levels, constituting 66% of the total flake collection from the site. There were four quartz crystal flakes, but the great majority of flakes were of vein quartz. The flakes were small: the size range extended from 33 x 19 x 9 mm to 7 x 7 x 3 mm, with the mode approximately 16 x 10 x 5 mm. Platforms when preserved were simple and relatively large, indicating a percussion technique.

Quartzite flakes constituted 19% of the total collection from the site. The nearest source of this material is 30 km to the south. Twenty-three percent of the quartzite flakes retained cortex, indicating a derivation from pebbles. Quartzite flakes ranged in size from 63 x 41 x 15 mm to 11 x 9 x 5 mm, with the mode approximately 28 x 20 x 5 mm. Platforms when preserved were simple and relatively large.

Limestone flakes constituted 14% of the total collection from the site. The flakes were relatively large, ranging in size from 75 x 48 x 18 mm to 14 x 6 x 4 mm, with the mode approximately 30 x 25 x 6 mm. Platforms were large and simple.

Chert was a very rare material in the flake collections from Toca de Manoel Latão. Only one unmodified flake was found, measuring 17 x 13 x 5 mm. The platform was simple and large.

DISCUSSION AND CONCLUSIONS

Despite not being able to provide radiocarbon dates, Toca de Manoel Latão yielded the best evidence for human occupation of the Central area before Pleistocene fauna became extinct locally. At first sight, this cave did not look promising at all because the chamber floors were well below the valley floor, quite damp except during a prolonged drought, and barely light enough to support a few plants inside. The presence of permineralized large mammal bone fragments with possibly artificial surface markings in the pile of backdirt left recently by local people who dug out a waterhole in the central chamber alerted us to the possibility of contemporaneity of man and Pleistocene fauna. When we found a quartzite hammerstone and flakes on the surface of the smaller, undisturbed eastern chamber, we decided to gamble on testing this cave that otherwise appeared so unpromising.

Many other similar caves with chamber floors lower than the valley fill were located during the initial survey of Central in 1983. After our success with Toca de Manoel Latão, we took another look at several of these *tocas*; but none looked quite as good. The major problem with most low-lying chambers, even if they have sufficient fill and sufficient light, is that flood waters occasionally run rapidly through them. Thus, although they may have been occupied at an early time, the cultural evidence would easily have been disturbed and quite possibly redeposited.

No evidence of disturbance was found in the eastern chamber of Toca de Manoel Latão. Rainwater pours down a chimney onto the boulder-strewn slope at the front and drips onto the floor near the rear of the eastern chamber, but water does not run across the level floor after it has hit the drip pools. As the floor in the eastern chamber is higher than the central chamber and the eastern chamber is completely walled in, water soaks into dry deposits; and thus the chamber simply fills up like a bathtub until it overflows over the lowest western wall into the central chamber. Outside the drip pools, no sedimentary structures were seen. Also, there was no evidence that stone or bone artifacts had been moved either horizontally or vertically from their original positions. The possibility that artifacts sank into saturated sediments from the surface is disproven by the fact that the heaviest stone artifacts were within the upper 20 cm of the deposit, and all artifacts were found only in the upper 60 cm of the clay/silt deposits.

Identifiable remains of extinct fauna *(Nothrotherium and Pampatherium)* were first encountered in the 10–20 cm level; and continued to the 50–60 cm level, in which a *Paleolama* tooth was found with a utilized fragment of exotic chert. Unquestionable evidence of association of extinct fauna and artifacts came from the 40–50 cm levels, in which a clearly butchered equid podial, a small mammal phalange apparently cut to form a bead, and half of a carefully shaped bone splinter bipoint were found with 12 stone flakes. The 30–40 cm level yielded two fragments of an equid astragalus, a utilized quartzite flake, four utilized quartz fragments, and six possible bone points. The 20–30 cm level yielded *Pampatherium* teeth and scutes; 15 possible bone point fragments; a scratched bone fragment; and a possibly worked large canine tooth; along with six utilized quartz fragments, one of which retains a red stain on a worn working edge; and a number of flakes without evidence of use.

A thin but nevertheless definite picture emerges from this evidence that people occasionally came into the chamber to process animal and probably vegetal produce obtained while foraging. Although large cats could have dragged in kills, no evidence of felid chewing was seen on the bone fragments. The definitely cut podial of a horse is the only clear evidence we encountered in the Central area for butchering a large animal. Probably the camelid tooth was also carried in by man, but the edentates could have crawled into the cave by themselves. At the time it struck us as unusual, however, that we were finding teeth of so many different kinds of animals and so few bones. We wondered if it were possible that people collected teeth. Although several bone fragments appeared to have been shaped into projectile points, conclusive evidence for deliberate fabrication of a projectile point was found on only one artifact, which came from the same level as the cut equid podial. However, this apparent association does not mean that these early people habitually hunted large animals. Most likely, they opportunistically took advantage of whatever game of any size that they encountered.

The foraging way of life continued after local extinction of the various large mammals. The uppermost zone, which also contained considerable rubble along the west wall of the chamber, yielded several spalls removed from hammerstones by heavy impact blows; and a complete hammerstone was left on the surface of an unexcavated square. People may have used the hammerstone to remove flakes from the large slabs of roof fall, or they could have been pounding vegetal material or possibly bones to include in a soup. Such bone crushing behavior could, of course, explain the paucity of bones relative to teeth.

At the conclusion of our work, the excavated area was partially backfilled; and a wall was built in front of the large slab of rockfall to try to retard erosion. The area under the slab probably contains more remains of extinct fauna and artifacts, and should be retained for future excavations.

Chapter 4
Abrigo da Lesma

INTRODUCTION

Location and Description of Site

The Abrigo da Lesma is located on the Fazenda de Solon Ribeiro da Souza, about 10 km north of the town center of Central. It is a small rock overhang situated at the northwest end of a small rock outcrop or *pedreira* about 10 m east of the Serra da Candeia. The *pedreira*, which is only about 10 m wide, 15 m long, and 12 m in maximum height, is separated from the *serra* to the west by a narrow chasm filled with heavy rock fall. There is also heavy rock fall to the east and north of the shelter area, just outside the overhang; and the rocky area is only partially covered with soil and *caatinga* vegetation. It is likely that the *abrigo* is part of the same cave system as Toca dos Ossos Humanos, a very large, deep, partially collapsed cavern in the *serra* just to the west. About 10 m directly to the west of the *abrigo* is a small irregular opening leading down into the Toca dos Ossos Humanos: this opening, a small rockshelter, has a wide shelf of breccia at a level about 150 cm above the level of the floor of the Abrigo da Lesma; and there are white pictographs on the ceiling.

The Abrigo da Lesma faces northeast. Its ceiling varies in height from about 2 to 2.5 m over a floor area measuring about 8 m long by 3 to 4 m wide (map, Figure 4-1). The *abrigo* is windswept; and in a storm rain probably enters it, as the floor is the same level as the valley. In October the east end of the shelter is exposed to sunlight in the morning, and for a brief period in late afternoon sunlight enters the west end. The floor area within the dripline is fairly level (Figure 4-2a). At the beginning of excavation there were several large rock slabs, roof fall, lying flat on the surface of the floor area. The ceiling of the shelter is horizontally fractured, and it is obvious that in the future more slabs will fall; but the rear wall of the shelter has a smooth surface, nearly vertical. As no roof fall was encountered within the deposits to the maximum depth of excavation at 240 cm below surface, formation of the shelter is not due to roof collapse. It is possible that the present *abrigo* was originally a side chamber, at a high level, of the Toca dos Ossos Humanos cave system.

Although there are no paintings on either ceiling or wall within the shelter itself, the walls of the Lesma *pedreira* to either side of the overhang have panels of red pictographs; and there are also some faded paintings in a narrow slit in the *pedreira* to the west of the overhang. The pictographs are lines of dots, starbursts, isolated circles, ovals or rectangles filled with lines, curving lines, and a few biomorphic figures (including a face with large ears that resembles Mickey Mouse).

The Excavations

The Abrigo da Lesma was first observed by Valdemar Fausto da Silva on the areal site survey in July 1983. He collected several artifacts from the surface, including a large thick keeled quartzite uniface tool which resembled a lesma or limace (slug). As such artifacts have been dated between 11,000 and 9000 yr B.P. at sites in Goiás and Piauí, the site was considered to have the potential of early occupation levels. The site had no name, so the title Abrigo da Lesma was assigned.

We carried out excavations in the Abrigo da Lesma for three weeks in October 1983. A simple topographic

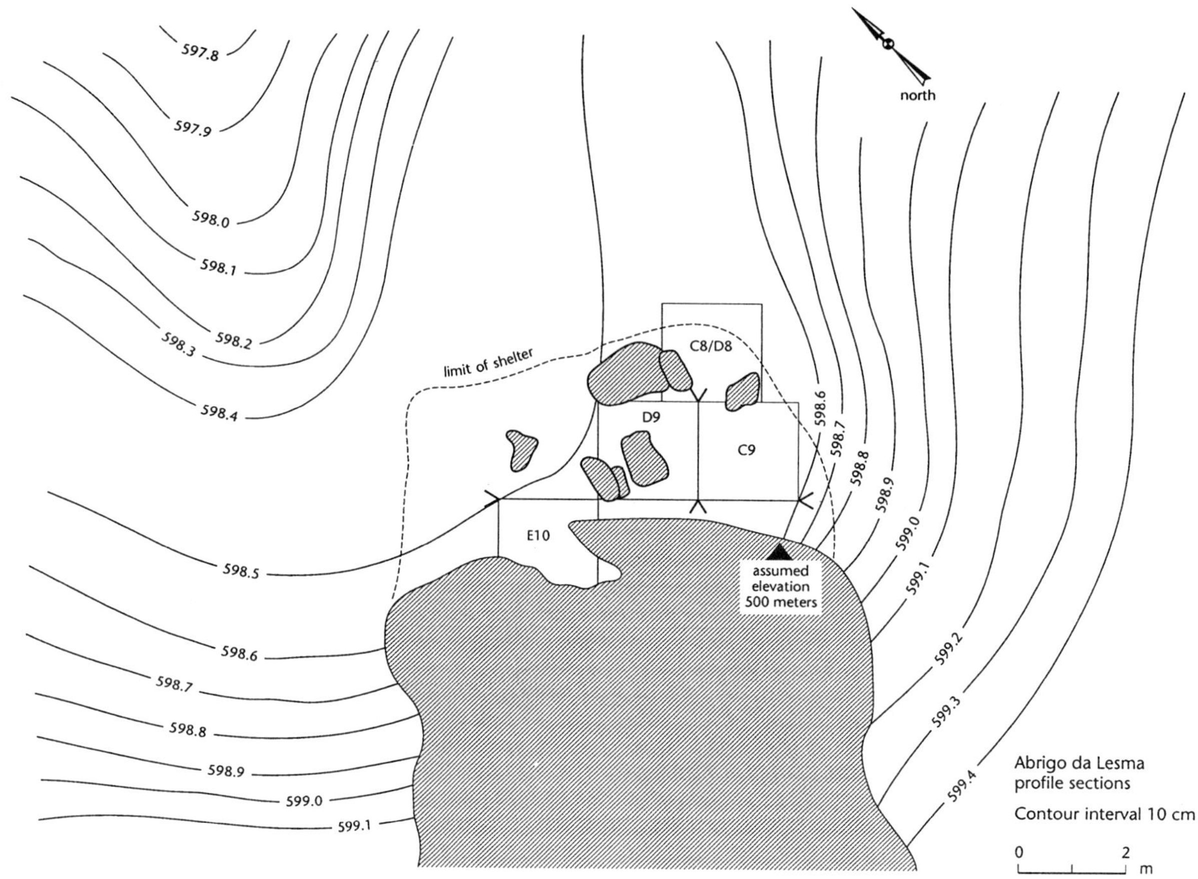

Figure 4-1. Plan of the Abrigo da Lesma.

map was made of the site and the area immediately surrounding it, and a grid system with 2-meter squares was imposed (map, Figure 4-1). Several large flat rock slabs resting on the floor of the shelter were rolled out of the way before excavations began. The first 2-meter square opened was Square C9, at the east end of the overhang. Subsequently, work began in Square C8/D8, a 2-meter-square area offset 60 cm west of the normal grid in order to avoid a tree. A 30-cm-wide baulk left between Square C8/D8 and Squares C9 and D9 was excavated at the close of field work at the site. Also excavated in October 1983 were Squares D9 and E10. A 60-cm baulk left between Squares C9 and D9 was excavated at the close of field work. Square E10 included the area of a small narrow alcove which extended into the *pedreira* at the west end of the overhang.

After artifacts and features were exposed, the deposits were removed in 10-cm levels. Excavation commenced with trowel and dustpan; but as the silt matrix became increasingly compact with depth, a geologist's pick was resorted to at the 30-cm level. By the 50-cm level a large heavy pick was necessary to loosen lumps of the deposit, subsequently broken up by a hammer. All excavated material was carried out by bucket and examined in a 4-mm sieve. All stone flakes and bone fragments were collected in level bags, and a sample of gastropod shell was preserved. Charcoal samples were also collected.

Excavation was carried to a maximum depth of 240 cm below surface in the southwest corner of Square C9 without encountering bedrock, although large rocks were exposed on the east side of this excavation unit at the 130-cm level. In other units, excavation was continued into the increasingly cemented silt deposit to levels more than 50 cm below the last flake or artifact recovered.

At the close of excavations profiles were drawn of the walls of all units excavated. Stratified series of soil samples were collected, but were left in Brazil to be analysed, and no report has been made. The excavated area was left open, with a fence built around it to protect livestock.

STRATIGRAPHY

Natural Stratigraphy

Field Description of the Sediments

The natural stratigraphic unit at the Abrigo da Lesma was a massive well-weathered silt deposit featuring gradual changes in color, texture, and consistency with increasing depth (profiles Figures 4-3, 4-4). In the upper 40–50 cm within the dripline, there was extensive cultural disturbance in the form of hearths and ash lenses, and human refuse. In addition, the soil profile was interrupted by a great fissure or vertical crack with secondary fill which ran across the central part of the site and extended in depth beyond the limit of excavation at approximately 200 cm.

The upper 50 cm of the silt deposit inside the dripline was the most complex in observable microstratigraphic details. In areas outside the dripline or with little cultural disturbance, the normal soil profile from 0–50 cm depth featured a well-marked crumb structure, brown to reddish-brown in color, dry and porous. Numerous small and large roots up to 10 cm in diameter crisscrossed horizontally as well as vertically through the sediment in this zone; and other elements of bioturbation of the deposits included several termite nests (cylindrical in form, with a hard shell about 10 cm in diameter and 20 cm in length), small insect cases, spider holes, and the occasional small rodent burrow. The major element of disturbance of the natural soil profile, to 50 cm below surface, however, was intensive human occupation of the shelter. Extensive irregular lenses of grey/white ash interpenetrated the silt sediment; and levels of occupation were littered by imported limestone fragments, stone flakes and artifacts, abundant gastropod shell fragments, and some fragments of riverine mussel shell, bone, and charcoal.

Below a depth of 50 cm, the massive silt deposit was reddish-brown in color and much more compact, difficult to excavate and break up for screening. Clay content increased, and below 70 cm a platy structure was apparent. At approximately this depth as well, small cemented nodules or irregular concretions of silt became frequent; and small spherical nodules of ironstone or manganese, up to 4 mm in diameter, became common. The degree of cementation of the silt deposit increased with depth; below the 150-cm level the silt was exceedingly hard. Below a depth of 130 cm in Square C8/D8 and the east part of Square C9, lumps, streaks, and ridges of a very hard yellow clayey silt appeared in the reddish-brown silt. This yellow clayey silt, which contained very hard cemented carbonate nodules and small manganese concretions, interpenetrated with the overlying reddish-brown silt; and appeared to be a soil horizon rather than a separate stratum. It was so cemented that a heavy pick could hardly flake it, and exposure of this zone in Squares C8/D8 and C9 effectively closed excavation. A few large rounded rocks had appeared on the east side of Square C9 at 130 cm depth, but bedrock was not reached.

Evidence of human occupation was found in the compact reddish-brown silt in the levels from 50 to 90 cm below surface in the form of scattered shell fragments, small charcoal fragments, stone flakes, and the

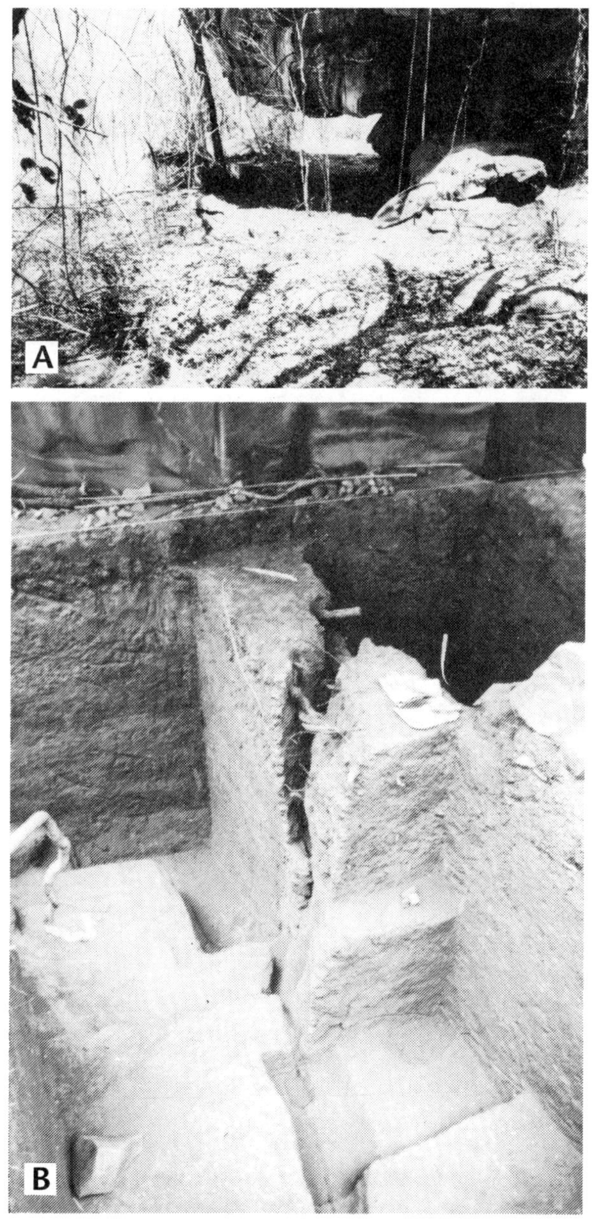

Figure 4-2. A) Abrigo da lesma from the west, with sheltered area in shade; **B)** excavations in the Abrigo da Lesma, showing massive silt deposit and the great fissure (in center of baulk).

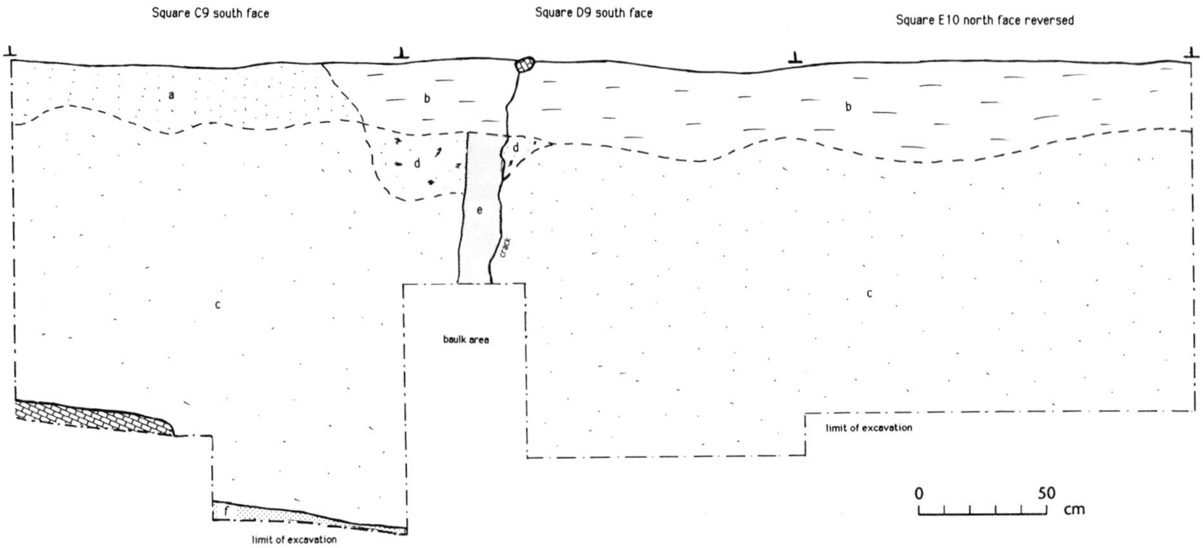

Figure 4-3. Profile of south face of main excavated area in the Abrigo da Lesma: **a,** reddish brown silt with crumb structure; **b,** reddish brown silt with abundant shell and charcoal fragments; **c,** compact reddish brown silt; **d,** compact reddish brown silt with large charcoal fragments; **e,** consolidated grey-brown silt with ash, charcoal, and shell fragments within fissure; **f,** mottled hard yellow clayey silt and reddish brown silt.

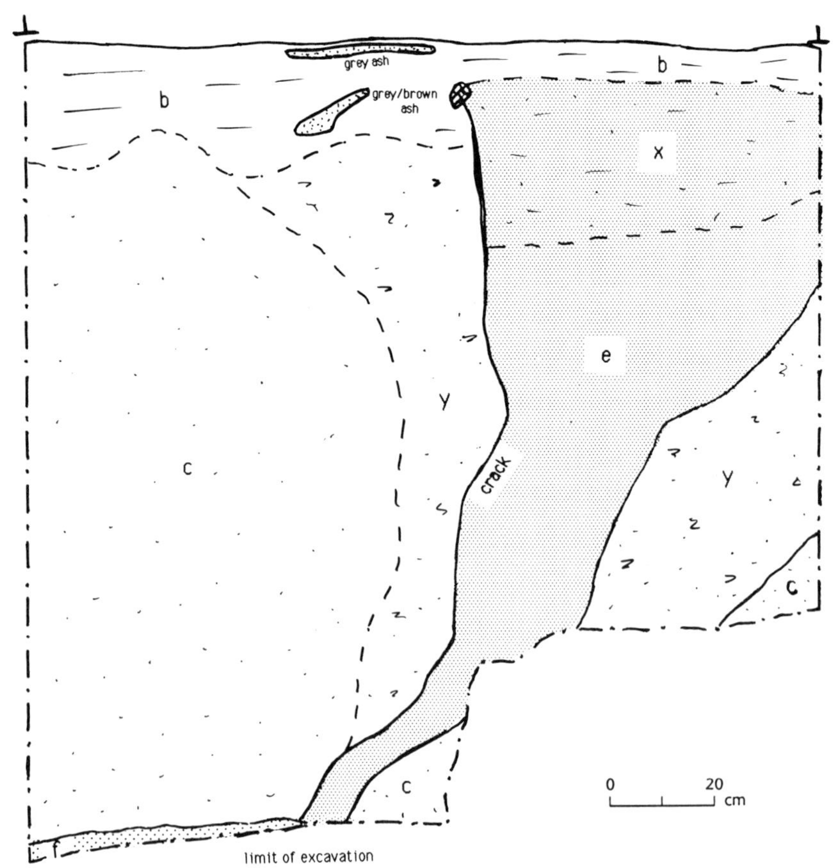

Figure 4-4. Profile of west face of Square C9, illustrating the great fissure:

- **b.** reddish brown silt with abundant shell and charcoal fragments;
- **c.** compact reddish brown silt;
- **e.** consolidated grey-brown silt with ash, charcoal, and shell fragments within fissure;
- **f.** mottled hard yellow clayey silt and reddish brown silt;
- **x.** loose grey-brown silt with ash, charcoal, and shell fragments;
- **y.** consolidated reddish brown silt with some charcoal flecks.

occasional artifact. Small charcoal fragments and the occasional flake continued to be found in the compact reddish-brown silt to a depth of 110 cm below surface. In Squares C9 and D9, some flakes were also found between 120 cm and 150 cm depth; and in the southeast quarter of Square C8/D8 a chert flake was recovered from the 160–170 cm level.

A notable feature of the reddish-brown silt deposit was the lack of rubble content. Angular limestone fragments were found only in the upper 20 cm or 30 cm; and all appeared to be closely associated with hearth areas, and often cracked *in situ*, evidently by heating. Within the dripline, there was no evidence of roof fall within over 200 cm of silt deposition. Small rounded pebbles of limestone or quartz were exceedingly rare within the massive silt unit.

At an early stage in the excavation of Square C8/D8 a great crack or fissure with soft grey/brown fill was found to extend north-south across the square, and subsequent excavation in Squares C9 and D9 demonstrated that it continued to the rear wall of the shelter. At first encounter this feature was thought to be an ash pit; then an animal burrow. However, as excavation proceeded to greater depths the fissure continued a narrow sinuous track across the shelter; and it was seen in profile to be a great natural crack in the sediment, extending to a depth of over 200 cm (Figure 4-2b), beyond the limit of excavation. The fissure was about 30 to 40 cm in maximum width at the top (about 10–15 cm below surface), narrowing to about 10–15 cm width at the limit of excavation. It was filled with fine brown silt and grey ash, containing abundant charcoal fragments and shell fragments above a depth of 120 cm below surface. The fill also contained a number of limestone fragments, usually in a vertical position, and ranging up to 40 cm in size. The occasional flake, bone fragment, or stone artifact was also found within it. In the upper levels, the grey/brown silt fill was soft and loose; but below a depth of about 120 cm the fill in the great fissure was well consolidated. The great fissure was found to be flanked on either side by a 20-cm-wide zone of consolidated reddish-brown silt containing small charcoal fragments. At the conclusion of field work at the site, the great fissure was thought to be possibly a desiccation crack or a tension crack, which may have filled and widened more than once, with material washed in, or deliberately deposited by the prehistoric human occupants of the shelter. The fill in the great fissure was excavated separately, and material found within was segregated from that recovered from the surrounding sediments.

Radiocarbon Assays

Four of the ten samples of charcoal collected from the sediments in the Abrigo da Lesma were submitted to Beta Analytic Inc. for radiocarbon dating. The ^{14}C ages in years B.P. reported are as follows:

Sample 5: Square E10, depth 0–20 cm: 940 ± 50 yr B.P. (Beta-8672)

Sample 4: Square D9, depth 20–30 cm: 2370 ± 60 yr B.P. (Beta-8671)

Sample 8: Square C8/D8, depth 48–58 cm: 2400 ± 70 yr B.P. (Beta-8673)

Sample 9: Square D9, depth 50–60 cm: 2260 ± 60 yr B.P. (Beta-8674)

Sample 4 consisted of scattered fragments of charcoal found in a matrix of compact reddish-brown silt in the southwest quarter of Square D9. Sample 5 was composed of large charcoal fragments collected from a hearth in the northeast corner of Square E10. Sample 8 consisted of a concentration of charcoal fragments found in compact reddish-brown silt in the south-central area of Square C8/D8 (in the C8/C9 baulk area). Sample 9 was a composite sample of small charcoal fragments found in an ashy zone on the east side of Square D9 (in the C9/D9 baulk area).

It may be noted that three of the dates (Beta-8671, Beta-8673, and Beta-8674) are within 200 years of each other despite a maximum stratigraphic range of 40 cm depth. In general, the series of dates suggests that deposition of sediments between 20 and 60 cm depth within the shelter occurred rapidly over a few hundred years. The 900-year-old hearth in the upper zone is associated with the ceramic occupation. No clear stratigraphic break marks a long hiatus in occupation. Unfortunately, charcoal samples collected below a depth of 60 cm were inadequate for conventional radiocarbon dating, so the age of the lower sedimentary zones and the traces of sporadic human occupation below 60 cm depth remains unknown.

Cultural Stratigraphy

There was abundant evidence indicating intensive human occupation in the upper 50 cm of deposit in the Abrigo da Lesma. In this zone occurred extensive ash lenses, several hearths, rock fragments, food refuse principally in the form of fragments of gastropod tests, fragments of charcoal, numerous stone flakes, and most of the 159 artifacts recovered from the site. The distribution of stone flakes is given in Table 4-2; the distribution of artifacts is provided in Table 4-3. Charcoal fragments, shell fragments, a small number of stone flakes, and the occasional artifact continued to be found between 50 cm and 90 cm depth; and there were several small concentrations of stone flakes between 120 cm and 150 cm depth, and a few flakes between 160 cm and 170 cm depth in the southeast section of Square C8/D8; but no definite occupation levels could be distinguished below 50 cm depth.

A significant cultural division is commonly drawn between ceramic and preceramic horizons. At the Abrigo da Lesma, eleven potsherds were found in the uppermost levels. Of the ten sherds with definite provenience, six were encountered in the 0–10 cm level and two in the 10–20 cm level. The two potsherds found between 20 cm and 40 cm below surface might easily be intrusive. The occupations in the upper 20 cm may also be distinguished by the preponderance of heavy tools, mainly of limestone but a few of quartzite, apparently used for chopping or pounding. However, small artifacts of quartz, chert, or quartzite, and fragments of utilized mussel shell, all abundant in the upper 20 cm, are artifact types which are found in lower occupation levels as well (see artifact distribution in Table 4-3); so the cultural break between ceramic and preceramic levels is not sharp at the Abrigo da Lesma.

Cultural features which could be distinguished in the upper 50 cm of the Abrigo da Lesma deposits were hearths and ash lenses. Hearth areas were zones that produced abundant large charcoal fragments as well as ash, and were underlaid by thin zones of reddish soil indicating burning in place. One such hearth in the extreme southwest corner of Square C8/D8, ranging from a depth of about 10–20 cm below surface, extended underneath a large slab of roof fall. This hearth was at least 45 cm in diameter. A smaller hearth, about 20 cm in diameter and 10 cm deep, was exposed in the 10–20 cm level in Square C8/D8 about 40 cm east of the large hearth. Another large hearth, about 50 cm in diameter, occurred at the 5–10 cm level in the east-central sector of Square D9 and the adjacent area of Square C9. There was also a small hearth with abundant charcoal, in an area about 20 cm in diameter, from a depth of about 5–20 cm in the northeast quarter of Square E10. Ash lenses, zones of white or grey ash with charcoal fragments and gastropod shell fragments, were very irregular in form. Numerous small and very thin lenses of grey/brown ash occurred mixed with the silt matrix to a depth of approximately 45–50 cm in the northern part of Square D9. In Square E10, ash and charcoal were well mixed with the silt matrix in the northern half of the square to a depth of approximately 50 cm.

Food refuse commonly occurred mixed with the ash lenses, but also in the reddish-brown silt matrix outside ashy zones. Fragments of gastropod tests were most abundant, particularly in the zone near the rear of the shelter. The northern part of Square E10, the southern half of Square D9, and the southwest corner of Square C9 were virtually shell midden in a reddish-brown silt matrix from 0–50 cm depth. Complete or almost complete tests of the giant gastropod *Megalobulimus* sp. were numerous in this zone, sometimes occurring in tight clusters of a dozen or more individual tests; and small fragments of shell of this genus were very abundant throughout the matrix. As well, there were numerous specimens of the medium-sized gastropod *Protoglyptus durus*, and the smaller *Cyclodontina* sp. (see Table 4-1). Several pockets of macerated and burned shell of the latter species, each pocket about 10 cm in diameter, were exposed in close association with the extensive hearth with grey/white ash in the east-central part of Square D9 and adjacent Square C9, at a depth of 5–10 cm below surface. As mentioned in the introductory section of this report, the simplest way to procure a snail is to force it to emerge by heating the shell near a fire; so that gastropod tests may be expected in close association with hearths.

Fragments of shell of the riverine mussel *Diplodon delodontus* were fairly frequent in the upper levels of the Abrigo da Lesma. This edible mussel lives only in fresh flowing streams found no closer than about 35 km away from the site, however; and it is possible that the mussels were not consumed at the site itself but rather that the fragments are pieces of shell utensils.

As noted earlier, bone fragments were relatively uncommon in the deposits at the Abrigo da Lesma. Most were of small mammals, and may be the food refuse of predators other than man; although there was a concentration of small mammal bones in the midden in the northern part of Square E10. The relatively few fragments of bone of large- or medium-sized mammals were very small in size, and well scattered within the deposits. Identified were deer and peccary (Table 4-1). One unidentifiable fragment of bone of a very large mammal was found in rotten condition in the north wall of Square C8/D8 at a depth of 38 cm below surface.

Rock fragments, cracked or shattered angular pieces

Table 4-1. List of Species Represented in Faunal Remains from the Abrigo da Lesma.

Mammals (identified by Martha Locks, Museu Nacional)

- *Mazama gouazubira*—caatinga deer
- *Tayassu albirostris*—peccary
- *Euphractus sexcinctus*—armadillo
- *Kerodon rupestris* —*mocó*, a rat-sized rodent

Molluscs (identified by Norma Campos Salgado and A. C. S. Coelho, Museu Nacional)

- *Diplodon delodontus*—large fresh-water bivalve
- *Megalobulimus* sp.—very large terrestrial gastropod
- *Protoglyptus durus*—medium-sized terrestrial gastropod
- *Cyclodontina* sp.—small/medium-sized terrestrial gastropod
- *Anctus* sp.—small terrestrial gastropod
- *Helicina* sp.—very small terrestrial gastropod
- *Leptinaria* sp.—very small terrestrial gastropod
- *Opeas beckianum*—very small terrestrial gastropod

of limestone averaging about 10 cm in size, were very numerous only in the northern part of Square E10 and the western part of Square D9, at depths of 0–30 cm below surface. A few rock fragments were also found at these levels on the west side of Square C8/D8 and on the west side of Square C9. In Square D9 the zone of rock fragments appeared to be largely in complementary distribution with the extensive zone of small ash lenses in the northeastern quarter of the square. It is notable that almost all of the heavy artifacts of limestone, choppers or pounding tools, occurred within these zones of rock fragments in the upper 20–30 cm of deposit (Figure 4-5a). As well, a high proportion of the small artifacts of quartz, chert, or quartzite with known coordinates were recovered from these zones.

The fragmentary remains of a human burial were exposed in the north-central part of Square D9 at the 40–45 cm level (Figure 4-5b). The bones occurred in a matrix of mixed ash and silt, but there was no visible evidence of a pit. The remains consisted of three sets of highly fragmentary long bones, extending approximately northwest-southeast, parallel to the rear wall of the shelter. About 10 cm to the west of the long bones was a line of three molar teeth with grinding surfaces facing east (as well, one molar was found in screening material from the area); and immediately underlying the zone of the teeth were some badly decayed phalanges or metapodials. All that could be preserved of the burial were the four molar teeth, a few phalanges, and fragments of the long bones. Their position indicated that the skull was to the west; and the body may have been in a crouched position or the long bones stacked. Study of the teeth indicates that the individual was a young adult, probably slightly over 20 years in age, to judge from the lack of wear on a fully developed third molar; and probably a female, to judge from the slenderness of the phalanges (Marilia Carvalho de Mello e Alvim, pers. comm). All of the teeth have caries, and the crown of one was broken transversely in life. No artifacts were associated with the burial.

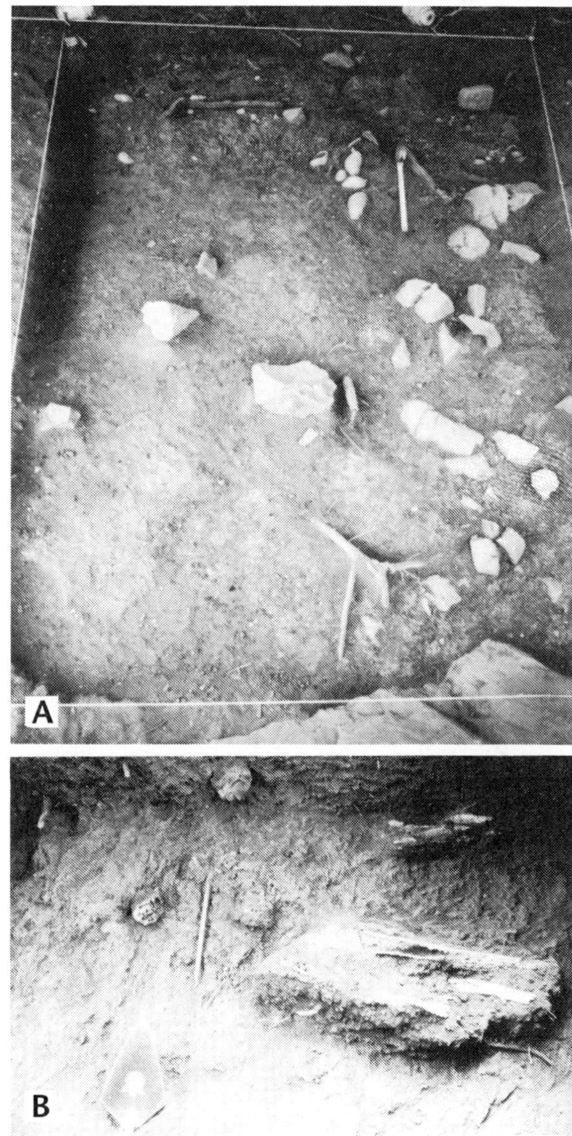

Figure 4-5. A) Occupational debris exposed in Square D9 at the 10–20 cm level, showing scatter of limestone rocks, lithic artifacts, and gastropod tests; **B)** fragmentary human remains exposed in Square D9 at the 40–50 cm level.

ARTIFACTS

Stone Artifacts

Flake Analysis

Approximately 638 flakes were recovered in the excavations at the Abrigo da Lesma. Distributional data on the flakes are presented in Table 4-2. Flakes were in high frequency in levels above 50 cm, and rare below 70 cm depth. Square D9 yielded the most flakes, about 42% of the total number recovered from the site. Square C9 yielded 25%, Square E10 17%, and Square C8/D8 16%. Materials flaked were quartz, quartzite, limestone, and several color varieties of chert. As these materials have different physical properties which affect flaking, the flakes will be described by category of material.

Quartz. Quartz flakes with no observable evidence of use constituted 27% of the total number of flakes recovered from the site. Ninety-two percent of the quartz flakes were of a translucent white/yellow vein quartz. Numerous fragments of this material, in blocks up to 30 cm in size, were seen over a 200-meter area on the

Table 4-2. Distribution of Unmodified Stone Flakes in Sediments of the Abrigo da Lesma.

	QUARTZ	QUARTZITE	LIMESTONE	CHERT	TOTAL
Square E10					
0–10 cm	2	2	24	5	33
10–20 cm	2	1	15	1	19
20–30 cm	5	0	13	0	18
30–40 cm	2	0	2	0	4
40–50 cm	2	1	18	2	23
50–60 cm	0	1	4	0	5
60–70 cm	0	0	0	0	0
70–80 cm	0	0	0	0	0
80–90 cm	1	0	2	0	3
90–100 cm	0	0	1	1	2
Total					107
Square D9					
0–10 cm	7	2	24	5	38
10–20 cm	11	4	19	5	39
20–30 cm	18	13	20	9	60
30–40 cm	23	2	25	9	59
40–50 cm	9	5	5	4	23
50–60 cm	7	2	11	5	25
60–70 cm	4	1	2	4	11
70–80 cm	2	2	1	4	9
80–90 cm	1	0	1	0	2
90–100 cm	1	0	0	1	2
100–110 cm	1	0	0	0	1
110–120 cm	0	0	0	0	0
120–130 cm	0	1	0	0	1
130–140 cm	0	0	0	0	0
140–150 cm	1	0	0	0	1
Total					271
Square C9					
0–10 cm	15	6	9	8	38
10–20 cm	5	6	4	4	19
20–30 cm	10	2	4	11	27

surface of a low depression between limestone ridges less than half a kilometer southeast of the Abrigo da Lesma; this area may have been a source of the material. Eight percent of the quartz flakes from the Abrigo da Lesma were of clear quartz crystal, the source of which is unknown.

Approximately 65 irregularly shaped blocks of vein quartz recovered, ranging in size from 39 x 27 x 13 mm to 8 x 5 x 4 mm, show a few poorly developed flake scars. Quartz flakes recovered in excavation ranged in size from a maximum of 48 x 24 x 13 mm to a minimum of 7 x 4 x 1 mm. Characteristically, quartz flakes were very irregular in form; and often relatively thick in cross-section. Striking platforms, when preserved, were often very poorly defined. Platforms tended to be large in proportion to the size of the flake; and plain, rarely facetted. Platforms and bulbs of percussion were most clearly defined on quartz crystal flakes. Many flakes of vein quartz featured two opposing bulbs of force, evidence of the bipolar flaking technique commonly used by the occupants of the Abrigo da Lesma. A number of quartz flakes and blocks were utilized as simple scraping or gouging tools, described below.

Quartzite. Flakes of quartzite composed 10% of the total number of flakes recovered from the Abrigo da Lesma. Most of the material was brown or grey in color. About 18% of the flakes retained a smooth cortex on one surface, indicating derivation from a pebble or cobble. The nearest known source of quartzite is the Serra Azul,

Table 4-2 (continued).

	QUARTZ	QUARTZITE	LIMESTONE	CHERT	TOTAL
Square C9 (continued)					
30–40 cm	7	1	11	2	21
40–50 cm	3	0	5	2	10
50–60 cm	2	1	7	4	14
60–70 cm	1	0	0	1	2
70–80 cm	4	0	5	1	10
80–90 cm	2	1	3	1	7
90–100 cm	2	0	5	0	7
100–110 cm	0	0	0	0	0
110–120 cm	0	0	1	0	1
120–130 cm	0	0	0	0	0
130–140 cm	0	0	1	0	1
Total					157
Square C8/D8					
0–10 cm	6	2	9	0	17
10–20 cm	1	1	4	0	6
20–30 cm	2	2	8	0	12
30–40 cm	0	1	2	2	5
40–50 cm	2	0	7	1	10
50–60 cm	0	0	9	2	11
60–70 cm	3	1	6	3	13
70–80 cm	1	0	5	0	6
80–90 cm	1	0	2	0	3
90–100 cm	2	1	2	0	5
100–110 cm	1	0	1	1	3
110–120 cm	1	0	2	0	3
120–130 cm	0	0	3	0	3
130–140 cm	3	0	2	0	5
140–150 cm	0	0	0	0	0
150–160 cm	0	0	0	0	0
160–170 cm	0	0	0	1	1
Total					103
Total flakes: 638					

about 20 km southwest of the Abrigo da Lesma. The quartzite recovered from the site is well silicified; relatively fine-grained; and flakes well, with clear conchoidal fracture.

Quartzite flakes recovered in excavation ranged in size from a maximum of 66 x 43 x 24 mm to a minimum of 10 x 9 x 2 mm. There was considerable variation in form. On large and medium-sized flakes, striking platforms tended to be large in proportion to the size of the flake; and plain or flat, suggesting a direct percussion technique. On very small flakes, the striking platform was frequently relatively small, suggesting detachment by pressure; but possibly through use. As described below, several very large quartzite flakes feature small irregular flake scars along utilized edges.

Limestone. As soon as excavation began in the Abrigo da Lesma, it became readily apparent that the prehistoric occupants had made extensive use of limestone as a material for stone flaking. Approximately 48% of the flakes recovered from the site are of local limestone. The limestone in the immediate area is very dense and fine grained, and flakes of this material show clear conchoidal fracture. There was virtually no natural deposition of rubble in the silt deposits within the rockshelter, so each piece of rock was examined carefully for evidence of alteration; and the flakes of limestone tabulated in this report could be clearly identified as products of human work by the presence of distinct striking platforms and/or bulbs of percussion.

Limestone flakes recovered in excavation ranged in

size from a maximum of 67 x 41 x 8 mm to a minimum of 8 x 7 x 1 mm. Many of the flakes were side-blow flakes; that is, the width of the flake was greater than its length from striking platform to distal end. Limestone flakes characteristically featured very large platforms, flat and plain; and a direct percussion technique is indicated. Limestone flakes often show strong lines of force. A number of the flakes were struck at a high angle. Very small flakes, with small platforms, may have been detached by pressure in use of the working edge of a core tool. As described below, heavy tools of limestone are prominent in the collection of artifacts from the upper levels of the site.

Despite the high frequency of limestone flakes, few utilized limestone flakes could be identified in the artifact collection (see description below). Experiments with the use of limestone flakes in scraping bone indicated that the edge of the flake is too soft for such work, and very quickly becomes worn down and blunted by friction against a dense material. It is possible that sharp limestone flakes were employed to cut very soft material such as meat, and such work has left no trace of wear on the edge of a flake. However, with the lack of any observable evidence of utilization on all but a few limestone flakes, it may be hypothesized that most of the limestone flakes found in the deposits at the Abrigo da Lesma resulted from the manufacture or resharpening of limestone core tools, or the utilization of such tools in scraping or pounding.

Chert. Chert flakes constituted 15% of the total number of flakes recovered from the deposits in the Abrigo da Lesma. There were several color varieties of fine cryptocrystalline material. The most common (60%) was a cream/white chert. In addition to the flakes, seven small irregular blocks of this material, with indistinct flake scars on one or more surfaces, were recovered from the deposits; and most of the chert artifacts described below are of this color. In lower frequency in the deposits were flakes of a shiny black chert (25%), a translucent chert (8%), and a dark red chert (7%). In addition, there was one small flake of a grey chert, and a large flake of a brown chert. The sources of the chert have not been located, although a few small chunks of weathered cream-colored chert were seen in a field about 9 km west of the Abrigo da Lesma; and there is also an outcrop a few kilometers west of the Rio Verde, about 30 km from the site.

Chert flakes recovered in excavation ranged in size from a maximum of 44 x 25 x 12 mm to a minimum of 10 x 7 x 1 mm. Most chert flakes on which the striking platform was preserved featured a plain flat striking platform which was large in proportion to the width of the flake; and these flakes appear to have been derived by a direct percussion technique. A few flakes with small platforms may have been detached by pressure. No flakes show evidence of a bifacial flaking technique. Chert artifacts recovered from the deposits are retouched or utilized flakes, and small core tools.

Quartz Artifacts

The primary objective of describing artifacts should be to reveal as much as possible about what the people were doing at the site in question. With this objective in mind, the quartz artifacts from the Abrigo da Lesma will be described by their method of manufacture, by evidence of use, and by evidence of intentional shaping. As there are no formal types (i.e., artifacts formed by the knapper into preconceived shapes such as projectile points or endscrapers) amongst the quartz artifacts, the usual archaeological description by form is not relevant and will not be attempted. When pertinent, the angles of the retouched working edges will be recorded, as they were probably significant in the use of the tool by the prehistoric people, and may be significant for archaeological analysis.

None of the quartz chunks or flakes in the assemblage show any evidence of being shaped into diagnostic tools. All the flakes and chunks were probably handy tools used to process other materials (e.g., wood, bone, meat, and hide) into food or other tools. Undoubtedly, most of the artifacts shaped into objects at the Abrigo da Lesma were made of easily shaped wood or other vegetable fibres (e.g., basketry, cordage, netting), while a few were made of bone or other animal products (e.g., sinew, hide, feathers). Unfortunately, most of these artifacts have perished. The non-perishable stone artifacts used to fashion the perishable artifacts constitute a very simple but effective flake industry with minimal edge retouch.

Experimental scraping of hard cow bone with chert flakes and quartz flakes and chunks showed that quartz was superior, as it held its sharp edge longer without breaking. In fact, on many of the quartz flakes we used, there was only minimal evidence of use retouch which is very difficult to see even with a hand lens. However, the difference between a freshly flaked edge and a worked edge can usually be felt, as the worked edge is dulled. Grooving or sawing bone with the intention of controlled breaking of the bone does create considerable edge retouch of the quartz flake. There appears to be no reason intentionally to retouch a sharp scraping edge. A worked dull edge would continue to scrape bone, while the natural retouching caused by grooving kept the edges usefully sharp. The only evidence for intentional retouch was on a piece which indicated a process of retouching on one side of the edge, flipping the piece over to work the other side, and thereby creating a projecting graver spur or nose between the retouched areas. The resultant sharp spur or nose is useful for grooving bone. It would be equally useful for grooving wood or cutting skin.

Only two obvious concentrations of quartz flakes

and chunks were excavated within the Abrigo da Lesma. Probably, therefore, most quartz pieces were broken up at or near the quarry source, where the most useful pieces were selected for transportation to the occupation site. If this was the case, then probably most quartz flakes and chunks had been preselected before they were brought to the site for use. In a sense these flakes and chunks could rightfully be considered as artifacts. However, flakes were described as artifacts only if they exhibited evidence of use, or illustrated the method that had been used to break the piece apart. Very likely, the former inhabitants of the site would be appalled at the way the most useful flakes (those with sharpest edges) were not identified as artifacts. Our experiments suggested that if these flakes had been used to work soft vegetable materials or to cut meat there would be no visible evidence of such use.

Whether or not they have bulbs, sharp-edged quartz flakes are tougher and much more durable for working other materials than are flakes of cryptocrystalline material like chert, chalcedony, or obsidian. Prehistoric people must have preferred quartz because of its durability; but as evidence of workmanship is very difficult to see, the job of the archaeologist trying to discover how the piece might have been used is severely hampered. The problem of analysis is particularly handicapped when most quartz artifacts were chosen simply for the usefulness of their natural working edges, rather than being intentionally retouched for any reason. At the Abrigo da Lesma, the only discernible pattern of intentional retouch was to form a projection (e.g., a spur or a nose) which would be useful for grooving or gouging some other material like wood or bone. Most other retouching was probably simply from use. Unfortunately we have no photographs of quartz artifacts from the Abrigo da Lesma, as drawings were planned but were not done. In fact, however, flaking and use wear are very difficult to illustrate on quartz artifacts by any means: the artifacts must actually be inspected in the hand.

Two water-worn milky quartz pebbles evidently were split by striking them with a hammer while holding them on an anvil, but they lack any impact marks or lines of force because they broke along crystal facets. One oval rounded stream pebble (BA-CE-3/98), measuring 27 x 22 x 18 mm, evidently was laid flat on an anvil and lightly struck near the middle. The 75° angle edge appears to be slightly worn, but not retouched. This artifact was recovered from the 0–10 cm level in Square E10. The outer surfaces of the other pebble (BA-CE-3/49) are only slightly waterworn, retaining some crystal facets. This specimen, which measures 49 x 29 x 26 mm, also broke along immature crystal facets. The longest broken edge, with an angle of 75°, appears to be more worn than the other edges. This specimen was found at a depth of 23 cm in the northwest quarter of Square E10. Both of these artifacts could have been used as small scraper planes for working wood or bone, although small quartz pebbles are obviously not good material for knapping because it is difficult or impossible to control how they will break.

Quartz crystals or even chunks of vein quartz have many more useful edges than broken quartz pebbles. With care, quartz crystals can be broken (or quartered, to use a knapper's term) so that they will yield several artifacts with tough and efficient working edges. Large chunks of vein quartz can be broken up simply by throwing a rock at them and picking out pieces with useful edges. More homogeneous cryptocrystalline mineral forms, such as chert, chalcedony, or obsidian, would have been preferred by the knapper because material without crystal planes or with minute crystals can be quartered with considerable control if the knapper understands and utilizes the physical principle of the cone of percussion. A homogeneous rock held in the hand and struck with a hammerstone at the proper angle will produce a decortication flake with a bulb of percussion which is a segment of the cone of percussion. On the other hand, a crystal or a rock containing large crystals will tend to break along crystal faces. However, it is possible to obtain normal bulbs of percussion when breaking up large clear crystals; but only after the crystal is carefully broken on an anvilstone. Vein quartz, however, will break along the many crystal faces that are present throughout the material. These distinctive differences will become clearer as the artifact description proceeds.

Quartz crystals must have attracted the attention of the earliest people because of their beauty. Also, the sharp pointed apex of a well-formed clear crystal is obviously a very useful natural tool for many purposes, including engraving, scoring, or grooving bone or wood, or perforating a hide. All decapitated crystal heads at the Abrigo da Lesma, as well as at most other sites, exhibit considerable use of the apex in the form of battering, dulling, or flaking. The production of small use flakes from the apex or other crystal edge undoubtedly prompted people to experiment with flaking crystal in order to increase the number of useful edges.

Artifact BA-CE-3/111 is a fairly clear complete crystal which was too small (21 x 12 x 11 mm) to try to break up. The apex has been battered and ground by heavy use, and a flake was removed from it by use. Other apical crystal edges also show rounding and polishing, and have a few tiny flakes removed from them. This well-used natural crystal was finally discarded after all useful edges and the apex had become too dull. It was found on the surface of the site in August 1983.

Vein quartz chunks were readily available to the inhabitants of the Abrigo da Lesma. Many broken pieces are scattered on the surface of a newly cleared (burned) field about 200 meters south of the shelter. Much vein quartz was also seen along the trail on the north side of the Serra da Candeia. About 7 km west-southwest, at Maxixe, the same kind of milky quartz was observed as deformed crystals which had intruded into calcite veins in the limestone. Very likely the local source on the other side of the valley along the northern margin of the Serra da Pedra Branca was a similar calcite/quartz vein, which had eroded out of the limestone, leaving the scatter of angular quartz chunks, many of which appeared to have been intentionally broken up in place. Useful pieces were selected and carried to nearby occupation sites, such as the Abrigo da Lesma. The few clear quartz crystal flakes and chunks were carried in from sources outside the limestone area. Because there was a local source, the occasional small chunks of vein quartz that apparently had been transported by water and never subsequently broken were considered to have been deposited in the rockshelter naturally. Only sharp-angled pieces or pieces showing differential wear on edges were considered in the artifact analysis.

The simplest way to break up a large chunk of vein quartz is to lay the piece on a rock and throw another rock at it. One can then pick out the most useful pieces. To judge from the lack of patterned breakage on the remnants found along the northern base of the Serra da Pedra Branca, this simple method had been used there, as well as on some of the pieces at the Abrigo da Lesma.

However, this is not an efficient way to break up quartz crystals, whether they are the cloudy and poorly formed crystals that occur in calcite veins or the more perfect clear crystal forms. To avoid unnecessary wastage of the most useful sharp edges requires that the natural plan of the crystal faces be studied to determine how the flaking blows should be directed. In order to obtain a clean flake scar and not an irregular break along immature crystal planes, the initial blow(s) must be quite forcefully applied. Probably considerable experimentation was necessary before a knapper, especially one who might be accustomed to quartering homogeneous blocks of chert or other similar cryptocrystalline material, realized that it is essentially impossible to break apart a hand-held crystal. One must place an edge or face of a crystal on an anvil and forcefully strike an opposing crystal edge or face. This method is similar to the bipolar technique for breaking apart a small water-rounded pebble.

The usual result of a forceful bipolar blow using a relatively heavy hammerstone to strike a crystal or a pebble held on an anvilstone is to split the cone of percussion, so that the bulb of percussion is fractured or entirely absent on the resulting flake and flake scar. If the force bulb is absent, the surface is flat but nevertheless exhibits lines of force emanating from the point of impact. Occasionally, if the force is very great, one or more spalls can peel away, sometimes on both sides, leaving an excurvate face (or faces) and a broad battered edge where the hammer struck, and also often another straight or nearly straight crushed edge caused by the counter-blow from the anvil. If the original pebble surfaces or crystal faces have been entirely or mostly removed by the splitting and peeling action, the resultant piece with opposing straight crushed platform edges is known as a *pièce esquillée.* These pieces, which have battered bits at one or both ends, can be useful woodworking wedges; but the bits are usually too crushed to be able to demonstrate such use. *Pièces esquillées* are, however, useful to the archaeologist who is attempting to analyse how the flaking was accomplished.

The bipolar anvil technique was clearly used to break up crystals found at the Abrigo da Lesma. Few of the flaked pieces at the shelter have bulbs of percussion. Instead, the visible lines of force indicate that forceful blows were directed at carefully selected spots while the opposing crystal edge or face was held on an anvil. The paucity of flakes or flake scars with bulbs on crystalline quartz pieces at the Abrigo da Lesma is directly related to the paucity of flakes from clear crystals which have developed in unrestricted environments and are therefore more homogeneous in structure because they have few immature crystal planes. Once most of the crystal faces on a large clear crystal have been removed by carefully directed blows, it is possible to remove a series of flakes from the resultant core in the normal hand-held method which produces bulbs of percussion on the resulting flake. Workshop sites located near an abundant source of large clear crystals can contain hundreds of normal flakes with negative and/or positive bulbs.

At the Abrigo da Lesma, five apical heads of quartz crystals had been intentionally removed by holding a crystal face on an anvilstone and forcefully applying a carefully directed blow with a hammerstone to a directly opposing facet or edge of a facet (e.g., a place where opposing crystal facets are parallel or nearly parallel to each other). In all cases the resulting flake surface is irregular and lacks a well-developed bulb of

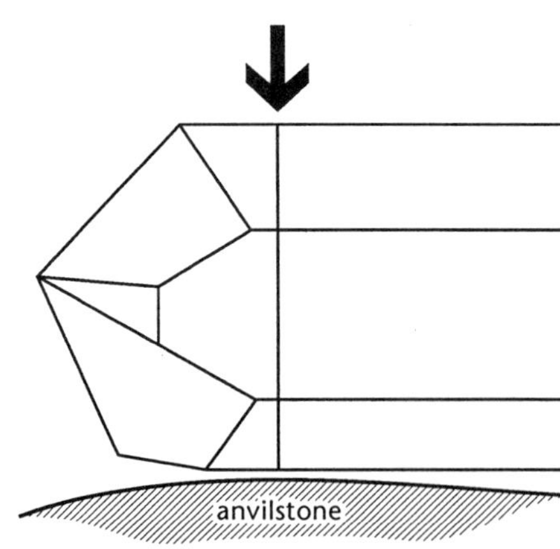

Figure 4-A. Decapitation of crystal head.

percussion because a normal cone of percussion cannot penetrate the network of immature crystal faces that are present near the apical end of a quartz crystal. However, the clearest crystal head (BA-CE-3/115), measuring 29 x 19 x 10 mm, exhibits a poorly developed bulb extending from the crushed platform on a crystal facet. In this case the opposing impact area has broken away, but the lines of force indicate that the anvil platform was quite broad and created a rebound flake that split the distal end of the bulb (partial cone) from the opposite direction. The split portion of the bulb illustrates what usually happens with a forceful bipolar blow: the force of the blow is applied equally and essentially simultaneously in opposite directions to split the cone, creating a flat flake scar, which is identifiable only by the lines of force extending toward the middle from both platforms. In this case the poorly formed bulbar surface was used as a platform for removing a few flakes (probably by use) from the high-angled edges (80–85°). Thus the piece could have been used as an endscraper. The crystal apex has also been blunted by use. The piece was found on the surface of the site in August 1983.

Artifact BA-CE-3/104, which measures 20 x 21 x 8 mm, is similar in that a very poorly developed bulb appears to have developed from the crystal face, which was used as a hammerstone platform. Actually, however, what happened is that, apparently because the two points of impact were not really opposite, the rebound blow from the anvil platform started to create a bulb in a different plane, so the opposing forces did not intersect in a straight plane to split the cone but instead caused a separate flake to peel off, creating a very irregular positive flake scar. A small lateral nose was also created, which may have been used, although it is possible that this piece was simply discarded after decapitation. It was recovered from the 0–10 cm level in Square E10.

Artifact BA-CE-3/94, which measures 53 x 30 x 7 mm, is a very irregular crystal head which exhibits a split cone with intersecting lines of force creating a nearly flat but slightly concave face. The resulting pyramid-shaped piece probably served as a keeled scraper, although few use flakes have been removed from the sharp flake edge, which has an edge angle varying from 60° to 85°. The apex and apical edges also appear to have been blunted by heavy use. Two negative flake scars from one apical edge (75°) may have been removed by such use. The artifact was recovered from the 0–10 cm level in Square E10.

Artifact BA-CE-3/47, measuring 48 x 32 x 28 mm, is also a pyramidal scraper. This vein quartz chunk was struck bipolarly in such a way that it split along immature crystal faces, creating an irregularly flat face with two useful ends, with edge angles of 45° and 70°. The 45° angle end has an incurvate/excurvate edge which shows considerable use as a steep endscraper. This tool was found at a depth of 14 cm in the north-central part of Square E10.

Another pyramidal scraper, BA-CE-3/43, measures 30 x 26 x 18 mm. In this case the hammer platform precipitated a positive bulb while the opposing broad anvil platform started with two negative bulbs, all of which converged into a very irregular split cone. The piece was decapitated in such a way that the apex of the crystal forms a lateral nose with a useful overhanging lip (70°) which exhibits considerable use-wear, including removal of a large curving use flake from the crystal surface. The three other corners also appear to have been used. Thus this decapitated crystal head was useful as an endscraper and perhaps a grooving tool. It was found at a depth of 16 cm in the northeast quarter of Square E10.

Artifact BA-CE-3/1 measures 38 x 36 x 15 mm. The apex has been much battered, possibly by use. It was decapitated with a nearly flat split cone which was used as a platform for removing several flakes, creating a short spokeshave concavity with a working angle of 45°. A projecting nose was then created next to the spokeshave edge by removing a large irregular flake from the other face, using an adjacent crystal facet as a platform. Elsewhere, another use flake was removed at a 90° angle from the split cone surface. Thus this crystal head was made into a useful combination spokeshave/graver/grooving tool. It was found on the surface near the rear wall of the shelter in Square C10 (unexcavated unit). This artifact is unusual in that the projecting nose evidently was intentionally formed by retouching from alternate faces. Intentional shaping of a portion of an artifact suggests that this kind of artifact may be a diagnostic tool type, although this hypothesis must be confirmed by finding more examples at other sites.

Two other flaked quartz artifacts from the Abrigo da Lesma exhibit intentional retouch from opposite faces in order to create a useful nose. Artifact BA-CE-3/32, found at a depth of 19 cm in the south-central area of Square D9, measures 33 x 29 x 18 mm; and artifact BA-CE-3/106, found on the surface in August 1983, measures 44 x 40 x 28 mm. Both pieces are simply chunks of vein quartz apparently selected from a pile of fragments broken by throwing a rock at a larger chunk. A useful edge was created on BA-CE-3/32 by removing two flakes at a 65° angle from a freshly broken flat surface, creating a nosed projection between the two negative flake scars. Subsequently, a shallow flake was carefully removed from the opposite face to sharpen the working edge of the nose, which shows considerable evidence of use. On BA-CE-3/106 a retouch flake was removed from the opposite face by using the split cone edge (a 75° angle) as a platform in order to sharpen a nosed projection which shows evidence of use. On both pieces, flaking from the alternate face was intended only to sharpen the working edge of a nose (not to create it), so the artifact demonstrates an even simpler kind of obvious intentional retouch.

A square flake scraper (BA-CE-3/108), a surface find

which measures 20 x 19 x 9 mm, appears to have been a crystal head which was decapitated bipolarly; but all crystal faces have subsequently been obliterated by steep retouch, creating four edge angles ranging from 80° to 90°. All edges and corners exhibit heavy use, although they are not completely dulled. Another heavily used segment of a clear quartz crystal head (BA-CE-3/138), which measures 20 x 12 x 13 mm, looks like it was repeatedly retouched from the flat decapitation flake surface to the extent that it was no longer useful because the edges had become oversteepened, to angles of 85° to 90°. This steep keeled scraper came from the 10–20 cm level in Square E10.

Artifact BA-CE-3/137, which measures 28 x 20 x 9 mm, is an ovoid flake scraper with a biconvex cross-section created by intersecting split cones. The lines of force on this piece, which lacks crystal faces, suggest that it was originally struck bipolarly along the longitudinal axis and later again struck bipolarly along the lateral axis. The latter step removed the original anvil platform but sharpened the edges (at 45–55° angles), which were subsequently much used. This artifact was recovered from the 10–20 cm level in Square E10.

Artifact BA-CE-3/103, which measures 26 x 15 x 12 mm, appears to be another example of a piece with a biconvex cross-section that was bipolarly struck twice, although in this case the second bipolar blow from the lateral edges split the cone in such a way that most of the lines of force from the previous blow were removed. The result is a rectangular *pièce esquillée* with some evidence of use on the sharp longitudinal ends, which have an angle of 60°. This artifact was recovered from the 0–10 cm level in Square E10.

Two chunks of what appears to be the same irregularly crystallized vein quartz were recovered from the 10–20 cm level in Square D9. Another chunk lacking describable features came from the same level, suggesting that the crystal was broken up on the site. The artifacts, BA-CE-3/141, measuring 33 x 23 x 21 mm, and BA-CE-3/143, measuring 39 x 27 x 15 mm, had been flaked in the same unusual manner by holding one edge on an anvil while striking the opposite crystal face twice before the cone split. The projection between the two flake scars (at an 85° angle) and the sharpest lateral point on the corner of the crushed anvil edge (at an 80° angle) on artifact BA-CE-3/141 both feel quite worn.

Artifact BA-CE-3/22, which measures 39 x 22 x 20 mm, is a thick chunk of vein quartz which appears to have been split bipolarly by striking the apex of the decapitated head of a large crystal while holding the opposing broken edge on an anvil, creating a straight crushed edge. The hammer blow created a ridged split cone scar from which three flakes had spalled off. The two straight lateral edges, with an angle of 70–80°, are worn; and one is flaked. The artifact was found at a depth of 4 cm in the southwest quarter of Square D9.

Another peeled split cone created by a sharp hammer blow is present on artifact BA-CE-3/142, which measures 39 x 27 x 15 mm. Much of the anvil-crushed edge was evidently removed by a subsequent bipolar blow from the opposite face. Two sharp edges, at angles of 50–60°, show minimal use-wear. This artifact was recovered from the 10–20 cm level in Square D9.

Two triangular segments were caused by split cones which peeled off spalls from both faces when struck on their pointed ends. Artifact BA-CE-3/97, which was recovered from the 1–10 cm level in Square E10, measures 31 x 15 x 8 mm; and artifact BA-CE-3/16, which was found in the 30–40 cm level in the northwest quarter of Square C8/D8, measures 28 x 18 x 10 mm. In each case the opposite end exhibits short crushed edges where the pieces were held on an anvil. The lateral edges of BA-CE-3/97, which have an angle of 70°, feel use-worn. On BA-CE-3/16 there is a bi-bevelled projecting nose created by the anvil rebound. This rounded nose, with an angle of 55°, appears to have been use-retouched after it was crushed by the anvil.

Artifact BA-CE-3/127, which measures 34 x 18 x 15 mm, is a bipolarly split vein quartz *pièce esquillée* because it has crushed wedge-shaped edges at opposing ends. This piece exhibits several flake scars on the faces between the two bits where split cone spalls peeled off. The wedge-shaped ends, with angles of 60–75°, appear to be worn, perhaps by use as a wedge or gouge. This artifact was recovered from the 0–10 cm level in Square D9.

Artifact BA-CE-3/74, which measures 30 x 29 x 18 mm, is a very similar *pièce esquillée* except that one end broke off. The remaining nearly straight wedge-shaped bit, with a 45° angle, would have been a useful woodworking wedge; but there is no definite evidence of such use. This artifact was found at a depth of 75 cm in the northeast quarter of Square D9.

Artifact BA-CE-3/18, a pyramid-shaped vein quartz chunk measuring 38 x 39 x 24 mm, was split bipolarly, creating a slightly incurvate crushed edge from the anvil rebound. This edge, with a 60° angle, appears worn and use-retouched, perhaps by use as a spokeshave. Interestingly, a series of spall scars from a crushed 95° angle edge evidently was caused by an earlier unsuccessful attempt to split the chunk bipolarly. This artifact was found at a depth of 1 cm in the northwest quarter of Square D9.

A split cone flake (BA-CE-3/95), measuring 37 x 37 x 12 mm, was forcefully struck bipolarly on its apex. The anvil platform has broken off squarely, but a sharp lateral edge has been retouched from the flat split cone face intentionally to create a denticulated edge with one especially prominent graver spur. This edge, with a 65° angle, could have been used as a scraper/graver or a saw. The artifact was recovered from the 0–10 cm level in Square E10.

Two flakes removed bipolarly from crystals exhibit crushed platforms where they were struck forcefully, splitting the cone. The crushed anvil platform edge is present on artifact BA-CE-3/188, which was found in the 0–10 cm level in Square C9, and measures 26 x 17 x 7 mm; but is not visible on artifact BA-CE-3/55, which was found on the 50–60 cm level in Square D9, and measures 21 x 19 x 6 mm. All sharp edges, with angles ranging from 30° to 55°, show some evidence of use as scrapers.

Artifact BA-CE-3/125, which measures 27 x 15 x 14 mm, is a vein quartz crystal fragment which was bipolarly struck twice, first by holding a remnant of a crystal face on the anvil and forcefully striking an old broken edge; and the second time by striking the same broken edge while holding another broken edge on the anvil. A projecting nose at one end and an adjacent excurvate edge with a 55° angle are retouched, probably by use as a steep endscraper. This artifact was recovered from the 30–40 cm level on the east side of Square D9.

One broken excurvate end on artifact BA-CE-3/113, a surface find which measures 36 x 26 x 15 mm, appears to be bifacially retouched; but the lack of any platform remnants suggests that instead the 50° bi-bevelled bit was created simply by holding it on an anvil and lightly striking the opposite end. Thus careful application of the bipolar technique evidently was occasionally used for the rapid creation of a bi-directionally retouched edge with one blow. The bit of this artifact has been dulled by use.

Artifact BA-CE-3/26 is a fragment of a larger split cone flake measuring 33 x 22 x 13 mm. It broke apart along immature crystal faces in such a way that it appears to be a flake blade with a dorsal ridge. This piece has a sharp lateral edge with a 40° angle which exhibits use retouch as a side scraper. It was found at a depth of 10 cm in the southwest quarter of Square D9.

The remaining artifacts are all chunks of vein quartz which lack any diagnostic features of manufacture. They appear to have been selected mainly for their useful pointed projections, which show evidence of use at one or both ends. These artifacts (BA-CE-3/99, 101, 102, and 117) range in size from 45 x 20 x 13 mm to 26 x 12 x 7 mm. All of these pointed fragments would have made useful perforators, grooving tools, or punches. Artifact BA-CE-3/117 is a surface find, artifacts BA-CE-3/101 and 102 were recovered from the 0–10 cm level in Square E10, and artifact BA-CE-3/99 was found at a depth of 50–60 cm in Square C8/D8.

Chert Artifacts

Evidently the cryptocrystalline materials (cherts, chalcedony, or agate) available to the inhabitants of the Abrigo da Lesma were of very poor quality for flaking. Every piece found in the excavations was saved because people must have transported it to this shelter. Several of the pieces selected as having some evidence of use are simply chunks of a patinated cream-colored chert retaining portions of the original nodular surface. Useful edges and projections on several pieces appear to have been selected from naturally sharp-edged pieces, and a few from pieces created by throwing a rock at a large nodule. Several of the remaining pieces were flaked bipolarly. Evidently this bipolar anvil technique was used to quarter nodules of chert and even chalcedony when the nodules were too small to flake by holding them in the usual way. Although there are numerous unused chert flakes in the level bags (see flake analysis), only three chert flakes with bulbs of percussion were segregated as artifacts. In addition, one portion of a core and the distal end of what appears to be a flake-blade removed from a polyhedral core appear out of place in the otherwise crude assemblage.

A fragment of a polyhedral core (BA-CE-3/2), which measures 47 x 39 x 29 mm, is of an opaque black chert with many inclusions; however, the material does have a very shallow weathering rind and flaked quite well despite inherent flaws. A fairly flat undulating surface was used as a platform for removing several stepped flakes along one face (Figure 4-6a). The portion of the original core was broken off by a forceful blow which created an undulating hinged face which intersects the original platform face at right angles. There is no evidence of use of the sharp stepped flake edge (60° angle); but the broad excurving 90° angled edge and another shorter 90° angled edge both feel worn and have several small use flakes removed, evidently by back-and-forth scraping. This artifact was found at a depth of 5–10 cm in the south-central area of Square C9.

The only other worked piece of black chert (BA-CE-3/133), which measures 16 x 15 x 3 mm, came from 50 cm deeper in the same square, C9. It appears to be the broken distal end of a thin flake-blade, the dorsal face of which exhibits several narrow negative flake scars. The excurvate edge, use-nibbled but still sharp, has the lowest working angle (15°) of any utilized flake from the site; its distinctive features suggest that it also was not flaked by the usual occupants of the Abrigo da Lesma.

There are two possible explanations for the presence of a foreign technology as illustrated by these black chert artifacts at the Abrigo da Lesma. One is that local people looking for stone with useful edges transported foreign artifacts fashioned with a different flaking technology. The alternative explanation is that members of a different cultural group occasionally occupied the Abrigo da Lesma. Hopefully, excavations at other late prehistoric sites in the area will confirm one of these hypotheses, both of which imply that there were people with a different flaking technology who lived in the general vicinity either as contemporaries or at an earlier time.

The usual technology at the Abrigo da Lesma is illustrated by the artifacts of cream-colored chert, the most abundant color variety of chert found at the site. Four utilized flakes of cream-colored chert with normal bulbs

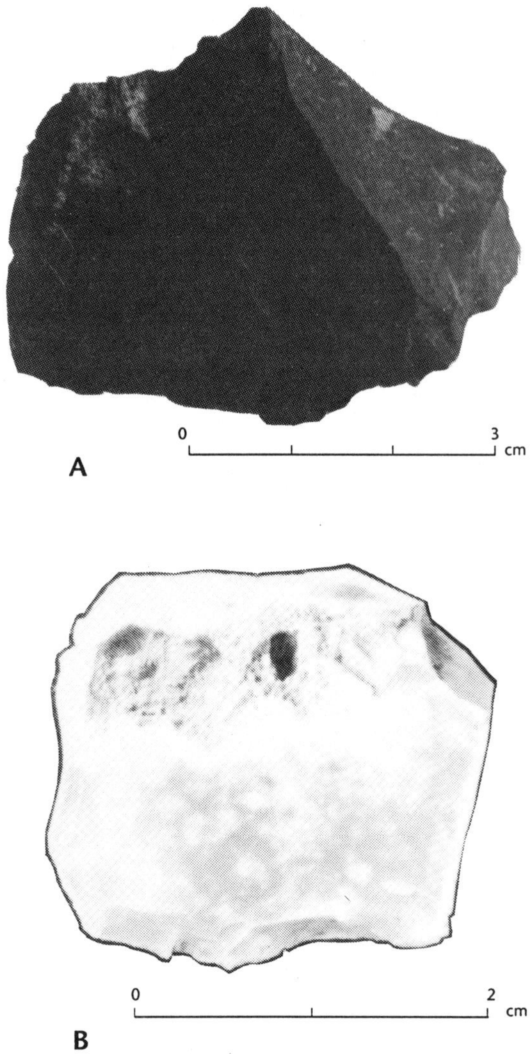

Figure 4-6. A) polyhedral core of black chert (BA-CE-3/2); **B)** translucent chert endscraper (BA-CE-3/14).

of percussion were excavated at different levels in Squares C9 and D9. Artifact BA-CE-3/93, which measures 34 x 22 x 8 mm, has a high-angled (125°) platform; and exhibits use-nibbling on one straight lateral edge with a 25° angle. Heat-crackling and a thermal spall scar indicate that this piece was subsequently heated. This artifact was found at a depth of 10–20 cm in Square D9. Artifact BA-CE-3/132, which measures 29 x 20 x 17 mm, was detached from its core only after several battering blows had been applied. A low-angle lateral edge (30°) and an adjacent projecting nose exhibit use-nibbling. This artifact was found at a depth of 60–70 cm in Square C9. Both lateral edges of BA-CE-3/62, a tiny flake measuring 17 x 18 x 3 mm with missing distal end, exhibit crushing and unifacial stepped flaking at an angle of 25°, probably by use. This is the only chert flake which lacks any cortex; however, this feature could be a function of its small size. It was recovered from a depth of 70–80 cm in the central section of Square D9. Artifact BA-CE-3/75, which measures 24 x 17 x 7 mm, also appears to be a normal decortication flake that hinged, but the bulbar end is missing. One lateral edge, with a 25° angle, exhibits minimal retouch, which includes a tiny graver spur which may have been deliberately formed. The artifact was found at a depth of 90 cm in the west-central part of Square D9.

Two chert flakes were formed by bipolar flaking, using the same techniques as were applied to break up quartz crystals. Artifact BA-CE-3/144, which measures 43 x 22 x 7 mm, is a blade-like flake with a dorsal ridge. It was created by holding a broken edge on an anvil and forcefully striking the opposite edge. The single blow removed a split cone flake from both faces, leaving a remnant of the platform containing the point of hammer impact, and an adjacent sharp edge where the two flakes scars intersect. The only sharp lateral edge, with a 35° angle, has been nibbled by use. This artifact was found at a depth of 10–20 cm in Square D9. Another artifact, BA-CE-3/14, which measures 22 x 21 x 11 mm, is a square endscraper, one edge of which was crushed on an anvil while the opposite edge was forcefully struck with a hammer (Figure 4-6b). Subsequently two flakes were removed unidirectionally to resharpen the crushed anvil edge (35° angle), which appears to have been used. This piece is of a better quality translucent chert. It was found in the great fissure, at a depth of 40 cm in Square C9.

The best quality material found at the Abrigo da Lesma is represented by two pieces of what appears to be agate. There is no cortex remnant on either piece. Both were bipolarly struck, so probably the original nodules were small. Artifact BA-CE-3/59, which measures 28 x 12 x 5 mm, looks like a flake-blade with a dorsal ridge; but actually it is one of a series of spalls that were removed simultaneously when the distal end was held on an anvil and the apex was struck. Both lateral edges, with angles of 20° and 40° respectively, exhibit use-flaking. The crushed anvil platform may also have been used. This artifact was found at a depth of 60–70 cm in the northwest quarter of Square D9. Artifact BA-CE-3/15, which measures 35 x 20 x 13 mm, is an unusually large chunk of agate which served as a keeled scraper. Evidently the smallest end was held on an anvil, and formed a crushed wedge-shaped bit when struck at the thick end. The blow removed two other missing spalls. One irregular lateral edge, with a 60° angle, exhibits considerable use-flaking, as does the anvil bit, with a 45° angle. This artifact was found at a depth of 46 cm in the southwest quarter of Square C9.

Five cream-colored chert chunks appear to have been selected for their useful edges. The surfaces of BA-CE-3/124, which measures 41 x 27 x 13 mm, are almost all nodular. Two very useful working edges, with angles of 55° and 60°, exhibit unidirectional stepped use flaking from the flattest face. Using the same platform, a single retouch flake was removed from the corner between these edges in order to create two sharp graver projections. This artifact was found at a depth of 20–30 cm in Square C9. Artifact BA-CE-3/9, which measures 31 x 25 x 13 mm, exhibits stepped use-flaking along a steep incurvate/excurvate edge with a 75° angle and a concave edge of 60° with lateral projecting noses. This tool could be classified as a double endscraper/spokeshave, although it lacks an intentional form. It was also recovered from a depth of 20–30 cm in Square C9. A translucent chert chunk (BA-CE-3/96), which measures 34 x 27 x 9 mm, exhibits use-nibbling and dulling on three edges with angles ranging from 35° to 60°. It is impossible to tell if this piece was broken apart by man or by thermal spalling. The artifact was recovered from the 0–10 cm level in Square E10. Two blocky chunks of cream-colored vitreous chert appear to have broken apart by thermal spalling. On artifact BA-CE-3/120, which measures 13 x 13 x 10 mm, one lipped edge with a 55° angle exhibits stepped flaking, such as would occur on an endscraper. Possibly this was an endscraper which split apart by thermal action. It was recovered from the 40–50 cm level in Square D9. The other thermally broken chert chunk (BA-CE-3/134), which measures 15 x 15 x 12 mm, also exhibits stepped flaking on a short straight edge with a 75° angle. It was found at a depth of 20–30 cm in Square C9.

Artifact BA-CE-3/100, which measures 27 x 15 x 15 mm, is a rectangular chunk of the very rare brown chert of jasper. It exhibits stepped use-flaking from naturally flat faces on three edges with angles ranging from 60° to 70°. Two of these edges are straight; the third appears to have been resharpened by removing a flake from the center of a fairly straight edge in order to create a spokeshave concavity with two lateral noses. This artifact was recovered from the 0–10 cm level in Square E10. A larger natural chunk of brownish-red chert (BA-CE-3/11), which measures 65 x 45 x 20 mm, has been unidirectionally retouched along one excurvate edge to create a bi-bevelled bit with a 40° angle (Figure 4-7a). This piece, which retains a weathered nodular surface on all faces except the bit, is shaped like a bi-bevelled axe; and may have been used as an axe or an adze, although it could have been a scraper of knife. Use retouch on the bit is largely unidirectional (same direction as the intentional flake scars); however, one use flake was removed from the opposite face. This artifact was found at a depth of 32 cm in the southwest corner of Square C9.

Quartzite Artifacts

Quartzite does not occur naturally anywhere in the limestone area north of Central. The closest known source is the Serra Azul, about 25 km south of the Abrigo da Lesma. People carried quartzite to the Abrigo da Lesma in two forms: angular blocks and water-rounded pebbles. Pebbles with pecked areas were used as hammerstones, while pebbles with polished faces and facets were probably used to prepare some other material. One pebble was flaked into a scraper/graver. In addition to the pebbles, suitable natural fragments of angular pieces were selected from outcrops of homogeneous quartzite. There is evidence that the block-on-block technique was used to quarter large cobbles. Also, decortication flakes were removed from the edges of weathered angular quartzite blocks in the same way that limestone blocks were used as a source of flakes.

Three quartzite artifacts from the Abrigo da Lesma have one flat face which superficially looks like a cleavage plane. However, despite the fact that the points of impact are missing, the presence of weak lines of force combined with a pattern of tiny incompletely removed flakes (similar to eraillure scars), the opened edges of which are directed toward the point of impact on most quartzite flakes, suggests that a block-on-block or anvil technique was used at quarry sites to quarter cobbles

Figure 4-7. A) retouched chert fragment (BA-CE-3/11); **B)** quartzite *lesma* (BA-CE-3/107).

and boulders. Experiments conducted elsewhere with quartzite cobbles demonstrated the effectiveness of the block-on-block technique, which can be used to quarter water-rounded cobbles or outcropping blocks. Simply placing the rock to be split on an anvil and throwing another rock at it might accidentally break the rock into useful pieces. However, a more efficient method which yields controlled results is to place the block to be split on an anvilstone and pack them both in sand, leaving only the tip of the piece to be split exposed. If another large cobble or boulder is thrown straight down at the exposed apex, the piece will normally split down the middle. What happens is that the cone of percussion splits because of the extreme force. The same thing happens when the bipolar technique is used to split small pebbles or quartz crystals that are held on an anvil. Surprisingly large boulders and blocks can be split with the block-on-block technique. The split cone face makes a perfect flat platform for the removal of ordinary flakes with bulbs of percussion (i.e., segments of cones of percussion). If the split cone face intersects at a useful angle with a naturally flat plane (e.g., cleavage plane, bedding plane, or thermal spall), an effective sharp-edged tool is immediately created without any intentional retouch or bulb of percussion.

Artifact BA-CE-3/105, which measures 82 x 81 x 22 mm, is such a tool. It is a square tabular chunk which looks like a uni-bevelled axe blade; and may have been so used, as there is considerable bi-directional use-flaking and wear along the excurvate bit edge, with a 25° edge angle. The bevelled face of the bit is a natural cleavage plane (it lacks the pattern of incompletely removed microflakes directed toward a point of impact). The poll half of this face exhibits a natural thermal fracture, as do three of the edges which naturally broke at right angles to the faces. The other face, which intersects the cleavage plane, creating the 25° angled bit, was evidently deliberately created by splitting the cone with the block-on-block technique. It is impossible to say if the knapper intentionally split the block so that the split cone face intersected with the cleavage plane face at this most useful angle. Perhaps the shape of this axe was accidentally created, but the piece was selected for its obviously useful shape. It was found on the surface in August 1983.

The only stone artifact with a definitely intentional shape from the Abrigo da Lesma is the *lesma* or slug-shaped object (BA-CE-3/107) found on the surface under the dripline in the unexcavated square E9 (Figure 4-7b). Although not a classic *lesma* because it is too thick (dimensions 82 x 47 x 23 mm) and was not made on a flake-blade, it appears to have been used in the same way for scraping. The dorsal surface retains an old weathering rind which subsequently attracted a thick coating composed of iron and calcium carbonate. Some of this coating adheres to the adjacent flaked surfaces as well. The ventral surface is a nearly flat split cone face which was used as a platform for removing steep flakes from both sides and from the rounded end. This continuous steeply retouched edge (70° angle on the sides and 65° angle on the end) exhibits stepped retouch flaking and evidence of wear polish, especially on a 3-cm-long section of the left side (as seen from the dorsal face) about a third of the distance from the apex to the base, which was squared by removing three right-angled flakes from the split cone platform. The squared base was then used as a platform for removing flakes in an unsuccessful attempt to thin the piece by removing the weathered dorsal face. The artifact can be described as a steep end- and side-scraper which obviously was intentionally shaped into a predetermined form. It evidently was most often held in the right hand so that the left edge could be applied to scrape something with a back-and-forth motion.

The only other intentionally retouched quartzite artifact that appears to have been made from a chunk by splitting the cone to create a flat ventral surface is BA-CE-3/30, which measures 32 x 33 x 11 mm. Actually, this square object appears to be the central segment of a flake-blade with two dorsal ridges flanked by a negative flake scar. In fact, it could be a central segment of another *lesma,* snapped squarely at both ends. Unfortunately, however, the lateral edges have been resharpened so the extreme wear on typical *lesmas* is not visible. The split cone face was the platform used to step-flake one quite sharp edge (with a 40° angle), while the other edge was retouched from the dorsal face. The latter edge, with a 50° angle, feels worn. The artifact was found at a depth of 17 cm in the southeast quarter of Square D9.

Artifact BA-CE-3/10 is a thick end/side scraper/graver made on a thick flake struck from a flat high angle (120°) unfacetted platform which is probably the remnant of a split cone face (Figure 4-8a). The artifact measures 55 x 44 x 21 mm, and it was found on the surface in the northeast quarter of Square B9 (unexcavated unit). Much of the dorsal face exhibits a series of hinged negative flake scars caused by previous attempts to remove flakes from the same platform. Half of the distal end of the dorsal face retains the original water-rolled pebble cortex. The excurving edge of the distal end (with a 50° angle) and the most prominent parts of the irregular ventral surface are covered with a dark purple/black stain from some unidentified substance. A small (5 mm wide) retouch flake was intentionally removed from the center of the distal end, using the ventral face as a platform, in order to create two sharp graver spurs, which are still sharp. This negative retouch flake scar is less stained than the other surfaces, confirming that the flake was removed soon before the artifact was discarded. At least three earlier retouch flakes were removed from the ventral face to create graver spurs, which are worn. Evidently this thick flake with a conveniently convex end was used to prepare

A

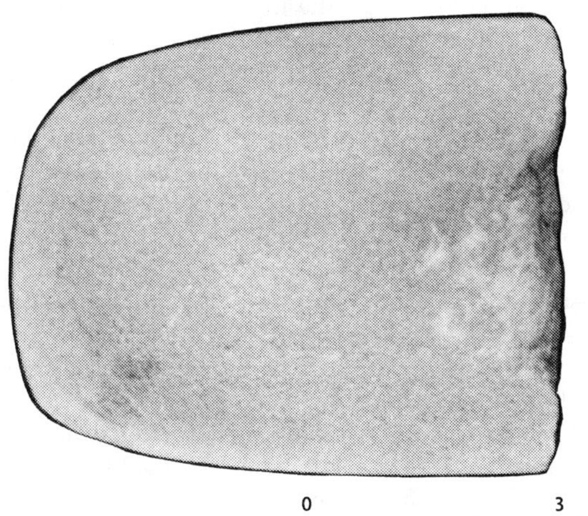

B

Figure 4-8. A) quartzite end/sidescraper/graver (BA-CE-3/10); **B)** shaped quartzite pebble (BA-CE-3/50).

something (probably a plant product) by rubbing the ventral surface over the material. The graver spurs could have been used to groove and cut the material.

Three percussion flakes retaining some weathered cortex (not water-rolled) were removed from flat unprepared platforms at the same high (120°) angle. On artifact BA-CE-3/110, which measures 58 x 42 x 17 mm, the sharpest lateral edge was retouched by two flakes from alternate sides to create three prominent noses flanked by two spokeshave concavities. This edge (with a 50–60° angle), especially the noses, and the distal end (with a 60° angle) are use-retouched and worn. This artifact was found on the surface in August 1983. The sharpest lateral edge (60°) of artifact BA-CE-3/123 (dimensions 33 x 24 x 10 mm) is slightly worn, as is a prominent graver spur on the edge of the platform end. Although this spur may have been created by previous attempts to remove a series of stepped flakes from the flat platform, the projection probably was intentionally resharpened by removing a small retouch flake. The artifact was found at a depth of 20–30 cm in Square C9. On artifact BA-CE-3/64, which measures 38 x 28 x 11 mm, the sharpest edge, with a 30° angle, appears to have been denticulated and worn by use. The artifact was found at a depth of 20 cm in the south-central part of Square C8/D8.

Two naturally angular chunks of quartzite had been picked up and used as scrapers at the Abrigo da Lesma. Most of the edges of artifact BA-CE-3/116, which measures 46 x 45 x 24 mm, are smoothed, perhaps while it was being transported. One short (15 mm) wedge-shaped edge apparently was steepened to a 60° angle by removal of one large flake from one direction and later resharpened by removal of a small flake from the other face. This artifact was found on the surface in August 1983. Artifact BA-CE-3/112, which measures 105 x 60 x 28 mm, is a natural peeled segment of a weathered block of quartzite created by thermal spalling. Large portions of both ends have later been snapped off; but a short (21 mm) bitted end was resharpened by unidirectional flakes to create a 45° angle edge, which is much worn. A short unbroken segment of the opposite end is a worn negative flake scar. One long lateral edge with a 50° angle is also much worn; while the other lateral edge, with a 35° angle, is less worn because it was resharpened by removing at least two unidirectional flakes. This artifact was also a surface find in August 1983.

Water-rounded quartzite pebbles were used as hammerstones. Artifact BA-CE-3/119, which measures 34 x 20 x 8 mm, is a hinged flake with a heavily pecked area around the point of impact. Obviously this flake, with a broad flat bulb, was unintentionally removed from a pebble by heavy pounding. It was found at a depth of 1–10 cm in Square C9. Artifact BA-CE-3/50, which measures 56 x 53 x 49 mm, is the distal end of an elongated pebble with one end pecked to a square shape (Figure 4-8b). Several use-flake scars are present around the periphery of the battered end. Subsequently one face has been flattened and polished by apparent use as a mano or polishing stone. There are no visible grinding striations, so seeds were evidently not ground. The object was broken by heavy battering concentrated near the center of one face; then the piece appears to have been intentionally split by holding the opposite edge on an anvil. The broken edge of the polished face exhibits many steep use flakes evidently removed by unidirectionally dragging the sharp right-angled edge as if it were the bit of a plane. The opposite, more weathered edge was also worn and bevelled by similar use. As the polished face and retouched edges are less weathered than the other faces and the pecked end, it is probable that the weathered hammerstone was recycled by deliberately splitting it for reuse as a rubbing tool and scraper plane. It was found at a depth of 20 cm in the northwest quarter of Square E10.

Artifact BA-CE-3/109, which measures 52 x 45 x 28 mm, is the rounded tip end of a hammerstone which probably broke by thermal action in a fire. The tip has been heavily pecked and battered. Two pecked areas on adjacent faces were truncated by the break. The broken edge of one pecked area, with an edge angle of 90°, is polished and worn by use. The other edges, with angles of only 50° or 70°, were not used. A roughly rectangular polished facet between the pecked end and the worn edge was created by rubbing. Again, it appears that the worn and polished areas were used more recently than the pecked areas. It is a matter of speculation as to what these recycled hammerstones were used for. This specimen was found on the surface of the site in August 1983.

Two ovoid water-worn pebbles exhibit much less evidence of use. Artifact BA-CE-3/46, which measures 80 x 47 x 25 mm, is a symmetrically flattened oval pebble which has clear evidence of slight pecking on both ends, near the middle of both edges and both faces. In addition, areas of slight polishing are evident on all faces and edges. This artifact was found at a depth of 8 cm in the northwest quarter of Square E10. Artifact BA-CE-3/114, which measures 53 x 33 x 25 mm, is an irregularly oval pebble which is considered to be an artifact only because it is a manuport. The only possible evidence of use is apparent differential staining, especially at one end. The artifact was collected from the surface in August 1983.

Artifact BA-CE-3/25 is a rectangular block of quartzite with a deep weathering rind on all surfaces except one end. The piece measures 96 x 73 x 39 mm, and it was found at a depth of 7 cm in the southwest corner of Square D9. As the rind is friable and disintegrating, any evidence for working has been obliterated. The squared edges and ends seem abnormal in form, and may have been pecked. A broad crushed edge and obvious point of impact on one corner of the least weathered end indicates that the piece was held on an anvil and bipolarly struck to split the cone and square that end. There appear to be a few negative flake scars created by using that squared end as a hammerstone.

Limestone Artifacts

In a cave site in which there is a great deal of angular rubble, the archaeologist does not have time to examine every rock closely; so it is often assumed that all of the broken limestone rocks are natural roof spalls. Even if a flake scar or a flake is noticed, it would be assumed that it was caused when the piece fell from the ceiling onto another rock. In other words, archaeologists habitually do not bother to look at limestone fragments to see if they exhibit any evidence of use. However, in a site in which there is very little if any rubble, each piece can be examined without difficulty. At the Abrigo da Lesma, sizable limestone fragments were encountered only in the upper 35 cm of the silt deposit; and they were concentrated in the northern part of Square E10 and the western part of Square D9. Most of the fragments were angular, shattered, and apparently fire-cracked. Some of the fragments, usually those with weathered surfaces, bore evidence indicating use as choppers, pounding tools, or hammerstones. In addition, a few limestone flakes also bore evidence of utilization.

A total of 25 limestone artifacts were identified from the Abrigo da Lesma. It is apparent that in some cases an Indian needing a tool would simply look around the immediate vicinity of the site for something that would serve the purpose without any intentional alteration. In most cases, however, the subangular weathered pebbles and cobbles were first broken open (quartered) in order to create more useful angular edges and projections. As will be described later, the bipolar technique was evidently the most successful method for quartering limestone pebbles. One reason for selecting subangular weathered rocks rather than angular rubble was because very few pieces of rubble were available, but a more important reason was that the rounded surfaces could be held in the hand with less danger of injury while the freshly made angular edges were used for tasks requiring heavy chopping and hammering. Unlike most of the siliceous stone artifacts, limestone rocks were not transported very far; and their average size is larger than the quartzite, chert, or quartz objects that had to be carried for some distance.

The easiest way to obtain a sharp-edged limestone flake to cut or scrape a soft material would be simply to strike a flake from a corner of one of the angular boulders near the shelter. However, there is no evidence that such was the practice at the Abrigo da Lesma; and the fact that utilization was identified on only four flakes among the approximately 300 limestone flakes excavated at the Abrigo da Lesma suggests that limestone flakes were rarely used for cutting or scraping. Probably most unused flakes were removed from blocks unintentionally by heavy use, or intentionally to reduce the size of a block, or to renew the worn edge of a chopping tool.

One of the utilized flakes, artifact BA-CE-3/6, is a thick flake (58 x 49 x 27 mm) with a lip on the platform and prominent force lines which created a denticulated distal edge at a 50° angle which was used as a scraper. A short right-angled edge also exhibits wear. This artifact was found at a depth of 5–7 cm below surface in the northwest quarter of Square C8/D8. Artifact BA-CE-3/53, which measures 84 x 45 x 25 mm, is a pyramidal flake which unfortunately is badly weathered. However, this flake was obviously struck from a weathered high-angled (130°) platform surface. Both lateral edges, with angles of 25° and 40°, exhibit negative use-flake scars from the tip end and on the dorsal surface, as well as other projections. This artifact was found at a depth of 33 cm in the northwest corner of Square E10. Apparently artifact BA-CE-3/131 is a decortication flake with a platform angle of 100°. This artifact, which was found at a depth of 10–20 cm in Square D9, measures 58 x 43 x 15 mm. The distal edge hinged, but a lateral edge with 20° angle is use-flaked on the bulbar side. Artifact BA-CE-3/54, which measures 88 x 58 x 29 mm, is a thick rectangular secondary flake exhibiting a broad positive bulb on the ventral face and a negative bulb on the dorsal face (Figure 4-9a). As both flake scars were produced by heavy hammer blows, probably the core was a large solid boulder. Two of the distal edges of this piece were unidirectionally trimmed by heavy percussion from the dorsal face. Four of the nosed projections on the trimmed edges (with angles of 30° and 50°) exhibit wear and use-retouch flaking, probably from chopping a soft material. This artifact was found at a depth of 34 cm in the northwest corner of Square E10.

Artifact BA-CE-3/38 is a thick natural slab of limestone which appears to be a core chopper, but probably what was desired were the steeply retouched projections along the flaked edges. This artifact, which was found at a depth of 5 cm in the northeast quarter of Square E10, measures 115 x 83 x 46 mm. A naturally flat surface was used as a platform to remove large flakes around the entire periphery, producing edge angles varying from 40° to 60°. A second generation of use-flaking at an angle of 85° to 90°, produced by use as a chopper, created step-flaked and worn prominences. The shape of this artifact suggests that it could be called a scraper-plane, but there is no evidence of either scraping or planing.

Artifact BA-CE-3/28, measuring 170 x 108 x 40 mm, is the largest and heaviest artifact from the Abrigo da Lesma. Three edges of this large thick naturally tabular chopper were trimmed to a 60° to 90° angle by removing a few large flakes alternately from both flat faces. Apparently the trimming was mainly in order to reduce the size and weight. The piece is rectangular in form, with rounded ends. The most prominent edges and corners on both sides exhibit much secondary stepped flaking at a 90° angle, and use-wear. This heavy duty chopper was probably used with both hands. It was found at a depth of 15 cm in the southwest quarter of Square D9.

The other limestone choppers found at the Abrigo da Lesma lack preliminary retouch. Most are unshaped subangular pieces of weathered limestone which were intentionally broken open and selected for their useful edges. At first it seemed that they had probably been broken simply by throwing another rock at them; however, careful analysis revealed that in many cases toolmakers used considerable care in quartering these rocks, based on a knowledge of how limestone breaks. Detection of patterned breaking in a few cases suggests that many pieces may have been produced by special techniques. A subcategory of four thin tabular choppers can arbitrarily be separated on the basis of shape. As naturally thin tabular rock fragments were not observed in the area of the shelter, these useful slabs were evidently intentionally selected for their potential tabular form, and transported to the site.

Artifact BA-CE-3/12, which measures 93 x 78 x 26 mm, is a rectangular slab heavily used on two irregularly parallel edges, which have angles of 10° and 30°. Battering flakes, some quite large, were removed bi-directionally by vertical pounding on the two edges and four corners (Figure 4-9b). Striking at some hard material vertically with the corners of this tool removed long shallow flakes, including a burin spall at one corner. There is no evidence that this angle burin was intentionally constructed. This artifact was found in the great fissure at a depth of 43 cm in Square C8/D8. Artifact BA-CE-3/41, which measures 97 x 97 x 19 mm, is a spade-shaped tabular chopper with a heavy coating of calcium carbonate. The rounded end and one square corner were used with the same vertical chopping motion, which removed shallow flakes bi-directionally

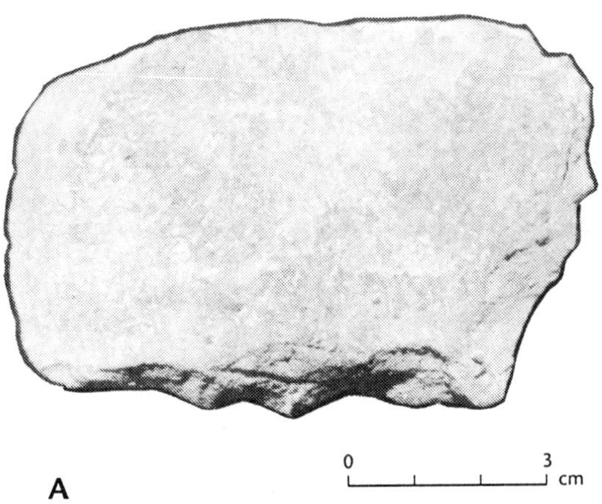

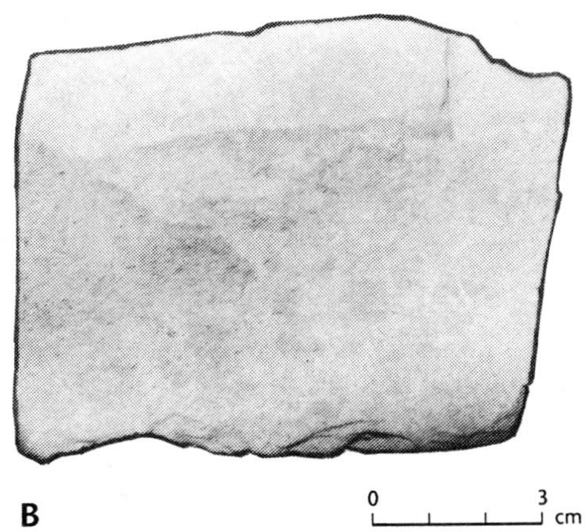

Figure 4-9. A) retouched limestone flake (BA-CE-3/54); **B)** utilized limestone slab (BA-CE-3/12).

from the rounded end and unidirectionally from the broadest corner at a 90° angle. This artifact was found at a depth of 17 cm in the northwest quarter of Square E10. Artifact BA-CE-3/7, which measures 95 x 68 x 14 mm, is a tabular chopper with one straight edge which is heavily battered and worn by vertical chopping which removed shallow flakes bi-directionally. Originally this chopper was probably larger; the lateral edges appear to have snapped off, perhaps by using the piece as an anvil. A concentration of short grooves near the center of one face could have been produced by holding a hard material on the face and gently striking it. Certainly, if this tabular piece had been used as an anvil for some purpose, such as for bipolar flaking, the vertical blows on the flat face could account for the geometrically snapped edges. Most forceful bipolar flaking was undoubtedly done at the quarry sites, but some bipolar retouching may have been done in the shelter. Therefore this artifact may be an old chopper that was recycled for use as an anvil stone. It was found at a depth of 5–7 cm in the northwest quarter of Square C8/D8.

A small triangular piece of limestone (BA-CE-3/67), which measures 65 x 48 x 12 mm, may be a fragment of a large chopper. Heavy unidirectional flaking is evident along one slightly incurvate edge, which has an angle of 45°. Lighter unidirectional flaking and wear are present on an excurving edge and the tip, which has an edge angle of 10° to 15°. The other end appears to have snapped off while it was being used as a chopper. This artifact was found in the great fissure at a depth of 12 cm in Square D9. Artifact BA-CE-3/24, which measures 140 x 108 x 53 mm, is a naturally pyramidal chunk which is probably a wall spall, as none of the surfaces are very weathered. Only the sharpest corner has a flake removed; but all three straight basal edges (with angles of 40°, 45°, and 70°) have been flaked by use as a chopper. This artifact was found at a depth of 1 cm in the central part of Square D9.

Artifact BA-CE-3/5, which measures 58 x 58 x 54 mm, is a roughly cubical chunk with only one weathered face. Two battered apices may be remnants of earlier attempts to break up the chunk. One irregular 90° edge is worn as well as battered, with at least three hinged flake scars made by heavy use as a chopper. All the other edges are quite sharp. This artifact was found at a depth of 5–7 cm in the northwest quarter of Square C8/D8.

Artifact BA-CE-3/27, which measures 100 x 86 x 42 mm, was a weathered limestone cobble found at a depth of 4 cm in the southwest quarter of Square D9. It was evidently intentionally split along a cleavage plane by vertically striking the surface parallel to a visible plane. A short negative flake scar was removed from this otherwise natural face. The opposite excurvate edge, with an angle varying from 20° to 35°, is battered, with use flakes removed bi-directionally by heavy chopping with vertically directed blows. Both corners show such use, with short shallow flakes removed. If the angles had been appropriate, the flakes removed would have looked like burin spalls. This artifact demonstrates that the knapper knew how to create a useful tool from very poor material with a minimum of effort. Some of the previously described tabular choppers may also have been deliberately cleaved, but the evidence is not visible.

The sharp ends and edges of several subangular chunks of limestone have been used. As most of these pieces appear to have been rounded pebbles and cobbles (not water-rolled) which had weathered outside the shelter, the angular edges and corners had to be artificially created. Limestone cobbles do not break apart as predictably as either cryptocrystalline rocks or quartz crystals. Nevertheless, as demonstrated by the previously described piece, toolmakers did attempt to break up limestone, after studying a rock to determine how striking it in a certain way might yield useful edges and corners. Undoubtedly toolmakers experimented with hand-held percussion; however, bipolar percussion seems to have been the most successful technique for quartering weathered limestone pebbles.

Artifact BA-CE-3/37, which measures 120 x 61 x 59 mm, is a pyramidal piece of limestone that evidently was very forcefully struck on its apex (perhaps by throwing a rock at it) after placing the opposing flat face on an anvil. Probably because of the nature of limestone, originally a massive mud deposit with occasional concretions, the cone did not split along a flat plane. Instead, a portion of a huge cone (with an eraillure scar) started to form; but it soon curved toward the force coming from the anvil, creating a peculiar curving ridge where the angle abruptly changed. Two basal corner projections, with angles of 50° and 60°, were then used for vertical chopping, which resulted in bi-directional flake scars. This artifact was found at a depth of 5 cm in the central part of Square E10.

Three weathered limestone pebbles have one unweathered face with unusual force lines created by breaking the rocks apart. Artifact BA-CE-3/72, which measures 89 x 68 x 42 mm, is a pyramidal pebble which evidently was struck on its apical ridge while the opposing face was held on an anvil. In this case, a cone segment carried only a short distance to a calcite vein, where it terminated. Evidently one flat end of the piece was then placed on the anvil and struck on the opposite apex. This time the partial cone intersected the previous crack, creating an unusual double-angled break. The only useful edge, with a 45° angle, is worn and use-retouched. One large flake was removed from this working edge. The artifact was found at a depth of 20 cm in the northeast quarter of Square D9.

Another broken elongated pebble, artifact BA-CE-3/29, which measures 141 x 66 x 65 mm, has a triangular cross-section. It features a peculiar undulating bulbar face which almost fits the positive bulb of the previously described specimen. The force lines on this face appear at first glance to indicate a thermal spall because they point to a fine concretion near the center of the concave portion of the face. However, the lines of force actually emanate from the two ends. Evidently one end was held on an anvil and the piece struck on the opposite end; but instead of splitting the cone, the force lines sought out the imperfection, creating the unusual undulating face. All three longitudinal edges (with angles of 40°, 65°, and 95°) and both ends were heavily battered and use-flaked. Two of the battered edges have been flattened by pecking, so this chopper was also subsequently used as a hammerstone to beat or pound something, rather than simply chopping some material into pieces. It was found at a depth of 7 cm in the northeast quarter of Square D9. Artifact BA-CE-3/71, which measures 90 x 47 x 44 mm, was found in the great fissure at a depth of 22 cm in Square D9. It is a rectangular weathered limestone pebble with flake scars on both sides of a weathered end produced by vertical pounding. The battered end was then placed on an anvil and the opposite end struck to split the piece. The hammer platform end (1.5 mm wide) was then used.

Artifact BA-CE-3/3, which measures 74 x 66 x 51 mm, is a chopper/hammerstone with three heavily battered edges and two ends flaked and pecked. Very likely, this broken weathered pebble was split bipolarly, perhaps twice from opposite directions; but there has been so much subsequent battering that it is difficult to be sure how the original pebble was broken apart. Eventually it was discarded after one end shattered during heavy use. It was found at a depth of 8 cm in the northwest quarter of Square C9.

Artifact BA-CE-3/51, which measures 78 x 65 x 63 mm, is a nearly cubical hammerstone made on a very homogeneous black limestone pebble. Unfortunately, it was heavily encrusted with calcium carbonate; and the acid used to remove this crust removed most of the evidence for working, including the lines of force from the straight unweathered face, which appears to have been split bipolarly. One 95° angle edge has obviously been heavily battered, with several use-retouch flakes removed. This artifact was found at a depth of 17 cm in the northwest quarter of Square E10.

Artifact BA-CE-3/39, which measures 65 x 58 x 32 mm, is a rectangular hammerstone made on a thick naturally tabular subangular pebble of limestone. One end is heavily battered and pecked, with several use-flake scars removed by vertical blows. The other end has an irregular break which may have been caused by using the piece as an anvilstone. Like the previously described tabular chopper (BA-CE-3/7), this thicker tabular hammerstone has a concentrated area of short grooves adjacent to the broken end. This artifact was found at a depth of 6 cm in the northwest quarter of Square E10.

Artifact BA-CE-3/66, which measures 73 x 61 x 55 mm, has assumed its quadrangular shape by heavy battering and pecking of a weathered pebble. Except for two concave faces, including old flake scars, nearly all edges and faces have been pecked. Flake scars, produced by earlier heavy battering, are evident, especially on one projection. Nearby, in a weathered concavity, is a small shallow pecked depression (8 x 11 mm in diameter) which may have been created by using the artifact as an anvil. This artifact was found in the great fissure, at a depth of 34 cm in Square D9.

Two small tabular pieces of weathered limestone exhibit unusual marks on one face. Artifact BA-CE-3/122, which measures 27 x 19 x 3 mm, has three fractured edges which might have been broken when the object was used as an anvil. Several nearly parallel scratches on one face were made recently, but four parallel incisions on the other face at right angles to a broken edge are definitely old. This artifact was found at a depth of 40–50 cm in the east part of Square D9. Several roughly parallel incisions on one face of artifact BA-CE-3/121, which measures 31 x 23 x 5 mm, are quite similar in appearance. It is not known what function such small thin pieces might have served. They would not have been closely examined except for the fact that their weathered surfaces indicated that they had been carried in from outside the shelter. This artifact was also found at a depth of 40–50 cm in the east part of Square D9.

Artifact BA-CE-3/129, which measures 50 x 35 x 19 mm, is another angular fragment of limestone with two weathered surfaces. It exhibits steep flaking along two opposing nearly 90° angle edges, as if they had been used for scraping. This artifact was found at a depth of 0–10 cm in Square D9.

Three subangular weathered pebbles exhibit short natural edges and points used for chopping. Artifact BA-CE-3/68, which measures 73 x 68 x 43 mm, has two adjacent battered edges; and several other short edges and projections have been battered and pecked. It was found at a depth of 40 cm in the great fissure, in Square D9. Artifact BA-CE-3/65, which measures 68 x 45 x 12 mm, is a naturally triangular tabular chunk which has been struck on one end at least three times, removing a burin spall with each blow. This burin shows no evidence of subsequent use, so it probably was not made intentionally. This artifact was found at a depth of 12 cm in the west-central part of Square D9.

Most heavy chopping and hammering was evidently accomplished at the Abrigo da Lesma with easily available and readily expendable chunks and cobbles of limestone. Although a few limestone flakes were evidently used for scraping, the sharper and more durable edges of quartz chunks and quartzite and chert flakes and chunks were normally used for the more delicate tasks of scraping and cutting. We do not know just what was being chopped and pounded with such effort, but it could have been a vegetable food.

Bone Artifacts

Greater weathering than in most shelters or caves is undoubtedly a major reason why few bone artifacts were recovered from the deposits at the Abrigo da Lesma. The weathering has obliterated most marks of workmanship from broken bone artifacts. But other factors must also have been operative to explain the paucity of bones of large and medium-sized animals. Evidence indicates that the Abrigo da Lesma was not a hunting station: the abundance of heavy-duty choppers, hammers, and scraping tools suggests that the products of gathering activities (plants and gastropods) and not game animals or birds were most often processed by the very small groups that could have occupied the shelter. For whatever reason, bone artifacts were very rare at the site. Only four bone artifacts were identified, and only one of these is complete.

Artifact BA-CE-3/88, which measures 26 x 5 x 4 mm, was evidently a cylindrical bone bead or pendant. It is a section of a long bone of a small mammal or bird, and each end had been intentionally squared and worn. Several parallel cut marks are visible on three faces parallel to one end, which was grooved and then snapped off squarely. The opposite end apparently was simply broken off roughly, and then the broken edges were ground and polished square. Another bone cylinder, slightly longer and larger in diameter, was found in the same screen load from the 20–30 cm level in Square E10. This object had been chewed at both ends by small rodents: also, two holes were gnawed into one face. Possibly this chewed bone had also been a bead, but all evidence has been obliterated.

Two broken bone artifacts exhibit longitudinal scrape marks made by a stone flake. One end of BA-CE-3/76, which measures 32 x 8 x 1 mm, was also evidently squared, probably by cutting an encircling groove and snapping; although any cut marks were subsequently obliterated by wear polish. Root etching is present in addition to the scrape marks on two parts of the external surface. All edges exhibit green bone breaks. This object, evidently made on a bird bone, could have been a larger pendant. It came from the 0–10 cm level in Square E10. Artifact BA-CE-3/91, which measures 18 x 7 x 2 mm, is a medium-sized mammal bone fragment which exhibits desiccation breaks. It has overlapping scrape marks and incisions over most of its external surface. This fragment is unusually well preserved. It was found in the 10–20 cm level in Square D9.

The surface of artifact BA-CE-3/4, which measures 38 x 15 x 19 mm, is covered with a thin coating of iron-stained calcium carbonate which proved impossible to remove. It is a segment of a medium-sized mammal ulna (?), broken at both ends, and lacking any marrow cavity. Some possible scrape marks are visible on the best-exposed surface. This artifact appears to be the central section of a solid bone projectile point with a triangular cross-section at the larger end and an oval cross-section at the smaller end. It was found at a depth of 15 cm in the northwest corner of Square C9.

Shell Artifacts

River mussel shells had to be imported into the Abrigo da Lesma from a great distance away. Only one whole left valve of a mussel was complete enough to be identified as *Diplodon delondontus.* Presumably all fragments belong to the same species, which lives in permanent watercourses. The nearest source to the Abrigo da Lesma is the Rio Verde to the west, which flows no closer than 30 km to the west of the site. Presumably shellfish would be eaten and the shells discarded near the place where they were collected; therefore, the shells must have been transported to the Abrigo da Lesma for some useful purpose. In this sense, all mussel shell fragments found at the site probably were artifacts; but 134 excavated fragments of shell were not included in the total artifact count because they exhibited no evidence of human alteration. In addition to the whole valve identified as to species (BA-CE-3/90), and which exhibits a short worn section on the outer edge as if it had been used as a knife, 44 other fragments of shell were considered as artifacts.

A large triangular shell fragment (BA-CE-3/165), found in Square E10 at a depth of 10–20 cm, exhibited a concave flaked edge which appears to be a portion of a perforation about 24 mm in diameter, near the center of the face of the valve, which measures 47 x 30 x 3 mm. The roughly flaked edge on the inner (concave) face, and slight smoothing on the opposite (outer) face was experimentally reproduced by Wesley Hurt in scraping roots with a pushing motion. This triangular shape was the most common type of mussel shell tool found in the Abrigo do Valdemar, excavated by Hurt. Another roughly triangular fragment (BA-CE-3/92), found in Square D9 at a depth of 10–20 cm, has an excurving edge which is flaked by heavy use. The outer edge has been steeply worn, and exhibits minute scratches on its inner surface. This piece, which measures 35 x 20 x 3 mm, may also have been used as a scraper. One rectangular shell fragment (BA-CE-3/128), found in Square D9 at a depth of 0–10 cm, exhibits some wear along the external edge, but a transverse break across the growth lines has been ground smooth on the inner surface, with visible striations created by external nibbling.

All mussel shell fragments were examined carefully with a 10-power hand lens. Evidence of use on the remaining fragments is limited to the outer edges of the valves, which may be worn, polished, flaked, or battered. The edges of a few fragments have been gnawed by rodents, a process which usually removed any previous evidence of use. Categories of evidence are limited to unusual wear, differential polish, and flaking or battering of the outer edges. Evidence of use was found on the edge of the external surface of 26 specimens, while only four fragments have flaked and worn inner surfaces of the edge. The edges of 14 other specimens were worn and battered by direct blows, which sometimes removed flakes from either the inner or outer surfaces. Two of the fragments with worn edges were calcined grey by extreme heat. A few pieces of shell not counted as artifacts were similarly burned.

The evidence for wear on these shell fragments does not suggest any particular function. The lack of striations suggests that the objects were not used to scrape anything gritty, such as a root. The only function that seems consistent with the variable evidence for wear, polish, and occasional flaking and battering of the edges is that the shells were probably used as cups and spoons; and the visible evidence for use was caused by normal wear and battering of such utensils while serving and eating food, and while being transported from one campsite to another. The few calcined pieces may have been tossed into a fire. In other words, most shell fragments are sherds of eating utensils which were discarded after they broke.

The distribution of utilized mussel shell fragments is given in Table 4-3. Square E10, an area highly productive of artifacts of all kinds, yielded 50% of the total of 45 shell artifacts. In vertical distribution, 31% of the shell artifacts occurred in the 0–10 cm level, 26% in the 10–20 cm level, and 15% in the 20–30 cm level. A scatter of shell artifacts was found in lower levels. Three specimens were recovered from the 70–80 cm level in Square D9; and one specimen was found at the 80–90 cm level in Square E10.

Ceramics

Potsherds

Eleven potsherds were recovered from the upper levels of the Abrigo da Lesma. All but two of the sherds were found in Square E10; the remaining two came from the adjacent southwest corner of Square D9. Six sherds were recovered from a depth of 0–10 cm; two sherds from a depth of 10–20 cm; one sherd from a depth of 20–30 cm; one sherd from a depth of 30–40 cm; and one sherd had no provenience. In other words, the occurrence of pottery is restricted to the upper levels in a small area of the site.

Two of the sherds, found at the 0–10 cm level, have a plain smooth brick-red surface and dark grey core, and are 5 mm in thickness. These sherds feature medium temper derived from an unidentified material but containing particles of angular quartz and grey calcite ranging up to 1 mm in diameter. An additional very small sherd found at the 20–30 cm level may pertain to this group.

The remainder of the sherds are distinguished by medium temper apparently derived from a micaceous schist, as mica particles up to 3 mm in size are prominent, and quartz fragments up to 2 mm in size are also present. One sherd, found in the 20–30 cm level, has a thin black slip on the interior and exterior surfaces; two additional sherds, from the 0–10 cm level, have a thin black slip on the interior (concave) surface. Four of the remaining sherds with micaceous temper have faint traces of dark material on a smooth brown surface, and may have originally also featured a black slip before surface erosion. There is one small rim sherd (measuring 34 x 32 x 5 mm) with micaceous temper. This sherd, with a smooth mottled grey/brown surface, features a pointed lip which is beveled on the exterior surface. It may be from a shallow bowl with large diameter.

The sherds with micaceous temper have an average thickness of 5 mm. One sherd, however, was 9 mm thick. This sherd was 63 x 58 mm in diameter, elliptical in form, perhaps with edges deliberately shaped. The exterior surface is smooth and reddish brown in color; the interior surface (concave) more greyish. On the interior surface of this sherd there are clear marks of the finishing tool in the form of shallow grooves up to 2 mm wide, running longitudinally and approximately parallel: the tool was probably the end of a small stick or cane. This sherd was found in an ashy zone adjacent to the back wall of the shelter at a depth of 40 cm below surface.

Examination of the small collection of sherds from the upper levels in the western part of the rockshelter, then, suggests two wares: a brick-red plain ware with temper of quartz and calcite grit, and a plain brown or black-slipped ware with micaceous temper. Excavation in the late prehistoric levels at more productive sites in the Central region should recover larger samples of potsherds which will permit definition of ceramic types.

Baked Clay Lumps

Four small rectanguloid lumps of baked clay were found in Square C9 at the 0–10 cm level. The largest specimen (broken) measures 20 x 18 x 10 mm. The surface of each lump is rough and reddish in color; the core of the broken specimen is grey. No temper could be observed. It appears as if the lumps were simply molded between the fingers.

Miscellaneous Artifacts

Six small pieces of soft hematite which may be lumps of red pigment were found at various levels in the silt deposits at the Abrigo da Lesma. All but one were recovered from Square E10: one from the 60–70 cm level, one from the 40–50 cm level, and three from the 10–30 cm level. One fragment was also recovered from the

Table 4-3. Distribution of Artifacts at the Abrigo da Lesma.

	Small Quartz Artifacts	Small Chert Artifacts	Small Quartzite Artifacts	Small Limestone Artifacts	Heavy Quartzite Artifacts
surface	7	0	3	0	4
Square E10					
0–10 cm	8	2	0	0	1
10–20 cm	4	0	0	0	0
20–30 cm	1	0	0	0	1
30–40 cm	0	0	0	2	0
40–50 cm	0	0	0	0	0
50–60 cm	0	0	0	0	0
60–70 cm	0	0	0	0	0
70–80 cm	0	0	0	0	0
80–90 cm	0	0	0	0	0
Total	13	2	0	2	2
Square D9					
0–10 cm	4	0	0	0	1
10–20 cm	5	2	0	1	1
20–30 cm	0	0	0	0	1
30–40 cm	0	0	0	0	0
40–50 cm	0	1	0	0	0
50–60 cm	1	0	0	0	0
60–70 cm	0	1	0	0	0
70–80 cm	1	1	0	0	0
80–90 cm	0	0	1	0	0
Total	12	6	0	1	3
Square C9					
0–10 cm	1	1	0	0	1
10–20 cm	0	0	0	0	0
20–30 cm	0	3	1	0	0
30–40 cm	0	1	0	0	0
40–50 cm	0	1	0	0	0
50–60 cm	0	1	0	0	0
60–70 cm	0	1	0	0	0
Total	1	8	1	0	1
Square C8/D8					
0–10 cm	0	0	0	1	0
10–20 cm	0	0	0	0	0
20–30 cm	0	0	1	0	0
30–40 cm	1	0	0	0	0
40–50 cm	0	0	0	0	0
50–60 cm	1	0	0	0	0
Total	2	0	1	1	0
Great fissure	0	1	0	0	0

Heavy Limestone Artifacts	Bone Artifacts	Shell Artifacts	Potsherds	Hematite or Ironstone	Total
0	0	0	0	0	14
3	1	8	5	1	29
2	0	7	1	0	14
0	1	2	1	3	9
0	0	4	1	0	7
0	0	1	0	1	2
0	0	0	0	0	0
0	0	0	0	1	1
0	0	0	0	0	0
0	0	1	0	0	1
5	2	23	8	6	63
4	0	1	1	1	12
2	1	2	1	0	15
1	0	1	0	1	4
0	0	0	0	1	
2	0	0	0	0	3
0	0	3	0	0	4
0	0	0	0	0	1
0	0	3	0	0	5
0	0	0	0	0	1
9	1	10	2	2	46
1	0	3	0	0	7
0	1	0	0	0	1
0	0	3	0	0	7
0	0	0	0	0	1
0	0	0	0	0	1
0	0	0	0	0	1
0	0	0	0	0	1
1	1	6	0	0	19
2	0	2	0	0	5
0	0	2	0	0	2
0	0	1	0	0	2
0	0	0	0	0	1
0	0	0	0	0	0
0	0	1	0	0	2
2	0	6	0	0	12
4	0	0	0	0	5

20–30 cm level in Square D9. The fragments range in size from 8 x 5 x 4 mm to 19 x 14 x 14 mm. They are ovoid or rectangular in form; and several have flat faceted surfaces, although no marks of grinding could be discerned. Probably they are remnants from painting designs on the walls of the *pedreira.*

Artifact BA-CE-3/136 is a small ironstone concretion, split to reveal a hollow in the interior from which red pigment may have been removed. The concretion was disc-shaped, with a diameter of 35 mm and a thickness of 20 mm. The lower surface was naturally flat. The hollow in the interior measures approximately 12 x 10 mm. The piece was found in the 0–10 cm level of Square E10.

Artifact BA-CE-3/70 is a similar but unbroken disc-shaped ironstone concretion which measures 57 x 54 x 22 mm. This concretion, apparently with a hollow interior, has a small hole about 3 mm in diameter in the flat surface; and little inventiveness or skill is necessary to produce a good whistle by blowing across the hole. This *possible* musical instrument was found in the northeast quarter of Square D9 at a depth of 10 cm below surface.

DISCUSSION AND CONCLUSIONS

We would not have excavated the tiny Abrigo da Lesma if the unifacial diagnostic *lesma* (*limace* or slug) had not been found on the surface. Excavation disproved our working hypothesis that the presence of this artifact, which in other parts of interior Brazil is recognized as an early-Holocene type, meant that we might uncover evidence for Pleistocene occupation. We were soon discouraged when we found potsherds up to 40 cm below the surface; and later our fears were confirmed when the radiocarbon dates indicated that the main occupation was between 2400 and 2200 yr B.P., with a later ceramic occupation after 900 yr B.P. Although a few deeply buried flakes and charcoal flecks suggest that earlier people occupied the site occasionally, we concluded that the great infilled fissure, which extended beyond our greatest excavated depth, quite possibly had intruded material from above; so it would never be possible to demonstrate earlier occupations.

The process of excavating this small rockshelter proved to be an instructive introduction to the complex problems involved in interpreting stratigraphy and identifying artifacts at cave sites in the Central area. Extensive excavations farther south in Minas Gerais had made us aware of the potential problem of subsequent infilling of dissected cave deposits, especially near cave walls. Redeposition within eroded channels is not easy to distinguish from original deposition in a region in which red-stained silt is massively redeposited by sheet wash. Possible the potsherds found at 40 cm depth near the rear wall of the Abrigo da Lesma were emplaced by erosion and subsequent redeposition.

We encountered a different feature which is more puzzling: the still incompletely understood phenomenon was a very deep fissure with a wedge-shaped cross-section which transected the rockshelter deposits from the dripline to the rear wall. Fortunately, the silt fill in the great fissure contained considerable wood ash and flakes of charcoal, so it was easy to excavate the fissure separately and to segregate all excavated materials. Nevertheless, we were puzzled by the fact that scattered charcoal flecks appeared to be concentrated in the vicinity of the fissure (but outside the ashy area) even at great depth, as if the crack has grown with periodic infilling similar to an ice wedge cast, with the youngest ashy material in the central core. The cause of the great fissure could be desiccation of the silt deposits; or possibly associated with sediment compaction in the partially infilled Toca dos Ossos Humanos cave system, which may have extended underneath the present rockshelter.

While the provenience of materials in the vicinity of the great fissure was suspect, the upper occupation of the rockshelter in the zone outside of the fissure did not appear to be badly mixed. The fact that there was practically no roof fall in the rockshelter sediments helped us immensely in the task of identifying artifacts, as we were able easily to recognize which stones had been picked up and used by the prehistoric occupants. The shelter floor was a continuation of the valley floor, so the clayey silt in the shelter has been deposited largely by sheet wash during rains; however, rocks of sizes useful to man evidently were not transported into the shelter by water. The paucity of stones in the deposits meant that it was possible to examine closely all pieces of limestone, vein quartz, quartzite, and chert that were encountered; and thereby evidence of use was recognized on many rocks. In fact, we suspect that many more rocks, especially limestone, would also show evidence of use if they had been collected in the excavations and examined under a binocular microscope. This kind of careful scrutiny of every rock encountered is not possible in rockshelters which contain a lot of rubble. Excavation of the Abrigo da Lesma gave us the opportunity to become familiar with the kinds of stones that were selected for use by local prehistoric people, so we were able to spot and examine more closely similar rocks in other sites.

Other than the addition of potsherds in the upper zone, dated about 940 yr B.P., there is little change in artifact assemblages from the various levels. The only formal shaped flaked stone artifact was the quartzite *lesma,* which may have been shaped by people belonging to an earlier cultural tradition. Almost all artifacts were selected for their useful edges or surfaces. High-quality flakeable stone was practically non-existent, although one black chert blade and a core of similar material were found.

Most vein quartz was evidently simply bashed on an

anvil and useful pieces selected from the resulting debris. Quartz crystal was more carefully flaked by holding the piece on an anvil and striking at approximate angles, but the primary purpose was still to create unshaped pieces with useful edges. Intentional retouch was very rare. Even use retouch was uncommon on the hard edges of quartz crystal. Vein quartz, chert, and limestone were available locally; but quartz crystal does not occur in the Central area, and quartzite was transported from sources at least 25 km away. Evidence of weathering on the limestone artifacts in the rockshelter suggests that fragments of this material were collected outside the shelter. Rounded quartzite pebbles were used for hammering, pounding, chopping, rubbing, and polishing other materials. Limestone was often used as anvils or blocks on which other material was processed. Both quartzite and limestone were also flaked to produce sharp edges, and projections were intentionally created on large blocky tools for tearing or grooving other materials. Surprisingly little evidence was found for utilization of quartzite or limestone flakes. Evidently there was little use of flakes as hand-held cutting or scraping implements. Rather, the material to be processed was rubbed on the sharp edges and projections, and rough surfaces of large quartzite or limestone blocks and pebbles.

Experiments by Wesley Hurt with utilized freshwater mussel shells (which had to be transported for at least 25 km to the Abrigo da Lesma) supports the hypothesis that most shell and stone artifacts were employed in processing vegetal materials. The Abrigo da Lesma, then, was a small campsite at which various tasks were performed; and the local plants, mammals, and gastropods were exploited.

Chapter 5
Abrigo do Pilão

Introduction

The Abrigo do Pilão, a large rock overhang located on the Fazenda Grota, is situated on the south side of the Serra da Pedra Branca; and faces south. The site is named for an old horizontal wooden mortar, made from a large log, which has lain in the western part of the rockshelter reportedly for many decades. In front of the level floor of the rockshelter there is a rampart of large limestone boulders, descending about 3 m to a broad level flat with *caatinga* forest. About 20 m to the west of the rockshelter is a low pass north over the bare limestone *serra*, and one can enter the rockshelter directly from this pass by climbing up a meter or so over heavy rockfall.

The Abrigo do Pilão is likely part of an extensive cave system, as there are large deep caves adjacent in the *serra* immediately to the east and west of the rockshelter. Two long low galleries leading off the eastern chamber of the rockshelter likely connect with the deep cave to the east.

The main part of the Abrigo do Pilão extends along the cliff face for a distance of about 17 m (Figures 5-1a, 5-2). Pictograph panels, with geometric designs mainly in red paint but also in yellow and black, extend the length of the overhang at an elevation of about 1.5 to 2 m above the surface of the fill (Figure 5-1b). About 4 m in front of the rear wall of the shelter is a zone of fallen rock, a low lip mound of large angular limestone boulders. The drip line, however, is situated only 3 m beyond the rear wall of the shelter; and if there is a wind, only a small alcove in the central area provides complete shelter. The floor of the main rockshelter sloped slightly downward from west to east, with a few large rocks protruding from the fill. The eastern and central areas featured a deposit of grey silt and ash, but in the western third of the shelter a deposit of yellow/orange travertine extended to the surface (Figure 5-2). In excavation of the eastern and central part of the main shelter,

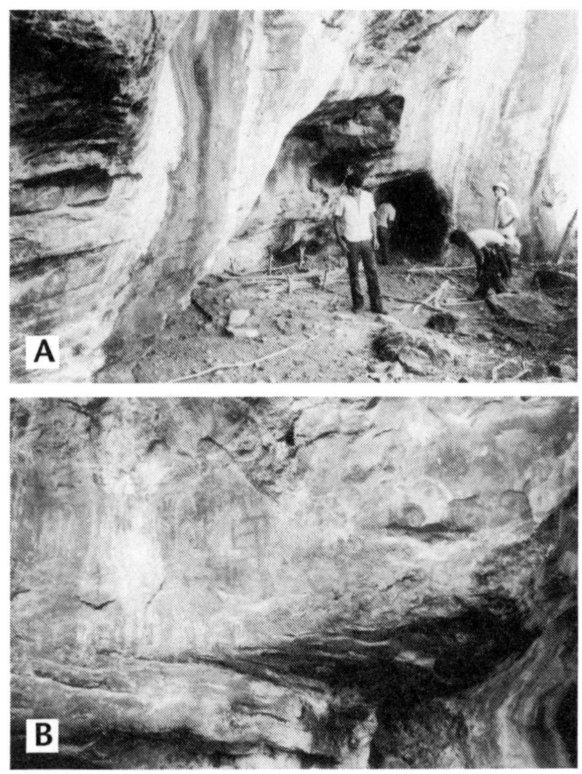

Figure 5-1. A) view of Abrigo do Pilão from west, in 1983. Entrance to eastern chamber is in shadow. **B)** pictographs on wall of main shelter.

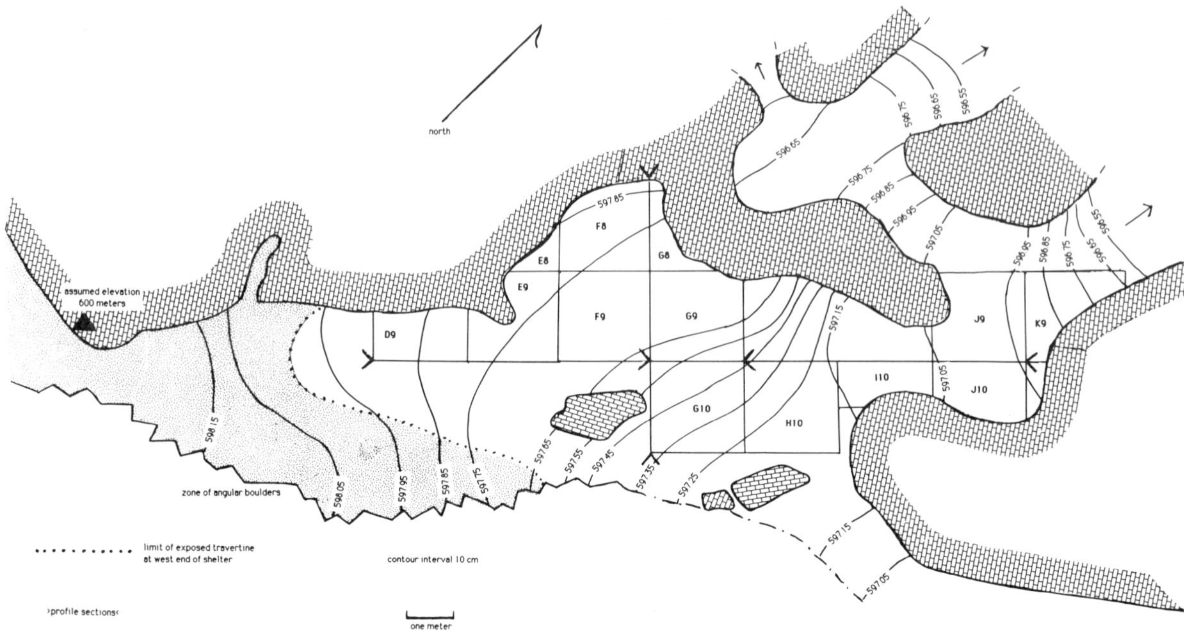

Figure 5-2. Plan of Abrigo do Pilão.

this travertine was found to underlie the silt and ash deposits.

At the east end of the shelter was a large opening into a covered chamber (see Figure 5-1a). A window in the rock of the south wall of this eastern chamber gave light to an area about 3 x 5 m in extent, and there was a level floor of silt and ash. There is adequate room to stand in this area, as the ceiling is about 2 m above the floor. Two very low long galleries with rock-strewn floors lead very steeply downward from the eastern chamber into darkness. Time and equipment to explore these galleries were lacking.

The Abrigo do Pilão was one of the largest rockshelters discovered in the limestone area during the 1983 Central survey. Its situation high above the surrounding country, and the artifact-strewn dry ashy silt floor of the main rockshelter and the eastern chamber, gave promise of deep stratified deposits containing a long record of prehistoric occupation of the area. The rock art high on the wall of the shelter is elaborate; and it was hoped that fragments of painted designs which had spalled off the wall above the floor were to be found incorporated into the underlying sediments in datable contexts.

With these expectations, excavation at the Abrigo do Pilão began on 7 May 1984. By May 21, ten 2-m squares had been excavated to sterile zones in the main rockshelter, and three 2-m squares in the eastern chamber (map, Figure 5-2). Baulks 20 cm wide were maintained in excavation of most of the units, and profiles of walls were drawn when excavation was suspended. Excavation was carried out in arbitrary 10-cm levels, using trowel and dustpan in the silt deposits, and picks in the travertine zone. All material was screened through a 4-mm mesh, and all shell and bone fragments were collected as well as flakes and artifacts. Ten charcoal samples were taken, at various levels in the ash and silt deposits in the main rockshelter.

At the close of field work the excavated area was left open, and a fence was built to protect livestock.

STRATIGRAPHY

Description of the Sediments

Only four major natural stratigraphic zones were encountered in the excavations at the Abrigo do Pilão (profiles, Figures 5-3, 5-4, 5-5). In the eastern and central sectors of the main shelter, there was a maximum of 60 cm of banded grey/white/pink ash and fine silt overlying a zone of friable yellow/orange travertine. In the eastern chamber, a deposit of fine grey/brown silt and ash about 50 cm thick overlay a massive deposit of coarse red silt with incorporated boulders.

The banded grey/white/pink ash and fine silt deposits were concentrated in the eastern and central part of the main rockshelter, petering out to the west: the ash and silt zone was little more than 10 cm deep in Square D9, and a few meters to the west of this excavation unit the yellow/orange travertine is exposed at the surface. The maximum depth of silt and ash was encountered in

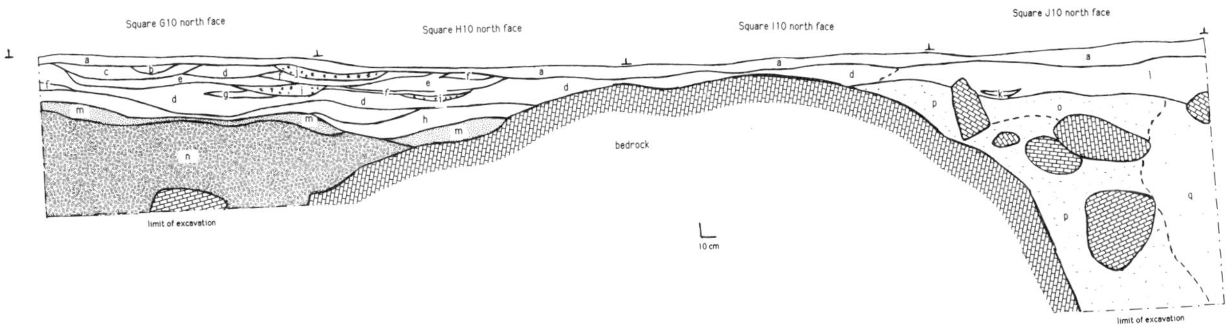

Figure 5-3. Profile of north face of Squares G10, H10, I10, and J10, Abrigo do Pilão. **a,** loose grey silt and ash; **b,** grey silt and ash; **c,** mottled pink and white silt and ash; **d,** mottled pink, white, and grey silt and ash; **e,** dark grey silt and ash; **f,** pink silt and ash; **g,** pink and grey silt and ash; **h,** white/grey ash and silt; **i,** grey ash and charcoal; **j,** white ash and charcoal; **k,** white ash; **l,** grey/brown silt and ash; **m,** coarse orange silt with travertine rubble; **n,** friable orange/yellow travertine; **o,** red silt; **p,** red silt with rubble; **q,** mottled reddish brown silt.

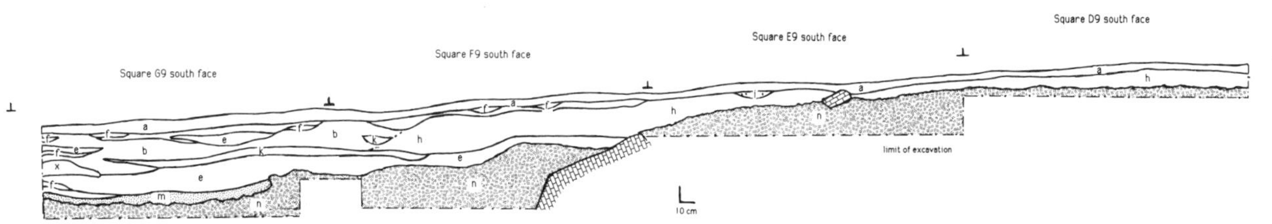

Figure 5-4. Profile of south face of Squares G9, F9, E9, and D9, Abrigo do Pilão. **a,** loose grey silt and ash; **b,** grey silt and ash; **e,** dark grey silt and ash; **f,** pink silt and ash; **h,** white/grey ash and silt; **i,** grey ash and charcoal; **k,** white ash; **m,** coarse orange silt with travertine rubble; **n,** friable yellow/orange travertine; **x,** root disturbance.

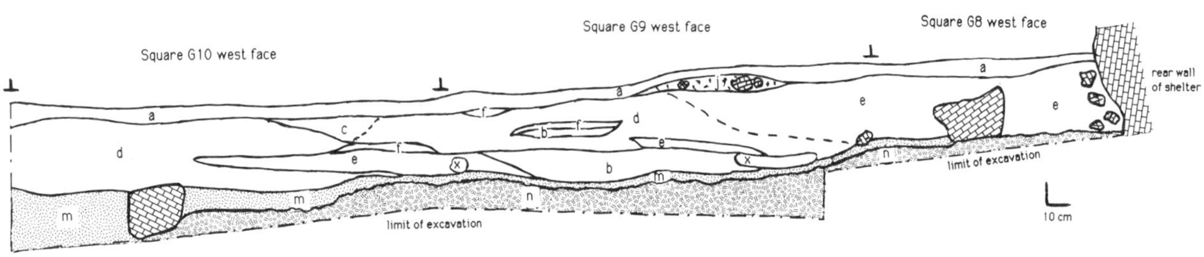

Figure 5-5. Profile of west face of Squares G10, G9, and G8, Abrigo do Pilão. **a,** loose grey silt and ash; **b,** grey silt and ash; **c,** mottled pink and white silt and ash; **d,** mottled pink, white, and grey silt and ash; **e,** dark grey silt and ash; **f,** pink silt and ash; **j,** white ash and charcoal; **m,** coarse orange silt with travertine rubble; **n,** friable yellow/orange travertine; **x,** root disturbance.

the alcove area (Squares G8 and F8), where the deposit was 55 to 60 cm thick; elsewhere in the eastern and central part of the rockshelter the thickness of the ash and silt deposit was about 45 to 50 cm (Figures 5-6a, 5-6b).

The zone of banded grey/white/pink ash and fine silt in the main part of the rockshelter is clearly the product of innumerable firehearths built by the prehistoric occupants. Indeed in a sense the deposit is almost totally cultural in origin, the product of intensive human occupation. Wall profiles (Figures 5-3, 5-4, 5-5) show a complex series of thin interlocking lenses of varicolored ash, and charcoal fragments were abundant in many areas. In general, the upper 10 cm of the deposit was a dry and unconsolidated mixed grey ash and silt zone. Underlying, to a depth of 30 to 40 cm below surface, was a compact zone of interlocking thin lenses of grey, white, or pink silt and ash. The lowermost silt and ash zone was usually a dark grey in color. In the area outside the dripline, and also in the zone with low

Figure 5-6. A) excavation in progress at Abrigo do Pilão, with view of west face of Squares G10, G9, and G8, showing ash and silt zone overlying friable travertine. **B)** view of north face of Square G10, excavated to surface of friable travertine.

ceiling just under the rear wall of the shelter, the entire ash and silt zone was a more uniform grey/brown in color, with individual lenses of ash much less distinct. Along the rear wall of the main shelter, grey/brown silt with high limestone-rubble content was found to fill former cracks or fissures which extended down the wall to as much as 20 cm below the normal level of the silt and ash deposit. Away from the wall, rock fragments were rare in the ash and silt zone.

In the main shelter there was a sharp unconformity between the ash and silt deposits and an underlying zone of friable travertine, which varied in color from red through orange to yellow. The upper 5 to 10 cm of this zone was a very coarse orange silt, apparently disintegrated travertine. The travertine was very friable and fragmented, but increasingly hard with depth; and a heavy pick and rock wedge were required to loosen it. Since this deposit was sterile and very difficult to excavate, it was penetrated to great depth only in Square G10, where it proved to be about 50 cm thick over bedrock.

In the eastern chamber a 50- to 60-cm-thick deposit of grey/brown silt and ash is the apparent equivalent of the silt and ash zone in the main part of the rockshelter, as silt and ash deposits extend across a high rock sill at the entrance to the chamber (profile, Figure 5-3). In the eastern chamber individual thin lenses of ash could rarely be discerned in the silt and ash deposit; and although fine ash was abundantly mixed in the silt matrix, there were no charcoal fragments. In the zone adjacent to the south wall of the eastern chamber there was a deep deposit of reddish-brown silt which apparently filled a former crack or fissure which extended to a depth of 130 cm below surface.

The grey/brown silt and ash zone in the eastern chamber was underlain by a deep deposit of coarse red silt. The massive deposit of coarse red silt incorporated large rounded and subangular boulders of limestone (profile, Figure 5-3). The red silt deposit became increasingly cemented with depth, with an increasing abundance of small ironstone nodules. Below a depth of 80 cm below surface a pick and rock wedge were necessary to loosen the material, and it was excavated to a maximum depth of 170 cm below surface in Square J9.

Faunal and Floral Remains

As reported in the Introduction to the Research, the entire collection of bones from the Abrigo do Pilão was misplaced in the Museu Nacional before study. This loss is especially unfortunate, in that the site yielded by far a larger quantity of bones than any other excavated in the Central area. The only information presently available, therefore, is drawn from the field notes of the excavation. In terms of species represented, remains of deer and peccary were readily identifiable from teeth and mandibles, and also common were scutes of armadillo. Bones and teeth of rodents and marsupials, and remains of birds were also noted.

Fortunately the field notes indicate the relative abundance of bones in the horizontal excavation units and vertical stratigraphic levels. It was noted that bone fragments were relatively uncommon at the 0–10 cm level in the front part of the shelter, but abundant at this level in the eastern chamber and in the alcove at the rear of the main shelter (in Squares E8, F8, and G8). At depths of 10–40 cm below surface, bone fragments were abundant in all areas of the site. Below 40 cm depth in the silt and ash zone, bone was relatively rare in the main shelter; but was still common in the eastern chamber. Only a few small bone fragments were found in the travertine in the main shelter, and in the red silt zone in the eastern chamber.

Gastropod tests were quite common in the ash and silt deposits at the Abrigo do Pilão; and a good sample was collected. Identified by the Setor da Malacologia of the Museu Nacional, species represented include the giant terrestrial gastropod *Megalobulimus* sp., the medium-sized *Protoglyptus durus*, the small *Cyclodontina* sp., and the medium-sized *Anctus* sp. Gastropod shell was most abundant in the ash and silt zone in the eastern chamber and in the alcove of the main shelter, and much less common in the front part of the main shelter. Only a few shell fragments were found in the travertine and the red silt zones. Concentrations of up to a dozen complete tests of *Megalobulimus* were sometimes found in the ash and silt sediments directly adjacent to the cave wall; these are likely individuals which did not survive a dry-season hibernation period after burrowing into the sediment. Most of the gastropod shell, however, can be attributed to human collecting activities. As noted, the giant gastropods have high protein content; and are easily procured by heating the shell near a fire so that the snail is forced to emerge.

There were also some fragments of freshwater mussel shell (of the species *Diplodon diplodontus)* throughout the ash and silt deposits in the Abrigo do Pilão. The nearest source of these mussels is the Rio Verde, about 30 km west. It is likely that these fragments originally pertained to shell artifacts transported to the site.

The dry upper 10 cm of the ash and silt deposits yielded plant remains. These were also misplaced in the Museu Nacional collections before study. The field notes report a variety of seeds and two corn cobs at the 0–10 cm level in the front part of the shelter. However, there is evidence of historic occupation of the site—remains of a wooden bed frame in the alcove of the main shelter, and a wooden mortar at the west end of the site—and the upper 10 cm of the deposit is quite loose and unconsolidated, so the plant material collected might be modern. On the other hand, the upper 10 cm of the deposit produced ceramics, mullers and pestles, and stone axes, artifacts often associated with horticulturalists in interior eastern Brazil. It would certainly have been worthwhile to analyse the floral remains recovered from the site. Hopefully the floral as well as the faunal collections from the Abrigo do Pilão will be located some day, and very valuable quantitative analyses can be carried out.

Finally, some human remains were noted in the ash and silt deposit in the alcove at the rear of the main shelter. A worn human incisor was found along the shelter wall in Square G8 at 10–20 cm depth, and in Square F8 a human molar was found at a depth of 50–60 cm along the shelter wall. A fissure at the rear of Square E9, adjacent to the shelter wall, yielded a human molar and some possible cranial fragments. In Square E9 as well, a human molar was found in brown silt directly overlying the travertine zone at 40 cm depth. These sparse and scattered human remains are unexplained, and the material was not studied.

Cultural Stratigraphy

Artifacts and flaking detritus were distributed throughout the ash and silt zones in the main shelter and the eastern chamber of the Abrigo do Pilão. A total of approximately 400 artifacts were recovered, and approximately 1860 stone flakes. The eastern chamber, despite a much smaller surface area than the main shelter, yielded 46% of the artifacts from the site. The stratigraphic distribution of artifacts is presented in Table 5-2.

The 0–10 cm level in both areas of the Abrigo do Pilão was most productive of artifacts, with approximately 50% of the total number from the site. In highest frequency were fragments of utilized mussel shell (53), utilized vein quartz flakes or fragments (35), and utilized chert flakes or fragments (27). Other common artifact types included utilized quartz crystal flakes (19), utilized quartzite flakes (14), heavy tools of limestone (12), utilized limestone flakes (8), and quartzite pebble hammerstones (7). Unique artifacts from the 0–10 cm level included fragments of two bifacially flaked quartz crystal projectile points, a stone lip ornament, a small engraved axe blade, two polished stone axe blades, a fragment of limestone possibly with red paint, and a small limestone block with a fine rectangular grid design in black paint. The 0–10 cm level also featured ceramics: all but two of the total of 120 sherds from the site came from the upper 10 cm of the silt and ash deposit.

The artifact yield from the silt and ash zone decreased progressively with depth below 10 cm. The 10–20 cm level yielded 77 artifacts, mainly utilized quartz flakes or fragments, utilized chert fragments, and fragments of utilized mussel shell. The 20–30 cm level produced 35 artifacts of similar types. The 30–40 cm level yielded 45 artifacts, mainly utilized flakes or fragments of quartz or chert. Thirty-two artifacts were found in the silt and ash zone below a depth of 40 cm, including several distinctive edge-trimmed flake tools, a few quartzite pebble tools, and a few limestone choppers.

Traces of earlier occupation in the Abrigo do Pilão are sparse. Some limestone flakes and heavy limestone tools were found embedded in the coarse orange silt zone immediately overlying the travertine in the main part of the shelter, and there were also some limestone flakes and flaked limestone fragments in the upper part of the red silt zone within the eastern chamber.

The most intensive occupation of the Abrigo do Pilão, then, occurred on the ceramic horizon, with an abundance of artifacts of various kinds left along with abundant charcoal, shell fragments, and bone fragments in the silt and ash matrix at the 0–10 cm level. Earlier occupations of the shelter produced fewer artifacts. While many major artifact types are found throughout the sequence in the ash and silt zone at the Abrigo do Pilão, some sort of cultural break is indicated at the 0–10 cm level, not only by the appearance of ceramics but other special artifacts such as polished stone axe blades, engraved or painted stones, and a stone lip ornament. It is possible that an economic shift occurred as well at this time, with less emphasis on hunting of medium-sized mammals, and perhaps the appearance of horticulture.

Radiocarbon Dates

Six of the ten samples of charcoal collected from the ash and silt zone at the Abrigo do Pilão have been radiocarbon-dated. The results are presented below, in stratigraphic order.

F9/G9 baulk, 0–10 cm	800 ± 60 BP (Beta-10016)
Sq. H10, 10 cm	860 ± 60 BP (Beta-10604)
Sq. G9, 10–20 cm	9610 ± 90 BP (Beta-10015)
Sq. G9, 20–30 cm	8790 ± 80 BP (Beta-10014)
F9/G9 baulk, 30–40 cm	9390 ± 90 BP (Beta-10017)
Sq. G10, 40–45 cm	9450 ± 90 BP (Beta-10605)

The two samples from the 0–10 cm level correlate to indicate the initiation of the ceramic horizon about 900 yr B.P. The dates from below 10 cm, however, do not correspond to an expected gradual progression to the ceramic horizon. Two explanations are possible at this time. One is that the deposits below 10 cm are very mixed, and charcoal from the basal deposits of silt and ash has been moved up into higher levels. The sample from the 10–20 cm level in Square G9, assaying at 9619 ± 90 BP, almost 8800 years older than the samples from the 0–10 cm level above, could be the result of mixture of much older charcoal at the 10–20 cm level. However, the stratigraphic profiles, with fine bedding of the ash and silt lenses, give no indication of disturbance. The second possibility is that the lower 40 cm of ash and silt in the main part of the shelter accumulated quite rapidly, due to intensive human occupation, over an interval of only a few hundred years in the early/mid Holocene. A similar situation was encountered by the authors at Lapa Pequena, a small well-stratified Minas Gerais rockshelter (Bryan and Gruhn 1978) in which 160 cm of ash and silt lenses accumulated in 600 years, between 8200 and 7600 yr B.P. At the Abrigo do Pilão there is no evidence in the natural stratigraphy of a great hiatus—an old surface, or an erosional interval—between deposition of the lower silt and ash lenses and the 0–10 cm level of the deposit, although the upper 10 cm is different in being drier, much less consolidated, and greyer in color. In any case, the radiocarbon dates suggest that intensive occupation of the shelter began by about 9500 years ago and lasted less than a millennium before the site was abandoned, not to be reoccupied until the ceramic horizon. The several limestone flakes and artifacts recovered from the upper part of the red silt deposit in the eastern chamber must indicate an even earlier occupation than is represented in the overlying ash and silt zone.

STONE ARTIFACTS

Flaking Debitage

A total of 1861 unmodified flakes of quartz, quartzite, limestone, or chert were collected in the excavations in the Abrigo do Pilão. The general characteristics of these materials will be discussed first, followed by a description of the distribution of flakes within the site (Table 5-1).

Raw Materials and Flaking Techniques

Approximately 28% of the total number of flakes collected from the site are of quartzite, which ranges in color from grey to red, with a small minority of white. The nearest bedrock source of quartzite is the Serra Azul, about 20 km to the southwest; other possible sources in the quartzite area to the north of the Central area are much farther away. Approximately 31% of the flakes retain an area of smooth water-polished cortex, indicating derivation from stream-rolled pebbles; and a few flakes were clearly derived from tabular fragments of quartzite. Unmodified quartzite flakes recovered range in size to a maximum of 78 x 70 x 19 mm, with a mode of about 24 x 22 x 5 mm. Of the 68% of quartzite flakes retaining the platform area, the vast majority feature a plain flat platform which is relatively large in relation to the width of the flake. Percussion flaking with a hammerstone is indicated as the major technique employed in flaking quartzite.

Approximately 25% of the total flakes from the site are of chert. The sources of chert in the Central area have not been definitely identified. Outcrops of light-colored chert fragments were seen on the ground in level limestone areas west of the Rio Verde, about 30 km west of the Abrigo do Pilão; and also at a locality in the *caatinga* about 50 km to the north. The Abrigo do Pilão cherts vary considerably in character. Most of the chert is white, yellow, or grey in color; but a small minority of the flakes or fragments are dark brown, dark red, black, or translucent (agate). The yellow/white/grey chert is of very poor quality for flaking, with numerous inclusions and flaws which facilitate shattering under percussion, and thermal spalling when exposed to fire. Many of the chert pieces recovered in excavation were angular fragments; only 47% displayed a striking platform, and most flakes were irregular in dimensions. The dark cherts and the agate were of better quality and less subject to shattering, producing more regular flakes. The great majority of the striking platforms were simple and relatively large: only 13% were small in relation to the width of the flake. Direct percussion flaking with a hammerstone is indicated. Chert flakes were for the most part relatively small: although the largest non-utilized specimen recovered measured 77 x 39 x 17 mm, the mode is about 20 x 15 x 4 mm.

Approximately 24% of the total number of flakes from the Abrigo do Pilão are of limestone, a material available on the spot. The limestone of the *serras* in the northern part of the *municipio* of Central is dense and fine grained, with good conchoidal fracture. Most limestone flakes have clearly defined platforms and prominent bulbs of percussion. The platform area is large in relation to the width of the flake, and platform angles are often very high. Many limestone specimens are side-blow flakes, with width much greater than length. A direct percussion technique is indicated, with use of a hammerstone. Non-utilized limestone flakes tend to be relatively large, with a maximum size recorded of 88 x 49 x 18 mm; the mode is about 30 x 20 x 7 mm.

Approximately 23% of the total flakes recovered from the Abrigo do Pilão are of quartz. Most of the quartz is a yellow/white or white vein quartz. Outcrops of fragments of such vein quartz were seen at some localities on the level soil-covered areas between limestone *serras* in the northern part of the Central area, and there is a known source within a few kilometers of the Abrigo do Pilão. However, approximately 16% of the quartz is clear crystal which does not occur in the Central area: the nearest known source, near Gentio de Ouro in the Chapada Diamantina, is over 100 km to the south. With fewer internal facets, the clear crystal flakes with much better control (once the crystal is quartered) than the vein quartz, which easily fractures into angular fragments. Only 34% of the vein quartz flakes display striking platforms, which are large and broad, indicating the application of direct percussion by a hammerstone. Non-utilized vein quartz flakes reach a maximum size of 42 x 28 x 15 mm, with a mode of about 18 x 10 x 5 mm. The maximum size of an unutilized quartz crystal flake was 35 x 18 x 6 mm, with a mode of about 16 x 10 x 4 mm.

Distribution of Flakes

A total of 1820 flakes were collected from the ash and silt zone in the Abrigo do Pilão (Table 5-1). Of this total, approximately 42% were recovered from the 0–10 cm level, the ceramic horizon. The greatest number of flakes found on this level came from Square G10 in the front of the main shelter (11% of the total) and from Square J9 within the eastern chamber (22% of the total). The 0–10 cm level in Square G10 yielded a very high proportion of limestone flakes; in Square J9 chert flakes were very numerous at the 0–10 cm level. The relative proportions of the total collection of flakes of different materials on the ceramic horizon were chert 27%, limestone 26%, quartz 25%, and quartzite 22%.

The upper preceramic levels, from 10 to 30 cm depth within the silt and ash zone, yielded approximately 42% of the total number of flakes from this zone. The front area of the main shelter was most productive at these levels, with Square G10 yielding 23% of the total and Square H10 14%. The entire area of the eastern chamber produced only 20% of the total of flakes from these levels. The relative proportions of the total collection of flakes from the 10 to 30 cm levels in the silt and ash zone were quartzite 32%, chert 24%, quartz 23%, and limestone 21%.

Only 16% of the total flake collection from the silt and ash zone came from depths below 30 cm. Most productive were Square G10 and G9, each with 12% of the total number of flakes from these lower levels; and Square E8, with 13% of the total. The relative proportions of the total collection of flakes from levels below 30 cm in the silt and ash zone were quartzite 34%, limestone 24%, chert 24%, and quartz 18%.

In general, then, in the occupation areas within the preceramic levels of the silt and ash deposit, there was a gradual increase in the quantity of flakes with time. Occupation of the site culminated on the ceramic horizon, with the greatest proportion of flakes and artifacts left at the site in the 0–10 cm level of the silt and ash deposits. The ceramic horizon was the period of most intensive utilization of the eastern chamber, with a great number of flakes and artifacts left in the 0–10 cm level of the silt and ash zone within this enclosed area. Earlier preceramic peoples seem to have preferred the main shelter for flaking activity.

Throughout the silt and ash zone there seems to have been relatively limited variation in raw material selected for flaking. There is a slight increase in the proportion of chert, from 24% below 30 cm to 27% on the ceramic horizon; and in the proportion of limestone from 24% from below 30 cm to 26% at the 0–10 cm level. Over this span of deposition, however, quartzite dropped in proportion from 34% to 22%; and quartz increased from 18% to 25%.

Flakes were rare but definitely present in stratigraphic zones below the silt and ash deposits. The large and deep fissure filled with reddish brown silt along the south wall of Square J10 in the eastern chamber yielded 24 flakes, scattered to a depth of 130 cm below surface. Eleven of these flakes were chert, eight limestone, four quartzite, and one quartz. The material in the fissure fill is likely derived from the upper silt and ash zone, but a few of the limestone flakes had red stains indicative of an origin in the adjacent zone of coarse red silt.

This coarse red silt zone in the eastern chamber yielded seven definite flakes, scattered to a maximum depth of 140 cm below surface. Six of the flakes found to a depth of 80 cm were limestone, and featured large platforms with prominent bulbs of percussion; and there was one vein quartz flake found below 90 cm depth. Several heavy limestone tools also recovered from the red silt zone will be described below. As well, an extensive lens of coarse orange silt (evidently disintegrated travertine) below the silt and ash zone in Square G10 yielded ten flakes: seven limestone, two chert, and one quartzite. A few stone artifacts also found embedded in this zone will be described below. These definite flakes and artifacts from the top of the coarse orange silt zone in the main shelter and from within the upper part of the red silt zone in the eastern chamber indicate very early occupations of the Abrigo do Pilão.

Table 5-1. Distribution of Unmodified Stone Flakes in Sediments of the Abrigo do Pilão.

	QUARTZ	QUARTZITE	LIMESTONE	CHERT	TOTAL
Main shelter					
Ash and silt zone					
0–10 cm	128	102	116	89	435
10–20 cm	92	117	80	60	349
20–30 cm	48	96	68	44	256
30–40 cm	36	66	38	32	172
40–50 cm	3	12	17	15	47
50–60 cm (Sqs.F8 & G8)	1	0	0	0	1
60–70 cm (Sqs.F8 & G8)	3	2	0	2	7
totals	311	395	319	242	1267
Coarse orange/red silt (disintegrated travertine) in Square G10					
40–50 cm	0	1	7	1	9
50–60 cm	0	0	0	1	1
totals	0	1	7	2	10
Eastern chamber					
Ash and silt zone					
0–10 cm	61	67	80	120	328
10–20 cm	20	21	7	45	93
20–30 cm	13	10	6	31	60
30–40 cm	10	15	11	17	53
40–50 cm	2	5	4	4	15
50–60 cm	0	1	2	1	4
totals	106	119	110	218	553
Red silt zone					
30–50 cm	0	0	1	0	1
50–60 cm	0	0	1	0	1
60–70 cm	0	0	2	0	2
70–80 cm	0	0	2	0	2
90–100 cm	1	0	0	0	1
totals	1	0	6	0	7
Infilled fissure in Square J10					
40–70 cm	0	1	0	1	2
70–80 cm	0	1	6	5	12
80–90 cm	0	2	1	1	4
90–100 cm	0	0	0	0	0
100–110 cm	0	0	1	0	1
110–130 cm	1	0	0	4	5
Totals	1	4	8	11	24

Projectile Point Fragments

Perhaps the most significant characteristic of the flaked stone industry from the Central area is the absence of any evidence of bifacial flaking. All stone artifacts are unidirectionally flaked, and there are no characteristic lipped flakes of the kind removed when finishing or retouching a bifacially flaked edge. Nevertheless, two carefully pressure-flaked fragments of projectile points of clear quartz crystal were recovered from the eastern chamber or its entrance (Figure 5-7a). Both exhibit clear evidence that they were utilized as scrapers for working something hard, like bone. Evidently both fragments, which are parts of different points, were picked up

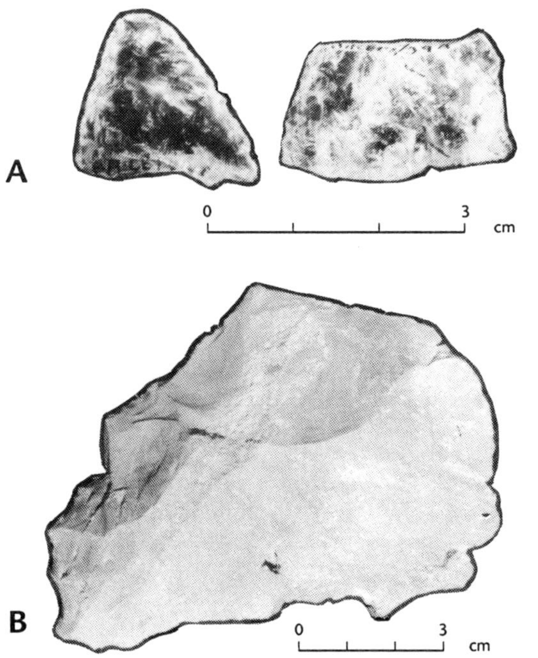

Figure 5-7. A) quartz crystal biface fragments BA-CE-17/18 (left) and BA-CE-17/398 (right); **B)** large brown jasper flake scraper (BA-CE-17/235).

elsewhere and transported to the Abrigo do Pilão, in order to put their useful edges to work. As both fragments came from the 0–10 cm level in adjacent squares it is possible that the same person recovered the useful fragments from an old workshop with discarded broken pieces. So far, the only whole crystalline quartz projectile points reported in Bahia are several tanged and barbed (pedunculated) points collected by various people in the São Francisco valley. It appears that bifacial projectile points were distributed along the river but rarely penetrated far inland.

The point tip (BA-CE-17/18) was found in the 0–10 cm level of the silt and ash zone in Square J10, inside the eastern chamber. This beautifully pressure-flaked point was bifacially shaped into a thin lenticular cross-section. The tip end, as well as both corners and both edges of the right-angle break, have subsequently been use-retouched, crushed, and worn by scraping and perhaps grooving. Most retouch flake scars are short, but one long narrow flake was driven halfway up the face from one broken edge. The dimensions of this artifact are 21 x 20 x 5 mm.

The point midsection (BA-CE-17/378), which measures 27 x 17 x 8 mm, was found in the 0–10 cm level in Square I10 at the entrance to the eastern chamber. This point had been bifacially pressure-flaked into a thick lenticular cross-section. All four corners and two edges with angles of 50° and 60° have been use-retouched and crushed. The heaviest use was near the center of the 60° edge. This stone has many crystal faces which may have caused it to break during manufacture. Two adjacent corners on one edge are broken along crystal planes; however, the broken projections, with edge angles of 40° and 50°, were subsequently unidirectionally use-crushed.

Flake Tools and Core Tools of Silicates

Artifacts made on intentional flakes of silicates with prominent bulbs of percussion are uncommon in the Abrigo do Pilão collection. Most of the quartz and chert artifacts were made on thick fragments, many of which had been broken naturally. Most utilized quartzite flakes had broken off during use of quartzite hammerstones or choppers. Thus most of the artifacts which can be categorized as flaked stone to distinguish them from the category of pecked, ground, and polished stone are not made on flakes removed intentionally from prepared cores; but rather are fragments selected for their useful edges which had been created either naturally or accidentally by man.

The main reason for this seemingly degenerate flaked stone industry may be the lack of good flakeable stone in the vicinity. The local cherts and vein quartz are of poor quality. The local limestone was flakeable, but edges of such flakes were weak and easily dulled, and there are very few utilized limestone flakes (described later in this report). Most of the flake tools are of quartzite, the source of which is 20 km or more from the Abrigo do Pilão. Actually, then, the Abrigo do Pilão collection should not be termed a flake and core industry but rather an industry of utilized fragments and chunks of silicate and limestone materials.

Chert, quartz, and quartzite each exhibit quite different flaking behavior. The local chert is either of poor quality, with many flaws and inclusions; or it occurs in nodules too small to be very useful. Most flake artifacts were made of better-quality cherts (brown or red jasper, translucent agate) obtained elsewhere. The nearest source of fairly good chert that we encountered was near the Rio Verde about 30 km northwest of the Abrigo do Pilão. Most of the vein quartz could have come from within a few kilometers of the site, as outcroppings of vein quartz were frequently seen eroding out of weathered limestone, in which it occurs within calcite veins. Agate probably was formed at the same time, when silica intruded through old calcite veins in the local limestone. No sources were seen in the Central area, however; and it is possible that the agate, a superior material for flaking, was transported from some other area, like the brown or red jasper. Also, clear quartz crystal, the most desired form of quartz for flaking, does not occur locally. The rarity and small size of the quartz crystal flakes found on the site are explained by the fact that the material had to be transported from a considerable distance. Quartz crystal requires special flaking techniques to be able to utilize it economically, so artifacts of this material will be described in a separate subsection.

Edge-trimmed Flake Tools

Only a few flake tools with prominent bulbs of percussion and intentionally trimmed edges occurred at the Abrigo do Pilão. Interestingly, all but one of these edge-trimmed flake tools were recovered in the lowest occupation levels in the silt and ash zone.

Two flake scrapers made of jasper are noticeably different from the remainder of the collection, and both came from adjacent squares at or near the base of the silt and ash zone. One (BA-CE-17/235) is a large relatively thin flake scraper of brown jasper, measuring 100 x 69 x 18 mm (Figure 5-7b). It is made on the kind of flake that is frequently encountered at a quarry site. The positive bulb has a lip, but the platform surface appears to be unprepared original cortex. One irregular lateral edge, measuring 85 mm in length with a 30° edge angle, has been unidirectionally use-flaked except for one small flake removed from the opposite positive bulbar face in order to resharpen a projection or graver spur, which is much used. This flake scraper was lying on the surface of the coarse orange silt (disintegrated travertine) at 50 cm depth in Square E8. The other flake scraper (BA-CE-17/324) is much smaller (Figure 5-8a), measuring 53 x 37 x 12 mm, partly because half of the periphery has been unidirectionally step-flaked to create edge angles of 50° and 30°; these edges are much used. Some of this use-flaking on the steepest edge was done at a later time, evidently when several retouch flakes were removed from the opposite face of another edge, revealing a brown jasper interior beneath a dark red exterior. This sidescraper came from the 30–40 cm level in Square E9, near the base of the silt and ash zone.

From the same lower zone in the silt and ash came what appears to be the broken end of a scraper of green jasper with step-flaking and wear around a convex end, which has an edge angle of 50°. This artifact (BA-CE-17/143), with orange silt adhering, measures 38 x 28 x 17 mm.

A tabular fragment of dark green jasper which is unidirectionally step-flaked on a convex edge (85° angle) came from the 0–10 cm level in Square E8. Orange silt adhering to its flaked surface suggests that it was picked up a few meters farther west, where the travertine surfaces. This steep scraper (BA-CE-17/218), measuring 47 x 37 x 19 mm, has been broken in half and one prominent corner subsequently reused (Figure 5-8b).

Three quartzite scrapers made on secondary flakes with step retouch came from the early occupation level at the very base of the silt and ash zone. The underlying coarse orange silt still adheres to these artifacts. Artifact

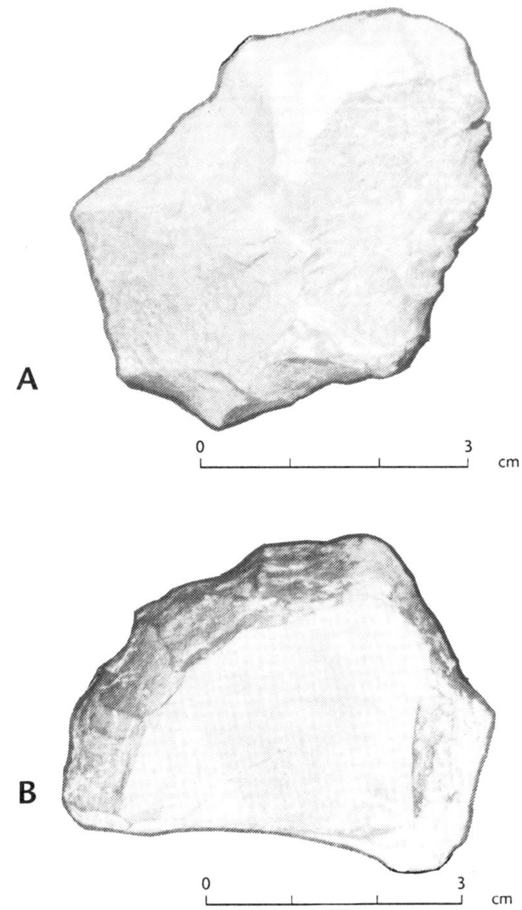

Figure 5-8. A) chert flake scraper (BA-CE-17/374); **B)** green jasper steep scraper (BA-CE-17/218).

BA-CE-17/329, from a depth of 40 cm in Square E9, is a pointed flake with an outline like a knife; but both lateral edges (one straight and one excurvate), have been unidirectionally retouched from the same bulbar face to form steep scraping edges with angles of 65° and 70° (Figure 5-9a). The artifact, of banded white quartzite, measures 74 x 54 x 16 mm. A white quartzite flake scraper (BA-CE-17/232) came from the 30–40 cm level in neighboring Square E8. This scraper, which has a prominent bulb and a prepared platform, measures 60 x 50 x 18 mm (Figure 5-9b). The distal end is broken, and both 90° edges are use-worn. One lateral edge with a 70° angle is unidirectionally step-flaked, while the other lateral edge, with a 40° angle, is unidirectionally trimmed from the opposite bulbar face. The last flake scraper of quartzite evidently also pertains to the early assemblage because orange silt adheres to one surface. This artifact (BA-CE-17/166) was found under the wall of the main shelter in Square F8 at a depth of 20 cm. The dimensions of this triangular red quartzite flake are 73

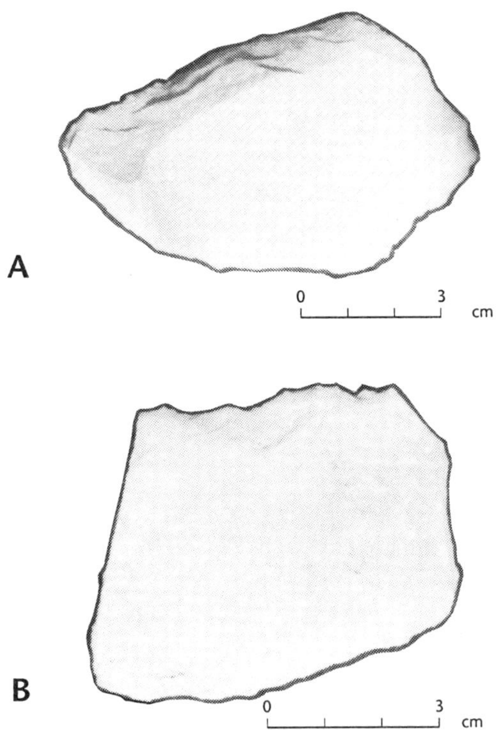

Figure 5-9. Quartzite flake scrapers. **A)** BA-CE-17/329; **B)** BA-CE-17/232.

x 54 x 21 mm. A portion of the original pebble cortex is present adjacent to the bulb of percussion, most of which was subsequently removed by steep unidirectional retouch from the opposite dorsal face, producing an edge angle of 70°. Several flakes were removed from the opposite bulbar face on this straight edge to create a pointed end. Two lateral projections have a black substance adhering to their worn surfaces. Another excurvate/incurvate edge, with an angle of 40° to 50°, has been unidirectionally retouched except for one resharpening flake. The third excurvate edge, with an angle of 15° to 25°, appears to be unidirectionally use-flaked.

Utilized Quartzite Flakes

Other intentionally struck flake tools in the Abrigo do Pilão were simply utilized, as their edges are not intentionally trimmed. They all came from the silt and ash zone. Four blade-like quartzite flakes with dorsal ridges have use-worn straight lateral edges. The convex end of BA-CE-17/341, from the 20–30 cm level in the G9/G10 baulk, is also worn. This white quartzite artifact measures 56 x 28 x 16 mm. The dorsal ridge of BA-CE-17/372, from the 0–10 cm level of Square G9, is differentially worn; and one platform corner is use-flaked. This red quartzite flake measures 44 x 26 x 12 mm. Another white quartzite flake (BA-CE-17/404) has one use-flaked and heavily worn lateral edge, with a 45° angle. The other edges and the tip are also worn. The dimensions of this artifact are 62 x 33 x 13 mm. This artifact came from the 0–10 cm level in Square E8. Both lateral edges, with angles of 35° and 45°, and both dorsal ridges of a large flake (BA-CE-17/213) are differentially worn. This artifact, which measures 87 x 57 x 27 mm, came from the 40–50 cm level in Square K9. Another large banded pink quartzite flake (BA-CE-17/76), which measures 70 x 56 x 31 mm, has a prominent bulb. The distal end is broken off squarely, and the resulting 90° edge and the bulbar platform edge (115° angle) are heavily worn. The other platform edge, with an 85° angle, is use-flaked and extremely worn; but there is only slight wear on the other edges. This artifact came from a depth of 20 cm in Square J9.

Two small flakes of white quartzite came from the 0–10 cm level in Squares E9 and F9. They measure 42 x 24 x 13 mm and 47 x 28 x 12 mm respectively. The smallest (BA-CE-17/298) is use-flaked on one convex lateral edge (angle 15°), while use-retouch and wear is evident on one broad straight edge of the other flake (BA-CE-17/131), which was made by a side-blow. The prominent bulb of BA-CE-17/373, from the 20–30 cm level of Square G9, is differentially worn as if it had been used to groove something. This white quartzite flake measures 48 x 32 x 15 mm. The distal convex edge (30° angle) of a grey quartzite flake (BA-CE-17/121), from the 50–60 cm level of ash and silt in Square J9, has been use-flaked and worn. A grey quartzite flake fragment (BA-CE-17/345) came from the 20–30 cm level in Square J10. One concave edge (20° angle) of this piece, which measures 34 x 18 x 7 mm, has been use-retouched.

A secondary flake of white quartzite (BA-CE-17/357) from the 0–10 cm level in Square K9 is coated with red ochre on the dorsal ridge and the worn convex distal edge (15° angle), which is also use-flaked. There is also wear and use-flaking on a straight lateral edge (15° angle) of this artifact, which measures 50 x 47 x 16 mm. This flat flake could have been used as a paint spatula.

Several quartzite flakes with flat bulbs or fragments lacking bulbs also show evidence of use. Most of these flake artifacts were unintentionally removed from pebbles by heavy use as hammerstones or choppers. For convenience, a few fragments and apparently natural spalls will be included in the same category because all were expediency tools selected because they had useful edges. Spalls removed from hammerstones that lack evidence of subsequent use will be described with the hammerstones.

Peck marks on the external surfaces of two pebble flake tools show that they definitely are pieces of broken hammerstones. Although the characteristic peck marks are not evident on the remaining six spalls or fragments, the presence of flat bulbs of percussion, often multiple, and other characteristics identify them as probable broken pebble hammerstones. Both lateral edges (angles of 20° and 30°) of BA-CE-17/272 exhibit differential use-wear and use-nibbling after the piece spalled off a hammerstone. It was found in the 10–20 cm level of Square J9, and measures 40 x 35 x 13 mm. The long wedge-shaped irregularly straight edge (angle 25°) of BA-CE-17/406 is worn and use-nibbled. This flake, probably used as a scraper, came from the 20–30 cm level in Square K9; and it measures 56 x 37 x 20 mm.

Another artifact (BA-CE-17/323) is a spall from a quadrangular white quartzite pebble that exhibits peck marks on one worn surface, showing that it broke by use as a hammerstone. Hematite stains part of an adjacent external face, which probably had been used as a palette. After breaking, one lateral edge (35° angle) and an adjacent squarely flaked end (40° angle) were differentially worn and stained by red ochre. Evidently the stained end of this broken artifact, which measures 79 x 58 x 19 mm, has also been used as a spatula. It was found in Square E9 in the 20–30 cm level. A second flake (BA-CE-17/364) evidently spalled off a white quartzite pebble hammerstone. Both the original pebble surface and the flaked surface are stained red as if the artifact had been dipped in a pot of liquid paint. In addition, there are many roughly parallel striations concentrated on the polished excurving pebble face, which shows that the piece had been used to grind something, most likely paint. This distinctive little flake, which measures 35 x 37 x 10 mm, came from the 0–10 cm level in Square E9.

Artifact BA-CE-17/350 looks like a fragment of a heavily weathered white quartzite-pebble hammerstone which was subsequently use-flaked and worn along one long lateral edge, which has an angle of 20°. The artifact measures 65 x 33 x 18 mm. It was recovered from the 20–30 cm level in Square J9. Another probable red quartzite hammerstone fragment (BA-CE-17/161) was found in the 0–10 cm level of Square F8. A short straight edge (40° angle) adjacent to the point of impact and a projecting spur at the opposite distal end have been worn. The artifact measures 25 x 28 x 8 mm. The straight edge (30° angle) of a fragment of a white quartzite hammerstone (BA-CE-17/348) has been use-nibbled and worn. The artifact came from Square F8 in the 30–40 cm level, and it measures 44 x 28 x 13 mm.

The excurving edge (25° angle) of another probable fragment of a red quartzite hammerstone (BA-CE-17/279) is heavily worn and use-flaked. Wear is also evident on one straight edge (25° angle) of this piece, from the 10–20 cm level in Square H10. The fragment, which measures 37 x 30 x 11 mm, evidently broke again and was no longer used.

Most of the bulbar end of artifact BA-CE-17/78 was flaked away to create two projections on a convex edge (50° angle) which was subsequently worn and use-flaked. Before the projections were created, this edge had been use-flaked and another 120° angle edge had been heavily worn and polished. This reused red quartzite scraper, measuring 54 x 43 x 21 mm, came from the 10–20 cm level in Square J9. A brown quartzite-pebble spall (BA-CE-17/22) with lines of force emanating from several points of impact later was used as a chopper, with use-flakes removed from several sections of the periphery, producing edge angles of 30° to 75°. This unique spall chopper, measuring 76 x 53 x 22 mm, was found in Square J10 at a depth of 20 cm. Another distinctive artifact is the end of a small white quartzite pebble (BA-CE-17/37) which broke, perhaps naturally, with a curving hinge. The artifact measures 42 x 35 x 18 mm. Both the 90° edge and the 10° edge of this little tool are use-flaked and worn. It was found in the 0–10 cm level in Square G9.

Several utilized flakes and natural spalls of white quartzite appear to have been collected from a bedrock quarry source where thermally spalled pieces with useful edges were available without the necessity of breaking up the stone. Similarly spalled material was observed in the Serra Azul south of Hidrolândia, about 30 km south of the Abrigo do Pilão. Two large thermal spalls of white quartzite came from on or near the surface of Squares K9 and D9. The former artifact (BA-CE-17/123), a blade-like spall with a dorsal ridge, is use-retouched on both lateral edges (angles of 25° and 30°) and the smallest end (edge angle of 60°). This artifact measures 98 x 58 x 18 mm. The other pyramidal spall (BA-CE-17/159) with a concave base exhibits wear and use-flaking on all four edges bordering the concave base. The artifact measures 74 x 49 x 24 mm. Three edges have angles of 20° to 25°; and the fourth edge is 90°. Dark brown material adheres to the 90° edge and three corners where the artifact was used to scrape some unidentified material.

Two similar-sized quartzite fragments have projecting corners and steep edges which have been heavily used for scraping or gouging. Both came from Square E8. The artifact (BA-CE-17/354) from the 0–10 cm level is a small keeled end/side scraper, measuring 32 x 22 x 15 mm, with step-flaking and wear on two 85–90° edges. The sharp projecting apex is also worn, and an unidentified brown substance adheres to the apex and several less-prominent projections. The polygonal artifact (BA-CE-17/230) from the 30–40 cm level superficially appears to be a tiny core, but actually the intentional unidirectional steep retouch on four 90° edges evidently was intended to create as many projecting spurs and steep corners as possible. A dark brown substance adheres to several other spurs and corners of this much-used artifact, which measures 32 x 28 x 16 mm.

A larger pyramidal fragment (BA-CE-17/343), measuring 49 x 32 x 19 mm, came from the 0–10 cm level in Square J9. Use-flaking on this artifact is evident on three basal edges, with angles of 85°, 40°, and 25°. Most of the latter edge was later steepened to 60° by retouching to create a projection which does not appear to have been used. Before retouching, however, both corners of the edge appear to have been used to work some red pigment, which still adheres.

The last quartzite fragment (BA-CE-17/343) looks like a broken pyramidal core; however, the series of flakes removed from the flat platform may have been intended to create a 45° angle scraping edge, which is slightly worn. This artifact, which measures 24 x 33 x 18 mm, was found in the 20–30 cm level of the G9/G10 baulk.

Chert and Agate Flakes, Cores, and Fragments

Although the kinds of artifacts flaked of chert, agate, and vein quartz are very similar to each other, it is easier to describe chert and agate separately for two reasons. First of all, the lack of crystal faces means that regular flakes can be removed from cores, which can be prepared from large nodules. Unfortunately, however, chert and sometimes agate has a tendency to explode when overheated; and this event occurred frequently in the Abrigo do Pilão because so many fires were built near or above where artifacts had already been deposited. Thus a great many chert fragments analysed separately among the flakes and fragments that lack evidence of use are probably pieces of some of the shattered chert artifacts and cores to be described below. Heat shattering may be useful for thermoluminescence dating, but this factor greatly hinders artifact description.

Most of the chert at the Abrigo do Pilão is of too poor quality to hold a thin cutting or scraping edge. Flakes are most useful for cutting because of their sharp low-angle edges, but the scarcity of utilized flakes suggests that cutting materials which would cause use-retouch or wear was not a particularly important activity at the Abrigo do Pilão. Also, the fact that retouch is always unidirectional suggests that the small flake tools were used for scraping rather than cutting.

The most-modified agate flake in the collection came from the 20–30 cm level in Square E8. This burinated flake (BA-CE-17/387), which measures 33 x 27 x 7 mm, is unidirectionally step-flaked around a convex end (edge angle 35°) which was resharpened to form two graver spurs, which are also worn. The remainder of the convex edge, with a 30° angle, is unidirectionally retouched from the opposite face except for the tip, which was resharpened by intentionally removing a burin spall, and was use-retouched in the same direction as the opposite end.

Two white chert flakes may have been intentionally pointed by breaking the sides off straight; however, there is no evidence that the points were used. In both cases a short straight edge has been use-nibbled. Both came from the 0–10 cm level in Square E9, and they measure 22 x 16 x 5 mm (BA-CE-17/299) and 25 x 24 x 6 mm (BA-CE-17/303).

Three flakes from the 30–40 cm level have edges steepened by retouch and heavy use. The entire convex edge of the chert flake from Square K9 (BA-CE-17/207), which measures 22 x 22 x 4 mm, has been retouched. One lateral edge (45° angle) of another chert flake (BA-CE-17/390) from the 30–40 cm level of Square E8 has been use-flaked. This artifact measures 24 x 23 x 13 mm. The straight edge (angle 30°) and spur on the distal end of an agate flake (BA-CE-17/106) from the 30–40 cm level in Square J9 has been use-retouched. In addition, an intentionally formed nose *(bec)* on the lateral edge (30° angle) of this artifact, which measures 33 x 30 x 12 mm, is much worn. The distal concave end of an agate flake (BA-CE-17/325) from Square E9 has been steepened to a 45° angle and worn. The short straight edge adjacent to the platform on this artifact, which measures 33 x 23 x 7 mm, has been use-nibbled.

The remaining nine utilized flakes of chert or agate simply have been unidirectionally use-retouched on edges that vary in angle between 10° and 45°. Two (BA-CE-17/64 and BA-CE-17/388) may have been removed from prepared cores, but the remainder are simply utilized flakes. The nine artifacts (BA-CE-17/64, 388, 27, 60, 67, 270, 271, 363, and 382) range in size from 45 x 33 x 11 mm to 27 x 17 x 7 mm. Four were recovered from the 0–10 cm level, three from the 30–40 cm level, one from the 40–50 cm level, and one from a depth of 70 to 80 cm in the fissure fill along the south wall in Square J10.

Only one intentionally prepared core of chert was identified in the Abrigo do Pilão collection, perhaps because the original nodules were small and because they were reduced beyond recognition. However, it is also possible that the production of polyhedral cores and the application of core-rejuvenation techniques were methods unknown to most of the occupants of the Abrigo do Pilão. The one polyhedral core (BA-CE-17/416), of white chert, was almost overlooked because it had thermally spalled into many fragments, four of which, from the same 30–40 cm level of Square F8, were reconstructable into the major part of the core, which now measures 57 x 55 x 30 mm. Only small sections of the original nodule were not flaked. At least three platforms had been prepared, from which several flakes were removed at nearly 90° angles before oversteepening caused stepping to occur. There is no evidence of subsequent use of this polyhedral core, so its purpose was evidently to produce useful flakes. It constitutes the best evidence that at least one person who visited the site was a skillful flint knapper.

One agate flake (BA-CE-17/346) from the 20–30 cm level in Square J10 evidently was removed from a similar core in order to rejuvenate a step-flaked platform. Three 90° edges of this rejuvenation flake, which measures 46 x 33 x 13 mm, feel smoothed by use; and one 35° corner is unidirectionally use-retouched.

The remainder of the chert cores and core fragments are multi-facetted; however, there is no real evidence of platform preparation, and in fact their primary purpose appears to have been for use as tools rather than for removal of flakes. Thus the term "core tools" refers to chunks that evidently were deliberately flaked to create useful high-angled edges, sharp projections (spurs), and noses *(becs)*.

The largest and most-complete core tool (BA-CE-17/160), which measures 64 x 53 x 38 mm, is of white chert. Most of its surface is flaked with three high-angle ridges and six projections showing much wear. In particular, a steep ridge (with edge angle from 90° to 115°) and nose (with 80° edge angle) at one end is heavily worn and stained black. Several worn edges were retouched to form sharp-edged projections. As with most core tools, evidently this much-used artifact from the 0–10 cm level in Square F8 was used for scraping hard materials, like wood or bone.

One small core (BA-CE-17/275), which measures 23 x 20 x 18 mm, exhibits step-flaking from two 90° platforms; and the resulting sharp spurs and edges are worn. One side of this white chert core tool appears to be stained black while the other side is stained red. Possibly this core tool, from the 0–10 cm level in Square J10, was used in pigment-processing.

A heat-spalled chert core tool (BA-CE-17/405) from the 20–30 cm level in Square K9 has been step-flaked from one platform to create a useful 90° edge. A sharp projection was created and rejuvenated at one end, which has an 80° edge angle. All projecting edges and corners of this broken core tool, which now measures 42 x 33 x 20 mm, are use-worn and nibbled.

Two small agate tools from the 0–10 cm level have been steeply retouched on one edge. Artifact BA-CE-17/48, which was recovered from Square J9 and measures 23 x 14 x 9 mm, has a much-worn 55° angle edge. The more angular tool (BA-CE-17/115), from the G9/G10 baulk, measures 27 x 23 x 12 mm; and has a 50° working edge and corner.

A thick discoidal flake or fragment of green chert (BA-CE-17/227) from the 10–20 cm level of Square E8 has been bi-directionally flaked around most of its periphery to create sharp edges (angles from 55° to 75°) and projections, all of which are worn. The projections along one undulating edge of this core tool, which measures 38 x 34 x 16 mm, have been ground smooth and striated by heavy use.

Two agate core tools from the 0–10 cm level of Squares E9 and F9 have many use-worn edges and projections. Artifact BA-CE-17/287 from the west side of Square E9 was thermally spalled after unidirectional flaking, and now measures 37 x 28 x 23 mm. Interestingly, two of the thermally broken corners (with edge angles of 65° and 75°) evidently were later used; and some black substance adheres to the most-projecting corner, which has an edge angle of 65° The chert core tool (BA-CE-17/127) from Square F9 has two step-flaked and much-worn 90° corners. The other corners, with edge angles of 90° and 55°) have also been rejuvenated and use-flaked. An unretouched but worn edge (70° angle) of this much-used core tool, which measures 38 x 32 x 21 mm, has a brown substance adhering to it.

Both ends of a multi-facetted agate core tool (BA-CE-17/81) from the 10–20 cm level in Square J9 have spalled off by heat. Two straight flaked edges (with angles of 70° and 85°) and three 90° corners are worn and use-flaked on this broken tool, which now measures 28 x 28 x 26 mm.

A completely flaked white chert core tool (BA-CE-17/223) with a triangular cross-section (dimensions 44 x 24 x 22 mm) came from the 0–10 cm level in Square E8. All three ridges, with edge angles of 70°, 70°, and 50°, have been bi-directionally flaked several times to create useful projections on this unusually shaped piece.

A multi-facetted white chert core tool (BA-CE-17/399) from the 0–10 cm level in Square I10 has been step-flaked and much worn on both projecting ends, which now have edge angles of 80° and 85°. Several edges of this artifact, which measures 46 x 27 x 32 mm, are worn and use-nibbled, in particular a long ridge with a 65° edge angle. One whole side of this much-used tool is covered with an unidentified dark-brown substance.

Three small white chert core tools from the 0–10 cm level in Squares F8 and F9 exhibit less evidence for use. One of these tools (BA-CE-17/130) from Square F9 is step-flaked on one short 90° edge so it could be a rejuvenation flake, which now measures 24 x 24 x 14 mm. Two 90° edges and one overhanging 70° edge feel differentially worn. One 65° edge of artifact BA-CE-17/162 has been step-flaked by use. This small tool measures 28 x 24 x 18 mm. The other little tool (BA-CE-17/132), measuring 24 x 18 x 13 mm, has four use-retouched and worn edges with angles of 65° to 90°, and one step-flaked 90° corner.

A discoidal thermally spalled white chert fragment from the 30–40 cm level in Square K9 looks like a graver (BA-CE-17/214), measuring 43 x 36 x 18 mm, with a sharp spur at one end; however, there is no clear evidence of use on this spur. Before spalling, an 85° edge was use-flaked.

In the Abrigo do Pilão industry, useful projections are often formed by unidirectionally flaking concave edges on either side. Later a rejuvenation flake is often removed from the opposite face to resharpen the projection. Both of these subtle techniques are present on a small agate tool (BA-CE-17/282) which measures 23 x 21 x 12 mm. The much-worn nose *(bec)* has an angle of 50°. This small tool came from Square J10 between 80 and 90 cm depth in the fissure fill next to the wall of the eastern chamber. A similar white chert tool (BA-CE-17/417) from the 0–10 cm level of Square H10 has a projecting nose (edge angle of 55°) which has been resharpened by removing a flake from the opposite direction. Only one concavity is present on this heat-spalled fragment, which measures 26 x 26 x 13 mm. Two shallow concavities and an intersecting nose on BA-CE-17/184 have been step-flaked and much used, but the nose was not rejuvenated. This small tool, from the 0–10 cm level in Square K9, measures 27 x 27 x 12 mm. Two concavities (45° edge angle) were flaked to form two spurs on artifact BA-CE-17/157 from the 0–10 cm level in Square F8. A corner of this small tool, which measures 27 x 18 x 11 mm, has also been step-flaked and use-worn.

Single step-flaked concavities with 90° edge angles, perhaps for use as spokeshaves, are present on one edge of two small chert core tools. One agate tool (BA-CE-17/91) collected from the surface measures 25 x 15 x 8 mm. The other chert spokeshave (BA-CE-17/98), from the 0–10 cm level of Square J9, measures 18 x 19 x 12 mm.

An agate core tool (BA-CE-17/168) has a 90° spur created by step flaking on one side, and a much-worn projecting nose (35° edge angle) formed at one end by unidirectional flaking on either side. This small tool, measuring 37 x 22 x 12 mm, came from Square F8 in a collapsed wall section somewhere between 10 and 40 cm below the surface. A heat-crazed white chert core tool (BA-CE-17/414) from the 10–20 cm level in Square G10 has been use-nibbled along one concavo-convex 90° edge. It measures 35 x 25 x 9 mm. Another small chert tool (BA-CE-17/185), which measures 26 x 25 x 14 mm, has been step-flaked on a projecting 90° nose and worn on other 90° edges. It was found in the 0–10 cm level of Square K9.

An agate tool (BA-CE-17/375), perhaps a broken flake, found in the 10–20 cm level in Square J10, has been use-nibbled on one concave edge (with an angle of 50°) and a contiguous spur (25° edge angle). This small graver measures 22 x 18 x 8 mm. Step-flaking is present on one 90° concave edge and particularly the contiguous corner of a small chert tool (BA-CE-17/320) which measures 34 x 16 x 13 mm. This artifact came from the 20–30 cm level in Square E9. Although little used, the projecting tip (70° angle) of a chert chunk (BA-CE-17/228) from Square E8 in the 20–30 cm level of Square E8 has evidently been step-flaked and broken by use. This possible graver measures 37 x 28 x 22 mm.

The remaining eight chert and agate core tools exhibit only use-nibbling or wear on edges that vary between 30° and 90°. These eight tools (BA-CE-17/41, 50, 105, 178, 191, 206, 344, and 349) range in size from 44 x 23 x 16 mm to 22 x 13 x 11 mm. Three came from the 0–10 cm level, one from the 10–20 cm level, two from the 20–30 cm level, and two from the 30–40 cm level in the silt and ash zone.

Quartz Crystal Flake Artifacts

The sharp apices of natural quartz crystals were useful for graving or grooving wood or bone; but once the tip was worn, people must have tried to rejuvenate the useful pointed edge. The problem of breaking open a small crystal is quite formidable because there are so many crystal faces and many more incipient facets in the interior to impede normal conchoidal fracture. The knappers at Lapa Pequena (Bryan and Gruhn 1978) near Montes Claros in Minas Gerais had mastered the problem by removing the head of the crystal by carefully directing a bipolar blow from one longitudinal facet to another just below the head. The new flat flake surface could be used as a platform for removing longitudinal blade-like flakes.

One example of such a decapitated crystal head (BA-CE-17/117) came from the 0–10 cm level of the G9/G10 baulk. The opposing crushed edges (angles of 35° and 40°) of this artifact, which measures 18 x 20 x 8 mm, were probably later used for scraping. Another flake (BA-CE-17/47) with opposed crushed edges, one of which is a crystal surface, came from the 0–10 cm level in Square J9. The crushed edges of this *pièce esquillée,* which measures 15 x 13 x 5 mm, could have been used. There are also two small blade-like flakes from Square K9. One of these blades (BA-CE-17/170), from the 0–10 cm level, was driven off using the decapitated surface of the crystal as a platform. A central flake had already been removed, leaving a parallel crystal ridge on both sides. The distal end of this small tool, which measures 18 x 8 x 4 mm, has been retouched to form a pointed spur with a 15° angle edge. The distal end of the other blade (BA-CE-17/198), with two dorsal ridges, is broken off squarely, probably by heavy downward pressure. A crystal face was used as an oblique-angled platform to strike off this flake, so the original crystal was probably very large. Use-nibbling is present on both lateral edges (35° angles) of this unusual piece, which measures 13 x 12 x 5 mm. It was found in the 10–20 cm level in Square K9.

The probability that large clear crystals were sometimes reduced by the occupants of the Abrigo do Pilão is verified by the presence of a large thin flake with part of a crystal face remaining on the platform. The convex lateral edge (15° angle) of this hinge flake (BA-CE-17/208), which measures 35 x 28 x 7 mm, is use-retouched and worn, as are both 15° edges converging toward a broken projection (90° edge angle) which is use-nibbled. Even a hinged ridge from a previous flake scar parallel to the lateral ridge has been use-retouched, evidently by planing some material. This much-used crystal flake came from the 30–40 cm level in Square K9. A similar but smaller hinged flake (BA-CE-17/356), measuring 19 x 17 x 4 mm, was recovered from the 0–10 cm level in Square E8. It has been use-retouched on one straight edge, which has an angle of 15° The adjacent portion of the hinge on this artifact has been carefully retouched to form a steep edge (with 85° angle) and corner, which are worn smooth. The opposite corner and adjacent concave edge (15° angle) has been use-retouched.

Most of the rest of the flaked artifacts probably made from large clear crystals are either broken, or are thick and multi-facetted with many useful high-angled edges and corners. They will be considered after reviewing the flaked fragments that retain several crystal faces, because the latter specimens help to explain the technology used to flake smaller crystals.

One nearly complete small milky quartz crystal (BA-CE-17/415), which measures 24 x 7 x 7 mm, has been broken obliquely at both ends to create a boat-shaped longitudinal cross-section. Both ends (edge angles of 30° and 40°) have been retouched on this piece, which came from the 0–10 cm level in the G10/H10 baulk. Apparently the procedure used was to hold the crystal flat on an anvil with the root end hanging over the edge of the anvil, and strike off the root at an oblique angle. Then one repeats the procedure by obliquely striking the base of one of the crystal facets at the head end. Although an anvil is used, the method is not bipolar and does not result in opposing crushed edges. One end of this artifact is stained black, and there is a red stain along a worn crystal ridge as if it had been used to prepare pigment. This artifact illustrates a somewhat less efficient method of breaking open a crystal than the technique of removing the head at right angles to the longitudinal axis, because the oblique angle does not produce a platform from which blade-like flakes can be removed. It would be possible, however, repeatedly to rejuvenate the piece by removing new segments, perhaps simply by sharply striking the piece on another stone, much as burins are rejuvenated.

Ten oblique-angled flakes are the results of obliquely-decapitated crystal heads. Occasionally the remnant striking platform retains part of a crystal face; but more often the platform has been prepared by removing previous crushing flakes, perhaps removed while the whole crystal was used as a tool. The working edges vary in angle from 25 to 90°. The ten crystal flakes (BA-CE-17/36, 46, 55, 100, 165, 273, 278, 384, 380, and 381) vary in size from 38 x 18 x 5 mm to 11 x 10 x 6 mm. Seven flakes were recovered from the 0–10 cm level, and four from the 10–20 cm level in the silt and ash zone. In addition, four flakes and fragments of crystal evidently were removed from the roots of crystals by oblique blows. These artifacts (BA-CE-17/49, 352, 365, and 413) show evidence of use-flaking or wear on edges which vary in angle from 30° to 85°. They range in size from 27 x 22 x 15 mm to 14 x 10 x 5 mm. These four flakes were well dispersed through the silt and ash zone, with one example from the 0–10 cm level, one from the 20–30 cm level, one from the 30–40 cm level, and one from the 40–50 cm level. Evidently this special flaking technique persisted for some time.

People experimented with other ways of reducing quartz crystals. A fragmented clear crystal (BA-CE-17/362), which measures 28 x 9 x 7 mm, apparently exhibits an unsuccessful attempt to remove a large crystal head by striking it too near the apex. The piece, which was recovered from the 0–10 cm level in Square K9, simply shattered with the attempt; and negative flakes were removed from both sides. However, the knapper was able to recoup a useful 85° step-flaked edge of this rectangular artifact. Another artifact, a curving spall (BA-CE-17/391) which could have been removed from another aborted attempt to decapitate a crystal, was turned into a useful little tool by using a 40° convex edge. It came from the 0–10 cm level in Square H10, and measures 18 x 8 x 5 mm.

Three irregular crystal heads of vein quartz were also altered for use. One bipolarly decapitated head (BA-CE-17/359) from the 0–10 cm level in Square K9 has been retouched on one 85° edge, evidently through use as a scraper-plane. This artifact measures 24 x 17 x 15 mm. Another artifact (BA-CE-17/397) is the apex of an irregular short crystal which has had four flakes removed by direct blows to the apex, probably to rejuvenate the 50° to 60° edges. Two 90° root edges of this artifact, which measures 27 x 22 x 18 mm, have also been use-retouched and worn; and there is a dark stain on the corner between these steep-angled edges. This artifact was recovered from the 30–40 cm level in Square E9. Another short complete crystal (BA-CE-17/54), which measures 24 x 21 x 10 mm, has a flake removed, probably by use, from a projecting nose (the apex). This artifact came from the 0–10 cm level in Square J9.

One thin flake of clear crystal (BA-CE-17/79) from the 10–20 cm level in Square J9 appears to be a rejuvenation flake removed from an 80° corner which had previously been flaked and worn. The flaking on this artifact fragment, which measures 16 x 10 x 2 mm, is unusual in that three invasive flakes were removed at an 80° angle; and then many tiny flakes were removed by use-nibbling.

Four small thin flakes of milky quartz exhibit enough unilateral retouch to be classified as flake scrapers. Artifact BA-CE-17/20, which measures 23 x 17 x 6 mm, features a lateral edge with a 35° angle retouched to form a graver spur, which is worn. This artifact was recovered from the 0–10 cm level in Square J10. Artifact BA-CE-17/126, which was found in the 0–10 cm level in Square F9, has use-retouch and wear on a 30° convex edge, a 30° straight edge, and a corner. It measures 24 x 13 x 5 mm. Artifact BA-CE-17/209, which measures 26 x 18 x 4 mm, features a 20° straight edge which is use-retouched. It was recovered from the 30–40 cm level in Square K9. Artifact BA-CE-17/342, from the 20–30 cm level in the G9/G10 baulk, has a 15° lateral projection which is retouched and worn, and use-nibbling on a 20° edge. It measures 22 x 14 x 4 mm.

Nine fragments of clear crystal, most of which lack

crystal facets, exhibit use-retouched edges and corners, with edge angles varying between 35° and 90°. The higher-angled edges were probably more desired, as they are not as apt to break under pressure as the thin flakes. The nine artifacts vary in size from 28 x 14 x 8 mm to 13 x 12 x 8 mm. Six were recovered from the 0–10 cm level, two from the 10–20 cm level, and one from the 20–30 cm level in the silt and ash zone.

Three quartz artifacts were made from water-rounded pebbles. Although pebbles can easily be split open with the bipolar technique, it is difficult if not impossible to predict in advance where the crystal planes are within a quartz pebble. A heavy hammer blow was used to split open artifact BA-CE-17/295, which measures 27 x 19 x 14 mm. The resulting platform was then used to drive off two flakes, one of which was a burin-like spall. The projecting platform edges (45° and 60° edge angles) of both flake scars appear to have been use-flaked. This artifact was found in the 0–10 cm level of Square E9. Use-retouch and parallel striations are evident on a 30° edge of a small clear crystal pebble fragment (BA-CE-17/74) which measures 16 x 17 x 6 mm. This artifact was found in the 0–10 cm level in Square J9. One end of another utilized pebble fragment (BA-CE-17/97) was evidently broken by heavy use. Portions of three flaked ridges on this piece, which measures 25 x 17 x 10 mm, were crushed and worn before it broke apart. This artifact came from the 0–10 cm level in Square J9.

Vein Quartz Fragments

Because vein quartz crystals normally grow in a compressed environment, vein quartz is characterised by many interlocking crystal faces which make it impossible to control flaking in a regular manner. Nevertheless, broken fragments of vein quartz provide excellent working edges which are both hard and durable, so quartz fragments were highly desired as tools. Vein quartz occurs in the vicinity of the Abrigo do Pilão, and very small naturally weathered fragments were found incorporated in the red silt deposit in the eastern chamber. As most of these showed no evidence of flaking, presumably they were deposited in the cavern by natural means.

A quartz fragment that has been rounded by water or chemical weathering lacks useful edges, so it must be broken to obtain a working edge. The easiest way to break up a large chunk of quartz is to lay it on a rock and throw another rock at it. Useful pieces can then be picked out of the resulting debris. A more refined version of this ancient knapping technique is known as the bipolar method, which is less wasteful and probably essential if the piece to be broken apart is small or has a rounded surface. The bipolar method involves holding a flat face of the stone to be broken on an anvil stone and forcefully striking an opposing flat face in order to split the piece. Actually, what happens is that the cone of percussion is split, rather than producing a normal conchoidal fracture. The split face can be slightly concave or convex, or the broken piece may look like a section of an orange if more than two pieces break off with the same blow. This kind of segment often terminates in an elongated pointed projection with angular cross-section which could become a useful tool.

A bipolar quartz flake can usually be identified by following the lines of force back to the point of impact and to the opposing rebound platform. If one or both platforms have subsequently been removed it is very difficult to identify a bipolar flake. Also, sometimes the flake splits along a crystal plane without leaving clear lines of force. It is also difficult to tell if a crushed projecting end or straight crushed edge caused by the forceful hammer blow has subsequently been used.

Several quartz fragments in the Abrigo do Pilão collection were clearly bipolarly flaked, while several more probably were as well. Undoubtedly bipolar flaking was used to break up other fragments as well, although the evidence is not obvious. It can be assumed that the bi-directionally crushed straight edges and projecting ends created by bipolar flaking were actually used. This assumption can be demonstrated on one artifact (BA-CE-17/269) because a black substance is adhering to the projecting point of impact where the projection was used to gouge or scrape something. A lateral convex edge (45° angle) of this artifact has been unidirectionally use-nibbled, and a resharpening flake has been removed from the opposite face. This artifact measures 33 x 28 x 13 mm, and it was recovered from the 30–40 cm level in Square J10.

Another bipolarly flaked quartz fragment (BA-CE-17/389) has useful projecting noses created by bipolar crushing at both ends. Again a lateral edge (with 50° angle) of this multipurpose artifact exhibits use-flaking and wear. This artifact, which measures 38 x 18 x 11 mm, was found in the 30–40 cm level of Square E8. Another bipolarly flaked quartz fragment (BA-CE-17/312) from the 10–20 cm level in Square E9 was probably used on both opposing chisel-like points of impact. A red stain on one end of this semilunar-shaped artifact, which measures 34 x 22 x 7 mm, may indicate that it was used to gouge hematite nodules.

The projecting end of artifact BA-CE-17/385, created by a heavy hammer blow, appears to have been used. This quartz fragment, from the 0–10 cm level in the G10/H10 baulk, measures 23 x 16 x 12 mm. A bipolarly struck fragment of vein quartz crystal (BA-CE-17/83), which measures 42 x 24 x 17 mm, has two use-flaked lateral edges of 55° and 65° created by using the flat split cone face as a platform. This artifact was found in Square J9 at 20 cm depth in the silt and ash zone.

Three vein quartz artifacts have opposing straight crushed edges caused by the hammer and anvil rebound of bipolar flaking. These artifacts are classifiable as *pièces esquillées* (scaled pieces), which experiments have shown serve admirably as small wood-working wedges (Ranere 1978). The fact that there are two opposing sets of straight crushed edges on artifact BA-CE-17/85 supports the hypothesis that it served as a wedge. An impact blow on the tip end has also removed a flake of the kind that could have been made if the piece had been used as a wedge or chisel and struck on the opposite crystal face. This much-used tool, measuring 28 x 22 x 8 mm, was found in Square J9 at a depth of 20 cm in the silt and ash zone. Directly associated was another small pyramidal vein quartz tool (BA-CE-17/84) which may be a crystal head that was decapitated with a bipolar blow. Probably both crushed platform edges (with angles of 50° and 55°) were used; and the piece, which measures 33 x 28 x 10 mm, has also been step-flaked on the 65° apex. One *pièce esquillée* (BA-CE-17/268) may have been a small wedge. It measures 22 x 12 x 6 mm, and came from the 20–30 cm level in Square F9.

Several vein quartz pieces exhibit less definite but probable evidence of bipolar flaking. A rectangular block (BA-CE-17/302) appears to have been squared on both sides by bipolarly striking off flakes that appear to be burin spalls removed to resharpen the 90° edges and corners. One sharp corner of this artifact, which comes from the 0–10 cm level in Square E9, has a dark stain while an adjacent worn edge is stained red. This unusual burinated quartz fragment, which measures 33 x 27 x 13 mm, may have been used to prepare pigment. A tiny rectangular vein quartz fragment (BA-CE-17/369), which measures 21 x 8 x 7 mm, appears to have been squared off in a similar way by removing one bipolar spall. One end appears to be differentially worn, and the opposite end intersects a previously retouched 40° edge. This artifact came from the 10–20 cm level in Square E8. Artifact BA-CE-17/14, which measures 24 x 22 x 22 mm, exhibits the kind of dorsal ridge that forms from a bipolarly struck blow on a thick flat platform, in this case a weathered crystal facet. The distal end of this flake tool, recovered from the 0–10 cm level in Square J10, has been resharpened by subsequent bidirectional retouch to form a bi-bevelled working edge (50° angle). Two corners of this artifact, with edge angles of 80° and 90°, have been removed by step flaking.

A triangular vein quartz fragment (BA-CE-17/120), exhibiting a split cone point of impact on two corners, was evidently bipolarly struck twice. One anvil edge of this piece, which measures 28 x 22 x 7 mm, broke off; but the other convex edge is apparently unidirectionally use-flaked. This artifact was recovered from the 50–60 cm level at the base of the silt and ash zone in Square J9.

A subangular weathered vein quartz fragment (BA-CE-17/420) has one crushed and step-flaked 90° edge which appears to be an aborted attempt to flake the piece bipolarly. The artifact measures 27 x 19 x 15 mm. It was recovered from the red silt in Square J10 at a depth between 120 and 150 cm. A pyramidal vein quartz tool (BA-CE-17/400) from the 0–10 cm level in Square I10 appears to be a vein quartz crystal head that was finally decapitated by placing a crystal face on an anvil and striking a previously battered edge (with a 65° edge angle) that had been repeatedly beaten in previous attempts to break it open. Both lateral edges (with angles of 65° and 80°) of the split plane and the projecting end (with an angle of 70°) have been use-retouched. This piece measures 35 x 27 x 17 mm.

The remainder of the vein quartz fragments do not exhibit any evidence of being flaked by special techniques. Some may have been carefully broken apart; but most appear to be simply fragments that were selected for their useful edges, corners, and projections. Many appear to have been created by throwing another rock at them, but others are weathered fragments which have steeply flaked edges. Some of these artifacts exhibit much evidence for use, while others apparently were used very little before being discarded. The pieces will be grouped together according to the characteristics of their useful edges and projections.

Two pointed angular fragments with plano-convex cross-sections of vastly different size appear to have been used as perforators. The largest artifact (BA-CE-17/229), which comes from the 30–40 cm level in Square E8 and measures 82 x 45 x 23 mm, has a much-used pointed end which may have been created by a direct heavy hammer blow. Both converging edges (with angles of 90° and 50°) and the convex face have been smoothed by use. The 90° angle edge was previously step-flaked. A projecting nose (with 80° angle) on one side is also use-flaked and smoothed. The smaller tool (BA-CE-17/102), from the 10–20 cm level in Square G10, measures 23 x 13 x 8 mm. The pointed projection has been differentially smoothed. Both of these tools would have made excellent hide perforators.

Another plano-convex fragment of vein quartz (BA-CE-17/146) looks like it has a graver spur on one corner, but there is no good evidence that it was so used. The entire convex edge, with an angle of 55°, has been retouched; and some of it step-flaked by heavy use. This endscraper, which measures 28 x 20 x 18 mm, came from the 30–40 cm level in Square F9. Another artifact (BA-CE-17/319) with a plano-convex cross-section is shaped like a thick endscraper (Figure 5-10a) and may have been such before most of the 65–80° edge broke off during heavy use. Part of the edge (75° angle) retains use-flaking, and a projecting nose (65° angle) at one end has been resharpened by removing a flake from the planar face. This artifact, from the 10–20 cm level in Square E9, measures 38 x 33 x 19 mm. Another vein quartz core tool (BA-CE-17/140) with a resharpened projecting nose (60° angle) and two step-flaked straight edges (angles of 80° and 85°) came from the 30–40 cm level in Square G8. This artifact measures 38 x 34 x 27 mm.

Two multipurpose core tools with several used steep-angled edges came from the 10–20 cm level in the

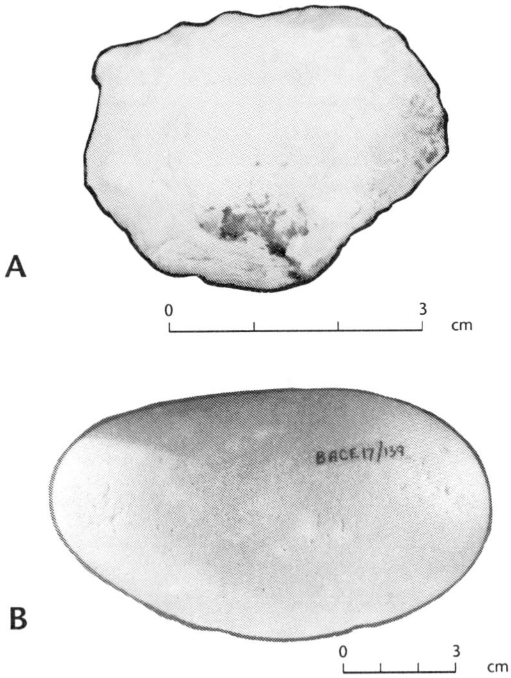

Figure 5-10. A) quartz retouched flake (BA-CE-17/319); **B)** quartzite hammerstone (BA-CE-17/ 139).

silt and ash zone. A tabular vein quartz fragment (BA-CE-17/402), which measures 43 x 24 x 21 mm with a rhomboidal outline, has been use-retouched on all ten edges, with angles of 75° to 90°. Flaking on four edges of this artifact occurred after the tool broke. It was found in Square I10. A multi-facetted core tool (BA-CE-17/80) which measures 48 x 33 x 32 mm has at least seven corners that have been smoothed by use. One 90° angle edge is use-flaked and smoothed, and one end is polished and stained red where it presumably was used to scrape hematite. This artifact was recovered from the 10–20 cm level in Square J9.

Seven thick vein quartz fragments (BA-CE-17/71, 156, 238, 361, 377, 379, and 418) were simply retouched on one or more steep-angled edges which vary in edge angle from 60° to 90°. The seven artifacts range in size from 48 x 34 x 22 mm to 19 x 13 x 12 mm. Three were recovered from the 0–10 cm level, two from the 10–20 cm level, and two from the 40–50 cm level in the silt and ash zone.

Another similar group of thick vein quartz fragments are completely stained orange, a feature suggesting that they lay in the orange or red silt for a long time. Three of these tools (BA-CE-17/154, 290, and 376) were retouched after as well as before staining, indicating that people collected useful quartz fragments from elsewhere in the site and reused them. Several uniformly stained tools (BA-CE-17/133, 148, 151, and 353) from the silt and ash zone probably had been picked up by later occupants but not reused. The rest of the stained tools (BA-CE-17/40, 122, and 419) were found very deep in the sediments of the eastern chamber. The smallest of these artifacts is 28 x 18 x 13 mm; unfortunately the largest size was not recorded, so the size range cannot be given. All have been use-retouched or worn on one to three edges, varying in angle from 60° to 95°. Six were recovered from the 0–10 cm level, one from the 10–20 cm level, one from the 50–60 cm level in Square J9, and two from between 120 and 150 cm in the red silt zone in Square J10.

Seventeen vein quartz fragments have lower-angled working edges that are similar to those found on flakes. Two of these may have been flaked with special techniques. Artifact BA-CE-17/66, which measures 23 x 9 x 8 mm, is tabular in form; and use-retouched and worn on one convex 25° edge. It might be a core rejuvenation tablet struck off to remove an older 90° concave edge which appears to be use-retouched and much worn. The other artifact (BA-CE-17/350) is a rectangular fragment with a triangular cross-section, measuring 33 x 13 x 8 mm. It may have had a burin spall removed longitudinally from the thick edge. The thin 20° edge and one end (with 35° angle) of this artifact, which comes from the 20–30 cm level in Square J9, feel use-worn. The other fifteen thin angular quartz fragments have used edges and corners, with edge angles ranging from 25° to 90°. They range in size from 53 x 22 x 8 mm to 17 x 17 x 11 mm. Seven were recovered from the 0–10 cm level, three from the 10–20 cm level, one from the 20–30 cm level, three from the 30–40 cm level, and one from the 40–50 cm level in the silt and ash zone.

Two angular vein quartz fragments exhibit ochre staining along the angular intersection of crystal facets with flaked surfaces. There is no use retouch on these 90° to 110° angle edges, which would have been overlooked if they were not stained red. Use retouch is present on another 90° edge of artifact BA-CE-17/407, from the 40–50 cm level in Square E9. This artifact, indicating the use of hematite in the lowest occupation zone within the silt and ash, measures 28 x 24 x 8 mm. The other vein quartz fragment (BA-CE-17/68) comes from the 0–10 cm level in Square J9. It is small and rectangular, measuring 24 x 9 x 8 mm. There is a red stain along a 90° intersecting edge between a crystal facet and a flaked surface. One narrow end of this artifact has been step-flaked, crushed, and stained black, perhaps by using it to scrape a black mineral pigment.

Pebble Tools of Quartz, Quartzite, or Chert

A tiny quartz pebble tool (BA-CE-17/421), measuring 24 x 18 x 14 mm, looks like it became subrounded by weathering. It has been unidirectionally flaked along one 45° angle edge, and has some use flakes removed from the same edge in the opposite direction. This artifact was found in Square J10 between 120–150 cm depth, possibly in the filled fissure along the wall of the eastern chamber.

Two possible small pebble tools of quartzite came from near the base of the silt and ash zone. Both are quite small pebbles which split longitudinally. One is a small brown quartzite pebble (BA-CE-17/234) which measures 33 x 28 x 15 mm. It was split longitudinally, perhaps by use as a hammerstone after two flakes had been removed unidirectionally from the bit end. There is no conclusive evidence of use of the bit for chopping. This artifact, found under the rear wall of the main shelter in the 30–40 cm level in Square E8, is deep enough to be stratigraphically associated with the early edge-trimmed tool complex. A grey quartzite pebble (BA-CE-17/202) came from the 30–40 cm level in adjacent Square F8. It is somewhat larger, measuring 61 x 44 x 24 mm; but it also appears to have split longitudinally by use as a hammerstone. In fact, two burin-like flake scars extend from the pointed poll end. The bit end is composed of two straight edges (45° angle) which converge to a triangular point near the center. In addition to these quartzite pebble tools, a larger water-rounded pebble of yellow jasper (BA-CE-17/328) has been steeply flaked to create three 90° edges which have been step-flaked by use. This pebble chopper/scraper, from the 30–40 cm level in Square E9, may have looked like a classic pebble chopper before it was step-flaked. It measures 52 x 48 x 40 mm.

Six other quartzite artifacts evidently were used for chopping, although they lack the characteristic unretouched butt ends and opposing flaked bits. All but one retain part of a rounded pebble surface which may have been caused by exfoliation or by stream rolling. The completely flaked chopper (BA-CE-17/172) is an angular chunk of grey quartzite which was found in the 0–10 cm level in Square K9. Although this discoidal chopper, which measures 79 x 76 x 38 mm, is heavily coated with calcium carbonate, bidirectional retouch is readily evident on one nearly straight edge (45° angle) and unidirectional retouch on the opposite convex edge (45° angle). One heavily weathered white quartzite pebble may have been split bipolarly with a heavy blow; however, the rebound platform was subsequently removed by steep (90°) step flaking, creating a 90° working edge. This artifact (BA-CE-17/396) came from under the wall of the shelter in Square E9 at a depth of 30 cm. It measures 81 x 52 x 54 mm.

The planar face of a similar tool (BA-CE-17/305) of banded pink quartzite appears to be a natural break, but a nearly parallel face was formed by a heavy blow which created a flat bulb of percussion. The original natural 80° edge was step-flaked and heavily worn, with battering flakes removed in both directions. The resharpened 70° edge and projecting corner (45° angle) also exhibit much wear. Finally, this artifact, which now measures 82 x 54 x 33 mm, was broken in half and discarded. This much-used tool was found in the 0–10 cm level in Square E9.

At the other extreme in amount of use, artifact BA-CE-17/366 appears to be a broken fragment of a white quartzite chopper which shows remnants of limited unidirectional flaking along a 60° edge. The present dimensions of this fragment are 47 x 47 x 21 mm, and it was found in the 10–20 cm level of Square E8. The upper level of Square J10 (0–10 cm) yielded a tabular grey quartzite pebble (BA-CE-17/21) with both ends flaked and battered by corner blows. This artifact measures 84 x 57 x 30 mm.

The last artifact classified as a chopper (BA-CE-17/25) forms a logical transition to the category of hammerstones because this fine-grained red quartzite (or argillite) pebble broke along a natural cleavage plane when it was used as a hammerstone. Peck marks are present, especially on the corners of the angular waterworn face. After breaking, a straight edge with 35° angle was unidirectionally retouched for use as a chopper; and use flakes subsequently were removed bidirectionally by downward blows. A projecting corner of this chopper, which measures 67 x 62 x 33 mm, is most heavily battered and worn. This artifact was collected from the surface by the discoverer of the site, Valdemar Fausto da Silva, who could not recall exactly where he found it.

Quartzite or Sandstone Hammerstones, Mullers, and Rubbing Stones

Among other uses, the hammerstones lacking any pigment stain probably were used for flaking other stones. Most are quartzite pebbles with pecked areas. A few artifacts appear to be sandstone, but they may be actually weathered quartzite.

A discoidal white quartzite pebble (BA-CE-17/24) has two waterworn flat faces, near the center of which are shallow pecked depressions. Both sides exfoliated naturally, but the resultant four 90° edges, as well as both ends, have been heavily pecked. This artifact, collected from the surface of the site, measures 84 x 65 x 53 mm. A smoothly waterworn elongated oval white quartzite hammerstone (BA-CE-17/139) came from Square F9 at a depth of 30 cm. This artifact, which measures 110 x 64 x 38 mm, exhibits patterned pecking on both faces near each end, and slight pecking near the center of each face (Figure 5-10b). One side is flattened by pecking, while two pecked depressions are on the other side. An irregularly oblong white quartzite pebble with heavily pecked areas on both ends, two edges, and near the center of one face was found in Square G10 at a depth of 20 cm. This hammerstone (BA-CE-17/3) measures 107 x 55 x 56 mm (Figure 5-11a). A red quartzite hammerstone (BA-CE-17/23) which split along an old bedding plane was found at 20 cm depth in Square J10. Both ends and both edges of this piece, which measures 67 x 63 x 42 mm, are heavily pecked; and there is light pecking elsewhere on parts of the pebble surface.

A white quartzite pebble hammerstone (BA-CE-17/226) which apparently had broken along a bedding plane by heat, was recovered from the 10–20 cm level in Square E8. There are pecked areas near the center of one face near each end and on the other flatter face. This broken hammerstone measures 75 x 40 x 36 mm. A fragment of a banded pink quartzite hammerstone (BA-CE-17/189) that was shattered by heavy blows directed to one end came from the 10–20 cm level in Square K9. This fragment measures 67 x 49 x 28 mm. A bulbless spall removed from a red quartzite hammerstone (BA-CE-17/33) by heavy pounding was found in the 0–10 cm level of Square G9. This fragment, which measures 34 x 33 x 7 mm, exhibits a pecked and battered end; but there is no evidence of use after it broke off.

Two tabular pieces of sandstone appear to have been used for hammering more than for rubbing or grinding. A grey pebble (BA-CE-17/188) has been split along a bedding plane by a heavy blow to one end. The opposite end of this artifact, which measures 84 x 48 x 27 mm, has been battered and flaked by heavy use. It was recovered from the 10–20 cm level in Square K9. A coarse white sandstone slab (BA-CE-17/221) from the 0–10 cm level in Square E8 appears to have been pecked or perhaps rubbed on the ends and convex edges. It measures 55 x 54 x 19 mm. Another white sandstone pebble fragment (BA-CE-17/203), from the 40–50 cm level in Square F8, has been pecked on one previously use-battered end; but the remnants of both faces appear to have been used previously for grinding. This broken muller/hammerstone measures 68 x 61 x 39 mm.

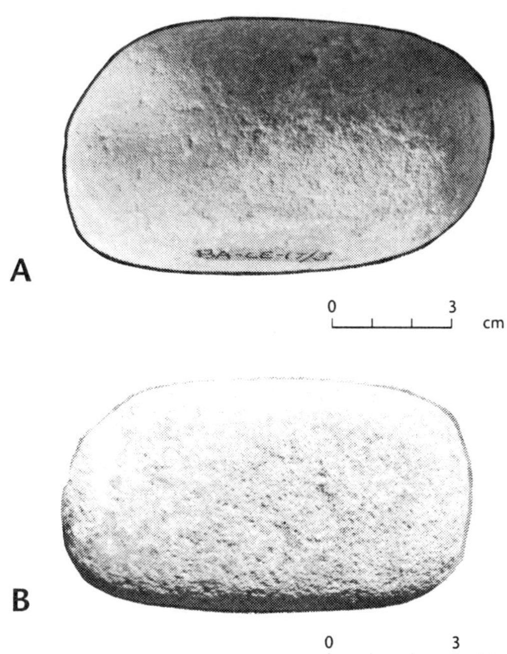

Figure 5-11. A) quartzite hammerstone (BA-CE-17/3); **B)** quartzite muller/hammerstone (BA-CE-17/173).

The only definite muller (BA-CE-17/173) was also used as a hammerstone. Apparently after being completely pecked into a symmetrical quadrangular shape (73 x 55 x 38 mm), both faces were smoothed and one face was facetted by grinding (Figure 5-11b). Both ends, both sides, and the centers of both faces have been further pecked. This rare shaped artifact was recovered far within the eastern chamber, from the 0–10 cm level in Square K9, where it may have been cached along with several shaped pestles and axe blades.

Four small water-rounded quartzite pebbles came from the silt and ash zone at the 10–20 cm level. Only one (BA-CE-17/316). from Square E9, was obviously used as a hammerstone, as it has been pecked on both ends. This pebble, which measures 48 x 39 x 29 mm, is a dull red color which may be due to hematite staining; but the stain is so uniform it is impossible to be sure. Another oblong quartzite pebble (BA-CE-17/190) from Square K9 is naturally pecked over its entire surface, but it was later deliberately pecked on one end. This little-used hammerstone measures 63 x 42 x 32 mm. A small spherical quartzite pebble (BA-CE-17/116) measuring 26 x 23 x 21 mm shows no obvious evidence of use. It was recovered from a depth of 12 cm in Square J10.

A symmetrically oval red quartzite pebble hammerstone (BA-CE-17/17), which measures 87 x 74 x 49 mm, exhibits red-stained areas which are also more polished by use than the pecked areas around the periphery and in the center of both faces (Figure 5-12a). This artifact came from a depth of 3 cm in Square J10. Another pigment-processing tool (BA-CE-17/201) came from the 40–50 cm level in Square F8. This artifact is half of a quartzite hammerstone which was pecked on the end and on both broad faces near the end. On one face near the broken end is an area in which the high spots are stained by red ochre. There are no grinding striations, but interestingly the portion and size of the stained area would be appropriate if someone who picked up the pebble to hammer something had pigment on his thumb. The artifact measures 85 x 65 x 61 mm.

The last quartzite pebble tool to be considered appears to have been a rubbing stone (BA-CE-17/15) perhaps used for polishing pots. It came from a depth of 10 cm in Square J10, and it measures 53 x 39 x 27 mm. This artifact has a polished black stain concentrated on one face and part of one edge.

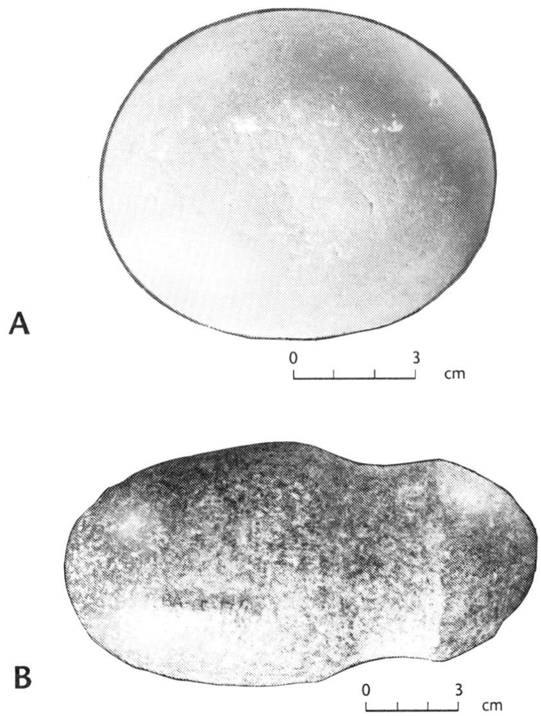

Figure 5-12. A) quartzite hammerstone (BA-CE-17/17); **B)** grooved and polished axe blade (BA-CE-17/1).

Greenstone Pestles, Mauls, and Axe Blades

Six artifacts ground out of exotic igneous rocks are clearly separable in the Abrigo do Pilão collection, not so much because of the material but because they all appear to have been deliberately shaped by grinding and pecking. The concept of deliberately shaping an artifact was rarely applied to materials from the Abrigo do Pilão. As all artifacts that were shaped were made of materials that must have originated at localities a significant distance from the rockshelter, it is quite possible that the concept of shaping involved technologies foreign to the local inhabitants, and these artifacts are imports or trade pieces. Certainly the complete polished axe blade must have been an especially prized possession. The fact that all three axe blades are of different types suggests the probability that they were made by different groups of people, probably far distant from the Abrigo do Pilão.

A broken pestle-shaped maul/hammerstone (BA-CE-17/231) was found in the 30–40 cm level of Square E8. It appears to have been ground and polished into an oblong cylinder which broke at both ends, and it now measures 73 x 65 x 55 mm. The edges, especially both sides and one end, were subsequently pecked by use as a hammerstone and battered and flaked by use as a maul; but there is no evidence that this broken piece was actually used as a pestle to grind something in a mortar. A greenstone flake (BA-CE-17/378) removed by a heavy blow from a polished maul like the one just described came from the 30–40 cm level in neighboring Square E9. This fragment, which measures 24 x 20 x 3 mm, was not used subsequently.

A quadrangular quartzite paint pestle (BA-CE-17/297) had previously been broken at least twice while hammering. The 90° edges of the originally flat break were subsequently battered and flaked by heavy use. The end and both lateral faces are flattened by light pecking, and the two broader faces exhibit round pecked areas. The pecked end and the unmodified portions of both broad faces are stained by hematite. This much-prized artifact, measuring 72 x 53 x 48 mm, was found in the 0–10 cm level of Square E9.

The symmetrically rounded butt end of a ground and polished greenstone axe blade (BA-CE-17/136) with a flattened oval cross-section was found in Square F9 at a depth of 18 cm in the silt and ash zone. After polishing, this artifact, which measures 54 x 68 x 39 mm, was use-pecked on the end and both edges. Evidently it broke by heavy hammering blows applied to a face as if it were used as an anvilstone.

A ground and polished serpentine axe blade (BA-CE-17/90) has a flattened oval cross-section and nearly straight sides. The bit is missing. This artifact, which measures 108 x 58 x 31 mm, was found on the surface of Square K9 far within the eastern chamber. After shaping, the entire butt end was battered and pecked by use as a hammerstone; and the bit apparently broke off by a heavy side blow. One irregular edge of the broken end of this artifact was subsequently facetted and polished by apparent use as a scraper-plane. In fact there is no actual evidence that this piece was used as an axe.

A broken tabular fragment of serpentine (BA-CE-17/392), evidently polished by use but not ground, came from the 0–10 cm level in Square H10. This artifact might be the butt end of a small axe or chisel which broke off and shows no evidence of subsequent use. The artifact measures 28 x 22 x 6 mm.

Certainly the most magnificent artifact from the Abrigo do Pilão was a complete polished and grooved axe blade (BA-CE-17/1) found on the surface of Square K9 well within the eastern chamber less than a meter from the serpentine axe blade. Both axe blades must have been carefully placed for safekeeping along the wall of the inner chamber where the ceiling was very low. This greenstone axe blade, which measures 158 x 78 x 48 mm, was very skillfully ground and polished into a bilaterally symmetrical ovoid outline with flattened oval cross-section with bi-bevelled edges around the entire periphery (Figure 5-12b). Then a broad hafting groove (38 mm wide) was carefully pecked around the periphery at a point about a third of the distance from the butt end. Areas within the pecked groove have been stained black by the hafting cement. The bit exhibits use striations, but only one nick has been removed by use. Obviously much care was observed in using as well as fabricating this splendid piece.

Limestone Artifacts

Limestone is the only lithic material readily available in the immediate vicinity of the Abrigo do Pilão. As they did not have to be transported, usefully shaped pieces could be used as expediency tools for a few minutes and then discarded. Most objects used for a short time probably show no clear evidence of use at all, and were overlooked among the natural limestone rubble. If evidence for flaking was seen, however, the rock was examined more carefully. If only one or two flakes had been removed without apparent pattern, the piece was usually discarded as possibly having been flaked naturally when stones spalled from the wall or ceiling. Several flake scars or evidence of patterned flaking, chopping, or scraping were necessary criteria to separate pieces as artifacts or probable artifacts. The category of "expediency tools" is highly debatable among archaeologists, but we believe that no archaeologist could deny the artifactual nature of most of the items to be described; and although the remainder might be debatable because they show minimal evidence of use, we feel that it is best to describe them for the record.

All shapes of the heavy limestone artifacts from the Abrigo do Pilão are natural, but people were able to select rocks with the most useful shapes and working edges. Limestone usually is bedded, so tabular pieces were commonly selected because they fit the hand or they had useful flat faces and high-angle edges. To judge from the differences in weathering, many of the tabular pieces were carried into the rockshelter from outside.

Among the pieces that evidently were picked up elsewhere for their useful shape and transported to the shelter are three naturally quadrangular pieces. All three are rectangular in plan and nearly square in cross-section, and comfortably fit the hand. They conform to a commonly desired size and shape for hammerstones or pounders made of any material. Several long unidirectional battering flakes have been removed from one 90° angle edge at one end of BA-CE-17/31, which came from the surface of Square I10. Shorter battering flakes have been removed from three 90° edges and one corner of the opposite end of this hammerstone, which measures 89 x 63 x 55 mm. A similar but less used hammerstone (BA-CE-17/292) came from a depth of 5 cm in Square E9. One long battering flake has been removed from a 90° corner at one end. One 90° edge of the opposite end and a contiguous 90° angle longitudinal edge have been heavily use-flaked and battered. This hammerstone measures 115 x 56 x 47 mm. The same kind of high-angle edge battering is present on BA-CE-17/192, which came from the 10–20 cm level in Square K9. All four edges, of each end, with angles of 90° to 115°, and two longitudinal 90° edges have been unidirectionally step-flaked and battered by downward-directed blows (Figure 5-13a). This artifact measures 93 x 48 x 47 mm. All three of these artifacts would be excellent percussion flaking hammers, as the relatively soft limestone would "bite" into the rock to be flaked. Probably many of the hundreds of flakes analysed separately were removed by these three much-used artifacts.

The desire for sturdy right-angle edges for percussion flaking probably accounts for many of the other less shapely artifacts of limestone. Several fragments with similar unidirectionally battered right-angle edges are probably hammerstones that broke during heavy use, and there is no evidence or minimal evidence for use after they broke. Artifact BA-CE-17/367 appears to be one end of a weathered quadrangular hammerstone that spalled off by a heavy corner blow. This battered flake was found in the 10–20 cm level of Square E8, and it measures 75 x 62 x 22 mm. All three 90–95° edges were use-battered and step-flaked before the flake spalled off. Two opposing 90° edges of another fragment of a weathered tabular piece of limestone have been use-flaked. This hammerstone fragment (BA-CE-17/77), which now measures 53 x 49 x 36 mm, came from the 10–20 cm level in Square J9. Three 90° edges and two 90° corners of another fragment of a weathered tabular piece from the 30–40 cm level of Square E9 have been use-battered and step-flaked. This broken hammerstone (BA-CE-17/327) now measures 74 x 53

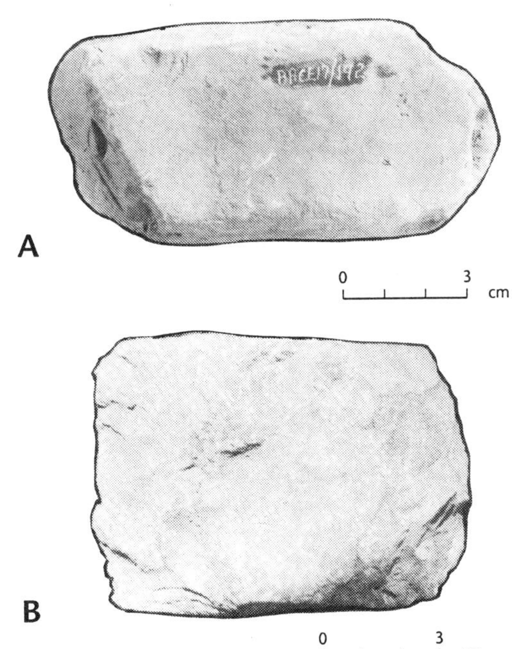

Figure 5-13. A) limestone hammerstone (BA-CE-17/192); **B)** flaked limestone fragment (BA-CE-17/112).

x 48 mm. Two opposing edges (with angles of 90° and 70°) of a similar tabular fragment (BA-CE-17/110), now measuring 87 x 52 x 46 mm, have been use-flaked and battered. This artifact came from the 30–40 cm level in Square J9. Use flaking and battering is present on one excurving 90° edge of another tabular fragment, which measures 77 x 46 x 43 mm. This hammerstone (BA-CE-17/317), from the 10–20 cm level in Square E9, has a few flakes removed from other 90° edges. Heavy use flaking and crushing is present on two 90° weathered edges and two 110° broken edges of a tabular weathered fragment (BA-CE-17/5) from 20 cm depth in Square G10. This tabular hammerstone measures 108 x 78 x 58 mm.

Three artifacts with much-altered high-angle edges may not be flaking percussors. One tabular fragment (BA-CE-17/112), rectangular in cross-section and plan, has been unidirectionally step-flaked on one 80° angle edge (Figure 5-13b). The lack of crushing and the lower edge angles make the function of this artifact uncertain. There is some use battering on other 70–80° edges. This artifact, which measures 104 x 72 x 34 mm, came from the 40–50 cm level in Square J9. Another similarly shaped artifact (BA-CE-17/321), which measures 92 x 76 x 40 mm, has been heavily battered and use-flaked on one 80–90° end. The edge crushing appears to have been made by heavy downward chopping rather than by the glancing blows of a percussor. This artifact was recovered from the 20–30 cm level in Square E9. Similar downward battering and crushing is present on one longitudinal edge (with a 55° angle) and both ends (with 90° angles) of a weathered piece of limestone from the 30–40 cm level in Square J9. This chopper (BA-CE-17/108) measures 93 x 73 x 47 mm.

The presence of bipolar flaking on the small quartz and chert artifacts means that anvil stones must have been used. Any of hundreds of rocks with a flat surface could have been used as anvils, so perhaps there should be no concern about the lack of obvious anvilstones. However, a few tabular limestone pieces that could have served as anvils evidently were split by downward blows such as might be applied if one were holding another rock on top and forcefully striking its opposite end. A very large flake with three points of impact was removed from the 90° edge of a thick tabular limestone fragment (BA-CE-17/10), which measures 111 x 70 x 63 mm. This possible anvilstone came from between 45 and 50 cm deep in Square G10. A similar thick tabular limestone fragment (BA-CE-17/197) has several scattered flake scars on several 90° edges and some possible points of impact on one surface. This artifact, which could be a core, came from the 10–20 cm level in Square K9; and it measures 104 x 84 x 57 mm. A triangular fragment of limestone (BA-CE-17/322) appears to be a flake removed from the corner of a similar thick tabular piece. It spalled off with a flat negative bulb from a downward blow such as might be applied to an anvilstone. The distal edge of the flake curved slightly, creating a useful overhanging 90° angle edge which is step-flaked and worn by use as a draw knife or scraper. This artifact, which measures 93 x 61 x 43 mm, came from the 20–30 cm level in Square E9.

Two thin tabular choppers with use-flaked and crushed convex edges can be grouped together. One (BA-CE-17/34) is semilunar in outline, and appears to have been notched for hafting in a manner similar to an Inuit woman's knife. This artifact, from the 0–10 cm level in Square G9, measures 89 x 64 x 12 mm. The unilateral notch evidently matches a naturally concave edge on the opposite side. The area on one face which would have been beneath the haft exhibits scratches parallel to the haft. The convex bit edge of this hafted chopper is crushed and bidirectionally use-flaked by downward-directed blows. There is no evidence of hafting on the other similar chopper (BA-CE-17/224), which measures 87 x 72 x 25 mm, and comes from the 10–20 cm level in Square E8. The bi-bevelled working edges of both choppers are approximately *45°*. Another artifact (BA-CE-17/28), which measures 93 x 62 x 17 mm, is also a thin weathered tabular limestone piece; but the use-flaking has created a concave working edge of 30°. This artifact came from the 30–40 cm level in the G10/H10 baulk.

Three limestone choppers made on natural fragments that fit the hand can be grouped together because they each have one unidirectionally flaked edge with working angle varying between 40° and 50°. They would be called pebble choppers if they had been made on pebbles, and all but one came from deep within the silt and ash zone in apparent association with the two small quartzite pebble choppers described separately. One of these tools (BA-CE-17/107), which measures 105 x 87 37 mm with a rectangular cross-section, has three large negative flake scars and several tiny step flakes removed from an excurvate edge which has an angle of 50° (Figure 5-14a). This artifact came from the 30–40 cm level in Square J9. Another chopper (BA-CE-17/174) with a rectangular plan may have been made on a flake (as there is apparently platform preparation), but the platform end has subsequently been heavily use-flaked and battered to form a rounded edge (Figure 5-14b). This opposite chopping edge naturally forms a straight bi-bevelled bit (with 50° edge angle) which is unidirectionally flaked. This tool, which measures 77 x 65 x 28 mm, came from the 20–30 cm level under the rear wall in Square F8. The third chopper (BA-CE-17/237) came from the 40–50 cm level in neighboring Square E8. This chopper, which measures 108 x 64 x 38 mm, has many short unidirectional flake scars on one long excurving edge, which has an angle of 50°.

Four similar choppers differ only because the working edges are bidirectionally flaked; and therefore, if they were made on pebbles they would be called chopping tools. Two of these tools came from deep levels, so they were stratigraphically associated with the

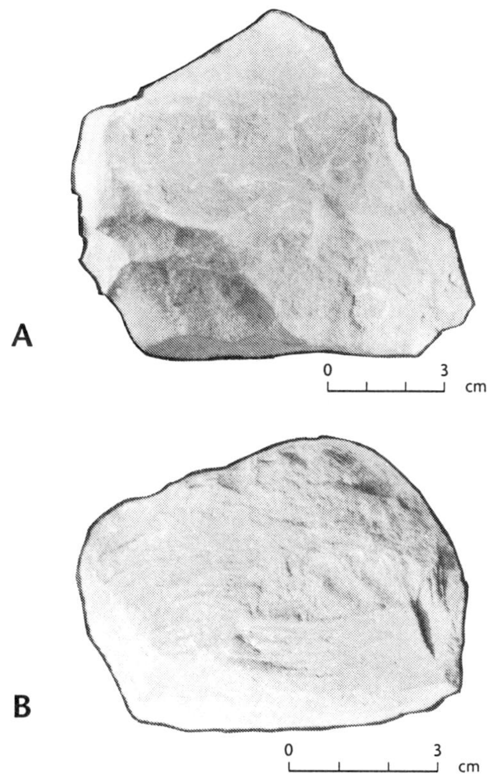

Figure 5-14. Limestone choppers. **A)** BA-CE-17/107; **B)** BA-CE-17/174.

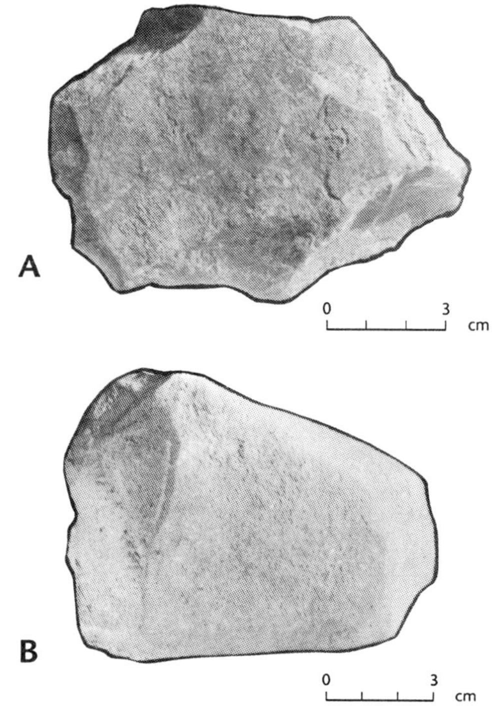

Figure 5-15. Limestone chopping tools. **A)** BA-CE-17/109; **B)** BA-CE-17/187.

choppers described above; the other two tools were recovered from the eastern chamber in the 10–20 cm level. One tool (BA-CE-17/109) has two planar faces which converge to a convex wedge-shaped bit end (with a 40° edge angle), part of which subsequently broke off (Figure 5-15a). This rectangular chopping tool measures 112 x 69 x 32 mm, and it came from the 30–40 cm level in Square J9. The same level in Square E9 yielded a tabular fragment of limestone with a truncated triangular outline and bifacial flaking on the broad end, which has an edge angle of 45°. This artifact (BA-CE-17/108) measures 112 x 69 x 27 mm. Another weathered triangular fragment of limestone (BA-CE-17/187), which comes from the 10–20 cm level in Square K9, also has a triangular outline which has been deliberately truncated by step-flaking and crushing, probably to help the tool fit the hand (Figure 5-15b). The broad bit end of this chopper, with a 45° edge angle, has been unidirectionally flaked; but subsequent heavy battering has removed short flakes from both directions. The artifact measures 111 x 73 x 38 mm. A weathered rectangular limestone fragment (BA-CE-17/195) is bifacially flaked on the broadest end (with a 45° edge angle), and there is some use-flaking along a lateral scraping edge (Figure 5-16a). This artifact, which measures 85 x 63 x 24 mm, also came from the 10–20 cm level in Square K9.

Three angular fragments of dense limestone found in the surface debris were much used for heavy chopping on 60–65° edges. They all have acquired thick coats of calcium carbonate, but flaking is nevertheless very evident. Artifact BA-CE-17/141, from Square F8, has been unidirectionally flaked along one excurving 60° edge. Several heavy battering flakes have been removed from other edges of this thick discoidal chopper, which measures 87 x 64 x 47 mm. Square G10 yielded a similarly shaped chopper (BA-CE-17/2) which also fits the hand very well. Heavy use-battering is present on one bifacially flaked end (edge angle 60°) as well as on three corners and adjacent 90° edges. Many scratches are visible on three smooth faces of this chopper, which measures 79 x 77 x 52 mm. Square F8 yielded what appears to be a broken fragment of a similar chopper (BA-CE-17/142). Flakes have been removed unidirectionally from one short edge (65° edge angle) of this piece, which now measures 79 x 52 x 30 mm.

A weathered limestone fragment (BA-CE-17/179) with a rectangular outline has been heavily battered and use-flaked on one end (80° edge angle) and a contiguous side (also 80° edge angle). This hammerstone/chopper, which measures 92 x 57 x 56 mm, was found in the 0–10 cm level of Square K9. The same level in Square E8

A

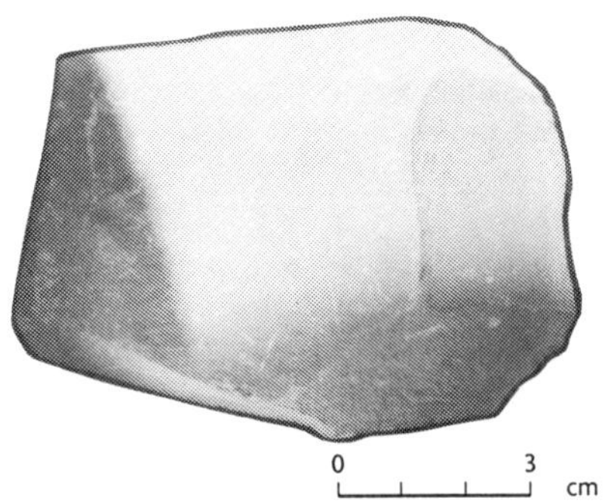

B

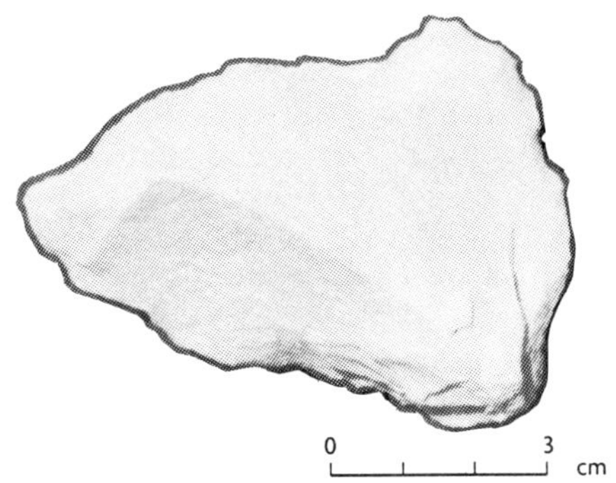

Figure 5-16. A) flaked limestone fragment (BA-CE-17/195); **B)** utilized limestone flake (BA-CE-17/169).

yielded an oval weathered limestone pebble (BA-CE-17/217) with a triangular outline, two corners of which have been heavily battered and flaked by use as a hammerstone. This tool measures 107 x 73 x 53 mm.

Four tabular limestone fragments with triangular outlines exhibit heavy battering on at least one apical end. The largest hammerstone/chopper (BA-CE-17/152), which measures 112 x 112 x 61 mm, is use-flaked and crushed on one end (75° edge angle) and along one 90° edge. Isolated flake scars are present on other edges of this artifact, which was found in the upper part of the G9/G10 baulk. A similar limestone hammerstone/chopper (BA-CE-17/193) came from the 10–20 cm level in Square K9. Battering flakes have been removed from the edges of two apices (with edge angles of 50° and 65°) and along two opposing 90° edges. A few flake scars are evident on the other apex (80° edge angle) of this chopper, which measures 98 x 87 x 61 mm. A less-used triangular chopper (BA-CE-17/315), from the 10–20 cm level in Square E9, exhibits use-battering along one continuous 60° edge, which includes an apex and one long edge. This tabular chopper measures 82 x 68 x 44 mm. Another triangular chopper (BA-CE-17/216), which measures 80 x 55 x 56 mm, features use-flaking on two apical edges, with angles of 60° and 70°. Two large flakes have been removed from the other apex of this chopper, which was found at 50 cm depth in Square K9.

A limestone artifact (BA-CE-17/310) from the 0–10 cm level in Square E9 was apparently used as a paint pot. It is a large chunk, measuring 118 x 108 x 107 mm, that probably spalled off the wall, as portions of one surface contain a natural polished iron oxide coating that occurs on the shelter wall. One end exhibits three negative flake scars from heavy battering blows. A natural depression (75 x 35 x 20 mm deep) on one side is coated with red ochre. There is no evidence of grinding, but the depression could easily have been used as a container for previously mixed pigment.

A weathered tabular fragment of limestone (BA-CE-17/401) from the 0–10 cm level of Square I10 appears to have a coating of orange pigment applied to one edge and the high spots of one face. A large flake scar is present on one end of this artifact, which measures 53 x 48 x 25 mm.

Several flaked limestone pebbles and fragments which do not fit into other categories can be described together. A tabular fragment of dense limestone (BA-CE-17/196), which measures 118 x 86 x 33 mm with a triangular outline, has been use-flaked along one concave 45° edge. A few flakes were also removed from two 90° edges of this artifact, which was found in the 10–20 cm level in Square K9. An irregular weathered fragment of limestone (BA-CE-17/119), which measures 113 x 112 x 54 mm with a square outline, has been battered along one 65° edge. This artifact was recovered from the 50–60 cm level of the silt and ash zone in Square J9.

A small weathered tabular fragment (BA-CE-17/26), which measures 56 x 47 x 42 mm, has flake scars on two opposing 90° edges. It was found just below the surface in the G10/H10 baulk. A weathered tabular limestone pebble (BA-CE-17/194) has had flakes removed from five corners. This artifact, which may have been used as a hammerstone, measures 58 x 46 x 34 mm; and it was found in the 10–20 cm level in Square K9. A small rounded limestone pebble (BA-CE-17/236), which measures 40 x 38 x 33 mm, has a large negative flake scar created by striking one corner. Possibly this artifact, which came from the 40–50 cm level in Square E8, was intended to be made into a pebble tool.

A weathered flattened cylindrical limestone fragment (BA-CE-17/138) from the 20–30 cm level in Square G8 has been truncated at one end by flaking, and broken at the other end. The flattest weathered face of this artifact, which measures 52 x 22 x 13 mm, appears to have been used to rub something. A small tabular fragment (BA-CE-17/6), which measures 50 x 28 x 8 mm, has been striated and polished on a concave 90° edge and contiguous sharp projection by rubbing something, such as wood. It was found at a depth of 40 cm in Square H10. Another small tabular fragment (BA-CE-17/311), which measures 47 x 41 x 13 mm, has a natural wedge-shaped edge (35° angle) which has been unidirectionally flaked. This artifact came from the 10–20 cm level in Square E9. A flat tabular fragment (BA-CE-

17/39) from 20 cm depth in Square G9 has a rhomboidal outline, measuring 87 x 82 x 7 mm. A flake has been removed from one corner, and two other corners appear to be crushed by similar use as a lightweight chopper.

Although over 400 limestone flakes were identified from all levels of the silt and ash zone at the Abrigo do Pilão, only 12 limestone flakes exhibit evidence of use, a fact suggesting that most flakes had been unintentionally removed from pebbles and fragments used as hammerstones or choppers. All but one of the 12 utilized flakes, now to be described, came from the 0–10 cm level in the silt and ash zone. Apparently sharp low-angle edges were not in great demand at the Abrigo do Pilão. Thin limestone flakes were not particularly useful because the edges were not durable enough when used for heavy-duty jobs such as working hard wood.

Four thick flakes with durable high-angle edges came from the 0–10 cm level in the silt and ash zone. Two of these are apparently steep sidescrapers with stepped flaking. The only whole scraper (BA-CE-17/300), from Square E9, is step-flaked on one convex corner (edge angle 50°) and one concave edge (angle 40°) The convex corner of this artifact, which measures 88 x 62 x 31 mm, was resharpened by removing a flake from the opposite bulbar face. A broken tabular flake (BA-CE-17/222) with a flat bulb is step-flaked around a concave end (70° edge angle) to resharpen a previously dulled edge (80° angle). The present dimensions of this scraper, which comes from Square E8, are 67 x 38 x 22 mm. It is difficult to tell if the stepped flaking and battering on a short straight edge of a broken flake (BA-CE-17/355) from Square E8 is due to scraping/chopping action or platform preparation. A lateral straight edge of this artifact, which measures 48 x 24 x 17 mm, is differentially use-polished and bevelled.

A distinctive pyramidal flake (BA-CE-17/169) from Square K9 superficially looks like a "ridge-back core" made with the special technique identified in the Yuha Desert of southeastern California (Childers 1979). In this case, however, there is no clear evidence that the four flake scars forming the pyramid were removed from the apex, as is the case with "ridge-backs"; rather, the surfaces may be natural, or some may have been removed by corner blows, as was the flake forming the base of the platform. Use flakes were subsequently removed from three corners and two edges (with edge angles of 65° to 85°) as well as along one convex end (with a 60° angle) of this artifact, which measures 87 x 55 x 37 mm (Figure 5-16b).

A small triangular limestone flake (BA-CE-17/153), which measures 42 x 21 x 7 mm, has had a burin-like spall removed from its pointed end, which is smooth and polished, as is the opposite concave gouge-like base and the high spots of both faces. This much-used artifact, which could have been mounted as a point, came from the 0–10 cm level in Square F8.

The convex bulbar face of artifact BA-CE-17/360, a limestone flake, is covered with longitudinal striations where the flake had been rubbed on something—perhaps a pot. A straight edge of this flake, which comes from the 0–10 cm level in Square K9 and measures 55 x 25 x 8 mm, is also polished by use. A notch unidirectionally flaked onto a lateral edge of a long narrow flake (BA-CE-17/69) from the 0–10 cm level in Square J9 has been use-polished. This spokeshave measures 52 x 25 x 8 mm.

One straight edge of a secondary limestone flake (BA-CE-17/38) from the 0–10 cm level in Square G9 has been use-flaked. This flake scraper measures 42 x 27 x 9 mm. A secondary blade-like flake (BA-CE-17/333) with two dorsal ridges came from the 0–10 cm level in the F9/G9 baulk. Both corners of the platform end of this artifact, which measures 52 x 38 x 13 mm, have been used, perhaps for grooving wood. The lateral edge of another flake (BA-CE-17/96) has been unidirectionally step-flaked to form an endscraper with a 45° edge angle. This artifact, from the 0–10 cm level in Square J9, measures 26 x 22 x 7 mm. Step-flaking is also present on one 45° edge of a secondary flake (BA-CE-17/199) from the 10–20 cm level of Square K9. This scraper measures 27 x 25 x 7 mm. Although it is a natural blade-like fragment that probably spalled off the wall, artifact BA-CE-17/70 will be included here for convenience. Use-flaking is evident along one straight sharp edge (with a 45° angle), and there are many random scratches on an adjacent weathered surface. This spall, which measures 105 x 54 x 18 mm, was recovered from the 0–10 cm level in Square J9.

Several flaked limestone pebbles and fragments found below the silt and ash zone will be described separately here because they came from below an unconformity and therefore they could have considerable antiquity. Several edge-trimmed quartzite and chert flakes, and several quartzite and limestone pebble tools from the lowest part of the ash and silt zone have previously been described separately as possibly representing a distinguishable early industry in the Abrigo do Pilão. Several of the artifacts from the underlying red silt in the eastern chamber might also be considered as pebble tools because most of them are made on pebbles that have been rounded, but evidently not by stream action. Much of the surface of these rounded pebbles is covered by a coating of calcium carbonate which when removed mechanically reveals a smooth polished surface but no semilunar hemicones such as would appear if the pebbles had been rolled in a stream. Similar polished limestone pebbles can be found in drip pools within caves in the area. Although the flaked surfaces are also weathered, it is clear that the flakes were removed after the pebbles had become rounded.

The limestone artifacts found in apparent associations with each other in the coarse orange silt in Square G10 will be described separately from the flaked pebbles found in the red silt inside the eastern chamber in Square J10. Possibly the two deposits had temporal correspondence, but unfortunately they are not stratigraphically connected across the rock sill in Square I10 at the entrance to the eastern chamber.

Two angular limestone fragments found next to each other embedded in the top of the orange silt between 45 and 50 cm below surface in Square G10 were not rounded by weathering. One is a thick tabular chopper (BA-CE-17/9) which measures 165 x 74 x 67 mm. It exhibits unidirectional use-flaking along one 120-mm-long excurvate edge which varies in angle from 40° to 90°. The other tabular fragment of limestone (BA-CE-17/8), which measures 119 x 68 x 35 mm with a rectangular outline, has been flaked unidirectionally along the shortest end, which has an edge angle of 60°. A large flake has more recently been removed to sharpen an otherwise use-battered edge.

A more-weathered subangular limestone fragment (BA-CE-17/12) was found in the coarse orange silt in Square G10 at a depth of 50 cm below surface. This rectangular tabular piece, measuring 125 x 83 x 40 mm, has several flake scars along a longitudinal 90° edge, and a few scars on two corners. At a higher level (40 cm below surface) but well embedded in the coarse orange silt in Square G10 was an oval subrounded limestone pebble (BA-CE-17/7) with a large flake removed from the pointed end. Four flake scars are present along an edge near the other end of this artifact. Many scratches are visible on one polished edge of this hammerstone, which measures 172 x 80 x 62 mm. A subrounded pebble chopping tool (BA-CE-17/13), found at a depth of 52 cm in the coarse orange silt in Square G10, has several flakes removed bifacially from the broadest convex edge. A blow on the pointed end of this well-used artifact, which measures 73 x 68 x 63 mm, removed a long blade-like flake.

Unfortunately the most obvious limestone pebble tool from great depth in the eastern chamber was recovered from near the wall in Square J10; and although found at a depth of 100–110 cm below surface, it could have fallen down the fissure that was present in this area. This rounded pebble chopper (BA-CE-17/32) is unifacially flaked and then use-battered at one end, which has an edge angle of 60°. The opposite end of this artifact, which measures 70 x 58 x 32 mm, also exhibits two flake scars. Another discoidal pebble tool (BA-CE-17/30) probably also came from the same zone at 90° cm depth in Square J10. Several flakes have been removed bidirectionally from the broad excurvate edge (with a 50° angle) of this artifact, which measures 107 x 87 x 37 mm.

The other flaked pebbles of limestone from the eastern chamber were found in the red silt deposit away from the area of the fissure. A weathered discoidal pebble tool (BA-CE-17/124) was bidirectionally flaked along one excurvate edge, and to a lesser extent on the opposite end. This artifact, which measures 83 x 68 x 26 mm, came from the 50–60 cm level in the red silt in Square J9. A similar tabular pebble chopper (BA-CE-17/125) of weathered limestone was found nearby in the same level within the red silt. This artifact, measuring 87 x 74 x 27 mm, has been flaked unidirectionally along one broad 40° edge to create a triangular outline. A rounded ovoid limestone pebble (BA-CE-17/134) has been flaked unidirectionally at both ends. The original weathered surface under the calcium carbonate coating is smooth and polished. This artifact, measuring 109 x 69 x 53 mm, came from the 70–80 cm level in the red silt in Square J9. A similar ovoid pebble from the same level has been intentionally split in half. The resulting thick flake (BA-CE-17/137), which measures 87 x 72 x 32 mm, appears to have been used around most of its periphery.

Stones Altered for Artistic Purposes

Several objects, the largest category of which are faceted chunks of ochre, can be described together as pieces representing artistic expression. The beautifully finished grooved axe, and the two fragmentary crystal projectile points which were originally bifacially flaked with great care, also could legitimately be included in this category; but they are described with other ground stone and flaked stone artifacts.

Probably the most distinctive object in this category is a lip ornament pecked and ground out of a calcite crystal. This artifact (BA-CE-17/42) was recovered in the upper 10 cm of the silt and ash deposit in Square J9, inside the eastern chamber; and it measures 14 x 8 x 7 mm. Originally it was rectangular in outline and cross-section, with parallel crystal facets at both ends. Although all surfaces have been ground, the rectangular cross-section was retained at the largest end. However, over 10 mm of the total length, the cross-section has been squared to a diameter of 7 mm, with rounded edges, produced first by careful pecking and then by grinding. The complete object is neither symmetrical nor polished, so it is possible that the piece was lost before it was finished.

An engraved but broken limestone object (BA-CE-17/75), measuring 26 x 23 x 11 mm, was found nearby in the same square and level in the eastern chamber. It appears to be the bit half of a tiny (ceremonial?) axe blade with use-flakes removed from both sides of the naturally bi-bevelled bit. One straight bi-bevelled edge is worn smooth. Evidently the suggestive shape of the object is natural; but the weathered surfaces were deliberately stained red, probably with hematite, after both sides had been engraved rather irregularly with basically the same design: a deep diagonal line extending from the same corner of the bit and presumably to the diagonally opposite corner before the object broke in half. Sets of roughly parallel irregular lines were then incised on either side of the center line at a different oblique angle. The design on one face was more deeply incised than on the other face. This carefully engraved object was then used and broken.

The most abundant evidence of artistic expression in the shelter is provided by the impressive panels of pictographs. Part of a panel of red designs over Square G10 apparently had spalled off, so everyone was alerted to look for painted limestone fragments in the sediments during excavation. One tabular fragment (dimensions 36 x 29 x 3 mm) was found in the 0–10 cm level in the G10/H10 baulk. Concentrated areas of powdered hematite adhere to the high spots on the most weathered face of this probable piece of painted wall spall (BA-CE-17/29).

A tabular limestone fragment measuring 68 x 40 x 27 mm, possibly a wall spall, was recovered from the silt and ash zone in the 0–10 cm level of Square E9; and this artifact (BA-CE-17/306) has a cross-hatched design in black applied with a pencil or crayon. This type of pictograph is common on the walls at the west end of the Abrigo do Pilão, but fine line black designs are not visible immediately above Square E9. Evidently the artifact had been transported as a piece of mobile art. The original cross-hatched design appears to extend beyond the margins of the rock. Subsequently a straight line applied with a thicker crayon was drawn diagonally across the original design.

Another tabular fragment marked with black crayon was found in the 30–40 cm level in Square E8. This artifact (BA-CE-17/233) weathered on both faces to a wedge-shaped edge which was notched by flaking. One end has also been unidirectionally notched from the opposite direction. A small part of one face between the flaked areas exhibits a few apparently random lines drawn with a black crayon after the piece was flaked. Some reddish orange pigment adheres to the high spots on the same face and especially along the worn wedge-shaped edge. The opposite face appears to have some randomly incised lines. Probably this artifact was used as a piece to test pigments.

Pieces of black pencil or crayon have never been identified in the excavations, although there is a locally abundant form of crystalline limestone which creates a black streak. Manganese nodules could have been used if mixed with a binding material. The paint is too dark and durable to be pure charcoal; although charcoal mixed with another ingredient, perhaps wax, might yield the desired consistency.

Five facetted pieces of red ochre and one of limonite were excavated. Very likely these materials were used for mixing the pigments for the red and yellow pictographs on the walls. The paint could also have been applied to decorate the body. The rhomboidal piece of light-orange limonite with a triangular cross-section has four ground flat facets with clear parallel striations, and one broken end. This artifact (BA-CE-17/284) which measures 23 x 10 x 8 mm, was found in the 10 cm level of the silt and ash zone in Square D9, in the central part of the main shelter. The irregular hematite chunks vary in hue from a dark metallic red to an orange-red. The darkest piece (BA-CE-17/274), found in the 20–30 cm level of Square H10, exhibits some sorted bedding on a broken edge. Two faces of this chunk, which measures 31 x 16 x 12 mm, exhibit striations and parallel sets of scratches. A roughly rectangular dark red chunk (BA-CE-17/371) measuring 31 x 20 x 13 mm was found in the 0–10 cm level in Square G9. This artifact has short grooved and polished facets on four edges and a larger area of one convex face. The rest of the surfaces are unaltered. A small irregular fragment of reddish orange hematite (BA-CE-17/280), which measures 14 x 7 x 4 mm, was found in the 10–20 cm level of Square H10. This artifact exhibits a small scraped facet on one convex edge. A small tabular piece of hematite (BA-CE-17/158) measuring 13 x 12 x 5 mm was found in the 10–20 cm level in Square F8. All edges and faces of this piece are worn smooth, although there are no surface marks. A larger tabular hematite chunk, measuring 23 x 25 x 8 mm, has one flat face exhibiting cross-hatched grinding striations and polished edges. The surface of the more irregular face has been gouged with a high-angled flake. The edges of this artifact (BA-CE-17/394), from the 10–20 cm level in Square G9, are unaltered.

OTHER ARTIFACTS

Ceramics

Approximately 120 potsherds were collected at the Abrigo do Pilão, and all but two came from the 0–10 cm level. Potsherds were most abundant in Square F8 (23% of the total collection) near the rear wall in the alcove of the main shelter; in Square F9 (11% of the total), also in the alcove; and in Square H10 (9%) in the main shelter adjacent on the west.

The major group of sherds (84% of the total collection) are distinctly thick in section (range 14 mm to 8 mm; mode 12 mm). The pots were incompletely fired: cores of sherds are dark grey or black, with oxidation penetrating only 1 to 2 mm from the exterior and/or interior surfaces. Some cores appear to be platy in structure, but most are homogeneous. The temper appears to be a fine quartz grit, with particles homogeneous in size; the tempering is very light. The surfaces of many sherds were blackened by fire and ash, and it may be assumed that vessels were used in cooking. Surface finishing was somewhat irregular: a few sherds have broad shallow irregular grooves obviously left by shaping fingers. Apparently all sherds were originally slipped; and in cases where the slip has flaked off, one can see marks of heavy brushing of the surface underneath, apparently with grass in irregular strokes, which often dragged fragments of temper. Vessels were slipped on the interior and exterior surface, and some sherds have traces of stick polishing. Due to the discoloration caused by ash or burning, it is difficult to determine the original color of the slip. One sherd is orange/red, nine are a mottled orange/grey/black (indicating smudging in the firing stage), about 25 sherds have a buff slip, and the others are too grey from burning to determine the previous coloration of the slip. One sherd has a black slip, and one sherd is painted black on buff.

For this thick ware, three sections of rim indicate wide-mouthed jars or bowls with incurving rim (Figure 5-17a). These rims are simple, with rounded lips. A more complex rim was thickened on the exterior. One rim, outward-turning, is likely from a narrow-mouthed large jar. One body sherd preserves a small pointed lug about 5 mm wide, 18 mm in length, and 5 mm high.

The remaining 19 sherds in the Abrigo do Pilão collection were first sorted out on the basis of relative thinness. Differences in temper and surface finish led to further sorting. Two sherds with pocked surfaces appear to have fine calcite temper. They are both unslipped, with smoothed interior surface and rough exterior surface. The larger and thicker sherd (8 mm in thickness) has a reddish interior surface and grey exterior surface which has been roughly smoothed with a stick. The smaller sherd, only 4 mm thick, is grey on the interior and exterior surfaces, with smooth interior and brushed exterior. Two other sherds have light micaceous temper. Both are dark grey, with smooth interior surface and eroded exterior surface. They range in thickness from 5 to 7 mm. The remaining 15 sherds have a light grit temper, with angular particles of quartz up to 1 mm in diameter. Seven have a well-polished interior and exterior slip varying from light orange to grey in color. Finishing was rough, however, with most sherds showing grooves and pits from dragged particles of temper. Cores are grey. The thickness varies from 6 mm to 5 mm. One rim sherd is simple and incurving, with rounded lip; another is simple and straighter (Figure 5-17b). One basal sherd indicates a ring base about 5 mm high. Four of these sherds, including the ring base, were found in the 0–10 cm level in Square I10, at the entrance to the eastern chamber. The remaining five sherds are similar in thickness, temper, and core color. Two have a fine grey slip on the interior, and the rest have smoothed interiors; but the exterior surface of all five sherds is unslipped and brushed, with fine shallow horizontal grooves. Two of these five sherds came from below 10 cm in the ash and silt deposit: one from the 10–20 cm level; and one from the 40–50 cm level in fissure fill at the rear wall, in Square G8. The latter is a large rim sherd, a simple incurving rim with pointed lip, suggesting a large open bowl (Figure 5-17b).

Three unusual fired clay objects found in the ash and silt deposits may have been baked accidentally. A small cylindrical fired clay coil (BA-CE-17/267) with fingerprints on it was found in the 20–30 cm level in Square F9. The coil measures 18 x 8 x 6 mm. The other two fired clay specimens are roughly rectangular fragments with

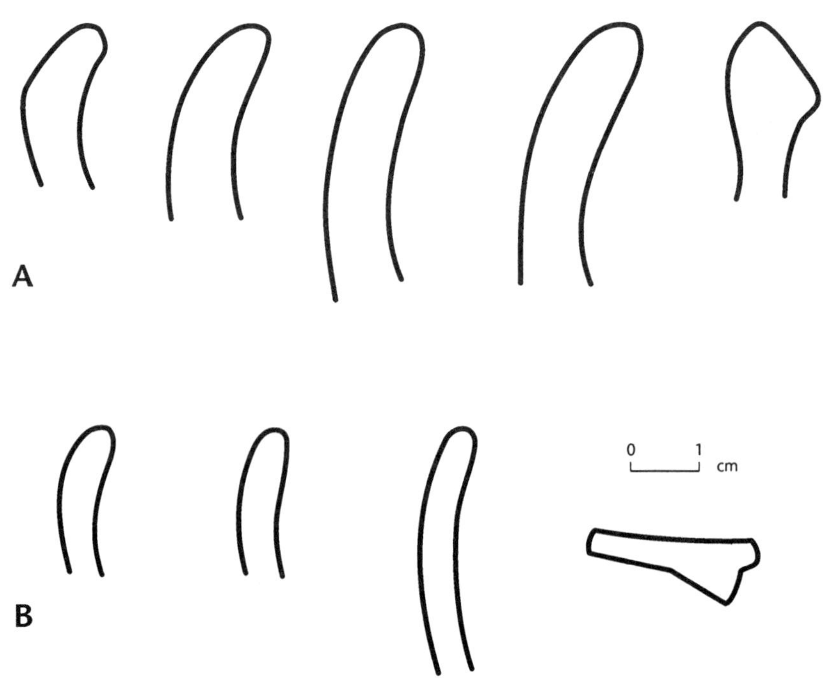

Figure 5-17. Ceramics. **A)** profiles of rim sherds of thick ware; **B)** profiles of rim sherds and basal sherd of thin ware.

one concave face that has been striated or brushed. The opposite, more-irregular face of each specimen exhibits striations and some wear. One (BA-CE-17/86) came from the 10–20 cm level in Square J9, the other (BA-CE-17/374) from the 30–40 cm level in the same square. The former specimen measures 16 x 12 x 5 mm, the latter specimen 26 x 13 x 8 mm. Their function is a mystery.

Shell Artifacts

Utilized Mussel Shell

Freshwater mussels *(Diplodon diplodontus)* require permanent water. The nearest permanent stream with mussels is the Rio Verde, about 30 km west of the Abrigo do Pilão. Many small fragments of mussel shell were encountered in the ash and silt deposits of the Abrigo do Pilão. Of these, 73 were selected as exhibiting some evidence of use, and were called artifacts (distribution in Table 5-2). Undoubtedly all of the shells had been transported to the site for use. They could have served as cups and spoons, but their primary function may have been scraping roots. Wesley Hurt performed some experiments using mussel shells for scraping the skins from roots; and he was able to replicate the wear patterns he observed on the valves from the Abrigo de Valdemar, where a larger number of classifiable specimens was recovered. The shells would wear out quite rapidly, through heavy use; but useful edges could be regenerated by knocking a hole in the center of a valve and later by snapping the worn shell into segments. Triangular segments were commonly found; and if these triangular segments have worn concavities on their apices, probably the shell had previously been perforated.

Thus it is possible to establish a series of types of shell artifact based upon the stages of utilization. Class 1 is whole valves with one worn edge (six examples). Class 2 is heavily worn whole valves with concave worn edges (three examples). Class 3 is perforated valves (one example). Class 4 is snapped fragments not exhibiting subsequent use (six examples). Class 5 is triangular segments with worn edges or apices (28 examples). Class 6 is triangular segments with worn concave apices (15 examples). Class 7 is miscellaneous fragments showing wear (14 examples). Class 8 is small fragments too broken up to exhibit use (not counted as artifacts).

Only 14 valves in the collection were complete enough to make a count of left and right valves. Interestingly, there are equal numbers of each. There is a significant variation in size, showing that valves of all sizes, at least from a minimum of 53 mm long with 2-mm-thick margins, were useful. Some of the thick-walled fragments (up to 6 mm thick) must have belonged to valves at least twice as large as the minimum size. In fact, valves with thick-walled margins may not have been as useful as the thinner valves because the external surfaces on the large valves are not as rough. For scraping, the overlapping growth lines of the broad end opposite the umbo were most useful. The valve was held with the thumb inside the concave surface, and the external surface of the broad end was pushed along the surface of the root in order to scrape off the skin. The margin of the broad end and adjacent growth layers on the external face gradually flake off with such use. Very few specimens exhibit the expectable sets of striations on the external face extending from the broad end toward the umbo. As the striations were probably caused by grit adhering to the root, the paucity of striations suggests that the roots were washed before they were scraped. Thus the 10–20 cm level of Square F9 yielded a snapped and subsequently unused fragment of a broad end of a shell (BA-CE-17/129) which exhibits the clearest striations as well as typical flaking of the growth layers on the external surface. Only one completely perforated valve (BA-CE-17/225) was found, in the 10–20 cm level in Square E8. It also exhibits a few striations and heavy marginal flaking.

The remainder of the outer margins of many valves also are often worn. Such wear could have been caused by use as spoons or containers before the shells served as root scrapers. Such wear could also have been caused during transport from the river. Some of the margins of shells also exhibit characteristic rodent gnaw marks. Several of the shell artifacts have been calcined grey, but subsequent fires situated near them in the sediments probably account for such alteration.

Utilized Gastropod Shell

For a short while after some scratches were noted on the external surface of a fragment of a large gastropod shell (BA-CE-17/45) from the 0–10 cm level in Square J9, other similar fragments were carefully examined and collected. The edges of four small fragments (BA-CE-17/61, 62, 63, and 72), all from the 0–10 cm level in Square J9, seemed to show evidence of wear, as if they also might have been used for scraping something. However, after continued observation it was concluded that a great many gastropod shell fragments exhibit the same characteristics. As the gastropod shells do not have overlapping growth lines that create a useful rough scraping surface, they probably would not serve as root scrapers; although they could have been used for some other purpose. The catalogued fragments have been saved for further study and comparison, although it was decided that examination of all the thousands of gastropod shell fragments was too time-consuming for the present. Such a study could be made, however, as all gastropod shell was collected at the request of the Setor de Malacologia of the Museu Nacional as a stratigraphically complete series from a major prehistoric occupation site.

Table 5-2. Distribution of Lithic, Bone, and Shell Artifacts in Sediments at the Abrigo do Pilão.

	Utilized Vein Quartz Fragments	Utilized Quartz Crystal Flakes	Utilized Chert Flakes and Chunks	Utilized Quartzite Flakes	Utilized Limestone Flakes
Main shelter					
Ash and silt zone					
0–10 cm	19	8	16	9	3
10–20 cm	9	5	1	3	0
20–30 cm	4	1	3	4	0
30–40 cm	6	0	5	4	1
40–50 cm	5	0	2	0	0
50–60 cm	0	0	0	0	0
totals	43	14	27	20	4
Red/orange silt (disintegrated travertine) in Square G10					
40–50 cm	0	0	0	0	0
Eastern chamber					
Ash and silt zone					
0–10 cm	16	11	11	5	5
10–20 cm	6	2	4	3	1
20–30 cm	3	0	3	4	0
30–40 cm	4	4	5	0	0
40–50 cm	1	0	1	1	0
50–60 cm	2	0	0	1	0
totals	32	17	24	14	6
Red silt zone	0	0	0	0	0
Infilled fissure in Square J10	1	0	1	0	0

Bone and Antler Artifacts

The main reason for selecting for excavation rockshelters formed in limestone rather than in non-calcareous rock is because bone should be better preserved. Unfortunately, although much bone was preserved at this site, peculiar conditions in the Abrigo do Pilão made it impossible to examine the original surfaces of most bone fragments for evidence of workmanship. Certainly, many more than 13 bone artifacts, all that could be identified, must be present among the thousands of bones, mostly fragmented, that were recovered from the ash and silt zone. The problem is that wood ash and limestone dust, which constituted the bulk of the cultural deposit, became baked onto the surfaces of most stones and bones by the heat from subsequent nearby fires. Coated silicious stones are easy to clean by soaking them in a bath of muriatic acid; but limestone must be dipped very quickly; and experiments with dipping coated bones resulted in erosion of the original surface of the bone. Attempts to remove the coating mechanically with a fingernail sometimes flaked off the outer layer of bone. Surface alterations, including cuts, scrape marks, and grinding marks, are visible on eight artifacts, half of which happened to escape the process of coating; while relevant small sections of the other four artifacts were successfully cleaned mechanically. Five completely coated pieces tentatively were called artifacts because of their suggestive shape.

In addition, one of several segments of long bones of medium-sized mammals (probably deer or peccary) exhibiting green-bone spiral fracture, was called an artifact (BA-CE-17/411) because it retains three negative flake scars on one edge where the bone was forcefully struck to break it open. This fragment, which measures 81 x 14 x 6 mm, came from the 20–30 cm level in Square F8. Deliberate fracturing of long bones could serve for marrow extraction and/or to create segments useful for the manufacture of bone artifacts. The baked coating on the outer surface prevents identification of any alteration marks which would have been created if the piece were detritus of manufacture.

One probable phalange fragment (BA-CE-17/410) from the 0–10 cm level in Square K9 exhibits two short

Limestone Pounders or Choppers	Flaked Limestone Fragments	Pebble Hammerstones	Mullers or Pestles	Axes	Utilized Mussel Shell	Bone Artifacts	Misc.	Total
7	1	4	2	1	31	3	3	107
4	4	1	2	0	8	2	3	42
1	3	1	1	0	1	1	2	22
2	2	1	1	1	0	0	0	23
2	6	1	1	0	2	0	0	19
1	0	0	0	0	0	0	0	1
17	16	8	7	2	42	6	8	214
1	2	0	0	0	0	0	0	3
5	1	3	1	2	22	2	8	92
6	3	4	1	0	3	2	0	35
0	0	0	0	0	1	2	0	13
4	1	0	0	0	2	1	1	22
3	0	0	0	0	2	0	0	8
1	0	0	0	0	0	0	0	4
19	5	7	2	2	30	7	9	174
0	4	0	0	0	0	0	0	4
1	1	0	0	0	1	0	0	5

deep transverse cuts (6 mm long) near the articular end, which has been chewed by rodents. One V-shaped cut looks like a butchering cut, but the fact that the other incision was caused by a series of saw strokes suggests the possibility that someone was trying to cut off the articular end to use the hollow section for some purpose. However, the artifact, which measures 37 x 12 x 7 mm, fragmented longitudinally with a desiccation break before the end could be severed. Another artifact (BA-CE-17/35) is a segment of rib, measuring 76 x 16 x 2 mm, which was cut squarely and snapped at both ends. One thin edge looks slightly chewed. This uncoated artifact, from the 0–10 cm level in Square G9, is the remains of someone's meal.

Artifact BA-CE-17/403 is a fragment of a medium-sized mammal bone which measures 18 x 11 x 3 mm. It exhibits many short scratches against the grain of the outer surface of the bone. One end of this artifact appears to have been flaked by impact, as if it were a projectile-point fragment. The bone, subsequently calcined, came from the 10–20 cm level in the G9/G10 baulk. A somewhat more definite projectile point (BA-CE-17/116) came from the 0–10 cm level in the same baulk area. This bone, which measures 42 x 10 x 4 mm, is fresh and uncoated, so all evidence of workmanship is clearly visible. It broke with a curving spiral fracture obliquely across the grain. The opposite broken edge was then carefully scraped to make a symmetrical pointed end, the tip of which subsequently broke off with an impact blow. The unaltered base and basal edges retain green-bone breaks. The external surface and both edges near the tip end are polished by use.

A probable base of another bone splinter point (BA-CE-17/200), from the 10–20 cm level in Square K9, was recognized by the presence of a set of grooves across the grain on both broken edges at a point 10 mm from a symmetrically broken pointed tip, as if the fragment had been jammed into a socket as far as it would go. This entire pointed tip is more worn and eroded than the remainder of the piece, the dimensions of which are 28 x 6 x 2 mm. The opposite end is roughly broken, perhaps by impact. There is no evidence of grinding or scraping, although possibly the edges had been flaked in order to fit the socket.

One cylindrical projectile point (BA-CE-17/4) evidently was scraped carefully into shape. It measures 46 x 8 x 7 mm. The relatively freshly broken tip of this piece from the 10–20 cm level in Square H10 reveals solid dense bone. The entire base end was heavily coated with baked ash/silt after the base was roughly broken. The 20–30 cm level in Square J9 yielded another bone point (BA-CE-17/88) with a flattened oval cross-section, and measuring 48 x 9 x 3 mm. Although cancellous bone is present at the base end, a relatively fresh broken tip end reveals solid bone. The remaining surface is coated with baked ash/silt. A similar coating covers the entire surface of artifact BA-CE-17/89, which was found in the same area and level. It also appears to have been scraped into a flattened oval cross-section, but the presence of an asymmetrical single shoulder and a blunt point suggests that it is the base end of a point. The remaining fragment measures 28 x 8 x 3 mm. Although completely coated with ash/silt, artifact BA-CE-17/44 appears to be a symmetrical point tip which split longitudinally upon impact. Its original cross-section would have been oval, and its present dimensions are 22 x 15 x 3 mm. It was recovered from the 10–20 cm level in Square J9.

The remaining three bone artifacts are evidently awls. Two right ulnae of deer exhibit evidence of workmanship despite the extensive baked ash/silt coating. Artifact BA-CE-17/104, which measures 62 x 21 x 8 mm, was recovered from the 30–40 cm level in Square J9. The dorsal ridge appears to have been bevelled to create a pointed tip which broke during use and again during excavation. Two parallel longitudinal incisions are present on the lateral surface near the broken tip.

The use-broken tip of the other ulna awl (BA-CE-17/412) exhibits two sets of parallel oblique incisions on the medial side of the dorsal ridge near the broken edge. The remainder of the surfaces of this calcined artifact, which measures 49 x 21 x 7 mm, are covered with a coating of baked ash/silt. It was found in the 0–10 cm level of Square E8. The remaining bone artifact (BA-CE-17/409) is a short but apparently complete deer antler tine measuring 57 x 7 x 7 mm. It features overlapping scrape marks near the tip end, the only surface not coated with baked ash/silt. It came from the 0–10 cm level in Square K9.

DISCUSSION AND CONCLUSIONS

At the time of discovery, Abrigo do Pilão was thought to be the most likely site in the Central region to provide a long occupation sequence because it appeared to have considerable depth of deposit, and it was a large overhang set high enough above the valley floor so as not to be subject to periodic inundation by valley floods during storms. Also it was easy to enter, and the living area was not only ample but quite level. The fact that it was within a few meters of a low pass across an otherwise formidable limestone *serra* would also have been an important consideration for groups of people who might plan to rendezvous somewhere in the area. In addition, the eastern chamber provided extra shelter and a convenient hiding place to cache valuable objects.

Excavation seemed to confirm our expectation that we had a long occupation sequence, although there was surprisingly little evidence for technological change throughout the main zone of occupation, which consisted largely of culturally deposited wood ash mixed with silt and some rubble. There was no evidence of natural stratigraphic breaks; and there seemed to be little else than the addition of potsherds, polished stone axes, and evidence for art (painting and engraving) to distinguish the upper thin ceramic zone from the much-thicker preceramic deposits.

We were also aware that the evidence for hunting medium-sized mammals was largely restricted to the preceramic zone of ash and silt. Our working hypothesis in the field was that the occupants of the shelter were always mainly foragers, but that in late prehistoric times an emphasis on hunting available game gave way to supplementing the foraging subsistence with crops; although only circumstantial evidence for horticulture, like the stone axes, seemed definite, as the corn cobs found in the surface dust on the site may be historic in age. We were surprised, however, when the radiocarbon dates indicated that there was a very intensive occupation between 9600 and 8800 yr B.P., after which time the shelter apparently was not used until about 900 years ago. It remains a mystery why for such a long time people did not use this previously favored locality. The question of a middle-Holocene hiatus in the occupation of cave and rockshelter sites in the Central area will be discussed in the final Review and Discussion section of this report.

The primary purpose of the Projeto Central was to locate evidence for human occupation during the Pleistocene. The most intensive occupation of Abrigo do Pilão was during the early Holocene, but some evidence was found for earlier occupations. Unfortunately, however, these earlier occupations are not datable except by relative stratigraphy because few organic remains were preserved in the orange zone of disintegrated travertine stratigraphically beneath the silt and ash zone in the main sector of the shelter, or in the red silt zone beneath the silt and ash zone in the eastern chamber.

The limestone bedrock in the Central area is quite dense and homogeneous. As the only fossils are a few algae and there are few bedding planes, the rock flakes with a good conchoidal fracture. Although the flaked edges are much softer than any silicate, steep edges nevertheless would have been quite useful for many purposes, including cutting meat, bark and other plant fibres, and preparing hides and sinew. As usually sharp-edged rubble was readily available for many purposes without flaking, most artifacts were undoubtedly expediency tools picked up and used at the spur of the moment. Obviously, especially when a fair amount of roof fall is present, it would be difficult to recognize most limestone expediency tools, especially after chemical weathering had eroded the surfaces. Gradually, however, we became aware of limestone fragments which did not appear to be roof fall; and which often had elusive but sometimes suggestive and occasionally conclusive evidence for use.

Most of the limestone artifacts, many of which were crudely flaked, came from the dry silt and ash zone which retarded chemical weathering and allowed recognition of conclusive evidence. In the underlying orange silt in the main part of the shelter, carbonic acid had attacked the flaked surfaces more severely; and we were often unsure whether or not an object had been flaked, although two chert flakes and one quartzite flake were definite. As it turned out, in the case of the red silt zone in the east chamber, we were at first perhaps overly careful as we often discarded questionable pieces that looked like they might have been flaked. Gradually, however, we began to recognize limestone flakes with definite force bulbs, and several rounded pebbles with relatively sharp flaked edges. Later our hunch that these were flaked pebble tools appeared to be confirmed when we discovered that the red silt in the eastern chamber contained several rounded limestone pebbles covered with a calcium carbonate coating, which when removed mechanically revealed smooth polished cortical surfaces, which probably had been formed in drip pools in caves. Flakes clearly had been removed from one edge and/or an end to form pebble choppers and chopping tools. However, clear evidence of use for chopping or pounding was found on only one of these pebble tools from the red silt zone. The stratigraphic separation plus the fact that it is a distinctive pebble and flake-tool industry which did not persist into the overlying ash and silt zone combine to suggest that the limestone pebble tools from the red silt zone were used significantly earlier than the early-Holocene occupation 9500 years ago. Future archaeologists working in the area should test our hypothesis that there was a Pleistocene occupation of the region which was characterised by pebble tools and flakes. Meanwhile, it may be possible to obtain a uranium/thorium date on the calcium carbonate coatings of the pebble tools from the red silt zone.

Evidence was also found for another early occupation on the surface of the orange silt immediately underlying the ash and silt zone in the main area of the shelter. Intentionally edge-trimmed flake tools are rare; however, eight large jasper or quartzite flakes with prominent bulbs had been unidirectionally trimmed to form scrapers. With two exceptions, all came from near the base of the ash and silt zone, or were lying in the orange zone of disintegrated travertine. Most of these distinctive flake tools, including the two found in higher levels, had orange silt adhering to their surfaces, indicating that they had been moved from their original orange silt matrix by later occupants of the ash and silt zone. Although the sample is quite small, evidence suggests the possibility that all of these artifacts originally belonged to a single assemblage deposited on the weathered surface of the travertine before the ash and silt zone began to accumulate. Evidently later occupants, accustomed to using expediency tools rather than carefully flaking their own artifacts, often picked up and reused the large flakes with such useful edges.

The flaked tools in the main early-Holocene occupation, dated between 9600 and 8800 yr B.P., are quite different in character. The working edges of these small flakes and chunks were never intentionally trimmed, even when the material was of good-quality quartzite or quartz crystal. The sharp edges of these artifacts were simply utilized, a practice which sometimes removed flakes irregularly in an unpatterned manner. Utilized flakes and chunks of quartz, quartzite, chert, and limestone, in addition to limestone pounders, choppers, and hammerstones, constitute the undistinguished lithic industry during this period. Utilized river mussel shells and a few bone artifacts complete this early assemblage. To judge by the deposition of 40 to 50 cm of wood ash in a complex series of overlapping and intermixed hearths, occupation of the shelter was quite intensive for about 800 years.

The simple flaked-lithic industry shows no improvement in the much-later ceramic level. There is still no evidence of intentional retouch, although ground stone axes, pestles, and mullers were added to the artifact assemblage, as well as pottery. The penchant for reusing artifacts also continued. Two beautifully bifacially retouched but broken quartz crystal projectile points were collected elsewhere and put to use as scrapers.

The significantly higher yield of artifacts in the ceramic zone does not necessarily mean that occupation of the shelter was even more intensive. Several of the most impressive ground stone artifacts appear to have been deliberately cached in the rear, and not broken or lost. Perhaps the shelter was used only occasionally by horticulturalists who camped in the shelter as a very temporary residence, in contrast to the earlier more intensive occupation of the shelter which resulted in massive deposition of wood ash.

In sum, four discrete occupations of the Abrigo do Pilão have been recognized. The final occupation, about 900 years ago, was probably by horticulturalists. The most intensive occupation, between 9600 and 8800 years ago, was by hunters and collectors. Two proposed earlier occupations were also presumably by hunters and collectors during the very early Holocene and/or late Pleistocene.

Chapter 6
Toca do Cosmos

INTRODUCTION

Toca do Cosmos is located in the southeastern part of the large *municipio* of Xique-Xique, approximately 10 km north-northeast of the community of Rio Verde, and about 1 km east of the small settlement of Guaxanim (identified as São José on the Rio Verde 1:100,000 topographic map, Folha SC-23-Z-B-VI). The *toca* is in an area of dry *caatinga* forest; but situated less than 2 km west of the Rio Verde, a small but permanent stream (Figure 6-1a) which flows from a canyon west of the Serra Azul through a low valley to the Rio São Francisco, which it entered about 50 km to the north, before construction of the Sobradinho dam flooded the lower reaches.

Toca do Cosmos, one of the few cave sites known in the Rio Verde area, was first located and named by the authors at the end of their field season in nearby Central in July 1984. The site is named for the spectacular rock art which graces the flat white ceiling of the eastern sector of the cavern, with designs in red, pink, purple, or orange colors portraying an apparent comet, a number of rayed or spoked discs, starbursts, and other probable celestial elements (Figures 6-5a, b). The rock art, recorded in 1984 by Museu Nacional personnel under the field direction of Tania Andrade Lima, is to be reported upon elsewhere.

Toca do Cosmos is situated on the edge of an open wooded depression about 150 m in diameter, apparently formed by collapse of part of a low flat horizontal outcrop of ancient weathered cherty limestone which extends as an open, very sparsely vegetated landscape for a distance of about 1/4 km to the south and southwest of the *toca*. The site is a solution cavern, actually part of a large and very complex cave system which is enclosed within the limestone outcrop. Access to this cave system is not only through the broad overhang at Toca do Cos-

Figure 6-1. A) the Rio Verde, near the crossing of highway BA-052. **B)** cave sites in the Rio Verde area. The high trees in the distance to the left mark the vertical shaft into Toca da Gameleira; the entrance to Toca do Cosmos is marked by the trees on the right edge of the limestone outcrop.

mos but also through the vertical-walled opening of Toca da Gameleira, which is situated within the limestone formation about 100 m to the southwest (Figure 6-1b). The two *tocas* are connected by an irregular partially silt-filled and dark but passable tunnel which leads off southwestward from a ledge between the upper and lower shelters of the Toca do Cosmos. It appears that the cave system was formed by water solution acting upon a thick bed of friable vesicular limestone underlying a 3-meter-thick bed of harder limestone which forms the upper edge of the overhang. Although there are many tunnels of varying size and the cavern roof and floor are deeply eroded by water, no stalagmites or stalactites occur in the cave system.

Toca do Cosmos, which faces northeastward into the depression, consists of an upper shelter and a lower shelter, roofed by the same rock overhang at the edge of the limestone outcrop (map, Figure 6-2; Figure 6-3a), and joined by a narrow rock ledge which drops off vertically (about 4 m) on the west side of the lower shelter. The upper shelter is the larger area. It has a maximum length of approximately 34 m and an average width of 14 m, with several broad low-roofed and silt-choked tunnels leading southwestward from the rear. The rough irregular ceiling of the upper shelter is very low, much less than 2 m above the sediment fill in most places; and most of the upper shelter is dark, as the front or north side of the upper shelter is walled off by very large vertical-standing limestone blocks (Figure 6-3b). The main access to the interior, providing the most light, is an opening about 3 m wide, with a short talus slope, at the east end of the upper shelter. There are two other openings in the wall of limestone blocks to the west; but they are very narrow, and lead down very steep talus slopes into dark areas. The surface area of the sediment fill in the lower shelter, about 4 m lower in elevation than the surface of the fill in the upper shelter, was smaller in area, with the sediment extending into a low-roofed and progressively narrowing and darker funnel-shaped tunnel about 20 m long and 6 m wide at maximum; but a high and broad opening to this lower sector of the cavern provides light to a large area in front of this tunnel (Figure 6-4a, b). Access to the level silt-covered floor of the lower shelter is down a steep rock talus at the entrance. The flat horizontal white ceiling of the lower shelter provided the easel for the rock art, reached from irregular shelves of light-colored vesicular limestone on either side of the sediment-filled tunnel.

The authors conducted excavations in Toca do Cosmos from 14 June until 1 July 1985. Although most of the

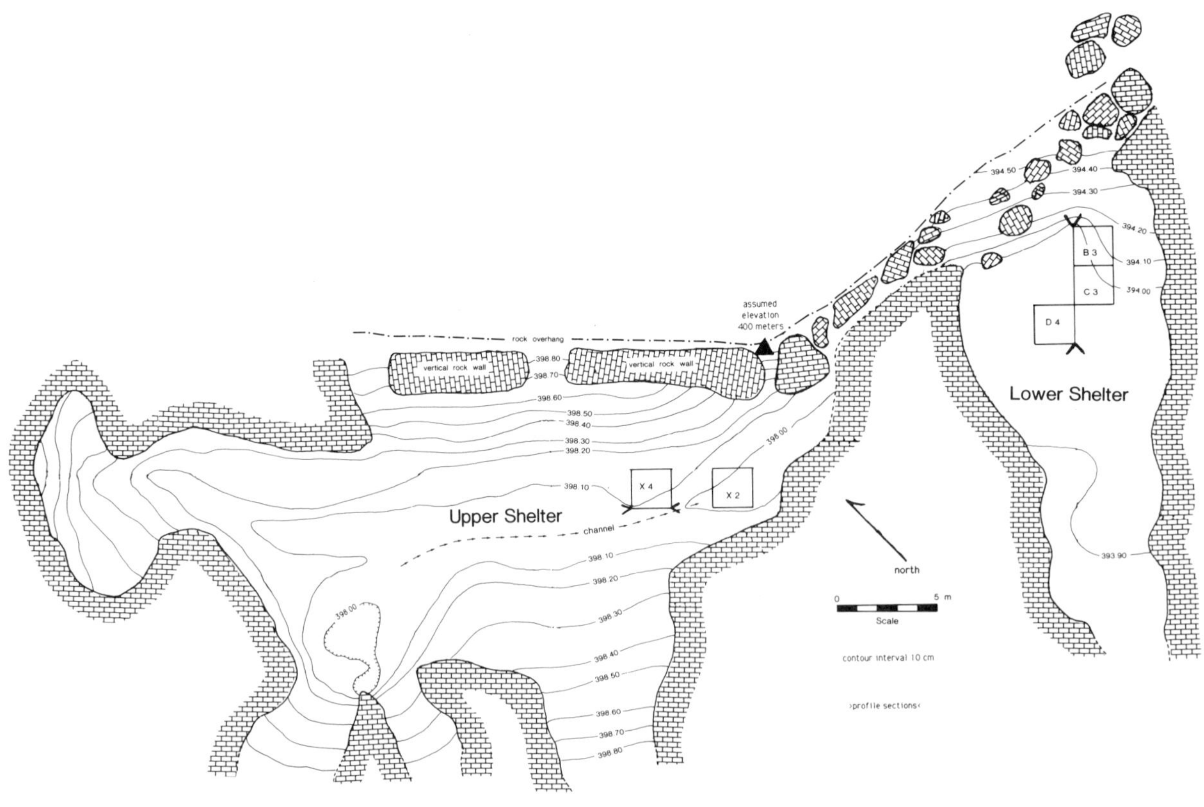

Figure 6-2. Plan of the sediment-filled areas of Toca do Cosmos.

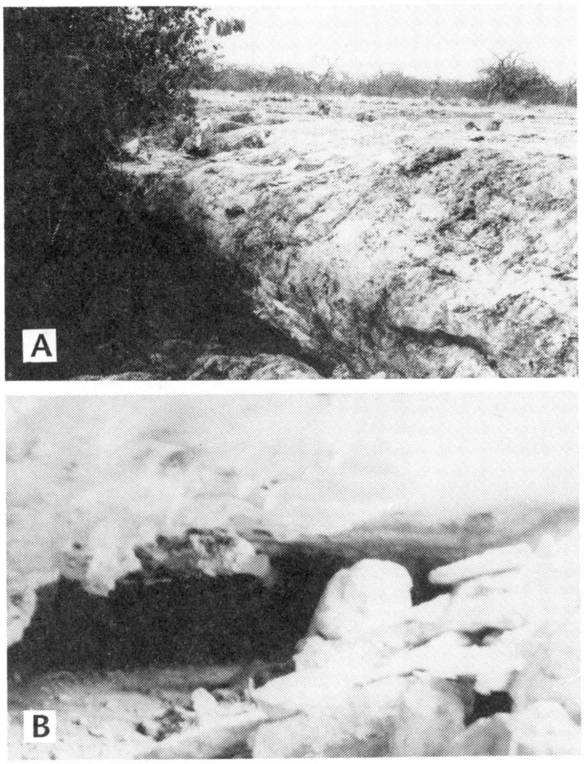

Figure 6-3. A) entrance to Toca do Cosmos, on the edge of the limestone outcrop. **B)** interior of the upper shelter.

upper shelter appeared too dark and cramped to favor habitation, there was abundant evidence of human occupation in shallow washed channels on the surface of the fill: numerous valves of freshwater mussels brought from the river, a few heavy quartzite artifacts, and a few potsherds. In mid-June, just after the close of the 1985 rainy season, the fill in the upper shelter appeared drier than the lower shelter, so the Toca do Cosmos excavations were begun in the former area. A baseline was laid out the length of the upper shelter, to parallel its north wall; and the sediment-filled area of the upper shelter was mapped. Five 2-meter squares were laid out along this baseline in the best-lighted area, near the east entrance. It was originally planned to excavate the five squares in alternate order; but sterile deposits were soon encountered in Squares X2 and X4; and the focus of work moved to the lower shelter, where four squares were laid out in the level area at the foot of the rock talus at the entrance (map, Figure 6-2). Three of these squares (B3, C3, and D4) were excavated.

Excavation of the squares in both the upper and lower shelters was carried out to bedrock in arbitrary 10-cm levels, using a trowel in soft deposits and a hand-pick in the more consolidated zones. In Squares X2 and X4 a pick was used to excavate the compact sediments in the deeper levels. All material was examined on a 4-mm screen. Mussel shell, gastropod shell, and bone fragments were collected as well as flakes, potsherds, and lithic artifacts. At the conclusion of the work the walls of excavation units were profiled and photographed.

STRATIGRAPHY

Natural Stratigraphy

Sedimentary deposits in the upper shelter and the lower shelter at Toca do Cosmos proved to be quite different in character. In the upper shelter excavation units (Squares

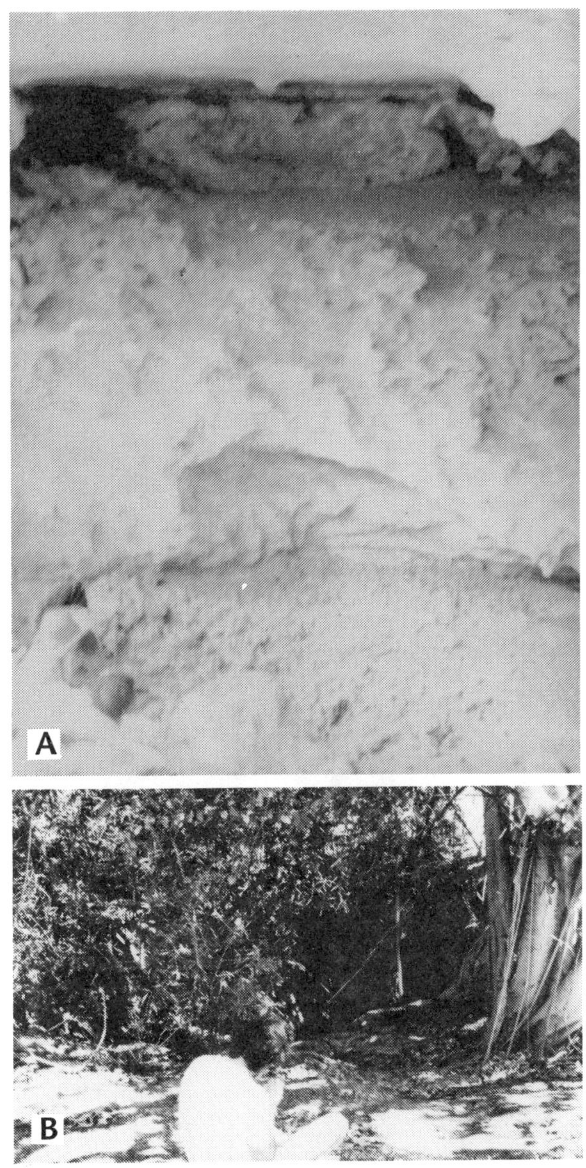

Figure 6-4. A) interior of the lower shelter of Toca do Cosmos. **B)** entrance to the lower shelter.

X2 and X4), there was a zone of brown silt about 25 cm in maximum thickness overlying a deep deposit of sterile compact orange/brown silt. In the lower shelter excavation units (Squares B3, C3, and D4) a talus slope of rock fragments sloping steeply from the mouth of the cavern extended under a zone of brown silt with scattered rock fragments.

In the upper shelter excavation units, an irregular undulating bedrock floor was reached at depths averaging between 110 cm and 150 cm below surface, although in some areas the rock floor was deeply fissured, in one case to a depth of 230 cm below surface. The rough rock floor was coated with a deposit of compact coarse grey sandy silt, apparently disintegrated rock. This coarse grey sandy silt filled the deepest and narrowest fissures in the bedrock floor.

Over this bedrock floor in the upper shelter was a massive deposit of hard dry compact porous orange/brown silt which varied in thickness from 110 cm to 200 cm (profile, Figure 6-6). This deposit appeared fairly homogeneous, although small ironstone nodules and calcareous concretions increased in frequency with depth more than 70 cm below surface. There were also some scattered small fragments of chert, deeply weathered. A few very large subangular limestone slabs appeared in a horizontal position in the basal zones, below 100 cm depth. The dry compact orange/brown silt was sterile of cultural material and even organic remains: no bone or gastropod shell was found in this zone. The upper surface of the orange/brown silt zone was irregular in contour; and in Square X4 a deep narrow fissure,

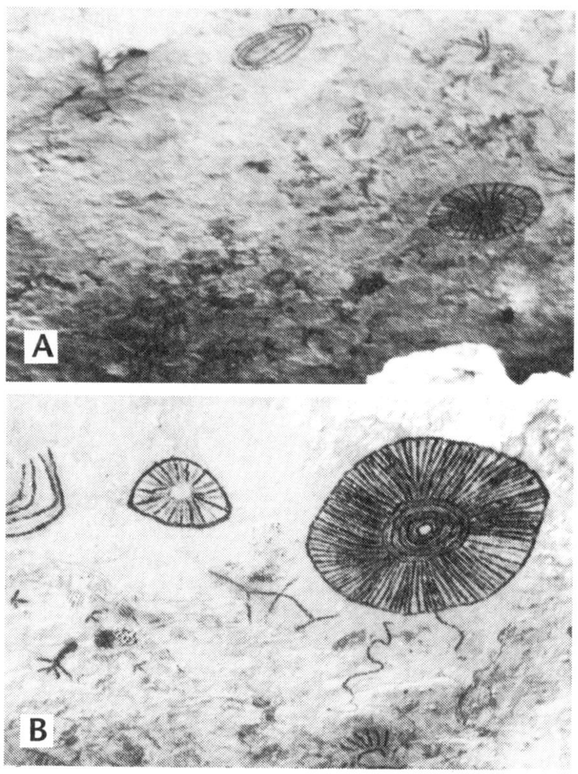

Figure 6-5. A) pictographs on east ceiling of the lower shelter of Toca do Cosmos. **B)** detail of pictographs. The large spoked circle is over 1 m in diameter; and painted in red, pink, and purple.

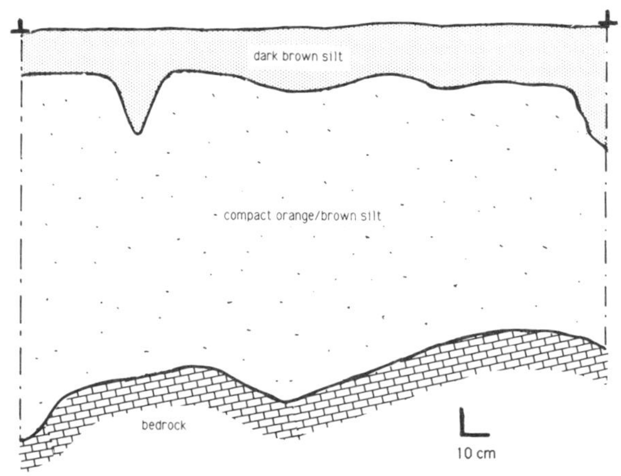

Figure 6-6. Profile of south face of Square X4 in the upper shelter, Toca do Cosmos.

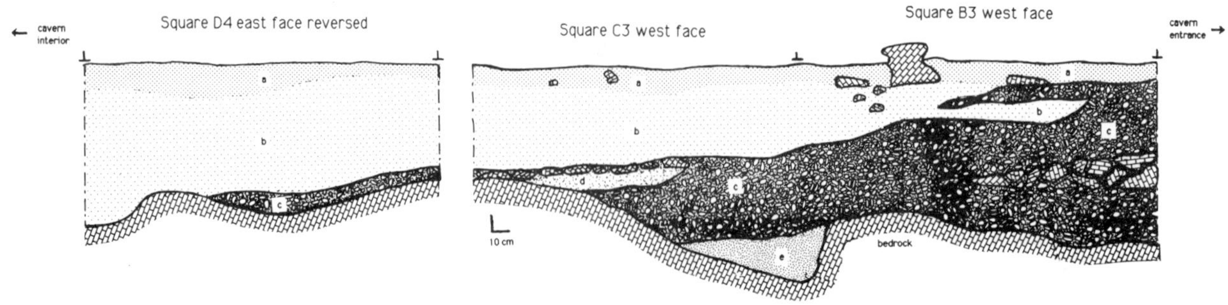

Figure 6-7. Profile of deposits in the lower shelter, Toca do Cosmos. **a,** dark brown silt; **b,** light brown silt; **c,** brown silt with abundant rock fragments; **d,** lens of brown silt; **e,** cemented coarse grey/white sandy silt.

probably a desiccation crack in the orange/brown silt, extended across the square, reaching a depth of 70 cm below surface. This fissure was filled with brown silt from the uppermost stratigraphic zone.

The brown silt zone in the upper shelter was about 10 to 25 cm thick (Figure 6-6). It was dark brown in color, and relatively loose and fine in texture. The upper surface was channelled by shallow rills, in which had accumulated some rock fragments and quantities of riverine mussel shell. Mussel-shell fragments were abundant throughout this deposit, and there were also numerous fragments of gastropod shell; but bone fragments were relatively rare. A small lens of charcoal fragments and ash with rock fragments associated in the southeast quarter of Square X4 apparently marked a hearth at the 10–20 cm level.

In the lower shelter there were two major sedimentary zones (profile, Figures 6-7). A deposit of brown silt with abundant rock fragments, evidently a continuation of the entrance talus, extended down into the interior at a steep angle from the mouth of the cavern; and this zone was covered by a deposit of brown silt apparently derived from the broad tunnel to the rear of the cavern (Figure 6-8a, b).

The zone of brown silt with rock fragments is clearly a continuation of the steep rock talus exposed at the entrance to the lower shelter. In the excavation units, the upper surface of the zone appeared at a depth of approximately 5 cm below surface on the north side of Square B3; and the upper surface extended to a depth of approximately 60 cm below surface on the south side of Square C3, a slope of approximately 25° over a horizontal distance of 3.8 m. In Square D4, farther inward from the mouth of the shelter, the zone of brown silt with abundant rock fragments was not encountered until a depth of 70 cm was attained on the north (exterior) side of the square; and this sedimentary zone did not extend more than 130 cm south in Square D4.

This rock talus contained abundant unsorted fragments of limestone, ranging in size up to 35 cm or more. The limestone fragments feature a chalky-white surface; and were subangular in form, features indicating some degree of chemical weathering. The rocks were enclosed in a matrix of compact brown silt. The color of the matrix became lighter with depth. In Square B3 the upper 20–30 cm of this zone yielded riverine mussel shell, pockets of gastropod shell, and some bone fragments; but faunal remains were sparse in other areas. In the basal levels of the brown silt and rock zone in Square B3 a few small highly mineralized fragments of bone of a large mammal were found.

The zone of brown silt with rock fragments was overlain by a massive deposit of brown silt containing few rock fragments. This deposit was thickest within the cavern: in Square D4, the most interior excavation unit, it attained a maximum thickness of 110 cm, extending right to bedrock on the south (interior) side of the square; whereas on the north side of Square B3, nearest the cavern entrance, it was only 5 cm in thickness. The surface of this silt deposit rises to the south, into the tunnel (map, Figure 6-2); and an origin of the silt in the tunnel extending south from the cavern entrance is indicated. The brown silt was compact, increasingly cemented with depth. The upper 20 cm was darker in color than lower zones. Subangular weathered rock fragments occurred very scattered within this zone and were more

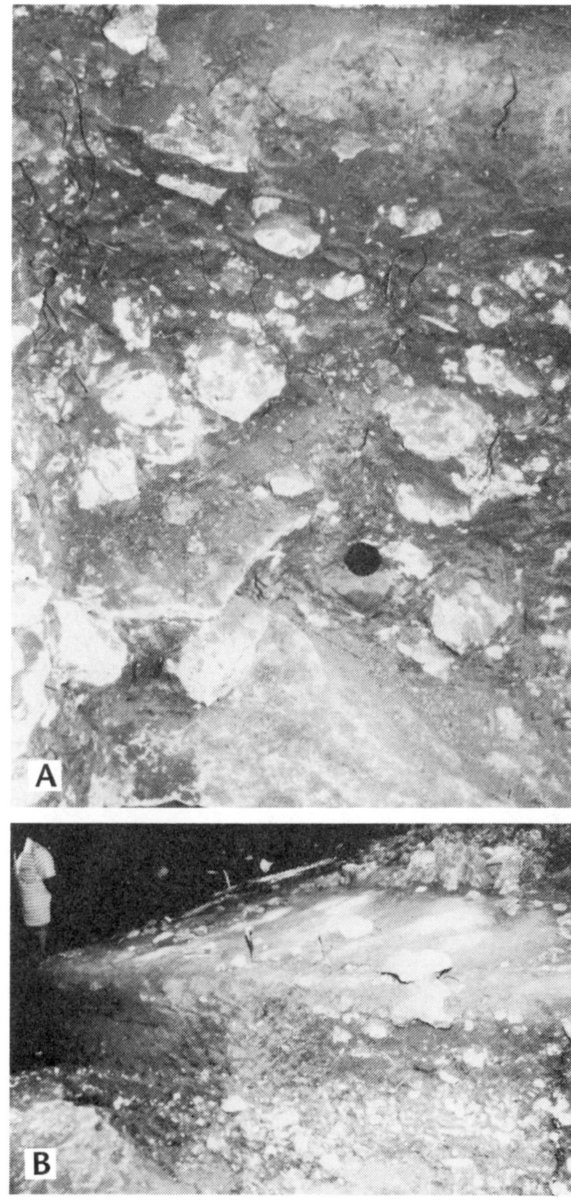

Figure 6-8. A) east face of Square B3 in the lower shelter. Camera lens cap rests on an embedded quartzite chopper just above bedrock. **B)** west face of Squares B3 and C3.

common toward the entrance to the cavern. Fragments of riverine mussel shell were relatively sparse, but numerous gastropod shells occurred in concentrations in the upper 30 cm; and there were also some scattered fragments of bone of large and small mammals. Some scattered charcoal fragments were collected at the base of the brown silt zone in the southeast quarter of Square D4.

The bedrock floor of the lower shelter was exposed at depths averaging between 70 and 100 cm below surface, but it was very irregular in contour; and there were some deep hollows and fissures extending to a maximum depth of 120 cm below surface. The surface of the bedrock was very rough and coated with coarse grey/white sandy silt, evidently disintegrated limestone. This coarse grey/white sandy silt, very cemented, also filled the basal part of deep hollows and fissures in the bedrock.

Faunal Analysis

The most obvious faunal remains at the beginning of excavations in Toca do Cosmos were the abundant shells of riverine mussels, *Diplodon diplodontus.* The mussels were readily obtained in the Rio Verde, less than 2 km to the east of the site. The distribution of riverine mussel valves within the cavern sediments is indicated in Table 6-1. To estimate the number of mussels, the number of valves with the umbo preserved were counted; half that number indicates the minimum number of individuals.

The upper levels of the brown silt zone in the upper shelter were most productive of riverine mussel shells. Square X2 produced 140 minimum number of individuals at the 0–10 cm level, due to accumulation of shell fragments in a shallow channel in the upper part of the brown silt zone. Without accumulation in a channel, the 0–10 cm level in Square X4 yielded 66 minimum number of individuals. Clearly riverine mussels were an important part of the diet of the occupants of the upper shelter.

A similar pattern is seen in the distribution of riverine mussel shell fragments in the upper levels of the lower shelter (Table 6-1). Shell fragments were most common in the upper 30 cm of the zone of brown silt with abundant rock fragments in Square B3; but they also occurred in the 0–40 cm levels in Square C3, most commonly in the brown silt and rock zone at the 10–30 cm level. Mussel shell was relatively rare in the upper part of the brown silt zone in Square D4. Fragments of riverine mussel shell were not found below 40 cm depth, possibly because of poor preservation but also possibly because the earlier occupants of the lower shelter made little use of this food resource.

Gastropod shells were also commonly found in the upper levels in both the upper and lower shelters at Toca do Cosmos (Table 6-2). A sample of tests collected was identified by the Setor da Malacologia of the Museo Nacional. Tests of the giant terrestrial gastropod *Megalobulimos* sp. were in highest frequency in the 0–20 cm levels of the brown silt and rock zone in Square B3, and the 10–30 cm levels in the brown silt and rock zone in Square C3 in the lower shelter; in the upper shelter there was only a concentration of seven tests in the 0–10 cm level, the shallow channel accumulation, in Square X2. This gastropod is highly nutritious, so the animals were likely collected by the late prehistoric occupants for food.

Table 6-1. Stratigraphic Distribution of Minimum Number of Individual Fresh Water Mussels *(Diplodon diplodontus)* in Deposits in Toca do Cosmos.

Upper shelter	
Square X2	
0–10 cm	140
10–20 cm	33
Square X4	
0–10 cm	66
10–20 cm	29
20–30 cm	2
Lower shelter	
Square B3	
0–10 cm	45
10–20 cm	52
20–30 cm	25
30–40 cm	1
Square C3	
0–10 cm	5
10–20 cm	23
20–30 cm	28
30–40 cm	5
Square D4	
0–10 cm	4
10–20 cm	1
20–30 cm	1
30–40 cm	1

The most common gastropod genus in the upper levels of sediment in Toca do Cosmos was *Cyclodontina* spp. Tests of this gastropod are quite abundant now on the limestone plateau, where they accumulate by water action in fissures or low spots. Small in size, they were not likely a food resource. Another genus, *Anctus* sp., is medium-sized; but remains were relatively sparse in the cavern deposits. Other genera of gastropods, occurring in relatively low frequency, were very small and of no food value. It is interesting that two genera, *Pomacea* and *Drepanotrema,* are riverine: they were likely carried into the cavern attached to the shells of the river mussels.

Bone fragments were uncommon in the sedimentary

Table 6-2. Stratigraphic Distribution of Gastropod Tests in Deposits in Toca do Cosmos.

	MEGALOBULIMOS SP.	*ANCTUS* SP.	*CYCLODONTINA* SPP.	*POMACEA* SP.	MINOR SPECIES[1]
Upper shelter					
Square X2					
0–10 cm	7	3	132	12	8
10–20 cm	0	2	131	2	40
20–30 cm	0	2	28	1	8
Square X4					
0–10 cm	1	1	105	0	16
10–20 cm	1	3	88	3	2
20–30 cm	0	0	12	1	0
Lower shelter					
Square B3					
0–10 cm	19	5	94	7	1
10–20 cm	28	2	27	7	0
20–30 cm	6	2	10	2	0
30–40 cm	0	0	2	0	0
40–50 cm	0	0	1	0	0
Square C3					
0–10 cm	11	0	16	2	0
10–20 cm	20	1	19	7	1
20–30 cm	20	0	15	5	3
30–40 cm	1	0	3	1	0
Square D4					
0–10 cm	2	0	100	0	6
10–20 cm	5	0	55	0	6
20–30 cm	2	0	18	0	0
30–40 cm	1	0	2	0	0

[1]*Drepanotrema sp., Oxystila sp., Helicina sp., Streptatermon sp.*

deposits in both the upper and lower shelters. Most fragments were small and unidentifiable. The most notable find was a complete peccary mandible discovered in an inverted position in the brown silt and rock zone at the 10–20 cm level at the north end of Square C3; several cranial fragments and fragmentary limb bones found at the same level in Squares B3 and C3 may pertain to the same individual. Isolated teeth as well as other fragments of bone of large mammals may pertain to peccary, and the upper levels of sediment in both the upper and lower shelters also yielded some bones of small mammals and birds yet to be identified. At the very base of the zone of brown silt with abundant rock fragments, below 100 cm depth in Square B3, a few fragments of heavily mineralized bone of a large mammal were found. These resemble iron-stained fossilized bone fragments in Toca da Gameleira and probably were carried from that site by human transport, as some traces of utilization are present on the specimens.

Radiocarbon Dates

Only two concentrations of charcoal occurred within the sediments in Toca do Cosmos. Charcoal Sample #1, from a depth of 10–20 cm in the brown silt zone in Square X4 in the upper shelter, provided a date of 1230 ± 60 yr B.P. (Beta-13928). Charcoal Sample #2 was a very small sample which was given additional counting time to produce a date of 3230 ± 210 yr B.P. (Beta-13929). This sample consisted of small fragments of charcoal found in the basal levels of the brown silt deposit, just over bedrock in the southeast quarter at a depth of 91 cm in Square D4 in the lower shelter.

Even though Charcoal Sample #2 (3230 ± 210 yr B.P.) was collected from a zone just overlying bedrock, it could be questioned whether the oldest sedimentary zone in the lower shelter has been dated, as the brown silt as a major stratigraphic unit overlies the zone of brown silt with abundant rock fragments which is part of the rock talus at the opening of the cavern. However, there is some intertongueing of the two deposits (profile, Figure 6-7), suggesting that they may have accumulated in step. The natural stratigraphic situation suggests that material at depth in the zone of rock talus should be older than the base of the brown silt zone; but how much older is difficult to say. Cultural stratigraphy may aid in interpretation.

CULTURAL STRATIGRAPHY

A ceramic horizon may be defined at Toca do Cosmos in the brown silt zone of the upper shelter, and in the upper 30 cm of deposits in the lower shelter (Table 6-3). Sherds were found throughout the brown silt zone in the upper shelter. In the lower shelter, sherds occurred to a depth of 30 cm in both the rock talus zone of brown silt with abundant rock fragments and the zone of brown silt which originated in the rear of the cavern, a distribution suggesting that the upper sections of these two different deposits are contemporary. One sherd was found as deep as 40–50 cm in the brown silt zone in Square D4. Also associated with the ceramic horizon are 38 modified riverine mussel shells; a bone bead from the upper shelter; and from the lower shelter, two utilized flakes, six hammerstones, two choppers, and two flaked pebbles. Only one flaked stone artifact, a small quartz scraper, was recovered in excavations in the upper shelter.

The preceramic horizon consists of a scatter of stone artifacts found in the lower shelter deposits to bedrock (Table 6-5). In Squares B3 and C3, there was a notable concentration of choppers, hammerstones, and scraper/planes at the 40–80 cm level in the zone of brown silt with abundant rock fragments. In Square D4 artifacts were less common; but 12 of the total of 13 stone artifacts, including hammerstones and choppers, occurred at levels between 50 and 100 cm in the deep brown silt deposit in this inner excavation unit. There is very tentative evidence, then, of a possible correlation of an early occupation in the rock talus zone with artifacts in the brown silt zone below the 40 cm level. The cultural stratigraphy thus suggests that the deposition of the brown silt zone in the lower shelter might have been approximately in step with the expanding accumulation of the rock talus.

ARTIFACTS

Ceramics

A total of 127 potsherds were collected from Toca do Cosmos. Approximately 65% were recovered from the upper shelter, and 35% from the lower shelter; but types of pottery were not equally distributed between the two areas (Table 6-3).

The most abundant class of pottery (41%) was a plain thin ware featuring heavy calcite tempering and a rough surface finish. The surface color on the exterior or interior of the sherds ranged from a dull pale red (most common) through buff to dark grey (23%). Surfaces were rough and uneven, poorly finished by hand-smoothing or light brushing which dragged particles of temper and often tore the fabric. The surface of many of the sherds was pocked by erosion and loss of temper particles. The most distinctive feature of this class of pottery is the white or grey calcite temper fragments obvious in abundance on the surface of the sherds. The fragments are angular and unsorted, with size ranging up to 2 mm, although the mode is 1 mm. Examination of the sherds also shows a moderate amount of grit in the paste, mainly quartz particles up to 1 mm in size. The ware is relatively thin: thickness of sherds ranges from 4 mm to 7 mm, with the mode 5 mm. Most sherds appear to have been well fired, with complete oxidation, although some sherds have a grey interior. The sherds nevertheless are somewhat friable, and a platy structure is observable in the core. Five small rim sherds were recovered (Figure 6-9a). One rim was slightly bevelled on the interior; but the other four rims were simple, with a pointed lip. One rim sherd has a shallow fine incised horizontal line 2 mm below the lip.

This coarse red/grey ware with abundant calcite temper was found in both the upper and lower shelters; but 71% of the sherds came from the lower shelter, in which the ware was distributed to a depth of 30 cm below surface (although mostly in the upper 20 cm), occurring in both the brown silt deposit and the zone of brown silt with abundant rock fragments. One sherd

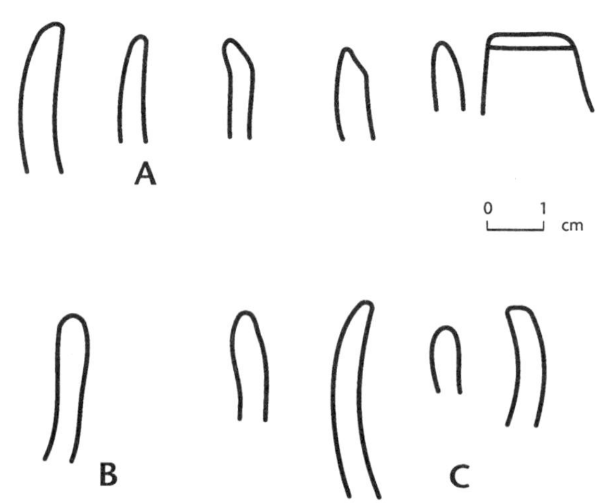

Figure 6-9. Ceramics. **A)** rim sherds of coarse thin red/grey ware; **B)** rim sherd of smooth grey ware; **C)** rim sherds of smooth red ware.

Table 6-3. Stratigraphic Distribution of Potsherds in Deposits of Toca do Cosmos.

	Ware Type					
	COARSE THIN RED/GREY	SMOOTH GREY	SMOOTH RED	DARK MICACEOUS	THICK DARK	TOTALS
Upper shelter						
Square X2						
0–10 cm	3	8	6	5	0	22
10–20 cm	4	5	6	4	0	19
20–30 cm	1	0	1	1	0	3
Square X4						
0–10 cm	2	6	6	0	0	14
10–20 cm	3	11	4	0	0	18
20–30 cm	2	3	2	0	0	7
Lower shelter						
Square B3						
0–10 cm	13	1	0	2	0	16
10–20 cm	6	1	0	0	0	7
20–30 cm	3	0	0	0	0	3
Square C3						
0–10 cm	6	1	0	0	0	7
10–20 cm	8	0	1	0	0	9
20–30 cm	0	0	0	0	0	0
30–40 cm	0	0	0	0	1	1
Square D4						
40–50 cm	1	0	0	0	0	1
Totals	52	36	26	12	1	127

was found at a depth of 40-50 cm in brown silt in Square D4. In the upper shelter, sherds were concentrated in the upper 20 cm; with only three sherds below 20 cm, likely in fissure fill.

The second most common class of pottery (29%) was a grey ware with smooth surface finish and moderate calcite tempering. The surface color ranged from buff to grey to dark grey. Ten sherds were black on the interior. The surface finish is very smooth, with careful hand-smoothing or light brushing; but some sherds show a torn fabric. However, surfaces are not pocked by loss of temper fragments. The temper is a moderate amount of subangular white or grey calcite fragments, with particles ranging up to 1 mm in size. A light amount of quartz grit is also present in the paste. The ware is relatively thin: sherds range in thickness between 4 and 6 mm, with the mode 5 mm. Sherd cores are buff in color, with complete oxidation; and the core features a platy structure. Only one rim sherd was recovered: it displays a simple direct rim form with pointed lip (Figure 6-9b).

Nearly all (92%) of the sherds of this class of smooth grey ware were recovered from the upper shelter; only three sherds were found in the lower shelter, two in the 0–10 cm level in the brown silt and rock zone and one at the 10–20 cm level in brown silt. In the upper shelter, 14 of the sherds were found in the 0–10 cm level and 16 in the 10–20 cm level, with three at the 20–30 cm level and three recovered from fill in a fissure.

The next most-numerous sherd class (20%) was a red ware with smooth surface finish and moderate calcite tempering. The surface color is a dull pale brick red on the exterior and interior. The surface finish is very smooth and even, well smoothed by hand or by fine brushing. As cores are buff in color, a thin red slip may have been applied. The tempering material is sometimes visible on the surface; but the surface is not pocked, and tearing of the fabric is rare. The temper is a moderate amount of subangular white or grey calcite fragments, ranging up to 1 mm in size. Very little quartz grit is observable in the paste. Thickness of sherds ranges from 4 mm to 7 mm, with the mode 4 mm. Cores are buff in color, with complete oxidation; and a platy structure is evident. Four rim sherds present a simple direct form, with three of the lips pointed and the fourth rounded or slightly flattened in form (Figure 6-9c). The largest rim sherd suggests a wide-mouthed bowl.

All but one of the sherds in this class of smooth red ware were recovered from the upper shelter. The one sherd identified from the lower shelter came from the 10–20 cm level in the brown silt zone. In the upper shelter, 12 of the sherds were found at the 0–10 cm level, 10 at the 10–20 cm level, and three sherds were found at the 20–30 cm level.

A highly distinctive minority ware (9%) in the Toca do Cosmos sherd collection is heavily tempered with micaceous grit. The surface color is a very dark grey or dark brown/grey on both the interior and exterior. The surface finish is very rough and uneven, with only light smoothing or brushing; and the surface is very gritty to the touch. Vessels were heavily tempered with a highly micaceous fine sand, with angular particles of quartz and mica ranging up to 2 mm in size. The thickness of sherds ranged from 4 to 6 mm, with the mode 5 mm. Sherd cores are dark in color; and the sherds are very friable, with a platy structure. It appears that vessels were poorly constructed, with breaks common at coil junctures. No rim sherds were recovered.

All but two of the 12 sherds of this micaceous ware were recovered from Square X2 in the upper shelter, where they were distributed to a depth of 30 cm. Two sherds were identified from the 0–10 cm level in Square B3 in the lower shelter.

Finally, one body sherd of a thick dark ware was found isolated at a depth of 35 cm in the brown silt zone in Square C3 in the lower shelter. This sherd, dark grey to dark brown/grey in color, features a very rough surface finish, with torn fabric and temper particles protruding to give a gritty feel to the surface. The interior surface is significantly smoother than the exterior. There is heavy grit temper, with subangular particles of quartz up to 2 mm in size: some mica is also present. The ware was distinctively thick; the sherd has a thickness of 9 mm. The core is dark in color, and friable.

Several pottery wares are thus identifiable in the ceramic collection from Toca do Cosmos. The presence of calcite fragments in the temper relates the coarse red ware to the finer red and grey wares, although the latter types are distinctive in terms of proportions of temper and fineness of surface finish. The micaceous ware is quite distinctive; and the sherd of thick plain grit-tempered ware found at depth in the brown silt deposit in the lower shelter may be significant.

Stone Artifacts

The cultural zones in the Toca do Cosmos yielded relatively little flaking debitage: only 71 unmodified flakes were recovered from the sediments in the entire site, 32 (45%) from the upper shelter and 39 (55%) from the lower shelter (Table 6-4). In the upper shelter, flakes were concentrated in even distribution in the upper 30 cm of the brown silt deposit in Square X2; only three flakes were found scattered in the brown silt zone in Square X4. In the lower shelter, flakes were scattered at very low frequency throughout the zone of brown silt with abundant rock fragments in Square B3, with a marked concentration at the 70–80 cm level. In Square C3, flakes were also most numerous in the brown silt

Table 6-4. Stratigraphic Distribution of Unmodified Stone Flakes in Deposits in Toca do Cosmos.

	CHERT	QUARTZITE	QUARTZ	TOTAL
Upper shelter				
Square X2				
0–10 cm	4	0	0	4
10–20 cm	10	0	0	10
20–30 cm	10	0	0	10
30–40 cm	5	0	0	5
total	29	0	0	29
Square X4				
0–10 cm	0	1	1	2
10–20 cm	0	0	0	0
20–30 cm	0	0	0	0
30–40 cm	1	0	0	1
total	1	1	1	3
Lower shelter				
Square B3				
0–10 cm	0	2	0	2
10–20 cm	0	0	0	0
20–30 cm	0	0	0	0
30–40 cm	0	0	0	0
40–50 cm	1	1	0	2
50–60 cm	0	0	0	0
60–70 cm	0	1	0	1
70–80 cm	3	10	0	13
80–90 cm	3	0	0	3
90–100 cm	0	3	0	3
100–110 cm	1	1	0	2
total	8	18	0	26
Square C3				
0–10 cm	0	1	0	1
10–20 cm	0	0	0	0
20–30 cm	0	0	0	0
30–40 cm	0	2	0	0
40–50 cm	0	2	0	2
50–60 cm	0	0	0	0
60–70 cm	2	2	0	4
70–80 cm	0	4	0	4
total	2	9	0	11
Square D4				
80–90 cm	1	0	0	1
90–100 cm	0	1	0	1
total	1	1	0	2
TOTAL	41	29	1	71

and rock zone at a depth of 60–80 cm, with only a scatter in the deposit of brown silt overlying. In Square D4 only two flakes were found, in the basal levels of the section at the 80–100 cm level.

The Toca do Cosmos flakes were predominantly of chert (41, or 58%) or quartzite (29, or 42%); only one small quartz flake was recovered from the site. Chert flakes were concentrated in the upper shelter, in Square X2, which yielded 29 chert flakes. In the lower shelter, quartzite flakes were predominant (74% of the total collection from this area of the site), with notable concentrations in the brown silt and rock zone at the 70–80 cm level in Square B3 and the 60–80 cm level in Square C3.

Chert is readily available in the immediate vicinity of Toca do Cosmos, as irregular nodules outcrop from the limestone matrix. The local chert nodules, however, are very irregular in form, with a rough cortex. When freshly broken, the chert is a translucent grey or cream-white; but it weathers to a yellow color when enclosed in sediment, and may become deeply patinated. Chert flakes recovered in excavation ranged in size from 13 x 7 x 2 mm to 72 x 29 x 19 mm, with a mode of 29 x 23 x 6 mm. Only 14 of the 41 chert flakes (34%) retained cortex. Striking platforms when preserved (on 65% of the chert flakes) were simple and large relative to the size of the flake, indicating derivation by direct percussion.

Quartzite pebbles ultimately derived from the quartzite beds forming the Serra Azul about 25 km to the south occur scattered in the area on and around the limestone outcrop, and may be derived from ancient fluvial deposits. Twenty-one of the 29 quartzite flakes (72%) retained cortex, indicating derivation from pebbles. Quartzite flakes ranged in size from 19 x 9 x 3 mm to 59 x 46 x 15 mm, with a mode of 38 x 35 x 11 mm. Striking platforms when preserved (on 72% of the quartzite flakes) were large and simple, indicating detachment by direct percussion.

Quartz was rarely utilized in Toca do Cosmos. Only one unmodified quartz flake was found; and there was a sparsity of quartz artifacts, although small quartz pebbles could be readily collected in the immediate vicinity. The one small quartz flake recovered was derived from a pebble.

A total of 82 stone artifacts were recovered from Toca do Cosmos (Table 6-5). Most are modified pebbles. With one exception, a small retouched water-rolled chert pebble tool (BA-XX-1/271) which will be described with similar quartz pebble tools, all of the chert artifacts are made from nodules readily available from the local limestone. These nodules are broken naturally into thick angular chunks of chert. Spalled surfaces of the chert nodules are generally creamy white, although the surface has usually been stained orange by the sediment matrix. Evidently flaking of this chert was difficult to control, perhaps because of a high water content, which caused the material to break along what appear to be thermal spalls. Although the spalls may be conchoidal, they often lack most characteristics of true flakes. These chert artifacts have at least one high-angled (75–90°) step-flaked working edge, which makes them superficially look like cores from which flakes have been repeatedly removed. However, the chert is very poor quality; and the interiors of the artifacts and flakes have all weathered to a soft powdery consistency. Thin-edged flakes of this material were not a desired commodity.

Almost all chert flakes with good bulbs came from the upper 40 cm in Square X2 in the upper shelter, whereas all of the chert artifacts came from the three excavation units in the lower shelter. Evidently people did occasionally knap chert in the east end of the upper shelter, but there is no indication what they may have been making. The step-flaked nodules and fragments thereof from the lower shelter evidently were made and used there for some special purpose. Evidently at first the desired edges were intentionally created by removing a few large flakes using a natural plane face as a platform. Most of the subsequent step flakes may have been removed to resharpen the denticulated working edge; however, many of the short nibbling flakes were probably removed unintentionally by use. For convenience, these artifacts will be called scraper-planes, although their exact function is unknown. They are of a shape and size which could readily be grasped in one hand, with the working edge and projections protruding for grooving and sawing as well as planing wood.

The largest (61 x 54 x 51 mm) of these scraper-planes (BA-XX-1/245) came from a depth of 79 cm in the brown silt zone in Square D4. The undulating 75–85° step-flaked edge has three projections which are use-nibbled and more worn than the intervening concavities (Figure 6-10a). The projections are less pronounced on the other examples. BA-XX-1/262, from a depth of 96 cm in the brown silt zone in Square D4, has a concavo/convex edge with small denticulations (Figure 6-10b). Two spurs on the edge are slightly worn and use-nibbled. A separate 80° edge of this artifact, which measures 71 x 54 x 32 mm, has a much worn nose fashioned by step-flaking on both sides. Square B3 yielded two more examples. BA-XX-1/267, from the 90–100 cm level in the brown silt and rock zone, measures 56 x 55 x 36 mm, and has two step-flaked working edges at right angles to each other (Figure 6-10b). One irregularly excurving edge (with a 70° angle) has a few worn spurs. The steeper edge (75–80°) evidently has more recently been renewed to create a denticulated edge with three slightly worn spurs. The smallest (62 x 34 x 24 mm) whole scraper-plane (BA-XX-1/286) came from the 60–70 cm level in the brown silt and rock zone in Square B3. Most of its undulating step-flaked edge (with an 85° angle) was unfortunately scraped by a trowel, exposing the chalky weathered interior. The undamaged portion of the edge is worn and use-nibbled.

Two small chert chunks are evidently fragments of broken scraper-planes. Square B3 yielded BA-XX-1/292

Table 6-5. Stratigraphic Distribution of Non-Ceramic Artifacts in Deposits of Toca do Cosmos.

	Utilized Flakes	Hammerstones	Choppers	Scraper/ Planes	Flaked Pebbles	Misc. Stone
Upper shelter						
Square X2						
0–10 cm bs	1	0	0	0	0	0
Square X4						
0–10 cm bs	0	0	0	0	0	0
10–20 cm bs	0	0	0	0	0	0
total	0	0	0	0	0	0
Lower shelter						
Square B3						
0–10 cm bs	0	0	0	0	0	0
0–10 cm bsr	1	2	0	0	1	0
10–20 cm bsr	0	2	1	0	0	0
20–30 cm bsr	0	0	1	0	0	0
30–40 cm bsr	0	0	0	0	1	1
40–50 cm bsr	1	1	2	0	0	0
50–60 cm bsr	0	0	2	0	1	0
60–70 cm bsr	1	0	2	1	1	2
70–80 cm bsr	2	1	0	2	2	1
80–90 cm bsr	1	0	0	0	1	0
90–100 cm bsr	0	1	0	1	2	0
100–110 cm bsr	1	0	0	0	0	0
total	7	7	8	4	9	4
Square C3						
0–10 cm bs	0	0	0	0	0	0
10–20 cm bs	0	1	0	0	0	0
20–30 cm bs	1	1	0	0	0	0
20–30 cm bsr	0	0	0	0	0	0
30–40 cm bs	1	1	1	0	0	0
40–50 cm bs	0	0	0	0	0	0
50–60 cm bsr	1	4	3	0	0	0
60–70 cm bsr	3	2	4	1	0	0
70–80 cm bsr	1	2	1	0	0	0
total	7	11	9	1	0	0
Square D4						
0–10 cm bs	0	0	0	0	0	0
10–20 cm bs	0	0	0	0	1	0
20–30 cm bs	0	0	0	0	0	0
30–40 cm bs	0	0	0	0	1	0
40–50 cm bs	0	0	0	0	0	0
50–60 cm bs	0	1	0	0	1	0
60–70 cm bs	0	1	0	0	0	0
70–80 cm bs	0	1	0	1	1	0
80–90 cm bs	0	0	1	1	1	1
90–100 cm bs	0	0	0	1	0	0
90–100 cm bsr	1	0	0	0	0	0
Total	1	3	1	3	5	1
Totals	16	21	18	8	14	5

bs = brown silt zone; bsr = zone of brown silt with abundant rock fragments.

Modified Hematite	Bone Artifacts	Modified Shells	Total
0	0	11	12
0	0	12	12
0	1	5	6
0	1	17	18
0	0	7	7
0	0	0	4
0	0	2	5
0	0	0	1
0	0	0	2
0	0	0	4
0	1	0	4
0	0	0	7
0	0	0	8
1	0	0	3
1	0	0	5
0	0	0	1
2	1	9	51
0	0	1	1
0	0	0	1
0	0	0	2
0	0	2	2
0	0	0	3
0	0	0	0
1	0	0	9
0	0	0	10
0	0	0	4
1	0	3	32
0	0	0	0
0	0	0	1
0	0	0	0
0	0	0	1
0	0	0	0
0	0	0	2
0	0	0	1
0	0	0	3
0	0	0	4
0	0	0	1
0	0	0	1
0	0	0	14
3	2	40	127

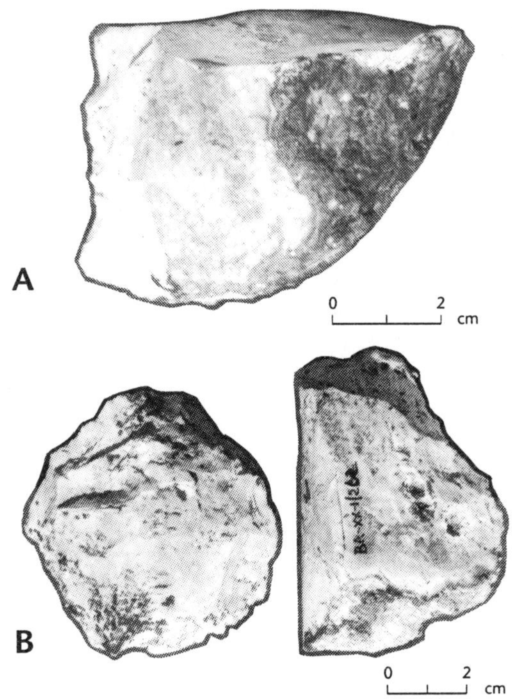

Figure 6-10. Chert scraper/planes. **A)** BA-XX-1/245; **B)** BA-XX-1/267 (left and BA-XX-1/262 (right).

in the brown silt and rock zone at the 70–80 cm level. A short (16 mm) 90° edge has been step-flaked and slightly worn on this angular chert piece, which measures 54 x 28 x 24 mm. A separate projecting corner has been struck forcefully, but the edge shows no evidence of use. One edge of BA-XX-1/293, from the brown silt at the 80–90 cm level in Square D4, has a series of incomplete hinge scars of stepped flakes. Evidently this fragment, which measures 47 x 24 x 12 mm, spalled off the working edge during use. Another small (58 x 32 x 19 mm) angular chunk of chert (BA-XX-1/290), from the 60–70 cm level in brown silt in Square C3, may also be a fragment of a scraper-plane; however, the step-flaked edge (with a 65°angle) is very narrow (6 mm), and confined to a projecting corner. A separate 90° edge is use-nibbled but not intentionally step-flaked.

Two chert flakes with steep-angled step-flaked edges appear to have been removed from the working edges of scraper-planes, probably to renew the edges. One hinged flake (BA-XX-1/294), from the brown silt and rock zone at the 80–90 cm level in Square B3, has a prominent bulb removed from the working edge at a 100° angle, as were previous flakes. At first, artifact BA-XX-1/294 was catalogued as a burinated flake, as one long side of this thin flake (38 x 24 x 6 mm) with a shallow negative bulb has a concave face created by an end blow from the same platform as adjacent step flakes. Subsequent analysis, however, indicated that the burin-like scar was created by the same kind of vertically-directed blow to the platform as created the hinge flakes. The edge of this unintentionally burinated flake is not worn.

A small (59 x 36 x 23 mm) unbroken chert nodule (BA-XX-1/287) has a natural projection near the center of one longitudinal edge (with a 75° angle) which has been step-flaked to resharpen it. This nose of this expediency tool, found in the brown silt and rock zone at the 60–70 cm level in Square B3, was much used.

Only two of the waterworn quartz pebbles proved to be of good quality quartz crystal. A pointed oval quartz flake (BA-XX-1/12) with a plano-convex cross-section and a prominent bulb, and measuring 38 x 22 x 10 mm, came from the upper 10 cm level in brown silt in Square X2. It was evenly retouched on the excurvate platform edge, (with an angle of 40°) to form a tool which could be used as a scraper or perhaps a projectile point. A sharp spur had been created at the tip end by slight retouch on the otherwise unretouched hinged edge of the flake. The other flaked quartz chunk (BA-XX-1/231), from brown silt at the 30–40 cm level in Square D4, is of absolutely clear crystal; however, it has no apparent formal shape (Figure 6-11a). It measures 27 x 13 x 12 mm. One 80° angle edge has been steeply flaked and crushed by use. The adjacent beaked tip is broken, also perhaps by use; but the flat break was used as a platform to remove more than one hinged burin spall. Several closely packed impact scars left by a pointed object are present on the steeply-flaked face near a 3/4 impact cone which created a useful projecting nose with a 65° edge, which is use-nibbled. Another narrow chisel end (with an 80° angle) has also been use-flaked. Although this crystal chunk has no deliberate shape, several useful edges were carefully created by a craftsman who appreciated the strength as well as the beauty of clear quartz crystal.

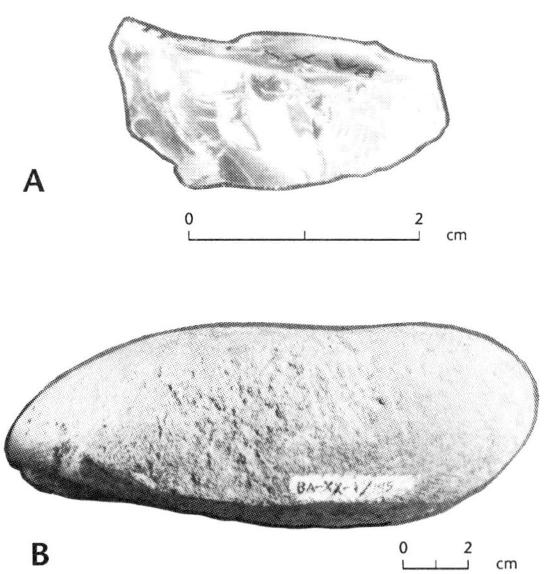

Figure 6-11. A) flaked quartz fragment (BA-XX-1/231); **B)** quartzite pebble hammerstone (BA-XX-1/195).

Flaking of vein quartz pebbles can be only minimally controlled. A few Toca do Cosmos specimens appear to have been held on an anvil or struck against another rock in order to split off an end or to remove a flake to create one or more useful high-angled working edges. In many cases the flake scars appear to be very old and worn, so perhaps these flakes had been removed naturally by stream action. These indefinite artifacts, usually with one single flake scar, have been retained in level bags for possible future studies; but are not described as artifacts.

A number of flaked vein quartz pebbles were definitely artifacts, however. One end of a quartz pebble (BA-XX-1/268) from the brown silt and rock zone at the 90–100 cm level in Square B3, had been removed with a single blow. The opposite pointed end of this small (19 x 13 x 9 mm) pebble has been flaked and battered as if used as a punch. Another subangular quartz pebble (BA-XX-1/255) has had crushing flakes removed from both pointed ends, also possibly by use as a punch. This subangular pebble, which measures 27 x 21 x 18 mm, came from the brown silt and rock zone at a depth of 85 cm in Square B3. One weathered quartz pebble (BA-XX-1/269) has peck marks scattered over the ends and edges. The naturally rough weathered surface of this oblong pebble, which measures 77 x 31 x 19 mm and came from the brown silt and rock zone at the 90–100 cm level in Square B3, would make a good flaking hammerstone, although perhaps someone had repeatedly attempted to break it open without success.

Peck marks are also visible on the surface of BA-XX-1/256, the largest (57 x 54 x 54 mm) quartz pebble found in Toca do Cosmos, in Square D4 at a depth of 89 cm in the brown silt zone. In this case three flakes were removed from different edges. All of these useful high-angled edges (with angles of 85–90°) are somewhat worn. Two adjacent flakes have been removed in opposite directions to create a concave 75° edge, which is worn, on another flaked quartz pebble (BA-XX-1/232), which measures 24 x 20 x 11 mm, and was found in the brown silt and rock zone at the 50–60 cm level in Square B3. One large flake was removed from a corner of BA-XX-1/163, which came from the 0–10 cm level in the brown silt and rock zone in Square B3, and measures 54 x 31 x 29 mm.

Several unidirectional flakes have been removed from the ends of three small pebbles with plano-convex cross-sections to create straight steep scraping edges with angles of 85–90°. One of these tools, measuring 22 x 16 x 14 mm, is a banded chert pebble (BA-XX-1/271) from the brown silt and rock zone at the 90-100 cm level in Square B3. One quartz pebble (BA-XX-1/247) came from the brown silt and rock zone at a depth of 76 cm in Square B3, and measures 31 x 27 x 17 mm. The other quartz pebble (BA-XX-1/210) came from Square B3 in the brown silt and rock zone at the 30–40 cm level. As the flaked surface of this pebble, which measures 31 x 26 x 23 mm, is as darkly stained as the cortical surface, the flake may have been removed naturally in a stream. Also the entire edge is quite battered and worn, so it may not be an artifact.

Many of the smaller quartzite pebbles are also minimally flaked and/or pecked. With the exception of BA-XX-1/230, which has a flake scar created by a carefully placed blow to one corner with a small pointed object, quartzite pebbles with only one flake scar were retained in level bags but not considered to be demonstrable artifacts. BA-XX-1/230, the exception, measuring 33 x 26 x 18 mm, came from a depth of 10–20 cm in the brown silt zone in Square D4.

A tiny (22 x 16 x 10 mm) quartzite pebble (BA-XX-1/250) with a triangular cross-section, from the brown silt zone at the 70–80 cm level in Square D4, has single flake scars on one end and on two sides opposite each other. A tabular quartzite pebble (BA-XX-1/240) with a square outline (55 x 54 x 23 mm), from the brown silt zone at 60 cm depth in Square D4, has light pecking marks on all corners and a large flake scar removed by a heavy blow from one corner. Another tabular quartzite pebble (BA-XX-1/242), from the 60–70 cm level in the brown silt and rock zone in Square B3, has a triangular outline and measures 36 x 35 x 17 mm. A narrow flake has been removed with a side blow from near one corner by a small pointed object. A flake scar carefully positioned in this manner creates a projecting corner which would be useful for grooving wood. A similar blow removed a flake from both faces of another corner. A single pick mark is present in the same position on the third corner. It appears that someone was using a carefully placed punch, such as the tip of a quartz crystal, to resharpen projecting corners. This technique is also seen on BA-XX-1/244, found at a depth of 79 cm in the brown silt and rock zone of Square B3. One end of this tabular quartzite pebble (38 x 34 x 24 mm) had naturally split off; and a similar narrow flake was removed from near a corner, using the split face as a platform. The opposite end has been removed from the same platform by a side blow to a corner. The 90° angle edge is much worn. Light peck marks are present on both flat cortical faces, as if the artifact had been used as an anvilstone. One quarter of a quartzite pebble (BA-XX-1/236), measuring 39 x 38 x 21 mm, from a depth of 53 cm in the brown silt zone in Square D4, has a concentration of peck marks on the flattest cortical face, where it was apparently used as an anvilstone. The quartering may have occurred accidentally while hammering.

Two naturally broken quartzite pebbles have been flaked at both ends, probably by use as hammerstones; and pecked on their faces. BA-XX-1/130, from a depth of 16 cm in the brown silt and rock zone in Square B3, is a weathered quartzite pebble, measuring 54 x 37 x 22 mm, with irregular flake scars at both ends. Several peck marks are present on the flattest cortical face where it was used as an anvil. A fire-broken quartzite pebble (BA-XX-1/252), measuring 58 x 53 x 21 mm and found in the brown silt zone at a depth of 60-70 cm in Square D4, has one battered and use-flaked end (with a 90° angle) as well as a flake removed from the opposite corner. Several peck marks are present on the nearby rounded end.

A long spall has been removed from one face of a flattened quartzite pebble (BA-XX-1/220) by a heavy blow to a corner which has been heavily pecked. This pebble hammerstone, which measures 70 x 57 x 35 mm, was found at a depth of 48 cm in the brown silt and rock zone in Square B3. One corner of BA-XX-1/215, a tabular pebble with a triangular outline, measuring 68 x 57 x 28 mm, has been heavily battered by hammering. This quartzite hammerstone came from the brown silt and rock zone at the 60-70 cm level in Square C3. An elongated quartzite pebble (BA-XX-1/200) has been lightly pecked on both ends and a flake removed from near a corner as well as from one end. This hammerstone, measuring 61 x 37 x 22 mm, was recovered from a depth of 59 cm in the brown silt and rock zone in Square C3. A larger (77 x 43 x 43 mm) elongated quartzite pebble hammerstone (BA-XX-1/216), from a depth of 77 cm in the brown silt and rock zone in the same square, has side-blow flakes removed from flat-faced corners at both ends. One entire end of this hammerstone has been removed by a large flake scar and an overlapping small flake scar, which created two projecting edges (with 80° angles) which are use-flaked and worn. Peck marks are present on three other corners, while one projecting corner lacks peck marks but is stained by hematite.

A similar-shaped quartzite pebble (BA-XX-1/241), which measures 94 x 81 x 30 mm and was recovered from a depth of 76 cm in the brown silt and rock zone in Square B3, has a concentration of relatively recent peck marks on one corner. Heavily stained areas at both ends also appear to have been pecked at an earlier time, although it is possible that these old rough surfaces are due to differential weathering. A small (47 x 34 x 28 mm) oval quartzite pebble (BA-XX-1/169) with a weathering rind was found in the brown silt zone at a depth of 27 cm in Square C3. It appears to have been pecked all over one face and a bit elsewhere. Although these look like artificial peck marks, it is possible that they are the result of weathering. Two other pebbles with this unusual kind of weathering rind appear more definitely to have been used. BA-XX-1/186 was found at a depth of 38 cm in the brown silt zone in Square C3. This tabular quartzite pebble, which measures 72 x 58 x 31 mm, has pecked areas on the two flattest faces and three edges. Another side has weathered off naturally. Both faces of another tabular quartzite pebble (BA-XX-1/251), which measures 82 x 64 x 33 mm and was found at a depth of 71 cm in the brown silt zone in Square D4, have been completely pecked, leaving all four sides untouched. The high spots of one face, with a shallow pecked depression, have been smoothed by use as an abrading stone, while the other face is still rough.

A quadrangular quartzite pebble (BA-XX-1/162) with both ends broken off has also been used as an abrading stone. The high spots of the flattest cortical face and the flattest broken end have both been smoothed by heavy use. All but one 90° angle edge of this artifact, which measures 71 x 62 x 61 mm and was found at a depth of 10 cm in the brown silt and rock zone in Square B3, have been battered and pecked by use as a hammerstone. The cortical surface of the smallest end has been removed by pecking.

Three large elongated quartzite pebble hammerstones were recovered from Square C3. BA-XX-1/167, measuring 112 x 59 x 53 mm, was found at a depth of 18 cm in the brown silt zone. Pecked facets are present on both ends, on two central projections, and along one edge. Large pecked facets are present on two projecting longitudinal edges and on both ends of BA-XX-1/195, which measures 165 x 58 x 54 mm, and was found in the brown silt and rock zone at a depth of 60 cm (Figure 6-11b). A large spall has been removed from one end by a heavy blow. Likewise, a large spall has been removed from one end of BA-XX-1/192, which measures 133 x 67 x 63 mm. The resultant 90° angle edge of this artifact, which was recovered from the brown silt and rock zone at a depth of 55 cm, has been battered and worn by heavy use. In addition, the central portion of the narrowest edge has been unidirectionally step-flaked and subsequently worn. Also, the high spots on the two flattest faces are smoothed, and exhibit faint parallel striations.

An elongated quartzite pebble (BA-XX-1/129) has been roughly broken in half longitudinally, probably by thermal action. The apex of the cortical surface of this broken pebble, which measures 122 x 71 x 55 mm, had been pecked over an area of ancient impact cone marks. One 80° angle end and adjacent 70° angle broken edge of this artifact, from a depth of 12 cm in the brown silt zone of Square B3, has been battered by use as a chopper, as has another 65° angle edge.

Battering of 90° angle split pebble edges is present on two other hammerstone/choppers. Three corners and three right-angled edges of a large (118 x 98 x 74 mm) quadrangular quartzite pebble (BA-XX-1/184) with one side split off, have been battered and step-flaked by heavy chopping. Other cortical edges of this heavy pebble, recovered from a depth of 37 cm in the brown silt zone in Square C3, also are battered.

Similar evidence of heavy use is present on BA-XX-1/139, which has been split in half across the bedding planes. Two of the three 90° angle edges of the split face are battered and step-flaked, as is one 90° angle cortical edge of this quartzite hammerstone, which measures 79 x 57 x 56 mm. A clearly pecked facet extends along a cortical ridge, and peck marks are scattered elsewhere on this hammerstone, which was found at a depth of 15 cm in the brown silt and rock zone in Square B3. The 90° angle edges of another split quartzite pebble (BA-XX-1/217), from a depth of 70 cm in the brown silt and rock zone in Square C3, show less evidence of use. Several peck marks are present on the cortical surface near the large stepped concavity caused by the heavy impact that split this piece, which measures 73 x 50 x 49 mm. Several deep peck marks from use as an anvilstone are present on the apical face. One of these heavy blows evidently peeled off the weathering rind from the other end of the pebble.

Two hammerstones are fashioned of extraneous exotic materials. A quadrangular hammerstone of igneous rock (BA-XX-1/197) was shaped by pecking. Three faces of this artifact, which measures 58 x 58 x 57 mm and was recovered from a depth of 55 cm in the brown silt and rock zone in Square C3, are quite smooth. The other face and the two ends have been roughened by pecking. A spall was removed from one end, but the surface evidently was pecked again. A flattened limestone pebble hammerstone (BA-XX-1/174) obviously weathered outside the cave into a nearly square outline measuring 87 x 82 x 38 mm. It has been battered and use-flaked along one edge. Other edges of this artifact, which was found at a depth of 10 cm in the brown silt and rock zone in Square B3, show some evidence of use; and both faces appear to have been pecked by use as an anvilstone. All surfaces, including the flaked surface, have subsequently been etched by acid.

Two quartzite pebbles were retained because they appear to have an unnatural coating of some identifiable material on them. The 90° angle edge of one pebble (BA-XX-1/259), split across the bedding planes, probably by a heavy impact blow, has a few flake scars. The pebble measures 70 x 58 x 30 mm. The split face and adjacent cortical surfaces of this pebble, recovered from a depth of 90 cm in the brown silt zone in Square D4, have a shiny chocolate-brown coating which may be of some vegetal material. The other pebble (BA-XX-1/254), measuring 57 x 54 x 38 mm, has strings of a black gummy substance which appears to be spattered on one edge and the ends. It was recovered from a depth of 70–80 cm in the brown silt and rock zone in Square B3.

The category of hammerstones merges into the category of more classic pebble tools with steeply flaked edges which are generally referred to as choppers. Evidently, the most desirable working edges were between 80° and 90° in angle; however, repeated resharpening by step-flaking can create 90° angle edges. All but one of these pebble choppers are manufactured of quartzite. One side of an exotic granite pebble (BA-XX-1/288) from the 50–60 cm level in the brown silt and rock zone in Square B3 had spalled off, probably along a cleavage plane, to produce an 80° edge, which subsequently was use-battered. Use-flaking continues onto a contiguous 90° angle edge of a thermal spall scar. The working edge of this pebble, which measures 77 x 69 x 54 mm, exhibits several clearly visible points of impact and associated lines of force. Although the edge of this pebble tool was not intentionally flaked, it served well enough without flaking so that the artifact was apparently transported a considerable distance from its source.

The intentionally unidirectionally flaked quartzite pebble tools often have prominent noses or spurs, usually near the center of the working edges. On most examples these projections have been resharpened by step-flaking, using the original cortical face as a platform; however, in two cases the projecting edge has been resharpened by removing thin flakes from the original platform face in the opposite direction, using the edge itself as a platform. The best example of this resharpening technique is on BA-XX-1/193, found at a depth of 60 cm in the brown silt and rock zone in Square C3 (Figure 6-12a). The original 70° angle edge, with a broad central projection, was created by removing one or more long flakes from the flattest face. The central projecting edge was then resharpened by removing flakes in the same direction lateral to the projection, and a series of thin flakes in the opposite direction, using the projecting edge as a platform. The working edge is much worn; and there are scattered peck marks present on various cortical surfaces of this pebble chopper, which measures 68 x 63 x 55 mm.

The 70° angle working edge of BA-XX-1/198, found

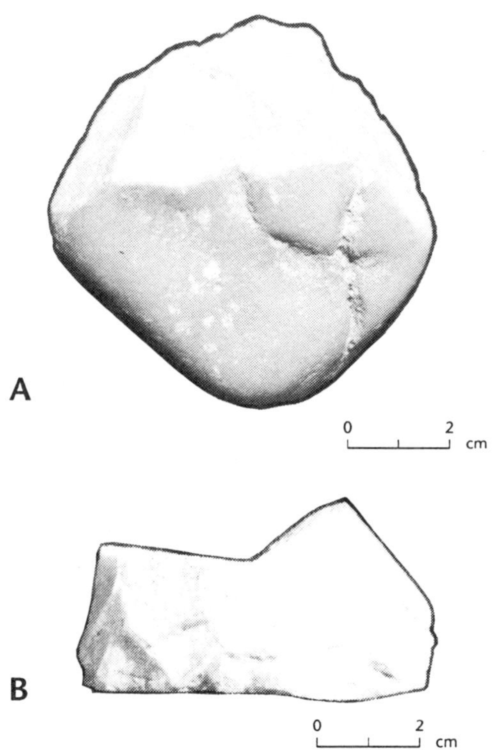

Figure 6-12. Quartzite choppers. **A)** BA-XX-1/193; **B)** BA-XX-1/239.

at a depth of 57 cm in the brown silt and rock zone of Square C3, is much straighter, although there is a small projecting nose near the center which has been resharpened by lateral step-flaking; and removal of a thin flake from the opposite face on one side of the nose, which is much smoothed by use. This quartzite pebble tool measures 63 x 53 x 36 mm.

The excurvate edge of BA-XX-1/239 has been step-flaked to create a denticulated edge (75° angle) with several projections, which are crushed and polished by use (Figure 6-12b). This artifact, which now measures 61 x 55 x 34 mm, was broken into three pieces by heat spalling. The least important dorsal piece was never found. The other two fragments recovered were both found in Square B3 but at significantly different depths in the brown silt and rock zone (one at 45 cm depth, 21 cm south and 90 cm west of the northeast stake; and the other at 68 cm depth, 125 cm south and 153 cm west of the northeast stake), due to the southward slope of the rock talus zone in this excavation unit.

The working edge of a weathered tabular quartzite pebble chopper (BA-XX-1/221) with an excurvate projecting edge has been used and step-flaked so much that the battered working edge reached a 90° angle, at which time the piece evidently was discarded. Scattered thin step flakes have also been removed by heavy use from the flat platform edge of this artifact, which was recovered from a depth of 42 cm in the brown silt and rock zone in Square B3. It measures 77 x 62 x 33 mm.

BA-XX-1/273 (Figure 6-13a) has an irregularly straight edge with a small central projection, which has been resharpened by step-flaking on one side; however, the impact for an attempted step flake on the other side was too strong, so a large flake spalled off, making that portion of the edge too fragile for use as a chopper. The previous working edge is somewhat worn, but the fragile portion of the edge is sharp; so this chopper, which measures 74 x 62 x 50 mm and was recovered from a depth of 59 cm in the brown silt and rock zone in Square C3, evidently was discarded.

A small (66 x 56 x 36 mm) quartzite pebble chopper (BA-XX-1/258) with a triangular outline, found at a depth of 87 cm in the brown silt zone in Square D4, has been flaked on the broad end to create an irregular 65° angle edge with two projections (Figure 6-13b). The low-angled edge of this flaked pebble does not appear to have been used; however, the wedge-shaped narrow end has been flaked into a short 80° angle edge, which is heavily worn. Scattered peck marks on the surface may be from aborted attempts to remove flakes from the pebble.

Another double-edged pebble tool (BA-XX-1/291) was exposed in the east face of Square B3 at a depth of 75 cm in the brown silt and rock zone (Figure 6-14a). This originally quadrangular quartzite pebble, now measuring 65 x 64 x 61 mm, has been steeply flaked to create two opposing chopping edges which are somewhat

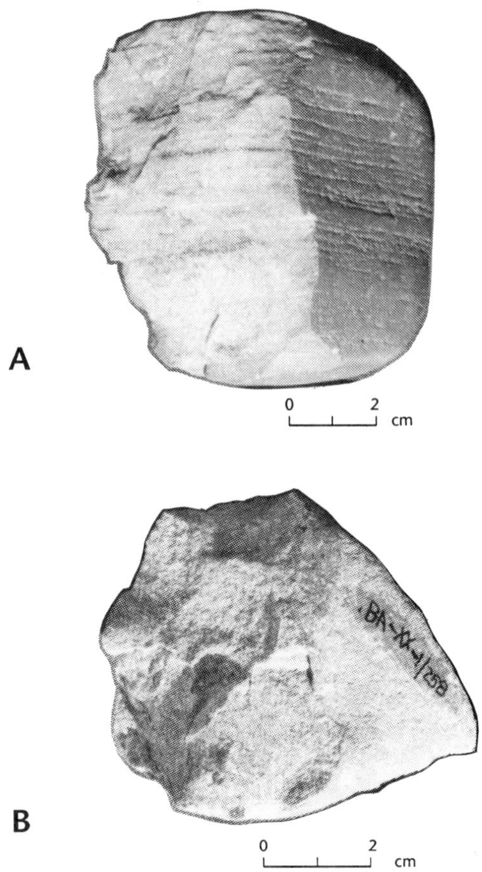

Figure 6-13. Quartzite choppers. **A)** BA-XX-1/273; **B)** BA-XX-1/258.

worn. One 70° angle edge is fairly straight but denticulated by step-flaking; the other edge, with a 75° angle, has a central projection. Some hematite adheres to the high spots of the flaked surfaces, so the piece evidently was used during the preparation of red ochre. Several accidental hand-pick marks are present on the flaked surfaces.

A much-used quartzite chunk (BA-XX-1/237) will be described here because it also has two main working edges, including one excurving denticulated edge with a 70° angle formed by removing long flakes from a slightly concave surface to create a steep endscraper. If the piece is flipped over, there is a broad excurving denticulated 45° angle edge created by removing small flakes from the cortical surface. The latter edge of this piece, which measures 58 x 49 x 25 mm and was found at a depth of 66 cm in the brown silt and rock zone in Square B3, is much worn.

Three flaked quartzite fragments appear to be portions of the step-flaked and battered edges of pebble tools which broke off, either accidentally or intentionally during attempts to renew the chopping edges. BA-XX-1/227, recovered from a depth of 56 cm in the brown silt and rock zone in Square B3, measures 56 x 42 x 35 mm. It appears to be the much battered and rounded excurvate working edge (75° angle) of a pebble tool which had already been resharpened several times by removing step flakes from the flat cortical face. It is difficult to tell if the fragment spalled off by accident or by intention; however, one 65° angle spalled edge is slightly use-flaked and worn.

Another possibly heat-spalled pyramidal quartzite fragment (BA-XX-1/201) was recovered from a depth of 60 cm in the brown silt and rock zone in Square C3. It measures 49 x 42 x 41 mm. The 80–90° angle step-flaked excurving edge is much worn. A prominent ridge extending at right angles to the main working edge is also battered by heavy use. This battered ridge may be the original projecting nose of a pebble tool. Another quartzite fragment (BA-XX-1/203), measuring 57 x 39 x 38 mm, was found in the brown silt and rock zone at a depth of 65 cm in Square C3. Several step flakes have been removed from a prominent nose using a plane surface as a platform, and the remainder of the 90° angle working edge is worn on this artifact.

Two irregular quartzite fragments that fit together at an odd angle were found near each other in Square C3 at a depth of 71 cm in the brown silt and rock zone. One edge of the cortical surface with the broken surface is much battered by heavy chopping or hammering, which evidently shattered the tool (BA-XX-1/275). The combined fragments measure 60 x 43 x 22 mm. Flaking is also present on some broken edges.

A small (41 x 25 x 12 mm) quartzite flake (BA-XX-1/211) from the 30–40 cm level in the brown silt and rock zone in Square B3 has been removed from a battered 90° angle hammerstone or chopper edge by a heavy blow. Chopping edges can also be present on thick flake spalls. The foremost example is BA-XX-1/188, from a depth of 22 cm in the brown silt and rock zone in Square B3. This thick (88 x 38 x 76 mm) quartzite flake was removed by a strong blow which created a broad bulb from an 110° angle platform. The broad excurving distal edge of this flake has been crushed and battered by heavy use as a chopper (Figure 6-14b). Several large flakes have been removed from the cortical surface, probably by heavy use, but possibly by intention to resharpen the working edge. Another 90° angle edge adjacent to the platform has also been battered and step-flaked by heavy hammering.

A thick flake (BA-XX-1/183) with a prominent bulb has had all cortication surfaces removed, so it could have come from a bedrock quarry. Most edges of this flake, which measures 92 x 69 x 31 mm, have been broken off squarely. These 90° angle edges show little use; however, a straight 60° angle edge has been worn and use-flaked. The artifact was found in the brown silt zone at a depth of 32 cm in Square C3. An irregular quartzite flake (BA-XX-1/206), measuring 83 x 66 x 27 mm, was evidently removed from a hammerstone, as the original cortical edge and part of one face are flattened by pecking. A long excurvate edge has been pecked and battered, and several flakes have been removed by use as a chopper, This artifact was recovered from the brown silt and rock zone at a depth of 68 cm in Square C3.

Most of the edges of a thick quartzite flake (BA-XX-1/274) with a flat bulb have been broken off, although evidence of use is present on portions of three 90° angle edges. An S-shaped 65–85° angle edge has been created by two intersecting flake scars removed by blows from opposing edges. This excurving edge has been use-flaked and worn. This thick flake chopping tool measures 62 x 57 x 34 mm. It was recovered from a depth of 68 cm in the brown silt and rock zone in Square B3.

The edges of two large decortication flakes with prominent bulbs show some use retouch. BA-XX-1/261, recovered from a depth of 86 cm in the brown silt and rock zone in Square B3, appears to have been used slightly along the distal 30° angle edge, and the 90° angle bulbar edge also appears to have been smoothed by use. This flake tool measures 67 x 63 x 23 mm. Another large rectangular flake (BA-XX-1/208), measuring 72 x 53 x 24 mm, was recovered from a depth of 69 cm in the brown silt and rock zone in Square C3. Four corners of this flake, varying in edge angle from 50° to 85°, have been smoothed and slightly use-flaked.

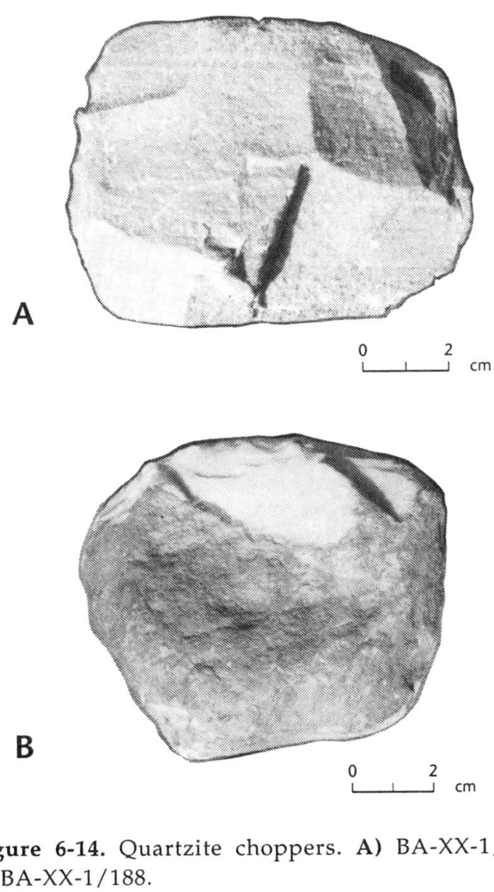

Figure 6-14. Quartzite choppers. **A)** BA-XX-1/291; **B)** BA-XX-1/188.

The edges of five flaked quartzite chunks show some evidence of use. BA-XX-1/196 is a flake that probably spalled off a hammerstone, as the cortical surface exhibits some pecking near the flat bulbar end. The rounded distal end of this flake, which measures 70 x 54 x 25 mm, and was recovered from a depth of 58 cm in the brown silt and rock zone in Square C3, has been worn smooth and use-retouched. A similar 50° distal edge on BA-XX-1/209, found at a depth of 69 cm in the brown silt and rock zone in Square C3, has been use-flaked. A small pecked area is present on a corner of this piece, which measures 81 x 37 x 30 mm. One excurvate edge with a 65° angle on BA-XX-1/264 from a depth of 92 cm in the brown silt and rock zone in Square D4 has been step-flaked; and wear is present, especially on an adjacent spur. Scattered peck marks are present on the surface of this fragment, which measures 68 x 38 x 26 mm. One 90° angle edge of a tabular quartzite chunk with a rectangular outline (BA-XX-1/207), from a depth of 69 cm in the brown silt and rock zone in Square C3, has been slightly smoothed and use-nibbled. The piece measures 65 x 54 x 23 mm. A blocky quartzite fragment (BA-XX-1/182) from 35 cm depth in the brown silt zone in Square C3 has no waterworn surfaces, so it could have come from a quartzite outcropping. All of the broken surfaces of this chunk, which measures 55 x 53 x 33 mm, appear to be natural. One end has been step-flaked and crushed to form a 90° angle edge, and the opposite corner of the same plane face is use-flaked and battered. A flat face, a concave face, and a ridged face may have been polished; however, it is possible that they were sand-blasted.

Nine flakes removed from quartzite pebbles show some evidence of use. The bulbar end of BA-XX-1/248, from a depth of 74 cm in the brown silt and rock zone in Square B3, appears to have been retouched to form a thick squared projection with worn edges (110° angle). The distal edge (45° angle) of this flake, which measures 56 x 31 x 12 mm, has been steepened by use as an endscraper. The bulbar end of another utilized quartzite flake (BA-XX-1/223) from the 70–80 cm level in the brown silt zone in Square C3 has also been reduced by removing four flakes in order to resharpen a projecting corner, the 80–85° edges of which are more worn than any thin edges. One of these flake scars created a burin-like spall on this flake, which measures 76 x 41 x 9 mm. The distal edge (15° angle) of BA-XX-1/272, from a depth of 105 cm in the brown silt and rock zone in Square B3, has been retouched to form two small protruding spurs which are use-worn. The lateral straight edge, with a 50° angle, has also been slightly worn and slightly retouched. This artifact measures 40 x 32 x 8 mm. BA-XX-1/213 has a long narrow projecting nose which is smoothed and use-flaked, possibly as a perforator or graver. This graver tip appears to have been renewed twice by removal of burin spalls. This unusual burinated quartzite flake was found in the 60–70 cm level in the brown silt and rock zone in Square C3, and measures 48 x 24 x 12 mm. A separate 40° angle straight edge appears to be use-nibbled. A pyramidal quartzite chunk (BA-XX-1/224) has a projecting corner which is smoothed by use, possibly as a perforator. This flake measures 39 x 31 x 22 mm, and it was recovered from the 40–50 cm level in the brown silt and rock zone in Square B3. Another quartzite chunk (BA-XX-1/234) with a triangular cross-section apparently has been retouched to resharpen a worn projecting corner, which has a 35° edge angle. This flake, recovered from a depth of 65 cm in the brown silt and rock zone in Square B3, measures 43 x 37 x 17 mm. The flat bulbar face and parts of the thin edge (10° angle) of BA-XX-1/140 has evidently been smoothed by use. This thin flake measures 52 x 41 x 14 mm. It was recovered from the 0–10 cm level in the brown silt and rock zone in Square B3. A 90° edge of BA-XX-1/253 has been step-flaked. Also, there is a dark waxy substance adhering to both ends and adjacent flaked surfaces of this flake, which measures 52 x 33 x 17 mm and was recovered from the 70–80 cm level in the brown silt and rock zone in Square B3. Hematite adheres to the convex edge (60° angle) and high spots on the adjacent bulbar face of BA-XX-1/289, which was recovered from the 60–70 cm level in the brown silt and rock zone in Square C3. The convex stained edge of this flake, which measures 51 x 39 x 14 mm, fits the concave face of the grooved hematite concretion (BA-XX-1/284) which was found in the 50–60 cm level in the brown silt zone in the same square.

Modified Hematite Fragments

One of the objectives of the excavations in Toca do Cosmos was to date the spectacular rock art which decorates the flat white ceiling of the lower shelter. However, the area with deep sediment fill was not directly underneath any design panels; and it was unlikely that a decorated segment of the ceiling would be found fallen into datable sediments. Most likely the modified hematite fragments and the hematite-stained pebbles and flakes found in the lower half of the stratified deposits were associated with the ceiling paintings; but it is always possible that pigment was produced for body painting or decoration of wooden artifacts, so their presence in stratigraphic context is not definite proof of the age of the rock art on the ceiling.

While small fragments of red ochre occurred scattered throughout the deposits in the lower shelter, the most definite evidence of use of hematite to obtain pigment was recovered relatively deep in the zone of light brown silt with rock fragments. The largest piece of modified hematite (BA-XX-1/284), measuring 92 x 37 x 41 mm, was found in this stratigraphic zone at the 50–60 cm level in Square C3. It is an irregular fragment of a dark red hematite concretion with a concave face approximately 8 mm in depth, with five fine line incisions and a number of fine striations running lengthwise in the concavity, and fine striations on an adjacent flat surface (Figure 6-15a). The piece must have been gouged, scraped, and ground in order to obtain the coloring material. Another large modified hematite piece (BA-XX-1/263) was found even deeper, at a depth of 82 cm in the light brown silt and rock zone in the northern sector of Square B3. This varicolored piece was tabular in form, measuring 67 x 48 x 14 mm (Figure 6-15b). Parallel striations from gouging form a broad longitudinal groove on one red face. There are several striations at right angles to the groove and adjacent to a squared edge, which exhibits oblique striations. There is a limonite coating on the opposite face, but no evidence of modification. The piece was worked for red paint by grooving and grinding. A less-modified hematite pebble (BA-XX-1/265) was found at a depth of 90–100 cm in the light brown silt and rock zone in Square B3. This piece, measuring 37 x 28 x 18 mm, was an irregular dark red hematite fragment with a set of fine parallel striations on a flat face. It was apparently ground to obtain the coloring material.

Bone Artifacts

Bone was relatively sparse in the deposits at Toca do

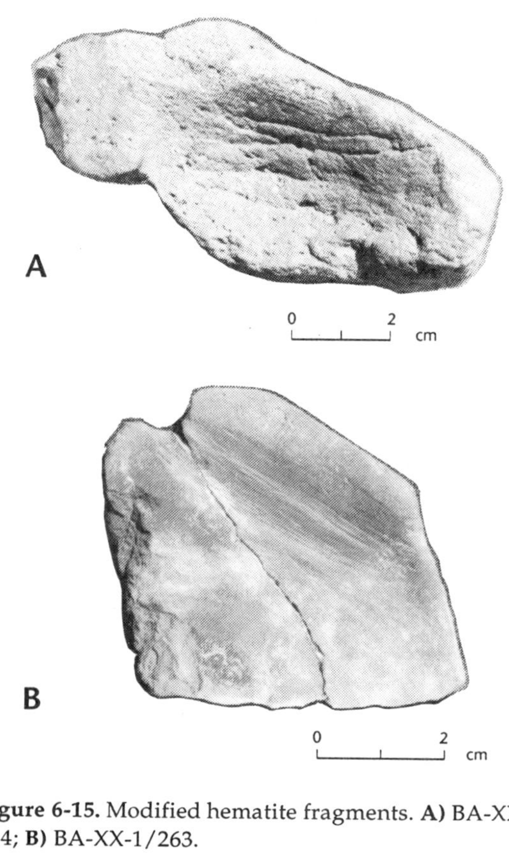

Figure 6-15. Modified hematite fragments. **A)** BA-XX-1/284; **B)** BA-XX-1/263.

Cosmos, and only three bones or teeth were found to be modified. There was a small bone bead, a possibly utilized large carnivore canine, and an incised fragment of a shaft of a long bone of a large mammal.

The bone bead (BA-XX-1/45) was recovered from the brown silt zone at a depth of 10–20 cm in Square X4 in the upper shelter. It is a cylindrical segment of a bird (?) bone, measuring 10 x 6 x 5 mm, with irregularly bevelled edges ground and polished (Figure 6-16a). The exterior surface displays some short parallel incisions or scratches.

The carnivore canine (BA-XX-1/243) is very large, measuring 61 x 18 x 13 mm; and may be that of a jaguar. It was recovered deep in the brown silt and rock zone, at the 70–80 cm level, in Square B3. Although much of the surface enamel is eroded, the remaining enamel surface shows fine scratches but no clear proof of human use. The tip has broken off.

The incised fragment of a mammalian long bone (BA-XX-1/229) was recovered from the brown silt and rock zone at a depth of 55 cm in Square B3. The segment measures 64 x 24 x 5 mm. The surface is badly eroded, but a set of short parallel cuts about 4 mm long may be observed on the exterior surface near one edge; and there are several very short parallel cuts near the opposite edge. These may be butchering marks.

It may be noted in addition that two highly permineralized fragments of bone of a giant mammal were found in the basal zone of the brown silt and rock zone at a depth of 100–110 cm below surface in Square B3. These large fossil bone fragments, measuring 98 x 53 x 33 mm and 73 x 43 x 12 mm, may have been collected in Toca da Gameleira nearby and brought to Toca do Cosmos for utilization, as each has a small flake or two removed from an end.

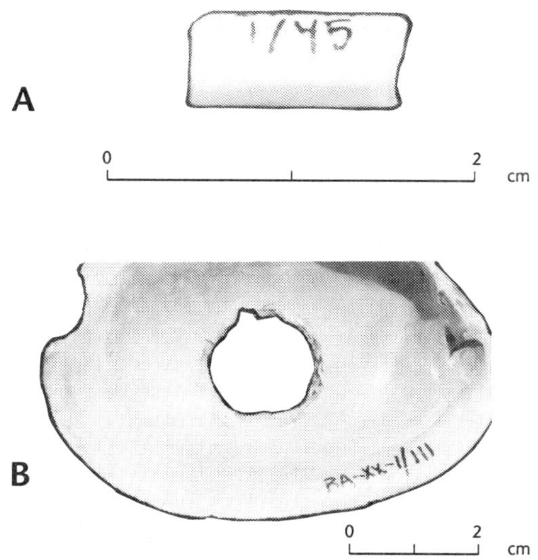

Figure 6-16. A) bone bead (BA-XX-1/45); **B)** modified mussel shell (BA-XX-1/111).

Mussel Shell Artifacts

Shells of the riverine bivalve *Diplodon diplodocus* were quite abundant in the brown silt zone in the upper shelter, although less common in the corresponding upper 30 cm of the deposit in the lower shelter. This mussel, found in the Rio Verde less than 2 km east of the site, was apparently a significant food resource for the late prehistoric peoples of the area. All shells were examined, and a total of 42 showed evidence of modification.

The most common type of modification (on 20 complete valves and 10 fragmentary valves) was the placement of an irregular perforation in the central part of a valve (Figure 6-16b). Valves were almost equally distributed in terms of left and right. The central perforations, which feature irregular edges (with flaking on the interior) and a generally elliptical form, vary in diameter from 28 x 17 mm to 10 x 6 mm; with the mode approximately 20 x 15 mm. There would seem to be no consistent relationship between size of valve (which varies from 68 x 56 mm to 48 x 36 mm) and size of the perforation other than that the thicker-walled shells tend to have the smaller holes.

When and why the perforations were made is still undetermined. In experiments, a small pebble hammerstone proved fairly successful in duplicating the perforations on a fresh shell; but dry shells shattered. The perforation may have been made to extract the animal, but it would be far easier to steam the mussels open or to force the edge of the shell than to knock a hole in its center. A local informant said that such a perforation might be made to suck the animal out once the soft parts had become liquified. It is thought that the perforated shells may have been used as special scrapers, but no clear evidence of use-wear is apparent on the inner edge of the perforation. The lack of wear on the edge of the perforation would also argue against the use of the perforated shells as stringed ornaments.

In terms of distribution, most of these artifacts were found in the brown silt deposit in the upper shelter: 10 in the 0–10 cm level of Square X2, 8 in the 0–10 cm level of Square X4, and 4 in the 10–20 cm level in Square X4. In the lower shelter, Square B3 yielded 5 perforated shells from the brown silt zone at the 0–10 cm level, and one from the 10–20 cm level in the brown silt and rock zone. Square C3 yielded one at the 0–10 cm level in brown silt, and one at the 20–30 cm level in a brown silt and rock zone. None were found in Square D4.

Three valves had one or more perforations significantly smaller than those on the artifacts described above. Two of these valves are small in size, measuring 46 x 36 x 2 mm (BA-XX-1/122) and 42 x 38 x 2 mm (BA-XX-1/102). BA-XX-1/102, recovered from the 0–10 cm level in Square X4, has an oblong perforation measuring 5 x 3 mm slightly off center; while BA-XX-1/122, from the 10–20 cm level in Square X4, features two small (4 mm diameter) perforations spaced 8 mm apart in a line about 11 mm from the broadest edge of the shell. In neither case do the perforations show evidence of wear from a string. The largest valve in this group (BA-XX-1/110), from the 0–10 cm level in Square X2, measures 59 x 48 x 4 mm. It has a small (3 mm diameter) incomplete perforation possibly made with a punch. The broad end of the valve is worn to a straight edge, possibly formed by scraping.

Three other shell artifacts (BA-XX-1/109, 112, and 117) all from the 0–10 cm level in Square X4, also show evidence of wear on the broad end of the valve. The valves range in size from 62 x 52 x 5 mm to 72 x 61 x 8 mm. On the two smaller specimens, the broad edge has been worn back, with flaking and irregular notching, about 5 to 7 mm from the original edge; on the largest specimen (BA-XX-1/117) the wear is less pronounced. These modified valves could have been used as scrapers, although no striations are apparent on either the interior or exterior face of the valves.

Finally, six valves or fragments of valves appear to have a small perforated notch on the short side of the umbo. The notch averages 2 to 3 mm in diameter, and may result from the use of a small punch or wedge. The complete valves range in size from 62 x 48 x 3 mm to 45 x 38 x 1 mm. Two specimens (BA-XX-1/83, 84) were found in the fill in a fissure in Square X4; two specimens (BA-XX-1/144, 148) in brown silt at a depth of 0–10 cm in Square B3; one specimen (BA-XX-1/178) in the brown silt and rock zone at a depth of 10–20 cm in Square B3; and one specimen (BA-XX-1/181) at a depth of 20–30 cm in a brown silt and rock zone in Square C3. Perhaps both the perforations and the notches were made to affix some sort of haft.

DISCUSSION AND CONCLUSIONS

Toca do Cosmos was chosen for excavation because of its spectacular rock art and its proximity to Toca da Gameleira. It was hoped that there might be a way to date the pictographs and perhaps to associate them with an early occupation. Unfortunately, no decorated wall spalls were incorporated in the sediments, so the rock art is not directly datable. Several hematite fragments and artifacts used for scraping and grinding hematite were found in the preceramic deposits between 50 and 100 cm below surface in the lower shelter. Most likely these modified hematite fragments and hematite-stained hammerstones and flakes relate to the rock art, because all were found in the lower chamber below the ceiling panels; but they could have been used to produce body paint as well. The evidence for pigment processing came from the lower half of the deposits, but a charcoal sample from just above bedrock that assayed only approximately 3200 yr B.P. indicates no great antiquity for even the oldest artifact-bearing deposits in the lower shelter of Toca do Cosmos. The occupation of the upper shelter was only on the ceramic horizon, with a radiocarbon date of about 1230 yr B.P. It may be that the upper shelter was closed and uninhabitable until then.

Assuming the date of 3200 yr B.P. from the basal levels is correct, it appears that the lower chamber of Toca do Cosmos filled quite rapidly during the last three millennia. The bulk of the fill was derived from roof collapse which formed a talus encroaching from the cave entrance. The expanding talus acted as a dam to retain the brown silt deposited from the recesses of the cave. Probably the rock talus expanded in spurts, as the roof of the cave entrance collapsed periodically. The brown silt washing in from the rear of the cave then gradually accumulated behind the rock talus dam. Thus artifacts deposited at the same time on the talus slope might roll downslope and be found at different depths, while contemporary artifacts deposited in the more horizontally bedded brown silt might be found at an even lower depth. The date of approximately 3200 yr B.P. came from the basal levels of the brown silt just above bedrock, so it should date the earliest occupation of the lower chamber. It is possible, of course, that earlier silt deposits had been flushed out, leaving heavy objects lying on the bedrock floor. The two minimally flaked fragments of permineralized large mammal bone, most likely of giant sloth, came from the brown silt just above bedrock. Although they could be referred to an earlier occupation, the fact that there were only two broken pieces that appear to have been used suggests that they had been selected from the eroded surface of the Toca da Gameleira for their useful edges and ends, and carried next door by later occupants of Toca do Cosmos.

The main reason people congregated in Toca do Cosmos may have been to express their artistic impulses on the smooth white ceiling of the lower chamber. They may also have performed rituals related to cosmological concepts portrayed on the ceiling. The thick chert scraper planes with denticulated edges, and quartzite pebble choppers with central projections, suggest that people probably also worked wood and perhaps processed other vegetable materials in the cool shade of the rock overhang. The main settlement, however, may have been outside the cave. An open settlement site, now marked by an extensive spread of shell fragments with some stone flakes on the rock surface of the limestone outcrop, was located on the edge of the limestone outcrop about 100 m south of the upper shelter.

Chapter 7
Toca da Gameleira

INTRODUCTION

Location and Description of the Site

Toca da Gameleira, the second cave site in the Rio Verde area, is located about 100 m southwest of Toca do Cosmos; and is part of the same cave system which extends under a low barren horizontal limestone outcrop in the *caatinga*. The entrance to the cavern is an elliptical vertical-walled opening in the limestone, with the surface of its sediment fill approximately 5 to 7 m below the surface of the limestone formation.

In terms of three dimensions, Toca da Gameleira is a very complex cave system, opening into irregular partially silt-filled tunnels at several levels. The main chamber of the cavern is guitar-shaped in plan, about 12 m long in an east-west direction, and 8 m in maximum width (map, Figure 7-1). The western half of the main chamber is sheltered by a high rock overhang. In the northwest part are irregular sloping shelves of rough vesicular cherty limestone at three levels. Small tunnels lead off the highest shelf. Two major tunnels, formed along joints or fissures in the limestone, parallel each other to the north and south of the main chamber (map, Figure 7-1). The south tunnel extends almost 20 m west of the main chamber before pinching out, and about 6 m east of the main chamber before the tunnel is blocked by a steep cone of silt. The north tunnel, connected to the main chamber by a narrow but open passage, extends about 6 m west before pinching out. The east branch of the north tunnel extends about 10 m into a large irregular silt-filled chamber which ultimately connects to an irregular silt-filled passage with opening situated between the upper and lower shelters of Toca do Cosmos, about 100 m to the northeast. At least two species of bat, one large and one small, occupy this tunnel of the cavern system.

The site, first discovered by the authors in July 1984, is named for a large *gameleira* tree *(Ficus doliara)*, whose thick complex root system occupies much of the northeast side of the main chamber, and provides access from the surface of the limestone outcrop to the cavern floor (Figure 7-2b). There is also another large tree, similar to a willow, locally called a *salgeira* (species unidentified) established on the north side of the vertical-walled opening. Both trees rain leaves and limb fragments into the vertical opening to the cavern in the dry season.

The tree roots are embedded in a low cone of limestone rock debris under the vertical-walled opening to the cavern (Figures 7-1, 7-2a). The rock-rubble cone features limestone fragments up to 2 m in diameter. It drops off in all directions from the vertical-walled opening to the cavern; but there is a more level rock-strewn floor under the overhang to the west. In the western branch of the south tunnel, however, the floor is covered with reddish brown silt.

Within the main chamber, and along the walls of the north and south tunnels, are low openings where the surface of the sediment fill slopes down and under the cavern wall. Debris at the mouth of these openings suggests they function as sinkholes for drainage during rains. The one excavation unit carried to bedrock, however, indicated that the sediment fill within the main chamber of the cavern may be only approximately 3 m in depth.

The Excavations

When the site was first examined by the authors in

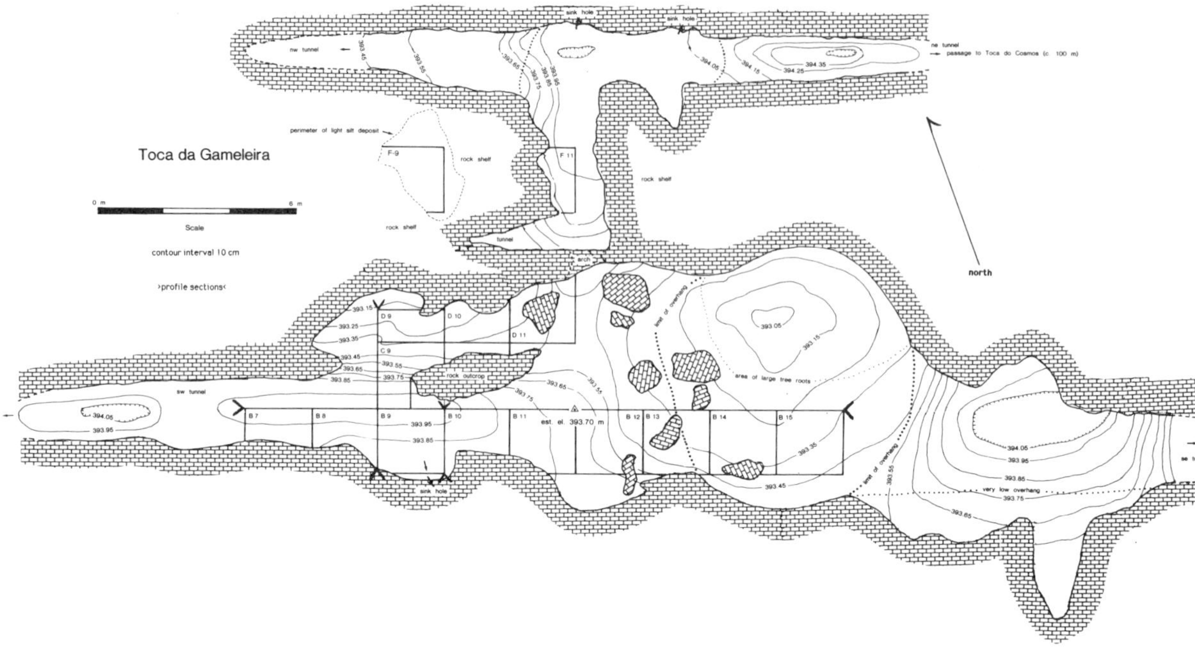

Figure 7-1. Plan of the sediment-filled areas of Toca da Gameleira.

1984, mineralized fragmented bones of giant ground sloth, as well as lithic artifacts including hammerstones and choppers, were observed on the surface of the sediment fill. In the hope that clear evidence would be found of a direct association of man with giant sloth, excavations were undertaken by the authors in Toca da Gameleira in late June 1985, and completed at the end of July.

The sediment-filled floor area of the cavern was first mapped, and a grid system laid out with a long trench extending from the west branch of the south tunnel to the east end of the rock-rubble cone (map, Figure 7-1). Nine adjoining 2-m squares were excavated in alternating sequence along this trench, to sterile deposits at a depth of 70 cm; one square (B15) at the east end of the rock rubble cone was excavated to bedrock at a depth of approximately 3 m. As well, a shallow fissure 1 to 2 m broad in the lowest rock shelf, adjacent to the main trench on the north (encompassing Squares C9, D9, D10, and D11), was excavated when it was found to contain quantities of fossil sloth bone fragments. Also, half a 2-m square (F12) was excavated in the narrow passage leading to the north tunnel.

All units were excavated by trowel or hand pick in 10-cm levels, and the material was examined on a 4-mm mesh screen. Concentrations of large fossil bone fragments were mapped in situ. All bone and modified lithic materials were collected. At the completion of excavation the walls of each unit were profiled.

STRATIGRAPHY

Natural Stratigraphy

Field Description of the Sediments

When Toca da Gameleira was first examined, rock rubble was the most prominent feature on the surface of the sediment fill. Directly underneath the large vertical-walled shaft opening of the cavern was a low broad cone of large limestone boulders and angular limestone rubble, with the roots of the two large trees intertwined. The surface zone of limestone rubble extended into the east wing of the south tunnel for a distance of about 10 m, but in the west wing of this tunnel a level deposit of reddish brown silt surfaced. Incorporated into the surface rock rubble was a scatter of fossil bone fragments and lithic artifacts, as well as small rounded or subrounded quartzite or quartz pebbles. In local areas bones of small mammals were abundant.

As excavation was undertaken in the main trench the rock rubble zone (Unit 2) was found to range in thickness from 15 cm at the west end of the trench to 40 cm at the east end (profiles, Figures 7-3, 7-4, 7-5). Most of the subangular or angular limestone fragments ranged in size from about 3 to 20 cm; but larger stones were common, especially in the east sector of the trench. The smaller fragments, under 5 cm in size, tended to be flat and scalar in nature, apparently wall spall. The surface of the limestone fragments was commonly chalky-

Figure 7-2. A) excavations in progress under the vertical shaft which provides access to Toca da Gameleira; **B)** entrance to Toca da Gameleira from surface of limestone outcrop.

white, a feature indicating weathering. Also incorporated into the unsorted deposit were rounded or subrounded pebbles of quartzite and quartz up to 4 cm in diameter. In the western sector of the main trench, fragments of a dark ironstone breccia also occurred in this zone, as well as rough nodules of chert. The matrix of the rock rubble was a very dark brown/black silt with crumb structure evident in the upper levels. Roots of varying size were very numerous in this zone. Both dark-stained fossilized and recent unaltered bone, and artifacts were found within it, as well as some riverine mussel shell and many small gastropod shells in the upper 10 cm. Some charcoal fragments were recovered at a depth of 10–20 cm in Square B15 at the east end of the main trench.

The stratigraphic zone (Unit 3) directly underlying this zone of dark brown/black silt with abundant rock fragments (Unit 2) varied in character from one end of the trench to the other (profiles, Figures 7-3, 7-4, 7-5, 7-6). At the east end of the main trench, directly underlying the zone of dark brown/black silt with abundant rock fragments (Unit 2), was a thin "transition zone" of lighter brown silt with fewer rock fragments (Unit 3a), only about 5 to 15 cm in thickness, grading into the underlying zone of yellow/brown clayey silt (Unit 3d). This transition zone contained large bone fragments and yielded some artifacts. At the west end of the trench (appearing in Square B12 and continuing west), the brown clayey silt directly underlying Unit 2 contained abundant unsorted fragments of a dark-colored friable breccia (in Units 3b and 3c). The breccia appeared to be composed largely of cemented ironstone nodules of varying size. Breccia fragments, usually rounded or subrounded, ranged in size up to 30 cm. The breccia fragments were especially concentrated in Squares B10, B9, B8, B7, and C9 (Figure 7-7b). Also abundant in this stratigraphic zone (Units 3b and 3c) in these areas of the site were unsorted irregular rough fragments of weathered chert, ranging in size up to 30 cm. Rounded or subrounded pebbles of quartz and quartzite were also incorporated. The matrix in Units 3b and 3c was a brown clayey silt, increasingly more clayey and lighter in color with depth, grading into the underlying zone of yellow/brown clayey silt (Unit 3d) at approximately 50–60 cm depth below surface. Fossilized bone fragments were abundant in Units 3b and 3c, and artifacts were also found.

The underlying zone of yellow/brown clayey silt (Unit 3d) contained fossil bone fragments to a depth of approximately 60 cm below surface; and small rough irregular chert fragments also occurred. In Square B15 at the east end of the main trench, where excavation was extended to bedrock (Figures 7-5, 7-7a), the clayey silt became an orange/brown in color below 60 cm depth; and rough irregular weathered chert fragments of varying size up to 20 cm in diameter increased in frequency. Small rounded or subrounded pebbles of quartz and quartzite were found scattered in the clayey silt to a depth of about 120 cm below surface. Below about 100 cm depth, manganese stains and small ironstone nodules occurred; and the clayey silt became increasingly clayey and mottled, orange/grey in color; and greyer in color with depth below 200 cm. The bedrock floor of the cavern, rough and weathered, was reached at a depth of approximately 310 cm below surface on the north side of Square B15. A few large weathered subangular limestone boulders were enclosed in the clayey silt directly above the bedrock floor. Throughout the 3-m section,

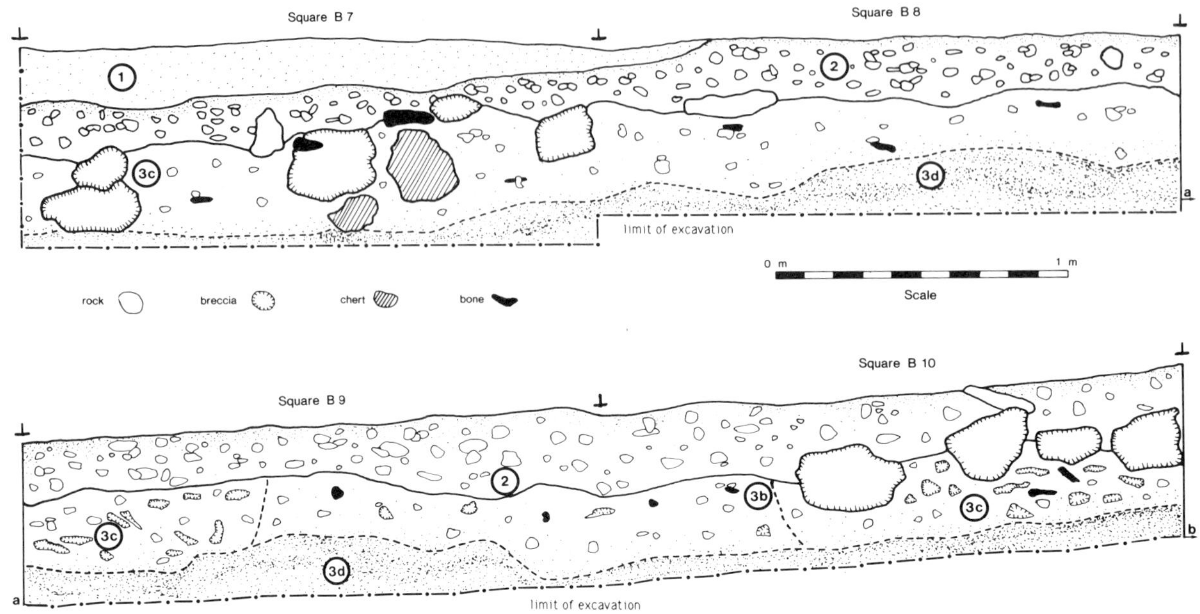

Figure 7-3. Profile of north face of Squares B7, B8, B9, and B10. **1,** reddish brown silt; **2,** dark brown/black silt with abundant rock fragments; **3b,** brown silt with breccia and chert fragments; **3c,** brown silt with abundant rock, breccia, and bone; **3d,** yellow/brown clayey silt.

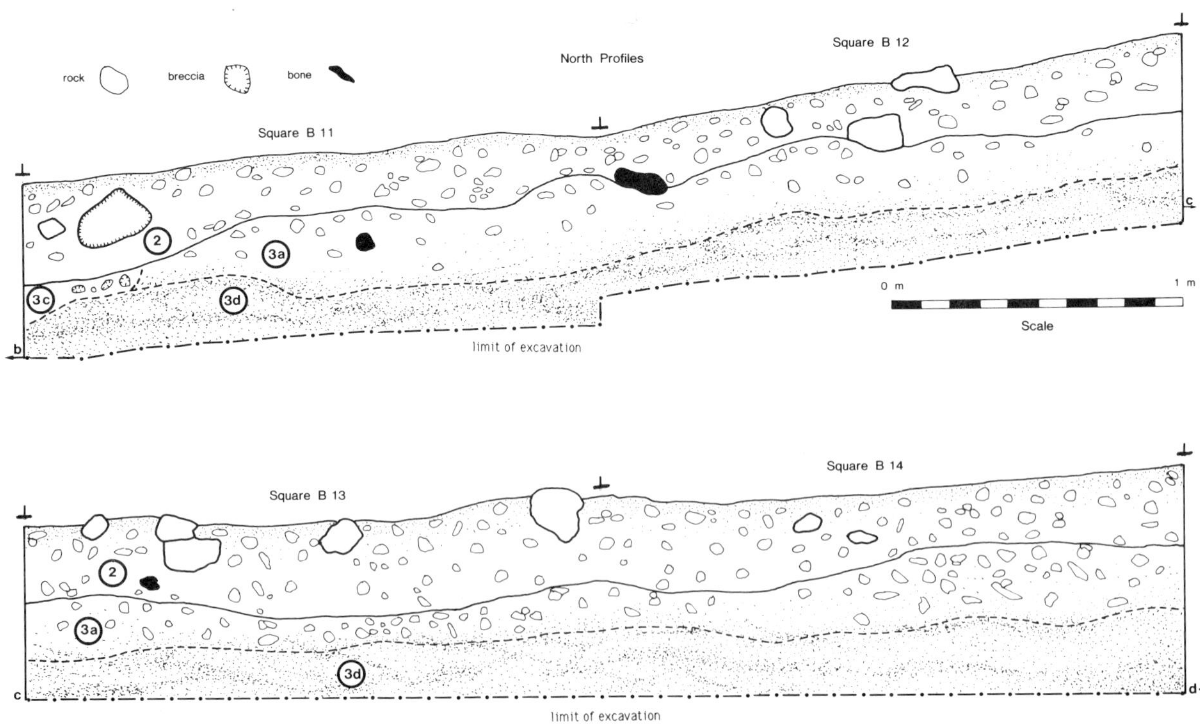

Figure 7-4. Profile of north face of Squares B11, B12, B13, and B14. **2,** dark brown/black silt with abundant rock fragments; **3a,** light brown silt with scattered rocks; **3c,** brown silt with abundant rock, breccia, and bone; **3d,** yellow/brown clayey silt.

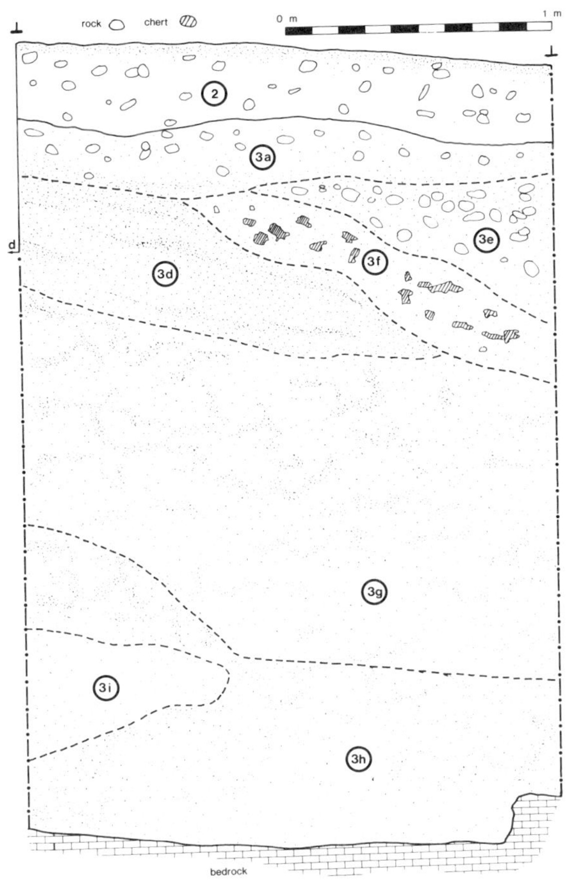

Figure 7-5. Profile of north face of Square B15, Toca da Gameleira. **2,** dark brown silt with abundant rock fragments; **3e,** light brown silt with scattered rocks; **3d,** yellow/brown clayey silt; **3e,** orange/brown silt; **3f,** orange/brown clayey silt; **3g,** mottled orange/grey clayey silt; **3h,** mottled grey/orange clayey silt; **3i,** grey/white clayey silt.

the clayey silt remained moist. No organic material was found below a depth of 60 cm below surface.

The two irregular shelves of light-colored vesicular limestone bedrock in the west and northwest sectors of the cavern were partially covered by deposits of dry light-brown silt. As it was originally planned to place a screen on the lower rock shelf, in the general area of Square D10, the sediment cover was excavated. A shallow rock channel containing an abundance of large fossil bone fragments was exposed. The upper 5–10 cm of the deposit in this area (comprising parts of Squares D11, D10, D9, and C9) was a fine loose light-brown silt containing abundant remains of microfauna as well as a few fragments of fossilized bone of large mammals; and much rock rubble. It appears to be a dry equivalent of Unit 2. The underlying zone was a compact light-brown silt with a polygonal blocky structure (polygons 4–6 cm in diameter), containing abundant unsorted subangular fragments of chert (up to 4 cm in size) and dark breccia (up to 10 cm in size) plus small scalar limestone fragments, with occasional small rounded or subrounded pebbles of quartz and quartzite. This zone appears to be a dry equivalent of Units 3b and 3c in the main trench. Fossilized fragments of giant mammal bone were abundant in this zone. About 5 cm above bedrock in this broad shallow channel in the lower rock shelf, at a maximum depth of 40 cm below surface, was a thin compact cemented layer of coarse reddish brown sandy silt containing abundant small ironstone nodules as well as some irregular chert fragments and the occasional fossil bone fragment and rounded quartz or quartzite pebble. In some areas bedrock was coated with a deposit of very coarse grey cemented angular sand. In the central part of Square C9 the bedrock channel in the lower rock shelf dropped off, below 70 cm depth below surface; but the zone of abundant bone fragments and rock rubble continued into the zone of brown silt with abundant breccia and chert fragments (Units 3b and 3c) prominent in Square B9 to the south (profile, Figure 7-6).

In Squares B8 and B7, at the west end of the main trench and at the entrance to the west wing of the south tunnel, a zone of reddish brown silt (Unit 1) about 20 cm in maximum thickness overlies the zone of dark brown/black silt with abundant rock fragments (Unit 2) which outcrops at the surface farther east in the cavern. The reddish brown silt zone (Unit 1) contained numerous bones of small mammals, some gastropod shells, and a few fragments of bone of large mammals, with sparse rock. Some charcoal fragments were collected at the 10–20 cm level in Square B8. This reddish brown silt deposit on the surface at the entrance to the west wing of the south tunnel appears to be derived from the silt deposits farther back within the tunnel. Below this surface zone of reddish brown silt the stratigraphic sequence in Squares B7 and B8 is the same as farther east in the main trench (profile, Figure 7-3).

Excavation was also carried out in a section of the narrow passage connecting the main chamber with the north tunnel of the cavern. In Square F12, numerous large fossil bone fragments were found in an unsorted deposit of brown silt with abundant limestone fragments. At a depth of approximately 40 cm below the estimated surface level, this zone gave way to an orange/brown clayey silt with numerous chert fragments but little bone. Excavation was suspended at a depth of 80 cm below surface as the rock wall of the passage curved in to the north.

Provisional Interpretation of the Natural Stratigraphy

The lowermost deposits in Toca da Gameleira are clayey sediments probably derived from disintegration

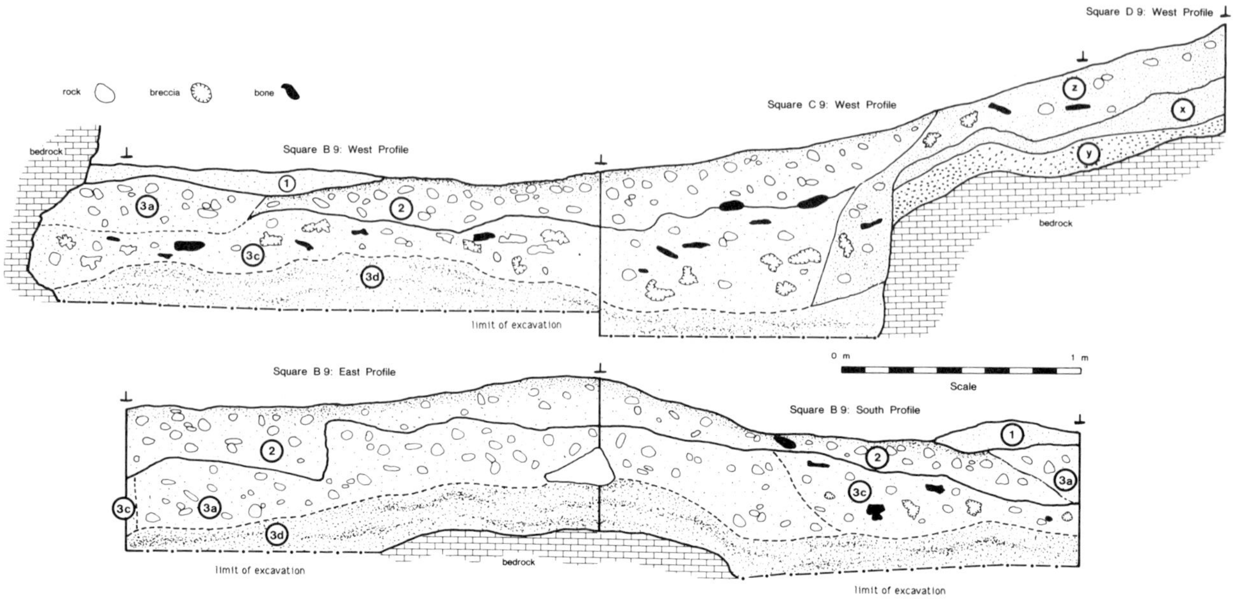

Figure 7-6. Profile of west face of Squares B9, C9, and D9; and south and east faces of Square B9. **1,** reddish brown silt; **2,** dark brown/black silt with abundant rock fragments; **3a,** light brown silt with scattered rocks; **3c,** brown silt with abundant breccia, rock, and bone; **ed,** yellow/brown clayey silt; **x,** reddish brown sandy silt; **y,** greyish angular sand; **z,** compact light brown silt.

of the limestone bedrock within the cavern, and the rough chert nodules enclosed in the cavern sediments likely weathered out of the local limestone as well. No organic material, specifically fossil bone, is found below 60 cm depth, and no exotic quartz or quartzite pebbles below 120 cm depth; a distribution suggesting that the cavern was not open to extraneous material for some time after its formation. Mammal bones and artifacts are found only in the upper 60 cm of deposit.

The presence of exotic quartz and quartzite pebbles in Toca da Gameleira was at first thought to be the result of human intervention; but the abundance of unaltered pebbles, especially in otherwise sterile lower levels, indicated natural derivation. Extremely weathered stream-rolled pebbles were also found scattered on the surface of the limestone outcrop outside the cave. Many of these quartzite pebbles were hollow ghosts; and several quartz pebbles were glazed, indicating long-term exposure to tropical weathering. Evidently the Rio Verde, now entrenched about 2 km to the east, traversed the area of the site at one time in the very remote past, leaving a scatter of quartz and quartzite pebbles as the only remnant of its former course.

In the upper zones of sediment, definite unconformities may be discerned between Unit 1, the reddish brown silt at the west end of the main trench and in the west branch of the south tunnel; Unit 2, the zone of very dark brown/black silt with abundant rock fragments making up the rubble cone and extending throughout the cavern; and the underlying clayey units 3a, 3b, 3c, and 3d. The latter deposits, with a matrix of brown clayey silt, grade into the underlying clayey silt which continues to bedrock. However, Units 3b and 3c incorporate an abundance of chert fragments, breccia fragments (of unknown origin), and fossilized fragments of bone of megamammals. These clasts are jumbled and unsorted, and deposition by strong colluvial water action is indicated; probably an intensive flooding of the cavern. The abundant clasts in Unit 2 are also unsorted, indicating strong water action during floods of short duration; but the matrix of dark brown/black silt is well weathered, with crumb structure and high humic content, and a chalky-white patina on enclosed limestone fragments. Unit 2 contains material—fossil bone fragments and some breccia fragments—derived from the underlying deposits, but deposition appears to have stabilized for some time. Unit 1, restricted to the west end of the main trench, seems to be a relatively recent deposit of reddish brown silt washed in from the west branch of the south tunnel of the cavern. Similar silt deposits fill the tunnels leading into the cavern from the upper rock shelf, and from the east wing of the north tunnel.

Radiocarbon Dates

Only two samples of charcoal were obtained in the excavations in Toca da Gameleira, unfortunately both very high in the stratigraphic section. A date of 470 ± 90 years B.P. (Beta-13930) was obtained on a sample of charcoal fragments collected in the northwest quarter of Square B15 at a depth of 10–20 cm in the zone of very dark brown/black silt with abundant rock fragments (Unit 2). A date of 1110 ± 80 years B.P. (Beta-13931) was obtained on a sample of charcoal fragments collected in the southeast corner of Square B8 at a depth of 10–20 cm, in the basal zone of the reddish brown silt deposit (Unit 1). As this reddish brown silt zone overlies the zone of very dark brown/black silt with rock in this area, a younger date was expected. It is possible that the rubble cone in the east sector of the cavern, under the vertical-walled opening, has continued to accumulate after deposition of the reddish brown silt zone in the far western area of the main chamber. It is also possible that the younger charcoal fragments in Square B15 filtered down or were dragged down among the rocks by roots.

In any case, the available radiocarbon dates for the Toca da Gameleira are quite recent. The transition zone of light-brown silt (Unit 3a) and the zones of brown silt with abundant breccia and chert fragments (Units 3b and 3c) remain undated; along with their content of fossil bones and artifacts.

Faunal Remains

An outstanding feature of Toca da Gameleira was the abundance of fossilized fragments of bone of giant mammals. Approximately 545 kg of fossil bone fragments was collected. Most of the bone, a dark grey or brown in color, was very highly mineralized, apparently by iron salts. The collection is yet to be thoroughly analysed, but it may be readily seen that almost of all this dark fossil bone is of giant ground sloth, *Eremotherium* and possibly *Megatherium* (identified by Diogenes de Almeida Campos). A count of clavicles indicated that at least five individual animals are represented. Also mineralized to the same high degree were a few bones of another large mammal, possibly *Toxodon,* as some highly mineralized fragments of the distinctive teeth of this genus were identified by Prof. Campos.

There were also a few bones and teeth of large mammals which were white in color, less mineralized, possibly by calcite. The white fossil bone specimens also await firm identification; but according to Prof. Campos, one molar may be *Macrauchenia,* another a large cervid, and another possibly horse.

In terms of vertical distribution, the fossil bone fragments occurred in all stratigraphic zones from the surface to a depth of 50–65 cm. They were most abundant, however, in the transition zone of light-brown silt (Unit 3a) and the zone of brown silt with abundant breccia and chert fragments (Units 3b and 3c): 76% by weight of the total of dark-colored fossil bone fragments were found jumbled in these zones. All of the white, less mineralized fragments of bone of large mammals recovered also came from these zones. Fossil bone fragments in the overlying zone of dark brown/black silt with abundant rock (Unit 2) were fewer in number, generally smaller in size, and more scattered: 23% by weight of the total of fossil bone fragments were found in this upper zone. A few large bone fragments were found embedded in the upper part of the yellow/brown clayey silt zone (Unit 3d), lying horizontally or at a low angle.

In terms of horizontal distribution, there was a marked concentration of large fossil bone fragments in

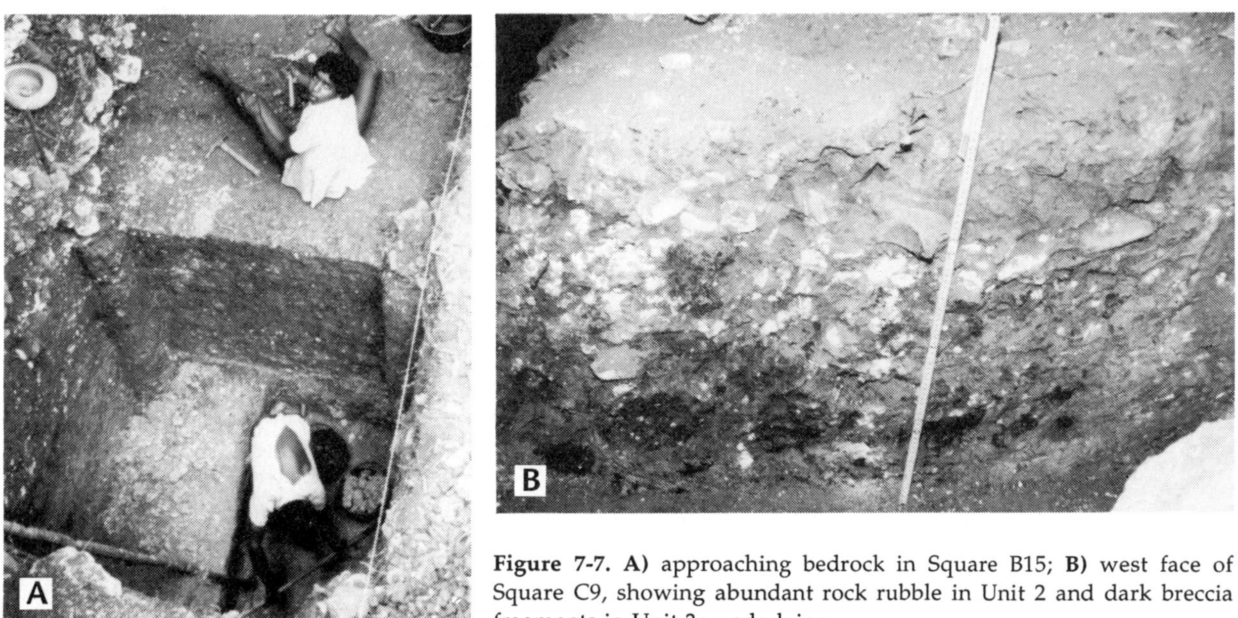

Figure 7-7. A) approaching bedrock in Square B15; **B)** west face of Square C9, showing abundant rock rubble in Unit 2 and dark breccia fragments in Unit 3c underlying.

the west sector of the cavern, in Squares A9 North, B7, B8, B9, C9, D9, D10, and D11. Approximately 67% by weight of the total of fossil bone fragments came from these excavation units. The shallow bedrock channel in the lower rock shelf (in the area of partial squares C9, D9, D10, and D11) was virtually filled with large fossil bone fragments. A high density of fossil bone fragments in the narrow passage leading to the north tunnel is indicated by the amount of fossil bone in Square F12, only a partial square in area excavated but yielding 5% by weight of the total of fossil bone fragments recovered from the cavern. Only 28% by weight of the total of bones were recovered in the entire eastern sector of the cavern.

In all areas, even with dense concentrations of fossil bone fragments, the bones were found jumbled with the rocks or breccia fragments, although in most cases the elongate bones lay approximately horizontal. No fossil bones were found in articulation, even within zones of very high concentration of large fragments in the bedrock channel in the lower rock shelf and in the excavated areas at the west end of the main trench (Figures 7-8a, 7-8b). The fossil bones were highly fragmented by desiccation: only a few bones—clavicles, podials, metapodials, and phalanges—were recovered in a complete state. Articular ends of humeri and femora were readily identifiable, but limb shafts were apparently shattered. Identifiable vertebra fragments were in low frequency. Very few fragments of pelvis, scapula, or cranium could be identified. A number of tooth fragments were recovered, but very few identifiable fragments of mandible or maxilla.

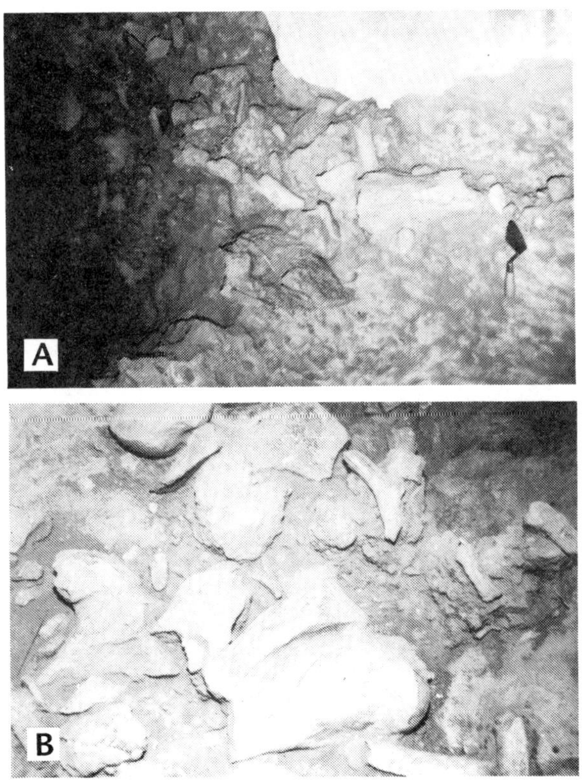

Figure 7-8. Jumbled bones of giant sloth exposed in silt deposits. **A)** in Square D10; **B)** in Square D9.

The extreme fragmentation of the fossil bones was evidently due to desiccation and subsequent movement by gravity and water action. It is clear that the bones had been transported subsequent to the death and decomposition of the animals, and the place of death can only be guessed. It is possible that the sloth denned within the cavern: the west side of the cavern, with limestone shelves, would furnish good shelter with light, provided that the animals could enter and leave the cavern safely. Possibly, however, once in the cavern, these giant animals could not escape; and eventually died on the west side of the cavern, where their bones are now concentrated. The skeletons may have lain exposed for some time, the bones desiccating and fragmenting before incorporation into the sediments which accumulated in the cavern.

The few highly mineralized bone fragments definitely not sloth are possibly *Toxodon,* as a few highly mineralized teeth of this genus were definitely identifiable. As there is no possibility of this kind of animal dwelling within the cavern, the bone fragments and teeth must have been transported into the cavern and incorporated into the sediments. The few less-mineralized, white-colored fragments of bone of large mammals were also likely transported from outside and incorporated into the cavern sediments.

The upper 10 cm of the deposits in all areas of the cavern yielded many fragments of bones of small mammals—rodents, marsupials, bats—and probably some birds and reptiles, all yet to be identified by species. These small bones were particularly abundant in areas near the walls of the cavern, and below the edge of limestone shelves; and are clearly the remains of owl pellets, deposited in late prehistoric and modern times. A large white owl fled the cavern when the excavation crew first arrived.

The upper 30 cm of the cavern deposits also yielded approximately 2300 gastropod tests and some fragments of riverine mussel shell (*Diplodon* sp.). The mussel shell fragments were very sparse, with only one or two small fragments being found in the 0–10 cm level of any excavation unit. These shells were transported from the Rio Verde, less than 2 km to the east. Among the identifiable gastropod shells, tests of *Cyclodontina* spp. constituted 95%. The small tests of this genus are abundant on the surface of the limestone outcrop surrounding the cavern; and probably they have washed into the cavern from above: the shells were notably most abundant in the excavation areas directly under the vertical shaft opening of the cavern. Notably very rare were tests of the giant edible terrestrial gastropod *Megalobulimos* sp.: only three were recovered.

Cultural Stratigraphy

Approximately 100 stone or bone artifacts were found scattered throughout the upper 50 cm of the cavern sediments. The artifact categories consist of modified fragments of bone and teeth, stone flake tools, chert nodule tools, flaked quartz pebbles, flaked quartzite pebbles, quartzite hammerstones, and potsherds. The stratigraphic distribution of stone and bone artifacts is presented in Table 7-1.

Seven quartzite pebble hammerstones and a flaked quartzite pebble were found on the surface of the deposits in the cavern. In excavation, Unit 1, the reddish brown silt zone restricted to the west end of the main trench, yielded only a modified sloth bone and a flaked quartz pebble. Unit 2, the zone of very dark brown/black silt with abundant rock fragments, yielded the most artifacts, with one modified sloth bone, one modified bone fragment not sloth, two modified sloth teeth, six stone flake tools, three chert nodule tools, nine flaked quartz pebbles, seven flaked quartzite pebbles, and 16 quartzite hammerstones. Ceramics were confined to this stratigraphic zone; with 22 potsherds recovered, almost all from the upper 10 cm. Also notable from Unit 2 was a fragment of a small quartz crystal biface, found at a depth of 20 cm; and a few fragments of brown bottle glass found to a depth of 10 cm below surface demonstrate that Unit 2 accumulated until modern times.

The more clayey sedimentary zones underlying (Units 3a, 3b, 3c, and 3d) yielded a number of artifacts. Unit 3a produced one modified white mineralized bone fragment and one modified sloth bone, four stone flake tools, two chert nodule tools, six flaked quartz pebbles, seven flaked quartzite pebbles, and one quartzite hammerstone. Unit 3b yielded two modified white mineralized bone fragments, two modified fossil bones not sloth, one modified sloth tooth, three chert nodule tools, and one flaked quartz pebble. Unit 3c produced one modified sloth tooth and two modified *Toxodon* teeth, two chert nodule tools, two flaked quartz pebbles, two flaked quartzite pebbles, and one quartzite hammerstone. Artifacts were very sparse in Unit 3d, the yellow/brown clayey silt, with only one chert nodule tool and one flaked quartz pebble recovered.

In general terms, modified fossil bone or teeth fragments were distributed in all sedimentary zones in the upper 40 cm of the cavern deposits; while chert nodule tools and flaked quartzite pebbles also were found in all sedimentary zones. The artifact assemblage from Unit 2, the uppermost stratigraphic zone in the eastern and central sectors of the cavern, featured ceramics as well as a number and variety of stone tools, including the only bifacially worked lithic artifact recovered from the site. The presence of ceramics and a bifacial tool indicates a relatively late dating for Unit 2.

The artifact yield from Toca da Gameleira is comparatively sparse, and human occupation of the cavern may have been sporadic because of the difficulty of access to the floor through the vertical-walled opening. There is no evidence of hearths in any area of the cavern, and artifacts are not concentrated in restricted zones. A major interpretive problem is posed by the clear evidence for redeposition and disturbance in all sedimentary zones containing artifacts. Artifacts occur in the same sedimentary zones with fossilized bones of megamammals, but the character of the deposits indicates that colluviation and mixture had occurred. Any case for association of man with extinct fauna must depend upon evidence of modified fossil bone fragments, to be discussed in the next section of this report.

ARTIFACTS

Introduction

Aside from the ceramics, all artifacts from Toca da Gameleira are made of bone (including teeth) and stone. The description and classification will be by alteration, including process of manufacture, rather than by form. In order to try to understand the processes of fabrication or unintentional alteration of materials, it is useful to categorize artifacts as (a) deliberately shaped, (b) shaped by use or accident, or (c) unshaped but utilized. The vast majority of artifacts from Toca da Gameleira are unshaped, although a small percentage of stone artifacts attained a typological form because the fabricator consistently tried to obtain useful working edges. Such artifacts gradually attained their patterned shape during the process of repeated use, rather than by direct intentional shaping by the fabricator. A formal classification by shape alone would fail to encompass the majority of artifacts. A formal classification of useful edges, primarily edge angles, would come closer to reality; but there is a great deal of variation among the finished products. A functional classification would be even better; but in most cases the archaeologist ends up assuming function, such as scraping or planing, without the means of being certain that his assumptions are correct. Therefore, it is concluded that the most accurate means of descriptive classification is on the basis of the process of manufacture or alteration of the artifact.

Assumptions about function are inherent in the description when an object is referred to as a scraper, a spokeshave, or a scraper-plane; but these terms are used simply as handy nomenclatural devices. The original implement being described may have been used in the manner indicated by the term; but it is suspected that many artifacts served various purposes, perhaps at different times. Also, a great many objects with altered edges are probably expediency tools: a convenient object that was picked up and used once to perform a

Table 7-1. Stratigraphic Distribution of Stone and Bone artifacts in Toca da Gameleira.

	Modified Sloth Bone	Modified Sloth Teeth	Modified Non-Sloth Bone or Teeth	Bifacial Stone Tools	Stone Flake Tools
surface	0	0	0	0	0
Unit 1	1	0	0	0	0
Unit 2	1	2	1	1	6
Unit 3a	1	0	1	0	4
Unit 3b	0	1	4	0	0
Unit 3c	0	1	2	0	0
Unit 3d	0	0	0	0	0
total	3	4	8	1	10

necessary task at hand. The useful edge of such an artifact may be altered only slightly; and in fact, most expediency tools were probably overlooked during excavation. Although everything from definitely non-sterile areas was screened, most of the common rocks, including limestone rubble and natural chert nodules, were discarded by the excavator before screening. At first, all quartz and quartzite pebbles were kept; but after discovery that these pebbles are common on the eroded limestone surface in the vicinity of the site, only pebbles clearly exhibiting flaking or pecking were retained; and only those having more than one flake or pecking scar were numbered as artifacts because it was assumed that minimal flaking and pecking could have occurred naturally at some time during the history of a pebble. Nevertheless, many unnumbered pebbles have been kept with the collections for the possibility of future study.

Bone Artifacts

The only possibly intentionally shaped bone artifact from Toca da Gameleira is what appears to be a symmetrically ground bone splinter projectile point (BA-XX-2/51), but unfortunately the surface is so badly eroded that no marks of fabrication are visible; therefore it can only be termed a possible bone point. It is made of a splinter of bone of a medium-sized mammal, and measures 51 x 12 x 3 mm (Figure 7-9a). The base is broken irregularly, although the sides converge regularly to a thin tip. The bone is permineralized white, and the specimen came from Unit 3a at a depth of 30–40 cm in Square B13.

The only fossilized white bone artifact that exhibits clear evidence of alteration is a roughly cylindrical piece (BA-XX-2/127) from Unit 3b at a depth of 30–40 cm in Square B9 (Figure 7-9b). It was broken by troweling; but may be nearly complete, measuring 37 x 12 x 10 mm. Possibly it is the base of a projectile point; however, there is no evidence of shaping because the surface is badly eroded. A deep intentional groove 7 mm long and 1 mm wide at an oblique angle on one side preserves a set of expanding striations which appear to be tool marks.

A large (194 x 53 x 7 mm) fragment of a thick-walled (10–15 mm) long bone fragment (BA-XX-2/123) is the only other permineralized white bone which may have been altered (Figure 7-10a). As with the other two specimens, the surface is badly eroded; and unfortunately the specimen was hit several times with a hand pick and trowel before it was realized that the piece was bone and not a limestone fragment. Nevertheless, there are two cuts and two gouges on one face at the weathered oblique angle that seem to be older than the recent obvious blunt marks. Also, there appear to be old eroded flake scars along both longitudinal external edges. The specimen came from Unit 3b at a depth of about 30 cm in Square B8.

These three bone pieces catalogued as artifacts are from larger-sized mammals than those which were gen-

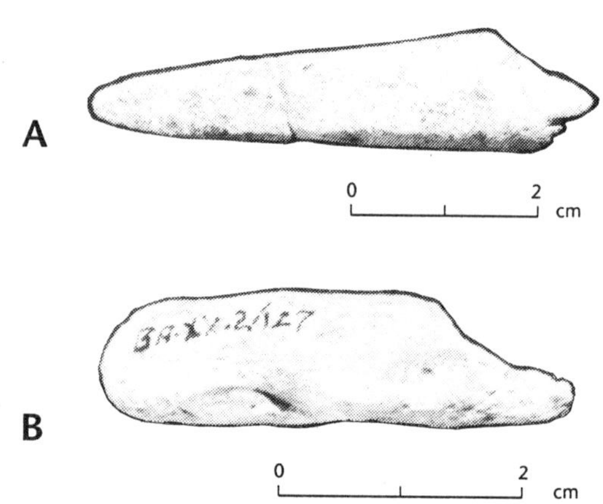

Figure 7-9. A) possible fossil bone point (BA-XX-2/51); **B)** possible fragment of fossil bone point (BA-XX-2/127).

CHERT NODULE TOOLS	FLAKED QUARTZ PEBBLES	FLAKED QUARTZITE PEBBLES	QUARTZITE HAMMERSTONES	TOTAL
0	0	1	7	8
0	1	0	0	2
3	9	7	16	46
2	6	7	1	22
3	1	0	0	9
2	2	2	1	10
1	1	0	0	2
11	20	17	25	99

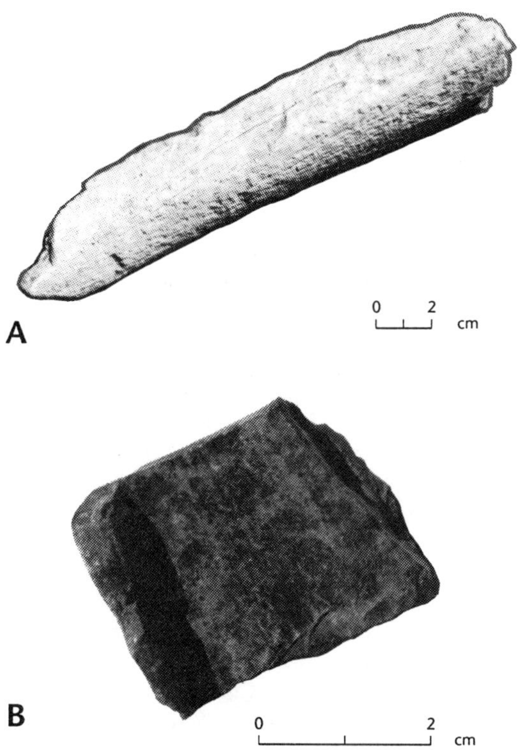

Figure 7-10. A) possible worked fossil bone (BA-XX-2/123); **B)** flaked sloth tooth (BA-XX-2/115).

erally available in the area during the Holocene. Evidently they were permineralized under different environmental conditions than the bones of either recent mammals or the giant sloth. Similar chalky-white permineralization is present on a *Macrauchenia* molar from Unit 3c at a depth of 40–50 cm in Square B8. A tooth of a large cervid was retrieved in the screen from Unit 2 in the 10–20 cm level in Square B7. It may also have come originally from Unit 3. Most of these white bones and teeth came from the same sector of the cavern in the two squares at the mouth of a tunnel where the deposits are quite level; only one came from the rubble cone which had accumulated under the entrance to the cavern.

Sloth bones were generally recognized by dark-brown or orange-brown staining, complete permineralization by iron salts, and exceptionally rough surfaces from muscle attachments. The color difference is due to the sediment color change with depth. All bones appear to have been stained dark brown originally, but became orange-brown when they remained in the yellow/brown sediment matrix for a prolonged time. It was disappointing to discover so little evidence of human alteration of sloth bones. In the hope of finding evidence of alteration, all bones and fragments were washed and examined. No definite evidence for alteration of green bone was found, although a fragment (BA-XX-2/97) with the shape of a flake (40 x 26 x 12 mm) with a prominent bulb was found in Unit 2 at a depth of 23 cm in Square B8. The platform may have been prepared; however, all flaked (?) surfaces are "pebbly", and apparently broke after fossilization and not when the bone was fresh. The eroded surfaces do not retain any definite evidence of intentional flaking.

Another sloth bone fragment (BA-XX-2/98), from Unit 1 at a depth of 10–20 cm in Square B8, has been bidirectionally step-flaked on one 80° angle edge at one broken end. The flaked surfaces have differential amounts of use polish; so the piece, which measures 64 x 24 x 19 mm, apparently was flaked while being used for chopping. A few small flakes were also removed from a 90° longitudinal edge. This specimen could be a small fragment of a larger chopping tool. Another sloth bone fragment (BA-XX-2/47), from Unit 3a at a depth of 35 cm in Square B13, has been unidirectionally step-flaked and polished on one end, probably by direct impact blows to the slightly excurvate 90° angle edge. It measures 51 x 49 x 16 mm.

Flakes have been removed from one end of several

other fossilized fragments of long bones and rib sections. However, when it was realized that most of the flaking was on the uppermost end of bones found in an upright position, probably placed there because of redeposition by colluvial action and not by intention, it seemed possible that the flaking was the result of natural impact blows during colluviation. Examples of two upended flaked rib fragments were retained but not numbered as artifacts.

The only other flaked fossil bone retained as an artifact is a long bone fragment (BA-XX-2/70) which measures 156 x 42 x 26 mm, with large flakes removed from both ends, and a small flake from each longitudinal edge. The old flaked edges of this piece, from Unit 2 at a depth of 10–20 cm in Square B9, are polished. Most of one end was broken during excavation.

The most conclusive evidence for use was found on four broken sloth teeth, and several other sloth teeth were retained because they seem to follow the same pattern. The best evidence is a patterned set of use flakes along the 90° angle internal enamel edge of a central tooth fragment (BA-XX-2/115) protected from natural flaking by retention of a lateral corner, the edge of which is flaked bidirectionally, as is the opposite corner (Figure 7-10b). The flake scars on the 90° angle edge were evidently removed unintentionally by an oblique push-planing action. The bidirectional flakes could have been removed while grooving something. This artifact, which measures 32 x 27 x 9 mm, came from Unit 3c at a depth of 30–40 cm in Square A9 North.

The occlusal end fragment of another sloth tooth (BA-XX-2/130) has been battered and step-flaked by vertical chopping impact blows, which removed the entire natural chewing surface. A flake scar is also present on one lateral 90° angle edge. This artifact, which measures 33 x 32 x 15 mm, was found in compact brown silt at the 0–10 cm level in Square D9 South. Another large (48 x 45 x 20 mm) occlusal end fragment of a sloth tooth (BA-XX-2/129) was found nearby in the same square and level. A few small use flakes have been removed from the naturally worn central enamel ridge, which has not been battered; however, parallel sets of striations extend across the grain beyond the flaked surfaces on both sides of the ridges. Parallel striations and large use flakes have been removed from the broken lateral 90° angle edge. Some flake scars are more worn than others, evidently by a planing action. The other lateral edges also appear to be differentially polished. The entire outer enamel appears to have peeled off and subsequently been worn and polished naturally before the central enamel ridge of another broken sloth tooth (BA-XX-2/56) was bidirectionally flaked by vertical chopping. This tooth, which measures 51 x 44 x 19 mm, is stained light brown because it came from the light-brown silt zone at a depth of 24 cm in Square C9 North.

A small (38 x 20 x 14 mm) broken sloth tooth fragment (BA-XX-2/131), found in loose brown silt at a depth of 0–10 cm in Square F12, has one flake scar on the external enamel edge. As the scar exposes the white interior, it could be a recent pick flake; however, part of the flaked surface is polished. The rest of the 90° angle edge appears to be use-nibbled and polished. Another fragment, not catalogued as an artifact, was found in Unit 2 at a depth of 10–20 cm in Square B12. A large and a small flake had been removed from the lateral enamel edge. Isolated flakes were also removed from three worn edges of another tooth fragment from the same level and square. It is not possible to demonstrate that these two flaked tooth fragments were expediency tools, although they were kept with the artifacts for further study.

Two non-occlusal tooth fragments from a large mammal other than sloth (and apparently *Toxodon)* have evidently been used, and another tooth fragment might have been used. A slightly incurvate 90° angle edge of dentine on BA-XX-2/57 has been use-flaked and polished, and several deep parallel oblique scrape marks extend against the grain onto the adjacent enamel surface from the flaked edge. This artifact, which measures 59 x 23 x 28 mm, came from a compact light-brown silt zone at a depth of 10–30 cm in Square C9/D9. A smaller tooth fragment (BA-XX-2/95) came from Unit 3c at 20–40 cm depth in Square B9. Many deep parallel oblique cuts and scratches extend across the grain on the flat enamel surface. The adjacent edge of this piece, which measures 33 x 19 x 6 mm, is not polished; and may have broken off after use. Both of these artifacts apparently were used for scraping and/or planing. Another tooth fragment, from Unit 2 at a depth of 0–10 cm in Square B9, has some tiny flakes removed from both the enamel and dentine edges of a worn 90° angle break. The evidence was not definite enough to call this piece an artifact.

Although a great deal of time and effort was spent in washing thousands of bones and examining their surfaces for incisions and scratches, only four unidentifiable fossil bone fragments exhibited patterned incisions. Only one of these fragments (BA-XX-2/77), which measures 97 x 44 x 27 mm, has the rough surface characteristic of sloth bone. A rather protected concave edge (about 85° angle) exhibits a 12-mm-wide band of five parallel scratches extending across the grain of the bone onto an external face where the pattern reappears as far as a broken edge 47 mm away. This piece came from Unit 3c at a depth of 30–40 cm in Square B9.

Three rib fragments have regular smooth surfaces and cross-sections which indicate that they are not sloth bones. The longest fragment (BA-XX-2/84), which measures 155 x 29 x 19 mm, with a flattened ovoid cross-section, was found in compact brown silt in Square D10, where it occurred with sloth bones at a depth of about 20 cm. A set of parallel incisions occurs at an oblique angle near a broken end, and a single deep cut occurs at the same angle about 2/3 of the distance to the opposite end. Another set of incisions occurs at nearly right angles to the first set, and near the center of the medial (incurvate) face. Sets of fainter scratches occur elsewhere on the internal surface. Another rib fragment (BA-XX-2/96) with a thick lens-shaped cross-section (71 x 38 x 19 mm), from compact brown silt at a depth of 10–30 cm in Square C9 North, has several sets of short parallel oblique striations on the medial surface and a set of very short shallow striations on the external surface. A small (57 x 29 x 20 mm) rib fragment (BA-XX-2/128) with a flattened oval cross-section came from Unit 2 at a depth of 10–20 cm in Square B12. A set of three deep parallel oblique incisions occurs on the external face. A set of short shallow parallel oblique scratches and an isolated deeper cut occur on the medial face. All of these cuts and scratches could be interpreted as butchering marks, although the possibility cannot be excluded that the marks were made later while the ribs were used as tools. The fact that only four of thousands of fossilized bones exhibited striations and cuts suggests that it is unlikely that the bones had been altered by trampling.

Stone Artifacts

Unmodified Flakes

Chert nodules, quartz and quartzite pebbles, and limestone were raw materials for flaking available in the immediate vicinity of Toca da Gameleira. A white/yellow chert, relatively brittle with internal flaws, outcrops in the bedrock; and small rough nodules were seen on the surface of the limestone formation around the cavern entrance. Small pebbles of quartz or quartzite were also seen on the ground surface near the cavern. Unlike the limestone in the Central area, the local limestone is of very poor quality for flaking, and no definite limestone flakes were identified in the collection.

Only 54 unmodified stone flakes were recovered in excavation in the cavern. The distribution is presented in Table 7-2. There was a concentration of eight flakes in Square B7 at the 30–40 cm level (Unit 3c), and a clustering of five flakes at the 0–10 cm level (brown silt) in Square D10; but otherwise flakes were very scattered in distribution, with most excavation units and stratigraphic units yielding only a few. Most of the flakes may have been removed from artifacts in use through wear, or by resharpening of working edges. No flakes were recovered below 40 cm depth in the sediments.

Of the total of 54 unmodified flakes, chert flakes were of highest frequency (46%). Unmodified chert flakes ranged in size from 19 x 12 x 3 mm to 52 x 36 x 18 mm, with a mode of 30 x 20 x 5 mm. Rough cortex was present on 56% of the chert flakes, indicating derivation from nodules; while 68% of the chert flakes featured a large, simple platform, suggesting direct percussion. Thirty-nine percent of the total of 54 unmodified flakes were of quartzite. Quartzite flakes ranged in size from 16 x 12 x 3 mm to 77 x 64 x 23 mm, with a mode of 34 x 30 x 7 mm. Smooth cortex indicating derivation from pebbles is present on 48% of the quartzite flakes. Forty-nine percent of the quartzite flakes retained evidence of a large simple platform, a feature which suggests direct percussion.

Only 15% of the unmodified flakes were of quartz. Small pebbles of vein quartz were seen on the surface in the area of the cavern, and 88% of the quartz flakes retained cortex indicating derivation from water-rolled pebbles. Only a few quartz flakes retained clear evidence of the striking platform, large and simple in character. Unmodified quartz flakes ranged in size from 16 x 14 x 3 mm to 47 x 35 x 13 mm, with a mode of 23 x 16 x 8 mm.

General Observations on Flaked Stone Artifacts

Most stone artifacts were altered by flaking; although a few were pecked, and often unintentionally flaked as well, by hammering and chopping. Most modified flakes have been removed from quartzite or quartz pebbles, although a few came from chert nodules. In addition there are flaked quartzite and quartz pebble artifacts, and several flaked chert nodules.

Contrary to expectations, the abundantly available nodular chert was not a desirable flaking material, evidently because it was too brittle even before the interior had been altered to a white powdery substance by weathering. This leaching process occurred after flaking, as the flake surfaces often retain a high sheen characteristic of good quality chert. There are no chert cores, and most identifiable chert flakes have unusual points of impact which suggest that they were unintentionally removed from nodules being used as choppers or scraper-planes. In fact, apparently there are only a few flakes that were intentionally removed from quartzite or quartz pebbles.

Flake Tools

Intentional pressure flaking is present on only one artifact (BA-XX-2/22), which came from Unit 2 at a depth of 22 cm in Square B11. This bifacially retouched quartz crystal fragment, which measures 25 x 20 x 8 mm, has two broken edges; but the other excurving edge exhibits invasive pressure flaking extending over both faces. Subsequent nibbling and step-flaking may have been caused by forceful use as a scraper on the 45° angle edge. One unretouched surface appears to be the naturally irregular surface of a crystal root and not a waterworn pebble. Quite likely, a pressure-flaked artifact, perhaps already broken, was picked up elsewhere

Table 7-2. Stratigraphic Distribution of Unmodified Stone Flakes in the Deposits of Toca da Gameleira.

	CHERT	QUARTZ	QUARTZITE	TOTAL
Square B7				
0–10 cm	0	0	0	0
10–20 cm	0	0	0	0
20–30 cm	2	0	0	2
30–40 cm	5	1	2	8
total	7	1	2	10
Square B8				
0–10 cm	0	0	0	0
10–20 cm	0	0	0	0
20–30 cm	1	0	0	1
total	1	0	0	1
Square B9				
0–10 cm	0	0	0	0
10–20 cm	2	0	2	4
20–30 cm	1	0	0	1
total	3	0	2	5
Square B10				
0–10 cm	1	0	0	1
10–20 cm	0	0	0	0
20–30 cm	0	0	0	0
30–40 cm	0	0	1	1
Square B11				
0–10 cm	1	0	0	1
10–20 cm	0	0	1	1
20–30 cm	0	0	1	1
30–40 cm	1	2	0	3
total	2	2	2	6
Square B12				
0–10 cm	0	0	2	2
10–20 cm	0	0	2	2
20–30 cm	0	1	0	1
total	0	1	4	5
Square B13				
0–10 cm	0	0	1	1
10–20 cm	1	0	0	1
20–30 cm	1	0	3	4
total	2	0	4	6
Square B14				
0–10 cm	0	0	0	0
10–20 cm	0	0	0	0
20–30 cm	0	0	0	0
30–40 cm	1	0	0	1
total	1	0	0	1
Square B15				
0–10 cm	0	0	0	0
10–20 cm	1	0	0	1
20–30 cm	0	0	2	2
30–40 cm	1	0	1	2
total	2	0	3	5
Square A9				
0–10 cm	0	0	0	0
10–20 cm	0	0	0	0
20–30 cm	0	0	0	0
30–40 cm	0	2	0	2
total	0	2	0	2
Square C9				
0–10 cm	0	0	0	0
10–20 cm	0	0	0	0
20–30 cm	1	0	0	1
total	1	0	0	1
Square D9				
0–10 cm	1	0	0	1
Square D10				
0–10 cm	2	0	3	5
10–20 cm	1	0	0	1
total	3	0	3	6
Square D11				
0–10 cm	0	1	0	1
10–20 cm	0	0	0	0
20–30 cm	1	1	0	2
total	1	2	0	3
total	25	8	21	54

and transported to the cavern, where it was used for scraping.

The only clearly intentional flakes retaining bulbs are of quartzite, the best available flaking material. An elongated flake (BA-XX-2/55) with a flat crushed bulb evidently was removed from the end of a weathered quartzite pebble by a forceful hammer blow. This flake, which measures 55 x 32 x 11 mm, came from Unit 2 at a depth of 10 cm in Square B9. A parallel-sided blade-like flake (BA-XX-2/25) with both positive and negative bulbar faces came from Unit 3a at a depth of 30–40 cm in Square B15. It measures 35 x 20 x 8 mm. A small concavity was retouched on a 30° angle lateral edge. A small quartzite pebble (BA-XX-2/133) with a pyramidal form (47 x 32 x 30 mm) was found in compact brown silt in the 0–10 cm level in Square D11. Probably it was split by holding the base on an anvil and striking near the apex. Evidence for use is lacking.

An exotic brown banded quartzite/argillite flake with a prominent lipped bulb (BA-XX-2/45) exhibits definite evidence of use only on the slightly weathered dorsal face, the high spots of which are differentially polished by scraping or planing adjacent to a 90° angle hinged edge, which was prepared by step-flaking from blows directed vertically onto the platform on the dorsal side of the bulb. This unusual retouched flake, which measures 53 x 37 x 11 mm, has snapped and nibbled thin edges (with angles of 10 to 15°) which are probably the result of blunting rather than retouching for use. This piece, from Unit 3a at a depth of 33 cm in Square B11, is an excellent example of the preference for high-angle edges even when low-angle edges were available for use.

The high-angle edges of three thick flakes had desirable strong working edges. One flake (BA-XX-2/32) has a positive bulb and a separate nearly complete cone (possibly split) created by forceful direct impact blows to a pebble. This large double-sided flake, which measures 75 x 63 x 23 cm, with a thick platform and an excurvate distal edge (30° angle), has been unidirectionally retouched at one end to create a 60° angle working edge and a sharp projection which is worn by use. This flake came from Unit 3a at a depth of 25 cm in Square B11.

A thick decortification flake (BA-XX-2/121) was unifacially retouched by percussion on the cortical pebble surface to create a crude *lesma* or *limace* form with a blunt (unretouched) tip and a fairly straight right lateral edge (60° angle) which is more worn than the undulating left lateral edge (45–50° angle), which has only three large flake scars (Figure 7-11a). This artifact, which measures 67 x 47 x 20 mm, is the only flaked artifact which may retain an intentional form. It came from Unit 2 at a depth of 18 cm in Square B8.

A thick quartzite chunk (BA-XX-2/16), with a rectangular outline measuring 50 x 42 x 27 mm, came from Unit 3a at a depth of 37 cm in Square B15 (Figure 7-11b). Most of the cortical pebble surfaces have been removed by heavy percussion which created several useful high-angled edges (about 90°), a beaked nose, two other projecting noses, and four concavities, all of which show different amounts of wear. Another thick flake (BA-XX-2/82) was fashioned into a rectangular piece measuring 52 x 43 x 19 mm, with several useful working edge (Figure 7-12a). This much-used artifact came from Unit 2 at 30 cm depth in Square B7. Negative flake scars created by a side blow to the thick platform opposite the high-angled (120°) positive bulb created a beaked working edge which was subsequently resharpened by removing shallow flakes from the cortical surface of the platform as well as parallel to the negative flake scar. This beaked scraping edge (with a 45° angle) is heavily worn. One lateral working edge was created by a side

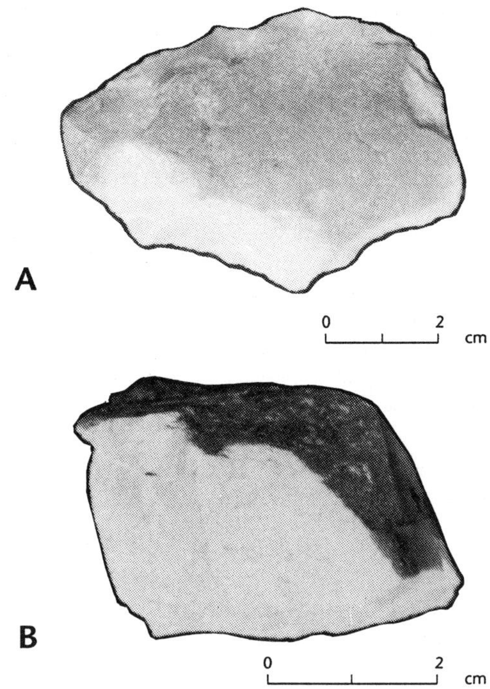

Figure 7-11. A) retouched quartzite flake (BA-XX-2/121); **B)** flaked quartzite fragment (BA-XX-2/16).

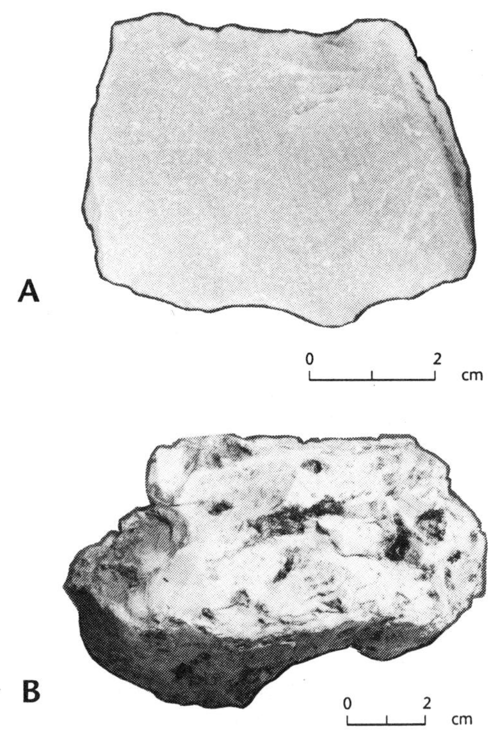

Figure 7-12. A) retouched quartzite flake (BA-XX-2/82); **B)** battered chert nodule (BA-XX-2/18).

blow to the thick platform, which removed a long flake from the cortical surface. The lateral edge was then unidirectionally step-flaked on the bulbar face to create an irregularly incurvate working edge (65° angle) with spurred projections at both ends. Both spurs were resharpened by removing small flakes from the opposite direction. This edge is not as worn as the opposite lateral edge, from which two large flakes were removed in opposite directions to create an S-shaped undulating edge (with a 60° angle) with a broad central projection which is heavily worn. The thick distal end has been flaked from various directions to create and resharpen two 90° angle working edges. One of these edges has a projection which is worn and resharpened by removing a flake in the opposite direction. This much-used tool illustrates how desirable high-angled working edges were created and repeatedly resharpened by carefully considered removal of high-angled retouch flakes.

BA-XX-2/78 from Unit 2 at a depth of 17 cm in Square B12 may be a broken piece, now measuring 37 x 28 x 16 mm, of a similar object flaked from a quartzite pebble, as many flakes have been removed from various directions, creating high-angled working edges. Stepped flaking, possibly created by one heavy impact blow to a 90° angle edge, made a useful edge which could have been used as a spokeshave. Two projecting spurs (with angles of 40 and 50°) on an adjacent incurvate edge are more worn than any other edges.

Chert Artifacts

Two weathered chert flakes were numbered as artifacts. BA-XX-2/99, from Unit 2 at a depth of 30–40 cm in Square B7, has a prominent positive bulb which is slightly shattered. The flake measures 48 x 40 x 12 mm. A separate bulb is present on one corner of the broad platform. The presence of several points of impact on the platform suggests that this flake may have been removed unintentionally from a nodule used for chopping or hammering. The only evidence of use is at the distal end, where possible unintentional retouch and some polish is present on a 20° angle edge. Part of the retouched edge was broken during excavation. Another chert flake (BA-XX-2/24) appears to have been burinated. It measures 35 x 19 x 8 mm, and came from Unit 3a at a depth of 30–40 cm in Square B15. There is no evidence of use, and the negative burin flake scar appears to have been created with the same impact blow as the main flake rather than an intentional burin blow.

Most of the chert artifacts are weathered chert nodules with one or more edges evidently selected for the preparation of some material which had to be chopped. The two flakes described above could have been unintentionally removed from the working edges of such tools; and another angular chert chunk (BA-XX-2/80), from Unit 2 at a depth of 20–30 cm in Square B7, also appears to be a flake (measuring 48 x 40 x 20 mm) removed accidentally from a nodule by a chopping blow on a 90° sinuous edge.

A fragment of a chert chopper (BA-XX-2/90), which measures 29 x 26 x 16 mm, was found in Unit 3a at a depth of 20–30 cm in Square B12. This white chert exhibits a peculiarity found on some nodules wherein the cracks caused by incompletely removed flakes have been filled with a black substance (iron?) that highlights the direction and extent of impacts. The unidirectionally retouched edge (90° angle) is step-flaked and worn by use. Possibly the fragment was intentionally removed in order to renew a worn edge, as the chert piece was broken off by a direct impact blow to the surface opposite the step-flaked edge. An angular chert chunk (BA-XX-2/125) with thermally spalled faces has been flaked on three corners to create graver spurs. Two spurs are worn out, but one 90° angle edge was step-flaked to create and renew a sharp graver spur. This artifact, measuring 74 x 55 x 39 mm, was recovered from Unit 3c at a depth of 30–40 cm in Square B8.

No complete chert nodule artifacts with unidirectional step-flaked edges were found in Toca da Gameleira. A different form of bidirectional stepped flaking, caused by vertical chopping blows to high-angle ridges (usually with 90° angle edges) appears to have been unintentionally made by heavy chopping, whereas the unidirectional flaking appears to have been intentionally done to make a sharp scraping or planing edge with many denticulations.

The five battered edges (varying from 30 mm to 67 mm long) on BA-XX-2/18 (Figure 7-12b) are undulating, suggesting the possibility that some hard material, like wood, was struck against the edges of this chert nodule as part of some preparation process. Some quite large flakes were removed during this process, leaving marks of vertical blows such as those found on the two flakes described above. The fact that several exposed edges of this piece are not battered proves that the object was not naturally battered by rolling. The piece measures 101 x 59 x 58 mm, and came from Unit 2 at a depth of 10 cm in Square B11.

At first, the largest (273 x 189 x 92 mm) and most solid flaked chert nodule (BA-XX-2/104) was thought to have been a potential core cached 5 cm below the surface under the overhanging cavern wall in Square A9 North. However, several small use flakes were removed in the same direction from the 70° angle edge of a flat thermal spall. Although this most exposed edge is not battered, portions of several other projecting edges have been differentially battered by direct 90° angle blows, similar to the edges on artifact BA-XX-2/18. Again, the lack of flaking on some of the most exposed edges proves that the piece was not flaked naturally. Also, the differential battering could have been caused by beating a material like wood on certain 90° angle edges. This nodule is large and heavy enough that it could have been imbedded in the ground or wedged between other rocks, and some resistant material was struck and/or rubbed over the exposed edges during a preparation process.

Two smaller chert nodules may simply have been used as choppers. BA-XX-2/120 has been bidirectionally battered along one 90° angle edge. This nodule, measuring 83 x 69 x 44 mm, was recovered from Unit 3a at a depth of 20–30 cm in Square B10. The other angular chert nodule (BA-XX-2/83), from a depth of 20 cm in compact brown silt in Square D10, has apparently been slightly use-flaked along one excurving 90° angle edge. The nodule measures 82 x 77 x 64 mm. A small (42 x 29 x 22 mm) naturally angular chunk of chert (BA-XX-2/39), from Unit 2 at a depth of 10–20 cm in Square B15, has been unidirectionally step-flaked on two 90° angle edges, each about 25 mm long. One of these edges includes a beaked graver spur which is worn smooth.

Projections and noses were made on even smaller chert nodules. A slightly stream-worn exotic blue chert nodule (BA-XX-2/30) has been unidirectionally flaked, probably by holding this small pebble (27 x 20 x 17 mm) on an anvil, to create projecting graver spurs on two edges. One spur is worn smooth, the other is less worn. This piece came from Unit 3d at a depth of 40–50 cm in Square B15. Another small (44 x 38 x 18 mm) exotic chert pebble (BA-XX-2/66), tabular in cross-section, has been unidirectionally step-flaked at one broad 90° angle end, as if it were a tiny pebble tool (Figure 7-13a). The working edge of this piece, from Unit 3d at a depth of 46 cm in Square B13, has been differentially worn and crushed by chopping or planing. These two small chert pebble tools were among the few artifacts found in the upper part of the yellow/orange clayey silt (Unit 3d). BA-XX-2/40 is a small chert nodule (27 x 17 x 12 mm) unidirectionally step-flaked at one end to form a beaked nose with a 65° angle edge. This artifact came from compact brown silt at a depth of 20–30 cm in Square D10. Another small (36 x 21 x 11 mm) nodular chert fragment (BA-XX-2/50), from compact brown silt at a depth of 0–10 cm in Square D9, has been step-flaked along one 70° angle edge to create a central projection, which was later resharpened by removing shallow flakes from the natural platform surface at right angles to the step-flaked edge.

Figure 7-13. A) flaked pebble of exotic chert (BA-XX-2/66); **B)** flaked quartz pebble (BA-XX-2/108).

A larger (62 x 47 x 31 mm) chert nodule (BA-XX-2/15), from compact brown silt at a depth of 22 cm in Square D10, has been unidirectionally retouched along two edges (60° angle) from opposite directions to form a graver spur at the tip end. The edges and graver spur are all worn. Another chert nodule (BA-XX-2/126), from Unit 3c at a depth of 30–40 cm in Square B8, has a nearly flat natural face used as a platform to remove three flakes from a 26-mm-long lateral edge (80° angle). The other lateral edge (90° angle) has been battered by direct blows, and one large flake has been removed from the 65° angle end. This piece measures 67 x 44 x 28 mm. Another tabular chert nodule (BA-XX-2/132), from Unit 3b at a depth of 20–40 cm in Square D9, measures 68 x 48 x 20 mm. Both lateral edges (with angles of 80° and 90°) and one end have been unidirectionally step-flaked from opposite directions to form undulating working edges with projections which are worn.

Flaked Quartz Pebbles

Subrounded and rounded vein quartz pebbles were bipolarly split if they were too small for hand-held flaking or for direct use as choppers or hammerstones. Unlike the limestone *serra* area north of Central, where unrolled vein quartz was locally abundant in some places, there is no evidence that quartz was simply smashed by throwing rocks at chunks of quartz lying on rocks.

One small (27 x 25 x 17 mm) flattened quartz pebble (BA-XX-2/31) from Unit 3d at a depth of 40–50 cm in Square B15 has been split transversely; but the 90° angle edges and projections are uniformly worn, so it is not possible to prove that the edges were used. A quartz pebble (BA-XX-2/112) from Unit 3c at a depth of 32 cm in Square A9 North was bipolarly split along a cleavage plane. The artifact measures 43 x 26 x 14 mm. The proximal end was shattered by the impact, but the 90° angle edge could have been used. Another bipolarly split quartz pebble (BA-XX-2/29), from Unit 2 at a depth of 10–20 cm in Square D11, also lacks any definite evidence of use. It measures 39 x 28 x 15 mm. A tiny (21 x 15 x 13 mm) rounded quartz pebble (BA-XX-2/134), from Unit 2 at a depth of 20–30 cm in Square B11, has been split transversely, creating a concave face. The beaked edge (with an angle of 60°) has been steeply retouched to form an endscraper with a lateral graver spur. A quartz flake (BA-XX-2/46) with a split bulb and a crushed hinge at the other end has been steeply retouched, probably by use, on a 10-mm-long section of an 80° angle lateral edge. This utilized flake, which measures 45 x 38 x 12 mm, came from Unit 3a at a depth of 35 cm in Square B11.

Three bipolarly flaked vein quartz fragments came from Unit 2 in Square A9 North. Two of these fragments (BA-XX-2/109 and 117), from a depth of 30 cm, fit together to form a specimen which measures 26 x 24 x 7 mm. The thickest lateral edge (with an 80° angle) has been steeply retouched unidirectionally to form a central graver spur, which is worn. The bulbar corner also has a sharp spur which may have been used. The other small (22 x 15 x 6 mm) quartz fragment (BA-XX-2/113), from a depth of 32 cm, could be part of the same specimen; but it does not fit. One irregularly excurving edge (with a 70° angle) has been step-flaked by use.

Waterworn vein quartz pebbles, ranging in form from subangular to rounded, have often been flaked at one or more ends. Although the flaking may sometimes have been unintentional, by impact blows while the pebble was used as a hammerstone, steep-angled edges frequently were utilized. Some broken fragments may have been flaked bipolarly, although the evidence is indefinite.

A broken quartz pebble (BA-XX-2/73), from Unit 2 at a depth of 10 cm in Square B14, has several flake scars along an 80° angle edge. One of several projections along the edge has been resharpened by removing a tiny flake from the cortical face. The pebble measures 38 x 35 x 25 mm. A smaller (21 x 18 x 13 mm) quartz fragment (BA-XX-2/135), from Unit 3a at a depth of 30–40 cm in Square B14, has a crushed concave edge (with a 90° angle) that could have been used as a spokeshave. An attempt to fashion a projecting corner by removing two flakes from a flat surface was aborted when the projection broke along a crystal face. Another subangular quartz pebble (BA-XX-2/86), from Unit 3c at a depth of 37 cm in Square B9, was probably flaked bipolarly from end to end and transversely. The pebble measures 41 x 18 x 16 mm. One pointed end, created by a split cone, and the opposite end, which has a 70° angle excurvate scraping edge, appear to have been used.

The remainder of the quartz pebble artifacts were not intentionally split before use; rather, the steep edges of flake scars or of natural breaks along crystal faces were used and sometimes rejuvenated by removing flakes from another direction. A projecting nose (with an angle of 80°), on one steeply flaked end of BA-XX-2/118 from Unit 2 at a depth of 20–30 cm in Square B10, has been resharpened by removing a flake from the naturally spalled face. The artifact measures 23 x 18 x 15 mm. A lateral 90° angle steeply flaked corner has also been resharpened by removing a flake from another spalled face. One excurvate edge of BA-XX-2/100, from Unit 3a at a depth of 20–30 cm in Square B14, has been retouched to form a steep endscraper edge (80° angle) with a projection, which was resharpened by removing a flake from a flat spalled crystal face. The artifact measures 27 x 20 x 17 mm. A naturally spalled crystal head (BA-XX-2/67) has a steeply retouched 80–85° edge with projections which were not resharpened after they became worn. This steep scraper, which measures 28 x 27 x 8 mm, was found in screening material from Unit 3g at the 90–100 cm level in Square B15. As this zone of the deep pit was generally devoid of exotic pebbles, very likely this specimen fell from a higher level. Two flakes have been removed from the end of a quartz pebble (BA-XX-2/38), using a worn flat spall as a platform. A concave 80° angle edge and an adjacent projection are worn on this piece, which measures 46 x 32 x 29 mm. It came from Unit 3a at a depth of 30 cm in Square B13.

Four subrounded quartz pebbles have been forcefully struck on or near corners, possibly by use as hammerstones, removing flakes bidirectionally. It is impossible to be certain that the crushed irregular edges (with angles of 70–90°) of three of these flaked pebbles (BA-XX-2/21, 63, and 108) were used as scrapers or spokeshaves. Their respective dimensions are 51 x 52 x 22 mm, 57 x 39 x 34 mm, and 51 x 44 x 26 mm (Figure 7-13b); and they came from Unit 2 in Square B11 at 18 cm depth, Unit 2 in Square B9 at 15 cm depth, and Unit 1 in Square B8 at 10 cm depth. A similar quartz pebble (BA-XX-2/94), from Unit 2 at a depth of 28 cm in Square B8, has a 60° angle undulating edge which has been rejuvenated and subsequently worn slightly. It measures 46 x 41 x 26 mm.

Three minimally waterworn angular vein quartz pebbles (BA-XX-2/17, 81, and 122) have flakes removed from one end, probably by use as hammerstones. They measure 68 x 37 x 26 mm, 59 x 51 x 41 mm, and 60 x 48 x 29 mm; and respectively came from Unit 3a in Square B15 at a depth of 37 cm, Unit 3a in Square B14 at a depth of 33 cm, and Unit 3b in Square B8 at a depth of 27 cm. The first specimen (BA-XX-2/17) may not be demonstrably an artifact; but the steeply flaked edges (with angles of 85 and 100°) of the other two are worn, probably by use.

Flaked Quartzite Pebbles

Quartzite as well as quartz pebbles were locally available on the eroded limestone surface in the vicinity of Toca da Gameleira. Most of the quartzite pebbles seen scattered on the surface are small and highly weathered in a peculiar manner. A fairly thin, sometimes shiny external rind, possibly caused by an ancient desert varnish, is resistant to decomposition; however, if the rind is broken, the interior of the pebble erodes to sandstone and ultimately sand. At first, many such pebbles with small areas of erosion were thought to be artifacts when excavated in both of the Rio Verde cavern sites. Later, after many similarly weathered pebbles were found on the surface, it was realized that only rarely can such a weathered pebble be determined to be an artifact. Therefore, most of these eroded pebbles were discarded, although some were retained for further study. A few were kept as artifacts because they have clear evidence of pecking and flaking as a result of hammering.

Another peculiar kind of weathering occurs in which the outer rind on the pebble evidently peeled off, revealing a rough surface. The center of these more solid subangular pebbles is much less friable, and will flake with a conchoidal fracture. The rest of the quartzite pebbles have normal weathering rinds, which occasionally peel off naturally like an orange skin; but nevertheless usually will flake conchoidally. When used as hammerstones, many exhibit pecked areas only; but occasionally flakes were removed unintentionally by heavy hammering. Other pebbles were intentionally flaked pebble tools.

The first category, hammerstones with broken rinds and decomposing interiors, includes three flattened ovoid quartzite pebbles with single flakes removed from one or both ends. BA-XX-2/5, which measures 50 x 33 x 25 mm, was found on the surface of Square B15; while BA-XX-2/6, which measures 67 x 44 x 17 mm, came from compact brown silt in the upper 10 cm of Square D10; and BA-XX-2/53, which measures 78 x 42 x 22 mm, was found in Unit 2 at a depth of 10 cm in Square B9. Peck marks are also present on the faces of BA-XX-2/5 and BA-XX-2/53. BA-XX-2/119 is a larger (61 x 42 x 39 mm) ovoid pebble with a shiny weathering rind, found in Unit 3c at a depth of 43 cm in Square B8. One side was evidently peeled off along a cleavage plane by an impact blow to one corner. The opposite corner has battering flakes removed by heavier hammer blows. Several peck marks which removed the thin weathering rind are visible on another corner. Another small (52 x 46 x 39 mm) ovoid quartzite pebble, (BA-XX-2/12) from the surface of Square B10, has been pecked to a flat facet at one end; and scattered pecking marks have penetrated the weathering rind elsewhere, especially on one face (Figure 7-14a).

Three larger quartzite hammerstones were found in

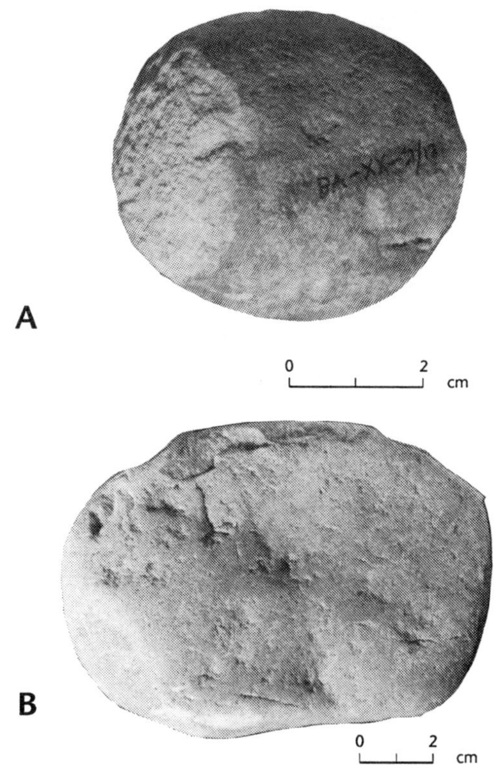

Figure 7-14. Quartzite pebble hammerstones. **A)** BA-XX-2/12; **B)** BA-XX-2/3.

Unit 2. BA-XX-2/23, which measures 78 x 70 x 45 mm, came from a depth of 36 cm in Square B15; BA-XX-2/72, which measures 102 x 77 x 66 mm, was found at a depth of 3 cm in Square B14; and BA-XX-2/74, which measures 66 x 60 x 58 mm, was recovered at 20 cm depth in Square B14. Large pecked areas are present on one edge and a corner of BA-XX-2/23, and a large flake has been removed from one end. Both ends of BA-XX-2/72 have been battered by heavy hammering. A flake removed from one end of BA-XX-2/74 also removed a spall along a bedding plane. Pecking also helped spall off the opposite end. A large battering flake has been removed from near a corner of BA-XX-2/61. The crushed concave edge could have been used as a spokeshave, although there is no proof of subsequent use of this small hammerstone (48 x 36 x 22 mm), which was found in Unit 2 at a depth of 16 cm in Square B9. Hammering flakes were removed from near both corners of an 80° angle edge of BA-XX-2/35, which was recovered in Unit 2 at a depth of 26 cm in Square B13. This quartzite pebble measures 64 x 28 x 24 mm. A well-rolled quartzite pebble (BA-XX-2/75) with a flattened cross-section (68 x 54 x 23 mm), found in Unit 3a at a depth of 30 cm in Square B14, has one end removed squarely, probably by striking the piece while it was held on an anvil. A few use-nibbling flakes have been removed from the cortical surface of one of the slightly smoothed 90° angle edges. An adjacent 60° angle flaked edge is smoother, and has two use flakes removed from it. The opposite end has several impact marks, some of which removed flakes.

The remainder of the quartzite hammerstones have pecked areas, which are often pecked facets. Occasionally flakes have spalled off by heavy hammer blows. The best example of the latter process is BA-XX-2/27, from Unit 2 at a depth of 32 cm in Square B13. This large (94 x 80 x 59 mm) hammerstone, with a triangular outline and a rough surface (possibly created by pecking), has been facetted by vertical pecking on one broad corner. A large hinged spall has been removed from each face by direct impact blows. Artifact BA-XX-2/41 is an impact spall with a pecked apex and nearly right-angled broken hinge at the opposite end; it is a spall that was removed from another pebble by the same pounding process. The spall, measuring 69 x 38 x 24 mm, came from Unit 2 at a depth of 10–20 cm in Square B11.

A large fine-grained quartzite pebble hammerstone (BA-XX-2/3) with a flattened cross-section (108 x 80 x 48 mm) has a smooth flat facet on one edge (Figure 7-14b). Evidently the working edge of this unusual artifact, which was found on the surface of Square B15, was originally steeply flaked like a pebble chopper; but later it was used for vertical chopping or pounding, which created vertical impact scars extending parallel to the flattest face. Some of these vertical flakes spalled off in the manner just described. Finally the edge of this much-used artifact attained a smooth finish which lacks any evidence of pecking or abrasion.

Another unusual artifact (BA-XX-2/49) was found on the surface of Square B9. This quartzite pebble, with a rough surface, measures 58 x 56 x 66 mm. It was split in half by a vertical blow to one corner. The opposite end has also peeled off, possibly when a flake was removed from the tip end. A peculiar curving projecting ridge (15 x 5 mm) thereby created on the end may have been used for grooving, which created a small (3 x 4 mm) polished and striated facet on the cortical remnant between the flake scar and the spall scar. Probably this peculiar ridge was created accidentally, but an enterprising person put the useful projecting edge to use.

Four oblong quartzite pebbles, all found near each other, have been pecked by use as hammerstones. BA-XX-2/4, which measures 91 x 45 x 35 mm and was found on the surface of Square B15, has been pecked on both ends; and a rough flake was removed from one end. The other three quartzite pebbles each have a small pecked facet near the center (most projecting part) of one longitudinal edge. A flake was removed from near the end of BA-XX-2/9, which measures 107 x 48 x 41 mm and was found in Unit 2 at a depth of 2 cm in Square B15. Peck marks are visible on both ends of BA-XX-2/10, which measures 108 x 49 x 38 mm and was found in Unit 2 at a depth of 5 cm in Square B15. Another edge of this artifact has been battered by hammering. One end also has a smooth polished red stain, although there are no striations to indicate that the pebble had been used as a pestle to prepare pigment. On a face near an edge of BA-XX-2/2, which measures 83 x 43 x 39 mm, there is a circular depression (18 x 20 mm) which evidently was pecked and then the high spots smoothed, perhaps by use as a whetstone. This artifact was found on the surface of Square B15. A peculiar flattened ovoid quartzite pebble (BA-XX-2/68), from the surface of Square B14, may also have served as a whetstone. It measures 59 x 49 x 25 mm. The weathering rind of this pebble has been removed from both faces by gouging out shallow oval to circular depressions with a sharp-edged object, producing a fine grade sandstone whetstone which would be very useful for shaping wooden points. In fact it is possible that the pecked facets on the projecting edges of the three pebbles described above were fashioned to procure a rough sandy surface suitable for grinding wooden objects. One end and one side of a small (54 x 41 x 22 mm) flattened oval quartzite pebble (BA-XX-2/116), from Unit 2 at a depth of 10–20 cm in Square B10, appear to have been pecked; and then the roughened sandy edge was smoothed, perhaps by using the object as an abrading stone for working wood.

Four broken quartzite pebbles have larger pecked facets on edges. BA-XX-2/7, which measures 74 x 68 x 50 mm, may have been associated with the above set of facetted pebbles, as it came from 3 cm deep in Unit 2 in Square B15. One side (40 x 25 mm) has been flattened by pecking and then smoothed. One end was spalled off by heavy impact blows, and the 85° angle edge has been battered and smoothed by heavy use (Figure 7-15a). Unit 2 in Square B15 also yielded BA-XX-2/14, at a depth of 30 cm. This subrounded quartzite pebble, which measures 52 x 56 x 48 mm, appears to have broken in a fire. One flattened edge (50 x 27 mm) appears to have been pecked and then smoothed. The broken 90° angle edge may also have been used. BA-XX-2/43, from the 0–10 cm level of light-brown silt in Square F9, also appears to be fire-broken. It measures 73 x 45 x 41 mm. All four edges around a flat cortical side are pecked and/or battered. One end of BA-XX-2/105, from the 0–10 cm level in Unit 2 in Square B10, has been pecked into a flat facet (60 x 10 mm). Some pecking is present on a corner along another edge. This artifact measures 68 x 62 x 43 mm (Figure 7-15b).

A tabular quartzite pebble (BA-XX-2/52) with a rectangular outline (94 x 57 x 23 mm) from Unit 3a at a depth of 40 cm in Square B13, was kept mainly because of its unusual shape. The entire periphery has many undulations which could be worn flake scars, but the only definite flake scar is near a corner.

An ovoid quartzite pebble (BA-XX-2/107), which has original rolled cortex only on a portion of one irregular face, evidently has been pecked over much of the rest of that face, both edges, and the opposite flatter face, where there is a pecked central depression 12 mm

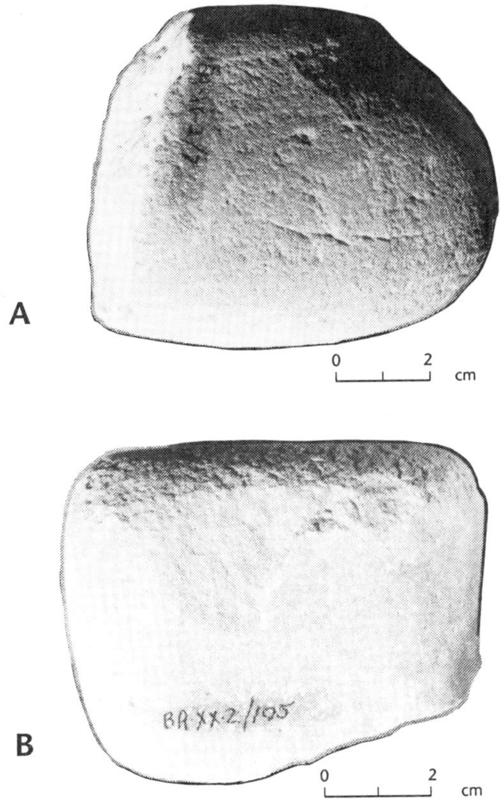

Figure 7-15. Pecked quartzite pebbles. **A)** BA-XX-2/7; **B)** BA-XX-2/105.

in diameter (Figure 7-16a). Evidently this artifact is a *quebra-coco,* a tool type never found in the Central sites, in an area where palms do not grow. *Carnauba* palms are present in the Rio Verde valley, about 2 km east of Toca da Gameleira. The artifact, which measures 108 x 75 x 48 mm, was found in Unit 2 at the 0–10 cm level in Square A9 North.

The rest of the collection can be categorized as flaked quartzite pebble tools, although only two are classic pebble tools with unidirectional flaking to create an excurvate working edge, which shows concentrated use. BA-XX-2/11, measuring 69 x 51 x 38 mm, came from Unit 2 at a depth of 12 cm in Square B15. The central projecting part of the excurving step-flaked 70–80° angle edge was resharpened by removing thin step flakes from the planar face at right angles to the main flaking direction (Figure 7-16b). The resharpened nose is battered but less worn than the remainder of the working edge, which would be excellent for grooving or planing wood. The naturally spalled opposite end has several unidirectional flake scars removed at an earlier time to create an excurving working edge with an 85° angle, which is worn and polished. The other really classic pebble tool (BA-XX-2/26), measuring 93 x 61 x 50 mm, came from the surface of Square C9. Unidirectional stepped flaking along one excurving side intentionally created a central projecting nose (90° angle) which is crushed and battered by heavy use (Figure 7-17a). One corner has been pecked and another flaked by use as a hammerstone. Impact marks are scattered elsewhere on the cortical and flaked surfaces. A 90° angle flaked edge opposite the main worked edge has also been battered by chopping in the same manner as the projecting nose.

Two small quartzite pebbles have been unidirectionally flaked from a flat face to create an off-center projection at the intersection of a straight edge (70° angle) and a steeper (85° angle) concave edge. The beak of the largest of these tools (BA-XX-2/89) is more worn than the other working edges (Figure 7-17b). One flake was removed from the opposite end. This artifact measures 63 x 41 x 19 mm, and was recovered from Unit 3a at a depth of 40 cm in Square B12. The other artifact (BA-XX-2/110), from Unit 3c at a depth of 28 cm in Square B8, has the same outline but the straight edge is natural. The 90° angle concave edge and beak are worn on this small tool, which measures 43 x 33 x 13 mm. A flake has been removed from the opposite end and another from a corner.

Two small quartzite pebbles, also with plano-convex

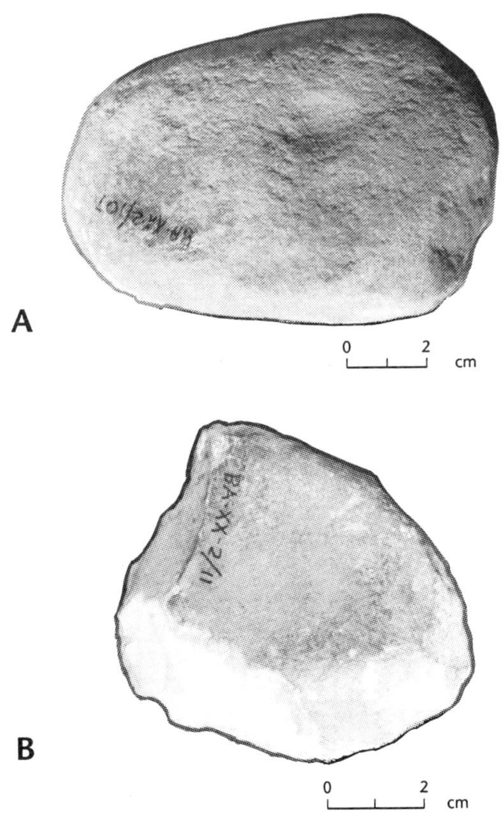

Figure 7-16. A) quartzite *quebra-coco* (BA-XX-2/107); **B)** quartzite scraper/plane (BA-XX-2/11).

A

B

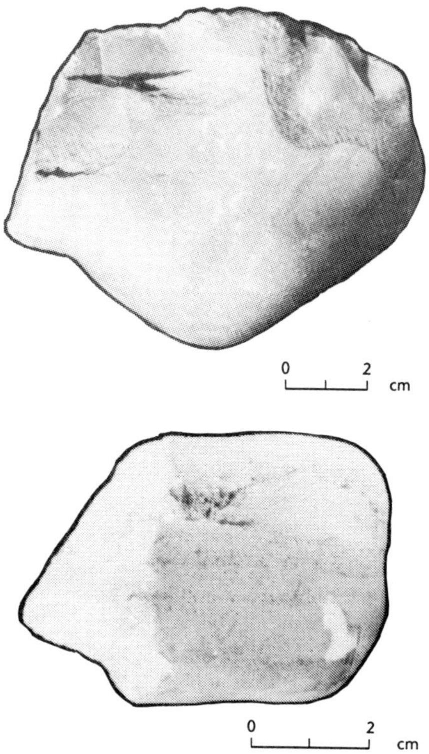

Figure 7-17. A) quartzite chopper (BA-XX-2/26); **B)** quartzite pointed tool (BA-XX-2/89).

cross-sections, have straight 90° angle working edges created by steep unidirectional flaking. The slightly denticulated edges of these steep endscrapers (BA-XX-2/106 from the upper 10–cm level in Unit 2 in Square B10, and BA-XX-2/124 from Unit 3b at a depth of 30–40 cm in the same square) are much used; and both have flake scars on the opposite pointed ends. BA-XX-2/124, which measures 43 x 32 x 16 mm, has been flaked straight across (Figure 7-18a); but BA-XX-2/106, measuring 67 x 43 x 30 mm, is flaked at an oblique angle (Figure 7-18b).

Three small elongated quartzite pebbles have been unidirectionally retouched along a longitudinal edge. BA-XX-2/48, the smallest (measuring 56 x 42 x 16 mm), came from Unit 3a at a depth of 35 cm in Square B13. The flaked edge (45–55° angle) has been resharpened by removing one flake from the opposite side to make a central projection more prominent. The nibbled edge appears to have been used for scraping. BA-XX-2/101, measuring 58 x 49 x 39 mm, is more steeply flaked to form a straight 80° angle chopping edge, which is step-flaked (Figure 7-19a). One end of this pebble tool, from Unit 2 at a depth of 33 cm in Square B8, has been battered by use as a hammerstone. The excurving 85° flaked edge of BA-XX-2/103, from a depth of 3 cm in Unit 2 in Square A9 North, has later been renewed to a 90° edge angle; and a flake was removed from a projecting corner in the opposite direction. Two other corners of this pebble tool, which measures 66 x 51 x 38 mm, have been pecked; and one of these is stained with hematite, although there is no indication of pigment preparation.

Unidirectional flaking was used to fashion a much-worn pointed tip with a 70° angle working edge on BA-XX-2/114, from Unit 3c at a depth of 40 cm in Square B7. The contiguous edges have been resharpened by flipping this quartzite pebble, which measures 66 x 48 x 23 mm, over and removing flakes in the opposite direction. These undulating S-shaped 60–70° angle edges are also heavily worn. An undulating longitudinal edge (80° angle) on BA-XX-2/37, from Unit 3a at a depth of 35 cm in Square B13, has been much worn and battered. This subangular quartzite pebble, with a triangular cross-section (72 x 40 x 23 mm), has also been battered on a portion of the apical ridge. In addition, flakes have been removed from a concave platform edge to form a beaked 85° angle edge 25 mm long near one end.

This kind of short beaked or lipped steep scraping edge with a concave platform seems to have been desired, because such an edge is present on five more quartzite pebble tools of highly variable shapes and sizes. A beaked working edge was first recognized on BA-XX-2/92, from Unit 3a at a depth of 40 cm in Square B14. On this pebble, which measures 98 x 63 x 54 mm,

A

B

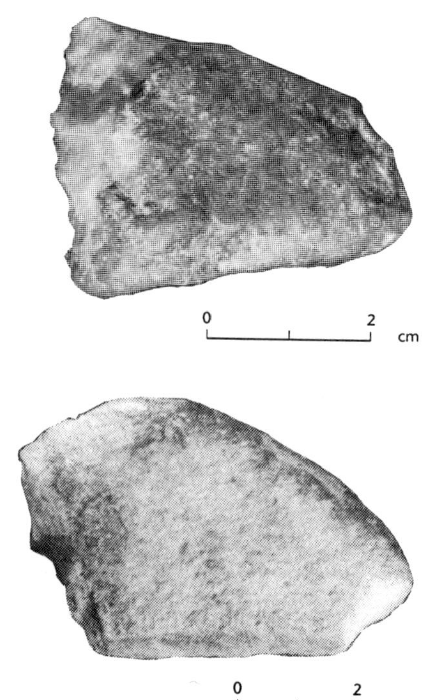

Figure 7-18. Flaked quartzite pebbles. **A)** BA-XX-2/124; **B)** BA-XX-2/106.

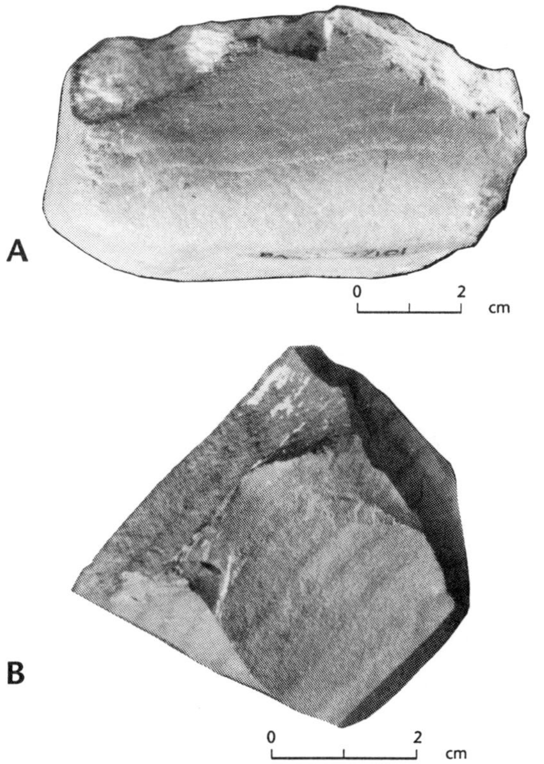

Figure 7-19. A) flaked quartzite pebble (BA-XX-2/101); **B)** flaked quartzite fragment (BA-XX-2/102).

the concave platform edge was fashioned by removing a large decortication flake with a broad flat bulb from one side. The resultant concave face was then used as a platform for removing three long flakes and several short flakes to create an undulating beaked 70° angle edge 29 mm long, and a contiguous but separate concave spokeshave edge with a 90° angle. Flakes were removed from the concave flake face to resharpen projecting portions of the main working edge and to fashion a graver spur between the two working edges. The 90° angle platform edge of the original decortication flake was also retouched to form a projection on the other end of the 20 mm long spokeshave edge. Both the platform edge (with a 90° angle) and the long incurvate distal edge (also with a 90° angle) have been battered and use-flaked. Although many edges of this pebble tool have been used, evidently the main working edge was intentionally fashioned into a beaked steep scraper which would be very useful for planing wood.

A similar beaked scraping edge is present on BA-XX-2/91, found in Unit 3a at a depth of 40–50 cm in Square B14. This quartzite pebble, measuring 67 x 65 x 38 mm, was first split along a cleavage plane; and then a decortication flake with a slightly curving bulb was removed at right angles. The desirable beaked end was then created by removing a flake from a corner of the concave edge. The beaked edge was then deliberately narrowed to 25 mm long by removing a large flake from the side of the same concave edge. Use flakes were also removed from three 90° angle edges, and one corner of the cortex has been pecked by hammering. The intended well-worn 90° angle scraping edge is very similar to the intentional edge on the tool previously described.

A similar beaked edge (with a 90° angle) is present on BA-XX-2/8, from a depth of 3 cm in Unit 2 in Square B15. This irregularly flattened quartzite pebble, measuring 60 x 61 x 29 mm, would not have been recognized as having any features except steeply retouched edges, if this pattern had not been noted on the previous two artifacts. Although the main working edge (with a 90° angle) is about the same length (20 mm), the concave platform is part of the natural waterworn cortical surface. A natural depression on one face was recognized as being useful when one end of the pebble was flaked off. The steep unidirectionally retouched edge is much worn, probably by planing.

A larger quartzite pebble (BA-XX-2/93), which measures 82 x 78 x 45 mm, has been split twice, creating two separate concave lipped edges. One of these lipped edges is long, and does not show any definite evidence of use, although the other 65° angle excurvate edge exhibits several flake scars from chopping. The other lipped edge was sharpened by removing a flake from the corner of the concave platform edge, and then narrowed to 23 mm long by removing a flake in the other direction, using the new face as a platform, with the same procedural sequences as with BA-XX-2/91. The slightly concave beaked scraping edge (with an 80° angle) and especially the spurs at either end are slightly worn. This artifact was found in Unit 2 at a depth of 30 cm in Square B8.

The last smaller (50 x 42 x 31 mm) quartzite pebble tool (BA-XX-2/102) has several thermally spalled edges (Figure 7-19b). A naturally concave spalled face was used as a platform for removing a flake at right angles in order to create a 28-mm-long beaked working edge, which has been step-flaked but not worn very much. Step flaking is also present around a corner on a contiguous 90° angle edge which lacks a lip. This pebble tool was found in Unit 2 at a depth of 5 cm in Square B10.

Miscellaneous Artifacts

A quadrangular pebble hammerstone (BA-XX-2/76) of an igneous rock, measuring 71 x 55 x 43 mm, was found in Unit 2 at a depth of 0-10 cm in Square B14. When partially cleaned of calcium carbonate in an acid bath, remnants of hematite powder remained cemented to one face with an irregular elongated, possibly pecked, depression measuring 35 x 15 mm. An adjacent end squared by pecking also has some hematite on it. Roughened pecking is also evident around the periphery of the opposite end, which also has some hematite adhering to it. This pebble, partially shaped by use, appears to have been used as a pigment preparation tool. There are no pictographs visible in Toca da Gameleira. Perhaps the paint was used for body ornamentation, or the pictographs in nearby Toca dos Cosmos.

An abraded piece of bottle glass (BA-XX-2/58) was found in Unit 2 at a depth of 10 cm in Square B9. Other pieces of the same bottle, including one that fits onto BA-XX-2/58, came from the surface of Squares B13 and B14. To judge from the reconstructed neck, the bottle was an early beer bottle with cruder molding ridges than are present on modern beer bottles. The thickness is also variable, and generally thicker than a modern bottle. Evidently someone, perhaps a *caboclo*, picked up a piece of a bottle that had been broken near the top of the rubble cone under the cavern entrance and carried it at least 6 m downslope, where a sharp-edged naturally rounded nose (forming half a percussion cone) was used to scrape or groove some object. Parallel striations extend from the external face across the entire broken edge of this fragment, which measures 61 x 34 x 4 mm. Also the 60° angle external edge is slightly ground for a length of 10 mm. Striations are lacking elsewhere on this broken edge or on the internal surface, and the pattern of parallel striations does not fit random striations on the adjacent broken fragment. Another bottle glass fragment (BA-XX-2/59), from the surface of Square B13, has a corner which has been burinated at least twice. As there is no evidence of use of this burinated edge, it was concluded that end shocks to remove one or more burin spalls from a corner can occur naturally when a bottle breaks. Archaeologists should always be aware that it is easy to remove burin spalls from a projecting edge of flakeable material.

Ceramics

Twenty-two potsherds were recovered from Toca da Gameleira. Most were found in the eastern sector of the main trench, under the vertical-walled opening to the cavern; and most at the 0–10 cm level, in Unit 2.

The most numerous class of pottery (68%) was a plain thin ware featuring heavy calcite tempering and a rough surface finish. The surface color of the sherds ranged from a dull pale red through buff to grey, on the interior and exterior. The surface finish is rough, with the fabric often torn; and the surface presents a pocked appearance due to the erosion and loss of temper particles. The pottery was heavily tempered with subangular grey or white calcite fragments, with the particle size ranging up to 2 mm. There is also a moderate amount of quartz grit in the paste. The thickness of the sherds ranged from 3 to 7 mm; the mode was 5 mm. Sherd cores are grey to buff in color, with complete oxidation; but the sherds are somewhat friable, with a platy structure. No rim sherds were recovered.

Of the 15 sherds in this class, 53% were recovered from the 0–10 cm level in the very dark brown silt and rock zone (Unit 2) in Square B15; and 20% were found in the same level and sedimentary zone in adjacent Square B14. Two sherds were recovered from the 10–20 cm level in Unit 2, one in Square B13 and the other in Square B11. One sherd was found in the 0–10 cm level in Square B12, and one in the 0–10 cm level in Square D11. Two sherds of a grey ware with smooth surface finish and moderate calcite tempering were found in close association in Square B15 at the 0–10 cm level in Unit 2. There was a very large rim sherd (found broken in five pieces) which indicates a shallow wide-mouthed bowl with mouth approximately 18 cm in diameter and a minimum depth of 10 cm. The rim is simple and direct, with a slightly rounded lip. The surface color is dark grey to dark grey/brown on the interior and exterior. The vessel was well smoothed on the interior and exterior, with some evidence of fine brushing in vertical strokes. The surface is somewhat pocked but the temper is not prominent. There is moderate calcite and quartz grit temper, with particles ranging up to 3 mm in size. Thickness ranged from 6 to 7 mm, with the mode 6 mm. Core sections indicate that the vessel was well fired, with complete oxidation; a platy structure is evident.

Three sherds of a red ware with smooth surface finish and moderate calcite tempering were found in the 0–10 cm level of loose silt on the rock shelves, on Squares D10 and F11. The surface color was a dull pale red to buff on the interior and exterior. The surface is well smoothed, with interior surfaces smoother than exterior. There was a moderate amount of tempering, with subangular calcite fragments up to 3 mm in size; no grit was observable. Sherds ranged in thickness from 5 to 6 mm, with the mode 6 mm. Sherd cores were buff in color, with complete oxidation; and a platy structure is evident.

Finally, one body sherd of a thick ware was found at the 20–30 cm level in Unit 2 in Square B14. The interior of the sherd was dark grey/brown in color; and the exterior brown. In terms of surface finish, the exterior surface was very uneven; the interior surface was much smoother. Some pock marks are visible due to erosion and loss of temper particles. There was heavy grit temper, with subangular quartz particles ranging up to 3 mm in size. The sherd was 9 mm thick.

The small sample of pottery recovered from Toca da Gameleira corresponds with other ceramic collections in the region. The same classes were found in the Toca do Cosmos nearby.

DISCUSSION AND CONCLUSIONS

Toca da Gameleira was found at the end of the 1984 excavation season during a short extensive survey to get acquainted with the region outside the immediate vicinity of Central. The cave was chosen for excavation because of the apparent association of artifacts with fossilized sloth bones in the surface deposits. The working hypothesis that people were contemporary inhabitants of the cave with giant sloths was disproven when excavation indicated that the original deposit containing the sloth bones had been subject to flood waters which had removed the finer deposits and exposed the rock-like bone fragments as part of a lag deposit composed largely of rock and breccia rubble. The lack of butchering marks or any other evidence of alteration by either man or nature before permineralization of the sloth bones confirmed that the association of sloth bones with artifacts was secondary. Evidently the sloths had lived and died in the cave long before human occupants occasionally picked up and used a broken sloth bone or more often a tooth having a useful working edge.

A case can be made, however, that people did occupy the cave before the end of the Pleistocene but long after the sloths had died. Several fossil bones and teeth of large mammals other than sloths were cut, grooved, and flaked in ways which would be very difficult to explain by trampling or other natural action. A few broken bones which lack the corrugated surface so characteristic of giant sloth bones were permineralized chalky-white, evidently by calcium rather than by iron. These bone fragments are of unidentifiable large mammals, although a single tooth of a large cervid and a *Macrauchenia* tooth with similar permineralization may belong to the animals whose bones were altered. Neither of these ungulates would have climbed into the vertical-walled cavern entrance; and if they had fallen in, their remains would have been much more abundant. Also, the lack of evidence for carnivore chewing suggests that these bones were not dragged in by felids. The simplest explanation is that people carried in the remains of scavenged animals, either for food or for use as tools, as they did in Toca de Manoel Latão and Toca dos Buzios.

With the exception of the giant cervid tooth, which came from Unit 2, all of the permineralized white bones and teeth came from upper parts of Unit 3, the brown clayey silt underlying. The upper portions of Unit 3 evidently had been mixed and moved by flood water action. Although the original provenience of altered bones and other artifacts from the upper part of Unit 3 has been lost, it is unlikely that many artifacts subsequently deposited with the silt and rubble to form Unit 2 could have intruded very far into Unit 3. Most if not all artifacts from Unit 3 should be older than the deposition of Unit 2 or the locally restricted and recent Unit 1, which yielded only two artifacts. Therefore, it is possible to divide the artifact assemblage from Toca da Gameleira into at least two components: the older including everything in Unit 3, and the younger in Units 2 and 1. Formation of Unit 2 continued for an unknown amount of time, and only the latter part of the deposit is datable by radiocarbon to about 470 years B.P.

The only intentionally shaped artifacts came from Unit 2. The fragment of a pressure-flaked quartz biface evidently was picked up elsewhere and carried into the cave, where it was used as a scraper. As at Abrigo do Pilão, the only bifacially flaked artifact had not been manufactured locally. Several water-rolled pebbles were partially shaped by use, including a *quebra-coco* with a centrally pecked depression on one face, an edge-ground cobble, and a quadrangular hammerstone; but the only intentionally shaped artifacts found in the cave were the potsherds and the exotic broken biface. However, graver spurs and noses often had been intentionally created on the edges of flaked artifacts from both the early and late components. Most likely, these spurs, usually found on high-angled edges, were designed for planing, grooving, and cutting wood. Quite likely, wooden artifacts had been shaped in the cave; but the intentional shaping of flaked stone artifacts was never part of the local cultural repertoire.

Only one cylindrical bone splinter projectile point appears to have been symmetrically shaped. This point, made from a permineralized white bone of a medium-sized mammal, came from the older component in Unit 3, along with two other cut bones of larger mammals, one of which may also have been a projectile point. A sloth bone that had been step-flaked and polished by use on one end was also found in Unit 3, along with a sloth bone fragment which exhibited patterned incisions restricted to a concave spokeshave-like edge. The inner broken edge of a sloth tooth differentially exhibited patterned flaking and polishing where it evidently had been used as a scraper-plane. Another tooth fragment from Unit 3c also exhibits cuts and scratches from scraping or planing. These four old fragments of heavily iron-permineralized sloth bones and teeth may have been picked up and used by the same people who worked the three calcium-permineralized bones of animals that evidently had died at the time of human occupation. These early people also flaked chert, quartz, and quartzite pebbles and the rare chert nodule which had not weathered to chalk. When available, people used naturally sharp and steep edges. They also intentionally created nose, beaks, projections and denticulations on steep flaked edges, all of which could have served as efficient wood-working tools. In total, the oldest component in Unit 3 contained four retouched flakes; a burinated flake; a nosed quartzite chunk; a step-flaked chopper; three chert nodules with denticulated and step-flaked edges; three split quartz pebbles; three quartz pebble scrapers; three quartz pebbles with steeply retouched edges; two exotic chert pebbles with step-flaked edges; three quartzite pebble hammerstones; and five quartzite pebbles with intentionally created beaks, projections, and lipped edges. A total of 29 stone artifacts and seven bone artifacts were recovered from the oldest component (in the upper part of Unit 3) which probably dates to the late Pleistocene, before *Macrauchenia* and a giant cervid became extinct.

Essentially the same kinds of artifacts were found in the later component (in Unit 2), although the artifact yield was more abundant. Even flaked iron-permineralized sloth bones and teeth were more abundant, although only one calcium-permineralized bone artifact was found in Unit 2. Possibly all of these artifacts of fossil bone had been derived from Unit 3. Some of the stone artifacts may also have been derived.

Most potsherds and all bottle glass came from the upper 20 cm of Unit 2. A *quebra-coco* and two pebbles with hematite stains, one of which is a quadrangular igneous pebble hammerstone, probably also relate to the recent ceramic zone.

Although people may have occupied the cave occasionally throughout the late Pleistocene and Holocene, as a place where perishables could be processed in a cool shady retreat from the sun, the complete history of occupation of Toca da Gameleira has irrevocably been disturbed by flood waters and colluvial action. For us, then, the site was intriguing but disappointing.

Chapter 8
Review and Discussion

Our Record of Prehistoric Occupation in the Central Area

The archaeological record in the Central area of interior Bahia is still very sketchy at present. Only six excavated limestone cave or rockshelter sites are reported here. Nevertheless it is possible to draw some conclusions about the prehistory of the area, placing it in the context of the known archaeological record in interior eastern Brazil.

In that context, evidence for a late Pleistocene settlement of the Central area is to be fully expected. Central is only about 200 km due south of the region of São Raimundo Nonato, Piaui, where excavations in the well-stratified sandstone rockshelter site of Toca do Boqueirão da Pedra Furada have produced remains of human occupation, in the form of lithic artifacts and constructed hearths, dated back to over 40,000 years ago (Guidon and Parenti 1989; Delibrias et al. 1989; Parenti et al. 1990). Another rockshelter in the São Raimundo Nonato area, Toca do Sitio do Meio, has yielded radiocarbon dates on four hearths ranging from about 14,300 yr B.P. to 12,200 yr B.P., with stone artifacts associated (Guidon and Delibrias 1985:399). In the western Bahian *municipio* of Corimbe, southwest across the Rio São Francisco, evidence of early human occupation has been found in a limestone rockshelter known as Morro Furada, in ash beds with abundant shells of giant terrestrial gastropods, and charcoal radiocarbon dated at about 21,000–16,000 yr B.P. (Schmitz 1990:47). In caves in the Central area, however, none of the Pleistocene occupation levels have produced radiocarbon dates; so we have no firm indication of the precise age of our Pleistocene materials.

We must here make note of excavations by Beltrão and French associates in Toca da Esperança, which were carried out subsequent to our fieldwork in the Central area. Toca da Esperança is part of the same cave system as Toca dos Buzios, which is a higher, smaller chamber. It has been announced that fractured fossil bones recovered in association with three quartzite artifacts in a basal stratigraphic level under a cemented breccia zone in Toca da Esperança have yielded uranium-thorium dates ranging between 204,000 and 295,000 years ago; and a middle Pleistocene age for human occupation is suggested (de Lumley et al. 1988). Documentation of the context, in the form of presentation of detailed scale drawings and photographs of the natural stratigraphic profiles, and artifacts and bones in situ, is awaited; as well as presentation of the results of geological and sedimentological analyses to determine the origin and history of the sedimentary matrix. With our experience in Toca da Gameleira, we have to fear that the dated fossil bones may be ancient "lag gravels," fractured by natural processes, deposited and redeposited by internal flooding in the cave system, and eventually mixed with stone artifacts of much later age (although still very likely Pleistocene).

Is it possible that we have the same situation, then, at Toca dos Buzios, where we found fossil bone fragments, fractured by desiccation, in association with quartz artifacts in the basal yellow silt under a cemented flowstone/breccia floor? It may be noted that there is no evidence of colluvial reworking of the yellow silt matrix in the bedrock channel; and the edges of the bone fragments are still sharp, not rolled in redeposition. Microscopic study of a small number of the bone fragments indicated alteration of edges and surfaces by human use. Because of chemical weathering or encrustation, it was impossible to determine for certain in all cases whether the alteration occurred before or after permineralization of the bone; however, there are grounds for arguing that the modification occurred before the fossilization.

At Toca de Manoel Latão the evidence for a Pleistocene occupation is solid: an equid podial with two sharp cut marks clearly made while the bone was fresh, found with stone and bone artifacts in association with bones and teeth of other extinct fauna in a situation of slow, undisturbed deposition of clayey silt. It is frustrating that as at Toca dos Buzios, the bone from Toca de Manoel Latão was too altered to be radiocarbon dated; but a Pleistocene age for the artifacts is clearly indicated by the remains of extinct fauna associated.

At Toca da Gameleira, it is evident that people were not contemporary with the giant ground sloths whose bones were fractured by desiccation and were redeposited in the clayey silts and rubble zones, although later occupants of the cave utilized edges of fossilized sloth bone fragments and teeth. A few modified fossil bone fragments not permineralized in the same fashion as the sloth bones suggest that people were in Toca da Gameleira before the extinction of some Pleistocene species, and the stone and bone artifacts found in the clayey silt of Unit 3 may be early. However, it was not possible to obtain a radiocarbon date on any facies of Unit 3.

Similarly undatable are the few limestone pebble tools found in the red silt deposit underlying the ash and silt zone in the eastern chamber of Abrigo do Pilão. No identifiable bone fragments were found in this zone, but these artifacts must be older than the dates of about 9500 yr B.P. obtained on charcoal from the overlying ash and silt zone; and they are likely Pleistocene in age.

The artifact assemblages from our Pleistocene levels feature simple pebble tools or flake tools of quartz, quartzite, chert, or limestone with working edges or surfaces modified by utilization or minimal retouch, not deliberate shaping of the piece. Working edges were also modified on amorphous bone fragments or teeth in Toca dos Buzios, Toca de Manoel Latão, and Toca da Gameleira. These simple stone and bone tools may have been used to shape wooden artifacts. In Toca de Manoel Latão as well, there are fragments of simple bone projectile points; but no stone bifacial points are found in the Central area until the ceramic horizon, and even those three utilized fragments of points are apparently intrusive into the region. While bones of extinct fauna are associated with the artifacts in the Pleistocene levels, the tool kit popularly conceived by many archaeologists to be associated with "Paleoindian big-game hunters," featuring bifacial projectile points, is absent.

The preceramic levels in the ash and silt zone at Abrigo do Pilão represent the early Holocene, with radiocarbon dates ranging between approximately 9500 and 8800 yr B.P. The earliest assemblage, found mixed in the zone of disintegrated travertine and at the very base of the overlying ash and silt zone, features large jasper or quartzite flakes with edge trimming. It is notable that large flake tools are components of the earliest Holocene Itaparica tradition, first defined in Goías rockshelters by Schmitz and his associates (Schmitz 1980, 1986; Schmitz et al. 1976, 1989), and now known to be widely distributed in the dry zones (*cerrado* or *caatinga*) of interior eastern Brazil. *Lesmas* or *limaces*, the marker for the Itaparica tradition, are absent from the Abrigo do Pilão assemblage, however.

The flaked-stone industry throughout the early-Holocene ash and silt zone at Abrigo do Pilão is characterised by small utilized or minimally retouched amorphous flakes or fragments of quartz, quartzite, chert, or limestone. A similar early-Holocene flaked-stone industry, with small scrapers and pointed tools made on amorphous flakes or fragments of quartz and chert, is known from the rockshelter GO-JA-01 in southwest Goías, defining the Serranópolis phase, which dates back to 9000 yr B.P. (Schmitz 1980, 1986; Schmitz et al. 1989); and from the rockshelter of Lapa Pequena in northern Minas Gerais, where preceramic occupation levels were dated between ca. 8200 and 7600 yr B.P. (Bryan and Gruhn 1978). At both sites there was an emphasis on the collection of palm nuts and large terrestrial gastropods. At Abrigo do Pilão, abundant mammal bones indicate an emphasis on hunting of medium- and small-sized mammals; as well, large terrestrial gastropods were collected. Quartzite and limestone choppers and pounders, however, may have been used to process plant food at Abrigo do Pilão. Mussel shell artifacts also occur in the early Holocene deposits.

Between the latest radiocarbon date of about 8800 yr B.P. from the preceramic ash and silt zone at Abrigo do Pilão and the radiocarbon date of about 3200 yr B.P. from the base of the brown silt deposit in the lower shelter of Toca do Cosmos, there is a substantial gap in our archaeological record for the Central region. Wesley Hurt (pers. comm. 1985) has a radiocarbon date of about 3300 yr B.P. from a lower preceramic level at the Abrigo de Valdemar in the southwest part of the region of limestone *serras*, but nothing earlier is dated. There thus appears to be a middle-Holocene gap in the occupation of limestone caves and rockshelters in the Central region. We may possibly be seeing an archaeological reflection of the Hypsithermal climatic interval, with drought conditions too severe to permit habitation in the area, at least in the limestone caves. However, it must be stressed that there is no direct paleoenvironmental evidence of past climatic conditions in the region; and it must be admitted that the gap in the archaeological record may well be simply a sampling error.

It is interesting to note, however, that there are two other cave sites in interior eastern Brazil with the same kind of interrupted sedimentary record as Abrigo do Pilão. In southwestern Goías, the large rockshelter GO-JA-01 features thick lower preceramic sedimentary deposits dated between ca. 10,600 yr B.P. and 6700 yr B.P.; then, after a disconformity, a thin upper ceramic horizon (Jataí phase), dated at ca. 1000 yr B.P. (Schmitz et al. 1989:33–48). At Lapa Pequena in northern Minas Gerais, the thick preceramic deposits dated between 8200 and 7600 yr B.P. are also directly overlain by a much later ceramic horizon, dated at ca. 500 yr B.P. (Bryan and Gruhn 1978:Table 1). At the Gran Abrigo de Santana do Riacho in central Minas Gerais, however, there are preceramic occupation levels dated between 6000 and 4500 yr B.P. (Prous 1981, 1986), as well as later occupations. It may be that under severe climatic conditions during the middle Holocene, the population in interior eastern Brazil abandoned some local areas but persisted in others. With the excavation and radiocarbon dating of different types of sites in different microenvironmental zones, the situation will become clearer.

Our archaeological record in the Central area resumes at Toca do Cosmos and Abrigo da Lesma. At the latter small rockshelter in the area of limestone *serras*, the main occupation was radiocarbon dated between 2400 and 2200 yr B.P. Animal bones were rare; shells of giant terrestrial gastropods abundant. The lithic industry was a continuation of late-Pleistocene/early-Holocene tradition, characterised by utilized or minimally retouched amorphous flakes or fragments of quartz, chert, quartzite, or limestone; and heavy limestone or quartzite tools used for pounding and chopping. Mussel-shell scrapers may have also been used in the processing of vegetal materials. At Toca do Cosmos in the Rio Verde area, the oldest radiocarbon date of 3200 yr B.P. comes from the base of the brown silt deposit just above bedrock in the lower shelter. Again there is very little mammal bone. Most of the artifacts found in the preceramic levels were heavy tools: thick chert scraper/planes, and quartzite pebble choppers. Modified hematite fragments suggest that the painting of pictographs at this site began in the preceramic period.

The ceramic period in the Central area was represented at Toca do Cosmos, Toca da Gameleira, Abrigo da Lesma, and Abrigo do Pilão. Ceramics appeared in the region in late-prehistoric times. Sherds were concentrated in the upper 10 or 20 cm at all of these sites; and the radiocarbon dates for ceramic levels were about 1230 yr B.P. at Toca do Cosmos, about 1100 yr B.P. at Abrigo do Pilão, about 900 yr B.P. at Abrigo da Lesma, and about 500 yr B.P. at Toca da Gameleira. It is notable that the same lithic, bone, and shell industries continued from the preceramic period; with ceramic-horizon assemblages still featuring small tools made on amorphous flakes or fragments of chert, quartz, quartzite, or limestone with minimal retouch, heavy pounding or chopping tools of quartzite or limestone, mussel-shell scrapers, and simple bone points. A few polished stone artifacts, including axe blades, were cached at Abrigo do Pilão; and polished axes are also reported on the ceramic horizon at Abrigo de Valdemar (Wesley Hurt, pers. comm. 1984). Most of the polished stone artifacts are of exotic igneous stone, and may have been traded into the area. The three utilized fragments of bifacial projectile points may also have been trade items or collected outside the Central area.

The ceramic wares vary from site to site in terms of tempering material and vessel wall thickness; but all of the pottery is plain, very rarely decorated by incision or painting. Some wares were slipped red or grey; others plain or brushed. Rim sherds suggest simple vessel shapes. In all, our Central pottery appears to be affiliated with the Aratu tradition known to be widespread in northeastern Brazil in the late-prehistoric period (Schmitz et al. 1980:20–40; map:53); but its precise relationships must be determined by more detailed comparative studies.

It is not known whether the appearance of ceramics is to be correlated with the introduction of horticulture in the Central area. The non-ceramic component of artifact assemblages on this horizon at Toca do Cosmos, Toca da Gameleira, and Abrigo da Lesma indicates no change in technology from earlier times; and there is no direct evidence of a shift in economy. The plant remains preserved in the dry upper deposits at Abrigo do Pilão might have provided key information; but the collection, presently misplaced in the Museu Nacional, was not analysed; and as well, there is a good chance of mixture of materials from an historic occupation of the site. We can suppose that the latest prehistoric population in the Central area knew horticulture; but without direct evidence, that can be only a surmise.

Some Observations on Prehistoric Cultural Patterns in the Central Area

Certainly nothing conclusive can be said about settlement systems in the region of Central, as only a few selected cave and rockshelter sites in the limestone area have been explored. As discussed in the Introduction to the Research, the area has not been systematically surveyed for open habitation sites. It would be foolhardy, then, to devise formal models of settlement/subsistence systems for the area; but some ideas can be advanced.

As a base for considerations, we can certainly conclude that the subsistence economy of the prehistoric population was based on hunting and collecting. Even on the ceramic horizon, horticulture cannot be demonstrated; and in any case, it may well have been only a small segment of the subsistence economy. Remains preserved on sites indicate hunting of a variety of medium to small mammals (including deer, peccary, armadillo, rodents) and likely reptiles and birds as well; the collection of giant terrestrial gastropods; the gathering of freshwater mussels in the Rio Verde; and most likely the collection of a wide variety of edible or useful plants in the *caatinga* forest.

These economic pursuits must have been affected by the strong seasonality in the region: the marked difference between the wet and dry seasons, with the likelihood of frequent prolonged droughts affecting water supplies as well. Unfortunately, without a detailed ethnoecological study in the region, we do not know which plant foods and animals might have been seasonal in abundance or availability. One category of food which we do know is not available in the dry season is the giant terrestrial gastropod: the snails hibernate under ground. We may presume, then, that caves and rockshelters in which shells of giant terrestrial gastropods are abundant in occupation levels were principally wet-season campsites. In the region of the limestone *serras*, three of the four sites excavated—Toca dos Buzios, Abrigo da Lesma, and Abrigo do Pilão—clearly fall into this category. Only in Toca de Manoel Latão were gastropod shells uncommon. This low-lying cave may have been too damp for occupation in the rainy season. In the Rio Verde sites, giant terrestrial-gastropod shells were common in the occupation levels at Toca do Cosmos; but notably very rare at Toca da Gameleira, which was probably subject to severe flooding during heavy rains, and not as suitable for occupation as the nearby Toca do Cosmos.

One might speculate that at the very height of the dry season the limestone region was largely abandoned, as permanent waterholes are very few and far between in the region. A logical seasonal move for human groups would have been to the better-watered canyons and uplands of the Serra Azul and Chapada Diamantina to the west and southwest; or into the Rio Verde valley, where freshwater mussels could provide a staple food resource. If worse came to worse, with a truly prolonged and severe drought, groups could have repaired to the Rio São Francisco, about 70 km to the northwest. Like the present rural people of the Central region, who emigrate temporarily when drought conditions become severe, the prehistoric population may have returned quite promptly to the area as soon as conditions improved.

The archaeological record indicates that the basic technology and material culture of the prehistoric population in the Central region remained simple and stable from the late Pleistocene through the ceramic horizon. In the lithic industry, very few artifacts were formally shaped: pebbles, flakes, or fragments of quartz, quartzite, chert, or limestone were modified by utilization or minimal unifacial retouch of working edges or surfaces. Among hundreds of lithic artifacts recovered from the excavated sites, there are only three utilized fragments of bifacially shaped artifacts which were probably collected outside the Central area by the latest prehistoric people. The few polished axes and other shaped artifacts from the ceramic horizon at Abrigo do Pilão also appear exotic in the area. The traditional lithic tools in the Central region were always simple; essentially formless. Quite striking to North American archaeologists is the absence of stone projectile points: throughout the prehistoric sequence, weapon points were made of bone or wood. Indeed there were no bifacial artifacts of any kind at our sites. The lithic artifacts were utilized mainly to work vegetal materials: to shape wooden tools, weapons, and utensils; and to process plant food. Mussel-shell artifacts, a long-standing tradition in the area, may have been utilized as scrapers or containers. Bone artifacts, aside from simple projectile points, are notably rare.

The non-perishable material culture of the prehistoric population of the Central area, then, is quite unimpressive. What we do not have is a sample of the rest of the material culture: the weapons, tools, utensils, and ornaments made of wood, fibers, skin, or feathers. Ethnographic records of surviving aboriginal tribes of interior eastern Brazil indicate that the perishable material culture may have been quite rich and elaborate.

Certainly clear evidence of the creative capacity of the prehistoric population of the Central area is to be seen in the complex rock art, which graces the walls or ceiling of many caves and rockshelters, and cliff faces. Of the six sites we excavated, only one, Toca da Gameleira, lacked pictographs; and there were only a few at Toca de Manoel Latão. Both sites, it may be noted, produced evidence of only sporadic occupation; and not during the wet season. At Toca dos Buzios the dark walls and ceiling were covered with white pictographs in circular, geometric, and life form designs. At Abrigo do Pilão, the rock face above the shelter featured many pictographs in red, yellow, or black; unfortunately, most were indistinct. At Abrigo da Lesma, the walls of the rockshelter were bare; but just around the corner, on the vertical wall of the rock outcrop, were geometric and life forms in red. The polychrome pictographs on the white ceiling of the lower shelter at Toca do Cosmos were truly spectacular. Many other caves seen in the limestone *serras* in the Central area had pictographs, and the walls of the canyons in the Serra Azul feature spectacular geometric designs and life forms. The rock art of the Central area is to be analysed and reported upon by other researchers on the Projeto Central; but we may conclude here that it must reflect a rich and complex symbolic culture maintained by the prehistoric population of the region.

The Aboriginal Heritage in the Central Area

Aboriginal society in the Central area apparently collapsed very quickly with the entry of the first European explorers at the beginning of the 17th century, and the aboriginal peoples in the area are unknown by name.

The local historian (Duarte 1978b) makes only brief mention of tribes variously called Amoipiras, Massacarás, Pontás, or Aracujás recorded to the north, in the middle São Francisco valley; but the aboriginal groups in the Central area cannot be identified. On Curt Nimuendaju's ethnohistoric map of Brazil (IBGE 1981), the nearest tribes noted are the Tupi-speaking Amoipira along the Rio São Francisco, the Tupi-speaking Tobajara on the Rio Paramirim about 100 km southwest of the upper Rio Verde, and the Kariri-speaking Payayá or Sapuya at the headwaters of the Rio Salitre about 150 km east of Central. It is impossible to know whether the aboriginal population of Central was affiliated with any of these groups.

While Indian society is long gone in the Central area, one commonly observes Indian phenotypic features in the rural population. As well, Posey's very brief ethnoecological survey in 1985 indicates that much aboriginal knowledge has been maintained. It is hoped that our archaeological research in the area will contribute to appreciation of Indian history and heritage by the present citizens of Central.

References Cited

Ab'Saber, A. N.
1977 Espaços ocupados pela expansão dos climas secos na América do Sul, por ocasião dos periodos glaciais quaternários. *Paleoclimas* 3. Instituto de Geografia, Universidade de São Paulo.

Bryan, A. L., and R. Gruhn
1978 Results of a test excavation at Lapa Pequena, MG, Brazil. *Arquivos do Museu de História Natural* (UFMG) 3:261–325. Belo Horizonte.

Childers, W. M.
1977 Ridge-back tools of the Colorado Desert. *American Antiquity* 42:242–248.

Delibrias, G., N. Guidon, and F. Parenti
1989 The Toca do Boqueirão do Sitio da Pedra Furada: stratigraphy and chronology. In *Early Man in the Southern Hemisphere,* edited by John Prescott, pp. S3–S11. Supplement to Achaeometry: Australasian Studies 1988. Department of Physics and Mathematical Physics, University of Adelaide.

Duarte, A.
1978a *Geografia de Central.* Multilith. São Paulo.
1978b *História de Central.* Multilith. São Paulo.

Farrand, W. R.
1985 Rockshelter and cave sediments. In *Archaeological Sediments in Context,* edited by Julie K. Stein and W. R. Farrand, pp. 21–40. Center for the Study of Early Man, University of Maine, Orono.

Ferri, M. G.
1980 *Vegetação Brasileira.* Editora da Universidade de São Paulo.

Guidon, N., and G. Delibrias
1985 Inventaire des sites Sud-Américains antérieurs a 12 000 ans. *L'Anthropologie* 89(3):385–408.

Guidon, N., and F. Parenti
1989 Toca do Boqueirão do Sitio da Pedra Furada: escavações 1987. *Dédalo,* Publ. Av. no 1:57–67. Universidade de São Paulo.

IBGE (Instituto Brasileiro de Geografia e Estatistica)
1980 *Nomenclatura dos Alimentos Consumidos no Brasil.* IBGE, Departamento de Estudios do Consumo. Rio de Janeiro.
1981 *Mapa Etno-Histórico de Curt Nimuendaju.* IBGE, Secretária de Cultura do Ministério da Educação e Cultura. Rio de Janeiro.

Inda, H. A. V., H. D. Schorscher, M. A. Dardenne, C. Schobbenhaus, N. L. E. Haralyi, P. C. Azevedo Branco, and R. Ramalho
1984 O Cráton do São Francisco e a Faixa de Dobramentos Araçuaí. In *Geologia do Brasil,* pp. 193–247. Ministério das Minas e Energia, Departamento Nacional da Produção Mineral. Brasilia.

de Lumley, H., M. de Lumley, M. Beltrão, Y. Yokoyama, J. Labeyrie, J. Danon, G. Delibrias, C. Falgueres, and J. Bischoff
1988 Découverte d'outils taillés associés à des faunes du Pleistocene moyen dans la Toca da Esperança, Etat de Bahia, Brésil. *C. R. Academie de Science,* t. 306, Série II:241–247. Paris.

Parenti, F., N. Mercier, and H. Valladas
1990 The oldest hearths of Pedra Furada, Brazil: thermoluminescence analysis of heated stones. *Current Research in the Pleistocene* 7:36–38.

Prous, A.

1980 Minas Gerais. In *Temas de Arquelogía Brasileira 2: Archaico do Interior,* edited by P. I. Schmitz, A. S. Barbosa, and M. B. Ribeiro, pp. 32–39. Anuario do Divulgação Cientifica no. 6, Instituto Goiano de Pré-História e Antropologia, Universidade Católica de de Goías.

1981 Fouilles du Gran Abri de Santana do Riacho (MG), Brésil. *Journal de la Societé des Americanistes* 67:163–183.

1986 L'archéologie au Brésil: 300 siecles d'occupation humaine. *L'Anthropologie* 90(2):257–306.

Ranere, A. J.

1978 Toolmaking and tool use among the Preceramic people of Panama. In *Advances in Andean Archaeology,* edited by D. L. Browman, pp. 41–84. Mouton: The Hague.

Schmitz, P. I.

1980 A Evolução da Cultura no Sudoeste de Goías. *Pesquisas,* Antropologia 31:185–225. Instituto Anchietano de Pesquisas, São Leopoldo RS.

1986 Cazadores antiguos en el Sudoeste de Goías, Brasil. In *New Evidence for the Pleistocene Peopling of the Americas,* edited by A. L. Bryan, pp. 183–193. Center for the Study of the First Americans, University of Maine, Orono.

1990 O povamento pleistocénico do Brasil. *Revista de Arqueologia Americana* 1:33–68.

Schmitz, P. I., A. S. Barbosa, A. L. Jacobus, and M. B. Ribeiro

1989 Arqueologia nos Cerrados do Brasil Central: Serranópolis I. *Pesquisas,* Antropologia 44. Instituto Anchietano de Pesquisas, São Leopoldo RS.

Schmitz, P. I., A. S. Barbosa, and M. B. Ribeiro (editors)

1980 *Temas de Arqueologia Brasileira 5: Os Cultivadores do Planalto e do Litoral.* Anuario de Divulgação Cientifica no. 9. Instituto Goiano de Pré-História e Antropologia, Universidade Católica de Goías.

Schmitz, P. I. A. S. Barbosa, and I. Wust (editors)

1976 *Arqueologia de Goías em 1976.* Instituto Anchietano de Pesquisas, São Leopoldo RS.

Index